D0842154

GB

The Great Ideas

"The Hand of God," 1954, a sculpture by Carl Milles; in the Millesgården, in Lidingö, a suburb of Stockholm. Man confronting climate with his technology.

The
Great Ideas
Today

1982

Encyclopædia Britannica, Inc.

CHICAGO
AUCKLAND • GENEVA • LONDON • MANILA • PARIS • ROME • SEOUL • SYDNEY • TOKYO • TORONTO

"Minds and Brains: Angels, Humans, and Brutes" was delivered as the
1982 Harvey Cushing Oration to the American Association of Neurological
Surgeons at their Annual Meeting in Honolulu, April 26, 1982.
Published by the *Journal of Neurosurgery*. Reprinted by permission of the
Journal.

"The Red Wheelbarrow" by William Carlos Williams from *Collected
Earlier Poems*. Copyright 1938 by New Directions Publishing Corporation.
Reprinted by permission of New Directions.

"Synchophantasy in Economics" by Louis O. Kelso and Patricia Hetter
Kelso. Copyright 1982 by Louis O. Kelso and Patricia Hetter Kelso.
Reprinted by permission of the authors.

"Man a Machine," from *Man a Machine* by Julien de La Mettrie,
translated from the French by Miss Gertrude Bussey, revised by Professor
M. W. Calkins, 1927. Reprinted by permission of the publisher, Open
Court Publishing Company.

"The President of the United States" by Woodrow Wilson originally
appeared in *Constitutional Government of the United States*, published in 1908
by Columbia University Press.

Printed in the U.S.A. Library of Congress Number: 61-65561
International Standard Book Number: 0-85229-398-4
International Standard Serial Number: 0072-7288

A NOTE ON REFERENCE STYLE

In the following pages, passages in *Great Books of the Western World* are referred to by the initials '*GBWW*,' followed by volume, page number, and page section. Thus, '*GBWW*, Vol. 39, p. 210b' refers to page 210 in Adam Smith's *The Wealth of Nations*, which is Volume 39 in *Great Books of the Western World*. The small letter 'b' indicates the page section. In books printed in single column, 'a' and 'b' refer to the upper and lower halves of the page. In books printed in double column, 'a' and 'b' refer to the upper and lower halves of the left column, 'c' and 'd' to the upper and lower halves of the right column. For example, 'Vol. 53, p. 210b' refers to the lower half of page 210, since Volume 53, James's *Principles of Psychology*, is printed in single column. On the other hand, 'Vol. 7, p. 210b' refers to the lower left quarter of the page since Volume 7, Plato's *Dialogues*, is printed in double column.

Gateway to the Great Books is referred to by the initials '*GGB*,' followed by volume and page number. Thus, '*GGB*, Vol. 10, pp. 39–57' refers to pages 39 through 57 of Volume 10 of *Gateway to the Great Books*, which is James's essay, "The Will to Believe."

The Great Ideas Today is referred to by the initials '*GIT*,' followed by the year and page number. Thus '*GIT* 1968, p. 210' refers to page 210 of the 1968 edition of *The Great Ideas Today*.

Contents

Preface

I n keeping with our plan to stay abreast of current developments in the arts and sciences—developments in physics, biology, the humanities, and social studies, of which we have given regular accounts in the past and will continue to report on in the future—we devote a portion of this year's *Great Ideas Today* to new disciplines, or aspects of old ones, which we have not previously taken up.

One of these, in the field of the social sciences, is the American electoral process, specifically the way in which every four years there is chosen a president of the United States. This is a matter of concern at present owing to the decline of political parties, the power of television, and the growth of single-issue politics. That as a result of these and other new factors the best candidates for the office are not selected, or if they are, are subjected to inhuman rigors of campaigning, is widely accepted, but it is not so clear what if anything can be done to improve the situation. The possibilities, and the fundamental constitutional questions they involve, are considered here in an article by Douglass Cater, of the Aspen Institute for Humanistic Studies, who has experience in presidential politics.

To a quite different area belongs the science of climatology, which is discussed following by F. Kenneth Hare of the University of Toronto. A relatively new science, or at least a fresh amalgam of old ones, climatology comprehends much of what nowadays we have come to regard as the life-support system of the earth—the conditions, as we may say, of our existence, including airs, waters, winds, temperature—in their complex, shifting patterns. Such a science would hardly have been possible before the age of the computer, so large are the quantities of data that are required to make even modest predictions as to long-term trends, and even so the predictions are subject to dispute, as Professor Hare acknowledges. But an immense amount is known now as compared with any time in the past.

Next will be found a report on recent biblical scholarship, by Raymond Brown of Union Theological Seminary, who reports on textual discoveries and archaeological finds that have increased our understanding of the Bible as an historical document. Work in this field—involving the examination of stones and tablets, archaeological digs in Palestine, and so forth—has been going on for a long time, of course, and while there are perhaps no altogether startling discoveries since those of the Dead Sea

Scrolls some years back, the sum of what has turned up and its implication for biblical scholars is in many details highly suggestive, as Father Brown indicates.

Finally, among our long articles this year will be found an account of the theories of literature and literary criticism that have been proposed, both in this country and in Europe over the past sixty years. Harvey Goldstein, who reports on this abstruse subject, is himself a scholar of literary theory in the seventeenth and eighteenth centuries, which had its own complexities. Its contemporary equivalent will be found to reflect twentieth-century philosophical thought, of which it is an extension, at many points.

In another part of the volume we repeat the feature of book reviews introduced last year in the belief that we should give some account of books that readers of *The Great Ideas Today* may find especially worthwhile. Reviewed this year by Mortimer Adler are Robert Nozick's *Philosophical Explanations,* a work that has caused much comment elsewhere, and *After Virtue,* by Alasdair MacIntyre. Also, reviewed by Charles Van Doren, are three works on computer theory, or, more exactly, what has come to be called Artificial Intelligence: *The Mind's I,* edited by Douglas Hofstadter and Daniel Dennett; *Brainstorms,* which is by Dennett alone; and *Mind Design,* edited by John Haugeland. Last but not least appears a review by Louis O. Kelso and Patricia Hetter Kelso of George Gilder's *Wealth and Poverty,* which has been accepted as a manifesto of the conservative economics of our day in this country and elsewhere.

In connection with Mr. Van Doren's report here on what may or may not become thinking machines, we publish in addition the text of an address given by Mr. Adler to the American Association of Neurological Surgeons this year, at the Association's invitation, on the mind and the brain in angels, humans, and brutes—this by way of comment on what is obviously a current topic, the whole question of whether it is possible or not to construct machines that will match or even surpass human thought processes.

We have included as well a discussion by Otto Bird, our consulting editor, of the *Pensées* of Pascal, which will serve to bring our readers up to date on recent editorial researches into that work. These researches demonstrate that while the bulk of what we know as the *Pensées* are, and must remain, in random sequence, all of them were intended by Pascal to have a certain order, and this can now be reconstructed for approximately one-third of them, including the famous no. 233 (in the usual numbering), called The Wager.

As in other years, many of the "Additions to the Great Books Library" in the volume are included for their relevance to the original articles and essays. Thus, J. O. de La Mettrie's *Man a Machine,* an eighteenth-century forerunner of works in behavioral psychology, is prophetic of the vision of mechanical intelligence discussed by Charles Van Doren. So, too,

Matthew Arnold's essay, "The Function of Criticism at the Present Time," and the story by Henry James called "The Real Thing," will be recognized as having reference to Professor Goldstein's discussion of literary theory. And Woodrow Wilson's description of the office of president of the United States, which is taken from his book, *Constitutional Government*, first published in 1908 when Wilson himself was president of Princeton University, is of interest in connection with Mr. Cater's piece on the electoral process that, in fact, quotes from it.

The longest "Addition" here, Boethius's *Consolation of Philosophy*, is offered merely for its own sake, however, and in recognition of its importance for ancient philosophy, of which during the Middle Ages it constituted a kind of digest before the works of Plato, Aristotle, and others had appeared again during the Renaissance, and of which, derivative though it may be, it is a moving personal account. Boethius, who died in A.D. 524, and who saw the last of the thousand-year period of classical culture that began with the rise of Athens and ended with the fall of Rome—a period far longer and more intellectually connected than anything Western culture has achieved since—spent much of his life trying to preserve, through translations and commentaries, the learning of those centuries, with the idea of making this available to generations yet unborn. It was a task that must have seemed immense in that age of destruction and decline; indeed, it must sometimes have appeared to Boethius, as it did to Saint Augustine, that his pen could hardly move fast enough, given that the barbarian was at the gate. But fortunately they both had time to save much, if by no means all, of what had come down to them.

This issue of *The Great Ideas Today* also includes, in response to requests from some of our readers, a Note to the Reader in which connections are suggested, chiefly by means of the *Syntopicon* to *Great Books of the Western World*, between the works in that set and contents of this volume—a service we have performed piecemeal, with one or more brief Notes, in past issues, but which is here attempted on a more comprehensive scale.

The editors are indebted, as always, to the editorial copy department of Encyclopædia Britannica, Inc., for seeing the volume through the press; also to the company's art department, to which are owed the illustrations, photographs, and diagrams that appear at various points; to the editorial typesetting staff, listed on another page; and to other departments whose services have been required.

PART ONE

Current Topics

Minds and Brains: Angels, Humans, and Brutes

Mortimer J. Adler

Editor's Introduction

As the review of recent books about artificial intelligence elsewhere in this volume will serve to indicate, that subject is very much with us at the moment, when we hear—not for the first time, it is true—that machines with the operational capacity of the human brain (or conceivably much more than that), and even perhaps with similar chemical constituents, are within the realm of possibility, will likely enough in time be made.

The question, supposing this in fact is done, is whether the resulting mechanism, having presumably the powers of a human brain, would in effect be one—whether the old dream of a thinking machine, the Faustian homunculus, can after all be realized. This is cousin to another question, of late not quite so insistently put as it was a few years ago, whether chimpanzees or dolphins can be taught some form of language, in which case it can be argued, as indeed it has been argued, that they are of the same order as ourselves, that the difference between their brains and ours, however large, is but a matter of degree along the same continuum.

It was at any rate with these possibilities in mind that Mortimer J. Adler accepted the invitation of the American Association of Neurological Surgeons to give the Harvey Cushing Memorial Oration at the Association's annual meeting in Honolulu this year, in an effort to distinguish as clearly as possible the philosopher's view of such matters from that of the physician and the scientist. This lecture, which is reprinted here with minor changes, will recall, to those familiar with Mr. Adler's writings, his earlier book, *The Difference of Man and the Difference It Makes* (1967), as well as the "Symposium on Language and Communication" in *The Great Ideas Today* 1975, to which he was a contributor.

Introduction

I am honored by your invitation to deliver the Harvey Cushing Memorial Address—or Oration, as it is referred to. An address I hope it will be; but an oration, I think not. More than honored, I am awed, coming as I do from the soft science of psychology and the even softer discipline known as philosophy, and standing before you who are leading representatives of a science that is hard down to its core.

When first approached, I was hesitant to accept such an assignment. I do not know whether it was the eloquence expected of an orator that frightened me, or the eminence of Harvey Cushing that made me hesitant. What overcame my scruples on these two counts were the many memories that soon crowded into my mind—not only the recollection of my great admiration for Dr. Cushing, but also the memory of how far back in my life and how deep in my intellectual interest lay the study of neurophysiology.

I recalled that while a young instructor in psychology at Columbia University in the early 1920s I went down to the College of Physicians and Surgeons, then located at 59th Street near 10th Avenue, to take a course in neuroanatomy with Professors Tilney and Elwyn.

Professor Elwyn was the anatomist who gave us most of the lectures and supervised our microscopic examination of slides of spinal sections. Dr. Tilney was one of the great neurologists of his day. I remember vividly his coming in a dinner jacket to an evening lecture to tell us about his diagnosis of brain pathology and about the surgical procedures involved in its therapy.

As a student and teacher of psychology, I could not help but be interested in the workings of the brain and central nervous system. The early chapters of William James's two-volume *Principles of Psychology* were filled with speculations about the relation of mind and brain, as were Ladd and Woodworth's *Elements of Physiological Psychology*. Both books, if you were to read them today, would greatly amuse you by the extent of the ignorance that then passed for scientific knowledge. In more recent years, my reading in this field included many books of much more recent vintage. Let me just mention a few in passing: C. S. Sherrington's *The Integrative Action of the Nervous System;* C. Judson Herrick's *The Brains of Rats and Men;* J. C.

Eccles's *The Neurophysiological Basis of Mind;* Ward Halstead's *Brain and Intelligence;* Warren McCulloch's *Embodiments of Mind;* K. S. Lashley's *Brain Mechanisms and Intelligence;* Wilder Penfield's essay on "The Physiological Basis of the Mind," in *Control of the Mind.*

Even more recently, the rise of experimental researches and technological advances in the field of artificial intelligence has opened up another vein of interest in the physical basis of mind; and I have turned to such books as John von Neumann's *The Computer and the Brain; Minds and Machines,* a collection of papers edited by A. R. Anderson; A. M. Turing's essay "Computing Machinery and Intelligence"; J. Z. Young's *Programs of the Brain;* Daniel C. Dennett's very recent *Brainstorms.*

Please forgive me for what may appear to be pretension to some erudition in a field in which you are all experts. I mention my excursions into the literature of neurophysiology and of artificial intelligence in order to allay the suspicion that may arise in your minds when I proceed now to deal philosophically—even metaphysically—with the problem of the relation of mind to brain.

You might suspect that my philosophical speculations reflect ancient and venerable theories that no longer stand up in the light of the facts uncovered by the most advanced scientific research. You might even suspect that since I am going to talk to you as a philosopher, I might feel justified in doing so in cavalier ignorance of relevant scientific knowledge bearing on the matters to be considered. I would like to assure you that neither suspicion is justified. I may not be as well-informed with regard to the most recent advances in neurophysiology as I should be, but I hope you will find that my philosophical consideration of mind and brain does not fly in the face of facts that must be taken into account.

The two main questions that I would like to consider with you can be stated as follows: (1) Will our knowledge of the brain and nervous system both central and autonomic, either now or in the future, suffice to explain all aspects of animal behavior? (2) On the supposition that the answer to that question is affirmative, then the second question is: Does this mean that we will also succeed in explaining human behavior, especially human thought, in terms of what we know, now or in the future, about the human brain and nervous system?

You will observe at once, I am sure, that the answer to the second question, in the light of an affirmative answer to the first question, depends on one crucial point: whether the difference between human beings and brute animals is a difference in kind or in degree.

To probe and ponder the answers to these two questions, I propose to proceed as follows. First, briefly to explain the distinction between difference in kind and difference in degree, and especially the two modes of differences in kind—radical and superficial. Second, to illustrate a radical difference in kind by considering humans in relation to angels and to eliminate what I hope you will agree is an erroneous view of the relation of mind to brain. Third, to consider humans in relation to brutes and also in relation to machines devised to represent artifical intelligence. And, finally, to propose what I hold to be the correct view of the relation of the human mind to the human brain—correct, that is, until future experimental research in neurophysiology and in the sphere of artificial intelligence succeeds in refuting it.

Differences in kind and in degree

A difference in degree exists between two things when one is more and the other is less in a given specified respect. Thus, for example, two lines of unequal length differ only in degree. Similarly, two brains of unequal weight or complexity differ only in degree.

A difference in kind exists between two things when one possesses a property or attribute that the other totally lacks. Thus, for example, a rectangle and a circle differ in kind for one has interior angles and the other totally lacks them. So, too, a vertebrate organism that has a brain and central nervous system differs in kind from organisms that totally lack these organs.

A difference in kind is superficial if it is based upon and can be explained by an underlying difference in degree. Thus, for example, the apparent difference in kind between water and ice (you can walk on one and not on the other) can be explained by the rate of motion of their component molecules, which is an underlying difference in degree. Similarly, the apparent difference in kind between humans and other animals (things that human beings can do that other animals cannot do at all) may be explainable in terms of the degree of complexity of their brains. If that is so, then the apparent difference in kind is superficial.

A difference in kind is radical if it cannot be explained in terms of any underlying difference in degree, but only by the presence of a factor in one that is totally absent in the other. Consider the difference between plants and the higher animals. This appears to be a difference in kind, for the animals perform operations totally absent in plants. If this difference in kind can be explained only in terms of the presence in animals and the absence in plants of brains and nervous systems, then it is a radical, not a superficial, difference in kind.

Angels and human beings

Let me begin by saying that I wish you to consider angels only as possible beings—as purely hypothetical entities. Whether or not there is any truth in the religious belief that angels really exist need not concern us. As possible beings, angels are purely spiritual. Our interest in them here arises from the fact that they are conceived as minds *without* bodies. As minds without bodies, angels know and will and love, but not in the same manner that we do. Their lack of bodies has a number of striking consequences. They do not learn from experience. They do not think discursively, for they have no imaginations or memories. Their knowledge, which is intuitive, derives from innate ideas implanted in them at the moment of their creation. They speak to one another telepathically without the use of any medium of communication. Their minds, which are infallible, never go to sleep.

In all these respects, minds without bodies differ from the human mind precisely because the latter is associated with a body and depends upon that body for some if not all of its functions.

You may question the possibility of angels—of minds without bodies, minds without brains. If so, let me defend the possibility of angels against the materialists who think they have grounds for denying that angels are possible. I do so because, as you will see presently, the error of the materialists has a critical bearing on of my treatment of the problem of minds and brains.

The argument of the materialists runs as follows. They assert that nothing exists in reality except corporeal things, from elementary particles up to the most complex organisms, from atoms to stars and galaxies. But angels are said to be incorporeal. Therefore, they conclude, angels are impossible, as inconceivable and impossible as are round squares.

The argument is weak in one respect and faulty in another. Its initial premise (that nothing except corporeal things exist) is an unproved and unprovable assumption. It may be true, but we have no grounds for asserting its truth, neither with certitude nor even beyond a reasonable doubt. It is as much a matter of faith as the religious belief in the reality of angels. Even if we were to grant the truth of that initial premise, the argument is faulty, because the conclusion does not follow. If the premise assumed were true, the valid conclusion to be drawn from it is that angels—incorporeal beings—do not exist in reality. But the conclusion that angels cannot exist—that they are impossible—does not follow at all.

In fact, there are many positive arguments to support the conceivability and possibility of angels, though I am not going to take the time to set them before you. For our present purposes, let it suffice for us to recognize that the exponents of materialism cannot validly deny the possibility of angels. This being so, neither can they deny that the human mind may be a spiritual—an immaterial—factor associated with the brain as a corporeal factor, both of which are needed to explain human thought.

This brings us to a view at the opposite extreme from materialism, a view that looks upon the human mind as an immaterial substance, an immaterial power, that does not need a brain for its unique activity, which is rational thought. This is the view taken by Plato in antiquity and by Descartes at the beginning of modern times. It commits what I have called an angelistic fallacy, for it regards the rational soul or human intellect as if it were an incarnate angel—a mind that, in humans, may be associated with a body, but one that does not depend upon or need a body for its intellectual operations.

I do not have to persuade you, in the light of all you know about the dependence of human mental operations upon brain functions and processes, and all you know about the effects of brain pathology upon human thought, that this Platonic and Cartesian view of the human mind as an incarnate angel flies in the face of well-attested evidence and must therefore be rejected. I wish only to add that, on purely philosophical grounds, the dualism of mind or soul and body does not stand up. It denies the unity of the human being. It makes us a duality of two independent substances—as independent as a boat and the person who is rowing it. Either of these can cease to exist without the other ceasing to exist. They are existentially distinct and separable, as our own mind and body are not. If they were, we should be left with the inexplicable mystery of why they were combined—why the human mind should have any association with a human body.

Human beings, other animals — and intelligent machines

There is no question that in many behavioral respects we differ from other animals only in degree. Nor is there any question that the human brain differs from the brains of the higher mammals in degree—in complexity and in the ratio of brain weight to body weight.

There may be some question as to whether human and animal brains also differ in kind. I would like to leave this question for you to answer. For example, is the asymmetry of the human brain's left and right lobes uniquely human? Is the absence in animal brains of anything like the motor center for speech, which seems to be connected with cortical asymmetry, a difference in kind? Is the special character of the very large frontal lobe of the human brain another indication of a neurological difference in kind?

Whatever answers you give to these questions should be considered in the light of what I am now going to say about behavioral differences in kind between humans and brutes. Here are the differences between humans and brutes that I think are differences in kind, not in degree. Whether these differences in kind are superficial or radical remains to be seen.

So far as we can tell, animals are capable only of perceptual thought, whereas humans are capable of conceptual thought, which appears totally absent in animals. Conceptual and syntactical speech, with a vocabulary of words that refer to imperceptible and unimaginable objects, together with the way in which humans learn speech, is one indication of this. It is unrefuted by all the recent work on so-called speech by chimpanzees and bottle-nosed dolphins. So far as we can tell, animal perceptual thought, involving perceptual abstractions and generalizations, cannot deal with any object that is not perceptible, or that is not perceptually present. Human conceptual thought, in sharp contrast, deals both with objects that are not perceptually present and with objects that are totally imperceptible—with angels, for example.

This basic difference between perceptual and conceptual thought, and the fact that man alone seems to possess the power of conceptual thought, explains many other differences between human and animal behavior. Man is the only animal with an extended historical tradition and with cultural, as opposed to merely genetic, continuity between the generations. Man is the only animal that makes laws and constitutions for the associations he forms. Man is the only animal that makes machinery and that produces things by machinofacturing. None of these things, and others like them, would be possible without conceptual thought and conceptual speech.

If I am right concerning the existence of behavioral differences in kind between humans and brutes, we must face the question that still remains: Is this difference in kind superficial or radical? Can it be explained in terms of differences in degree between human and animals? If so, it is only superficial. If not, it is radical.

One other condition must be satisfied in order for us to conclude that the difference is only superficial. The differences in degree between human and animal brains must itself provide us with an adequate explanation of the apparent difference in kind between human and animal behavior.

Let me table that question for a moment in order, first, to consider the human mind in relation to the machines that are supposed to embody artificial intelligence and are supposed to differ in degree only from human intelligence. I do this because it will have a critical bearing on the ultimate question to be resolved.

Here the most important things to point out are that the difference between the human brain and the artifacts supposedly endowed by their makers with intelligence lies in the fact that the latter are purely electrical networks, whereas the human brain is a chemical factory as well as an electrical network, and that the chemistry of the brain is indispensable to its electrical operation.

The extraordinary researches of the last thirty years have shown us how important the chemical facilitators and transmitters are to the operations of the human brain. These are absent from the functioning of artificial intelligence machines so far, though there is now some movement in the direction of creating what are called "wet computers." Until that is fully realized, there will remain a difference in kind between the human brain and computers, one that would not be removed even if machines could be constructed that had electrical units and connections in excess of ten raised to the eleventh power.

The Turing game

If the dream of wet computers is not fully realized, neurophysiology may some day be able to explain human thought, but we will never be able to construct a machine, no matter how complex and refined electrically, that will think the way that human beings do. We can train dogs and horses to do very complicated and remarkable tricks that have nothing to do with their possessing intelligence of the sort that any human being has. So, too, we can program computers to do even more complicated and more extraordinary tricks that are amazing counterfeits of human thought, but this does not mean that they have the power of human thought, or that they are reflexively aware *that* they are thinking and know *what* they are thinking.

If the only difference between men and brutes was the relative size and complexity of the nervous machinery, aided and abetted by the products of brain chemistry, then wet computers might be constructed to think as well as men, if not better, especially if future computers exceed the human brain's componentry by some power greater than ten raised to the eleventh power and if something analogous to all the human brain's chemical agents is operative in a so-called wet computer.

However, if the difference between men and brutes is not purely a quantitative difference in brain weight and complexity, relative to body size and weight; if, instead, the difference between the perceptual power of brutes and the conceptual power of humans stems from the presence in man of an immaterial factor—the human intellect that cooperates with the brain but whose operations are not reducible to brain processes— then no computer, regardless of how extensive its componentry and how chemically assisted its electrical circuitry is, will ever be able to think, to engage in conceptual thought as human beings do.

As Descartes said centuries ago, *matter cannot think.* The best computer that ever can be made by man will always be, electrically and chemically, nothing but a material thing. That is why the test proposed by A. M. Turing—a test to discover whether computers will ever be able to think in human fashion—is so interesting and so significant. It is an answer to Descartes's challenge to the materialists of his day, defying them to build a machine that could think intellectually.

The Turing game is the only critical test that I know whereby to determine whether computers can think in the way in which human beings think, A. M. Turing, by the way, was the somewhat mad English genius who broke the German enigma code.

The Turing test is based on the following game as a model. An interrogator stands in front of a screen behind which are a pair of male and female human beings. The interrogator, by asking them questions and considering the answers they give in written form, must try to determine which one of the persons is a male and which a female. The persons behind the screen must do their intelligent best to deceive the interrogator. If they do their intelligent best, they will succeed. The interrogator's determination will be no better than a guess on his part—fifty percent right, fifty percent wrong.

Now, says Turing, place a human being and a computer behind the screen, and let the computer have what Turing calls merely infant or initial programming.

Infant programming can be of two sorts. (1) Our own infant programming consists of the relatively small number of spinal or cerebrospinal reflexes with which we are born. Other animals, with more or less elaborate instinctive patterns of innate preformed behavior, have much more elaborate infant programming of this sort than humans do. Analogous to such infant programming would be the programming of a computer to give preformed responses to certain definite stimuli.

Let us suppose that the computer's infant programming greatly exceeded man's infant programming in the form of innate reflexes. No matter how large the number of preestablished responses to stimuli programmed into the computer, that number—N—would never be large enough for the computer to pass the Turing test to be described below; for though the computer could be programmed to answer N questions, there would always be the $N + 1$ question, and more after that, which the computer would be unable to answer.

(2) The other sort of infant programming that humans have consists in their innate abilities to learn, among which, for example, is their ability to learn to speak any language whatsoever, or their ability to think about any subject whatsoever within the range of all possible thinkables. To pass the test proposed by Turing, a machine would have to have this second kind of infant programming, and have it to a degree that at least equalled its possession by human beings.

No computer yet built has such programming. All have much more infant programming of the first sort than humans have, but none yet has the second kind of infant programming. Until a computer does, it will fail to deceive the interrogator. By asking questions beyond the range of N, no matter how large N is, the interrogator will always be able to detect which answer came from a machine and which from a human being.

I am betting that a machine with programming of the second sort will never be built and so no machine will ever successfully pass Turing's test. If I turn out to be wrong about this—and only the future will tell—then I will concede that machines can think the way human beings do, and that physical processes, whether merely electrical or electrochemical, can provide us with an adequate explanation of human conceptual thought as well as of animal perceptual thought.

Before I go on, let me call your attention to three matters that are connected with or emerge from our consideration of the Turing test.

The first is the historic fact that the seventeenth-century philosopher, Descartes, anticipated Turing by proposing a similar test to show that machines—and animals, which he regarded as machines with senses and brains but without intellects—cannot think. It was a conversational test. No machine will ever be built, Descartes said, that will be able to engage in conversation in the way in which two human beings engage in conversation that is infinitely flexible and unpredictable in the turns that it will take.

Second, whether or not a Turing machine, contrary to Descartes's prediction, will ever be built, it is certainly clear that no talking chimpanzee or dolphin, using its sign language, could ever pass the Turing test of being indistinguishable from a human being behind the screen.

Third, whether you think that the difference in kind between humans and brutes is only superficial depends on your predicting that neurophysiology will someday be able to explain how human beings perform distinctively in the Turing game. Does the power of the human brain account for their distinctive performance? Or is some other factor—some immaterial factor, such as Descartes thought the human intellect to be—needed to explain it?

Minds and brains

We have already encountered two extreme views of the relation of the human mind or intellect to the human brain. At one extreme, there is the materialist who denies not only the reality but also the possibility of immaterial beings, powers, or operations. On this materialist view, brain action and processes provide the necessary and also the sufficient conditions for all mental operations, human conceptual thought as well as animal perceptual thought. This view has come to be called the identity hypothesis. The word *identity* signifies that mind and brain are existentially inseparable. The word *hypothesis* concedes that it is an unproved—and, I think, also unprovable—assumption.

The identity hypothesis takes two forms, one more extreme than the other. The more extreme form is known as "reductive materialism." It claims that there is not even an analytical distinction between the action of the mind and the action of the brain. The less extreme form—in my judgment much more in accord with the indisputable facts—admits that any description of brain processes is always analytically distinct from any description of mental processes; we do not use the same terms in both cases, and cannot. This is just as true of animal perceptual thought as it is true of human conceptual thought. Conceding the analytical difference between brain processes and thought processes, this less extreme form of materialism nevertheless insists that mind and brain are existentially inseparable, and so brain action should be able to explain all acts of the mind, both conceptual and perceptual. On this hypothesis, tenable in its less extreme form, neurophysiology should be able to succeed in explaining all aspects of human intelligence as well as all aspects of animal intelligence. The furthest reaches of human thought should not escape its explanatory powers.

At the other extreme, there are the immaterialists who deny that brain processes can now, or will ever be able to, explain human thought. On this view, brain action is not even a necessary, much less a sufficient condition, for thought. This immaterialist view takes its most extreme form in the philosophy of Bishop Berkeley, who denied the very existence of matter and, therefore, regarded humans as purely spiritual creatures, no less spirits than the angels in heaven.

The extreme form of immaterialism flies in the face of indisputable facts, just as the extreme form of materialism does. We should, therefore, have no hesitation in rejecting both of these extremes. The less extreme form of immaterialism is, as we have already observed, the Platonic and Cartesian view of the rational soul or the human intellect as an incarnate angel, somehow incarcerated in a human body—a purely spiritual substance dwelling in a body that it in no way needs for its essential operation, which is rational thought. Just one fact—and one negative fact is always quite sufficient—casts grave doubt on the Platonic and Cartesian view. Angels, as I pointed out, never sleep. Their intellects are always active. Human beings do fall asleep and wake up. Their intellects are sometimes inactive. We may dream from time to time, but we are not always thinking. That fact is inexplicable on the Cartesian and Platonic view of the intellect's relation to the human body and brain.

In between these two extreme views, each in its several forms, lies the only view that recommends itself to me as fitting all the facts we know. It fits everything we know about the nature of human thought and about the limitations of matter and its physical properties. I would describe this middle view as a moderate materialism combined with an equally moderate immaterialism.

Its moderate materialism consists in its accepting two tenets held by the less extreme form of the identity hypothesis. The first of these tenets is that brain processes and mental processes are analytically distinguishable. No description of the one can ever be substituted for a description of the other. It also agrees that brain processes are at least a necessary condition for the occurrence of mental processes—something that is denied by the extreme forms of immaterialism.

The middle view that I espouse is also materialistic to the extent that it concedes that every aspect of perceptual thought, in humans as well as in other animals—all the acts of sense perception, imagination, and memory, as well as emotions, passions, and desires—can be or will someday be explained entirely in neurophysiological terms. There is nothing immaterial or spiritual about any of the behavioral or mental operations that are common to human beings and other animals.

What is immaterialistic about this middle view—and quite moderately immaterialistic, in my judgment—can be summed up by saying that human thought (that is, distinctively conceptual thought) cannot now, and never will, be explained in terms of brain action. Nor can the freedom of the human will—the freedom of choice that is distinctively human—ever be explained in terms of physical causation or the motions of material particles.

In other words, without the acts of perception, imagination, and memory, all of which are acts of the sense organs and the brain, conceptual thought cannot occur. Mental pathology and disabilities, aphasias of all sorts, senile dementia, and so on, indicate plainly the role of the brain in the life of the mind. But that is a limited role.

Perhaps the most precise way of summarizing this middle view is as follows. We see with our eyes and with the visual cortex of the brain. We hear with our ears and with the acoustical cortex of the brain. But what organ do we think with? What is the organ of conceptual thought? The middle view answers: *not with the brain.* We do not think conceptually with our brains, even if we cannot think conceptually without our brains. In short, the brain is a necessary, but not the sufficient, condition of conceptual thought. On this one crucial point, the middle view differs from the less extreme form of the immaterialist or the non-identity hypothesis—the view of Plato and Descartes.

This means that an immaterial factor or power—the human intellect and will—is involved in cooperation with the human brain in the production of conceptual thought and free choice. And this if true, as I think it is, means that the difference in kind between human beings and other animals, not to mention machines, is a radical, not a superficial, difference in kind.

It also means that mankind occupies a position on the boundary line between the whole realm of corporeal creatures, and the realm of spiritual beings, the angels and God, whether these be regarded as mere possibilities or are believed in as actual. But mankind, in this middle position, does not straddle the line that divides the material from the spiritual, with one foot in each realm, as Plato and Descartes would have us think. Mankind is mainly in the realm of corporeal things, but by the power of his immaterial intellect, he is able to reach over into the spiritual realm.

Concluding reflections

Permit me a few concluding reflections. I am relatively certain of only two things. One is that failure to concede the indispensable role of the brain in human thought is an angelistic fallacy that must be rejected. The other is that the materialistic denial of the possibility of spiritual substances and of immaterial powers, such as the human intellect, must also be rejected.

With somewhat less assurance, I am persuaded by everything I know that brain action by itself does not and cannot suffice to explain conceptual thought, because the essential character of such thought involves transcendence of all material conditions. The reach of the human mind to objects of thought that are totally imperceptible and totally unimaginable is the clearest indication of this.

Where does this leave us? As I see it, with these three conclusions: (1) All aspects of animal behavior, animal intelligence, and animal mentality—all below the level of conceptual thought—can be or will be satisfactorily explained by our knowledge of the brain and nervous system. (2) Such knowledge can now contribute—and in the future it will do even more to contribute—to the explanation of the acts of the human mind. But neurophysiology will never provide a completely satisfactory explanation of conceptual thought and freedom of choice. (3) Programmed machines, at their very best, may simulate acts of animal or human intelligence; but, since they are clearly not living, conscious organisms, such simulation is never more than a counterfeit of perceptual or conceptual thought. It is thought that the machine itself does not experience, thought of which the machine is not reflexively aware. It is never the real thing.

PART TWO

Current Developments in the Arts and Sciences

Electing the U.S. President

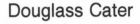

Douglass Cater has had a distinguished career in journalism and public affairs. For many years on the staff of *The Reporter Magazine,* he was its national editor when in 1964 he was made special assistant to President Lyndon Johnson on education and health policy. In this position, collaborating with James Killian, John Gardner, and others, he helped to develop programs that led to the Elementary and Secondary Education Act of 1965, the Public Broadcasting Corporation, the International Education Act, and the Teacher Corps.

A founding fellow of the Aspen Institute for Humanistic Studies, Mr. Cater was director of its program in communications and society, which has made studies of television and its impact, and has been in charge of designing its Center for Governance at Wye Plantation in Maryland, to which he has contributed a paper on the U.S. presidential electoral process.

The recipient of numerous grants and awards, he has taught at various colleges and universities and is the author of *The Fourth Branch of Government* (1959), a study of the role of the press in American politics; *Power in Washington* (1964), delineating "sub-governments" in American politics; and other works.

In February of this year Mr. Cater was appointed president of Washington College, the tenth oldest chartered college in the United States, in Chestertown, Maryland.

Paradox now haunts our presidential selection process. In the continuing effort to extend the popular franchise, latter-day developments in the way we choose our nation's leader appear to be threatening the "legitimacy" (i.e., the capacity to govern) of the president who emerges from the contest. This has been accompanied by further decline in the effective role of the political parties and, measured by public opinion polls and voter turnout, widespread citizen disillusionment with the workings of the electoral process. The 1980 election brought the lowest percentage of voters to the polls since 1948; during the past two decades the trend has been steadily downward.

The time has come as an urgent priority of governance to consider how the presidential electoral process can better serve its intended purposes in a free society: to identify and call forth the most worthy candidates, to engage the serious interests of the electorate, and to choose a leader while least disrupting the ongoing conduct of government in a time of sustained challenge at home and abroad.

I

During the long, hot summer of 1787, no issue provoked more vacillation among the Constitution drafters at Philadelphia than the choosing of the chief executive. They had little difficulty in defining the president's duties and even determining how he should be addressed—"His Excellency" seemed appropriately respectful but non-monarchical. Deciding on the electoral process, however, stirred continuing dispute. A perception widely shared among the delegates was that the method of picking the president would greatly influence the power structure they were striving to create. Their dispute did not arouse the familiar antagonisms of big state versus small or northern states versus southern. Instead, this was a struggle over the very nature of American government.

Edmund Randolph of Virginia began the debate within the first fortnight of the convocation at Philadelphia by offering a resolution to allow the first branch of the national legislature to choose the president. James Wilson of Pennsylvania responded that "at least . . . in theory" he favored election by the people, since the experience of New York and Massachusetts showed this to be a "convenient and successful mode." He entered a resolution to divide the states into districts in which qualified voters would choose electors. He was opposed by Roger Sherman of Connecticut who thought the appointment should be made by the national legislature so that the national executive would be "absolutely dependent on that body." Executive independence, he argued, would be "the very essence of tyranny." Elbridge Gerry of Massachusetts, opposing both Randolph and Wilson, submitted a resolution to permit choice by the governors of the various states. Randolph objected. "The governors," he said sarcastically, "will not cherish the great Oak which is to reduce them to paltry shrubs."

George Mason of Virginia felt that most objections would be obviated by placing executive power in the hands of a triumvirate: "Under a single Executive," he reasoned, "the Government will, of course, soon degenerate into a Monarchy." James Madison favored a single executive who would be aided by a council to advise him but not to control his authority. Randolph suggested a seven-year term; Sherman, three years; Mason, at least seven but without eligibility for a second term. Others proposed eleven and fifteen years. Possibly with tongue in cheek, Rufus King of New York suggested twenty years, noting that this would represent "the median life of princes." Wilson took him seriously and protested that a president entering office at age thirty-five would be at age fifty-five "in the very prime of life . . . cast aside like a useless hulk." Gerry observed sadly, "We seem to be entirely at a loss on this head."

By midsummer, the argument was in full flower. Still no progress had been made on the method of selection. On July 17 the Committee of the Whole, by a vote of 10–0, opted for a unitary executive and, by 9–1, struck out Randolph's proposal that the choice be made by the national legislature, substituting somewhat vaguely: "by the citizens of the United States." Then after defeating, 2–8, a resolution to allow the state legislatures to choose the electors, the convention reversed itself and restored, 10–0, presidential selection by the national legislature. Comparing this method to the election of the Pope by the Conclave of Cardinals, Gouverneur Morris of Pennsylvania offered the dour opinion that such an arrangement would soon reduce itself to the work "of intrigue, of cabal, and of faction." Charles Cotesworth Pinckney of South Carolina argued on the other hand that a popular election would be dominated by "a few active and designing men." And Colonel Mason dismissed the notion of popular election with his famous rejoinder: "It would be as unnatural to refer the choice of a proper character for Chief Magistrate to the people, as it would, to refer a trial of colours to a blind man. The extent of the Country renders it impossible that the people can have the requisite capacity to judge the respective pretensions of the Candidates." In the subsequent roll call, only Pennsylvania cast a favorable vote for popular election.

Two days later, the delegates voted in favor of a six-year term after hearing Ellsworth's argument that the executive by too frequent elections would "not be firm eno'. There must be duties which will make him unpopular. . . ." Williamson of North Carolina made the practical point that election expenses would be considerable and ought not to be unnecessarily repeated. Shorter terms, he added, would be unattractive to the best men while those "of an inferior character will be liable to be corrupted."

On July 24 the Committee of the Whole affirmed once again that the president would be chosen by the national legislature (7 aye, 4 no) and then, on Wilson's suggestion, specified that the choice would be made by not more than fifteen legislators selected "by lot." These electors were to retire immediately and not separate until they had reached a choice. "By this mode intrigue would be avoided in the first instance, and the dependence would be diminished," Wilson concluded.

Still the controversy raged. Ellsworth proposed that the president's first election be made by the national legislature, but that reelection should require the support of the state legislatures. Madison argued there would be "very little opportunity for cabal or corruption" if the electors were to meet at some place distant from the rest of the government. Gerry objected that a popular election would put power in one set of men, such as the Society of the Cincinnati, acting in concert. On July 26 the convention voted once again for a unitary president, chosen by the national legislature, to hold office for a single term of seven years duration. The state roll call was 6 aye, 3 no, 1 divided, 1 absent.

At one point in the proceedings, Benjamin Franklin, much the oldest delegate, made a lengthy speech urging that the chief executive should receive no salary but be reimbursed for "necessary expenses" as General George Washington had been compensated during his eight years as Commander-in-Chief of the Continental Armies. Otherwise, argued Franklin, the combining of ambition and avarice would attract "men of strong passions and indefatigable activity in their selfish pursuits." Already being touted for first president, presiding officer Washington made no comment. Madison records in his journal that Franklin's proposal was "treated with great respect, but rather for the author of it than from any apparent conviction of its expediency or practicality."

The end of August found the delegates still at odds over presidential selection. Dispute arose about whether the national legislature should choose by a single or joint ballot. Once again, Morris attempted to promote an amendment substituting popular elections. On August 24 he was defeated by a vote of 5 to 6.

The breakthrough finally came on September 4 when the Committee of Eleven, appointed to come up with a solution, reported to the assembled delegates a plan remarkably close to the final one. Each state would choose its electors in a manner to be determined by its own legislature

"During the long, hot summer of 1787, no issue provoked more vacillation among the Constitution drafters at Philadelphia than the choosing of the chief executive." Pictured here are some of the delegates who helped decide on our electoral process.

James Madison

Benjamin Franklin

Gouverneur Morris

George Mason

Rufus King

Charles Cotesworth Pinckney

Elbridge Gerry

and equal in number to its combined senators and representatives. These electors would convene in their respective states (to avoid the cabals and corruption of a national gathering) and cast ballots for two persons, at least one of whom would have to be the inhabitant of another state. No member of Congress or federal officeholder could serve as elector. In the absence of a clear majority on the first ballot, the U.S. Senate was to act immediately to choose the president.

Objections being raised to allowing a Senate "aristocracy" to make the choice, the delegates voted to move this responsibility to the House of Representatives with a proviso that each state's delegation would be counted as a single vote. The delegates decided also to fix the presidential term at four years with no hindrance to reelections. They voted down an effort by Madison to establish an Advisory Council for the President, thereby provoking Mason's lament, "He will be unsupported by proper information and advice, and will generally be directed by minions and favorites . . ." Because of this and other complaints, Mason subsequently felt constrained from signing his name to the new Constitution.

Consider the outcome of all the disputation: The miracle workers at Philadelphia decisively rejected the notion that citizens should pick their chief magistrate by direct vote. Though they decided not to allow the initial choice to be made by the U.S. Congress, they eventually gave the House of Representatives authority to break electoral deadlocks, which many felt would occur with fair frequency.* The electors themselves were to be distinguished citizens, though forbidden to hold federal office. They would not journey to the nation's capital but would meet in their respective states. Their balloting would not specify which vote was intended for president and for vice-president.† The electors would be allowed to ballot only once. If no one received a majority of the electoral votes, the U.S. House of Representatives would make the choice from the five (later amended to three) receiving the highest votes. It is clear that fear of faction, cabal, and intrigue was what moved the Constitution makers, leading them to impose a system of checks throughout the electoral process.

The authors of *The Federalist* treated the results as an unmitigated success. Consider the assessment made by Alexander Hamilton in Federalist Paper No. 68: "The mode of the appointment of the Chief Magistrate of the United States is almost the only part of the [Constitutional] system, of any consequence, which has escaped without severe censure, or which has received the slightest mark of approbation from its opponents. The

---

* In fact, the House has been obliged to act directly only twice so far, in 1800 and 1824. In 1876 Congress acted jointly to set up an Electoral Commission to adjudicate disputed returns from four states.

† In 1804 the Twelfth Amendment to the Constitution remedied this oversight following the tie vote between Thomas Jefferson and Aaron Burr in the election of 1800.

most plausible of these . . . has even deigned to admit that the election of the President is pretty well guarded."

Hamilton claimed four major benefits for the Electoral College: (1) It would permit the choice of a president to be made by persons who were "most capable of analysing the qualities adapted" to the station of the presidency and who would be "most likely to possess the information and discernment requisite to such complicated investigations." (2) It promised to make the executive "independent for his continuance in office on all but the people themselves." He would not be directly answerable to the Congress or to state governments. (3) It would reduce the opportunity for "tumult and disorder." The multiple members of the Electoral College and their convocation in the separate states would make it difficult for them to communicate their "heats and ferments" to the people. (4) The same "detached and divided situation" of the electors would raise an obstacle to "cabal, intrigue, and corruption," since the college would come into being for the sole purpose of choosing a president and vice-president and would dissolve when this task was accomplished.

Hamilton concluded: "The process of election affords a moral certainty that the office of President will never fall to the lot of any man who is not in an eminent degree endowed with the requisite qualifications. Talents for low intrigue and the little arts of popularity may alone suffice to elevate a man to the first honors in a single State; but it will require other talents, and a different kind of merit, to establish him in the esteem and confidence of the whole Union . . ."

II

The first two elections were the only times our nation's electoral system worked precisely as anticipated by our founding fathers. For the first, in 1789, some states had chosen their electors by popular vote, some by the state legislatures, and the rest by a combination of these two methods. New York failed to act because of a fight between the state senate and assembly while two states—Rhode Island and North Carolina—had not yet ratified the Constitution. George Washington received the unanimous vote of the electors on one of their two ballots; John Adams, with half as many votes, became vice-president. In 1792 Washington was elected to his second term by unanimous vote.

Undoubtedly, having such a widely acclaimed father of our country made the choice easier. But by 1796, the incipient Democratic-Republican Party was beginning to challenge the dominant Federalists, and Thomas Jefferson came within three electoral votes of defeating Adams. Partisanship was on its way, leading to the Jefferson-Burr victory in 1800. Since the electors had not specified which of their two ballots was for president and which for vice-president, their tie vote brought the first crisis of the electoral system and threw the contest into the House of

New York, 6th April, 1789.

Sir,

I have the honor to transmit to your Excellency the information of your unanimous election to the office of President of the United States of America. Suffer me, Sir, to indulge the hope, that so auspicious a mark of public confidence will meet your approbation, and be considered as a sure pledge of the affection and support you are to expect from a free and enlightened People.

I am, Sir, with sentiments of respect, your most obedient servant,

His Excellency
George Washington, &c.

"The first two elections were the only times our nation's electoral system worked precisely as anticipated by our founding fathers. . . . George Washington [left] received the unanimous vote of the electors on one of their two ballots; John Adams, with half as many votes, became vice-president. In 1792 Washington was elected to his second term by unanimous vote." Shown above is a letter to Washington informing him of his election as president.

Representatives. One roll call after another brought Jefferson to one vote shy of the necessary majority. Alexander Hamilton, though a staunch Federalist, made an impassioned plea to his fellow party members to support Jefferson, whom many considered a dangerous radical. "I trust the Federalists will not finally be so mad as to vote for Burr," he wrote at the time. "I speak with intimate and accurate knowledge of his character. His election can only promote the purposes of the desperate and the profligate. If there be a man in the world I ought to hate, it is Jefferson. With Burr I've always been personally well. But the public good must be paramount to every private consideration." Finally, on the thirty-sixth ballot, Jefferson prevailed.

It had been a disheartening experience in the House of Representatives. During the prolonged ordeal some sought to exploit the situation for special advantage. Jefferson wrote soon afterward, "Many attempts have been made to obtain terms and promises from me. I've declared to them unequivocally that I would not receive the Government on capitulation; that I would not go in with my hands tied." One cynical Federalist in Congress sent word to Hamilton: "The means existed of electing Burr, but this required his cooperation. By deceiving one man (a great blockhead) and tempting two (not incorruptible) he might have secured a majority of the states. He will never have another chance of being President. . . ." Instead, Burr served four years as vice-president, then, his enmity further stimulated, he challenged and killed Hamilton in a duel.

In 1804 Jefferson won reelection handily, as did successive representatives of his party, until in 1824 the Federalists did not even put up a presidential candidate, leaving four Democratic-Republican candidates to battle among themselves. This brought a different kind of crisis. When Andrew Jackson failed to receive a clear majority of electoral votes, the House of Representatives handed the victory to John Quincy Adams, who had received even fewer. Shortly before the House vote an anonymous letter was published, accusing Adams of promising to make Henry Clay secretary of state in return for his support. When Clay in fact was subsequently appointed to that Cabinet post, Jackson wrote a friend, "Was there ever witnessed such a bare-faced corruption in any country before?" The event did lasting damage to Adams's leadership. In 1828 Jackson avenged himself by winning a massive victory as head of the Democratic-Republican Party, trouncing Adams, who headed the newly formed National Republicans.

The first third of the nineteenth century brought steady movement among the states toward a standard system of choosing electors by popular vote. By 1832 only South Carolina relied on its state legislature. Other states employed the winner-take-all practice, which effectively eliminated free choice by the individual elector. Throughout U.S. history, individual states have split their electoral votes on less than a dozen occasions; the so-called "faithless elector" who breaks his pledge to a particular candidate has occurred even less frequently. Thus the Electoral College lost any pretense of being a deliberative body weighing the choice of president. Instead it has routinely, if somewhat imprecisely, reflected the outcome of the popular votes within each state. Only twice in the last century and a half—in 1876 and 1888—have the Electoral College results been different than the popular. More typically, the electoral votes exaggerate the size of the popular victory. On a number of occasions, a president has won with support of less than a majority of the voters.

The 1876 contest proved particularly unsettling to the electoral system. Early returns indicated that Tilden, the Democrat, led Hayes, the Republican, by more than a quarter million popular votes. But disputed returns in three formerly Confederate states threw the contest into the House of Representatives. The House appointed an electoral commission that voted 8 to 7, strictly according to party loyalty of its members, on each of the disputes. When the three states were assigned to Hayes, Democrats in Congress threatened to filibuster but were finally assuaged by Hayes's promise to withdraw federal troops from the South and thereby terminate the Era of Reconstruction.

Three times in this century—in 1912, 1948, and 1968—the prospect loomed of throwing the election into the House of Representatives: in 1912 former President Theodore Roosevelt tried to win a return to the White House as leader of a third party. Instead he helped Woodrow Wilson gain office with only a plurality of popular votes. In 1948 Henry Wallace and Strom Thurmond split the Democrats with third-party movements but failed to stop Harry Truman's reelection. In 1968 George Wallace (no relation to Henry) sought to become president-maker, if not president, by requiring affidavits from the electors pledged to him promising to vote for "whomsoever (Wallace) may direct." Wallace did not win enough electoral votes to prevent Richard Nixon's victory, but only a few thousand popular vote switches in border and Northern states could have made the difference.

III

In 1832 Tocqueville, after making his celebrated tour of the United States, observed: "For a long time before the appointed time has come, the election becomes the important and, so to speak, the all-engrossing topic of discussion. Factional ardor is redoubled, and all the artificial passions which the imagination can create in a happy and peaceful land are agitated and brought to light . . . It is true that as soon as the choice is determined, this ardor is dispelled, calm returns, and the river, which had nearly broken its banks, sinks to its usual level; but who can refrain from astonishment that such a storm should have arisen?"

Beyond the intent of the founding fathers, who feared the rise of "factions," the struggle for the presidency soon extended to the earlier stage of party nominations. By 1800, nominations were being made by incipient party groupings in Congress. "King Caucus" dominated candidate choice for three decades. Then, in 1831, as an expression of popular discontent, eighteen states sent delegates to the first National Republican Party Convention, which nominated Henry Clay. The Democratic Party held its first convention in May 1832, with the purpose of finding a vice-presidential candidate to replace incumbent John C. Calhoun, who had lost favor with President Jackson. Over 200 delegates from twenty-three states nominated Martin Van Buren, Jackson's hand-picked choice. That same year the Democrats adopted the unit rule, committing the whole of a state's delegation to a single candidate.

Several claims were made in favor of the institution of the party convention. It divorced nominations from congressional control, represented more directly the will of the people, and increased the independence of the nation's chief executive. Conventions helped achieve compromise among personal and regional rivalries. They brought a better formulation of the party's program. Delegates could be chosen in several ways: by state legislatures, state conventions, formal caucuses, or state party leaders. This was to remain the unbroken system of making nominations throughout the remainder of the nineteenth century. By 1876, the hard-fought rivalry of a two major party system had emerged. Republicans and Democrats went about their convention business somewhat differently. The Republican Party outlawed the unit rule of each state's delegation and never adopted a two-thirds majority requirement for nomination. Democrats kept the two-thirds requirement till 1936 and clung to the unit rule in one way or another until 1980.

IV

The Electoral College has proved remarkably impervious to change. In 1804 an amendment to the Constitution was ratified to take care of the predicament caused by the electoral tie vote in 1800. Henceforth, there would be separate electoral lists for president and vice-president. Hardly a year has passed since then without one member of Congress or another submitting other amendments for Electoral College reform. But no further changes have resulted. More recently, the close elections of 1960 and 1968, as well as Supreme Court rulings relating to apportionment and re-districting, provoked renewed interest in reform. President Nixon, in 1969, asked Congress to take prompt action on an amendment to make the Electoral College vote conform to the division of popular votes within each state. The House of Representatives promptly responded by passing a resolution to abolish the Electoral College. It would set instead forty percent of the popular vote to be sufficient for election, and provide for a runoff election between the two top contenders if neither received such a

Alexis de Tocqueville. *"In 1832 Tocqueville, after making his celebrated tour of the United States, observed: 'For a long time before the appointed time has come, the election becomes the important and, so to speak, the all-engrossing topic of discussion. Factional ardor is redoubled, and all the artificial passions which the imagination can create in a happy and peaceful land are agitated and brought to light . . . It is true that as soon as the choice is determined, this ardor is dispelled, calm returns, and the river, which had nearly broken its banks, sinks to its usual level; but who can refrain from astonishment that such a storm should have arisen?' "*

plurality. But the Senate failed to act. Both Houses of Congress failed to respond when President Carter made a similar proposal in 1977.

V

Almost from the birth of the Republic the democratic impulse in America has sought to expand the participatory process by which the president is chosen. The party nominating convention was a nineteenth-century innovation; the burgeoning of party primaries within the states came in the twentieth. In large part they represented a revolt against party bossism working in the convention's smoke-filled rooms. Party primaries began as an outcropping of the progressive movement. They were hailed as a "return to the people" and quickly spread from state and local elections to the presidential contests.

In 1901 Florida enacted the first presidential primary law. When Robert La Follette's progressive Republican delegation was rejected at the 1904 Republican Convention, he returned home and pushed through an act to establish the Wisconsin primary. This one required the direct election of delegates to the national convention. The next step—a preferential vote for president—took place in Oregon, with delegates legally bound to support the winner. By 1912, fifteen states had provided for some form of popular primary. That year former President Roosevelt won nine of twelve Republican primaries, polling approximately half again as many votes as President Taft. When the Republican Convention, reenforced by states without primaries, renominated Taft, Roosevelt broke ranks and ran as an independent Progressive.

After the initial wave of enthusiasm, interest in the primaries waned, and a number of states repealed their primary laws. Following the Second World War, however, candidates in both major parties began to cultivate such contests. By 1960, seven state primaries provided the crucial battleground for John Kennedy against Hubert Humphrey. In 1976 Democrats and Republicans conducted primary fights in thirty states. In 1980 thirty-six primary contests decided the fate of the two major party contenders and spurred a "third force" candidacy well before the nominating conventions had assembled. King Primary had clearly won dominion. Once the random jousting ground to test a candidacy already formed, the primaries have become a procrustean bed in which every candidate must be measured and molded.

National party conventions, despite their diminishing role, have doubled in delegate size over the last two decades. Growth has taken place in the formal campaigns that require more candidate miles traveled, more "events" staged earlier in the day to meet the deadline of prime-time news, and greater dependence on televised and radio commercials. At the same time, there has been shrinkage in the direct and unrehearsed confrontation between major party nominees—four televised "debates" in

1960, three in 1976, and only one between the two major contenders in 1980. James W. Ceaser, of the Woodrow Wilson Department of Government and Foreign Affairs at the University of Virginia, comments in a research paper prepared for the Twentieth Century Fund (September 1980):

In 1968, approximately 40 percent of the delegates to the conventions were chosen in primaries; the power over the nomination still rested in large measure with the leaders of the traditional party organizations. By 1980, nearly three quarters of the delegates were selected in primaries: and for all intents and purposes, the nominees were chosen by those who had elected these delegates regardless of the wish or will of the leaders of the parties.

Caucus procedures for selecting delegates in the Democratic Party were "opened" and made subject to strict national party rules. Convention delegates, most of whom retained at least the theoretical option of exercising a discretionary choice in 1968, had, for the most part, by 1980 been transformed into instructed messengers, bound to their candidates not only by state laws, but, in the case of the Democratic Party, by a controversial national rule as well. Most delegate contests in 1980 were settled in elections that allocated delegates among pledged slates in proportion to the voters' expression of candidate preference, not, as in 1968, by plurality contests in which delegates frequently ran as individuals. Finally, new Federal campaign legislation enacted in 1974 altered the methods of raising and spending funds, creating different incentives and new problems for potential and active candidates.

Taken together, these changes altered the strategic environment of the nominating process. Political parties have virtually ceased to exist; in their place are party labels, which individual aspirants now vie to capture in extended plebiscitary contests. New power centers, in particular the national media, have moved into the vacuum and assumed important functions once performed by party power-brokers. The candidates, compelled to fashion their campaign tactics to meet the new environment, now declare their candidacies earlier than before and pursue the nomination chiefly by courting the voters rather than the party leadership.

Theodore H. White, veteran chronicler of president-making, has described the transformation of this contest over such a brief time span. Among the signs of change he perceives are political bosses replaced by a new breed of professionals; disappearance of the old party hierarchies reaching downward into communities and neighborhoods; media market maps hanging alongside electoral charts in the campaign command posts, which are usually quite distant from party headquarters; carefully focused ethnic and special interest appeals. The candidate moves in a "cocoon"

Candidate John Kennedy listens attentively to candidate Richard Nixon's remarks during one of the celebrated 1960 television debates. Moderator, Frank McGee, sits between them. *"There has been shrinkage in the direct and unrehearsed confrontation between major party nominees—four televised 'debates' in 1960, three in 1976, and only one between the two major contenders in 1980. . . . Now*

that the TV set has become the hearthstone of the American home, it remains a
valuable ideal for the presidential finalists to engage in direct encounters so that
the citizens can watch, make comparative judgments, and be encouraged to
exercise voter choice. But a single clash . . . having the aspects of a sudden-
death football playoff, makes mockery of such an ideal.''

of police and secret service agents, further surrounded by reporters who have grown into "the mob that overwhelms its story."

Basic changes of law and regulation have contributed to the transformation. Abolition of the unit rule for state delegations at nominating conventions intensifies the fierce struggle in every primary and caucus. Party rules and court decisions reenforce the growing demand for minority group quotas among the delegates. Financing reforms impose requirements for full reporting, with tight ceilings on individual contributions and even tighter limits on candidate funds to be matched by federal subsidy. An unintended consequence has been the prodigious growth of Political Action Committees (PACs)—by tenfold in numbers—over the past eight years. Supreme Court ruling allows the PACs to support candidates outside the federal spending quotas so long as they maintain independent status from candidate and party. In the opinion of Gus Tyler, Assistant President, International Ladies' Garment Workers' Union, New York, who is a student of campaign finance:

"The Supreme Court's interpretation of the First Amendment is that anyone may run a campaign for anyone at any time so long as the sponsor is doing so independently of the candidate. So, no matter what the law says, my friends and I have the right to raise money, raise the flag, and raise Hell to promote a particular candidacy."

In early 1982 a commission established by the Miller Center at the University of Virginia and including a number from both main parties offered this perceptive analysis:

> Taken together these changes dramatically altered the strategic environment of the nominating campaigns and changed the way in which candidates could seek to become their party's presidential candidate. The power of state and local party organizations and of elected party officials also greatly diminished between 1960 and 1980; in their place stand the national party labels which the individual aspirants now seek to capture by strategies of intimate village politics in the first contests (Iowa and New Hampshire) and by mass popular appeals thereafter. New power centers, in particular the national media, have moved into this vacuum and have come to exercise considerable influence over the outcome of the nominating decision. The candidates, obliged to fashion their campaign tactics to suit this new environment, think chiefly in terms of activating certain mass constituencies and pay less attention to negotiating and forging links with party leaders. The knowledge that voters, not delegates, will decide the results, combined with the time-consuming task of raising money in small sums to qualify for public financing, has forced candidates to begin their active campaigns much earlier than before. The media and public follow these developments, extending the active campaign for so long that public interest can give way to public apathy.
>
> Considering these changes with hindsight, it might be imagined that they were part of a single, comprehensive plan to transform the

nominating process. In fact, this was not the case. The changes were undertaken by different authorities—national parties, state parties, state governments, and the federal government—acting at different times under differing impulses. Frequently, they were reacting to each others' decisions. Yet as often as not they were misinterpreting each other's intentions or responding to consequences that had been neither desired nor foreseen. So the system we have now is more the result of unintended consequences and mutual miscalculations than deliberate design. Moreover, no one claims responsibility for this system because no one ever wanted it to be as cumbersome, complex, and confusing as it is.

Nor does the nominating process reflect a consensus on the part of party officials or political leaders. In actuality, no two presidential campaigns since 1968 have been conducted under the *same* rules and laws. No sooner has one nominating campaign ended than legislators and party officials have initiated modifications for the next one. The effort to change the nominating process today cannot, therefore, be depicted as a threat to a settled institutional system. On the contrary it is another—although quite different—step in a continuing search to solve a problem that has vexed American politics for more than a decade.

Many of the recent changes have, of course, represented indisputable improvements. Certain undemocratic abuses in the selection of delegates, offensive to proponents of any legitimate system, have been abolished; groups, notably blacks and women, that in some instances were effectively shut out of·participation in the process have been included; and the pall of illegal campaign contributions and excessive financial dependence on a few sources has been lifted.

Yet the system as a whole, despite these improvements, has proven unsatisfactory. In testimony after testimony, the Commission heard the same litany of unstinting criticism: that the active public phase of presidential campaigns is too long, diverting the attention of the public and political leaders from the business of governing the nation; that the democratic appearance of the decision-making process is often specious, with participation low and with many voting after the nomination decision has already been made; that there are too many incentives for candidates to create factional divisions within the parties and not enough to promote consensus; and that the rules of campaign finance produce unnecessary burdens for the candidates and interfere too greatly with the expression of natural political forces.

VI

In the estimate of Austin Ranney, a scholar of presidential campaigns, "Presidential politics has become, in substance if not in form, something closely approaching a no-party system." Ranney speculates about the consequence during the 1980s: "The Republic would not have collapsed, at least not right away. The party labels would persist for a while and serve as cures for the dwindling number of voters for whom they were still meaningful. The candidate organizations, the women's caucuses, the black caucuses, the Right-to-Life leagues and the like would become the only real players in the game. The mass communication media would become the sole agencies for sorting out the finalists from the original entrants and for defining the voters' choices. And the societal functions of interest-aggregation, consensus-building, and civil war-prevention would presumably be left to the schools, the churches, and perhaps Common Cause and Nader's Raiders. Would they perform those functions as well as the parties? At the moment we can only guess the answer. But perhaps we shall learn it from first-hand experience in the 1980s."

It may be useful to examine the "best case" and the "worst case" arguments made about what has happened to the presidential selection process:

Best Case: The effort to extend citizen participation in the presidential contest represents a triumph of citizen democracy over the "elitism" of both the original electoral college and the party bossism of the old nominating conventions. The party primary offers an effective franchise to minorities hitherto lacking a genuine voice in politics. We approach the quadrennial event with confident expectations that the election will take place on schedule and a verdict will be rendered without excessive riot or bloodshed. The nation can be expected to close ranks behind its chosen leader in reasonably good spirit. No other free society has sustained such an accomplishment over so long a period.

Inevitably, according to the "best case," the way we choose leaders must adapt to the changing environment. Highways, railroads, airplanes—each brought basic change to the electoral process. The electronic revolution now tranforms the way we communicate politically. It brings the contest directly into every household and provides information to many more millions than in the past. Despite the frenzy of the extended campaign, larger numbers of citizens are getting greater opportunity to judge their candidates.

In an ideal republic one could perhaps devise superior ways for enabling the citizen to make these judgments. But the democratic contest is not a tidy business. The skillful marshaling of campaign resources and the disciplined uses of energy over such a long contest provide a reasonably good measure of leadership capacities. The primary has opened the contest to candidates lacking entrenched support or national name recognition. It has shaken up the hardened bureaucracy of politics.

Granted that the long road leading from primary to national convention to formal campaign to election is a grueling one for the candidates, yet those who go along on the campaign trail sense a certain rationale. For one thing, the many hurdles demand of the one who would be leader that he prove himself equipped physically and temperamentally to sustain the rigor of that high office. As Woodrow Wilson, prior to his own presidency, remarked, "Men of ordinary physique and discretion cannot be Presidents and live. . . . We shall be obliged always to be picking our chief magistrates from among wise and prudent athletes,—a small class." Also there is logic in the campaign's testing of how well a candidate can mobilize the resources that are essential. A president must become accustomed to dealing with men and money in large quantities and must also be capable of winning the kind of support that money and party loyalty alone cannot buy. One detects amid all the hurly-burly of campaigning a mysterious communion which establishes for the president-to-be closer ties with the people.

Worst Case: The worst case takes longer to describe. It holds that the presidential election contest, carried to its present excesses, no longer serves its intended purposes: It discourages tested leaders from entering the arena while it attracts inexperienced ones; it substitutes hasty handshakes and even hastier campaign rhetoric for what should be a sober and serious dialogue; it reveals a candidate's adaptability to expert manipulation but fails to measure his capacity to offer genuine leadership in times of challenge and crisis. By its marathon length and frenetic activities, it diverts the nation's attention from the serious business of governing. Within the highly charged partisan atmosphere during at least eighteen months out of every forty-eight, immeasurable damage is being done to U.S. relations with friends and foes alike.

Primary campaign demands are tending to limit the arena to the "professional candidate" who has few responsibilities to distract him from total immersion in the contest. The protracted primary season erects high barriers against any who postpone entering the competition to a later stage, effectively discouraging those who already hold demanding jobs. Pollster predictions, urgently publicized by the media, dismiss worthy contenders while the fight is still raging and effectively close off their opportunities for funding and support.

It is a curious contest in which the professional candidate must make his way. No athletic competition could be conducted with so much variation of rules from one state to another. A contestant is proclaimed by the media to have won a "landslide" victory in a particular state even when his vote margin may be counted in only a few thousands. Delegate slates, mandated to a particular candidate by a small fraction of the electorate, determine the nomination before the nominating convention actually meets. Media hype transforms the marathon into a combination horse race and Super Bowl as reporters proclaim who is winning and losing and solemnly announce the victor before voters finish going to the polls. All this tempts even the most conscientious contender to engage in cynical manipulations.

Consider the "worst case" of how the professional candidate must spend his time. Long before he declares his ambition openly, he must reach the audacious conviction that he ought to be president. Gone is the time for leisurely courtship of a reluctant prospect by his peers. He must have convinced himself and, if he is truly professional, must never entertain second thoughts as he charts the obstacle course ahead of him. There is no longer a gestation period when the candidate can quietly brood about how to fill a job grown exponentially more difficult during recent decades.

The professional candidate must not risk his chances by recruiting colleagues to share the burden of forming a government. Even the choice of running mate must be delayed unless sudden campaign exigencies dictate the publicity need to announce one in advance. The candidate plays a lonely game. He must reconcile himself to endless recital of his name and ambition, selling himself to every faction and single-interest group, while revealing as little as possible the substance of his prospective leadership. He would be foolish to waste much personal time in preparing the lengthy position papers issued *pro forma* to the media with little expectation that they will be seriously examined or communicated. That task can be delegated to subordinates. He must marshal his energies for the staging of events that will attract media attention. He cultivates the grass roots as one more stage setting in which to make his pitch for the precious moments of evening television coverage. He garners on the road the raw material to be shaped into campaign commercials. Much like the professional actor before his mirror, he must engage in absorbing preoccupation with his "image," recomposing word and gesture as well as hair and dress style to communicate such fundamental virtues as sincerity, determination, invincibility. He must be a quick student of the occult practices of image making. And he must never, never display doubt that he has the answer to every conceivable issue confronting a world in crisis.

Campaign priorities divorce him from strong party ties, make him a loner. Even as he is less beholden to others, so are they to him. Once elected, his support has shallow roots. He is required to be a performer on the high wire without reliable party backing or enduring coalitions. Through good times and bad, he is at the mercy of public opinion grown increasingly volatile in rendering swift judgment on his performance.

The "worst case" derides the notion that the hyperbolic campaign engages the serious interest of the citizen. While greater numbers may participate in volunteer activities during the primaries, they constitute only a handful of the electorate and are heavily weighted with single-issue zealots. Against them stand the dismal statistics of voter turnout. Not quite a third of those who actually voted in the 1980 general elections cast their ballots in the primaries. Only 54 percent of the franchised population cast a presidential ballot, representing a steady decline since 1960. In an era when television brings the contest into almost every living room, the nagging concern of politics is citizen apathy. The widespread discontent with the nominating process adds opportunity for the independent candidates who, unlikely of election success, increase the possibility that no candidate will achieve an electoral majority. This, in turn, raises the spectre of the contest being thrown into the House of Representatives where, by Constitutional edict, each state delegation, large or small, casts a single ballot—a divisive and undemocratic procedure. The prospect that only a minority of a minority in Congress will end up picking the chief executive poses a serious challenge to our nation's capacity to produce a credible mandate.

Finally, the "worst case" argues that the evolution toward the permanent campaign in the United States does grave damage to the nation's leadership. The evidence is most clear in the condition of our international enterprises. Friend and foe have become accustomed to lowered expectations during our traditional election period. But their capacity for understanding now grows strained, more especially when one of the candidates is the incumbent president. They read the news dispatches describing each move of the U.S. government in terms of cynical campaign strategy. Even crisis management of foreign affairs becomes hostage to the maneuvering for partisan advantage. There are no ground rules to impose restraints on the unseemly contest. The results can be measured in alliances weakened, opportunities neglected, peacekeeping stalled, and war risks heightened. For indefinite intervals, a great nation lies exposed and vulnerable.

VII

Within both the major parties there has risen concern of late over the shortcomings of the electoral process. But concern is tempered with caution, for it is realized that earlier reforms have had unintended consequences resulting in some of the contemporary excesses. The present tyranny of party primaries grew out of reformist zeal to combat bossism in the conventions. The efforts to put limits on direct campaign spending and to provide federal funding have led to a diversion of private contributions to political action committees in pursuit of special interests. Any further reforms in the process by which we choose our presidents should proceed with care.

A recent report by the Commission on Presidential Nomination, authorized by the 1980 Democratic National Convention, voiced alarm over contemporary conditions: "half of the new generation of voters declaring themselves 'independent' of party, increased ticket splitting at all levels, irregular patterns of cohesion in Congressional and legislative voting. . . . Executives and legislators alike have too often chosen to 'go it alone' electorally. . . . Party politics—the politics of personal contact, deliberative judgment, coalition and compromise—have too often been replaced by remote-control campaigns, single-issue crusades, and faceless government. The traditional role of party—as a mediating institution between citizens and government, as a guide to consistent and rational electoral choice, as a bond pulling the elements of government together

A typical scene on Election Day 1960. A gymnasium temporarily converted into a polling place, lines of voters, and harried election officials. *"While greater numbers may participate in volunteer activities during the primaries, they constitute only a handful of the electorate and are heavily weighted with single-issue zealots. Against*

them stand the dismal statistics of voter turnout. Not quite a third of those who actually voted in the 1980 general elections cast their ballots in the primaries. Only 54 percent of the franchised population cast a presidential ballot, representing a steady decline since 1960.''

for the achievement of positive purposes—no longer seems secure."

This commission, named after its chairman, Governor Hunt of North Carolina, issued a number of recommendations designed to build increased strength and public confidence in the presidential nominating process. It is expected that the Republican National Committee will proceed in a similar manner.

Among the Hunt Commission recommendations, one is to bring elected and party leadership more effectively into the nomination process. In 1968, 68 percent of the Democratic senators and 83 percent of Democratic governors were convention delegates or alternates. In 1976 the number of governors had fallen by half; of the senators, by nearly three-fourths. "Only 14 percent of our Democratic Senators, 15 percent of our House members, and a handful of our big-city Mayors participated as voting delegates at the 1980 Convention." Pressures have effectively driven away from the convention the party's regular leadership. The Hunt Commission proposed an increase in the 1984 convention of more than 550 seats specifically for unpledged delegates drawn from party and elected officials, some of these to be named by the House and Senate Democratic Caucuses.

In brief, the Hunt Commission would enlarge the number of party leaders from 8 percent to 22 percent of the entire convention; of the unpledged, to slightly over 14 percent. The purpose would be to increase "the convention's *representativeness* of mainstream Democratic constituencies. It would help restore *peer review* to the process, subjecting candidates to scrutiny by those who know them best. It would put a premium on coalition building within the Party prior to nomination, the forming of alliances that would help us campaign and govern effectively. It would strengthen the party ties . . . and the presence of unpledged delegates would help restore decisionmaking discretion and flexibility to the Convention."

Increasing the convention's unpledged party leaders would counterbalance the small number of voters in the state primaries who can now commit slates of delegates pledged to a particular candidate well before most voters are prepared to make such a choice. (In 1976, 26.4 million voted in primaries, compared to 81.6 million in the November elections.) Allowing a substantial number of delegates to remain unpledged ("thinking delegates," in the description of former Governor Terry Sanford) would help transform the convention into a deliberative rather than rubber-stamp forum. While the Hunt Commission would retain existing rules to govern the selection of pledged delegates, it recommends loosening the present bind on these delegates and substituting the more general provision that delegates "in all good conscience reflect the sentiments of those who elected them." The delegate's first loyalty would be to his constituency, not to his candidate.

The Hunt Commission makes a series of proposals to broaden participation and maintain a fair and open process. All state primaries would be
obliged to operate within similar rules, including a flat ban on participation by non-Democrats. National party policy should be to "encourage
more states to shift from primaries to caucuses so that a better overall balance might result."

The trend toward "front loading" of delegate selection—i.e., the competition among the states to hold primaries and caucuses earlier than
others—has stretched out the nominating process. In 1972 only 17 percent of the delegates had been elected by mid-April; in 1980, 44 percent
were. To prevent locking up the nomination prematurely, the Hunt Commission would set rules that no primary or caucus be held before the
second Tuesday in March or after the second Tuesday in June. (Iowa and
New Hampshire would be allowed their traditional lead-off privilege, but
by only a week or two before the rest.) This three-month "window" for
the primaries would shorten the pre-convention season considerably.
State primaries would likely be grouped in clusters on successive Tues-
days. It would reduce the excessive publicizing of triumph or defeat in a
single state's returns and might even reduce the media's preoccupation
with candidate tactics while encouraging increased attention to the more
substantive contest.

Delaying the onset of the primaries may handicap the "unknown"
candidate seeking to build name recognition. The present marathon
clearly works to screen out "known" political leaders who might otherwise be attracted.

The Hunt Commission does not propose to change the mushrooming
size of the national party convention. Indeed, its proposed add-on would
enlarge the overall number of delegates to 3,850 (550 more than in
1980). This would put "some strain on convention logistics and facilities
but not, we are assured, an intolerable burden." Others would argue that
by reducing its size and enlarging its serious purposes, the convention
might become more credible as a deliberative institution. Party conventions in other Western democracies manage to avoid circus atmosphere.
In Great Britain, cabinet officers as well as other party leaders remain on
the platform throughout most of the proceedings, engaging freely in the
give and take of debate. American conventions could be usefully scaled
down from Valhalla dimensions, with robust dialogue substituting for
stupefying monologue. Perhaps it might cause TV to pay more attention
to the main events rather than to seek out offstage buffoonery and dissi-
dence. To enhance the party convention as an important instrument of
decision-making requires that the citizen, watching from his hearthside,
get a better appreciation of its seriousness of purpose. It is time that the
transforming role of television coverage is better evaluated and
accommodated.

VIII

Some persons favor establishing a single nationwide primary as the most democratic way of exercising the popular choice. This would represent a radical extension of the so-called grass roots control over the nominating process and further erode the role of the party delegates gathered in national convention. Even if not absolutely binding, it would amount to a plebiscite, influenced heavily by "the little arts of popularity" and would weaken the effort of party leaders to reach consensus on the nominee best able to be elected and to govern.

A different, if equally radical, approach to the nominating process— labeled "approval voting"—would permit primary voters to select as many candidates as they wish in a multi-candidate contest. This would encourage citizens who have not reached a final decision on a single candidate. The tabulated votes might reveal that Candidate C has greater strength among the electorate than Candidate A even though A might have received a larger plurality in a single-choice election. Steven J. Brams, a proponent of "approval voting," argues that it will be a twentieth-century reform comparable in importance to the Australian, or secret, ballot in the election reforms of the nineteenth century. When applied to party primaries, it would prevent the premature hardening of nominee selection and enlarge the deliberative role of the party nominating convention.

IX

While the Hunt Commission limits its proposals to the nominating process, others suggest that the formal campaign period could become a more meaningful contest for presidential leadership. Perhaps the most persistent proposal is to relax or repeal the "equal time" provision of the Federal Communications Act in order to allow increased and more varied broadcast programming devoted to the electoral contest.

The autumn campaign would benefit if electronic communication were to take the place, in larger degree, of frantic jet-hopping. How many citizens actually manage to glimpse the nominees in the flesh or hear more than perfervid snatches of stump oratory? Touring the vast continent is a vital part of the total campaign, but it cannot be the substitute for essential development of argument. Televised forums, documentaries, and genuine debates have the potential, if utilized, for creating a Greek marketplace of political dialogue.

Now that the TV set has become the hearthstone of the American home, it remains a valuable ideal for the presidential finalists to engage in direct encounters so that the citizens can watch, make comparative judgments, and be encouraged to exercise voter choice. But a single clash between the two major party nominees, as in 1980, having the aspects of a sudden-death football playoff, makes mockery of such an ideal. More enduring ground rules must be established for such debates. Among them might be:

— to eliminate the journalist-interrogators, or at least minimize their role, allowing the debaters to determine for themselves how to square off;

— to provide adequate response time when the opponents challenge each other's facts and memories;

— to refrain from pronouncing instant verdicts that have the effect of turning the debate into simply another sports event.

Critics charge that debates provide inadequate measure of a candidate's capacity for leadership and that there is strong temptation for blatant demagogy before the nationwide audiences they attract. One can concede these points without abandoning the effort for genuine debate. What are alternative ways by which most citizens can manage to get a revealing view of those who seek to be their leader? The post-debate polling evidence is strong that viewers are judging how the candidates handle themselves under stress, not measuring all the fine points of forensic skill.

Televised debates can be valuable only in the context of much fuller television coverage dedicated to the presidential campaign. Removing "equal time" restrictions on the broadcasters will provide them a good-faith challenge to offer such a forum. This, in turn, may slow the growth of political "commercials." Some social scientists maintain that the sixty-second spot advertisement contains more information bits than the longer candidate speeches. But it is doubtful that democracy is served by information bits honed and polished so that they penetrate our consciousness without straining our thought processes. In that direction lies George Orwell's vision of 1984. It will require a great deal of maturity on the part of candidates, the media, and, above all, the public if electronic communication is to restore president-making to a less manipulative and a more human dimension.

X

At the end of the election road, should we reform or abolish the Electoral College? Critics of the Electoral College claim that it is unrepresentative to allot a state's entire electoral vote to a nominee who wins only a bare plurality of the popular vote. By capturing a few key states, a candidate can win with fewer popular votes than his opponent. John Quincy Adams, Rutherford B. Hayes, and Benjamin Harrison won the presidency while losing the popular election. Woodrow Wilson, Harry Truman, and John F. Kennedy received more votes than their chief opponents yet won by less than 50 percent of the total.

Among the approaches to reform, one proposes to select electors in each state by congressional districts, with two running at large, in conformity with the state's delegation to Congress. Supporters talk of achieving "balance and symmetry in the political roots of the government of the

John Quincy Adams

"At the end of the election road, should we reform or abolish the Electoral College? Critics of the Electoral College claim that it is unrepresentative to allot a state's entire electoral vote to a nominee who wins only a bare plurality of the popular vote. By capturing a few key states, a candidate can win with fewer popular votes than his opponent." Shown here are the three men in U.S. history who won the presidency while losing the popular election.

Benjamin Harrison

Rutherford B. Hayes

United States." But what they would really do is to fix the same bias in the presidency that exists in Congress, giving added strength to the rural-agricultural populations now over-represented in the House of Representatives. Instead of the power belonging to the key "swing" states, this system would allocate power according to the gerrymandering of the state legislatures. Presidential nominees would probably end up vying over the size of the farm subsidy.

A second proposal for reform is to apportion each state's electoral vote in accordance with its popular vote, an idea which at various times has attracted both liberals and conservatives in Congress. Former Senator Henry Cabot Lodge of Massachusetts, who ran as the Republican vice-presidential nominee in 1960, was a sponsor of such a Constitutional amendment. The late Senator Estes Kefauver, liberal Democrat from Tennessee, argued that it would contribute to progress in the South by invigorating the two-party system. Former Representative Ed Gossett, a conservative Democrat from Texas, predicted flatly that the Civil War would have been avoided had the amendment been in effect. It passed the Senate and was headed for passage in the House when Gossett publicly extolled the curbs it would impose on the National Association for the Advancement of Colored People and other agents of minority groups. As a result, Northern congressmen in droves turned against the amendment.

When the Lodge-Gossett reform came before the Senate a second time, Senator John F. Kennedy was among the principal opponents who succeeded in defeating it. His was a prophetic fight. If the amendment had been in effect in 1960, according to one careful estimate, Kennedy would have won 286.871 electoral votes and Nixon (with his running mate Lodge) 265.036. But the tabulation does not account for the likelihood that a third-party movement in the South, with the added hope of success, would have drawn a great many additional electoral votes away from the Democratic ticket. Even had Kennedy not lost, the outcome might have been in doubt for a considerable period of time. As one analyst commented shortly after the election, "The country might drift in torment and indecision for weeks while handfuls of votes were counted and recounted and the electoral vote then recomputed."

One other proposed reform keeps recurring: to eliminate the Electoral College and substitute nationwide popular elections. But this stands little chance of serious consideration, for the less populous rural states would never ratify an amendment giving added weight to the mass vote of the big cities. Probably that is for the best, since a nominee soliciting a purely popular mandate might be less concerned about reconciling the nation's sectional differences. The demagogue playing to the mob would have new incentives.

Contemplating the possibilities of the various Electoral College reforms leads to a defense of the status quo. There should be curbs on the elector's capacity to disregard his mandate, but to alter the system radically in a misguided effort to create "balance and symmetry in the political roots" would be Constitutional quackery. A president has reason to draw his inspiration from somewhat different roots than the Congress. It is fitting that he be obliged to show special concern for the underdog groups of the nation who congregate in our cities. His efforts to reconcile the treatment of these groups with the nation's ideals has seldom failed to contribute to the public well-being. The politics of the Electoral College is useful education for presidents.

Lord Bryce, describing The American Commonwealth seventy years ago, thought it proper to include a chapter inquiring "Why Great Men are not Chosen Presidents." He raised the question without much feeling of distress since, as he maintained, "four-fifths of his [the President's] work is the same in kind as that which devolves on the chairman of a commercial company or the manager of a railway, the work of choosing good subordinates, seeing that they attend to their business, and taking a sound practical view of such administrative questions as require his decision." Few American or foreign observers would adopt such a complacent attitude today. We live in an age when the hourly judgments of the man who holds the White House office can shape the future of all mankind—even determine whether mankind has a future.

XI

In Tibet, upon the death of the Dalai Lama, who is both spiritual and temporal leader, the priests commence a search for the infant boy to whom his soul has migrated. This weird and wonderful quest may go on for years. To the Westerner it is a highly mystical way of selecting a new head of government. Yet one might wonder whether a truly impartial observer would judge the American method of choosing a president any less mystical.

The election of 1984 began shortly after the polls closed in 1980. In secret places, the president-making cadres—money raisers, media experts, public opinion specialists, voter analysts, direct mail solicitors, et al—were gearing up. The candidates, consulting raw ambition and brute stamina, were deciding to take the plunge. For we have entered the age of the perpetual campaign in which, to borrow Henry Kissinger's wry description, "Only unemployed egomaniacs can afford to stand for the Presidency." From spokesmen at all points of the political spectrum have come expressions of outrage that picking the president should have reached such a hyperbolic condition.

One of the more thoughtful analysts of the American presidency, Richard E. Neustadt, wrote shortly before the 1980 election: "I agree with the 'worst case' analysis. Indeed, I take the worst case, in this instance, to be the reasonably likely one: Professional candidates, campaigning almost permanently in a mode quite unlike governing, spell cumulative trouble for a political system always prone—as Austin Ranney keeps reminding

"Art Buchwald, satirist, put the proposition succinctly when he wrote that unless Americans gather together every four years to choose a leader, the country will revert to the Indians. Buchwald was attempting to explain that there is more to our electoral process than choosing a president; in a mystic way, our nationhood itself comes up for reaffirmation."

us—to civil war and now under the constant, if repressed, threat also of a nuclear war by mutual miscalculation.

"Ours is a Constitutional monarchy, a real one, not a mere symbol; and it is as though hereditary chemistry condemned us to a series of defective kings. This is precisely what Republican institutions ought to spare us. It should not be beyond the wit of man to make them serve."

The essential choice is whether to move still further in the direction of direct democracy or to restore an appropriate balance for representative democracy. The electronic age encourages the notion that each citizen can learn and pass judgment for himself, so why interpose power brokers between him and decision-making? By 1984, if we push this concept and utilize new communications technology, we could conduct our plebiscites from the comfort of our homes without even going to the poll. The cynic could argue that we would not need a president, simply a daily tabulator of the people's mandate.

Once the "tumult and disorder" of the election pass, there is widespread disposition to forget our discontents. Why bother to change the nominating process? In the latest election, a decisive victory was declared even though the victor received the support of only 27 percent of the voting age population. More than 46 out of 100 potential voters failed to go to the polls. If the present no-show trend continues, we will soon exceed the halfway mark of citizen apathy.

How do we explore the options before we are once again locked into the marathon leading to the presidential elections? Sound public policy will be best served by the widest possible citizen debate. But it will also require the establishment of common cause among party and elected leaders. They will be obliged to examine anew the ancient tension between representative and direct democracy.

How well does the marathon selection process work, not only in selecting the wise and able leader but also in conditioning him for the job ahead? The increase not merely in cost but in the "tumult and disorder" of the modern campaign is leading to a preposterous situation. The tempo has become so frantic that genuine doubt arises whether the nominees can stand the pace.

This is not a condition to be remedied simply by statute. The greater restraints must be imposed by a public philosophy that frowns on the excesses and penalizes those who commit them. There must be wider recognition of what we are trying to accomplish as we run the candidates over the hurdles. We must be aware that the way in which we select a president not only determines who he will be but also helps shape the fundamental philosophy of leadership brought to that high office.

Art Buchwald, satirist, put the proposition succinctly when he wrote that unless Americans gather together every four years to choose a leader, the country will revert to the Indians. Buchwald was attempting to explain that there is more to our electoral process than choosing a president; in a mystic way, our nationhood itself comes up for reaffirmation.

In the way we pick our president, we will be determining for the future how well we rule our nation. To continue along the prevailing course will confront this nation with a perpetual campaign in which the quest to choose someone to govern does fundamental damage to the increasingly difficult task of governing.

Climate: Yesterday, Today, and Tomorrow

F. Kenneth Hare

F. Kenneth Hare is a geographer and environmental scientist who has long been active in movements to protect and conserve nature, and to understand how the natural environment works. His special interests include world climate, notably its future course as carbon dioxide builds up in the atmosphere. In 1977 he chaired a federal study group on nuclear waste management in Canada and has also been involved in the question in the Swedish program and in the United Nations Environment Programme. He has just finished a twelve-year term as a director of the Washington-based energy research organization, Resources for the Future, Inc., and has served briefly on the advisory committee of the Electric Power Research Institute. He is currently provost of Trinity College, Toronto, and chairman of the the Climate Planning Board of Canada.

English by birth and early education, Dr. Hare has been a citizen of Canada since 1951 and is an Officer of the Order of Canada. He holds the Patron's Medal of the Royal Geographical Society, the Massey Medal, and six honorary degress.

I f it be true," wrote Montesquieu, "that the character of the mind, and the passions of the heart are extremely different in different climates, the laws ought to be relative both to the differences of those passions, and to the differences of those characters." This creature of the Enlightenment can be said to have foreseen the north-south dialogue, as we now misleadingly call the conflict between rich and poor nations. It is still true, as it was in Montesquieu's day, that the rich nations live in the cool mid-latitudes, and the poor in the warmer tropics. There are still commentators who echo Montesquieu's remarks, though every serious investigator would reject them. Determinism is an easy fashion to follow.

The political view of climate has always been tentative and jejune. There is much awareness of climate today, among laymen and professionals alike. Yet that concern rarely penetrates the political mind. Climate is a neglected factor at both national and international levels. It is also ignored by most social scientists. At the recent World Climate Conference, sponsored by the U.N., but organized by the scientific community, it proved almost impossible to persuade ranking economists and sociologists to take part—even though the conference was about climatic impact, and not climate itself.

What accounts for the neglect? My tentative answer is twofold. The first part says that climatology is a physical science, which social scientists and politicians find it hard to grasp. The second part, and probably the more critical one, holds that uncertainty about climate is so great that even politicians, expert in handling confusion, cannot see a practical way of dealing with it. Droughts, floods, searing heat and congealing cold come upon us unannounced. If we could predict them—and so far we cannot—politicians would be forced to act. Meanwhile inaction can prevail; democratic politics easily becomes the art of avoiding action.

If politics and climate do not readily mix (and we shall argue this further), technology and climate interact rather nicely. A large part of human technology is adaptation to climate—not only to the ordinary events of the humdrum day but to the violent excesses served up on the rare occasion. All farmers are applied climatologists, and often very good ones. So are marine and aircraft navigators, architects and civil engineers, tailors and shoesmiths. Even though mankind has retreated indoors for so much of its livelihood and daily living, it still adapts to climate. It does so implicitly. Climate is taken for granted. The measures we take to exploit it (like using the right crops), or to protect ourselves against it (like insulating houses), are not called climatology. Substitute the word *climatology* for *treason*, and Sir John Harington put it exactly:

> Treason doth never prosper, what's the reason?
> Why, if it prosper, none dare call it treason!

From time to time, of course, a climatic extreme overwhelms us, and we suffer accordingly. We are not foolproof against climate's extraordinary variability. There are cultivators in north Africa and western Asia who optimistically plant their little patches even when experience tells them that there will be enough rain for harvest in only two or three years in five. Even these hardy souls are not proof against five rainless years in a row. If the worst happens, they abandon the land and move on. They rarely die now-a-days; relief schemes catch up with them in time, though not always. In the same way the wandering herdsmen, whom we now call nomadic pastoralists, may lose their herds to thirst or, far more often, starvation; but they themselves will generally survive. In fact the simple societies of the desert margin have an extraordinary capacity for life. In part the key is stoicism in the face of what they see as inevitable—the classic fatalism of many religions. But it is also a function of their hidden versatility—the ability to improvise alternatives, the freedom from costly impedimenta. Adaptability in the face of harsh climates has involved buying mobility at the cost of permanence—and thereby acquiring another sort of permanence.

Western societies react differently. We, too, lose our crops from time to time, though rarely our herds. But we are not, generally speaking, vulnerable subsistence farmers. Our agriculture sends its produce into an intricate commodity and food system, one of whose functions is to supply international trade. Elaborate technical and financial institutions stand between the farmer and failure. It was not always so. The droughts of the 1930s caused much suffering and abandonment of land. The institutions created to combat the drought—like the U.S. Soil Conservation Service, and Canada's Prairie Farm Rehabilitation Administration—have in many cases survived. They were the forerunners of the elaborate agricultural support system of today. We now accept the cost of climatic anomalies and keep the farmer on his land (which we also protect).

The old apathy about climate has begun to recede. All of a sudden, about 1972 or 1973, public curiosity and anxiety began to show themselves. The 1970s turned out to be the first decade in four in which climate made headlines. This is not mere rhetoric. Michael Harrison, of the Institute for Environmental Studies in the University of Toronto, has analyzed the column area devoted to climate in several major journals. That area increased fivefold or tenfold in a year or two in the early 1970s, reaching peaks between 1974 and 1976 in the *New York Times* and the

London *Times,* and holding at high levels into 1981. *Science,* the newspaper of professional science, peaked a little later, but the professional journals of the meteorologists and geologists were in step with the daily press. In other words, both the public news media and the technical literature awoke to climate in a striking fashion. The awareness still flourishes, as this essay proves.

There are now the beginnings of a literature about climate's role in human affairs. The earlier tradition cast this problem into a deterministic mold, very much in the wake of Montesquieu. The writings of Ellen Churchill Semple, Ellsworth Huntington, Griffith Taylor, and S. F. Markham were all in this tradition. They were exalted in tone, wide in reference, and largely lacking in the empirical proofs that we now demand. Within the past few years, however, more prosaic commentaries in book form have multiplied, mostly written by concerned scientists rather than by specialists on public affairs. The list includes LeRoy Ladurie's *Times of Feast, Times of Famine,* based essentially on monastic records of the date of planting the vine, and a remarkable attempt to explain the rise and fall of Harappā and Mycenae in *Climates of Hunger,* by Reid Bryson and T. J. Murray. Both books looked backward, but both were seen as bearing on our present situation.

The Genesis Strategy, by Stephen Schneider and Lynne Mesirow, brought matters up to date. The book summarized the state of the art in the atmospheric sciences, but a main thrust was to accuse the staff of the U.S. Department of Agriculture of ignoring warnings from their climatological brethren. The food crisis of 1973–74, in the wake of widespread, climatically-caused harvest failures in 1972–73, was due, they said, to an unwillingness to take adequate account of climatic factors in estimating world grain supplies. Much the same message came in *Food, Climate and Man,* edited by A. K. and M. R. Biswas. LeRoy Ladurie is a French historian, R. A. Bryson and S. H. Schneider are U.S. meteorologists, and A. K. and M. R. Biswas are Canadians specializing in environmental and resource issues. In other words, the books came, not from agriculturalists, not from political commentators, but from scientists close to atmospheric concerns. If climate was now big news, it was not the students of food production who were proclaiming the fact.

Now that the focus of interest has shifted into the future, the trickle of books continues. Much of it has come from Boulder, Colorado, where the National Center for Atmospheric Research (NCAR) now employs social scientists to investigate climate's role in public affairs. Michael Glantz, for example, has edited or written useful analyses of the Sahelian drought, and of natural resource issues generally. *The Climate Mandate,* by Walter Orr Roberts and Henry Lansford, spells out the obligation that lies on professional consciences in this area. Most recently, W. W. Kellogg and Roger Schware have collaborated in *Climate Change and Society,* which deals with how, in the future, we may adapt to the carbon dioxide effect. Of this list Roberts and Kellogg are atmospheric scientists associated with NCAR. Glantz and Schware are political scientists. Gradually the urge to write about climate is spreading.

It took a phone call from John Van Doren to make me pick up my own pen again. Like Roberts, Kellogg, Bryson, and Schneider, I am an atmospheric scientist who has tried to call public attention to what I see as a dangerous gap in political awareness. I have not lacked for invitations. I wrote the climatic background paper for the U.N. Conference on Desertification held in Nairobi in 1977, in the wake of disaster in the Sahel. I convened the group of twenty-six authors who did likewise for the World Climate Conference of 1979, organized by U.N. specialized agencies in Geneva. My phone rings constantly with enquiries. But I am conscious of two discouraging facts. One is that many of the enquiries from reporters are couched in sensational, flippant, or even derisive terms—the "rain washed out the meteorologists' picnic" attitude. And the other is that those concerned with the conduct of public affairs, with the security of the world's food system, and with energy supply, hardly ever call. Nor do their associated professionals; economists, engineers, agriculturalists don't think I and my colleagues have much to say. In these pages I shall ask: are they right?

Is climate changing?

To the question "Is climate changing?" I can only reply that I see no evidence for it. Yet as soon as I utter the words (typically cautious scientific jargon as they are) I feel that I have misled my interlocutor. Because in one sense climate is always changing; it is never still. L. F. Richardson, founder of numerical weather prediction, parodied Swift when he wrote:

> Big whirls have smaller whirls
> That feed on their velocity,
> And smaller whirls still smaller whirls,
> And so on to viscosity.[1]

It is the whirls in the free-flowing atmosphere that ultimately deliver climate. Such is that freedom that the atmospheric circulation can hardly have repeated itself since the world began, nor is it likely to do so however long the planet survives. From the Brownian movement of the molecules to the giant meridional overturnings first hinted at by George Hadley, F.R.S., in 1735, the atmosphere's motion is a continuous exercise of fresh initiative. Change is its very essence.

Much the same can be said of human behavior, especially of the individual. Yet we speak confidently of personality, as if we are sure that something constrains a human being to limit his range of actions. We claim free will and cherish freedom. Yet each of us voluntarily chooses a restricted but versatile behavior pattern that others recognize and come to expect. Such is personality. And such, in the atmosphere, is climate.

Climatic change, then, is what we experience when the sequence of weather events surprises us and goes on doing so. We underestimate, however, the length of time required to justify the use of the word *change.* Climate is inherently variable. Large departures from average conditions are normal to it. Moreover they can last for months, or years, or even whole decades, as the droughts of the 1930s did, and that of the Sahel did until 1980. We define climate in such a way as to include these aberrations. Otherwise we lose the sense that they are as much part of the climate as are the humdrum years. We talk of climatic change only when, even so, we realize that the basic patterns have undergone lasting change.

From long experience climatologists have decided to treat thirty years as the standard period for climatic statistics. This period is sufficient to render most of the statistical measures fairly stable. It is also the length of a human generation, and not far from the typical span of an adult person's period of independent decision-making. Otherwise the choice is wholly arbitrary; there is no rhythm or preferred period in the atmosphere suggesting a thirty-year standard. If there are real differences in climate on, for example, the century scale, with this standard they will appear as real climatic changes, i.e., the successive thirty-year averages will differ significantly. On the other hand, the interannual changes or even decade-long anomalies will be largely absorbed. Official statistics are prepared worldwide in thirty-year periods that are advanced each decade (e.g., 1931–60; 1941–70; and 1951–80, just put into use). Obviously this procedure, whose only justification is convenience, implies that the *present* climate is defined as the experience of the *past* three decades. Hence the numerical picture is always out of date and may be misleading. The recent past may not be the proper key to the present, but we have no better measure.

Conventionally, the thirty-year periods therefore include much variability. We express the normal state by calculating mean values of the key measures of climate (i.e., its *parameters*). To these we must add estimates of the variability of each parameter about its mean value. The characteristic variability is as important to the definition of a climate as the "normal" condition, which may occur rather infrequently. We also need statistics of extreme events, for it is these that determine the safety margins that we must use in designing our bridges, dams, clothing, and housing. We have to include, moreover, quite a long list of elements: mean rainfall and temperature, the old standby parameters, are not enough these days. We need such elements as solar and net radiation, humidity, wind velocity, and trace gas content, such as carbon dioxide. The idea of climate has broadened and will broaden still more.

An abandoned farmstead in the dust bowl district of Dalhart, Texas, 1938.
*"Climate is inherently variable. Large departures from average conditions are
normal to it. Moreover they can last for months, or years, or even whole decades,
as the droughts of the 1930's did. . . ."*

To determine the climate of a place we can turn to the archives of the remarkable observing network created by atmospheric scientists over the past three centuries (more especially in the past three decades). No science is better organized, none so international. Climate is a single, pervasive world system. Its study demands international coordination, communications, and standards. These are provided by the World Meteorological Organization, a U.N. agency much older (and vastly more effective) than its parent. The observational network includes many satellites, telemetered balloons, tethered and free-floating buoys, and tens of thousands of humble rain gauges and shade thermometers. The information from this vast system is gathered hourly, or every six, twelve, or twenty-four hours, and immediately exchanged between the nations. Much of it is used at once, in support of weather forecasting services. All of it, whether so used or not, then finds its way to a small number of permanent archives, one of which (the largest) is the Environmental Data and Information Service's center at Asheville, N.C. The data are stored on disks and tapes and can be recalled at will (and at a cost).

It is difficult to convey to the lay observer the complexity and versatility of the atmospheric circulation. Each of us sees the endless procession of daily weather changes, dramatic and stimulating in the mid-latitudes, subtle and subdued in the desert lands. Unless we watch this procession over at least a hemisphere, as the professional meteorologist can and must do, we tend to exaggerate the meaning of our own experience. We are struck, for example, by prolonged cold spells in winter and often ask whether they portend a colder climate. A world view shows that such cold is always brought by anomalies in the world's wind systems, reinforced by anomalous temperatures in the sea. Elsewhere, and as part of the same anomaly, the cold will be balanced by prolonged warmth. Twice during the 1970s North America's west had record warmth and lack of snow throughout winter. As part of the same pattern, the east had record cold. A single observer's view is hence highly misleading, and his or her memory is short-term and biased. To use the jargon of the world modelers, the atmosphere behaves counter-intuitively; it makes fools of those who trust their subjective impressions of what it is up to.

To detect and prove change we have to surmount this obstacle. We make use of elaborate statistical tests; we average over large areas, and over long periods; we seek to eliminate purely local and transitory influences. And when we do so, we arrive at an unpopular and unexpected conclusion: that there is no convincing evidence of *lasting* climatic change in progress *now*. We can detect past change, and tentatively we can predict future change. What we cannot do is to prove that present conditions are changing to a new and lasting state.

What, then, is the fuss about? Why has climatic change become such a talked-about thing in the 1970s? The answer lies in the internal variability of the existing climate. For some previous decades there had been few serious anomalies in places where anomalies hurt. India had had few failures of her monsoon rains. North America, and especially the grain-producing regions, had had few years of really bad climate. Great progress was made in those decades toward higher agricultural productivity; the introduction of new crop hybrids, of new strains of cattle, of more abundant and cheap fertilizers, had transformed world food production. The 1960s, in particular, was the decade of the Green Revolution, sponsored by the major U.S. foundations. In this atmosphere of progress the impression grew that technology had conquered climate. It was more nearly true that climate was behaving itself. If there were anomalies (and indeed there were), they were mostly avoiding the crucial areas.

The 1970s were different. The best evidence shows little world tendency toward greater variability. But the anomalies of rainfall and temperature were large, and in this decade they hit regions that were vulnerable and important. We shall look closely at some of these below. In terms of political and economic impact the key anomalies were the great Sahelian drought, which mobilized the powerful third world lobbies in the U.N., and the succession of serious crop failures in the Soviet Union. The latter, in which bad climate and poor policies competed with one another to frustrate the Kremlin's hopes, were especially important in the world grain trade.

At times during this turbulent decade, during which inflation began to rock the economic boat, and during which the world's energy situation was transformed by the actions of the OPEC cartel, there was heated public debate about the socioeconomic role of climate. I have detailed this debate elsewhere. It involved professional climatologists who for a time flirted with the idea that a new ice age was at our doorstep; politicians of the caliber of Hubert Humphrey who were daunted at the prospect of climate-induced famine; and the technical and scientific communities worldwide. The debate culminated in two U.N.-sponsored conferences that focused on climatic issues: the U.N. Conference on Desertification, a political conference held in Nairobi in 1977, and the World Climate Conference, in Geneva in 1979. The latter was sponsored by U.N. agencies rather than the organization itself, and was essentially a meeting of technical people representing both the victims and the students of capricious climate. Its *Proceedings,* unfortunately published by the World Meteorological Organization in a fashion guaranteed to bury them forever, are the definitive review of the subject of this essay.

In sum, we find no evidence of climatic change in progress now. But we have acquired a new understanding of how climate affects human society. And we have forebodings for the future. Before we give voice to these qualms, we shall look at the 1970s in more detail.

(Above) Photograph taken from a satellite of the eastern U.S. on July 25, 1975.
(Right) This photograph was taken of the same area six days later. *"It is difficult to
convey to the lay observer the complexity and versatility of the atmospheric
circulation. Each of us sees the endless procession of daily weather changes,
dramatic and stimulating in the mid-latitudes, subtle and subdued in the desert
lands. Unless we watch this procession over at least a hemisphere, as the*

professional meteorologist can and must do, we tend to exaggerate the meaning
of our own experience. We are struck, for example, by prolonged cold spells in
winter and often ask whether they portend a colder climate. A world view shows
that such cold is always brought by anomalies in the world's wind systems,
reinforced by anomalous temperatures in the sea. Elsewhere, and as part of the
same anomaly, the cold will be balanced by prolonged warmth.''

The turbulent seventies

(a) African stresses

It was in Africa—and especially in so-called sub-Saharan Africa—that the dramatic interplay between climate and human aspirations best displayed itself. In recent decades the interaction has been unhappy. Africa is unique among the continents in that *per capita* food-supply has not increased in recent decades. Colonial domination has been largely removed, but prosperity has not replaced it. Here, as everywhere, one must avoid blaming nature alone for economic failure. But there is no doubt that climate has been singularly cruel to the ambitions of this vast continent's people. In fact only the republic of South Africa, scarcely typical of the continent, has been fairly free from serious natural disasters in the past two decades.

Independence came to much of French north Africa in 1960–61. De Gaulle's strategy of disengagement was especially effective along the southern margins of the Sahara, the Sahel, where new republics bearing (in some cases) ancient names appeared on the map. Senegal, Mauritania, Mali, Upper Volta, Niger, and Chad joined the formerly Anglo-Egyptian Sudan to form a grouping of new and insecure states. At or about that time east African republics were also in the making out of former colonial territories: Ethiopia, Somalia, Uganda, Kenya, and Tanzania were facing their independent careers. The Sahelian group could not have achieved freedom at a worse moment, when drought was about to overwhelm their territories. The east African states began in better circumstances, but later in their history they, too, were to be plagued by drought. Nation-building in Africa has had to contend with appalling climate.

Research has established a considerable degree of coherence in the climate of the Sahelian zone. Drought or abundance is apt to occur simultaneously over a wide area. Sharon Nicholson of Clark University has laid special stress on this coherence, which has obvious political implications; it means that severe economic and social stress may afflict several of the Sahelian republics at the same time. In fact this happened in the great drought of the 1970s, at the peak of which the entire Sahel from the Atlantic to the Ethiopian Highlands was in dire straits. Nicholson grouped the available data (in all, 419 stations, 300 of which were opened before 1925) into roughly latitudinal bands:

Band	Approx. latitudes	Mean annual rainfall (normal)	Normal length of rainy season (mos)
Sahelo-Saharan	18–20	50–100 mm [2–4 in.]	1 to 2
Sahel	15–18	100–400 mm [4–16 in.]	2 to 3
Soudan	12–15	400–1200 mm [16–48 in.]	3 to 5
Soudano-Guinean	9–12	1200–1600 mm [48–64 in.]	5 to 8

A scene most people have seen photographed again and again; weakened by disease and hunger, African women and children wait for emergency feeding in Ethiopia. *"Here, as everywhere, one must avoid blaming nature alone for economic failure. But there is no doubt that climate has been singularly cruel to the ambitions of this vast continent's people."*

Her work and subsequent studies by Raymond P. Motha and colleagues have shown that the drought extended through all four of the zones and for much of the period covered all longitudes as well. Such coherence is rare in climate; far more often an area afflicted by drought can call on the help of neighbors who are better off. In the 1970s central Africa could in few ways help itself.

The spatially averaged record shows, in fact, earlier long fluctuations in sub-Saharan Africa. There was severe drought, and much distress, in the years 1910–15. Thereafter, to a crude approximation, rainfall rose to a peak in the 1930s, which were prosperous years for the region. The 1940s were far less benign; rainfall was variable, and there were some very dry years (especially 1949). The 1950s continued the high variability, but for much of the decade rainfall was well above average. Independence came to much of the Sahelian and Sudanian republics at a moment when the decision-makers could recall abundant summer rains, tall grass, exuberant growth, and rise in livestock numbers.

In retrospect we can now see that the ensuing desiccation began in 1957 or 1958. With minor fluctuations—a few better years in a bleak sequence—rainfall diminished progressively. By 1961 it was down to normal values. By 1968 the new republics were admitting that drought was widespread. The rainfall reached its lowest point in 1972 and 1973 in most areas. The desiccation spread into and around the flanks of the Ethiopian Highlands; Ethiopia itself, Somalia, and later much of Kenya and parts of Tanzania felt its effects, though conditions in east Africa were patchier and less severe as a whole. In the late 1970s much of the subsistence farming land of Uganda was affected, adding to the miseries imposed by Amin's atrocious regime.

Conditions improved in 1974, the year of the U.N. World Food Conference, and almost immediately there was a slackening of international attention; "the drought is over" was the cry. In fact it was not; from Upper Volta eastward it resumed in 1975. In no subsequent year has drought been absent from the whole Sahel and Sudan, and in few places or years has rainfall been adequate. In east Africa in 1961 there had been an abrupt increase in rainfall over the plateaus and highlands. Lake Victoria, the source of the White Nile, reached an extremely high level. Several years of good rain ensued, which created a mood of optimism for land settlement and agriculture. The arrival of drought from, as it were, the Sahel had a serious impact on public plans in Kenya, Tanzania, and Somalia; it was an unexpected and unheralded blow.

I first made the acquaintance of the Saharan margin climates during the droughts of the early 1940s, when for military purposes I analyzed the atmospheric circulation over west and north Africa. One of my then-classified reports—a piece of juvenilia—was published in the journal *Climatic Change* in 1977, very much as a disinterred fossil. We have learned much since then. Rainfall in west Africa comes almost exclusively in the northern summer. It falls through a shallow southwesterly current from the south Atlantic. In January the northern limit of this monsoonal south-westerly lies not far inland, about 7° to 9° north latitude. Clear, arid, but dusty northeasterlies—the *harmattan*—then cover the interior. Rain is almost unknown. In April, May, and June the monsoonal limit moves northward. By July it typically lies in 15° to 20° north, averaging near 18° north in a good year. The moist current gets as far east as The Sudan. Hot, humid, and thundery weather covers all west Africa and extends even on to the margin of the Sahara. By September the condition is break-ing down, and in October, November, and December the harmattan northeasterlies push irregularly southward to restore the dusty, rainless weather derived from the Sahara.

This annual rhythm controls much of west Africa's economic opportu-nity. In the far north, as Nicholson showed, there is enough of the humid air to allow only a few thunderstorms over a one–two-month period. On this flimsy and precarious base the migrant herdsmen have depended for centuries. Their mobility allowed them to choose their summer pastures according to the year's luck in rain. But in the far south rain can fall for much of the year, and rain forest or tall savannah grasses cloaked the land before mankind laid them waste. The usual tropical diseases, waterborne or swamp-fed, limited the usefulness of the rainfall. Among cattle the scourge of trypanosomiasis—sleeping sickness—meant that the nomads could not bring their herds far south (though they could and did sell the meat to the cities of the south). Among people schistosomiasis and on-chocerciasis (filariasis) plagued the region, as they still do. Yet the tradi-tional economies minimized the impact of these misfortunes. Through a long history of cultural conservatism, Sahara, Sahel, Sudan, and Guinea interacted effectively in a fashion to make this remarkable climate in some sense an asset—a resource that the livelihood systems could exploit.

We cannot with certainty explain the post-1957 desiccation, because we do not fully understand the west African climate even in its normal state. The shallow monsoonal current is overlain by deep easterlies that cross all Africa and are part of the planetary wind-systems. These easter-lies are unstable in the dynamical sense, because of the southward tem-perature gradient (the air over the Sahara being warmer than that over the Guinea coast). Westward moving disturbances in these easterlies create most of the thunderstorms and steadier rains of the wet season. If this train of disturbances is weakened, if the supply of available moisture is lessened, and if the whole system is shifted north or south by a degree or two of latitude, there are drastic readjustments of rainfall. Drought follows a southward shift, or a weakening of the easterly disturbances. Such changes appear local to the unfortunate sufferers, but in fact they arise from slight shifts of the global circulation of the atmosphere; there is nothing that a small nation can do but endure them.

65

We cannot predict such anomalies, nor could we make much use of a prediction even if it were forthcoming. But a massive effort has been made to overcome these difficulties. Major international experiments have been conducted to gain insight into the processes involved. Through much of the 1970s the Global Atmospheric Research Programme (GARP) has been going on—and still continues. This huge enterprise has been mounted by the collaborative effort of the World Meteorological Organization and the International Council of Scientific Unions, ICSU, whose secretary-general, J. C. Dooge, has recently served also as the minister of foreign affairs of Ireland. The first is a U.N. specialized agency, the second a combination of the world's professional scientific societies. GARP has involved the ships, aircraft, satellites, laboratories, and money of many nations, including the U.S., Canada, and the U.S.S.R. It has called for two major achievements—a permanent strengthening of the World Weather Watch, i.e., observations, and the conduct of several international experiments.

One major experiment, called GATE, was staged over West Africa and the tropical Atlantic. It allowed an intensive study of the easterly disturbances mentioned above, and how they progressed westward to become, potentially, the harbingers of storms and hurricanes in the Caribbean and tropical America. The dates, June to September 1974, coincided with both drought conditions and their partial breakdown. A second experiment, WAMEX, is focusing more closely on the nature of the monsoonal rainfall over west Africa. Yet a third (not part of GARP, but run by WMO) is attempting precipitation enhancement—"rain-making" to the media—in the semiarid areas.

Much has been learned about the tropical circulation over Africa, and more will emerge as the huge pile of data is worked over. But already it is clear that the fight against desertification and famine depends as much on the social and economic habits of the nations involved as on the prediction of climate. The 1977 Desertification Conference identified most of the problems. There is first the breakdown of the old traditional livelihood systems, as nomads have given up (or been deprived of) their mobility, or as cash crops have replaced the old food staples. There is population pressure, as human numbers increase, and with them the number of cattle, sheep, goats, and camels. The search for firewood, the hunger of drought-starved animals, and sheer carelessness have driven out the trees, shrubs, and grass that once protected the soil. There has been a decay of the climate-society linkage, which would have been fragile even if the climate had stayed kind. The desiccation of the 1960s and 1970s exacerbated what was already going on. In some ways the Sahel and the Sudan have survived this stress better than they did the drought of 1910–15. In other ways matters are worse. And there is no clear sign that they are about to get better.

This complex change in the map of Africa has been called the south-ward spread of the Sahara—an oversimplification that has been useful in awakening the human conscience. It has given rise to another anxiety, supported by several simulations on giant computers in the U.K., the U.S., and the U.S.S.R. This is the fear that desert feeds on desert, that the spread of desert surfaces discourages rainfall—a positive feed-back loop.

Two mechanisms are involved. One is that part of the rain of a typical summer falls from locally evaporated water (in west Africa, for example, from Lake Chad, or the Niger, Chari, and Senegal rivers); hence drought tends to compound itself. The other is more subtle. A desert is more reflective to sunlight than is grass or forest. Hence if a soil is nibbled, grazed, burned, or trampled till it is bare, it becomes more reflective. In the jargon of the climatologists the albedo increases. An Israeli meteorol-ogist, Joseph Otterman, noted in 1974 that the borders between Israeli and Arab territories in the Gaza strip and the Negev were clearly visible on satellite images made by the Landsat sensors. Israeli land looked darker. He ascribed the difference to the better control of grazing ani-mals, and hence vegetation cover, on the Israeli side. He also suggested that this ought to influence rainfall from convective clouds, which would form more easily over dark, heated surfaces.

Major experiments were launched to test this increased albedo hypoth-esis. The late Jule Charney, of M.I.T.,[2] a founder of numerical weather prediction in the 1940s, proposed that the effect of increased albedo would be to favor accelerated sinking motion (subsidence) in the overly-ing atmosphere. The natural aridity of the subtropics is caused by the worldwide tendency for such subsidence to occur, in both hemispheres. In effect, Charney's hypothesis (which he supported by ingenious nu-merical modeling exercises) was that if desert surfaces are spread by hu-man misuse, local rainfall will decrease. Large general circulation models at the Goddard Institute for Space Studies in New York City, at NCAR, in England, and in the Soviet Union confirmed that for very large albedo in-creases the Otterman-Charney hypothesis would indeed lead to further spread of desert conditions.

The fear that human society itself creates the desert is ancient and per-vasive. The dominance of subtropical Africa, the Middle East, and much of Australia by desert is unquestionably natural, though the work of herdsmen and cultivators along the margin of the old world deserts may indeed have allowed the arid surfaces to spread. It is conceivable that the albedo feedback just described has contributed to the deterioration. At the U.N. Conference on Desertification this forbidding prospect was in everyone's mind. Case studies were submitted by many countries to show that these effects are present on every continent. James Walls has summa-rized these studies in a brilliant book called *Land, Man and Sand.*

A convective storm over the tropical Atlantic off the coast of Barbados. The Global
Atmospheric Research Programme (GARP) conducted *"one major experiment,
called GATE, . . . over West Africa and the tropical Atlantic. It allowed an intensive*

study of the easterly disturbances . . . and how they progressed westward to become, potentially, the harbingers of storms and hurricanes in the Caribbean and tropical America.''

The Sahelian disaster has thus brought in its wake a massive scientific effort, and a U.N. Conference that was the first world political event directly aimed at lessening the adverse impact of climate on human affairs. A world program to combat the spread of deserts is now in progress, much handicapped by the poverty and political weakness of most of the powers affected. It will probably be in the rich nations—the U.S., the U.S.S.R., and Australia in particular—that the needed technological change will be most easily developed. Certainly it will be mostly in the advanced countries that climatic research will go forward. But the real life-and-death struggle is on the desert margin in countries where there is little wealth, little cash margin and little skill: only, in many areas, a folk-memory that things once were better.

(b) The world food and energy systems

In the advanced countries it is easy to identify the local effects of bad climate. We have all seen floods, withered leaves, and tied-up winter traffic. It is far harder to detect the impact of such anomalies on national and international economies. We respond very quickly to bad weather, both technically and economically. There is a network of institutions to cushion us against environmental stresses, climate included. Nevertheless there are parts of the larger economy that are still vulnerable. The 1970s brought these to light. The international food system is one instance. The energy economy of the industrial nations is another. Tourism and recreation are together a third.

The food crisis of the 1970s was triggered rather than caused by climate. For the west African nations it was, as we have seen, the result of their inability to absorb the stress of the Sahelian drought. For the advanced industrial nations it consisted of upsets to international trade, largely, but by no means entirely, caused by climate-induced crop or fisheries failures. Agricultural economists argue persuasively that such perturbations are easily absorbed, and that market factors quickly restore abundance after each shortage. This is narrowly speaking true, though it does not take into account the persistent malnutrition of perhaps a tenth of mankind. Nor is it likely to remain true through the 1980s as demand from burgeoning third world population increases.

If we take world grain production as our measure, output in 1982 is expected to reach 1,491 million tons. It has recently been increasing at an average of 30–40 million tons per annum, a figure to compare with the annual growth of the human population, about 80 million. More than nine-tenths of the grain is consumed within producing countries, or continental trading blocs. The rest supplies the international grain trade, chiefly in wheat, rice, and coarse grains (usually for cattle feed). India and China are almost self-sufficient in most years. Europe and the Soviet Union are not, often importing over 40 million tons. The grain trade has a determining effect on world prices, which are very volatile.

Climate-induced upsets of this system are mainly of two sorts. Poor crops in large consuming areas place a heavy demand on the grain trade (since stored grain is equivalent to only 30–100 days' world supply). Particularly serious during the 1970s were repeated crop failures in the Soviet Union, notably in 1972, 1975, 1977, and 1979–1981. In 1973–74 alone the Soviet Union imported 28 million tons of grain, chiefly from the U.S., causing a panic scramble for supply, and a trebling of world prices for wheat and rice.[3] Both India and China have from time to time needed large imports. The second kind of perturbation consists of crop failures in the handful of nations that now control grain exports. The U.S., Canada, Australia, and Argentina are alone capable of maintaining world flows in bulk, though other suppliers—France, Thailand, and Pakistan, for example—contribute to regional trade. North America is, in fact, absolutely dominant. Hence bad climate in the chief producing areas of the U.S. and Canada has rapid and unhappy repercussions for the world food situation.

The 1970s were scarcely unique. They saw much variability of temperature and precipitation, but that is a normal aspect of climate. What counted was that the droughts, floods, heat, and cold tended to hit key areas—either consuming regions which could not supply their own food needs, or producing regions whose crops fell short of expectation. In 1972 alone there was severe drought in Texas, Sahelian and southern Africa, central and southern Australia, India, Pakistan, China, northern and eastern Europe, and the western Soviet Union (where it was also cold, and there was a failure of snow cover in the winter wheat area). A worse bag of anomalies could hardly have been imagined, and the grain trade was thrown into chaos. The effect was compounded, in late 1973, by the first oil boycott that ultimately threatened energy prices, and hence farm and fertilizer costs.

As if this was not enough, the Peruvian anchovy fisheries collapsed, partly because of a climate-induced oceanic warming off the South American coast called *El Niño*. The high productivity of this fishery is maintained by the upwelling of cold, nutrient-rich waters off the coast. Every few years, in response to atmospheric pressure changes over the Pacific (the Southern Oscillation), warmer, more saline equatorial waters flood the coast, disturbing the fish schools, and hence the industry. The 1972 El Niño halted the Peruvian fisheries by June, since when operations have been much restricted. In 1970 Peruvian fish catch (chiefly anchovy) exceeded 12 million tons and was much the world's largest. In 1971 it fell to under 11 million, and in 1972 to barely 2 million. Since then the anchovy catch has remained below that level. Why all this fuss about a small, oily fish? Because it was the largest source of the vital animal protein feed called fish meal. In 1970, before the collapse, Peru supplied 42% of world

"In 1972 alone there was severe drought in Texas [shown here], *Sahelian and southern Africa, central and southern Australia, India, Pakistan, China, northern and eastern Europe, and the western Soviet Union (where it was also cold, and there was a failure of snow cover in the winter wheat area). A worse bag of anomalies could hardly have been imagined, and the grain trade was thrown into chaos. The effect was compounded, in late 1973, by the first oil boycott that ultimately threatened energy prices, and hence farm and fertilizer costs.*"

consumption. Other sources have since replaced the Peruvian catch, and soybeans have met some of the protein demand. But the impact of the Peruvian failure was large. We are still not sure why the 1972 El Niño was so drastically effective. Overfishing, and possibly biological processes, may well have overstrained the system. The climatic anomaly triggered the collapse.

The sensitivity of the world food system to climatic variability was thus reemphasized by the events of the 1970s. Both grain production and protein supply were affected. On a world scale, in easier times, things tend to balance out; drought in one area is offset by good growing conditions in another. If one balances the U.S. (the greatest supplier) and the U.S.S.R. (an erratic producer, making frequent large calls on external supplies) in any one year there is only an 8% chance that both countries will have poor wheat crops; and a recent study by Sakamoto, Strommen, and Steyaert could find no case where such simultaneous failures occurred in two or more consecutive years.

World grain production used to push ahead steadily because of these counterbalancing effects. All through the 1950s and 1960s it rose at an average close to $2\frac{1}{2}\%$ per annum. During the 1970s the rise continued but became erratic. There were four years—1972, 1974, 1977, and 1979—in which there were absolute decreases, chiefly because of shortfalls in the U.S.S.R. World population rises at the rate of 80 million per annum. To feed these new mouths alone an annual rise of 2% in food production is needed, and to get rid of malnutrition an annual rise of 3% to $3\frac{1}{2}\%$ is to be desired. Small though they were—the largest (1971 to 1972) was only just over a 2% fall—the years of decrease in the 1970s were hence of consequence. Carry-over stocks from year to year smoothed out the effects, but the mark of climate on the essential upward course was clear. More than any other factor this impact led to the reawakening of interest in the role of climate in human well-being.

The direct impact of these events on opinion in the western countries was considerable, thanks largely to media coverage of the visible distress of the affected peoples. Churches, foreign aid agencies, and the major foundations all responded quickly. It may well have been the last group, however, that listened most intently. The Rockefeller Foundation, in particular, held consultations (which I chaired) on the world's climate-food relationships in New York (January 1974) and at Bellagio, Italy (June 1975), out of which the World Climate Conference of 1979 emerged. But it was the realization that western countries were not immune from climatic hazards that aroused most interest. The cold winters of the late 1970s in the eastern United States and the 1975–76 drought in western Europe were especially effective.

The winter of 1976–77 displayed a persistent anomaly pattern in which the westerly winds[4] that control mid-latitude climates were seriously perturbed and displaced. These westerlies are circumpolar in both hemispheres, extending at sea level from 35° to 65° latitude (with some seasonal variation). They are strongest about 10 to 15 kilometers above sea level, where their cores are the westerly jet streams associated with the temperature gradient from warm tropics to cold polar areas. Jet aircraft operate at these levels, and eastbound aircraft get bonuses by having tail winds. The cyclonic storms that bring rain or snow are fast moving wave disturbances of these westerlies. Over North America in winter the latter blow strongly at high levels over the whole continent, with a tendency for a slight northwesterly component west of the Mississippi, and a southwesterly component off the Atlantic Coast.

In 1976–77 these small deviations from west to east flow were exaggerated, and their position altered. The result was that warm Pacific air penetrated deeply into the mountains and plains of western Canada, bringing record warmth to areas usually dominated by frigid Arctic airstreams. In the Yukon temperatures for the entire winter (December, January, and February to a climatologist) were 7–9 degrees Celsius (12–16 degrees Fahrenheit) above normal. Conditions were almost as warm over the Prairies and northern Plains. They were more or less normal, however, over the rest of the western U.S. In many Canadian and Pacific northwestern areas there was a much shorter and thinner snowpack, and the winter sports industry was badly hit. Severe drought affected wide areas. There were thus repercussions for hydroelectric power development and the forest industries. A similar lack of snow-cover has plagued the U.S. mountain areas in several subsequent winters, coupled with extraordinary midwinter warmth, drought, and bare soils in the Great Plains. On March 17, 1981, I had the rare experience of looking down on the Canadian Prairies and northern U.S. Plains not only bare of snow, but largely free of lake and river ice as well—and of walking across the bone-dry prairie scuffing up the soil at a temperature (near Regina, Saskatchewan) of 18° Celsius (64.4° Fahrenheit).

Yet 1976–77 was a winter of discontent in the east, because of persistent cold that affected the entire continent from the Plains eastward (except paradoxically for the Arctic). Conditions were especially severe in the U.S. east of the Mississippi. Mean air temperature for the winter was 5 degrees Celsius (9 degrees Fahrenheit) below normal from eastern Illinois across Indiana and Ohio into West Virginia. The Ohio River froze, and barge traffic in coal and petroleum products was halted for a period. The natural gas distribution system proved unable to cope; in order to meet domestic space-heating demands there were cutbacks to industrial consumers. This led to one million layoffs and to substantial production losses. The weather made headlines for weeks—and the headlines were the opposite of those in Pacific Canada.

This extreme winter was an excellent example of a prolonged climatic anomaly that made headlines, started rumors of climatic change, and yet misled its witnesses. The people of Ohio Valley cities, struggling with the coldest winter in years, came to very different conclusions from those of Edmonton, Alberta, or Whitehorse, Yukon Territory. The latter were bemused by a mildness that led to visions of a permanent relaxation of their severe winter climate. Actually both events—the warmth of the northwest, the cold of the east—were parts of the same gigantic, short-lived disturbance of the global westerlies. To see them for what they were one had to have, as it were, spaceship vision.

Much the same principle applied to the drought of 1975–76 in northwestern Europe. It was caused, on the global scale, by a persistent but limited anomaly in the wind systems. While it was in progress it caused many problems for farmers, water supply authorities, navigation channel managers, and sanitary engineers. Substantial short-term losses were incurred. Yet other parts of the economy benefited. In sun-starved western Europe a summer of Mediterranean brilliance and warmth tempted huge crowds on to the beaches, coastal seas, and rivers; it was a glorious time for tourism and recreation. The drought broke abruptly in September 1976. After a summer in which many regions had less than half their normal rainfall, with the soil exhausted of stored water available to crops, it rained so hard in many areas that soils were restored to full wetness earlier than usual. The autumn was so wet that 1976 turned out to have normal or above-normal annual rainfall in some of the worst affected districts.

Careful analysis in the United Kingdom showed 1976 crop yields well below those of pre-drought 1974. Wheat was down 22% in England and Wales, and potatoes 40%. Yet the overall effect was much smaller than had been feared; modern advanced farming techniques provide some protection, and farmers do not just wait for rain. Some strange by-products were reported. Rhododendrons, which blaze in springtime all over western Europe, failed to do so in 1976. Many appeared dead by midsummer. When the rain came back in September, they amazed gardeners by leafing out again and blooming in the autumn. The same heavy rains washed out excess nitrogen fertilizers added to fields during the drought, and dangerous levels of nitrate affected some local drinking supplies. But overall the effect was surprisingly small, and gains partially offset the real losses.

This litany of aberrations during the 1970s could be indefinitely extended. I have a filing-cabinet drawer full of cuttings, reprints, and photographs from the five continents. As I said before, the scale of disturbances was probably not abnormal to the climate. The anomalies made themselves visible by happening where people could not only see them but suffer from them too. Awareness grew, and as the decade ended climate had become a topic of substantial public interest. In 1970 climatology was a lowly part of the atmospheric sciences, and climate was a poorly understood word. By 1980 there was a World Climate Program in progress, and many national meteorological services have formed national programs as well. Climatology has become a central part of the discipline.

And yet, as I said, climate still makes little impact on politics and economics. We have not yet found a way of using the new interest to good effect. New questions now present themselves: will *future* climate change? And if so, what can we do about it, given our political incompetence?

Future climates

(a) The carbon dioxide effect

Professional opinion about future climate is swinging toward the view that the next century may indeed see large changes, larger perhaps than anything previously experienced by civilized beings. This is quite a change in itself. Ten years ago only professional mavericks took this view.

Who are these professionals? One group is made up of geologists and geochemists, some of whom were arguing, until recently, that the earth was cooling toward a new ice age. The 1960s and 1970s have provided new and powerful tools for reconstructing past climates. The best evidence has come from cores drilled through the soft sediments resting on the ocean floors. These materials accumulate quietly and slowly—often no more than a few centimeters in a millennium—and are made up largely of the deposited skeletal or fecal remains of tiny organisms living in the upper layers of the ocean. An internationally-supported deep-sea drilling project, largely using U.S. research vessels, has provided a re- markable series of cores through these sediments, giving a continuous record of conditions back many millennia. These cores have been patient- ly examined layer by layer. They yield a consistent picture of sea tempera- ture change, and of the volume of ice on land (the glaciers). Some detail is now available back for half-a-million years. The indicators used are the relative frequency of certain species of microorganisms having known sea temperature preferences, and the ratio of two isotopes of oxygen, ^{18}O and ^{16}O, which gives clues as to the volume of land ice.

These studies—coordinated internationally by universities and re- search institutes as part of a project called CLIMAP—have shown that for at least the past half-million years, and probably the past two million years, the world has undergone repeated cold glacial epochs roughly 100,000 years apart. These "glacials" were separated by warmer intergla- cials. The most recent glacial epoch culminated 18,000 to 23,000 years ago. By 10,000 years ago the continental glaciers that had covered north- ern North America and Europe had mostly melted, and climate was close to that of today. The Neolithic Age, when mankind developed agriculture and learned to build cities and divide labor, began as the ice melted. The ensuing eight to ten millennia are the whole span of civilized human soci- ety. And the warm phase has already lasted as long as some past interglacials. It is this fact that makes some geologists announce an impending return of the glaciers. They were aided and abetted in the early 1970s by climatologists who feared that the cooling that began about 1940 might be the glacial's early stages.

Oddly enough, the discussions of 1982 deal with a quite different prospect—that the next century may be much warmer. Most atmospheric scientists (like me) believe that the buildup of carbon dioxide in the atmosphere will have this effect, though again there are mavericks who say the reverse.

The buildup of carbon dioxide (CO_2) is an observed fact. Serious monitoring of CO_2 concentration began only in 1957, at the Mauna Loa Observatory in Hawaii. It was then about 314 parts per million of the air (ppm for short). It is now (1982) about 339 ppm, an increase of $7\frac{1}{2}\%$ in twenty-five years. In the past century the increase has probably been 16% to 18%. Currently the increase is almost 4% per decade. It is monitored at a network of stations around the world.

We believe that most of this added CO_2 is coming from the burning of coal, oil, and natural gas, the fossil fuels. In 1982 about 6 billion tons of carbon will enter the atmosphere in this form. About half will stay there, the rest going into the ocean by solution, or into plant tissues. It is possible that the clearance of forest, especially the tropical rain forest, and the cultivation of new land are also on balance transferring carbon to the atmosphere, though this is less clear.

If we can predict future use of the fossil fuels, we can hence make a shot at calculating future CO_2 concentrations. Energy policy and prices are themselves up in the air, but one can at least sketch their probable future course. Many groups have tried to do this, for example the U.S. Department of Energy, and the International Institute for Applied Systems Analysis at Laxenburg, Austria. Allowing for the rising cost of energy, such estimates now suggest that by the year 2025 (only forty-three years ahead) the CO_2 concentration will reach about 435 ppm and will double its present value some time in the second half of the twenty-first century. Such a carbon-enriched atmosphere will be eminently breathable and will be good for vegetation and crops. But what will it do to climate?

To answer that question the atmospheric scientist must resort to the computer. What is needed are numerical models—necessarily large and complex—that incorporate the factors controlling climate. These include the solar constant (i.e., the power of the sun's input of energy, averaging 343 watts per square meter at the top of the atmosphere); the rate of rotation of the earth; the distribution of land, sea, and mountains; and the concentration of gases in the atmosphere that absorb and emit radiation (CO_2, water vapor, and ozone chiefly). Allowance will have to be made for heat storage and transport by the sea, and for the effect of clouds, snow, and ice. And the model will need to be "run" for the equivalent of long periods of time. Within the past decade we have made great strides in

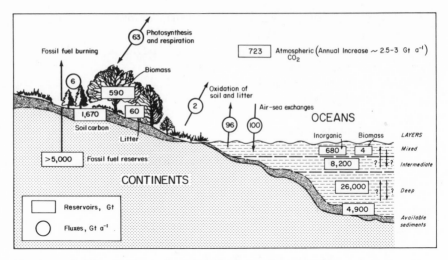

The storage (in billions of tons) of carbon in the main natural reservoirs (rectangles), and annual rates of transfer between reservoirs.

constructing adequate models. We started with single one-dimensional simulations referring to an average earth and ended the 1970s with several general circulation models that simulate the entire atmosphere and the surface layer of the ocean.

There is, as usual, some disagreement among the modelers, whose craft is arcane, and can be criticized only by other modelers; a little acerbity is not to be wondered at. But the leading groups have reached a fair measure of agreement as to the climatic impact: a doubling of carbon dioxide concentration will raise world surface temperatures by 2 to 3 degrees Celsius, the tropics having slightly smaller rises, and north polar latitudes having the greatest—of 8 degrees Celsius or more. A quadrupling (tested by only one or two studies) will produce approximately twice the effect.

Some of the studies—notably those carried out by Syukuro Manabe and his associates at GFDL Princeton—go much further. The Princeton exercises indicate for doubled CO_2 an appreciable increase in world precipitation (rain plus hail and snow), and hence soil moisture, except in a narrow mid-latitude band near 40° north, where a decrease of soil water is predicted. This is close to the most valuable agricultural land from which the world's wheat and coarse grain exports largely come. Unfortunately the models cannot yet say exactly where, on a longitudinal (east–west) basis, the effects will be most felt. The Princeton models also suggest that a quadrupling (but not a doubling) of CO_2 would lead to summer melting of the floating ice-pack sheet that now blocks the Arctic Ocean throughout the year. An exercise at NCAR by Claire L. Parkinson and W. W. Kellogg suggests that even a doubling will have such an effect. Hence it is conceivable that a century from now the Arctic Ocean will be open in summer—as navigable, in fact, as the Norwegian and Bering seas are today.

The dramatic force of these results is brought home if we realize that the 2 to 3 degrees Celsius warming predicted for a doubling, sometime after mid-twenty-first century, is greater than any temperature change in the past 10,000 years, the whole course of civilized history. Nothing like it has ever happened to modern humanity. And the Arctic Ocean, which may possibly clear of ice in a century, has probably not been open water for three-quarters of a million years. We are talking, that is to say, of a possible environmental revolution—brought on by human interference.

The carbon dioxide issue has become a leading research focus of the atmospheric sciences, supported by oceanographers, ecologists, and geo-chemists. In most informed eyes it outweighs the acid rain affair, which is regional, not global. Carbon dioxide is rapidly dispersed worldwide, and affects everyone. Sulfur dioxide and nitrogen oxides are precipitated nearer the source, being soluble in rain. The boom in CO_2 research has already produced some complementary results in related areas. We now realize, for example, that other gases, largely synthetic, can add to the CO_2 "greenhouse" action. Included are the fluorocarbons, the spray-can and refrigerant compounds that escape into the atmosphere (and which have been seen as threats to the ozone layer). Also suspected are nitrous oxide, a natural emanation from soil that may be increased by added fer-tilizer use, and methane, a product of decay of dead plant and animal tissues.

This greenhouse effect is a bit of a misnomer, since a greenhouse acts mainly by trapping warm air that would otherwise disperse. Carbon diox-ide and its companion gases act by absorbing and emitting certain wave-lengths of long-wave terrestrial radiation, the means by which the earth returns its sun-derived energy to space. If one adds these radiatively ac-tive gases to the existing store in the atmosphere, one increases the resistance to this return flow. For the energy to escape, the earth's surface and lowest atmosphere must get a little warmer, and the upper layers of the atmosphere a little cooler. Qualitative reasoning suggests this, and the models confirm it. In fact they suggest that today, since the increases in gas concentrations have been in progress for a decade, we ought to be able to detect temperature increases from .04 to .06 degrees Celsius each year, and much more in the north polar regions. In fact we cannot do so. Temperature varies much more than this from year to year because of cli-mate's natural, unrelated variability. The "noise" obscures the "signal," as the radio industry says when static from lightning makes it hard to tune in a distant AM station.

There are, moreover, some professional dissenters with excellent cre-dentials. For many years Reid Bryson and his associates at the Institute for Environmental Studies of the University of Wisconsin at Madison have argued that back-scattering of solar radiation to space by dust is

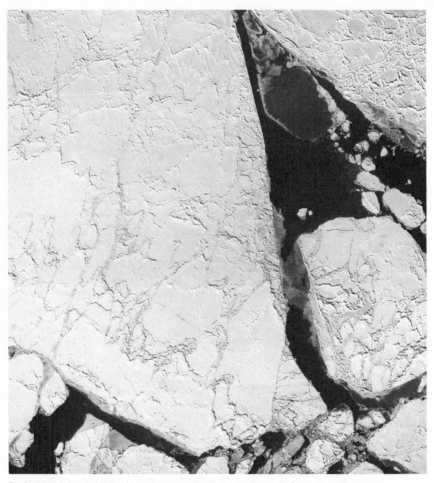

Broken pack-ice (white) with open water leads in the Hudson Bay. *"Leading groups have reached a fair measure of agreement as to the climatic impact: a doubling of carbon dioxide concentration will raise world surface temperatures by 2 to 3 degrees Celsius, the tropics have slightly smaller rises, and north polar latitudes having the greatest—of 8 degrees Celsius or more."*

offsetting the CO_2 warming. This dust, they have argued, is at least partly due to human interference, for example by land clearance and the burning of tropical vegetation. One can sometimes see such clouds of dust and smoke in satellite photographs. The rest of the dust comes chiefly from volcanic explosions, like that of Mt. St. Helen's. And these have increased since 1940. The Wisconsin school has published a model incorporating these effects that accounts quite well for temperature variation in the past century but predicts little change for the next. Dissent has also come from Sherwood Idso at the University of Arizona, and Reginald Newell at M.I.T.—ranking figures in the study of surface radiation and atmospheric circulation respectively. Their dissent has prompted vigorous rebuttals by the modelers. A consensus has not yet arisen, but a healthy debate is going on.

(b) Solar and ocean effects

Are there other ways for climate to change? There are indeed several, some internal, others external to the atmosphere and ocean. The internal possibilities include changes in the relation of atmosphere to ocean, and shifts of the system toward a new equilibrium without anything pushing from outside. External possibilities include a change in the sun's behavior, and other changes in the composition of the atmosphere.

The links between ocean and atmosphere are close but complex. The ocean has a huge capacity for heat storage. Its surface temperature fluctuates slowly, and currents and other mechanisms redistribute the stored heat about the globe. Such effects may, for example, delay the CO_2 warming by a decade or decades. A small anomaly of sea surface temperature can have quite an impact on winds and air temperatures thousands of kilometers away. Pioneered by Jerome Namias and his colleagues at the Scripps Institution of Oceanography, La Jolla (which also pioneered the CO_2 issue), the study of air-sea interactions has become another major focus of research. It leads to an understanding of short-term climatic fluctuations, rather than of climatic change. The problem is that we do not yet have models that adequately couple the atmosphere and ocean together, as nature does. Such models are in the making.

The possibility that climate may change without any change in forcing from outside is at first sight unlikely. But we have been aware for decades of such a tendency—for example, for unexplained anomalies to start suddenly and endure for long periods, like the droughts of the 1930s, or the sudden increases in rainfall in east Africa in 1961. Such impulsive changes argue that the atmosphere does have the ability spontaneously to alter its usual mode of behavior (which we have been calling climate).

In 1968 Edward Lorenz, of M.I.T., pointed out that the theory of the atmospheric circulation predicted the possibility of such impulsive changes. He argued from a purely mathematical standpoint that the system of equations describing the circulation—used in modified form in the models we looked at—had the property that the solutions in force at a given time were not unique. Other persistent modes of behavior were possible, and the atmosphere might pass from one mode to another without any external stimulus. The atmosphere, he said, was "almost-intransitive," a term borrowed from the mathematical field of ergodics. Lorenz's hypothesis has been widely accepted. It implies that the impulsive but long-lasting changes we observe in climate—but cannot yet predict—may arise from its own internal characteristics.

It may be easier to assess the effect of real external changes. Of these we have already mentioned the influence of volcanic dust. A big increase in the number and scale of explosive eruptions would indeed tend to cool the world down. Krakatoa did this in 1883, Agung (in Bali) in 1963. A rapid succession of such events would probably take us back to a glacial climate. Any other activity that led to a major increase in the particles carried by the atmosphere would also need close watching. And any human economic practice that adds long-lasting pollutants to the atmosphere has a possible climatic impact. Later in the essay we shall look at the so-called ozone problem, another discovery of the 1970s. Like the CO_2 effect, it has a role to play in future climate.

A final possibility—related to climate's first cause—is a change in the behavior of the sun, the source of nearly all atmospheric energy. A change in the solar constant, the power of the solar beam outside the atmosphere, is possible. So also is a change in the nature of the radiation, for example an increase in the ultraviolet component that creates ozone, or a change in the flow of particles into the upper atmosphere. Actually there is evidence that the sun is a quiet, constant star. But it does have variations in the number and size of sunspots, and periodic storms affect its outer surface, leading to marked changes in particle radiation.

Climatologists, dendrochronologists (tree-ring specialists), glacial geologists, and others have looked for decades for relations between the number of sunspots and the behavior of climate, especially temperature and rain. It is not hard to find apparently significant relationships between the eleven-year sunspot cycle (which is actually irregular) and climate. Longer sunspot variations, like the so-called Maunder Minimum of the seventeenth century, can also be related to climatic anomalies. The trouble with all such correlations is twofold: one, that no one has yet given a good physical reason for them; and two, that the correlations tend to disappear as time goes by.

Climatologists have been caught out so often in this way that they have a bias against cyclical variations. To identify a correlation between some natural rhythm and climate, they say, is to invite the correlation to disappear. The only rhythms they are really committed to are those of day and night, summer and winter—those imposed by the motion of the earth relative to the sun. In recent years they have cautiously admitted a so-called quasi-biennial cycle of 2–2½ years, weakly displayed in a great many records. These aside, the professionals are as skeptical of cycles as amateurs are prone to believe in them.

A real change in the solar constant remains, however, a possibility. Observations of the sun from satellites and high altitude observatories have recently shown apparent ups and downs in the constant of about 0.1%. Arguments about such light-sensitive pigments as chlorophyll, or those of the eyes of mammals, make it unlikely that large changes have occurred in the past, because the wavelength of the brightest sunlight depends on the sun's temperature, and so does the solar constant. The pigments are very nicely tuned to the present-day sun, yet they evolved ages ago, presumably in relation to a very similar condition. Nevertheless it is reasonable to think about fluctuations of 1 to 2% in the solar constant, just as we do about a doubling of CO_2. If such changes are applied to the big atmospheric models discussed above, they produce changes in temperature comparable with those due to a doubling of CO_2 concentration. We have no reason to expect a change in the sun. If it happens, however, it will certainly have rapid and pronounced effects on climate.

Even without variation in the output of the sun, small changes in the receipt of solar energy by the earth are known to occur. These are associated with minor but predictable changes in orbital behavior. Many years ago the Yugoslav authority M. Milankovitch calculated the effect of these changes on energy receipts by the earth. In our own time these calculations have been refined by A. L. Berger and applied to the geological record by J. D. Hays, John Imbrie, and N. J. Shackleton, members of the CLIMAP project. The interaction of the obliquity of the earth's equatorial plane and the precession of the equinoxes leads to cyclical variation of received solar radiation with periods of 19,000, 23,000, and 41,000 years. These lead to a redistribution of energy between northern and southern hemispheres. In addition the eccentricity of the earth's orbit has a period of about 93,000 years. Research in the past decade has shown that these cycles are detectable in deep sea sediments. Glacial periods have recurred at about 100,000 year intervals, not very different from the eccentricity's period. And the shorter cycles also show themselves in the sediments. Much of the climatic variation of the past two million years may thus be related to long-term irregularities in the earth's orbital behavior, though we are not yet clear as to the causal links.

(c) The ozone problem

The 1970s also produced two other newcomers to the list of possible climatic changes due to human action. Both have implications for future climate. They achieved widespread publicity because of their potential impact on health and the rest of the environment. These were the notion that the ozone layer was in danger, a scare that dates from 1971, and the other that acid rain is damaging lakes, streams, forests, and crops in northern Europe and North America. Both scares are still with us, though neither has yet gone beyond the stage of controversy.

The ozone layer is in the stratosphere. Ozone is most abundant at about 25 km above the ground, and the rest is largely found in the layer between 10 and 40 km. Small amounts are found at ground-level, especially in certain kinds of smog. But the real ozone layer is far above us—which is just as well, considering that our lungs can tolerate only about 0.5 ppm! Outside the jet aircraft in which we so often fly the air is not merely frigidly cold, $-40°$ to $-60°$ C. as a rule; it is also quite unbreathable, at least north of the westerly jet streams, where the ozone layer descends to its lowest levels.

Nevertheless this very toxic gas serves an essential purpose. It consists of molecules with three O atoms, O_3, whereas ordinary oxygen has two, O_2. What happens is that ultraviolet radiation from the sun breaks up the O_2, and the dissociated atoms have the opportunity to link up with other O_2 molecules to form O_3. This happens quite high up in the stratosphere, where the ozone itself can absorb further ultraviolet and be dissociated again. A considerable amount, however, is transported into the lower stratosphere, where it has a longer life expectancy. Hence the ozone layer lies mostly below the levels of most rapid ozone creation.

In the course of this activity much of the ultraviolet is converted into heat by ozone and oxygen absorption. Two consequences ensue: the air becomes warm, being almost as warm at about 50 km as at ground level; and the more damaging forms of ultraviolet, which would otherwise injure living cells, are filtered out. Hence the popular term "the ozone shield."

Nevertheless enough ultraviolet penetrates to ground level to have some biological impact. It is the kind called "soft" in the trade; it has relatively long wavelengths, all above 295 nanometers (nm = one billionth of a meter). The "hard" ultraviolet of shorter wavelengths does not penetrate. In the cells of living tissues, notably our own skins, the genetic material DNA is apt to be damaged by ultraviolet in the range 295–320 nm. The human skin synthesizes the dark pigment melanin to protect itself. Suntan in white skins, and the permanent dark pigmentation of other colors, is hence a defense mechanism. Evidence from epidemiologists shows that skin cancers—both carcinomas and melanomas—are much commoner in unprotected skin exposed to sunlight. If it were not for the ozone shield, the intensity of the damaging radiation would be much higher, as would the incidence of skin cancer.

In 1971 H. Johnston of the University of California suggested that oxides of nitrogen might reduce the ozone concentration in the stratosphere and thus allow more ultraviolet to reach ground level. The aircraft industry was at that time planning a large expansion of the fleet of supersonic transports (SSTs) which would operate right in the ozone layer. Their exhaust gases, rich in oxides of nitrogen, would mix directly with the ozone and attack it chemically. Johnston's results caused an immediate furor. The U.S. federal government launched the Climatic Impact Assessment Program (CIAP), involving twenty countries, to see whether the threat was real.

Only three years later, when it had begun to appear that SSTs would not, after all, be produced in numbers, a second threat was delivered. F. Sheridan Rowland and H. J. Molina, also of the University of California, suggested in 1974 that chlorofluoromethanes (CFMs)—compounds containing carbon, fluorine, and chlorine—might diffuse upward into the stratosphere, be dissociated, release chlorine, and thereby attack ozone. The CFMs are used as refrigerants, spray-can propellants, and plastic foam inflaters. Ultimately all will escape into the lower atmosphere. Indeed, as Rowland and Molina pointed out, the atmosphere already contains large amounts of these gases, which will probably stay there until they are destroyed in the stratosphere; no other good sink has yet been identified.

The analysis of these problems proved, as usual, difficult and complex. The chemistry of the atmosphere had been very much neglected. It was necessary quickly to develop ways of measuring the distribution of the gases involved, often at concentrations as low as parts per billion or even parts per trillion, and to do this at great heights in the atmosphere. This has been done in several countries, and many excellent measurements are now available. So also is a good, ground-based network of stations to monitor continuously the total ozone content of the atmosphere.

The chemistry that has been revealed is complicated. If ozone is continuously formed by solar ultraviolet, as suggested above, it must also be dissociated naturally. Otherwise the amount would build up. Three processes are dominant, all in the stratosphere. One is simple interaction of the ozone with oxygen atoms, which yields oxygen molecules. Another is interaction with oxides of hydrogen. And the third—much the largest—involves attack on ozone by nitric oxide. This is derived from the less active nitrous oxide that diffuses upward from the soil, where it is produced in the decay of organic material. This has been one of the fascinating discoveries, that a process vital to the functioning of ecosystems is also a part of the mechanism whereby the ozone shield is regulated—the shield that, in turn, protects the ecosystems from ultraviolet radiation. This is a good example of ecology's first law, that all things connect.

Many groups went to work on this problem. The epidemiologists showed that skin cancer was more common in regions with high ultraviolet radiation, chiefly the subtropics. It was more likely to affect light-skinned people, and was most often detected on exposed parts of the body. The mechanism appeared to be damage to DNA molecules in sunburned skin. For carcinomas in the U.S., the incidence doubled for each 8 to 11 degrees latitude toward south, where ultraviolet was stronger. Hence there was every reason to fear that a reduction in ozone concentration would increase skin cancer. A U.S. National Academy of Sciences report of 1979 said that a 16% reduction in ozone might induce "several thousand more cases of melanoma per year, of which a substantial fraction would be fatal; and several hundred thousand more cases of nonmelanoma per year." Also foreseen was significant damage to crops, marine microorganisms, and seafood species.

The atmospheric chemists did indeed predict such a large decrease in ozone, not from the oxides of nitrogen, but from the upward diffusion of CFMs. There has been speculation that increased use of nitrogen-rich fertilizers would add to the natural upward flow of nitrous oxide, the gas that currently underlies most of the required breakdown of ozone. But the usual view is that the main threat of an undesirable increase in the breakdown is due to chlorine from the CFMs. As usual, the probable effect is hard to calculate. One has first to work out how much of the CFMs will be manufactured in the future. Adding this to the load already in the atmosphere, and using inadequate estimates of the rate of vertical transport, one can then inject the estimates into a numerical model of the chemical reactions known to occur in the stratosphere, a list of many dozens. A recent estimate by the U.S. National Academy of Sciences gives a probable reduction of ozone somewhat smaller than had been feared as recently as 1979. The potential increase in skin cancer, however, was estimated to be rather larger.

U.S. investigators have not been alone in such exercises. Similar calculations have been performed in the United Kingdom, France, Sweden, and the Soviet Union. Qualitatively the results resemble those described by the National Academy of Sciences, but quantitatively they are generally smaller. U.K. investigators, in particular, tend to make more conservative assumptions and get more conservative answers—or so it seems to this conservative, British-born essayist!

There, for the moment, the matter rests. A few measures have been taken to reduce CFM use, but many governments and quite a few scientists remain skeptical. Even if they accept the validity of the threat, they are apt to argue that a decrease ofa few percent in ozone, and hence an increase in damaging ultraviolet, is less than the risk incurred in moving one's home from Toronto to Miami, from Copenhagen to Athens, or from Melbourne to Townsville.

Is there a resulting threat of climatic change? The answer is certainly yes. A persistent change in ozone content, or of ultraviolet radiation, is itself a change in climate, properly defined. More than that, however, the CFMs are among the gases that strengthen the greenhouse effect, thereby tending to raise surface temperatures, on the order of 10% of the CO_2 effect. Slight changes in stratospheric temperature, and of the level of the tropopause, may also occur. These effects should show themselves in the next half-century as additions to the expected CO_2 warming.

(d) Acid deposition

The carbon dioxide and ozone effects are alike in several ways. They are global, for example. Carbon dioxide, nitrous oxides, and the CFMs are all poorly soluble in water. If we add them to the atmosphere they stay there; rain does not scavenge them appreciably. Wind has the time to disperse the additions globally. The sources are unevenly distributed, but the effect becomes worldwide. All three gases, moreover, can affect climate by altering the heat balance of the atmosphere. And all three have effects on, or are affected by, living organisms.

Acid rain touches mankind regionally, rather than globally. Worldwide climatic impacts, if any, are subtle and hard to detect. But the effect on organisms is direct and easily seen, especially in lakes and streams. Acid rain is thus a problem of the kind to which the environmentalists are accustomed. They have made it widely known to the public.

The pollutants chiefly responsible for acid rain—more strictly for acid *deposition*—are sulfur dioxide (SO_2) and the oxides of single nitrogen, usually denoted by NO_x. Nitrous oxide, N_2O, important in the ozone problem, is not a source of acid deposition. Oxides of both sulfur and nitrogen are emitted as exhausts when fuels are burned. Coal and oil are the chief sources of SO_2, car exhausts of NO_x. The acidity of precipitation in North America and Europe is due more to SO_2 than to NO_x, but the latter has been gaining ground.

The acidity arises from chemical and physical reactions in the atmosphere. Some of the SO_2 and NO_x return directly to the soil, or to plant and building surfaces as dry deposition. What comes down is either gas or dry particles. The rest—and it is often the greater part—is dissolved in cloud particles, after some chemical changes. The rain and snow that fall from such clouds are weakly acidic. In general, the higher the concentration of SO_2 and NO_x in the atmosphere, the more acid is the falling precipitation. Acidity depends on the abundance of free hydrogen ions in the rain or melted snow. It is expressed in terms of the logarithm of the reciprocal of the ion concentration—the so-called pH scale. At 7.0, water is neutral. It is alkaline if pH is above 7.0, acid if below. As yardsticks, fresh tomato juice has a pH near 4, apple juice near 3, vinegar and lemon juice near 2. A decrease of 1 on this scale corresponds to a *tenfold* increase in acidity. Precipitation is, in fact, usually slightly acid, at pH = 5.6, because of dissolved CO_2 and other natural constituents of the atmosphere.

In recent decades precipitation (and, by inference, dry deposition) has apparently been getting more acid in many areas. Observations in northern Europe show this effect clearly. Similar changes have been reported from northern and eastern North America—and also disputed. The average pH of rain is now below 4 over parts of southern Scandinavia and parts of mainland Europe. It is almost as low over New York State and much of southern Ontario. Individual rainstorms on both continents may be much more acid. The regions affected are on the average downwind of densely populated and industrialized areas; in Europe's case these include industrial regions of Germany, the Low Countries, Britain, and France; in North America they are the great industrial belt of the northeast embracing southern Quebec and Ontario, New England, New York, Pennsylvania and the Ohio Valley, and the lower Great Lakes. The inference is inescapable that the burning of fossil fuels, chiefly oil and coal, especially in power generating-stations and metal-smelters, has been responsible for the growing acidity.

The most obvious effects have been in lakes and streams. Over much of the rocky, glaciated Laurentian Shield of eastern Canada and New York State, and in much of New England, there have been widespread reports

of the death of fish populations. The same has been even more dramatically shown in Scandinavia. In fact it was anger at the damage to their lakes and streams that prompted Swedish scientists to call for an international airing of the issue. This led to the summoning in 1972 of the United Nations Conference on the Human Environment at Stockholm, a landmark in world recognition of the interdependence of nations in the care of their natural endowments.

In Europe the Organization for Economic Cooperation and Development (OECD) and the U.N. Economic Commission for Europe (ECE) have both pressed for multilateral action to abate the problem and have sponsored far-reaching research. North America has followed suit. Canada and the United States have signed a memorandum of intent to proceed toward treaty regulation of the problem; only bilateral agreement can get results, since pollutants emitted in one country often fall into the territories and water bodies of the other. There is some difference of perception between the two countries. Canadian politicians loudly express the view that most acid rain in Canada originates from U.S. pollution and call for strong measures to reduce SO_2 and NO_x emissions. In fact, the world's largest single source for SO_2 is the Sudbury nickel smelting area of Ontario. Under the Reagan administration there have been moves to relax air pollution controls from both industrial plants and automobiles. It will be many years, if at all, before remedial measures can be fully effective in such an atmosphere of controversy.

Like the consequences of carbon dioxide buildup, the changes in precipitation chemistry associated with acid precipitation are themselves climatic changes, if one takes a wide enough view of climate. This is especially true if we consider the interaction between climate and living organisms, the bioclimate. The area of detectable impact is, however, more local. Acid rain has been called a rich man's disease, like gout and obesity. Indeed there are regions of the tropics and the southern hemisphere where soils do not have enough sulfur, and where a frequent sprinkling of acid rain would be welcome.

Regardless of perspective, the fuss about acid rain has undoubtedly added to public sensitivity to climatic impact. As the 1970s ended it was actually the most loudly debated of the climate-related issues. On a world scale most climatologists would give it less prominence. It is, in their view, unlikely to have major global effects on the other elements of climate.

Climate and society

I and my colleagues have thus felt the excitement, during the past decade, of new energy pulsing through our science, whose frontiers have been rolled back greatly. For the first time in decades, atmospheric scientists are being tempted to write books relating their work to the wide world beyond; Stephen H. Schneider and Lynne Morton have just published *The Primordial Bond,* an analysis of ". . . the intense and finely interwoven relationship between man and nature." It has taken a shock from outside to make us realize that our science is not a pleasant, private place but one of the disciplines that allows us to understand the things conditioning our lives.

We are now trying to develop a scientific way of showing how climate and the human economy interact. It is no easy job. Major projects are under way in several countries as part of the World Climate Program, or similar national plans. These ventures began in the wake of the 1979 World Climate Conference, or as a result of national anxieties about food and energy. International bodies have also got into the act. The World Climate Program itself, coordinated mainly by the World Meteorological Organization (WMO), is laying stress on four themes: research toward a better understanding of climate, and its long-range prediction; a better use of the huge volume of accumulated data about climate in economic decision-making; more imaginative applications of climatic understanding and foreknowledge; and a detailed analysis of climate's impact on specific sectors and on the global economy. The International Council of Scientific Unions (ICSU), world science's senior non-governmental body, is involved in the first and fourth of these undertakings, and the U.N. Environment Programme (UNEP) in the fourth.

The first of these objectives—a deeper understanding of climate—is obviously now an interdisciplinary affair. It is being tackled by WMO and

ICSU as a logical outgrowth of the Global Atmospheric Research Program, which indeed it is. If anyone had told me, however, when GARP was being designed a decade or two ago, that it would evolve into the core of a world climate program, I would have disbelieved it. I could not have conceived that my own profession could be so quickly converted to the notion that climate was the core problem confronting it. Nor would I have believed that biologists, agricultural scientists, foresters, oceanographers, geologists, and many others would be keen to join in. In my public addresses of the 1960s I kept announcing the change without believing it. I should have had more faith.

The second and third objectives are straightforward enough, if decision-makers will listen. Certainly the world's climatologists are united in wanting to be useful. Many of them have been pioneers in such applications. What they have been up against is the indifference to climate already stressed, and their own failure to devise ways and means of proving the importance of their data and ideas. Put baldly, the profession has not made a case in most countries for its own value. Here and there useful work is done, timely services performed. But all of us ache to do more, especially when we witness upsets like the imbroglios in the grain markets in 1972–73 and 1973–74.

The fourth objective of the World Climate Program aims to make this possible. It seeks an understanding of climatic impact and is mainly a research effort. WMO shrank from undertaking it, recognizing the limitations of a one-subject approach. Instead it farmed the responsibility out to UNEP, whose headquarters in Nairobi are in the midst of the continent most affected by bad climate in recent years. UNEP has had close associations with the fight against desert spread, but little contact with other climatic problems. So it turned to ICSU, and its Scientific Committee on Problems of the Environment (SCOPE), with headquarters in Paris. This list of acronyms is embarrassing, but inescapable. International science is organized into both inter-governmental and non-governmental bodies. Given the complexity of the subject it is surprising that the list is as short as it is.

Currently SCOPE's group of researchers around the world is trying to get an overview of what is going on in individual countries, and to originate studies of its own. The work is directed by Robert W. Kates of Clark University, Worcester, Massachusetts, a pioneer of hazard and risk studies. It brings together atmospheric scientists, economists, geographers, biologists, and systems analysts. Just a list of the countries from which the participants come demonstrates the worldwide nature of the study: New Zealand, Australia, France, Japan, Hungary, Federal Republic of Germany, Nigeria, Mexico, the Soviet Union, India, Tanzania, Canada, the U.S., and the U.K. Each of these countries has some special national competence as well as skills in a variety of sciences. The project is a good example of the quiet scientific initiatives that never make the front page.

(Top) Degraded, semi-arid, eucalyptus scrub with termite mounds in Queensland, a state of Australia. Such landscapes are vulnerable to desertification. (Bottom) Desertification; heavily eroded soils in semi-arid South Australia, due mainly to overstocking with sheep.

The problem turns out to be difficult, though not impossibly so. Some questions are comparatively simple. The yield of wheat, for example, is a resolvable function of summer rainfall, temperature, and variety of seed. The yield of a river system after specific rainstorms can also be predicted. There is a large body of such one-dimensional studies of climate-society linkages.

Obviously we need something more. Intuitively one feels that the energy problems of 1976–77, or the past three poor crop years in the Soviet Union, represent assaults by climate on the whole economic and social system. They ought to have had impacts well beyond food and energy supply. At the time, these aberrations caused headlines about widespread dislocations, economic losses and public incompetence. A feature writer for *The Economist*, for example, asserted that the repeated crop losses in the Soviet Union were due to technical and bureaucratic bungling. The Soviet leadership, he claimed, was merely blaming nature for its own failures, a view that I had to challenge, since I doubt if any agricultural system, however flexible, could have dealt with the climatic stresses recently faced by the Soviets. Surely, if the impacts are real, and are on the scale reported, they ought to show up through the whole economy? Can we not trace them into the socioeconomic fabric?

The answer has to be, not far! Economists are not in the habit of analyzing single external ("exogenous" they say) factors and their impacts. They treat items that are measurable in money terms, and which are traditional items of public accounting. They have a body of theory and practice that derives from inward-looking perspectives, most readily focused on economic statistics. In the past two decades they have had to devise new techniques to deal with problems of the environment, and it might be thought that these could readily be extended to climatic impact analysis. There have indeed been such attempts in the past few years, efforts that have enlisted the services of at least one Nobel prizewinning economist, Kenneth Arrow, who used to be a meteorologist. We have had analyses, for example, of the potential cost of the stratospheric ozone problem and of measures to overcome it, and of the potential impact on crop production of a 1 degree Celsius temperature rise or fall. But of overall macroeconomic analysis of climatic impact we have nothing.

The impression is growing, moreover, that the market economies of the west are largely immune from serious climatic impact. The headlines are about local dislocations and stresses, say the optimists; they ignore the almost immediate response of the sufferers to their own condition. Producers and consumers don't just sit down and endure a climatic stress; they react strongly to minimize its effects. Impact and reaction are almost simultaneous, and one never sees the direct consequences in a simple form. We have equipped ourselves with all kinds of devices to cushion the impact. There is the technical inventory, for instance: spare capacity in electrical systems, pending a hot summer or a cold winter; crop varieties that can meet all kinds of new climatic situations (or so the optimist says); irrigation systems; drainage systems designed to meet the hundred-year flood. And there are the institutional "fixes": bank-loans; insurance against hail, drought, flood, and frost; cooperative marketing; early warning systems; direct and indirect subsidies. All these devices and dozens of others shield the individual from the climatic threat. They also contribute to economic welfare, at least in prosperous countries. On this view an uncertain climate, like other forms of uncertainty, offers a challenge or even an opportunity rather than a threat, as long as the stress remains within bounds. All this is possible within economies that have income far beyond what is needed for bare necessities.

In effect, the strategy of advanced countries like the United States and Canada is to build into the system the technical competence to meet any sudden climatic problem by making sure that the tools and methods used are not too finely tuned to normal conditions. Elements of risk remain, and these are guarded against institutionally by the insurance companies, the banks, and government agencies. We think it worthwhile to absorb the cost of these measures and of the losses that still occur.

A curious result of this sophistication—of rolling with the punch—is that risk-taking seems to be on the increase in many western countries. In the Great Plains of the United States and the Prairies of Canada, for example, the high price of cereals in the past decade has pushed arable cultivation back toward the dry margin, from which it was driven in the 1930s. Much land is now cultivated in high risk areas, or by high risk techniques. I have seen the same process at work in semiarid Australia. In due course these areas will be stricken with prolonged drought and topsoil losses again. As Richard Warrick has shown, however, the farmer is now protected against most of the consequences. He is not risking his economic survival, as he was in the 1930s. Earlier drought in the Plains brought about wholesale abandonment of land, much of which is once again under the plough. It is unlikely that a future drought cycle will have such drastic effects on people. The soil, however, is still at risk. There is no guarantee that we shall avoid a physical dust bowl.

Risk-taking of another sort has confronted the electric utilities. In some large metropolitan areas, notably New York, the capacity of the electric generating and distributing system is severely stretched by prolonged summer heat, because air conditioning has become so widespread. Peak load tends to come in summer; one faces the paradox that one has to spend electric energy to get rid of heat, rather than to provide it. The hot summer of 1980 was a sustained nightmare in the large cities of the Middle West and South. Expansion of the electricity system to meet these demands has been hindered by many factors—environmental objections, high fuel costs, the poverty of municipal government, and, most recently, the high cost of money. So, many utilities have to coast through the heat waves of summer or the cold snaps of winter with little if any spare capacity. Failure means brownouts, "outages," or damage to facilities.

The impression that climate has been defeated is hence illusory. It remains in the near background from which from time to time it will emerge to embroil us. We are unlikely, on present form, to do much about it. Only when disaster strikes does a democracy move. I once complimented the chief executive officer of a major utility on how he kept so cheerful and asked: what was his strategy? He replied: "I'm waiting for disaster; nothing else works!"

Most social scientists who have worked on these problems would agree. It is not merely that hope springs eternal in the human breast. We are not simply forgetful of past injuries. Instead, we calculate that our gains from slightly risky enterprises are worth those risks. Our lives and livelihoods seem no longer at stake. We forget, perhaps, that millions of others are not as lucky. A serious change in our attitude toward environmental hazards as a whole has to wait, as a rule, on rude awakenings. Meanwhile the scientist and engineer will go on looking for ways of coping with the hazards.

The science of climate

(a) The climatic system

Repeatedly in the past pages I have argued that we must now take a broader view of climate. Climatologists have to think, in fact, of the climatic system—the way in which the atmosphere interacts with plants, animals, rocks, soils, water, snow, ice, the sun, and outer space. They have given up the idea that they are merely physicists or mathematicians, confining themselves to the atmosphere itself, and content with their instruments and computers. Nowadays at a world conference on climate one expects to see climatologists arguing with geologists, ecologists, hydrologists, geographers, oceanographers, and several other scientific groups. And the newcomers do not hesitate to write about climate as an important issue—which is just as well, because it turns out that they have much to say that would have never occurred to the older kind of atmospheric scientists.

Obviously the climatic system has much in common with the global ecosystem. In fact they are equivalent ideas. The first appeals to the climatologist, who puts the atmosphere at the center of the scene. The second is preferred by ecologists, who naturally put life in the middle. But these are only differences of stress; the system is the same system. Both are examples of how scientists have been brought to a holistic view of the natural environment. For two or three centuries science has evolved toward a never-ending subdivision of nature, so as to get a better look at it—reductionism, so-called. If one wants to look at nature as the stage on which human affairs are played, one needs a broader view. There are many who choose to study climate or natural ecosystems for their own sake, and they, too, need the holistic approach. In fact, the so-called first law of ecology, that all things are connected, cannot be escaped.

About the study of climate there is much, therefore, of what Stephen Toulmin calls "post-modern science." In his review in *The Great Ideas Today* 1981, Toulmin asserted that "the goals and methods of 'post-modern science' now rest on a recognition that, to a greater or lesser degree, all scientific understanding whatever involves uneliminable intervention by the scientist in the processes that he is seeking to understand. Instead of seeking to stand 'outside' those processes, scientists have now learned to accept their new status as participants within the very situations they are studying." Speaking of ecology as an example, he stressed that its theory and practice are unusually close, as in climate; that its methods focus on natural processes on the human scale, and in which human agencies may be effective, again as in climate; and that it has been able to achieve maturity and independence only during the last few decades, once more as in climate. The changes I have been describing are precisely those that Toulmin sees as advancing along an extended scientific frontier.

Certainly it has been necessary during the past decade, as in ecology, to bring human intervention into climatology. The climatic system that we study is man-altered, even to some extent man-adapted. We are now in a position to study the climates of other planets, thanks to space vehicles. The climates of Venus and Mars are still almost pristine. That of the earth, however, is significantly modified by our presence within it. The human environment envelops us even as we study it. Climate is a critical part of that envelope.

These changes have not happened without stress and discomfort for the professional atmospheric scientists. I can remember times when my own teachers and colleagues openly sneered at environmental ideas; they much preferred isolation and simon-purity. Yet the logic of events has dragged even the unwilling along toward the newer perspective. Ecology is mere birds-nesting, said a notorious skeptic, and to the cynical meteorologist climatology was mere number-crunching. Such sneers are now uncommon, and soon they will be forgotten. Climate has become, as we saw earlier, a central object of enquiry for these same cynics.

Climatology grew out of two main bodies of science—meteorology on the one hand, natural history, geography, and biology on the other. The latter came first. Among students of soils, vegetation, animals, and ecosystems it seemed obvious a century ago that climate played a key role in determining the natural history of the world; it was the core of any reasonable physical geography. Pioneers such as Augustin de Candolle, Wladimir Köppen and Warren Thornthwaite maintained, over a full century, the tradition of describing the regional climates of the earth, and of the role of climate in determining the character of soils and vegetation.

"Among students of soils, vegetation, animals, and ecosystems it seemed obvious a century ago that climate played a key role in determining the natural history of the world; it was the core of any reasonable physical geography. Pioneers such as Augustin de Candolle [above] . . . maintained, over a full century, the tradition of describing the regional climates of the earth, and of the role of climate in determining the character of soils and vegetation."

The descriptive element was large and necessary, and it is still needed. The forthcoming *Atlas of Historical Geography of Canada,* a major work by any standards, will base its physical regionalization on Köppen's classification of climates, now a half-century old.

Meteorologists are trained, as a rule, as mathematicians or physicists. Traditionally they turn up their noses at taxonomies and descriptions of natural events. The climatology of Köppen and Thornthwaite was, to the experimentally trained meteorologist, pretty poor stuff. They began to use the term *climatology* to describe the compilation of weather statistics, and *climate* became average weather. This usage persists, but it is weakening. Among meteorologists there have also been pioneers of the stuff we may now properly call climatology: William Ferrel, for example, who in the antebellum South reexamined Laplace's tidal theory, and in so doing discovered the essential mechanics of the general circulation of the atmosphere; Harold Jeffreys, whose 1926 paper on the general circulation demonstrated that its dynamics was in effect statistical in character; and Carl-Gustaf Rossby, on whose great achievements the present movement toward linking oceanic and atmospheric sciences depends.

All the sciences of the environment have one special quality that sets them off from the exact, experimental sciences. They deal with the actual world, which is enormously complex. They are observational: they need data about how things evolve. The experimental method, though not impossible, is usually difficult and of limited value. One can design rotating tanks or annuli, for example, in which water can be made to circulate in physical simulation of the atmosphere. But such methods are usually quite secondary to the main thrust of research, which depends on huge bodies of worldwide observational data, and on the ever-necessary computer with which to digest them. Number-crunching, the jibe of yesterday, has become the central method of the science.

Because the atmosphere varies in both space and time, the meteorologist has from the beginning been concerned to organize a network of observing stations, and a discipline of regular, unceasing observation. Weather maps began when it first became possible to collect observations at one place and plot them graphically—the so-called synoptic charts. At once it became apparent that the circulation of the atmosphere had patterns that moved about the earth. The wind might appear to blow where it listed, but it actually did so in an organized fashion. Superimposed on these patterns were less organized motions, the "turbulence" of present-day parlance.

Out of this experience came several of the attributes of the modern science. It was necessary, for example, to agree on a standardized list of things to observe, and ways of doing so. Instruments had to be made comparable in performance—cross-calibrated, in the jargon of science. A common numerical language had to be devised for the easy exchange of data, and systems of national and international communications had to be set up, because it was soon discovered that weather systems were larger than many countries and could move as fast as an express train. The electric telegraph made this possible, first in Europe, and then in North America.

By the beginning of our own century it had become obvious that observations were needed at high altitudes. Balloon soundings by Teisserenc de Bort in France demonstrated the existence of the stratosphere before the turn of the century. Developments in Germany and Scandinavia (especially Norway) led by the end of the First World War to the concept of moving, three-dimensional air masses, separated by sloping frontal surfaces on which moving cyclones formed. The use of high-altitude aircraft in the Second World War demonstrated the existence of westerly jet streams in the 10–15 km layer. The work of V. & J. Bjerknes in Norway, of E. Palmén (a Finn), and C. G. Rossby (a Swede) linked these ideas together and paved the way for the development after 1947 of solid dynamical theory to account for the behavior of the lower atmosphere.

In the postwar world the climatological system has become genuinely worldwide. The digital computer, first used in weather prediction at the

97

Institute for Advanced Studies at Princeton under the guidance of John von Neumann, transformed our ability to apply theory to the problems of prediction. Satellites began to add enormously to the observational resources of the science. By the 1970s it was possible to use the new technologies in moves toward a general comprehension of the atmospheric climate.

We have already seen that this evolution of the science required large-scale international organization and have sketched the outlines of the World Climate Program. We now face, however, a more formidable challenge. How do we carry matters further, so as to treat the whole climatic system, with human intervention included?

In a real sense, to do this flies in the face of established scientific method, not merely in the reductionist mode. It is a cardinal rule of the physical scientist not to mix apples and oranges. All physical equations balance, not only as regards numbers, but as regards "dimensions." Every term in such equations is like all its companions on either side of the equal sign. Thus every term in an equation about energy is expressed in energy units. Physicists, chemists, and mathematicians are used to such tidiness and logical precision.

Unfortunately one cannot apply such rigor to the propositions of the biologist, except in principle. Still less can one expect to do so with the affairs of human society. Only to a limited extent do the social sciences yield quantitative data, and only in economics is there a body of theory that in any way resembles that of the physical scientist. Economists achieve a measure of dimensional consistency by reducing as many things as possible to money terms. But most quantitative analysis in the social sciences is statistical and heterogeneous. Apples and oranges *are* mixed, and so are demographic data, social statistics, and even measures of humanity's physical and psychological attributes.

A full understanding of the climatic system with human intervention included will hence necessitate bridging a wide methodological gulf between the atmospheric sciences and the multitude of specialties that focus on human affairs. Already this is in full swing, especially in analyses of future energy requirements. Engineers are involved in much of the work. They have always been more ready to cut methodological corners than have physical scientists. Building a bridge, for example, calls for more than physical design; it requires such data as traffic counts, estimates of population growth, and climatic statistics. The discipline of engineering is being rapidly enlarged so as to encompass good environmental design; as I was writing this essay I was also at work on a chapter on the atmosphere for a textbook in environmental engineering. If human needs require a synthesis of disparate skills, the engineer will certainly try to provide it.

And so, too, will the atmospheric scientists. Already certain promising steps are being taken. It has become clear to some leading meteorologists that the climatic system is not merely a chimerical ideal; it offers a solid basis for new advances.

Interactive climatology and ecology

The science of ecology has offered the most obvious new insights. At the 1979 World Climate Conference a highly respected Swedish meteorologist, Bert Bolin, chose to deliver an address called *Global Ecology and Man*. It obviously startled the more conservative meteorologists in the audience. He laid major stress on the oddly named *biogeochemical cycles*, the mechanisms and pathways whereby living organisms and man exchange energy, nutrients, and materials with their physical surrounds. The study of these cycles, he maintained, was not only crucial for ecologists; it also gave important insight into climate and was indeed the proper way to link climate to the rest of nature, especially when human interference was at work.

Bolin himself has been one of the pioneers in the study of the carbon cycle in nature, as perturbed by man. He was among the first to see that the carbon dioxide problem in the atmosphere is really a gigantic disturbance of the overall system of exchange of carbon among air, sea, soil, rock, and living organisms. In the same way he showed that acid rain is properly seen as part of a disturbance of the natural sulfur cycle. Climatic processes are only part of the story in each case. Full comprehension requires knowledge of the whole cycle.

Nowhere is this interdependence of atmospheric, oceanic, terrestrial, and economic domains more obvious than in the energy cycle. Ecologists have become used to treating ecosystems in terms of their energy inputs and outputs. The teaching of George Evelyn Hutchinson at Yale University was a major factor in this change of outlook. In 1941 one of his doctoral students, Raymond Lindeman, published a remarkable paper called *Towards a Trophic-Dynamic Ecology*, in which he formalized the basis for an analysis of ecosystem energy exchanges and transformations. Lindeman was only twenty-six, and was dying of an incurable disease, but he was able to draw on earlier European traditions to move ecology toward an "energetic" basis. The International Biological Programme of the 1960s and 1970s was in many ways an outgrowth of his initiative and personal courage.

The energy of living organisms comes in the first instance from the conversion of solar energy (actually of visible light) by green plants in the act of photosynthesis. The energy so converted is then used to build up plant tissues and later flows up the food-web into herbivores, carnivores, and man. Large though it is, this metabolic energy flow proceeds at less than 1 percent of the rate of atmospheric energy processes; climatologists have usually regarded it as a minor and negligible term in their calculations. All life nevertheless derives its energy from this source, at first, second, third, or fourth hand (the trophic levels of Lindeman's system).

99

Photosynthesis proceeds freely on land, however, only if an abundant water supply is available in the green leaves, and if the temperature of those leaves is held within certain limits. Both conditions require a steady flow of water from the soil into the leaves and its evaporation to the atmosphere. This process of *transpiration* is in many humid areas the largest consumer of solar energy at the land surface. The transpiration of water from leaves to atmosphere is also the largest upward on-land component of the hydrologic cycle whereby the atmosphere's water content is exchanged with the surface. Hence the natural energy exchanges at the earth's surface—the energy climate—are heavily influenced by the requirements of plants and animals and also interlock with the exchanges of water and carbon between the same domains.

For generations scientific specialists managed to keep this unity sundered. Ecologists concerned with energy in ecosystems, for example, typically bothered only about metabolic energy, i.e., the tiny fraction that is actually involved in the biochemistry of organisms. The much larger fraction used in transpiration was often depicted in their work as "not used," in spite of the fact that photosynthesis would grind to a halt without transpiration. On the other hand, meteorologists persisted for decades in treating the upward flow of water vapor from land surfaces as evaporation in the purely physical sense. They neglected both the physics of soil water and the physiology of transpiration. Such neglect by ecologists and meteorologists of essential parts of the system's mechanics was due to imperfect methods of analysis, which are slowly and happily being replaced. Thus the big numerical models of the atmosphere now typically include estimates of both soil water storage and evapotranspiration in their inputs and outputs. But it will be a long time before the models of the ecologist and the atmospheric scientist are consistent with one another, and with what we need for a good understanding. Meanwhile we have to tackle the problem of human intervention with the imperfect tools in our possession.

What the ecologists have taught the atmospheric scientists is that all things are connected. One must study, not merely the atmospheric concentration of carbon dioxide, but the flow of carbon throughout the natural world, and into and out of the human industrial apparatus. In the water cycle, one must learn somehow that the upward flow of water from soil through plants into the atmosphere is as much a climatic process as the downward flow that we call rain. One cannot pick and choose according to the prejudices imparted by training. A scientific method that takes things apart—reductionism—may be necessary to an understanding of nature. But so also is the method—typically ecological—that seeks to comprehend whole systems.

The need to consider the work of man, and to repair some of the damage done to the environment, has been a spur to this movement towards synthesis and holistic thought. We have already seen that this is true of the carbon cycle. It is also true of energy, and of water. Irrigation, for example, is an intrusion into the natural hydrologic and energy cycles, and also tends to accelerate nutrient leaching. Hydrology is in many ways a sub-set of the larger body of knowledge called climatology. Yet its professionals, concerned almost wholly with water management, have developed their skills with only a weak and intermittent contact with the atmospheric scientists. Management demands a broader perspective.

Thus climatology, in its proper manifestation, must be seen as a body of knowledge continuous with, and not truly distinguishable from, its neighbors in ecology, hydrology, and oceanography. In its post-modern qualities it belongs, as Toulmin demonstrated, with all other sciences of the environment in which mankind is an actor as well as a student.

Conclusion

Like all essayists, I reach the heading "Conclusion" with mixed feelings—relief at having got there, guilt at perhaps not having arrived. I threw out numerous questions on the way. Have they been answered?

I began by asking whether politicians, social scientists, and engineers were right in attaching so low a value to the advice of climatologists, and to the facts of climate itself. I went on to suggest that there were many points at which existing climates touched human affairs, in some cases calamitously, in others trivially. Mankind, however, was highly adapted to normal climate and ordinary variability; it was only when extreme events produced dire consequences that there was political awareness of the need to do more. We were inclined to accept the risks involved in ignoring climatic hazards. They were a necessary cost incurred by our search for high economic return in good years. Advanced societies could afford such risks. The less developed world could not.

I find this a dissatisfying conclusion, and not merely because it is unflattering to my own profession. Throughout my scientific career—which has been diverse and has involved me in different fields—I have had the same sense that society makes poor use of science in its social and political processes, and in economic decision making. Like Toulmin, to whose own essay I referred, I remember the confident predictions of J. D. Bernal, whose colleague I once was, and the optimism in post-1945 decades that the golden age of useful science was finally upon us, notwithstanding the endless threat of nuclear war. What in fact we have done is to use science technologically; in the jargon of computer science, it provides our hardware. It makes much less impact when scientific knowledge takes the form of information, intelligence, or prediction.

The word *prediction* is the key. In socioeconomic and political affairs we still blunder into the future, which we cannot foresee. Investment decisions, commodity purchases, inventory control—all these and many others are made partly by hunch, partly after advice from so-called counsel, partly following scrutiny of the output of econometric models. Hunch is still a major factor. On the political scale it is certainly dominant. Within hours after our decision we know why we are so often wrong: the millions of other decisions taken almost simultaneously drive the markets, which make fools out of the pundits time after time and beggars out of average speculators.

Weather prediction has notoriously had the same failings (though it is far better than rumor and scuttlebutt allows). If all the satellites, radars, radiosondes, computers, and facsimile machines cannot make a forecast reliable, if events still ignore predictions for a few hours of weather ahead, how can we reasonably speak of prediction of climate? If we could, the effect on markets, for example, would be dramatic, and planning such things as wheat planting, installed electric capacity, and arctic sea navigation would become matters of reasonable precision. But the public knows that the weather forecaster is often wrong twenty-four hours ahead. How, then, can he be right about next year, next decade, or even next century?

The answer, surprisingly, is that it may be easier to predict long-range climatic change than it is to foresee next week's weather. Weather springs from very short-term processes having to do with the internal instability of the wind systems. Careful analysis shows that weather maps two to eight days ahead (depending on location) are essentially independent of present conditions. There is some controversy as to what this implies for predictability. But few professionals expect detailed, short-term weather forecasts to be extended very far. A few days or a week or two may be actually the upper limit of predictability, on present assumptions—though there are optimists who challenge this view. Climatic change, of the sort discussed above, arises from altered inputs to the system. If we can predict these, perhaps we can predict the consequences—as, in these pages, I have tried to do for the carbon dioxide buildup.

It is my conviction that only if we have predictive power, at a level of confidence that *justifies* confidence, can we hope for any major change in political attitudes toward climate. I am not optimistic that we shall quickly attain this power. But neither do I rule it out. And if we get it, then the potential use of that power will be highly significant for human welfare.

I end, then, on the familiar scientist's *credo:* we need more research! Research into climate's own mechanisms, into climate-society interaction, into the functions of the climatic system. Much is already happening, much more remains to be done. And in the scientific community, at least, the will is certainly there.

Bibliography
The following are the main books cited in the text

W. G. Dean, J. Warkentin, C. Harris, and others, eds., *Atlas of Historical Geography of Canada,* to be published.

A. K. Biswas and M. R. Biswas, eds., *Food, Climate, and Man* (New York: Wiley-Interscience, 1979), 285 pp.

R. A. Bryson and T. J. Murray, *Climates of Hunger* (Madison: University of Wisconsin Press, 1977), 171 pp.

M. H. Glantz, ed., *The Politics of Natural Disaster: The Case of the Sahel Drought* (New York: Praeger, 1976), 340 pp.

M. H. Glantz, ed., *Desertification: Environmental Degradation in and around Arid Lands* (Boulder, Colorado: Westview, 1977), 346 pp.

M. H. Glantz and J. D. Thompson, *Resource Management and Environmental Uncertainty: Lessons from Coastal Upwelling Fisheries* (New York: Wiley-Interscience, 1981), 491 pp.

W. W. Kellogg and R. Schware, *Climate Change and Society: Consequences of Increasing Atmospheric Carbon Dioxide* (Boulder, Colorado: Westview, 1981), 178 pp.

E. LeRoy Ladurie, *Times of Feast, Times of Famine* (New York: Doubleday, 1971), 426 pp.

National Academy of Sciences, *Protection against Depletion of Stratospheric Ozone by Chlorofluorocarbons* (Washington, D.C., 1979), 392 pp.

A. Rapp, H. N. Le Houérou, and B. Lundholm, eds., *Can Desert Encroachment Be Stopped?,* Ecological Bulletin 24, Swedish National Research Council, Stockholm (1976), 241 pp.

W. O. Roberts and H. Lansford, *The Climate Mandate* (San Francisco: Freeman, 1979), 197 pp.

S. H. Schneider and L. Mesirow, *The Genesis Strategy: Climate and Global Survival* (New York and London: Plenum Press, 1976), 442 pp.

S. H. Schneider and L. Morton, *The Primordial Bond* (New York and London: Plenum, 1981), 324 pp.

United Nations: *Desertification: Its Causes and Consequences,* U.N. Conference on Desertification Secretariat, Nairobi, 1977, published by Pergamon, Oxford, 448 pp.

J. Walls, *Land, Man and Sand* (New York: Macmillan, 1980), 336 pp.

World Meteorological Organization, *Proceedings of the World Climate Conference* (Geneva: 1979), 791 pp.

---

[1] So, naturalists observe, a flea
Hath smaller fleas that on him prey;
And these have smaller fleas to bite 'em
And so proceed ad infinitum.
Thus every poet, in his kind,
Is bit by him that comes behind.
Jonathan Swift, "On Poetry," 337

[2] Charney died in June 1981, the most influential meteorologist of his day.

[3] The U.S.S.R. imported 34 million tons in 1980–81 and is reported to be seeking 42 million tons in 1981–82. Their 1981 summer crop has been damaged by drought.

[4] In the lower atmosphere a wind is described by the direction *from* which it blows.

Recent Contributions to Our Knowledge of the Bible

Raymond E. Brown

Recognized by *Time* magazine as "probably the premier Catholic Scripture scholar in the United States," Father Raymond Brown is Auburn Professor of Biblical Studies at Union Theological Seminary in New York and the author of fifteen books on the Bible, among them a two-volume commentary on *The Gospel According to St. John* (1970) and *The Jerome Biblical Commentary* (1968), of which he was an editor—both of which won the National Catholic Book Award.

Father Brown, who was ordained a Catholic priest in 1953, holds doctorates in both theology and in Semitic Languages. He has been president of the Catholic Biblical Association (1971–72) and the Society of Biblical Literature (1976–77), which is the largest society of biblical scholars in the world. From 1972 to 1978 he served on the Roman Pontifical Biblical Commission, the only American among twenty scholars appointed to that body by Pope Paul VI as "outstanding for their learning, prudence, and Catholic regard for the Magisterium of the Church."

Besides his scholarly endeavors, Father Brown has been active in ecumenical work, having been the first Roman Catholic to address a Faith and Order Conference of the World Council of Churches (Montreal, 1963), and the only American Catholic appointed to the Commission, by agreement with the Council and the Vatican. From 1968 to 1973 by papal nomination he was also Consultor to the Vatican Secretariat for Christian Unity.

I n the title of this essay, "recent" covers a period stretching back to the era between the two World Wars, even if most attention will be given to the period after the Second War. Even more difficult to determine is the span covered by "knowledge." Most who read and study the Bible do so for religious and theological motives: they believe that it is the word of God and that a perception of divine revelation can be gained from its pages. Consequently "knowledge" could very appropriately cover what the Bible has come to mean for twentieth-century theology or religion(s), or for current spiritual and ethical issues (e.g., feminism, movements of liberation, disputed aspects of morality). Certainly relevant to biblical knowledge is the fact that in this century many Jewish and Christian scholars agree on approaches to the Hebrew Scriptures, and that since the Second World War most Roman Catholic and Protestant scholars use the same methodologies in studying the New Testament, even producing ecumenical commentaries on previously disputed passages.

Nevertheless, what is generally meant when one speaks of an increased biblical "knowledge" is what pertains to the other side of the twofold component in the Scriptures, the human side. A belief in the inspired character of the Bible does not make its pages any less a chronicle of the existence of people: Hebrews, Israel, the Jews,[1] and Christians. Covering almost 2,000 years and consisting of sixty-six to seventy-three different books[2] written at widely separate periods of time, the Bible may be perceived as the preserved library of those people, in particular, the Old Testament as the library of Israel, and the New Testament as the library of the early Church. Every research method that enlightens human activity is capable of throwing light on the Bible, not only those already employed earlier in this century (hermeneutics, linguistics, historical criticism, archaeology, sociology, comparative religion) but also chemistry, computer technology, etc. Indeed, the range of biblical research has so broadened that it is no small task to classify the methodologies, never mind the results.

Often, however, there is little agreement on how the methodologies (especially the more speculative) are to be applied. Most scholars would agree that one must study the literary genre of the various elements in a biblical book (form criticism), the traditions that have shaped the author's thought (tradition criticism), and the oral or written sources upon which he drew (source criticism), as well as the overall view that he has imposed as he shaped all this material into a new composition of his own (redaction criticism). Furthermore, many at least would agree that, once written, the author's composition became a piece of literature with its own existence, sometimes evoking responses he never dreamed of (literary criticism), and also that the author's work has become part of a sacred canonical collection which serves to interpret and qualify it (canonical criticism). Despite such agreement, scholars may and do differ widely on the relative importance to be given to each of these facets of interpretation, and as a result they produce commentaries that are very different in diagnosing the meaning of scriptural passages and their importance. No one can doubt that the twentieth century has seen great progress in the art of interpreting the ancient religious books that constitute the Bible. Yet the very diversity of speculative approaches suggests that this essay on new biblical knowledge should deal, as it does, with *agreed-on contributions of a more concrete type.*

Two areas of recent discovery illustrate concrete acquisitions of knowledge, namely, written material, hitherto unknown or unavailable, and physical remains of the culture, life, and worship of the biblical peoples insofar as those remains have been uncovered and deciphered by modern archaeology. This essay will be divided, therefore, into portions dealing with *written* and *archaeological* discoveries. While these discoveries will be discussed one by one, the main point of the essay is that taken together they increase almost every aspect of our knowledge of the Bible. The essay will cover:

I. Discoveries of tablets, scrolls, and other documents
   Ebla
   Ugarit
   Mari
   Nuzu (Nuzi)
   Hittite archives
   Amarna Egyptian archives
   Palestinian finds
   Elephantine
   Dead Sea Scrolls
   Nag Hammadi (Chenoboskion)
   Copies of the Bible
   Dubious finds
II. Archaeological discoveries
   Jericho
   Hazor
   Megiddo

I shall begin with the first of these two groups, taking up the listed materials in order.

I. Discoveries of tablets, scrolls, and other documents

One of the ways in which our knowledge of the Bible has been greatly expanded is by the discovery of pertinent writings. Sometimes these are copies of biblical books older than any copies hitherto possessed (Dead Sea Scrolls, Bodmer Papyri). Sometimes they are works reflecting biblical religion but not accepted into the canonical collection (Dead Sea Scrolls, Nag Hammadi). More often, the written discoveries cast light on the world in which the biblical peoples lived and on the languages and writing styles used in the Bible (Ebla, Ugarit, Mari, Nuzu). Empires, peoples, and cities previously little-known have left records (Hittites, Hurrians, Amarna), filling in the background of biblical history. The selection of writings below, meant to illustrate all this, moves in an approximately chronological order from the earliest historical period to the latest.

Ebla

Abraham, Isaac, Jacob, and Joseph, the patriarchs of the Book of Genesis, were migrants from Mesopotamia to Canaan, keepers of flocks, and merchants in contact with the kingdoms of Mesopotamia and Egypt. Most scholars would start the patriarchal history in the second millennium B.C. (Middle Bronze IIA by archaeological reckoning), but that is far from certain. Consequently there has been interest in the great civilizations of the last half of the third millennium (Early Bronze), either as an alternative earlier setting for the patriarchal period (below, pp. 142–144), or as the forerunner of the second-millennium cultures encountered by the patriarchs.

A recent discovery has uncovered an important third-millennium center in Syria (situated between Hama and Aleppo), closer geographically and linguistically to Canaan than were the Sumerian, Akkadian, and Egyptian civilizations hitherto known. Since 1964 an Italian archaeological mission of the University of Rome directed by Paolo Matthiae has

been excavating this center, known as Tell Mardikh (ancient Ebla), a city with a claimed population of a quarter of a million, which was destroyed by Naram-Sin of Akkad, a ruler known already through Mesopotamian finds. Between 1974 and 1976 the archives of Ebla came to light—over 16,500 inventoried items dating from the period 2400–2250 B.C. The epigrapher of the expedition, Giovanni Pettinato, estimates that 80 percent of these tablets are in Sumerian, a non-Semitic language of international import, while 20 percent are in a Semitic language (now dubbed Eblaite), seemingly of the same Northwestern branch as Hebrew.[3] This large tablet-find will be of prime importance for Middle Eastern history, religion, and sociology, as well as for our knowledge of the languages of the region (especially because of bilingual vocabularies found in it).

An acrimonious debate has taken place between Matthiae and Pettinato[4] over the import of the tablets for the Bible, the earliest passages of which date over 1,000 years later. It is a major difficulty that the cuneiform (wedge-shaped) signs in which the Eblaite tablets are written are capable of being read in several different ways. Nevertheless, in two respects the discovery promises to have biblical significance.

Clay tablets (opposite) found in Tell Mardikh (ancient Ebla) are covered with cuneiform script (left). *"This large tablet-find will be of prime importance for Middle Eastern history, religion, and sociology, as well as for our knowledge of the languages of the region. . . ."*

First, over 10,000 personal names appear in these tablets, which are largely commercial; and some of them can be read as forms of personal names hitherto encountered only or chiefly in the Bible: Adam, Eve, Jabal, Noah, Hagar, Bilhah, Michael, Israel (although decipherment will have to be debated by specialists in cuneiform transcription). Second, words that appear infrequently in Hebrew—there are some 1,700 words that occur only once in the Hebrew written before A.D. 70—are attested in Eblaite, often with meanings that cast new light on biblical passages. We must remember that poetry, including Hebrew poetry, often preserves ancient vocabulary and syntax, so that documents in a related Semitic language, even if written 1,000 or 1,500 years before the biblical text, can be informative about linguistic phenomena that were forgotten in a later period. Much less certain is the import of the Ebla discovery for the dating of the patriarchs (based on a partial misunderstanding that the kings and/or kingdoms of Genesis 14, an Abraham story, were mentioned therein), as well as the claimed Ebla reference to a form of the divine name of the God of Israel, Yahweh (so that there would have been a pre-Israelite Semitic deity named Ya).

Ugarit

On the Mediterranean coast some seventy-five miles west-southwest of Ebla lies Ugarit (modern Ras Shamra), excavated by a French expedition in over thirty campaigns since 1929, principally under the leadership of Claude Schaeffer. Although settlement at Ugarit goes back to the seventh millennium B.C., the flourishing period was in the Middle Bronze and Late Bronze period from 2000 to 1200 B.C., when Ugarit was in diplomatic relations with world powers like the Hittites, the Egyptians, the Mitanni, and the Mycenaeans. Ultimately, Ugarit fell to invaders from the Mediterranean, "Sea Peoples" related to the biblical Philistines.

The main importance of the site for biblical studies lies in another immense find of clay cuneiform tablets, some of them in Akkadian (the international language of that era), some of them in a northwestern Semitic language, related to Canaanite and an ancestor of Phoenician, henceforth dubbed Ugaritic. Written in an alphabetic system, the main body of Ugaritic tablets stem from the 1400s and 1300s, a period 1,000 years later than the Eblaite tablets, but still anterior to the Bible.

More literary than what has been found in the Eblaite tablets, Ugaritic writings preserved ancient Canaanite myths about the supreme father

Portion of a Ugarit clay tablet showing an alphabetic cuneiform script. *"Few will deny that the discovery of Ugaritic has proved an important background for the understanding of ancient Hebrew."*

god El, and the younger more active Baal who slew the sea god Yamm, as well as a sea monster, Lotan. (Hitherto the underlying myth was known in the Mesopotamian form where the god Marduk slew Tiamat.) Parallels to Hebrew Elohim and Yahweh have been claimed, especially since in some biblical poems God slays the sea monster Rahab or Leviathan (Lotan). Examples are found in Isaiah 27:1;51:9; Psalms 74:13–14;89:10; Job 26:12. In another legend (Aqhat) there figures Danel, possibly equivalent to the Danel (Daniel) of Ezekiel 14:14,20, who is associated with such primeval figures as Noah and Job. Even richer for biblical purposes than the religious symbolism of Ugaritic writings is the variety of poetic format and the wealth of vocabulary and syntactical construction, throwing light on Hebrew poetry. One scholar, the late Mitchell Dahood, composed a three-volume commentary on the Psalms[5] wherein he retranslates many of the obscure verses in the light of Ugaritic parallels and gives them almost entirely new meanings. (Dahood was influential in using Eblaite to throw light on Hebrew poetry also.[6]) The extent to which this is a valid procedure is disputed, but few will deny that the discovery of Ugaritic has proved an important background for the understanding of ancient Hebrew.

Mari

Let us turn our attention next to Mesopotamia, the land of the Euphrates and Tigris rivers, some 300 to 500 miles east from the Mediterranean, where the discovery of ancient documents has thrown light not so much on biblical Hebrew as on early biblical customs. One of the important sites is ancient Mari[7] (Tall Harīrī) on the Euphrates, dominating ancient caravan routes to the sea and to the northern river tributaries. Mari was excavated by another French scholar, André Parrot, in the 1930s and 1950s. Although settlement there goes back at least to the third millennium (contemporary with Ebla), the chief period of interest for our survey is the *floruit* of 1750–1697 B.C.

King Zimrilim of Mari in this period was a contemporary and, for a while, an ally of the illustrious Hammurabi of Babylon. The biblical patriarchs are often thought to have lived in the same era; and before the migration of Abraham to Canaan (subsequently Palestine), he and his ancestors were located in the region of Haran, an area at times under Mari domination. The Mari site yielded not only a magnificent temple and palace, a ziggurat (step-temple), and both statues and paintings, but more importantly 20,000 clay tablets of royal and business archives.

Despite the dominant use in these tablets of Akkadian (East Semitic), the majority of the population seems to have been Amorite, a West Semitic people (footnote 3) who overran and dominated Mesopotamia by the eighteenth century, becoming heirs of the great kingdoms of the third millennium. Abraham and his ancestors have sometimes been identified as Amorites, and in the Mari tablets the city Nahor appears, a name borne by Abraham's grandfather (Genesis 11:22–25) and by Abraham's brother (11:27–29). Zimrilim is described as struggling with the warriors of the Banū-Yamina, "Sons of the Right," a group bearing the same name as one of the subsequent tribes of Israel, Benjamin, also noted for military skills.

The curious designation of the Shechemites who dealt with Jacob as the "Sons of the Ass [Hamor]," (Joshua 24:32) may reflect the custom attested at Mari of killing an ass to seal an alliance. Indeed, one may wonder if Mari does not supply us with the example of a site where the great myths of the Sumerians and Babylonians were translated into West Semitic languages and underwent local variations. We may have here traces of the path from the great cultures of third-millennium Mesopotamia to the creation and flood narratives of the early chapters of Genesis.

Nuzu

Further east, near the Tigris, lay ancient Nuzu (Yorghan, or Yoghlan, Tepe), excavated in the late 1920s by an American expedition. Once again the chief biblical interest of the find comes from 5,000 cuneiform tablets written in Akkadian even though the population was of another stock. This time non-Semitic Hurrians were involved (biblical Horites and Hivites); for Nuzu lay in a province of the Mitanni Empire, dominated by an Indo-European aristocracy, an empire that in the 1500s and 1400s rivaled Egypt. The patriarchal ancestral region, Haran, was thickly populated by Hurrians and was a Mitanni center.

Although the Nuzu tablets date from several hundred years after the Mari tablets, they also enlighten the patriarchal practices,[8] even if the first scholarly claims about "parallels" were a bit overstated. At Nuzu, images of the household gods were important symbols of family unity and were generally passed on to the principal heir. The importance of such symbols makes intelligible Rachel's attempt to appropriate the household gods of her father Laban (Genesis 31:19,30). It was customary for childless people at Nuzu to adopt someone as son to serve them as long as they lived and to bury them after death; but it was understood that if eventually they had a natural child, this child would become the heir. We find the same situation in Abraham's adopting the slave Eliezer as heir (Genesis 15:2–3), only to have him replaced later on by the natural sons Isaac and Ishmael. A wealthy Nuzu wife who did not bear a child was expected to supply the husband with a slave concubine whose children would be counted as the wife's (*see* Genesis 16:2). Deathbed assignments of patrimony at Nuzu when the parent had "grown old" resemble the opening formula of the story of the struggle of Jacob and Esau for the birthright: "When Isaac was old . . . " (Genesis 27:1). These are but a few examples of how the tablet discoveries of Mesopotamia cast light on the biblical story. They also create some problems for dating the patriarchs, but that will be discussed later (below, p. 143).

ORIGINAL PICTOGRAPH	PICTOGRAPH IN POSITION OF LATER CUNEIFORM	EARLY BABYLONIAN	ASSYRIAN	ORIGINAL OR DERIVED MEANING
				BIRD
				FISH
				DONKEY
				OX
				SUN DAY
				GRAIN
				ORCHARD
				TO PLOW TO TILL
				BOOMERANG TO THROW TO THROW DOWN
				TO STAND TO GO

Table showing the development of cuneiform script from pictographs to Assyrian characters. The word cuneiform derives from Latin and means "wedge-shaped." It has been the modern designation, from the early 18th century onward, for the most widespread and historically significant writing system in the ancient Near East.

Hittite archives

When we move northwest from Mesopotamia, passing beyond the Mitanni/Hurrian regions, we come to another formidable empire, ruled by the Hittites with its capital at Ḥattusas (Boğazköy) in eastern Asia Minor. Neither Semite nor Indo-European in their distant origins (third millennium), the Hittites expanded their rule in the second millennium, sacking Babylon (1500s), crushing the Mitanni (1300s), and challenging Egypt and the formidable Pharaoh Ramses II at Kadesh (1285), only to have their own empire fall victim to invasions by the Sea Peoples and others ca. 1200.

The interpretation of cuneiform tablets in imperial Hittite (an Indo-European dialect) was begun in 1915 by B. Hrozný, a Czech scholar, and has now reached a satisfactory level, as has also our knowledge of another Hittite, Indo-European dialect written in hieroglyphics. The biblical "Hittites" (Neo-Hittites) are the mixed heirs of the old Hittite realms, especially Syria. They figure in the patriarchal story (Genesis 23:10), and intermarriage with Hittite women was evidently a major issue (Genesis 26:34; 27:46). Bathsheba was the wife of Uriah the Hittite when David took advantage of her. Ezekiel (16:3, 45) traces Jerusalem to combined Hittite and Amorite origin. However, we must be cautious, for Israelite memory may have confused Hittites and Horites/Hivites (Hurrians).

A major contribution of the Hittite archives to biblical knowledge involves the pattern of suzerainty treaties whereby the Hittite "Great King" made a pact with vassal kingdoms in his sphere of influence. (Such treaties were not unique to the Hittites, but their archives provide the best examples.) There are resemblances in format and wording to the covenant between God and Israel described in Exodus 20 and Joshua 24.[9] The Hittite king identifies himself in the treaty by name, titles, and attributes, even as the Bible gives the name of "Yahweh, the God of Israel" (Joshua 24:2; Exodus 20:2). This is followed in most Hittite treaties by a historical prologue where the Hittite king describes what he has previously done for the vassals, a prologue that constitutes implicit assurance of continued patronage. Similarly Joshua 24:3–13 describes what God did for Abraham and his descendants till Joshua's time. (Indeed, we may speculate that the covenant prologue and its recitation of history may have given shape to some of the narrative collections of the Pentateuch.)

Stipulations follow in the treaty, phrased as apodictic imperatives and indicating the king's expectations of his vassal; e.g., Mursilis II specifies, "Thou shalt seize all captives; thou shalt not leave any behind." The Ten Commandments of Exodus 20:3-17 (also in a "Thou shalt . . . shalt not" pattern) constitute the stipulations of the covenant between Yahweh and Israel. Sometimes, either explicitly or implicitly, there is a provision for the preservation of the treaty, just as Joshua 24:26 mentions the writing

A Hittite cuneiform tablet. *"A major contribution of the Hittite archives to biblical knowledge involves the pattern of suzerainty treaties whereby the Hittite 'Great King' made a pact with vassal kingdoms in his sphere of influence. . . . these archives exemplify for us the legal format in which the Israelites would have conceived their special relationship or covenant with God."*

of a law book. In fact, the Ark of the Covenant became the repository of the Decalogue for Israel (Deuteronomy 31:26). Witnesses to the treaty are listed, even as Joshua 24:22, 27 appeals to witnesses. Curses are leveled in case the vassal should break the treaty, and a blessing is promised if he keeps it—a pattern well attested in the Bible (Deuteronomy 27–28; Joshua 8:34). No one imagines that the Bible copied a specific Hittite treaty, but these archives exemplify for us the legal format in which the Israelites would have conceived their special relationship or covenant with God.

Amarna Egyptian archives

The Hittite archives came from a site some 750 miles north of Canaan; the archives of an Egyptian site about the same distance to the southwest of Canaan are equally informative. Amarna (sometimes Tell el-Amarna) is the modern name of ancient Akhetaton on the Nile roughly halfway between Thebes and Memphis. In the period 1375–1350 this city served as the capital for the Pharaoh Amenophis IV or Akhenaton, romantically dubbed the heretic pharaoh because he shifted the focus of Egyptian religion from Amon worshiped at Thebes to the god Aton, the sun disk, for whom he built a new city. It is debatable whether this worship was monotheism, but certainly the Egyptian hymn to Aton has parallels to Psalm 104. The religious reform was accompanied by a new realism in art (the bust of Akhenaton's wife Nefertiti is one of the most beautiful art pieces of antiquity) and by many social changes.

However, the negative aspect of the turmoil produced by Akhenaton is apparent in tablets discovered at Amarna in the last century and published in the first two-thirds of this century.[10] Written in cuneiform Akkadian, these tablets constitute some 350 items from the archives of the Egyptian kings who reigned at this site. Included is correspondence with other kings, and in particular a large number of letters *from* vassal rulers in Palestine and Syria. These latter attest to the decline of Egyptian control, not only because of international rivalry between Egyptians and the Mitanni or Hittite Empires, but also because of the incursion of peoples seeking to settle in more civilized regions. In over fifty letters from Byblos to the Egyptian court the peril from an Amorite leader is emphasized.

Even more interesting are the constant references to the Hapiru (Ḫabiru or 'Apiru), seemingly a mixture of unlanded vagrants, run-away slaves, and ill-paid mercenaries, who are invading the Canaan area, especially around Shechem. The similarity of name to "Hebrew" has raised the possibility that this correspondence in the early fourteenth century is describing *a phase* of the entrance of Hebrews into Palestine.[11]

In the correspondence, the vassal kings of the city-states of Canaan and Syria protest their "loyalty" to the Egyptian pharaoh and ask for protection; but it is quite clear that the monarch can do little. The return of the Egyptian seat of government to Thebes in or before the reign of Akhenaton's son, Tutankhamen (ca. 1350; the "Tut" of the famous tomb) marked the triumph of realism over romanticism as Egypt began to seek to restore political order throughout its sphere of influence.

Palestinian finds

The tablet or documentary discoveries discussed thus far have all been from outside the main territory of the Old Testament story, namely, that tiny geographical area at the east end of the Mediterranean called Ca-

Birds in a papyrus thicket: a painting on a wall of the North Palace of Akhenaton at Amarna. Some 350 tablets, written in cuneiform Akkadian were discovered in Amarna in the last century. From them it was possible to trace the decline of the Egyptian Empire in the 18th Dynasty.

naan, or Palestine, or Israel. The finds have also been anterior to the main era of Old Testament history which runs from the appearance of the tribes in Palestine (scarcely much after 1200) to the fall of the Judean monarchy (500s). Alas, when one turns to that main Old Testament territory and that era, major documentary finds are not forthcoming.

We may list some important but minor finds: a potsherd (ostracon) with an early example of the alphabet (from Izbet Sartah [Ebenezer?] ca. 1200 B.C.); a pendant with a poetic agricultural calendar (Gezer, ca. 900); a basalt stele of Mesha, King of Moab, describing his defeat of Israel (Transjordan, ca. 840); twelve Aramaic fragments of wall plaster from the 700s or early 600s at Deir 'Alla (Succoth?) in the Jordan valley, mentioning Balaam (Numbers 22–24); tax receipts inscribed in ink on potsherds from the capital of Israel during the reign of Jeroboam II (Samaria, ca. 750?); an inscription on the wall of the Siloam water passage, describing the tunneling process (Jerusalem, ca. 700); some twenty jar fragments inscribed in ink, describing a foreign invasion, perhaps that of Nebuchad-rezzar II against Jerusalem (Lachish, ca. 590?); some 200 ostraca inscribed in Hebrew and in Aramaic (Arad, 600s to 400s).

Illuminating the post-monarchical period of the Old Testament is an important find (early 1960s) of Aramaic fragments called the Samaria Papyri,[12] References to Persian Emperors date them to 375–335 B.C.; they were brought to a cave in the Wādī Daliyeh (nine miles north of Jericho on the Jordan) by refugees from Samaria, fleeing before Alexander the Great's destruction of the city in 332. These papyri help to fill in the biblical information about the names of the governors of Samaria and of the Jerusalem high priests.

Elephantine

A more important Aramaic papyri cache pertinent to the early post-monarchical period comes from Egypt. On Elephantine Island in the Nile (opposite Aswān, 100 miles south of Thebes) there was a colony of Hebrews (not necessarily Jews, i.e., of the tribe of Judah). The origin of this colony probably antedated the Persian invasion of Egypt (525), and it was terminated ca. 399 B.C. The papyri, found at the end of the nineteenth century and published in different lots throughout two-thirds of the twentieth century, are largely legal texts and contracts, reflecting the history of several island families.[13] But there are also letters bearing on the biblical history. These Hebrews had a temple to the God YHW (Yahu/Yaho) that was destroyed in 410 at the instigation of hostile Egyptian priests. Consequently, the Elephantine Hebrews wrote to Bagoas, governor of Judea, asking him for intercessory help. The names of Sanballat and of the high priest Johanan appear in this correspondence, throwing light on information in Nehemiah 12:22 and on the dating of biblical Ezra. These names, when combined with those found in the Samaria papyri, give us a sequence of Judean notables in the 400s and 300s. Evidently the request for help was successful and the temple rebuilt for at least a short period. Religion at Elephantine, practiced far from Jerusalem and the main Jewish centers, seems to have undergone considerable outside influence, even to the point of positing a female consort for YHW.

Dead Sea Scrolls

Let us move ahead chronologically to the Judaism of the period just before the birth of Jesus. As if by way of compensation for its previous failure to supply documentary finds, Palestine offers us perhaps the greatest single biblical cache of all time. For a decade beginning in 1947, in caves on the west side of the Dead Sea, Bedouin discovered scrolls and fragments of some 600 manuscripts.[14] The principal finds were in eleven caves near a site called Qumrān, ten miles south of Jericho. Excavations of the site by R. de Vaux and G. L. Harding between 1951 and 1956 uncovered a set of community buildings (water system, kitchen, dining room, pantries, pottery workshops, scriptorium) which were occupied from ca. 135 B.C. to ca. 31 B.C., and in a second period from ca. A.D. 1 to

Ruins at Elephantine, an island in the Nile opposite Aswan, Upper Egypt. *"Papyri, found at the end of the nineteenth century . . . are largely legal texts and contracts, reflecting the history of several island families. But there are also letters bearing on the biblical history."*

68. This agrees with the paleographic evidence dating most of the scrolls and fragments to the last two centuries B.C. and to the first century A.D.

It is now generally agreed that at Qumrān have been discovered the central settlement and the libraries of the Essenes, one of the three sects of the Jews by Josephus's reckoning (*Jewish Antiquities* 13.5.9 no. 171) whose city in the desert is described by Pliny the Elder (*Natural History* 5.17.73) as situated on the west shore of the Dead Sea, north of En Gedi. The Essenes, like the other two sects (Pharisees and Sadducees), were the offshoot of the Jewish revolt against Syrian dominance, a revolt which began under the leadership of the Maccabees in 167 B.C. against the hated Antiochus IV Epiphanes who had plundered the Temple and set up an altar to the Olympian Zeus. Eventually, ca. 152 Jonathan, brother of Judas Maccabeus, appropriated the high priesthood, in which office he was followed by his brother Simon (143), thus establishing the Hasmonean dynasty.

The Essenes seem to have been ultra-pious Jews who protested the Maccabean usurpation of the high priesthood, insisting on a purer Zadokite lineage and withdrawing to the Dead Sea area to separate themselves from the profanation of Jerusalem. Perhaps they were fueled numerically and theologically in their protest by Jews returning from Babylon who disagreed with Maccabean/Hasmonean religious innovation.[15] The Essene settlement at Qumrān was interrupted for part of the reign of Herod the Great (37–4 B.C.); an earthquake was the immediate cause, but the suspicions of Herod may have contributed. Resettled, the site was destroyed by Roman armies in A.D. 68 as part of the first Jewish war.

The biblical interest of the Qumrān or Dead Sea manuscripts is manifold. First, of the biblical books in the Hebrew canon (footnote 2), all but Esther are found at Qumrān. As we shall see below, hitherto our oldest complete Hebrew text of the Old Testament dated from the tenth century A.D. Now from Qumrān there come, at times, whole scrolls of biblical books 1,000 years earlier.[16] The Hebrew biblical text at Qumrān is not necessarily better than the standard Hebrew text already known (although in some cases it is; e.g., books of Samuel); but the diversity of the textual traditions now available helps to fill in our knowledge of how biblical books were copied and preserved. Some of the Hebrew fragments agree not with the standard Hebrew Bible but with the Greek translation (Septuagint) or with the Samaritan Pentateuch. In other words, for much of the Bible, Qumrān antedates the standardization process effected by the rabbis in the second century.

Second, deuterocanonical books (footnote 2) have been largely preserved in Greek; now Qumrān has yielded some of the Aramaic original of Tobit and the Hebrew of Sirach.

Third, targums or translations of the Hebrew biblical books into Aramaic (the spoken language of many Jews) were known to us previously from the second century A.D. and later. Qumrān supplies considerably earlier evidence, e.g., a *Targum of Job* from Cave 11 that may have been composed in the second century B.C. Targums are important for textual study, as a way of reconstructing the Hebrew text that underlies the Aramaic translation. They also enlighten the history of theology, since the translation betrays how a passage was understood at this early period.

Fourth, many manuscripts of well-known apocryphal books of pre-Christian Judaism (*Enoch, Jubilees,* some *Patriarchal Testaments*) have turned up in their original Aramaic or Hebrew. Hitherto we had been dependent on translations of translations, e.g., Ethiopic from Greek. These works are extremely important for reconstructing the variety of theological thought in intertestamental Judaism, a Judaism upon which Christianity drew.

Fifth, a considerable body of Qumrān literature consists of documents composed by the Essenes themselves: several editions of their rule of life; commentaries on the biblical prophets who, they thought, were writing about them and their history; hymns; visions of God's future plans, whether those involved a war between light and darkness or the perfect temple and state.

Relatively little "second-Temple" (pre-70 A.D.) Pharisee thought has been preserved, and virtually nothing of Sadducee origin, so that the Qumrān discovery of Essene literature is a major contribution to our knowledge of Judaism. But it is also significant for Christianity, since the Essenes and the early Jewish Christians had many common features. Both strongly emphasized the coming of the Messiah and the fulfillment of God's plans, along with the need to reform a nucleus of Israel for that moment. (An obvious difference is that one group thought the Messiah would come soon, the other that he had already come.)

Among common features shared by Essene and Christian theology and community life we may list the following: a basic appeal to Isaiah 40:3, "Prepare the way of the Lord . . . in the desert"; a firm sense of community and oneness, including some community of goods; entrance to the community on Pentecost; initiatory washing connected to the outpouring of the Spirit; a sacred meal of bread and wine; eschatological stress on celibacy; rejection of divorce; a dualistic view of humanity, divided into children of light and of darkness, children of truth and of falsehood (a view especially common in I John); an important place allotted to the Spirit of Truth; a special symbolism for Melchizedek; a community role given to a group of twelve; a supervisor (overseer, bishop) who cared for the common goods and inspected the doctrine of members, serving as a shepherd to his people; meetings of the members called "the Many" (*see* Acts 6:5; 15:12).

The Qumrān hymns and the hymns in Luke 1–2 (Magnificat, Benedictus, Gloria, Nunc Dimittis) have many similarities both in format and in the technique of rephrasing Old Testament passages. While there is no evidence of Qumrān knowledge of Christians or of direct Christian dependence upon existing Qumrān literature, the Dead Sea Scrolls offer important information about how Christianity may have developed from intertestamental Judaism and about the Palestinian thought-world in which Jesus lived.

Nag Hammadi (Chenoboskion)

Another find of manuscripts hidden in jars was made in Egypt at almost the same time (1945) as the Dead Sea discovery in Palestine. This time thirteen codices or books (with 1,240 inscribed pages) were involved, rather than scrolls, and the language was Coptic, a language descended from ancient Egyptian but heavily influenced by Greek.[17] The site is near the town of Nag Hammadi, on the bend of the Nile some seventy-five miles north of Thebes; in the fourth century A.D. the area was dotted with Christian monasteries. Chenoboskion (Chenoboskeia), where the great St. Pachomius (292–346) was converted and began his life as a hermit, was one of these, and the codices surely came from the library of such a monastery.

There are forty-six works (plus six duplicates, making fifty-two tractates in all), of which forty are nowhere else preserved. While the translation into Coptic took place at different times and in different regions (as we can tell from the dialects), the works were originally in Greek. There is

"Palestine offers us perhaps the greatest single biblical cache of all time. For a decade beginning in 1947 . . . Bedouin discovered scrolls and fragments of some 600 manuscripts. The principal finds were in eleven caves near a site called Qumran, ten miles south of Jericho" (above). (Left) Reconstruction of a Dead Sea Scroll. (Opposite) A page from the Isaiah Scroll, largest of the Dead Sea Scrolls and the only complete book of the bible found among them.

all the variety of a library: Plato's *Republic,* non-Christian writing on Seth, Jewish works, and Christian compositions from the second century to the fourth representing different theological views. What seems to unite such writing is that all these works could be read as giving special knowledge (Greek *gnōsis*) to those who know what to look for. Pachomius himself was an orthodox Christian, but there is evidence that gnosticism infiltrated Egyptian monasteries,[18] and we know of anti-heretical purges that took place under the influence of Epiphanius and of Athanasius (the famous fourth-century bishop of Alexandria). It may have been in fear of such a purge that the collection was buried for safekeeping or for posterity.

For the most part the importance of the library is for church history, augmenting our knowledge of how Christian gnostics of the second and third centuries thought and wrote, as distinct from a mirror image gained from what the Church Fathers wrote about them (especially Irenaeus and Epiphanius).[19] So far as that is true, the discovery might seem to lie beyond the biblical area that is the focus of this essay. But a few of the Christian works may contain authentic memories of Jesus not preserved in the canonical New Testament. The chief candidate for such preservation is *The Gospel of Thomas,* where occasionally there are sayings of Jesus in a more primitive form than that attested in the Synoptic Gospels. Moreover, certain strains of protognostic thought appear in the New Testament, and we may be finding in the Nag Hammadi treatises more developed forms of New Testament gnosticism.

Already, I Timothy 6:20 warns, "Avoid the godless chatter and contradictions of what is falsely called *gnōsis.*" I John 4:2 and II John 7 stress the importance of believing in Jesus Christ as one come "in the flesh." A full-scale denial of the fleshly reality of the crucified Jesus is found in several of the Nag Hammadi treatises. For instance, in the *Apocalypse of Peter* the crucifiers are torturing only the substitute fleshly Jesus, while the living Jesus stands off laughing at the whole process. II Timothy 2:18 attacks those who hold that the resurrection of Christians has already taken place. The late second-century Nag Hammadi *Letter to Rheginus (Treatise on Resurrection)* assures the addressee (Rheginus), "You already have resurrection." Titus 1:9 and Acts 20:28–30 give the presbyter-bishops of the Church the task of refuting the false teachers. A reaction from the other side may be heard in the hostility of the *Apocalypse of Peter* against "Those outside our number who name themselves bishop and also deacons, as if they have received authority from God." It is very clear that each side is charging the other with heresy and error. And if in II Peter 1:20; 3:2,15–17, Peter becomes the spokesman of apostolic authority guiding the faithful, in the *Gospel of Mary* (a work related to the Nag Hammadi find) Mary Magdalene is held up as the disciple whom Jesus loved more than he loved Peter and the others. She proclaims special revelation, disturbing Peter and Andrew for whom her teachings are "strange ideas." Thus we learn from the discovery of gnostic writings how complex the intra-Christian battles were.

The late second-century *Adversus haereses* of Irenaeus clearly diagnosed the gnostics as unorthodox. Many who read the abstruse reflections in the Nag Hammadi treatises may agree that gnostic views had traveled an enormous distance from Jesus of Nazareth. But these documents also make us realize that the decisions about orthodoxy and heterodoxy were easier in retrospect than in the heart of the conflict and that the opponents on each side had their integrity. One does not have to decide that Irenaeus and the writers of the Nag Hammadi codices were equally valuable for Christianity, or equally faithful to the New Testament, but both would have to be judged equally passionate in their devotion to what they regarded as truth.

Copies of the Bible

Besides documentary finds that cast light on the Bible, some discoveries (or rediscoveries) have increased our knowledge of how the Scriptures were preserved. The Hebrew Bible most used by students in modern times[20] is largely based on a vocalized text copied in A.D. 1008, known as the Leningrad Codex. A note at the end of this codex associates it with the tradition of the Ben Asher family, who lived at Tiberias in Galilee in the tenth century. An earlier copy of the Hebrew Scriptures by Aaron ben Asher, dated to about 930, had been kept by the Karaites (a Jewish sect) in Jerusalem. It was seen at Cairo by the great Maimonides, who maintained that it should serve as a model for copying scrolls of the Law. By the Middle Ages its presence was attested in Aleppo, whence the name Aleppo Codex; and in modern times it was thought to have been destroyed there during anti-Jewish riots in 1947. However, 600 of the 800 pages were preserved and smuggled into Israel in 1956. Now at last this superior manuscript, the oldest codex of the entire Hebrew Bible, has been published and can serve critical scholarship.[21]

Paradoxically, the Old Testament in Greek (Septuagint) has been preserved for us in earlier copies than the Old Testament in Hebrew. One of the oldest copies of the Septuagint is the fourth-century A.D. Codex Sinaiticus, part of which was discovered at St. Catherine's Monastery in the Sinai desert by Konstantin von Tischendorf in the middle of the last century. From a total of approximately 730 leaves, some 476 have been kept in London (British Museum) and some 43 in Leipzig. The rest were thought to be lost, until in 1975, in clearing debris beneath a church at the monastery, the monks found an old cell which contained manuscripts buried hundreds of years ago, perhaps by a collapsed ceiling. They are in several languages, but those in Greek are frequently in the uncial or capital letters characteristic of the most ancient Christian copyists. There seem to be ten complete codices and parts of what could be more. Some eight to fourteen leaves of Codex Sinaiticus are in the find. Publication is eagerly awaited.[22]

The great fourth- and fifth-century codices of the Bible were copied on vellum or skin. Fragments of even earlier copies of New Testament books on papyrus, mostly from Egypt, have been discovered in this century. In 1935 a fragment of The Gospel According to John, postage-stamp in size and known as the Rylands Papyrus (P[52]), was published; it was written about A.D. 135 and is very important for the dating of John. Another mid-second-century set of fragments (Egerton Papyrus 2), published in 1935, contains gospel passages resembling a mixture from the various canonical Gospels. A few scholars contend that this work is independent of the four Gospels preserved in the New Testament, but most think of it as a compilation.

In the 1950s and 1960s the Bodmer collection of early papyri was published.[23] It contained lengthy late-second-century copies of John (P[66]) and of Luke/John (P[75]). The latter agrees closely with Codex Vaticanus copied almost two centuries later, an agreement illustrating the fidelity of the scribes. The former papyrus has a somewhat different textual tradition from Vaticanus, closer at times to Codex Sinaiticus; this diversity

"One of the oldest copies of the Septuagint is the fourth-century A.D. Codex Sinaiticus, part of which was discovered at St. Catherine's Monastery in the Sinai desert by Konstantin von Tischendorf in the middle of the last century." (Above), Fourteenth verse from chapter one of I John from the Codex Sinaiticus.

shows that the different textual traditions of the later period already existed in the early centuries. In our modern libraries books printed in the last century are crumbling to dust; it is humbling to think that the dryness of the Judean desert near the Dead Sea and of the Egyptian desert near the Nile have preserved such papyri for almost 2,000 years.

Dubious finds

The documentary discoveries listed above explain some of the excitement prevalent in modern biblical studies. But it may be wise to close this section of the essay by some cautions about the care to be exercised in judging new "discoveries." If the west side of the Dead Sea has yielded remarkable scrolls in the middle of this century, a major find from the east side of that sea was already reported in 1883. M. W. Shapira, a Jerusalem antiquities dealer, tried to sell to the British Museum fifteen strips of parchment containing an early Hebrew text of Deuteronomy discovered in the Dead Sea area. The careful investigation by Clermont-Ganneau and others suggested that the strips were a forgery. A modern attempt to prove them genuine in the light of the Dead Sea Scrolls has had little success.

On the other side of the world at almost the same time another "discovery" was being made. In 1874, L. Neto, Director of the National Museum in Rio de Janeiro, announced that he had received a copy of what was alleged to be a Phoenician inscription carved in stone, discovered in northeastern Brazil. The text related how a group of Phoenician ships was blown off course to Brazil. Once again careful scholarship suggested a forgery, and a modern attempt to prove genuineness has had little following.[25]

In the early 1970s a Spanish Jesuit working in Rome, José O'Callaghan, thought that he detected a few letters of a passage from Mark's Gospel on fragments in Greek from Cave 7 of Qumrān. This identification implied a very early date for Mark (40s) and a knowledge of Christianity by the Dead Sea Essenes. However, the identification has been rejected by the majority of those who studied the evidence.[26] Such scholarly vigilance is reassuring to those who may wonder about the integrity of Bible study.

II. Archaeological discoveries

While documentary finds make the largest headlines, archaeological discoveries may tell even more about life in the biblical period. For instance, defensive walls and gates reveal military strength and the warlike character of the times; palaces reflect wealth, artistic accomplishments, and the ideology and grandeur of the monarchy; temples express religious aspirations and theological insights; streets and homes show the standard of life, how businesses were conducted and households were maintained.

Of course, even if we confine our report to archaeology in the Holy Land, the range of finds goes far beyond the biblical era. At one end it reaches back into the Stone Ages and to the beginnings of agriculture and of cities, as well as to civilizations in the land before the Israelites came. At the other end Palestinian archaeology uncovers post-biblical cultures. Among their remains are synagogues and cemeteries from the times of the early rabbis, and Christian churches from the times of the early bishops; Arab palaces reflecting the Islāmic conquest; magnificent crusader fortresses and churches, which are succeeded in turn by walls and structures indicative of Turkish supremacy. Thus, in what follows we are concentrating on the relatively short biblical period (1850 B.C. to A.D. 150) that is part of a 10,000-year archaeological record. Even then only a few outstanding sites can be given attention—those that illustrate the clarification and the confusion brought to the Bible by archaeological investigations.

Jericho

On a plain between the Judean mountains and the Jordan River, next to a spring that attracted settlers, the large tell (a mound raised by levels of settlement) that marks the site of ancient Jericho has been an example of the failures and achievements of Palestinian "digging." The father of Palestinian exploration, Edward Robinson, assumed in 1831 that the mound consisted of accumulated rubbish. Even the first major excavation, conducted by an Austrian/German expedition in 1907–9 (E. Sellin, C. Watzinger), represented an early stage in scientific knowledge when no accurate method had been devised for dating the finds.[27] The huge trench that was excavated cut across massive defensive walls, and inevitably the biblical description of the walls of Jericho (Joshua 6) was invoked in discussing these defenses.

Not until the 1920s and early 1930s, when the most distinguished American biblical-archaeological scholar of the twentieth century, W. F. Albright of the Johns Hopkins University, conducted an excavation at Tell Beit Mirsim (biblical Debir?), some forty miles to the southwest of Jericho, on the other side of the Judean mountains toward the Mediterranean, was a reasonably accurate Palestinian ceramic chronology developed.

Consequently, when the second major excavation of Jericho was conducted in 1936, this time under British auspices (J. Garstang), the scientific technology had improved. But the mound still proved infuriatingly complicated in terms of stratigraphy. For example, there were eighteen detectable layers of settlement, fallen walls lying almost horizontal, and dump pits from previous excavations which were poorly charted. Particular interest centered upon the large fourth city built on the site at a time when Palestine was under Egyptian dominance (Garstang's Layer III). The destruction of the walls of that city by a great conflagration was dated by Garstang to the Late Bronze period (1550–1200), specifically to 1400. Albright disagreed, for he dated the destruction closer to, or after, 1300.

After the Second World War Jericho was excavated once more (1952–58), this time by Kathleen Kenyon. She had worked in British archaeology with Sir Mortimer Wheeler and had developed an exquisitely minute system for noting stratigraphy.[28] This served her excellently in wrestling with the complicated occupations of Jericho, as did the new radiocarbon method of dating.

The site was already occupied in Mesolithic times, 8,000 years before Christ, but a major part of the mound consisted of Neolithic strata. Fascinating was the discovery of a huge tower and walls built before the art of pottery had been discovered, and admiration was evoked by the highly artistic plastered skulls and face masks of that supposedly primitive period. Cities rose and fell in the Early Bronze Age (3rd millennium), marked by seventeen phases of walls. By Middle Bronze IIA and B (1900–1650) there was a high point in the history of Jericho marked by a new culture resembling that of coastal Syria (Amorite?). In its final Middle Bronze stage the city was defended by an immense beaten-earth embank-

A section of the mound of Jericho. Jericho's great importance is that it provides evidence of one of the earliest known continuous settlements on earth and therefore of the first steps towards civilization.

ment or glacis, often associated with the military architecture of the Hyksos, the foreigners who dominated Egypt from 1675 to 1570. Here was Garstang's fourth city, but the violent destruction of that city clearly had to be dated to about 1560 when the Hyksos were expelled from Egypt—hundreds of years earlier than either Garstang or Albright had thought. Even more puzzling were the very scant signs of settlement during the Late Bronze period. While some allowance must be made for erosion, it seems indisputable that no great city occupied that site at the period (1300s or 1200s) fixed by most scholars for the Israelite invasion of Canaan. If the walls of Jericho came tumbling down, they did so centuries before!

The Bible reports that Jericho was cursed by Joshua (6:26), so there was seemingly no major reoccupation until that by Hiel in the time of Ahab (I Kings 16:34; ca. 850 B.C.). One may guess that such reoccupation was on a small scale and it may have been eroded by time; but, in fact, careful excavation has uncovered no signs of it. Archaeology has been kinder to the New Testament mention of a Jericho visited by Jesus (Mark 10:46–52). About two miles south of the mound of the older Jericho, an American expedition in the 1950s excavated magnificent pools, palaces, baths, and gymnasia, built by the Hasmonean priest-kings and by Herod in the 150 years before Jesus's ministry. Evidently the warm weather of the Jordan valley made Jericho a Herodian winter resort.

Hazor

Another great excavation marked the period immediately after the Second World War, when a new group of scholars entered Palestinian archaeology in force—the Israeli, now exploring the terrain of the new state they had carved out of Palestine. Between 1955 and 1958 and again in 1968 a distinguished Israeli soldier-scholar, Yigael Yadin, excavated the immense mound of Hazor on the west side of the Jordan rift valley, some eight miles north of the Sea of Galilee.[29]

Garstang had done five soundings in this mound in 1928 and had dated the final destruction of the site to 1400 B.C. As with Jericho, that dating seemed to fix the Israelite conquest of Canaan, for Joshua 11:10–13 describes how Joshua burned Hazor, "formerly the head of all these kingdoms." With more accurate methods, Yadin traced settlement at Hazor back to the Early Bronze Age and detected an immense expansion of city dwelling in the Middle Bronze Age, probably the era in which Hazor became the largest city in Canaan. Unlike Jericho, however, Hazor was a city in the Late Bronze Age as well. It was violently destroyed just before 1200, and the occupation in the following century was of another, less sophisticated type. Surely, the destruction marked the passing of the site into the hands of the Israelite invaders.

An important feature of the pre-Israelite era was a series of superimposed temples, representing rebuildings from the Middle Bronze into the

A circular tower (bottom left) is part of the Jericho city wall. *"Fascinating was the discovery of a huge tower and walls built before the art of pottery had been discovered, and admiration was evoked by the highly artistic plastered skulls and face masks of that supposedly primitive period."*

Section of the immense mound of Hazor. *"According to I Kings 9:15 Hazor was rebuilt by Solomon (ca. 950), along with Megiddo and Gezer; it was conquered two centuries later (732) by the Assyrians. This basic sketch has been confirmed at Hazor by [Yigael] Yadin's excavation."*

Late Bronze Age. The architecture of the last Canaanite temple consisted of a porch, a hall, and an inner sanctum. A similar architectural plan has been found in temples in other Canaanite and Syrian sites, and seemingly it inspired the architects of Solomon's Temple with its porch, holy place, and Holy of Holies. A rich find of cultic vessels and of an altar was made in the Hazor temple area; in particular, a large round basalt basin may have been the antecedent of the bronze "sea" of Solomon's Temple (I Kings 7:23–26).

According to I Kings 9:15, Hazor was rebuilt by Solomon (ca. 950), along with Megiddo and Gezer; it was conquered two centuries later (732) by the Assyrians. This basic sketch has been confirmed at Hazor by Yadin's excavation. There was a fortified city at Hazor in the tenth century (Stratum X) with gates and a wall structure similar to those found at Megiddo and Gezer; and there was a major destruction of the city at the end of the eighth century (Stratum V). Not mentioned in the Bible but

apparent in the excavation was the flourishing era of Hazor (Stratum VIII) under the dynasty of Omri and Ahab (875–850), hated in the Bible for their syncretistic religious policies, but among the ablest statesmen in the history of the Israelite monarchy. A large pillared storehouse, attributed wrongly to Solomon by Garstang, belongs to the Omri-Ahab era, as does a citadel and a complicated underground water system. Evidently Hazor had become for these kings an important defensive site against invasion from the east across the Jordan.

Parenthetically, it should be mentioned that at Samaria itself, the capital city built by Omri, earlier excavations in 1908–10 and 1931–35 showed the material elegance of the wealthy eighth-century dynasty.[30] (More recent excavations at Samaria in 1965 and 1968 enlightened chiefly the post-Exilic history of the city.) The buildings at Samaria were among the finest ever constructed in Palestine. Five hundred ivory fragments, mostly inlays from wall paneling, furniture and decorated boxes, illustrate the reference in I Kings 22:39 to the ivory house built by Ahab, and also provide background for Amos's prophetic words (6:1,4) addressed to "Those who feel secure on the mountain of Samaria" when he castigated "All those who lie upon beds of ivory."

Megiddo

Canaan or Palestine is divided in two by the great Plain of Esdraelon (Jezreel), running NW-SE from the Bay of Haifa to the Jordan valley. To the south of the plain are the mountains of Samaria and Judea; to the north are the mountains of Galilee. On the southern edge of Esdraelon were fortresses controlling passes from the mountains into the plain, passes through which armies had to travel as they moved from south to north, i.e., from Egypt toward Syria and Mesopotamia. One of these fortresses, Megiddo, has seen so many battles that its name has become synonymous with ultimate war: Armageddon (Revelation 16:16) reflects the *har* (Hebrew for "mountain") of Megiddo.

Curiously, in the early biblical story of Israel (Joshua 12:21; 17:11; 21:25; Judges 1:27; 5:19) Taanach, another of the Esdraelon fortresses, gets as much attention as, or even more than, Megiddo. But in the time of Solomon, Megiddo comes to biblical importance as a storehouse and a center for horses and chariots (I Kings 4:12; 9:15). Kings of Judah, such as Ahaziah in 842 B.C. (II Kings 9:27) and Josiah in 609 (II Kings 23:29–30), came to a bloody death at Megiddo.

Excavations were first done by the Germans (G. Schumacher) in 1903–5. As at Jericho, a huge trench that was cut through the mound showed many strata of occupation but offered little by way of exact dating. From 1925 until 1939 the Oriental Institute of Chicago conducted the largest expedition ever seen in Palestine, attempting to peel off the whole mound stratum by stratum. (Fortunately, that task proved too large, for some parts of a mound should be left to be excavated by future generations with improved technology.)

Twenty strata of occupation were uncovered at Megiddo reaching back to the Chalcolithic Age in the fourth millennium. Once again there were cities with immense walls in the Early Bronze and in the Middle Bronze Age, the latter period marked by palaces, temples, ivory treasures, and a Hyksos glacis. From the Late Bronze Age (1550–1200) were more strata of occupation showing Egyptian influence—not surprising since letters from the prince of Megiddo were found in the Amarna archives in Egypt (above, p. 116). The carved ivories discovered in the last phase of the pre-Israelite era were magnificent, and a massive temple has been uncovered similar to that found in Shechem (*see* below). There was a major destruction in the thirteenth century, presumably by the Israelites. American excavations under Paul Lapp between 1963 and 1968 at neighboring Taanach show a destruction in 1468 B.C. but no major consequent occupation until after 1300. One wonders why the biblical account of the Israelite wars with the Canaanites seems to feature Taanach more than Megiddo (Joshua 12:21).

In the "Chicago excavations" of Megiddo remarkable constructions in Stratum IV were attributed to the time of Solomon (900s)—a city wall, a

Remains of the stables at Megiddo. *"In the time of Solomon, Megiddo comes to biblical importance as a storehouse and a center for horses and chariots (I Kings 4:12; 9:15)."*

palace, a city gate, and stables for horses. There were other gates and walls, and so confusion with a later period was possible. Consequently, Yigael Yadin, fresh from the excavation of Hazor (a site mentioned together with Megiddo and Gezer in I Kings 9:15 as the site of Solomonic building), re-excavated Megiddo to straighten out the chronology of the monarchical period.[31] Some of the Solomonic structures (city wall with casemates, and a gate with four chambers) proved to be the work of the Omri-Ahab dynasty centered at Samaria, work that was completed a century after Solomon's time. Water systems thought to be pre-Solomonic were also redated with their later stage attributed to the period of Omri. However, a magnificent city gate with six chambers and two towers does belong to Solomon's era, as do similar gates at Hazor and Gezer. Like the campaigns at Hazor, the excavations of Megiddo confirm part of the biblical report about Solomon's building activity, but they also challenge the Bible's neglect of Omri and Ahab.

Shechem

South of Megiddo and near Samaria, the capital city of Omri, lies Shechem (adjacent to modern Nablus). This city controlled the pass where the road from Jerusalem to the north had to turn west to pass between the twin Samaritan mountain peaks named Gerizim and Ebal. In the patriar-

Remains of the triple gate at Megiddo. *"Remarkable constructions in Stratum IV were attributed to the time of Solomon (900s)—a city wall, a palace, a city gate, and stables for horses."*

chal narratives of Genesis, Abraham came to Shechem (12:6), as did Jacob (33:18) and Joseph (37:12–14); and the oak or terebinth of Shechem was a place of cult (35:4). Gerizim and Ebal were the sites of covenant promises and curses (Deuteronomy 27:12–13), and in the account of Judges 9, Shechem was the site of the first attempt at monarchy in Israel. There Abimelech ruled for three years, eventually seeking to eliminate those in the city who resisted his rule. These people of "the Tower of Shechem" took refuge in "the stronghold of the house of El-Berith" (the God of the Covenant). Later when Rehoboam, son of Solomon, went to receive support from the tribes of Israel (as distinct from Judah) he traveled to Shechem (I Kings 12:1). When Jeroboam succeeded in his revolt against Rehoboam (ca. 922 B.C.), he made

Beautiful carved ivories were discovered at Megiddo. This is a comb found there.

Shechem the first capital of the ten northern tribes (I Kings 12:25).

There had been a German excavation of Shechem (chiefly by E. Sellin) in 1913–14 and again in 1926–34, but the stratification of the site was left badly confused. A major American expedition began in 1956 and continued until 1973 (G. E. Wright, E. F. Campbell).[32] Traces of twenty-four periods of occupation were uncovered. After the oldest finds from the Chalcolithic era in the fourth millennium B.C., the excavation found a gap until occupation in the Middle Bronze Age (1900–1550). Seemingly the patriarchal visits described in the Bible would have to be localized in the latter era, when Shechem was a well-fortified city containing a sacred precinct with temples, which were eventually replaced by a massive fortress-temple. Late Bronze cities began about 1450 B.C. and lasted until a destruction in 1125. In this era the fortress-temple was replaced in the sacred precinct by a massive one-room temple. If one associates the destruction of 1125 B.C. with the Abimelech story of Judges 9, this temple may have been dedicated to El-Berith. However, such an identification would mean that there was no destructive break in the Late Bronze period between Canaanite and Israelite occupation. Outside the city, on the flanks of Gerizim, another sanctuary has been discovered, perhaps throwing light on the terebinth cultic place of the patriarchs and on the covenant renewal place noted by Deuteronomy.

Prosperity marked the monarchical period at Shechem when the city was continuously occupied, in the aftermath of King Jeroboam's patronage. This prosperity lasted even when, according to the Bible, the capital was shifted to nearby Samaria by King Omri. Destruction of Shechem by the Assyrians came in 724 B.C. In Hellenistic times a city flourished from 330 to 107 B.C.; for seemingly when Alexander the Great burned Samaria, Shechem became the center of the Samaritan community (Josephus, *Jewish Antiquities* 11.8.6; #340).[33] In the early part of this era the Samaritans built a temple to God on a section of Gerizim known today as Tell er-Râs. The temple was destroyed in 128 B.C. by the Jewish High Priest John Hyrcanus I who attacked from Jerusalem. Such destruction hardened the already bad relationships between Samaritans and Jews. The temple site would have been in ruins during Jesus's lifetime, although the tradition of worship on Gerizim was evidently still alive. The Samaritan woman reminded Jesus, "Our fathers worshiped on this mountain, while you people say that in Jerusalem is the place where one ought to worship" (John 4:20). An American expedition (R. J. Bull) began excavations at Tell er-Râs in 1964; it has discovered a magnificent temple enclave dedicated to Zeus, constructed by the Emperor Hadrian and approached by a monumental stairway of 1,500 steps. Hellenistic buildings from the third century B.C. have been discovered beneath the Roman temple; almost certainly they incorporate the remnants of the Samaritan temple.[34]

Arad

All the excavated Palestinian sites considered above after the discussion of Jericho have been to the north of that city. Yet even before the Israelites crossed the Jordan from the east to attack Jericho, they attempted to invade Canaan from the south through the Negeb. A figure who blocked their path was "the Canaanite King of Arad" (Numbers 21:1; 33:40). Confusingly, a defeat of Israel at nearby Hormah is recorded in Numbers 14:44–45 and Deuteronomy 1:44, while a victory over the King of Arad at Hormah is recorded in Numbers 21:2–3. The continuing importance of Arad is indicated in that after the conquest of Jericho, Joshua defeated the King of Arad as part of his conquest of the city-states of the south (Joshua 12:14, a passage which mentions a separate King of Hormah). The settlement of Arad by the Kenite allies of Israel is reported in Judges 1:16.

A valuable contribution of Israeli archaeologists has been the attention they have given to the Negeb or southern desert. In particular, in the 1960s and 1970s Y. Aharoni and Ruth Amiran conducted a major series of excavations at the huge Tell 'Arad,[35] eighteen miles east and slightly north of Beersheba. This Negeb site reflects the difficulty of desert living, for there is no spring, and the cities built there (sometimes as large as twenty-two acres) have had to depend for water on cisterns or storage basins facilitated by the presence of waterproof rock. Once again settlement at Arad reaches back to the fourth-millennium-B.C. Chalcolithic Age and to the first part of the third-millennium Early Bronze Age (with destruction about 2700 B.C.). Even in that early era the influence of the powerful southern neighbor, Egypt, is apparent. What is truly startling is the absence of settlements in the Middle Bronze and Late Bronze Ages, so that the site was unoccupied when, according to the Bible, the Israelites were supposed to be struggling against the King of Arad!

In the Iron Age a twelfth- or eleventh-century settlement, presumably Israelite-dominated from the start, arose at Arad, and six strata of occupation, covering as many centuries, have been found at a citadel-fortress there. Frequent destructions, culminating in a sixth-century catastrophe about the time of the fall of Jerusalem to the Babylonians, bear witness to the strategic importance of Arad for the southern defenses of Judah.

A fascinating find in the citadel-fortress is a sanctuary which existed from the 900s to the 600s B.C. On an east-west axis like the Temple of Solomon, this sanctuary had an anteroom with a square altar for burnt offerings. Further west, three steps led up to the Holy of Holies, and on one of the steps stood two pillar-shaped altars with a bowl concavity at the top for holding incense. Within the Holy of Holies stood a vertical stone about a yard in height, rectangular in shape with rounded ends—a massebah. One of the many ostraca found at Arad is a letter datable to about 600 B.C.; it mentions "the house of YHWH." Thus it would seem that a sanctuary to Yahweh, the God of Israel, existed at Arad throughout the reigns of the Davidic monarchs, despite the firm insistence of prophets and preachers in Judah that there should be only one place of worship, the Jerusalem Temple. A multiplicity of sanctuaries was part of the religious policy of the ten-tribe federation that constituted the Kingdom of Israel in the North (I Kings 12:29), but it is shocking to think that a sanctuary could survive in a royal fortress thirty-five miles south of Jerusalem. Moreover, in the Arad house of the aniconic Yahweh there stood one of the stone pillars condemned so vehemently in Deuteronomy 16:22; "You shall not set up a *massebah* which the Lord your God hates" (*see also* I Kings 14:23; II Kings 17:10; 18:4).

In the same vein, at Lachish, some thirty miles southwest of Jerusalem and northwest of Arad, recent excavations have uncovered a series of sanctuaries of Israelite/Jewish provenance, including another Israelite sanctuary of the tenth century B.C.,[36] with altar and lamps; a high place with a massebah stone; and a Jewish temple of ca. 200 B.C. When we combine this archaeological information with documentary evidence for the existence of a later Jewish temple at Elephantine (above, p. 118) where seemingly Yahweh was worshiped with a female consort, we begin to realize that the standardization of Israelite/Jewish worship was far from complete.

As for the Israelite conquest of Palestine, the formidable problem presented by the absence of second-millennium occupation at Arad before the 1100s has puzzled outstanding Israeli archaeologists. Aharoni, the excavator, argues that in Canaanite times Arad was not at Tell 'Arad but at Tell el-Milḥ (Malḥata), seven miles southwest of Tell 'Arad, while

Hormah was at Khirbet el-Meshash (Masos), three miles further west. Israeli excavations between 1967 and 1975 have shown that both these sites were occupied in the Middle Bronze Age with a destruction in the 1500s, and that at the second site there was a major Iron Age settlement in the 1200s. Another Israeli scholar, B. Mazar, argues that the Canaanite Arad mentioned in the Bible was an area and that Hormah was a city. He identifies Hormah with Tell el-Milḥ. While either of these solutions is possible, one cannot discuss the Arad issue without reflecting on information from other sites, some of them discussed above.

Archaeology and Old Testament dating

Perhaps, then, it is time to take stock of difficulties raised by the more accurate archaeological information made available since the Second World War. In particular, let us concentrate on the much debated chronology (and character) of two major biblical eras: the conquest of Canaan, and the time of the Patriarchs.[37]

The Israelite conquest of Canaan. A summary of the pertinent information supplied by the Bible may be useful. Hebrews under Jacob went down from Canaan to Egypt during a famine and were made welcome there because one of their family, Joseph, had become prime minister. Later, there arose a pharaoh who oppressed the people of Israel, making them do slave labor in building storage cities (Pithom and Raamses). Moses led them out of Egypt after a stay there of 400 or 430 years (Genesis 15:13; Exodus 12:40). After going to Mount Sinai, they wandered in the desert, with their activity centered at Kadesh-barnea about fifty miles south of Beersheba. They first tried to enter Canaan from the south, through the Negeb, but were defeated in whole or in part at Hormah by the Canaanite King of Arad. After forty years they came up the Transjordan on the eastern side of the Dead Sea, detouring further east around Edom and Moab, but conquering the rulers of Heshbon and Bashan. Joshua led them across the Jordan; he conquered Jericho and pushed into the highlands by conquering Ai. Seemingly without opposition, he went to Shechem to conduct a covenant ceremony at Mounts Ebal and Gerizim. Then Joshua made peace with the Gibeonites; but at Gibeon he defeated a coalition of southern Canaanite kings and conquered their cities, including Lachish, Hebron, and Debir. Next he defeated a coalition of northern kings led by the King of Hazor which he destroyed.

The first reference to Israel in external history is a stele of the Pharaoh Merneptah, ca. 1220 B.C., describing victories won in the Canaan area, an indication that by that date Israel was in Canaan. Working back from this reference, many scholars have proposed the following chronology. The Hebrews went to Egypt in the late 1700s at the beginning of the Hyksos era, at the same time foreigners descended from Syria into Egypt and ruled the country. Four hundred years later, the Nineteenth Dynasty (Ramses I, 1303–1302; Seti I, 1302–1290; Ramses II, 1290–1224)* moved the Egyptian capital to the delta area and began the building projects described in the Bible (city of Rameses), wherein the Hebrews were enslaved. The Exodus took place in early 1200s, and by the middle 1200s Israel was in Canaan, as indicated by Merneptah, successor of Ramses II. Albright's dating of the destruction of Jericho to just after 1300 B.C. fitted this theory.

Now, however, we are faced with confusing archaeological evidence, both supportive and contradictory of the biblical evidence. Let me list the archaeological data in the order of names mentioned in the above summary.

—There seems to have been no settlement at Kadesh-barnea before the tenth century.[38]

—The plausible sites suggested for Hormah were unoccupied from about 1500 to 1200 B.C.

—Tell 'Arad was unoccupied in the whole period from 2700 to 1100 B.C.[39]

—Heshbon was unoccupied in the second millennium before 1200.

—There was no major city at Jericho after the 1500s.

—Ai was unoccupied from the third millennium to 1200 or later.[40]

—Gibeon was unoccupied from 1500 to 1200 or later.[41]

—There was no major destruction at Hebron (Mamre) in the Late Bronze Age (1550–1200).

On the other hand, two of the Canaanite cities mentioned in the biblical story of the conquest of Canaan were violently destroyed ca. 1250–1200, namely Lachish and Hazor—also Debir, if it is to be identified with Tell Beit Mirsim. Even then, however, one must be cautious, for a late-thirteenth-century destruction followed by a twelfth-century Israelite occupation does not necessarily mean destruction by Israelites. About this same period the Pharaoh Merneptah was conducting a punitive expedition into Canaan; and there were raids by the Sea Peoples from the Mediterranean, anticipating the Philistine invasion of the next century (ca. 1180). One may also note that an important argument for a thirteenth-century date for the Exodus has disappeared. Surveys by N. Glueck in the 1930s indicated that Moab was not settled during most of the second millennium before the 1200s; consequently, Israel's avoidance of Moab en route to Canaan made no sense before the thirteenth century. Surveys in the 1970s now suggest that the Transjordan was occupied throughout the Late Bronze Age as well (1550–1200).[42]

Such an erosion of evidence for the thirteenth-century Israelite conquest of Palestine has led to much scholarly rethinking. A major figure in this has been G. E. Mendenhall of the University of Michigan.[43] In a radical rewriting of the "conquest" he maintains that there was a massive

---

*For alternative dating of the reigns of these Egyptian kings see *Encyclopaedia Britannica.*

breakdown of city cultural structure in Palestine at the end of the Late Bronze Age. Israelites did not conquer those cities; indeed, the twelve-tribal federation of Israel took place in Palestine about 1200 only *after* the destruction or collapse of Late Bronze culture. The Israelite "wars" were only guerrilla campaigns by people already on the scene, i.e., Canaanites influenced by a new religious ideology which led them to attempt a new social organization. Palestinian villagers and peasants were led to a struggle to fill in the vacuum created by the Bronze Age collapse; the leaders who purveyed the religious ideology consisted of a small band under the guidance of Moses.

Other forms of rethinking (not necessarily contradictory to Mendenhall's theory) adopt the expedient of interpreting the "conquest" as a composite narrative reflecting a series of events that actually took place over centuries. For instance, if the Hebrews came to Egypt with the Hyksos, many of them may have left with the Hyksos about 1570 B.C. The violent destruction of cities (e.g., Jericho) at the end of the Middle Bronze Age in the mid-1500s, as the shock wave of the Hyksos expulsion rolled back on Palestine, may have reintroduced Hebrews into the land. From the southern desert, tribes akin to the Israelites may have come up through the unoccupied and undefended Negeb in the Late Bronze Age, ultimately giving rise to the House of Judah. The Hapiru raids against the Canaanite city-states in the period 1375–1350 mentioned in the Amarna letters (p. 116 above) may have constituted another stratum of what would become Israel. Finally, a small band may have come from the Transjordan across the river in the 1200s to serve as a catalytic agent uniting these earlier related groups, somewhat as Mendenhall suggests. In any case, such complicated suggestions show how ambivalent is the claim that archaeology throws light on the Bible.

The Patriarchal Era. In the biblical account a chain of father-son relationships unites Abraham, Isaac, Jacob, and Joseph in four generations. Since Joseph was often seen as figuring in the Hyksos conquest of Egypt in the late 1700s, a date for Abraham in the 1800s was deemed suitable (Middle Bronze IIA). This dating fitted the theory that the patriarchs were part of the Amorite movement. In the east, Amorite waves took over the Sumerian kingdoms of Mesopotamia in the early second millennium, dominating virtually every city-state by the eighteenth century. Similarly in the west, Amorites brought to an end the great Early Bronze cities both of Palestine and of the Transjordan at the close of the third millennium. The Negeb features prominently in the patriarchal narratives, and Glueck's surveys indicated that the Negeb was occupied between 2000 and 1800, but not much later. Indeed, the picture of Semitic seminomads in an Egyptian tomb-painting at Beni Hasan (1800s) was thought to give an accurate idea of how the patriarch would have appeared.[44]

Today, the dating of the Patriarchal Era is so disputed that one cannot be sure there is a prevalent opinion any longer.[45] Of course, the intrinsic difficulties in gaining certitude about the biblical information are formidable. In the form known to us, the patriarchal narratives were committed to writing about the tenth century, and we can scarcely expect great historical precision to have been preserved over almost a millennium of popular storytelling. The patriarchs are presented in a family context, scarcely figures likely to leave traces on world history recoverable by archaeology. Virtually all scholars recognize the artificiality of the father-son relationship among the patriarchs. A group for whom Abraham was the revered ancestor may have become allied with a group for whom Isaac was a hero, and the family relationship attributed in the Bible to the patriarchs may thus be an expression of ancient tribal alliances.

If we move on to details, the Beersheba so prominent in the patriarchal narratives (Genesis 21:32; 26:23; 28:10) is not known to have been occupied to any great extent before the Israelite period about 1200. This late dating also affects the well of Beersheba, which is essential to the logic of patriarchal occupation. As for contact between Isaac and a King of the Philistines (Genesis 26:1), that is anachronistic for a period before 1200. On the other hand, in the first wave of enthusiasm over the Ebla finds, the names associated with Abraham in Genesis 14 were thought to be mentioned in an Early Bronze III context (above, p. 109), and some scholars seem willing to move the patriarchs back 500 years to the 2300s.[46] Others have used the Nuzu parallels to patriarchal practices (above, p. 112) to date the patriarchs to the era when Nuzu flourished, the 1500s,[47] even if that means the truncation of Israel's stay in Egypt.

In one form of nineteenth-century scholarship (J. Wellhausen) the patriarchal narratives of Genesis were thought to have minimal or no historical content. They were the compositions of a much later period, and the customs and features of that later period were unconsciously projected back on the distant past. Seemingly one of the contributions of twentieth-century archaeology was to put the stories of Abraham and his descendants on a more solid footing, so that the distinguished archaeologist and biblical scholar, W. F. Albright, could affirm that "there can be little doubt about their substantial historicity."[48] It is ironic that now some scholars, exemplified by T. L. Thompson,[49] would use the problems caused by archaeological discoveries to return to the Wellhausen position. Paradoxically (but with some exaggeration), in this approach much of the Patriarchal Era should be dated to the first millennium when the stories were being "created." However, there are many accuracies in these narratives of the distant past that cannot be so easily explained if the stories are much later creations without an underlying body of reliable tradition. Perhaps "the bottom line" of this discussion is the necessity of greater caution in the use of archaeology both to establish historicity and to dispute it.

If such caution must be exercised in regard to Genesis 12–50, chapters that have a contact with recognizable Middle Eastern and Egyptian history, what is to be said about the prehistory of Genesis 1–11, the stories of the creation and the flood? Some would try to use paleontology to disprove evolution (often on the assumption that the theory of evolution is incompatible with the thesis of a Creator God!). Closer to the theme of this essay are the 1955 and 1969 expeditions by Fernand Navarra, a French industrialist, designed to verify the medieval thesis that the resting place of Noah's Ark "upon the mountains of ARRT" (Genesis 8:4) refers to Mount Ararat on the Turkish-Russian border,[50] specifically to the extinct volcano called in Turkish Büyük Agri Dagi. (There are at least seven other old traditions about the resting place of the Ark, ranging as far as the Arabian peninsula or the mountains of the Tigris region. The Bible probably means the region of Urartu [modern Armenia]; and as the plural "mountains" indicates, it refers to no specific peak.)

The search for the Ark presupposes the historicity of the universal flood and the possible survival of a wooden structure from remote antiquity. Fragments of wood brought back from the two expeditions were subjected to radiocarbon dating. The most favorable dating of the 1955 specimens, reported by Navarra, from Spanish and French laboratories, is in the 4500–5000 year range. That means approximately 3000–2500 B.C.—the Early Bronze Age, when *we know* there was no universal flood or even one that covered much of the Middle East! Several English and American laboratories date the specimens from both expeditions much more modestly to A.D. 600–700. No wonder that most biblical scholars refuse to accept the claim that Noah's Ark has been discovered, or to change their view that the Genesis flood story, imaginatively based on local flood stories,[51] is a parable of theological insight.

Discoveries pertinent to the New Testament period

Discussions of archaeological contributions to biblical knowledge devote much more time to the Old Testament than to the New Testament. Israel was a people and a monarchy, leaving indisputable material traces that can be detected by uncovering ancient sites. In the first 100 years of Christian existence (the New Testament Era) the followers of Jesus of Nazareth left few remains that can be dug up. Consequently most New Testament archaeology illustrates only the ambiance in which Jesus and his followers would have lived and preached. Early in the twentieth century the travels of Sir William Ramsay[52] showed how the study of the ancient cities that were visited by Paul in his journeys (as described in Acts) and addressed by letter in the Book of Revelation (Apocalypse of John) clarified details of the biblical accounts. It should be emphasized, however, that the ambiance information is general in character. It is one thing to see the ruins or excavated remains of a town where Jesus, Peter, or Paul walked, but one must be more skeptical about specific indications related to the lives of these figures, for example, this is where Jesus multiplied the loaves, or there is a house in which Paul lived. The latter style of identification mostly indicates a place thought worthy by later Christians to recall the memory of such sacred events or persons.

Throughout this century, excavated inscriptions have been published mentioning by title or name some of the officials described in the New Testament. An inscription of special interest was discovered in an Israeli excavation in 1961 at Caesarea on the Mediterranean coast, a Herodian city that became the Roman administrative headquarters. Derived from a building dedicated to the Emperor Tiberius, the inscription has the designation "Pontius Pilate, Prefect of Judea" and thus confirms the suspicion of scholars that Tacitus (*The Annals* 15.44) was anachronistic when he called Pilate a procurator, a title not used for the Palestinian governor before the time of Claudius.

Often, too, the discoveries have cast light on customs mentioned in the New Testament. For instance, Mark 7:9–13 reports that Jesus criticized the Pharisees and scribes for freeing someone from an obligation toward a parent if the person said, "Anything of mine that might have been of use to you is *Qorban*." From later rabbinic usage, most scholars understood the statement to refer to dedicating gifts to God. Now the inscribed lid of a Jewish ossuary (bone box) discovered in the 1950s in a Kidron Valley tomb from the beginning of the Christian Era[53] has these words, "All that a person may find of profit in this ossuary is *Qorban* to God from the one who lies within it."

The New Testament (Matthew 16:18; Mark 3:16; John 1:42) agrees that Jesus changed the designation of one of his followers, Simon bar-Jona, to Kepha (Aramaic) or Petros (Greek), meaning "rock"; but we have never been certain whether this was a nickname or whether Simon was the first person to bear it. Now, J. A. Fitzmyer[54] has pointed to a pre-Christian reference to a Semite (probably a Jew) named "Aqab, son of Kepha" in the Elephantine documents (above, p. 118).

On a more sombre note, despite Jewish and Christian references to crucifixion, we have never had firsthand evidence of that gruesome punishment. Recently, there have been published two Dead Sea texts mentioning the hanging of men to die on a tree, the same expression used of Jesus in Acts 5:30, "whom you killed by hanging on a tree" (*see also* 10:39). More important is the discovery in 1968 of the bones of a crucified man[55] in a first-century A.D. tomb near Mount Scopus (Jerusalem). Although there is some debate about the exact position of the man during crucifixion as implied by the bones, it is clear that the two nails used for the hands were actually driven through the wrists. One nail seems to have been used to attach the two legs to the cross together through the heel bone, and the legs of the crucified were broken (John 19:32).

In this century there was published an inscription discovered at Nazareth containing an ordinance of the Emperor (probably Claudius, A.D. 41–54), insisting that graves must remain intact and instituting the death penalty for anyone who would violate a burial place. The time of the inscription and the locale where it was found raised in the minds of some scholars the suspicion that the charges and countercharges about stealing the body of Jesus of Nazareth (Matthew 28:11–15) may have contributed to such a governmental concern for tombs. Such finds cast general light on the death and burial of Jesus.

Much more problematic is the claim that the Shroud of Turin is the actual burial cloth of Jesus.[56] This curious image (almost the equivalent of a photographic positive) of a deceased man corresponds to the accounts of the wounds of Jesus preserved in *different* gospels. Careful modern tests show that it was not painted, and no one has been able to prove exactly how the image was produced. The Shroud can be traced with surety back to the Middle Ages (when returning Crusaders created a passion for relics from the Holy Land), but it is said to betray a knowledge of anatomy not available at that time. There are botanical signs that once the cloth had been in Palestine. Uncertain is the claim that the Shroud of Turin is identical with a much earlier cloth (seemingly lost by A.D. 1000) called the Mandylion of Edessa, which is said to have borne a facial image of the crucified Christ. There was first-century contact between Jerusalem and Edessa, so that a Jerusalem-Edessa-Crusader-France itinerary is possible. The Shroud has never been subjected to radiocarbon dating. The claim that a coin of Pontius Pilate covers one of the eyes of the figure on the Shroud of Turin is difficult to verify even when the photo is greatly magnified.[57] In the 1350s, when the Shroud appeared in France in the possession of Geoffrey de Charny, it was clearly thought by the local bishops of the area to be a reproduction rather than the actual shroud of Christ; and someone is said to have admitted making it.

Overall, two observations must be made about the Shroud. If it is a forgery, it is one of the cleverest of all times, baffling even the best tests of modern science. If it is genuine, it tells us virtually nothing about Christ's death that is not already known from the Scriptures. As for Christian faith, those who receive the blessing of John 20:29 for believing in Jesus without seeing his risen body will scarcely need the support of having seen an image of his dead body, however that image was produced.

Having surveyed some general contributions of archaeology to New Testament background, let us turn now briefly to some specific sites.

Jerusalem

Naturally, the most famous city in the Bible has attracted many excavators, beginning already in the 1860s with C. Warren. There is the usual problem that the half-dozen digs done before 1925 did not have the technical skills to interpret their finds correctly. Another difficulty is that Jerusalem has been continually occupied since its seizure by David ca. 1000, and constant rebuildings have made interpretation fiendishly difficult even for the most modern technology. Moreover, much of Jerusalem is sacred ground to three religions, Jewish, Christian, and Islamic, either because of holy places or of burials; and often the very area that would be the most interesting or the most necessary for clarifying stratigraphy cannot be excavated. Kathleen Kenyon[58] turned to Jerusalem (1961–67) after her extraordinary success at Jericho, only to be plagued by war. The 1967 campaign by Israel took Old Jerusalem from the Jordanians; this change caused Kenyon to interrupt her dig, never to resume it. Since 1967 Israeli archaeologists have been very active in different sections of the city.[59]

The most eye-catching feature of Old Jerusalem even today is the enclosure that once surrounded the Temple and now surrounds the beautiful Moslem sanctuary of the Dome of the Rock. The oldest section of the city (the Jebusite or Canaanite citadel conquered by David) lay south of this enclosure, and there has been a major archaeological effort[60] to unravel the complexities of that area, including the city defensive walls, the tombs of the kings of Judah, and the water supply channels.

Excavation has brought some clarity and inevitably some disappointments. The theory that the shaft discovered by Warren in the last century was the *ṣinnor* (tunnel?) by which David entered the Canaanite city has now been disproved. Many more campaigns may be necessary before scholars agree on the history of this portion of Jerusalem, and for the non-specialist its jumble of walls will probably always remain an unattractive mystery. When Solomon built the Temple, the city spread north on the east side flanking the Kidron Valley. The *exact* location of the Temple of Solomon (First Temple, ca. 960–587 B.C.), which has not left any physical remains, has been the subject of much discussion; but some light was cast by recent excavations on the location of the walls of the Second Temple (515–A.D. 70).[61] Seemingly, and surprisingly, this Temple was not under the present Dome of the Rock, but to the north of it.

A major historical question involves the date at which the city spread from the eastern side to the western hill which is actually the highest spot in Old Jerusalem and to which the name Mount Zion was eventually given. Apparently this major expansion, which made Jerusalem truly a city, happened in the eighth century, partly in connection with the fall of Samaria and the Northern Kingdom of Israel in 721 B.C.[62] Refugees streamed to the south and Jerusalem became their haven.

Without neglecting such finds from the older period of Jerusalem's history, one must admit that the most interesting recent discoveries have cast light on the last century B.C. and the first century A.D.[63] In particular, the buildings of the Hasmonean priests and of the Herodian kings have become more visible and are truly impressive. It was known that ca. 20 B.C. Herod the Great began reconstruction projects on the Second Temple; by the time of Jesus's ministry (John 2:20) the project had already been in progress for 46 years! Israeli excavations have uncovered the southern and western walls and the entrances of the Herodian Temple enclosure,[64] making it clear that Jesus's disciples were not exaggerating when they exclaimed, "Look, Teacher, what wonderful stones and what wonderful buildings" (Mark 13:1). Walls made of precisely fitted stones of immense size, colonnaded porticoes (stoa), double and triple gateways approached by monumental steps, a bridge over the valley dividing the eastern and western hills, and paved streets underneath have all been uncovered in whole or in part. It becomes apparent that Herod rivaled Solomon himself in the expenditure of wealth and grandeur of design. The warnings of Jesus and other first-century Jewish voices that all this could be destroyed seem audaciously prophetic now that we see the imposing solidity of what stood before their eyes.

Major remnants of a Hasmonean/Herodian fortress-palace (named the Antonia after Mark Antony) that was situated just north of the Temple area have been known since the last century. A pavement of massive stone slabs recalled the *lithostrotos* or "Stone Pavement" in John 19:13, and led some scholars to argue that the Antonia served as the praetorium (John 18:28) or Roman gubernatorial headquarters where Pilate tried Jesus. It now seems more likely the stone slabs are from the Roman city of Aelia Capitolina constructed on the site of Jerusalem a century later, in Hadrian's time. Another candidate for the praetorium is a palace-fortress on the west hill (Mount Zion), the Citadel near the Jaffa Gate;[65] here is where recent excavations have helped to clarify the extent of the palace and its impressive towers.

Connected to the identification of the Citadel towers is the issue of the northern wall of Jerusalem during Jesus's time. Josephus describes a history of three defensive walls (perhaps too modest a numbering!), the first of which was built long before by David and Solomon, and the third of which was begun by Herod Agrippa I in the 40s after Jesus's lifetime.[66] The Second Wall would have been standing during Jesus's ministry; it included more of the city than did the first but much less than did the third. Golgotha or Calvary, "the Place of the Skull" where Jesus died, stood outside that Second Wall, as did his nearby tomb (John 19:20, 41–42). In the early fourth century Constantine the Great built the Church of the Resurrection or Holy Sepulchre on the site then venerated by Christians as the place of death and of burial; it stands well within the modern (Turkish) city walls.

Some scholars who have identified those walls with the approximate line of the Second Wall reject the authenticity of the Holy Sepulchre. (From Edward Robinson on, discussions of the burial place of Jesus have not been uninfluenced by the dislike of many Westerners for the appearance of the Church of the Holy Sepulchre and for the religious rivalries that mar it.) Recent discoveries make it likely that the Second Wall came east from one of the towers of the Herodian Citadel and ran south of what now is the site of the Sepulchre which, consequently, was well outside the wall.[67] Indeed, it seems as if much of the area around the Sepulchre was a

From the oldest section of Jerusalem, the Jebusite or Davidic wall of the Ophel;
excavated by Kathleen Kenyon.

(Above and opposite) Ruins at the walls of the old city of Jerusalem.

quarry from which stones for the wall were hewed. The knoll called Golgotha may have been left unquarried because of the poor quality of the stone and/or because it was split by an earthquake. Tombs were frequently cut into areas left standing in a quarry, and one of the tombs thus cut could have belonged to Joseph of Arimathea, as the Scriptures report. Archaeology cannot verify the place of Jesus's death and burial, but the claim that archaeology has disproved the authenticity of the Holy Sepulchre Church may now be dropped.

Nazareth and Capernaum

Evidence about other sites of Jesus's life is hard to interpret. There has been considerable modern debate about the historicity of the infancy narratives in Matthew and in Luke, in particular about the likelihood of the birth at Bethlehem. In antiquity, however, those infancy stories would have been accepted and embellished. The Church of the Nativity was built by Constantine (A.D. 326) over a cave already venerated as the site of the birth events. Jerome (*Epistle 58, to Paulinus*) reports that in Hadrian's time (A.D. 135) the Romans had here a grove in honor of Tammuz (Adonis): "In the grove where the Christ-Child once cried they wept for Venus's lover." But even if the rival Roman cult shows that there was a Christian sacred site here some 140 years after Christ's birth, one must

California Organization of
Police and Sheriffs endorse

Bill Lockyer

for State Senate because

"Lockyer is <u>tough</u> on crime."

Lockyer Campaign Committee, 1213 A St., Hayward, CA 94541, I.D. 741735

still decide whether the site represented historical memory or was simply the localization of a pious belief.

At Nazareth important excavations have been conducted by B. Bagatti since 1955 in relation to the rebuilding of the Church of the Annunciation. Under a fifth-century Byzantine church there was an earlier church with the measurements attested elsewhere for Jewish synagogues. This similarity causes the excavators to speak of a church-synagogue frequented by Jewish Christians. At the same site several caves served as places of Christian devotion. The oldest known inscription with the Greek words for "Hail Mary" was found, as well as an inscription to "Christ, Son of God." It has been urged that such devotion probably reflects a memory of the house of Mary and of a cave which was the site of the angelic annunciation (Luke 1:26–27). What is certain from the excavations, however, is that this is a site in Mary's hometown where her memory was venerated by Christians from an early period.

The impressive synagogue ruins standing at Capernaum on the northern shore of the Sea of Galilee have been the object of debate. Is this the synagogue in which Jesus healed and preached (Mark 1:21; John 6:59), or is it a later synagogue perhaps built over the first-century synagogue? Many scholars think that the existing synagogue is of the third century A.D., but excavations since 1968 (V. Corbo) indicate an even later date (fourth century). Just south of the synagogue, closer to the lake, is an oc-

Details from the ruins of the ancient synagogue at Capernaum. *"The impressive synagogue ruins . . . have been the object of debate. Is this the synagogue in which Jesus healed and preached (Mark 1:21; John 6:59), or is it a later synagogue perhaps built over the first-century synagogue?"*

tagonal fifth-century church, but under it the excavators found signs of several centuries of buildings honoring Peter and going back to what they claim was a first-century house that was turned into a Jewish-Christian place of cult. In their judgment they have found the house of Peter mentioned in Mark 1:29 which Jesus entered when he left the synagogue. At least, one may judge that the excavations at Nazareth and Capernaum conducted by the Franciscan Fathers are revealing that a form of Jewish Christianity lasted in Galilee for several centuries with remarkable continuity.[68]

Rome

The Peter whose home was at Capernaum died in Rome in the sixties—almost all scholars would agree on that today. Under the site of the present Church of St. Peter, Constantine had a basilica built in A.D. 333. Excavations begun in the 1940s under the Constantinian level of the church have yielded fascinating discoveries.[69] This Vatican hill outside the ancient city was the site of the *Circus* of Nero; it was also a burial ground for rich and poor. The wealthy had mausoleums, but adjacent to the mausoleums was a place where burial was by simple inhumation. The Constantinian architects leveled part of the hill, and their buildings cut into the mausoleums.

Modern excavations have uncovered streets of a pagan necropolis going back as far as A.D. 70-100. The high altar of Old St. Peter's was over a spot where there were no mausoleums. About A.D. 160, a retaining wall, dubbed the red wall, was built in order to terrace the area. Near the center of that wall and directly under the subsequent high altar, there was a series of three superimposed niches, the upper two of which were part of the wall, the lowest of which was underground. The upper two formed a shrine or memorial consisting of a travertine stone slab resting on two marble columns. There is little doubt that this was the *tropaion* (trophy, memorial, perhaps tomb) referred to by the Roman presbyter Gaius, when ca. A.D. 200 he bragged about Rome's heritage from Peter and Paul: "I can show you the 'trophies' of the apostles. For whether you go to the Vatican, or along the Ostian Way, you will find the 'trophies' of those who founded the Church of Rome" (Eusebius of Caesarea, *Ecclesiastical History* 2.25.7).

Did the lowest niche once contain the bones of Peter?[70] One might guess that Peter was martyred in the *Circus* of Nero, that his friends exercised their legal right to ask for his body, and that they buried it nearby in an area where the poor were inhumed. They would have had to remember and even to mark the site of the burial and then 100 years later, when it was possible, to build a monument. Although bones (seemingly those of a woman) were found in an indentation under the red wall, no bones were found in the lowest niche. Accordingly, Pope Pius XII stated on Dec. 23, 1950, that it was impossible to identify the remains of Peter in these excavations. However, about A.D. 250 another wall was built, and in that supporting wall was inserted a marble box, near which is a graffito or inscription mentioning Peter. When this marble box was opened publicly, it contained only debris with minuscule bone fragments. Professor Margherita Guarducci claimed that it had previously been opened privately during the Second World War and that the bones of an elderly man which it contained had been deposited in another place in the Vatican. It was argued that these bones were originally in the lowest niche in the red wall and that they had been put in the marble box at the time of its insertion in the later wall. If that were the case, we would then both have the bones of Peter and know his original burial place, which was already venerated in A.D. 160. Pope Paul VI accepted this thesis on June 26, 1968.

Nevertheless, there are major difficulties facing it. (1) There is absolutely no way to verify the story that the marble box once contained bones. (2) It is not clear whether the *tropaion* of the second century marked the burial place, or the place of martyrdom, or was simply a memorial to Peter near where he died, the site of the monument being determined by availability instead of by historical memory. (3) There is a rival tradition at another place in Rome; on the Appian Way in antiquity there stood a "Basilica of the Apostles" at a site associated with St. Sebastian. Several inscriptions there mention Peter and Paul, but especially important is an inscription by Pope Damascus (ca. 375): "Whoever you are who seek the names of Peter and Paul, you must know that here the saints once dwelled." Since this site does not seem to have been a place for private dwelling, does the inscription refer to the resting place of the bodies of the Apostles? One might argue that the bones of Peter were taken from the niche in the Vatican wall in the mid-third century because of persecutions and were later returned to the Vatican, being placed in the marble box. But this theory raises as many problems as it solves in terms of motive and procedure.

Perhaps all that one can conclude is that Gentile Christians in Rome, even as Jewish Christians in Galilee, began very quickly to select memorial places where they could do honor to figures who surround Jesus in the Gospel narrative, such as Mary and Peter. The lives and sometimes the deaths of such figures had now become part of the Christian story and were to be commemorated by holy places.

*   *   *

This *selection* of documentary and archaeological discoveries illustrates recent gains in knowledge pertinent to the Bible. (As stated at the beginning, important gains in interpretative methodology, although less concrete and more disputable, may be added.) A review of the biblical applications suggested above shows how scholars, working inductively from such discoveries, have been able to cast light on almost every aspect of both Testaments: canonical collection, scribal transmission, languages, writing style, history, life-patterns, theology, worship, etc. To "cast light" on anything clarifies some features but brings out rough spots and awkwardness that otherwise would not have been visible. To some, the difficulties or problems uncovered by modern scholarship detract from the beauty of the sacred page which, in their view, should not be marred by human imperfections. To others, what has been uncovered by scholarship, including the problems, confirms the appropriateness of the Bible as the basic text of two religions, Judaism and Christianity, which in different ways have insisted that the truly human is a proper sphere or vehicle for the revelation of the truly divine.

The reader who seeks more technical information will find convenient the general articles on history, archaeology, canonicity, and texts and versions in *The Jerome Biblical Commentary,* ed. R. E. Brown *et al.* (Englewood Cliffs, N.J.: Prentice-Hall, 1968); also the four-volume *Encyclopaedia of Archaeological Excavations in the Holy Land,* ed. M. Avi-Yonah (London: Oxford, 1975-78); and the *Supplementary Volume* (5) to the *Interpreter's Dictionary of the Bible* (Nashville: Abingdon, 1976). Translated examples of many of the tablets and texts to be discussed may be found in J. B. Pritchard, *Ancient Near Eastern Texts,* (rev. ed.; Princeton Univ., 1955). Presupposing the more technical discussions, the footnotes facilitate further reading with references of a less technical character, especially to BAR (*Biblical Archaeologist Reader;* three paperback vols.; Garden City, N.Y.: Doubleday, 1961, 1964, 1970); and to the periodicals BA (*Biblical Archaeologist*) and BARev (*Biblical Archaeology Review*).

The following approximate dating may be helpful in reading even popular discussions of biblical archaeology (all are B.C.):

Chalcolithic 4000–3150

Early Bronze 3150–2200 (I=3150–2850; II=2850–2700; III=2700–2350; IV=2350–2200)

Middle Bronze 2200–1550 (I=2200–2000; IIA=2000–1750; IIB=1750–1550)

Late Bronze 1550–1200 (I=1550–1400; IIA=1400–1300; IIB=1300–1200)

Iron Age 1200–586 (I=l200–1000; II=1000–586)

[1] A common estimate of the extent of biblical history is from 1850 B.C. to A.D. 15Q. In the Old Testament period "Israel" is an appropriate title after the affiliation of the twelve tribes; "Jews" is a designation related to the tribe of Judah, the chief survivor of the tribal confederation in the post-Exilic period (after 539).

[2] The Hebrew canon, followed by many Protestant churches, has thirty-nine books; but Jews and Christians group these Old Testament books in a different order. On the basis of Jewish tradition in Alexandria, the Roman Catholic Church and some Orthodox churches recognize seven more books, often called deuterocanonical; some Oriental churches recognize even more. Christians are at one in acknowledging twenty-seven New Testament books.

[3] Semitic languages are often divided into *Northeastern* (Akkadian, Assyrian, Babylonian), and *Southeastern* (South Arabic, Ethiopic), as distinct from *Northwestern* (Amorite, Canaanite, Aramaic), and *Southwestern* (Arabic). By further specification, the Canaanite sphere includes Ugaritic, Hebrew, and Phoenician. Similar terminology is sometimes applied to the Semitic peoples.

[4] Articles have appeared in BA almost every year from 1976 through 1981, some of them polemical. Overall, one may compare P. Matthiae, *Ebla: An Empire Rediscovered* (Garden City, N.Y.: Doubleday, 1981) with G. Pettinato, *The Archives of Ebla: An Empire Inscribed in Clay* (Garden City, N.Y.: Doubleday, 1981).

[5] Anchor Bible volumes 16, 17, 17A (Garden City, N.Y.: Doubleday, 1966–70). For the applicability of Ugaritic to the Bible, *see* H. L. Ginsberg in BA 8 (1945) 41–58; reprinted in BAR 2. 34–50; for Ugaritic life and culture, *see* A. F. Rainey in BA 28 (1965) 102–25; reprint-

ed in BAR 3. 76–99.

[6] Dahood has an "Afterword" in the Pettinato volume (note 4 above), entitled "Ebla, Ugarit, and the Bible."

[7] G. E. Mendenhall in BA 11 (1948) 1–19; reprinted in BAR 2. 3–20.

[8] C. H. Gordon in BA 3 (1940); reprinted in BAR 2. 21–33; but *see* B. L. Eichler in the *Supplementary Volume* to the *Interpreter's Dictionary*, 635–36.

[9] On covenant forms, *see* G. E. Mendenhall in BA 17 (1954) 50–76; reprinted in BAR 3. 25–53; also D. J. McCarthy, *Old Testament Covenant: A Survey of Current Opinions* (Richmond: Knox, 1972); *Treaty and Covenant* (rev. ed; Rome: Biblical Institute, 1978).

[10] E. F. Campbell in BA 23 (1960) 2–22; reprinted in BAR 3. 54–75. About 375 items had been published by 1965.

[11] References to Hapiru are found in the Nuzu tablets as well, indicating a wide geographical presence; at most the biblical Hebrews would have been part of a much larger movement.

[12] F. M. Cross in BA 26 (1963) 110–21; reprinted in BAR 3. 227–39.

[13] E. G. Kraeling in BA 15 (1952) 50–67; reprintd in BAR 1. 128–44; also B. Porten 42 (1979) 74–104 (technical, after initial pages).

[14] For overall analysis *see* F. M. Cross, *The Ancient Library of Qumran* (2nd ed.; Garden City, N.Y.: Doubleday, 1961); best translation by G. Vermes, *The Dead Sea Scrolls in English* (2nd ed.; New York: Penguin, 1975); good survey by J. A. Sanders in BA 36 (1973) 110–48. For the recently published Temple Scroll, *see* J. Milgrom in BA 41 (1978) 105–20. Another important Dead Sea find was at Murabba'at, 12 miles south of Qumrān, pertinent to Bar Kokhba's revolt in A.D. 132–135; *see* articles by Y. Yadin in BA 24 (1961) 34–50, 86–95; reprinted in BAR 3. 254–78.

[15] J. Murphy-O'Connor in BA 40 (1977) 100–124.

[16] *See* P. W. Skehan in BA 28 (1965) 87–100; reprinted in BAR 3. 240–53.

[17] *See* BA 42 (1979) 206–56 (whole issue). For the texts: J. M. Robinson, *The Nag Hammadi Library in English* (San Francisco: Harper & Row, 1977).

[18] Christian gnosticism is not easy to define, since the Church Fathers of Alexandria (e.g., Clement) had strains of gnosticism that were not frowned upon as heterodox. Those gnostics ultimately deemed heretical were not of one mind among themselves; but prominent in one system or the other were such ideas as: a series of eons separating the Unknowable God from creation; the creator god of the Old Testament was evil or a demigod because he brought matter into existence; preexistent souls were entrapped in this matter; Jesus entered the world (even if he never really became part of it) in order to reveal to such souls their origin; such revealed knowledge (*gnōsis*) enables souls to escape the entrapment of matter.

[19] For the subtleties of the issue, *see* Pheme Perkins, *The Gnostic Dialogue: The Early Church and the Crisis of Gnosticism* (New York: Paulist, 1980).

[20] R. Kittel and P. Kahle, *Biblica Hebraica* (3rd ed.; Stuttgart: Wurtemberg. Bibelanstalt, 1937).

[21] M. Goshen-Gottstein guided the publication by the Hebrew University Bible Project; *see* BA 42 (1979) 145–63.

[22] J. H. Charlesworth in BA 42 (1979) 174–79; 43 (1980) 26–34; it is difficult to get clear information about what has been found.

[23] F. V. Filson in BA 22 (1959) 48–51; 25 (1962) 50–57; both reprinted in BAR 3. 304–14.

[24] *See* "The Shapira Affair" in BARev 5 (#4, 1979) 12–27.

[25] F. M. Cross in BARev 5 (#1, 1979) 36–43.

[26] For the basic fragments *see* the Supplement to the *Journal of Biblical Literature* 91/92 (1972) 1–20. J. A. Fitzmyer, *The Dead Sea Scrolls* (Bibliography; Missoula: Scholars Press, 1975) 119 comments: "Favorable reactions to the claims have come only from uncritical sources."

[27] For a perceptive history of the development of archaeological method in Palestine/Israel, *see* W. G. Dever in BA 43 (1980) 40–48. Also H. D. Lance, *The Old Testament and the Archaeologist* (Philadelphia: Fortress, 1981).

[28] K. M. Kenyon, *Digging up Jericho* (London: Praeger, 1957).

[29] Yadin's articles in BA from 1956 through 1959 are gathered in BAR 2. 191–224. Also Y. Yadin, *Hazor* (Schweich Lectures; London: Oxford, 1972) 191–224.

[30] G. E. Wright in BA 22 (1959) 67–78; reprinted in BAR 2. 248–57.

[31] Y. Yadin in BA 23 (1960) 62–68; reprinted in BAR 2. 240–47.

[32] A series of articles in BA from 1957 through 1963 are gathered in BAR 2. 258–300. *See also* G. E. Wright, *Shechem: The Biography of a Biblical City* (New York: McGraw Hill, 1965).

[33] For Mount Gerizim and the Samaritans, *see* R. T. Anderson in BA 43 (1980) 217–21.

[34] R. J. Bull in BA 31 (1968) 58–72.

[35] Y. Aharoni in BA 31 (1968) 1–32.

[36] Lachish had been excavated in the 1930s by J. Starkey, but Israeli archaeologists resumed excavation in the late 1960s (Y. Aharoni) and 1970s (D. Ussishkin).

[37] *See* the debate by E. F. Campbell and J. M. Miller in BA 42 (1979) 37–47.

[38] R. Cohen in BA 44 (1981) 93–107.

[39] *See* the posthumous article on Israel's conquest of the Negeb written by Y. Aharoni in BA 39 (1976) 55–76.

[40] On the 1964–72 excavations *see* J. Callaway in BA 39 (1976) 18–30. Bethel, near Ai, was destroyed about 1200, but the Bible does not mention a campaign of Joshua against Bethel.

[41] Gibeon was excavated by an American expedition in 1956–62; *see* J. B. Pritchard, *Gibeon: Where the Sun Stood Still* (Princeton Univ., 1962). Magnificent water systems were discovered, including an immense pool (*see* II Samuel 2:13).

[42] J. R. Kautz on Moab in BA 44 (1981) 27–35.

[43] G. E. Mendenhall, *The Tenth Generation: The Origins of the Biblical Tradition* (Baltimore: Johns Hopkins, 1973). *See also* BA 39 (1976) 154–57.

[44] W. H. Shea in BA 44 (1981) 219–28.

[45] N. M. Sarna, "Abraham in History," in BARev 3 (#4, 1977) 5–9.

[46] Some support this date from excavations in the Ghor, south of the Dead Sea, the most plausible site for the "Cities of the Plain" destroyed in the time of Abraham (Genesis 19:29); destruction there took place around 2350 and not in the Middle Bronze Age. *See* W. C. van Hattem in BA 44 (1981) 87–92.

[47] Important is the challenge by J. Van Seters, *Abraham in History and Tradition* (New Haven: Yale, 1975).

[48] BA 36 (1973) 10.

[49] T. L. Thompson, *The Historicity of the Patriarchal Narratives* (New York/Berlin: De Gruyter, 1974).

[50] L. R. Bailey in BA 40 (1977) 137–46; also his *Where Is Noah's Ark?* (Nashville: Abingdon, 1978).

[51] Flood stories are elaborated in various ancient Middle Eastern mythologies; e.g., *see* T. Frymer-Kensky in BA 40 (1977) 147–55.

[52] W. W. Gasque, *Sir William M. Ramsay* (Grand Rapids: Eerdmans, 1966). BAR 2. 313–420 gathers various BA articles on New Testament cities.

[53] J. A. Fitzmyer, *Essays on the Semitic Background of the New Testament* (London: Chapman, 1971) 93–100.

[54] J. A. Fitzmyer, *To Advance the Gospel* (New York: Crossroad, 1981) 115–18.

[55] Ibid., 125–46.

[56] I. Wilson, *The Shroud of Turin: the Burial Cloth of Jesus Christ?* (Garden City, N.Y.: Doubleday, 1978); Virginia Bortin in BA 43 (1980) 109–17; K. F. Weaver supplies excellent photographs in *National Geographic* 157 (June 1980), 730-52.

[57] *See* the debate in BA 43 (1980) 112, 197; 44 (1981) 135–37.

[58] K. M. Kenyon, *Digging up Jerusalem* (London: Praeger, 1979).

[59] *Jerusalem Revealed*, ed. Y. Yadin (New Haven: Yale, 1976).

[60] Articles by Y. Shiloh in BA 42 (1979) 165–72; 44 (1981) 161–70.

[61] A. S. Kaufman in BA 44 (1981) 108–15.

[62] M. M. Eisman in BA 41 (1978) 49–53.

[63] Very careful in evaluating evidence is J. Wilkinson, *Jerusalem as Jesus Knew It* (London: Thames and Hudson, 1978).

[64] B. Mazar in BARev 6 (#4, 1980) 44–59.

[65] M. Broshi in BA 40 (1977) 11–17.

[66] E. W. Hamrick in BA 40 (1977) 18–23.

[67] R. H. Smith in BA 30 (1967) 74–90; reprinted in BAR 3. 390–404; B. E. Schein in BA 44 (1981) 21–26.

[68] Both the archaeological evidence and its evaluation may be found in B. Bagatti, *The Church from the Circumcision* (Jerusalem: Franciscan Press, 1971).

[69] R. T. O'Callaghan in BA 12 (1949) 1–23; 16 (1953) 70–87.

[70] G. F. Snyder in BA 32 (1969) 1–24.

Theories of Literature in the Twentieth Century

Harvey Goldstein

Harvey Goldstein, who teaches English literature at the University of Southern California in Los Angeles, has specialized in the history of critical theory and the literature of the eighteenth century. Most of his publications, which include articles on the *Poetics* of Aristotle, the seventeenth-century doctrine of *discordia concors,* and the *Discourses on Art* by Joshua Reynolds (a work reprinted in *The Great Ideas Today* 1976), have been in those two areas.

A graduate of the University of Chicago and Northwestern University, from which he received his doctorate in 1960, Professor Goldstein taught at Williams College, Brandeis University, and the University of Rochester, before moving to California, where he now lives in Beverly Hills.

Notwithstanding his academic preoccupations, he regards himself as "most satisfied" by an extracurricular series of television lectures called "Ceremony of Innocence," which he gave on literary masterpieces from the Old Testament through Goethe's *Faust* for Station KNXT, in Los Angeles, in 1972–73.

The New Criticism

The commitment to theory in dealing with literature, which is among the characteristic features of our age, may be said to have begun about fifty years ago, with the New Criticism. "All of us who read seriously are, whether we like it or not, New Critics," was for a time among our critical commonplaces. So, a bit later on, was: "The New Criticism . . . has been dead for some twenty years." Still a third catchphrase, "the New Criticism died of its own success." And whatever that success amounted to, it was somehow bound up in the most bandied about critical slogan of the century: "A poem should not mean but be," which is itself a line from a poem by Archibald MacLeish.

I do not here attribute the rest of these quotations for, although their origins can be determined, they have become, in a sense, by endless repetition, public. It was Randall Jarrell who, in 1953, complained about the place of criticism in our age when he pointed out, with some justice, that students preferred critical analyses of *King Lear* or *The Turn of the Screw* to the works. But John Crowe Ransom had already said the same thing in a very different tone. In 1939 the first issue of *The Kenyon Review,* of which he was editor, proclaimed: "Now is the age of criticism. The living art decays . . . but the love of it quickens." "Our age," Ransom said, "is critical, and it has its own passionate enjoyments."

Such commonplace phrases raise troubling questions. For example, is MacLeish's famous *mot* itself "poetic" and therefore exempt from the need to mean? Still, despite various problems, the point is clear. Literary criticism has been a major enterprise in our century, and any study of twentieth-century criticism, especially in America, must confront the New Criticism, above all.

The phrase derives from the title of Ransom's 1941 collection of critical essays. But the work of such New Critics as Ransom, Allen Tate, Robert Penn Warren, and R. P. Blackmur (if he is a New Critic) goes back to the twenties, when a group of Southern writers, committed to agrarian politics and alienated from modern industrial and commercial culture, formed the "Fugitives." The group gets added identity from its association with such journals as *Hound and Horn, Southern Review,* Ransom's *Kenyon Review,* Tate's *Sewanee Review,* and from its connections with such institutions of higher learning as Vanderbilt, the University of the South, Louisiana State University, Kenyon College (especially its School of Letters), and later, Yale.

At mid-century, when there was academic conflict between critics of literature and historians of it, New Criticism quickly became synonymous with the critical movement as a whole. Perhaps that explains the recent stress on the divergences among the various New Critics. Some have, in fact, denied that there was ever a coherent body of ideas that justified the name for a whole group of critics. Blackmur had interests and used methods not shared by the others. Yvor Winters's moral concerns connect him with a different group known as the New Humanists. Kenneth Burke has so many critical concerns as to escape all labels. Tate is appalled by I. A. Richards's "scientism"; Ransom rejects Richards's doctrine of synaesthesis; Tate seems unhappy with Ransom's division of texture from structure, and so on. Yet despite such disagreements these men recognized grounds on which they came together as part of a significant literary movement.

Tate comments that the New Criticism is marked by "a hostility to, or neglect of, the 'historical method.'" This was certainly the charge that t enemies in the academies brought against the New Critics. And it has a kind of truth, although it is not true for the most part that they showed the historical ignorance they were accused of. René Wellek, whose *Theory of Literature* was a New Critical landmark, and whose discrimination of intrinsic from extrinsic approaches became a critical catchphrase, has argued that the New Critics were fairly careful historians. Tate's comment is not a manifesto of ignorance; rather, it locates the New Critical area of concern within the work itself. "Historical method" seems to be Tate's synecdoche for late nineteenth- and early twentieth-century discussions of literature that ignored the text in favor of sociological, psychological, and personal questions. The New Criticism was hostile to hedonistic impressionism and genteel moralism, to extrinsic and reductive approaches that had made literature a handmaiden of other disciplines. The issue also involved the teaching of literature; in the classroom the historical method had often degenerated into gossip, and knowledge about the work and its mileau seemed so nearly sufficient that the work itself was rarely dealt with.

The New Critics, then, developed approaches that would permit the study of literature as literature, not as a version of something else. Denying the separability of form from content, of style from matter, these critics practiced a close examination of the work's formal and stylistic qualities, which involved a strong emphasis on such devices of rhetoric as diction and imagery. Because form was declared to be meaning, these critics expunged the older view of literature as a prettified didacticism. If meaning was asserted, it was held to lie in literature's metaphoric, even symbolic, nature.

It is hard to determine the exact forces that brought about this "formalism." The doctrine of the inseparability of form and content goes back, of course, to Aristotle and his four causes, his awareness that a certain object is neither brass nor a ring, but rather a brazen ring. But why did such a notion seem so important in the first half of the twentieth century? The stress on form must, to some extent, be seen as poetry's defense against scientism. At the beginning of the century William Butler Yeats complained that the scientific movement intruded "externalities of all kinds" into literature and that, therefore, literature was losing itself "in opinion, in declamation."[1] Even earlier, Dostoyevsky's Underground Man had cried out against positivism's destruction of the things of the spirit, had felt that there was no place for sensibility in the world of the Crystal Palace. Allen Tate, himself, in 1940, argued that the importance of the New Criticism is in its way of combating positivism and the scientific attitude, the attitude which, he says, "has intensified if . . . not actually created our distress."[2] Tate, by the way, saw *historical* criticism as an imitation of the scientific method.

For reasons which are not too clear, World War I intensified the rejection of content in favor of form. What is known as Russian formalism developed in 1916 and continued as a movement until 1930, encouraging the literary experiments of Futurism and trying to "liberate poetic diction from the fetters of intellectualism and moralism."[3] It is doubtful, however, that this movement had any significant relationship to the New Criticism or to its immediate forerunners. Moreover, the Russian rejection of tefor things was really an attempt to make literature "scientific." Indeed, according to an historian of the subject, the movement's stress on concrete elements amounted to "a passion for scientific positivism."[4]

An early twentieth-century distrust of the didactic in America, England, and France seems much more directly connected to New Critical concerns. In 1924 George Moore's *An Anthology of Pure Poetry* claimed that "Shakespeare never soiled his songs with thought." Somewhat earlier, the Imagists had refused "to implicate the poem's effect in meaning."[5] Paul Valéry repeatedly examined the opposition of "Poetry and Abstract Thought" as he sought out his definition of "Pure Poetry," and he approvingly quoted Mallarmé's edict that poetry is made out of words, not out of ideas. American writers such as Marianne Moore and William Carlos Williams were making poems to show that poetry's concern is properly with things rather than ideas.

> So much depends
> upon
>
> a red wheel
> barrow
>
> glazed with rain
> water
>
> beside the white
> chickens[6]

Anti-didacticism, objectivity, impersonality were all important aspects of New Critical thought and deeply tied to its emphasis on form. Moreover, they raise issues which have been central in the history of Western critical thought.

The classical background

Formalism and anti-didacticism were significantly connected by Aristotle, and both positions ultimately derive from him. A glance at the *Poetics* makes it clear that the discussion is not about the "statements" that a poem might make. It can be assumed, therefore, that by turning the discussion from the content of poetry to its structure, Aristotle is able to "reply" to Plato's attacks on poetry's "pseudo-statements." Something of the same sort may well be going on in the work of I. A. Richards, one of the immediate sources of the New Criticism.

Horace's famous dictum to the effect that the aim of poetry is to "instruct and delight" returned attention to literature's cognitive content, and two millennia of writers paid at least lip service to literature's teaching. But the relation of poetry to knowledge was often seen as a complex one. Such sensitive and thoughtful critics as John Dryden and Samuel Johnson were both convinced that poetry's appeal was to the feelings, not to the intellect, and that good literature was not cerebral. If it "taught," it did so in a way that was peculiar to it. Coleridge distinguished science from poetry on the basis of truth and beauty. But it was Coleridge's source, Kant, who clearly separated the experience of art from conceptual knowledge. It was Kant who inspired the New Critical notion of artistic meaning as symbolic meaning. Moreover, by divorcing poetry from the cognitive, Kant helped solve the old problem of the relativity of response.

Among the reasons Plato attacked literature was that it opened itself up to a variety of private subjective responses, an *apeiron* of chaotic feelings. In the *Philebus* Plato discusses pure and impure pleasures. Impure pleasures are determined by the private states of mind of the spectator. Pure pleasures, on the other hand, are defined and shaped by the nature of the object which produces that pleasure. Whereas to Plato, tragedy provides the mixed and highly personal pleasure of "scratching an itch," pure pleasure derives from geometric forms and mathematical formulae: "These things are pleasurable in themselves and have nothing to do with the personal feelings of the individual viewer." Aristotle's disregard of the spectator and his emphasis on plot seem a way of dealing with a poem as a formalized object and therefore, because of its formal principle, place a poem among those things which are pleasurable in themselves.

After the epistemological revolution of the seventeenth century, when phenomenal reality came to be thought of as shaped by the perceiving mind, the problem of literary response intensified. "There is no more real beauty or deformity in one piece of matter than in another," Addison acknowledged. Thomas Rymer agonized: "How do I know that I am pursuing any man's maggot but my own?" Terrified by the subjective nature of response, and by the possible chaos of private tastes, critics for a century and a half tried to establish standards. The standard, however, was necessarily worked out in the area of response. Johnson tries to find some stability in "that which has pleased many and pleased long." He recognizes that it is a shaky and inadequate test. Hume's standard for taste is the nature of the man of taste. His argument is dazzling, but it seems circular.

The problem was somewhat solved when Kant separated the artistic experience from those other experiences that promote individual differences. Not only did Kant differentiate the judgment of taste from cognition, but also from sentiment and from use. The agreeable is, of course, a private matter determined by individual experience and temperament. But the response to art is disinterested and therefore transcends the personal; it is "a necessary and universal judgment." In this way, the nature of the experience, rather than the private history of the experiencer, becomes shaping. Kant established a precedent for the New Critics' turn away from historical and biographical concerns.

For the most part, the history of all criticism has been a search for objectivity and impersonality. There are, of course, exceptions, and it might perhaps be arguable that there are both flood and ebb tides. Some critics, even some eras, have celebrated the consciousness of the individual writer and reader. Stanley Fish for one, who has written on *Paradise Lost* from the reader's point of view, and many of the reader-response theorists might be cited. But the attempt to go beyond the person has dominated. Nietzsche declared that "the subjective artist is simply the bad artist." He advocated, in this matter, an essentially Kantian position: ". . . We demand above all, in every genre and range of art, a triumph over subjectivity, deliverance from the self, the silencing of every personal will and desire; since, in fact, we cannot imagine the smallest genuine art work lacking objectivity and disinterested contemplation."[7] Matthew Arnold demanded above all that the act of criticism be disinterested.

Forerunners: Eliot, Hulme, Richards

In some ways, the New Criticism, indeed twentieth-century Anglo-American criticism, begins with T. S. Eliot's "Tradition and the Individual Talent." This has been called "the single most influential essay in twentieth-century criticism in English."[8] It faces directly the question of impersonality and makes it central. And, in this respect at least, Eliot establishes one of the basic positions of the New Criticism. In a distinction that is somewhat reminiscent of Longinus on the "intrusive thyrsis," Eliot differentiates "emotions," which belong to the writer as a personality, from "feelings," which belong only to the language and structure of the work. His discussion of the transmuting of the artist's passions leads Eliot to an analogous observation about the spectator: "The effect of a work of art upon the person who enjoys it is an experience different in kind from any experience not of art." Literature itself becomes defined here as "a continual self-sacrifice, a continual extinction of personality."[9] Eliot's "complete separation" of "the man who suffers and the mind which creates" leads to such important New Critical statements of impersonality as "The Intentional Fallacy," and "The Affective Fallacy."[10] Does it not also become Structuralism's elimination of the person in favor of the linguistic code?

It has been said that Eliot here means only to banish the *idiosyncratic* personality, Horace's mad poet, as it were, the "unnatural" that Dr. Johnson associates with a wrong-headed pursuit of novelty. Perhaps. Eliot does attack the search "for novelty in the wrong place" of new human emotions. But it seems that he is also saying something about the ontological nature of literature. It is not merely that the civilized mind transforms the private mind out of its self-concern, but that form itself, in a successful work, so changes its content as to make it a part of form. The poet, says Eliot, has "only a medium" to express. Critical formalism and depersonalization are intimately tied.

T. S. Eliot, T. E. Hulme (pronounced "Hume"), and I. A. Richards are generally acknowledged the immediate sources of the New Criticism. Ezra Pound, although he denies Hulme's direct influence, nevertheless celebrates him: "I have no doubt that the bleak and smeary 'Twenties' wretchedly needed his guidance, and the pity is he wasn't there in person to keep down the vermin."[11] The vermin, of course, are those who dissolve the concrete particularity of poetry into abstractions or personal sentimentality. Hulme was the champion of "dry hardness." In his "Romanticism and Classicism," Hulme attacked both Arnoldian "high seriousness" and Carlyle's "circumambient gas," his fuzzy symbolism; and, like Eliot, he had located the defining and essential quality of poetry in its language, its craft. Poetry is a matter of images, of metaphors; that is the nature of its "accuracy." "Plain speech is essentially inaccurate. It is only by new metaphors . . . that it can be made precise." It is not subject—that "doesn't matter"—nor is "it the scale or kind of emotion that decides." Turning the Coleridgean distinction of fancy and imagination on its head, Hulme asked for "a cheerful, dry, and sophisticated" verse, and as this means a verse concerned only with "the exact epithet which hits it off, there you have a properly esthetic emotion."[12]

The similarities between Hulme and Eliot are striking. Further, Hulme anticipates the New Criticism not only in his linguistic concerns but also in his "metaphysics." In many ways both Eliot and Hulme prepare for

Ransom's attack on "Platonic" poetry, and, by their stress on the particularities of poetic language, perhaps, too, for Ransom's opposition of structure and texture. Certainly they, along with Pound, also establish the New Critical fashion of rejecting Romantic literature. Matthew Arnold, who had condemned the Romantics for their intellectual pretentiousness, had already begun that attack, which Irving Babbitt had continued. But Hulme goes beyond their Humanism. Humanism as well as Romanticism represents for him a failure of thought and tradition.

If there seems to be some kind of contradiction here, it is only apparent. Hulme makes it clear that poetry is a matter of craft, not of thought, yet he also indicates that certain intellectual positions either facilitate or prevent the achievement of that craft. A clear distinction between ethical doctrines and poetic composition, a recognition of proper limits, directs the poet to "that accurate description [which] is the legitimate object of verse." On the other hand, "a bad metaphysic of art" drags the infinite in and turns literature into "split religion."[13] Hulme's orthodoxy thus does not lead him to a didactic theory of art but locates art in its formal and textural qualities. In a sense he supplies a metaphysic for formalism.

Although I. A. Richards's influence on the New Criticism was also enormous, his positions differ somewhat from those of Hulme and Eliot. Because Richards engaged in a behaviorist psychologizing and focused on reader response and authorial attitude, both Ransom and Brooks criticized him. And Ransom criticized him too for his "scientism." Yet in his emphasis on close reading, his theory of irony, his discussion of poetic language and his discussions of poetry and science, Richards contributed to the development of the New Criticism.

Clearly his discrimination between the referential and emotive use of language was the forerunner of the New Critical distinction between coherence and correspondence. Richards pointed out that the scientific use of language is a matter of the truth or falsity which a scientific statement raises. Poetic statements, on the other hand, have no truth or falsity but effect emotions and attitudes—"This is the *emotive* use of language." Poetry therefore makes "pseudo-statements" which have no referential value. Poetic "truth" is a matter of inner coherence.

> The "Truth" of *Robinson Crusoe* is the acceptability of the things we are told, their acceptability in the interests of the effects of the narrative. . . . Similarly the falsity of happy endings to *Lear* or to *Don Quixote* is their failure to be acceptable to those who have fully responded to the rest of the work. It is in this sense that "Truth" is equivalent to "internal necessity" or rightness. That is "true" or "internally necessary" which completes or accords with the rest of the experience.[14]

Two aspects of this discussion troubled Richards's successors. Is Richards here making poetry inferior to science? Indeed, as Tate and Ransom suggest, is Richards arguing that poetry is no more than a kind of nonsense? Further, in his emphasis on the experience, is Richards performing an affective criticism that, in fact, locates the poem in the reader's response?

The relationship of poetry to truth is never an easy argument. Is there not always some fudging in it? What, for example, of Ransom's knowledge of universals and knowledge of particulars? How much does Eliseo Vivas solve with his concept of meaning that is not referential? In a sense, Richards may seem to trivialize *King Lear* when he says we must have no beliefs if we are to read the play. But is Richards here doing more than Kant had done? At any rate, Richards makes it clear that he does not in fact put poetry in a subordinate role. By 1934, science, too, for Richards seems to become a matter of coherence. The scientific view also turns out to be an hypothesis which cannot be verified. Poetry then is no more untrue than science, no more mythopoeic.

> If philosophic contemplation, or religious experience, or science gave us Reality, then poetry gave us something of less consequence, at best some sort of shadow. If we grant that all is myth, poetry as the myth-making which most brings 'the whole soul of man into activity,' and as working with words . . . and through them, in 'the medium by which spirits communicate with one another' becomes the necessary channel for the reconstitution of order.[15]

But Richards cannot quite count on that last remark. Though he accepts Coleridge in a way that neither Eliot nor Hulme can, he cannot follow Coleridge all the way into a distinct aesthetic universe.

Among Richards's other significant, and somewhat controversial, contributions to twentieth-century literary theory is the doctrine of synaesthesis. Richards had denied that the differentiating effect of literature was either beauty or empathy, for these may rise out of all kinds of nonliterary experiences. The doctrine of synaesthesis was to the effect that not all impulses arise properly from literature, but only a harmony and equilibrium of impulses. "When works . . . produce action or conditions which lead to action they . . . can not be called beautiful but stimulative."[16] Can we suggest that thesis leads to such stimulation, and that synaesthesis leads to the beautiful? At any rate, although Richards does not locate the emotions in the work, but in either the poet or the reader, it seems that he implies the qualities of the work as the necessary source of the emotional effects. "Thetic" responses have to do with facts and desires. Synaesthesis, on the other hand, resides in something like the balance and harmony of uncertainties.

Richards here is giving us a position very close to Kant's "disinterested interest" or to Keats's "negative capability." In fact the notion that good poetry—by being fuller, richer, "more inclusive"—results in an equilibrium seems to go all the way back to the aesthetic "lesson" that Homer carved on Achilles's shield. Certainly it seems to connect with the seventeenth-century notion of wit as a *discordia concors,* and to Nietzsche's "harmony out of every discord." It ties up with Eliot's stress on wit and leads to such New Critical terms of value as ambiguity, tension, the idea of irony as a principle of structure. Further, the doctrine of synaesthesis provides support to such other important notions as "purity," anti-didacticism, and impersonality. Impersonality is seen by Richards as an achievement of the inclusive poem, the synaesthetic poem, which offers not the "personality" of a single point of view but rather a multiplicity of points of view. And does not this emphasis on inclusiveness lead also to the New Critical values of complexity and coherence? It has been said that for Richards and his student William Empson there is a value in complexity itself.

Eliot had emphasized that every poem is dramatic, that someone is always talking to someone else. This had enabled him to argue the irony, impersonality, difficulty of good poetry. There is considerable agreement between Richards and Eliot. Their influence, along with that of Hulme and Pound, combined easily to form the New Criticism.

Deriving from this variety of influences, that criticism stressed the objective nature of the text and the possibility of an objective account of it. This had been Eliot's point, too, when he prefaced his description of "The Perfect Critic" with Rémy de Gourmont's "Eriger en lois ses impressions personnelles, c'est le grand effort d'un homme s'il est sincère." [To establish as laws his own personal impressions is the great aim of the sincere critic.][17] It might well be asked whether Gourmont's "sincère" is not kin to "disinterested." Criticism, quite as much as poetry, Eliot could have said, "is a continual self-sacrifice, a continual extinction of personality." Many of the New Critics suggested that criticism humanized precisely because it depersonalized the critical endeavor. Lawrence Lipking has suggested that criticism makes us healthily aware of our insincere emotions and faulty techniques.[18] "Approach . . . in humility,"[19] Ransom cautioned the critic.

Ransom, Tate, Brooks

Perhaps the first of the New Critics—after all, he was the first to use the term—John Crowe Ransom not only established many of the principles of the movement, he also carefully argued its "ethical" assumptions. Literature and literary criticism, in Ransom's view, were both antidotes to scientism, utilitarianism and egocentricity. Criticism is required to be humble before the poem; and because science, on the contrary, is aggressive, "the dualism between science and art widens." Ransom seems to employ here the Pauline opposition of love and pride. "The way to obtain the true *Dinglichkeit* of a formal dinner or a landscape or a beloved person is to approach the object as such, and in humility."[20] Science, on the other hand, "explores for properties," "manages," and because science is always "committed to a special interest," it destroys.[21] "People who are engrossed with their pet 'values' become habitual killers. . . . It is thus that we lose the power of imagination, or whatever faculty it is by which we are able to contemplate things as they are in their rich and contingent materiality."[22]

To Ransom, form is a complex concept that is intimately tied to forms (whether the forms of courtship or the forms of metre); and form, in this sense, increases our awareness of particularity. Ransom's opposition of the abstraction of structure and the concreteness of texture expands beyond poetry to all areas of human feeling and behavior. The dichotomy of science and poetry is paralleled in the difference between "prey" and "respect." When "every object is an object of prey . . . the real or individual object cannot occur."[23] On the other hand, respect for the object enables that object to "unfold at last its individuality; which . . . is its capacity to furnish us with an infinite variety of innocent experience."[24] Abstraction uses. "The fierce drives of the animals . . . are only towards a *kind* of thing, the indifferent instance of a universal, and not some private and irreplaceable thing."[25] Concreteness humanizes. "We . . . have sentiments; they are directed toward persons and things; and a sentiment is the totality of love and knowledge which we have of an object that is private and unique."[26]

Ransom's analysis of poetic qualities corresponds to his discussion of these activities. Because ideas have extension and are thin, and objects have intension and are thick, ideas prove inadequate to objects. Taking off from Allen Tate, Ransom classifies poetry of ideas as Platonic poetry, whereas poetry that deals with things is physical poetry. We perceive and experience physical poetry; it is objective in that the reader cannot reduce it to use or to thought. It is "given and non-negotiable." As the experience of the non-negotiable objectivity of a loved person diminishes our pride, so does the yielding to the physical reality of such a poem.

Nevertheless, though "all true poetry is a phase of physical poetry,"[27] there is no purely physical poetry. Percepts without concepts, after all, are empty. Ransom admits that human beings "are not quite constructed with the capacity for a distinterested interest."[28]

The poem then ought to have both a structure—its argument—and a texture. The texture is irrelevant to the argument of the poem and impedes that argument. But it is this very impedimenta of rich particularity that gives the poem its value. A third category of poetry ideally combines both. "Metaphysical" poetry develops "the volume of [such] percipienda or sensibilia" as meter, fiction, and tropes, and by so doing twists away from its own tough surface of discourse, "inviting perceptual attention, and weakening the tyranny of science over the senses."[29]

Although Ransom had rejected Richards's synaesthesis, denying that contrary experiences can fuse, his doctrine of structure and texture leads him into either a separation of form and content or to some sort of notion of the tension between the two which makes complexity of that tension a poetic value.

It seems, too, that Ransom's discussion of "metaphysical" devices leads him to a position similar to that of Eliot on the dramatic quality of poetry. The fiction transforms discourse into drama, so that Donne's "The Flea," for instance, becomes not an argument in behalf of sexual intimacy but rather the dramatization of a playful episode between two agents whose particular characterizations are the crucial elements of the poem. The arguments of most poems may well be dull affairs, but if they are fictional arguments, the particularities of character, setting, and language make them dramatically exciting.

Structure, in the sense of abstractable argument, of paraphrasable core, does not constitute the poem. And because a statement of the argument is frequently offered as an analysis of the poem, Cleanth Brooks, another of the New Critics, attacks "The Heresy of Paraphrase." If the reader is misled by paraphrase he "split[s] the poem between its 'form' and 'content'," he "raise[s] the problem of belief in a vicious and crippling form," he "misconceive[s] the function of metaphor and meter" making them decorative rather than organic.[30] A poem for Brooks is so thoroughly an organic whole that we cannot, in Yeats's famous figure, "know the dancer from the dance." The poem is "experience rather than any mere statement about experience." It is not the sign that says "Beware of the Dog," but something closer to playing with the dog—if not the act itself, at least a controlled enactment of the event, a "simulacrum of reality," as Brooks puts it. Brooks insists on both the "unity of experience" and its "contradictory and conflicting elements." By unifying these into a new pattern, the poem, it seems, gives us a new insight.

It is a unity, of course, very different from that of logic with its law of non-contradiction. "Experience," Allen Tate comments, "has decided to ignore logic" by combining disparate elements. Brooks establishes his organic criticism in terms of certain key concepts. Contextualism, "the primacy of pattern," makes every element in the poem "not a discrete particle of meaning but a . . . nexus or cluster."[31] The notion of every poem as drama assimilates all statements to a speaker and prevents their being turned into detachable propositions. Drama makes all poems "a pattern of resolutions and balances and harmonizations developed, through a temporal scheme."[32] Brooks's analysis and evaluation of poems, then, rests on the importance of such qualities as "ambiguity, paradox, complex of attitudes, and . . . irony."[33]

Much of this recalls the thought and language of the metaphysical writers who also celebrated *discordia concors.* And these poets, in turn, are celebrated by the New Critics. Although Brooks's collection of essays, *The Well-Wrought Urn,* demonstrates that this "ironic" structure emerges in poems as diverse as "The Rape of the Lock" and "Tears, Idle Tears,"

Brooks is, in fact, an apologist for metaphysical and modern poetry. Indeed, it has been suggested that the New Criticism as a movement emerged to confront the complexity, ambiguity, irony, and difficulty of such modern writers as Stevens, Pound, Hart Crane, and Eliot.

As much as anyone, Brooks was the codifier of the New Criticism. When Brooks, along with Robert Penn Warren, published *Understanding Poetry* in 1938 they began an approach to the classroom teaching of literature that would by the early fifties become firmly entrenched. A generation of American students quickly learned to deal with poems as if they were both anonymous and contemporary, to examine recurrent and developing images as a way of discovering the poems' substructure. A generation of students adopted the language of irony, ambiguity, tension, admired Donne and Eliot, disparaged Shelley. A good history of criticism could be written in terms of the shifting fashions in talismanic words and the changing popularities of the earlier writers.

The triumph of the New Criticism in the universities was neither immediate nor without resistance. The struggle between the New Critics and the historical scholars is well known. Writing in 1957, Yvor Winters recalls being warned that "criticism and scholarship do not mix." Nor did the New Criticism quite mix with older and somewhat more entrenched "extrinsic" modes such as social criticism and psychological criticism. Such careful readers as Edmund Wilson and Lionel Trilling felt that contextualism, by depriving the work of its human and cultural references, took too much away from literature. Moreover, looking at such complications to interpretation as William Empson offered in *Seven Types of Ambiguity,* Trilling also accused the New Critics of trying too hard.

But the New Criticism offered a teachable technique, and an apparently objective way to the analysis and evaluation of literature. It could be employed by any student. The era of the growth of the New Criticism was also the time when the G.I. Bill was expanding and democratizing the student body. To students who did not come out of the Great Tradition and who had no sense of belonging to the history and culture of England, the New Criticism presented a way of connecting to literature that they might not otherwise have had. This new student population may have contributed also to the growth in teaching modern literature. At the same time, there was being written poetry that in its complexity seemed to need the very methods of analysis the New Criticism presented. The growth of modern literature and the growth of the New Criticism reinforced each other. And, although the New Criticism began in anti-scienticism and anti-positivism, the possibility of reducing its methods, questions, and criteria to formulas and the appearance it gave of objectivity were reassuring to students who had been trained in the quantitative disciplines.

All these factors were at work in the period following World War II. By the early fifties the New Criticism was firmly established in the curriculum. In 1948, in *The Armed Vision,* Stanley Edgar Hyman expressed the hopefulness and excitement that students and teachers were beginning to feel about all the new criticisms. Walter J. Ong called the new method the first really adequate criticism ever to exist. In 1962 Brooks summarized its achievement as understanding the concrete literary work, fixing the limits of poetry, defining poetry's characteristic structure as well as the characteristic knowledge that poetry yields.

There were, of course, fraternal disputes. Yvor Winters, one of the group of four that Ransom first labeled as New Critics, was never quite comfortable with that label. Despite his early attack on the New Humanism, Winters did not give up its concerns. Though a close reader of the text, Winters stressed the importance of the text's content and the value of its message, insisting that poetry makes a rational statement about human experience. Indeed, Winters even defines poetic form in moral terms, as an imposition of order on matter, arguing that the poem's rational statement justifies and grounds its emotional content. Unlike Brooks, Winters demands that a poem be paraphrasable in at least general terms. This paraphrasable core is central, for it must motivate the kind and degree of emotions. In this way, Ransom's doctrine of irrelevant texture is denied.

R. P. Blackmur, also, was not at ease with the restrictions of the New Criticism, arguing that their techniques led to excess analysis, to oversimplification, and to excess application. He complained that skills hardened into methods and then into methodologies. By 1956, even Eliot worried about "the lemon-squeezer school of criticism."

Resisting the stiffness of methodology, Blackmur himself utilized many different positions, perspectives, and techniques until his commitment to openness and pluralism made him seem unsystematic. In a way, he is. The critic, he declares, is not a professional but a "master-layman of as many modes of human understanding as possible in a single act of the mind."[34] He must be aware of doctrine but reject doctrine and use the insight on which doctrine is based. Blackmur lists the determinants of criticism as "the presumed reader, . . . the general state of culture and knowledge, . . . the immediate history and tradition of critical and scholarly ideas and practice: all working unequally and incongruously together."[35]

Although Blackmur went beyond the work to the "life formed and identified" by the work, he still approached the poem through its technique and would not read a poem as a conceptual statement. The starting place is a linguistic and technical examination that then expands to the verbal, personal, and cultural contexts. In this way Blackmur tries to understand the forces that operate in the arts to transform our experiences. Questions about verbal form lead to a concern with symbolic form and to "the feeling of what life is about."

Rival formalists: The Neo-Aristotelians

Chief among the rival formalists, and perhaps most trenchant in their analysis of the New Critics, were the Neo-Aristotelians at the University of Chicago, led by R. S. Crane, Richard McKeon, and Elder Olson. In *Critics and Criticism,*[36] their collection of position papers, nearly one-third of the essays concern the New Criticism and its faults.

Despite the anti-scientism of many of the New Critics, the Neo-Aristotelians accuse the movement of blurring the necessary distinction between poetry and science. Elder Olson begins his assessment on an ironic note:

> The "new criticism" . . . [is] universally regarded as having at last brought literary study to a conditon rivaling that of the sciences. It has . . . established itself upon principles the scientific character of which is assured. . . . It has an over-all . . . unity of method, as well as an [established] doctrine [with] a list of "heresies" and "fallacies"; finally . . . it is still, like the sciences, in a happy condition of growth.[37]

This "unity of method" seems a central object of the New-Aristotelian attack which concentrates on two sorts of New Critical errors. The Chicago writers accuse the New Critics of a "monism," a rigid rhetorical analysis which looks for irony in poetry of various different kinds. They accuse them, too, of an exclusive concern with diction cut off from more important questions of genre, structure, and theme.

Olson points out that Empson reduces "all poetic considerations to considerations of poetic diction, and . . . reduc[es] all discussion of diction, even, to problems of ambiguities." This is similar to the grounds on which Crane attacks Brooks. In contrast, the Chicago writers affirm the primacy of structure: "the profundity and complexity in poetry which so much interests Empson is due primarily to action and character, which cannot be handled in grammatical terms, rather than to diction, which can." Poetic profundity, they argue, does not derive from verbal expressions—"We are in fact far less moved by the words as mere words than we think"—but from actions that "permit an extraordinary number of implications," in that they reveal many aspects of character and situation. "Where we can draw no such inferences [about character] where no such impression of humanity is conveyed, we remain largely indifferent in the face of the finest diction.[38]

The Chicago critics are not rigidly, but flexibly, Aristotelian, with a flexible framework of critical terms and critical concerns. Following Aristotle, they find a more significant *dynamis* in plot, character, and thoughts than in diction. Speech as action plays importantly on the emotions because speech provides the signs from which the audience infers those more powerful elements of plot, character, and thought. The role of speech and the meanings that derive from speech are significant areas of conflict between the Chicago writers and the New Critics. Writers such as Crane and Olson define "meaning" as indications of character, passions, and situations.

Viewing the poem as an object made by its artist in the way that it is rather than another, and concerned with the ways in which our emotions are determined by the object, the Chicago school tends to reject the intentional and affective fallacies. This does not imply that they deal with either artist or audience in psychological terms.

But these are, after all, disagreements between formalist schools—fundamental allies. Crane acknowledges the New Critics' "valuable contributions," and says he is almost inclined to let his gratitude toward them outweigh his misgivings. The misgiving that Crane insists on has to do with their failure to be pluralist. Despite the New Critics, he argues, "What we call poetry . . . is not all alike." It is not "one homogeneous thing"—it manifests itself differently in different genres. An adequate criticism will raise questions concerning those differences: "We value different poems for the different peculiar pleasures they give us, and we are aware that these differences are determined . . . by interrelated differences in language, subject-matter, technique, and principles of construction."[39]

Crane, who accepts and develops Aristotle's doctrine of imitation, demands of an adequate literary theory that it both maintain the integrity of the literary work (literary works are things "to which we attribute value for the intrinsic excellence of their making rather than any further utility they may serve") and also not cut that work off "from the life which it represents and tries to guide."[40] The spectator is a moral agent. The work represents a series of morally definable actions. Response is affected by this and by the formal qualities of the work—(Is it serious or otherwise?). As a formalist, Crane tries to discover, in the individual work, the devices in it which determine that it is read in one way and not another. "We understand by form that principle, or complex of principles, which give to the subject-matter the power it has to affect our opinions and emotions in a certain definite way such as would not have been possible had the synthesizing principle been of a different kind."[41]

Unlike the New Critics, whom they accuse of apriorism, the Neo-Aristotelians ask in each separate case what hypothesis about a work's form will best explain its effect on the reader's understanding. Their method apparently is both pluralistic and inductive. Form is determined by reasoning back from the observed effect to probable or necessary causes. The reasoning takes place with a group of terms and distinctions that derive from Aristotle's categories concerning the means, manner, and objects of "limitation."

Despite the emphasis on the emotional effect of the work, and the use of the language of "imitation," the Chicago critics do not seem either affective or "mimetic." Crane eliminates much of the notion of representation from his discussion of imitation: "The object imitated is internal and hence strictly 'poetic' in the sense that it exists only as the intelligible and moving pattern of incidents, states of feeling, or images which the poet has constructed in the sequence of his words."[42] The stress here is on the intrinsic nature of the object, the way in which it is constructed, the nature of the object as a pattern, that is, a form. It is the pattern itself that is intelligible and moving. Crane, himself, declares that his is not a theory of poetry as representation, where external reality makes demands upon the work. In my own view this is an entirely legitimate reading of Aristotle's doctrine, with Crane, like Aristotle, stressing not real possibilities but internal coherence. The work is not a replica of reality but an analogue, and as such it is autonomous.

What then do the poem's words point to? Olson makes a great deal of the fact that those words point to character, thoughts, and action which somehow are constructed, not real. Crane makes this specific, distinguishing between character and thought in life and character and thought in the poem. In his view the object of imitation—the pattern—does not imitate anything beyond itself; there is, after all, no tragic drama—no *Hamlet,* let us say—in nature, any more than there is an ode, or a sonnet. The imitation is quite a new creation. As such, it imposes its own character on the various materials—feelings, attitudes, incidents—it is made from, that its words depict. Yet, at the same time that the Chicago critics insist on this separation from reality, they do not let go of the "impression of humanity" that the work conveys.

In search of larger relevance

Two important books published in 1957 show a reaching beyond the work itself to a larger relevance. The epilogue of W. K. Wimsatt's *Literary Criticism: A Short History* still stresses formal study but looks for a unity of form and spirit in the "concrete universal." There is, says Wimsatt, a close relationship between form and values. He defines metaphor as just such a combination of concreteness and significance—"a way of facing and even asserting something serious while at the same time declining the didactic gambit."[43] He asserts that no theory of art can get along without the opposition and reconciliation of "making and saying." Of course, he reiterates that the two can never "come completely together without the collapse and loss of poetry," but he also says that they cannot be taken in strict dichotomy without the same loss. "It remains that a theory of poetic or fine art must do something yet different." Wimsatt's epilogue becomes a prologue to the next twenty years. He asks for a theory that will join coherence with correspondence, Aristotle with Plato, classic with romantic; "finally, and again basically, the work [with] either the author or the audience." Like Coleridge, Wimsatt at this point stresses art's mediating and reconciling power. This mediating becomes art's peculiar nature—poetry is the situation "where we see each member . . . only in and through its opposite."[44]

Northrop Frye's *Anatomy of Criticism* also appeared in 1957. It also, while remaining formalist in its emphasis, develops a context that goes beyond the individual work, a context that provides the work with its patterns of meaning and that defines its nature.

In his English Institute session on Frye, Murray Krieger argues that Frye is an alternative to the New Criticism. Ihab Hassan, on the other hand, labels Frye as a formalist and links him to the New Critics. At any rate, Frye has often been called the most significant theorist since the New Criticism, the most important critical voice of the late fifties and early sixties.

Like the New Critics, Frye continues to emphasize a Kantian disinterestedness: "The fundamental act of criticism is a disinterested response to a work of literature in which all one's beliefs, engagements, commitments, prejudices, stampedings of pity and terror, are ordered to be quiet."[45] Like the New Critics, he is opposed to explaining a literary work in terms of the nonliterary; he shares their belief that the work of literature should not be related to anything outside of itself. Yet he differs from them by shifting attention away from the single, discrete text to that text's relationship to the whole context of literature. Frye accuses the New Critics of a naive empiricism because they simply explicate "one work after another without paying attention to any larger structural principles connecting the different works explicated."[46]

At first, Frye looked for those principles of connection by putting the single poem in the context of the author's total output. But this did not afford principles reliable enough in their objectivity and significance. He broadened his method to investigate structural elements in the literary tradition as a whole where he looked for recurrent usages such as conventions, image clusters, forms, and genres. He found in these the formal principles of literature.

The experience of literature for Frye is both "centripetal" and "centrifugal." The reader approaches the reading of a poem with the assumption that it is a centripetally organized unity. The poem does not represent or reflect external events or ideas. Even the ideas which literature contains are not real ideas, for they are not involved with usefulness or verifiability—they are instead "hypothetical" ideas, parts of a centripetal whole. Frye employs his version of Aristotelian imitation at this point. For Frye, as for Crane, "the work of art is its own object [which] cannot be ultimately descriptive of something, and can never be ultimately related to any other system of phenomena, standards, values, or final causes."[47] Propositions in a poem, then, or descriptions, exist only as part of the image.

At the same time that the reader approaches the poem with this hypothesis of centripetality, his "first step in understanding it as literature is to

175

associate it with other literary experiences," and so the work is involved also and simultaneously in centrifugality. Elizabeth Bowen observes in one of her novels that there is no experience until it is reexperienced. Frye's point is similar: until we have gathered from our experience a pattern of qualities, conventions, similarities, and values, we do not have a way of experiencing what we encounter. An awareness of common properties is necessary for intelligibility. In order to experience literature, we must have a concept of literature which has been arrived at by discovering the qualities that literary works have in common. Lacking this kind of conceptual framework, criticism is nothing more than a crude and "subjective" induction.

Frye finds the New Critics guilty of this sort of subjectivity, and therefore, despite their claims, and the flashiness of their readings, the text they describe is for him indeterminate. Because they have "no sense of the archetypal shape of literature as a whole," the most they can come up with is "commentaries"—brilliant, ingenious, and futile.[48]

Only by recognizing and accepting the literary universe can the critic hope to achieve objectivity. The priority of the literary universe is a central point in Frye's argument. Because literary convention creates the poem, the poem can be objectively interpreted only by a critic who yields his own "originality" to a knowledge of literary "origins."

Frye denies the Romantic notion that the individual is prior to his society. In contrast, he accepts the view "that the new baby is conditioned by a hereditary and environmental kinship to a society which already exists." In the same way, he argues that "the new poem . . . is born into an already existing order of words, and is typical of the structure of poetry to which it is attached." This is close to Heidegger's protostructuralist observation that it is language, not man, who speaks. The formal conventions of literature, its generic and stylistic development, are the shaping spirit of the individual poem. "The true father . . . of the poem is the form of poetry itself, and this form is a manifestation of the universal spirit of poetry," Frye writes. The creative process is one of deindividuation. So is the critical process. "It takes a great deal of will power to write poetry, but part of that will power must be employed in trying to relax the will, so making a large part of one's writing involuntary." The critic gives up his solipsism in a somewhat different way—"by a study of conventions and genres, [he] attempts to fit poems into the body of poetry as a whole."[49]

In his joyous mid-century celebration of modern criticism, Stanley Edgar Hyman describes modern criticism as "qualitatively different from any previous criticism." Modern critics, he goes on, are doing something "radically different" with literature, and getting something "radically different" from literature. He defines that difference as "the organized use of non-literary techniques and bodies of knowledge to obtain insights into literature."[50] Primarily, modern criticism is characterized by the use of assumptions that derive from Darwin, Marx, Frazer, and Freud.

This hardly seems prophetic of the decade that followed Hyman's book. Nor does Hyman recognize the dominant place of the New Criticism at the time he was writing. His book was, however, an accurate vision of the diversity of forces that were to come to the surface at the end of the 1950s. Frye has been called the first important critic to replace the reign of the New Criticism. Frequently his contribution has been seen as bringing anthropology and Jungian psychology to bear on contextualism. René Wellek describes the *Anatomy* as combining "myth criticism with motifs from the New Criticism." He places Frye as a myth critic in the tradition of Jung and Maud Bodkin. Frye rejects the filiation: "I resemble [them] about as closely as I resemble the late Sarah Bernhardt."[51] He insists that he does not take his notions from either anthropology or psychology: "Criticism cannot take presuppositions from elsewhere, which always means wrenching them out of their real context, and must work out its own."

Such words as *myth* and *archetype* are key critical terms in Frye's system. We may anticipate their connection with anthropology and psychology. But such anticipations mislead. In Frye's usage, these words do not have extra-literary meanings. For one thing, *myth* to Frye is not content but form. Myths represent the structural principles of literature. The critic does an inductive survey of the literary field and arrives at its "interconnecting structural principles." The more we know about literature, the more clearly do these principles appear. Myths, then, are not patterns in either the individual mind or in the racial unconscious, but, because poems are made out of other poems, they are elements of the literary experience. Myths are literary conventions, or the conventional shapes of literature. In the *Anatomy,* Frye arranges these shapes according to four generic types: romantic, comic, tragic, and ironic or satiric.

"Myth is the archetype." But Frye sometimes qualifies that identity, distinguishing *myth* from *archetype* as narrative from significance, or defining *archetype* as a recurrently used literary symbol that becomes conventional. Recurrence establishes convention—and convention creates literary nature. For Frye, Homer and nature are the same. Any unit of literary structure which connects one work to another and integrates our literary experience is such a convention, an archetype.

Because Frye finds it a natural part of reading to expand beyond the text and to connect the individual work to the total experience of literature, he argues that just as an order of nature exists behind the individual, so too is there an order of literary nature, not just an aggregate, but an "order of words." He is fond of quoting Eliot's dictum that the monuments of literature form an ideal order and are not just a collection of the writings of individuals.

Although his stress is on the order of words rather than on the order of nature, on form rather than on content, on the conventional rather than the real, on literature rather than on life, Frye's system involves a fusion of both the centripetal and centrifugal concerns. In a recent book, *The Secular Scripture,* he defines form as "the shaping spirit, the power of ordering which seems so mysterious to the poet himself, because he often acts as though it were an identity separate from him." Content is another and perhaps equally mysterious otherness—it is, in fact, the fact of otherness itself, the feeling that there is something to be overcome and struggled with.

The imagination is identified with that shaping spirit which constructs "unities out of units." These elements are connected with each other rather than with the outer world. Imagination and its product, literature, is thus self-enclosed, self-referential, with its own internal systematic laws. "What the imagination, left to itself, produces is the rigidly conventionalized." But "left to itself, the imagination can achieve only a facile pseudo-conquest . . . meeting no resistance from reality."[52] The order of words must confront the order of nature, the imagination must adapt its structures to the demands of the external world. Frye describes this process: "In the course of struggling with a world which is separate from itself, the imagination has to adapt its formulaic units to the demands of that world, to produce what Aristotle calls the probable impossibility."[53] This adaptation creates a "roughly credible context" for these formulaic structures, but the underlying structure of nature remains unchanged by the process. Therefore the critic's task finally is not a break-through back to life; he must remain with the text and its internal self-reference.

French and continental criticism: Sartre

Recently, Geoffrey Hartman has examined the separation during the twentieth century of the continental critical tradition from the English. It goes back. Matthew Arnold had already, in the nineteenth century, cautioned the English against the Germanisms of Carlyle. To Hartman, 1919 is a significant year for determining America's twentieth-century direction. It was the year that saw the publication of both Eliot's "Tradition and the Individual Talent," and Ludwig Lewisohn's *A Modern Book of Criticism.* Lewisohn's ideal had been that of a transnational America that would not identify Americanization and assimilation. Eliot, on the other hand, sidelined the more intellectual and philosophical continental tradition. America went along with Eliot, and for fifty years American criticism was Anglo-American. With "the expatriation of the 1970s, the swerve of literary criticism [went] toward the Continent,"[54] observes Hartman. Perhaps this explains why, despite the French invasion of the 1940s, the popularity then of various "existential" catchwords and phrases, the cocktail party talk about Sartre and Camus, Jean-Paul Sartre did not significantly seem to influence literary theory in this country.

During the very period that the New Criticism, with its emphasis on the intrinsic nature of literature, its tendency to restrict criticism to certain types of imaginative literature, was establishing itself as the official criticism, Sartre, in such works as *The Psychology of Imagination* (1940), *Being and Nothingness* (1943), and *What is Literature?* (1947), was asserting the importance of reality over imagination, was arguing for a literature of engagement, was extending literature to include philosophical and political writings.

While American critics were establishing the doctrine of the "Affective Fallacy," Sartre was examining the dialectic of reading and writing and arguing that the literary object requires reading in order to exist, and exists only as long as the act of reading lasts. Reading is a necessary completion of the literary work; in a sense, reading is a kind of creation, for it is only by reading that the work is brought into being; indeed, it is only by reading that the work achieves objectivity.

A "chief motive of artistic creation is the need of feeling that we are in essential relationship to the world," Sartre says.[55] Each of our perceptions manifests some reality. With each of our acts the world reveals itself. Yet, each of us remains inessential to the thing revealed. The artist, however, is able to feel himself essential to his creation, for he has set up and condensed relationships, introduced order where there was none, imposed the unity of mind on the diversity of things. But the "results which [he has] obtained on canvas or on paper never seem to [him] objective."[56] These remain, for Sartre, merely a subjective discovery. If in perception the object perceived is essential, and we are not, we seek and obtain essentiality in creation, "but then . . . the object . . . becomes the inessential."[57] Only a reader brings objectivity to the artistic creation. For Sartre, this objectivity arises out of a kind of ignorance. The reader foresees and waits. He waits for the next sentence or next page to confirm or disappoint his foresights. The activity of reading is composed of hypotheses which are then confirmed or denied, dreams which are awakened, hopes which are fulfilled or disappointed, discoveries, deceptions. "Without waiting, without a future, without ignorance," concludes Sartre, "there is no objectivity."[58]

In the language of Sartre's phenomenology, to the writer his work is forever the *pour soi* (the subjective, the self-conscious), to the reader it is the *en soi* (the objective, the other, the real) and like the *en soi* always, it is somewhat beyond consciousness. To Sartre, the conscious, for all its importance, is a sort of fiction, and the real, by contrast, is privileged.

> It is not true that one writes for oneself. That would be the worse blow . . . But the operation of writing implies that of reading as its dialectical correlative and these two connected acts necessitate two distinct agents. It is the joint effort of author and reader which brings upon the scene that concrete and imaginary object which is the work of the mind. There is no art except for and by others.[59]

Reading, it seems, synthesizes the conscious and the real, perception and creation, and reading makes both the subject and the object essential. The object (the work of art) is essential because it imposes its own structures on the reader (It is, in Sartre's terminology, transcendent). The reader is essential because he makes it possible for there to be an object; he creates and discloses the object by his attentiveness, his effort, his thoughtfulness, and his willingness. "In short, reading is directed creation."[60] The author, it seems, guides the reader, but the reader goes beyond the author's guideposts. "In a continual exceeding of the written thing," the reader invents the density of the object.

Satre carefully investigates this relationship. The words of the work are already there. Each word "shapes our feelings, names them, and attributes them to an imaginary personage who takes it upon himself to live them for us."[61] On the other hand, the literary object has no other substance than the reader's subjectivity. "Raskolnikov's waiting is my waiting which I lend him."[62]

Creation can only find its fulfillment in reading. The writer, therefore, appeals to the reader to collaborate in the production of the book. The author appeals "politely" to the reader's "generosity"; that is, the author does not seek to overwhelm; and the reader is able to loan the author his feelings freely, and freely to accord his belief.

In a discussion that echoes Nietzsche's attack on Euripides, Sartre makes it quite clear that this collaboration would be destroyed if the author were to try to affect the reader with emotions of fear, desire, or anger. "Freedom is alienated in the state of passion." Literature, after all, is for Sartre an absolute end. The appeal to passion, on the other hand, turns the book into a means for feeding hate or desire. In the same way, if the reader were to suspect the author of having written out of passion and in passion, his confidence in the book would immediately vanish. The author's "decision to write supposes that he withdraws somewhat from his feelings . . . that he has transformed his emotions into free emotions as the reader does his."

The author and the reader trust each other; "each one counts on the other, demands of the other as much as he demands of himself; . . . if my demands are met, what I am reading provokes me to demand more of the author, which means that he demand more of me."[63] Despite Sartre's priority to reality over consciousness, the final goal of this exchange is to give the world "as if it had its source in human freedom." The reciprocal implications of author's and reader's demands upon each other enable the readaptation of being to man, the enclosing of the universe within man. Can it be that Sartre finally privileges consciousness over the real? If so, he has in mind only the special conditions by which the creation of the author's consciousness takes on objective reality in the eyes of the spectator.

The feeling of "aesthetic joy" is the sign that this end is achieved. "A complex feeling," says Sartre, forever denied the author, it is what the author aims at giving the reader. What are the elements of this complexity? The reader recognizes the work as an absolute end, and this recognition suspends, if only for a little while, "the utilitarian round of ends-means and means-ends." Henri Bergson's opposition of use and value re-emerges here. The object appears before the reader as a value. Also, inasmuch as the aesthetic object is, in fact, the world aimed at through the imaginary, it is the world, itself, that the aesthetic experience gives as a value. This experience enables us to internalize "that which is non-ego *par excellence.*" In it we transform fact into value and become able to perceive the world as both fact and value, as both "totally foreign and totally ours." Sartre adds, "the more ours as it is the more foreign."[64]

At the same time, inasmuch as reading is creative, the reader's consciousness perceives itself as being constitutive of the object. The act of reading, then, is a creation "where the created object is given *as object* to its creator," the only creation where the creator gets enjoyment from the object he creates, the only case where the consciousness is "conscious of being essential in relationship to an object that is itself perceived as essential." The authentication of the harmony between subjectivity and objectivity provides the aesthetic consciousness with a feeling of security, which, in turn, "stamps even the strongest aesthetic emotions with a sovereign calm."[65]

There is still a third, and rather Kantian, element in aesthetic joy. Not only does it present a joining of fact and value, and a harmony of subject and object, but it involves also an intersubjective harmony—the harmonious totality of all human consciousness. Kant had called the judgment of taste universal and necessary. Sartre picks this up, declaring the object "a universal confidence and exigency." Every man must feel the same pleasure in reading the same work.

Nevertheless, as would be expected, Sartre's aesthetics significantly diverge from Kant's. Although Sartre distinguishes prose as instrumental from poetry as a finality, even in the case of poetry, he rejects the Kantian "finality without end." Natural beauty, by presenting symmetry, harmony, and regularity tempts the spectator "to seek a finalist explanation for all these properties." But, Sartre argues, "the beauty of nature is in no way comparable to the beauty of art." The work of art, he asserts, does not have an end because it is an end. "The book presents itself as a task to be discharged"; from the very beginning it places itself on the level of the categorical imperative. "Although literature is one thing and morality a quite different one, at the heart of the aesthetic imperative we discern the moral imperative."[66]

Sartre's notion of the intersubjective world is less Kantian than it is Hegelian. It is Hegel's idea of other and otherness that permits Sartre to overcome solipsistic tendencies in his doctrine. By means of the notion of otherness, consciousness escapes from the isolation of the self and discovers its dimension of being-for-other-people, its place in an intersubjective world. Language, literature, and the languages of silence mediate mutual or inter-subjective consciousnesses. Unable to hear ourselves speak or see ourselves smile, we can never know our own language or our own bodies objectively—"as the other." But language is, in fact, "originally being-for-others," so in using language a subjectivity experiences itself as an object for the other.[67]

The writer is a being in language, a being in the world, a being within an historical time. Words are extensions of the writer's senses, they are dimensions of his body. "He maneuvers them from within, he feels them as his body; he is surrounded by a verbal body . . . which expands his impact upon the world." Because the relation of language to the world and to its historical moment is crucial, Sartre declares: "Art for the sake of Art . . . is sheer nonsense!"[68] Great writers, he points out, have always wanted to destroy, edify, and demonstrate.[69]

In light of Sartre's view of literature as "engaged," his distinction between prose and poetry is difficult to deal with. It seems to derive from Martin Heidegger's theory that our primary relation to the world is one of action and work, and that we first apprehend objects as tools and only later as things in themselves. For Heidegger, then, the work of art suspends our preoccupation with things as tools and lets us grow aware of them as vessels of Being. Sartre argues that the reader takes a utilitarian attitude toward prose. In prose, language functions as a system of signs, where the reader is involved not with the signs themselves but with the things signified. In poetry, on the other hand, language comes between the reader and meaning. In Heidegger's terms, the utilitarian attitude is suspended, and the poem is not a meaning, but a vessel of Being.

It is not easy to see how, for Sartre, poetry can be without significance altogether. Further, despite the moral dimension Sartre finds in all literature, despite his doctrine of engagement, the utilitarian nature of even prose literature is not directly utilitarian—aesthetic joy suspends the round of means and ends.

The artist both creates and negates a world. Any art, because it is creative, is necessarily imaginary, an imposition of essence upon existence, of style upon formless reality. After all, consciousness itself is a not-being, a nothingness, a withdrawal from the solid world of being. The *pour soi* is a rupture of the *en soi*. The world that the artist creates, by focusing attention upon itself, negates the real world. The imaginary, by definition, is the absent, and to apprehend the absent requires putting away that which is present. All our acts of consciousness, for Sartre, negate the world and its mindless passivity: "The real and the imaginary cannot coexist by their very nature."

Although Sartre clearly devalues the imaginary before the real, human freedom is itself a momentary victory of the imaginary over the real. Being imaginary, the art work is a nothing. But it discloses the world as if the world had its source in human freedom. Without such imaginary presentations of the world, we risk losing our humanity.

While the New Critics were closing the literary universe and even turning away from modern industrial society, Sartre was indicating a way out of that closed universe. Literature, he argues, is useful, though in an indirect way. "In the aesthetic modification of the human project, . . . the world appears [only] on the horizon," and never makes a demand on the reader's freedom. Yet the work of art, itself a product of both writer's and reader's freedom, demands that the world "be impregnated always with more freedom." Sartre argues that it would be inconceivable for the generosity provoked by the writer "to authorize an injustice," or that the reader could enjoy his own freedom while "reading a work which approves, or accepts, or simply abstains from condemning the subjection of man by man."[70]

"If the reader has lived this instant of freedom, if for an instant he has managed to escape—by means of a book—from the forces of alienation or oppression around him, you can be sure he won't forget it. Literature can have that effect."[71]

Merleau-Ponty

Sartre's friend, associate, and adversary, Maurice Merleau-Ponty, wrote much less than Sartre about literature. But he addressed just as directly the phenomenon of intersubjectivity in literature, the relationship of consciousness and perception, of consciousness and the world, the relationship of meaning and language.

Merleau-Ponty has been called "the philosopher of the ambiguous." Given, in his own style, to antithetical language, he is preoccupied with man's antithetical nature. The paradox of man is that he is a body-subject. He is a material being in a world of history and he is also the center of a subjective existence. The two contraries that define man are his situational and his subjective aspects. Merleau-Ponty keeps hold of both. They come together for him when we establish "communication with others and with ourselves for which our temporal structure gives us the opportunity" and our subjective structure gives us the power. The "I" streams forth in the world and this encounter establishes our categories of reality. But the grasp of reality that these give us is elusive. It does not afford us Descartes's clear and distinct ideas, only the possibility of charting my individual experience to present an analogue to another's experience. Merleau-Ponty thus stresses the intersubjective—mutuality, interdependence, interrelatedness. The communicative world mixes and intermingles consciousnesses and in that way establishes history. Merleau-Ponty therefore examines art only in history. For all art must express both the individual subjectivity and the community of shared meanings.

The act of reading, for him, is such an interchange between the individual and the history of the book's readings; it too is a community. Sartre had emphasized the private encounter between the individual subjectivity and the book, but for Merleau-Ponty the book is a "cultural object" and every act of reading is part of the cultural heritage. There is no interpretation outside the community of interpretation. My act of reading must involve "the book taken according to its conventional interpretation, the variations through time of that interpretation, and the way in which these layers of meaning accumulate, displace and complete each other."[72] No act of reading is separate and discreet. Every act of reading takes its place within the history of the work's interpretation and, in a way, recreates that history. "We imagine Julien Sorel, like a phantom traveler who haunts one generation after another, diffferent for each one, and we write literary history that attempts to connect these apparitions and to constitute the truth of Julien Sorel, the genesis of his total meaning."[73]

Language itself is born in community and it is also the founding act that creates community. It is by language that the "I" signifies its being in the world. It is language that connects the "I" with the world. And language makes us realize that "we are both indivisibly within and without."

Would there be perception of others without language? Dialogue is Merleau-Ponty's paradigmatic state of language. "In dialogue there is constituted between the other and myself a common ground; my thought and his are interwoven into a single fabric. . . . Our perspectives merge into each other, and we co-exist through a common world." Art and its audience, it appears, make such a dialogue. Art joins individual lives into a shared world.

Merleau-Ponty became interested in the works of Ferdinand de Saussure, and his distinction between the "spoken word" and the "speaking word" parallels Saussure's distinction between *langue* and *parole*—roughly, between language and speech. The spoken word is the inherited language, the language whose meaning has been established by custom and usage. Every man is taught to speak by the spoken word in him. This is the fundamental encounter of self and other, of subjectivity and the outer world, for here the objective—the spoken word—is itself (like the history of interpretations) a product of subjectivities. The "speaking word" is the individual's expression of his moment and consciousness built out of the acquired meanings of the spoken word. Tradition and consciousness, community and individual creativity act together here. And the "speaking word," in a way, recreates the "spoken word."

Merleau-Ponty's central concern with the paradoxical role of the individual in the confrontation between subjectivity and reality extends even to his consideration of literary forms and genres. The action of dialogue extends here also. For Merleau-Ponty, as for T. S. Eliot, innovation both defines itself against tradition and at the same time includes tradition. Every work, every artistic choice, involves a dialogue with the community of forms, and with those forms that were not chosen. Genre, in this respect, is analogous to language itself. The artist's subjectivity, expressing itself in forms, becomes the basis for a shared world. The expressive gestures of one human being establish a new manner of communal existence.

Merleau-Ponty, in effect, overcomes the paradox of self and otherness. He cites Hegel, asserting that "there is no choice between the *for-itself* and the *for-others;* . . . in the moment of expression, the other to whom I address myself and myself are linked without reserve."

All expressive activities are also linked. Merleau-Ponty can discuss Cezanne in the same terms that he discusses Proust, because painting and writing have the same source in the structure of human behavior. In an echo of Coleridge's discussion of the primary and secondary imaginations, Merleau-Ponty grounds expression in perception. "The expressive . . . was begun in the least act of perception, and has been amplified into painting and art." Because we are human we have a tradition of perceiving a universe and of constructing artifacts in a human way. Cultural meanings, then, are ingrained in the human personality; and the individual understands them without having to think about them. A speaker does not think before speaking; in speaking, his words are his thought.

The connection of perception and art is crucial for Merleau-Ponty. The work of art is a vehicle through which perception achieves a communicative form. Art "gives speech to perception." Consciousness, it seems, enters the world in perception and is, also, at the same time the ground of perception. The activity of perception simultaneously constructs the world in relation to the conscious self and creates consciousness of the self in relation to the otherness of the world. In this way perception finds form in the chaos of sensation. Art does too. And it is by finding form and giving language that art creates individual and communal meaning.

Although Merleau-Ponty often uses the terminology of signifier and signifieds, and talks about writing as a system of signs, his emphasis is not upon that system but upon the meaning that is given. He writes, after all, as easily about Cezanne as about Stendhal and writes about them in much the same terms. For him, the painter's colors and forms create the same meanings as does the writer's style. Perhaps, as has been recently argued, the painterly, because it is visible, is more basic to Merleau-Ponty than is the verbal. "Vision [is his] archetypal form of all perception."[74] In this regard, Merleau-Ponty reaches past Husserl to the empiricist thinkers of the seventeenth and eighteenth centuries. Thus he points out Husserl's connection to that tradition. In the seventeenth- and eighteenth-century discussions of *res et verba*, the linguistic sign, the *verbum*, is never treated as an end in itself. It is a medium that unites the subject with the world. Further, the empiricist tradition tended to look for an identity between the seeing subject and his sight and even between that sight and the world which it sees. That was an age, remember, that tended to identify poetry with its visual imagery. These same attitudes seem to hold for Merleau-Ponty. For him, too, signifier and signified tend to be in "a simple relationship of homonymy."

In contrast, the most recent structuralist and post-structuralist critics, as represented by Michel Foucault in *Les Mots et Les Choses,* emphasize the system of signs itself, give primacy to language, and stress the radical discontinuity and difference between words and things. For this reason, post-structuralist writers are hostile to the phenomenology of Sartre and Merleau-Ponty.

To Sartre, Merleau-Ponty, and their phenomenological forebearers like Husserl and Heidegger, language is representational. Not only can literature therefore represent reality, but the critic's work is also able to represent what is in the literature it is dealing with. Merleau-Ponty's description of the task of literary criticism fits into his overall philosophy. Criticism acts in the same way that art does. Both make valid intersubjective connections, each connects the subject to its object meaningfully. The job of the critic, says Merleau-Ponty, recapitulates the job of the artist. The critic is able to express the significance of the work just as the artist charts the significance of reality. Criticism, then, is one more way in which consciousness can undergo a meaningful encounter with reality. Because language does not seem to be a problem to Merleau-Ponty, the critic's language can be in the same kind of valid relationship to the work as the author's language is to the objectivity it is rendering. Language is, for Merleau-Ponty, an example of cultural meanings, and these, he argues, are part of our tradition of perceiving and expressing in a human way. They are ingrained in the human person. Language viewed this way need not distort the objectivity of the work, and a critical encounter with a text may therefore be objectively valid.

Can we say that, for the phenomenologist, language is reality? Heidegger had said that we are owned by language. Merleau-Ponty points out that the aphasiac's entire relation to the world is upset and his ability to perceive is changed. The aphasiac, it seems, does not see the same things in the world that other people do; he cannot find the same meanings.[75] Once again, modern phenomenology connects to the empiricist thinkers of the seventeenth and eighteenth centuries. John Locke's discrimination between real essences and nominal essences comes very close to attributing to language the prime power of meaningful perception. Phenomena are experienced and shared by virtue of language. Because the aphasiac cannot name the items of his experience, says Merleau-Ponty, he cannot perceive reality. Because he cannot name the items of his experience communal meaning is lost. Thought itself is not merely a subjective state, but is the very life of human relationships. And language, in this sense, is thought.

Merleau-Ponty tends to identify thought, perception, and emotion as being intentional acts. They are human ways into the world, all of which are identified with language. It is no wonder, then, that he rejects the formalisms that were current during the middle of the century: "One condemns formalism with good reason." He grounds that condemnation on formalism's separation of technique from reality. He argues, in fact, that its mistake is that it esteems form too little, "so little that it detaches it from meaning."[76] Because reality comes into being only with expression, a work of art is a unity in which the expression and what is expressed are indistinguishable. To write or to paint is not to make objects but to reveal the world.

To criticize is to reveal the world of the work. That, of course, does not mean that any critical analysis of a text is ever final, any more than any work of art is a final expression of reality. New subjectivities continue to stream into the world, "the speaking word" continuously alters "the spoken word," makes new perceptions, reveals new realities.

Philosophically, the aim of phenomenology was to establish the continuity between experience and reality. Descartes's melting of the beeswax, his separation of thinking substance from extended substance, may have been the first modern rupture in being, but it went on. The empiricists, it turned out, found themselves dividing sense data from perception—a much more profound division than that between the senses and the understanding. Kant's separation of *Ding an sich,* things in themselves, from phenomena merely reaffirmed the fact that the world was already dichotomized.

Perhaps none of these thinkers really left the world dual. A valid history of philosophic thought from the seventeenth to the nineteenth century could emphasize the attempts to overcome the duality. Hume, for example, moved the argument away from reason to human nature and found the ground of unity in faith and passion. And does not Kant bridge the unbridgeable chasm by means of the practical reason and the aesthetic judgment? But a constant pattern in the history of human thought involves overlooking earlier solutions to problems and stressing the problems themselves. Gerald Graff in his eloquent and witty studies of modern criticism has argued that entrepreneurship is the most important motive in modern criticism. It may well be a constant element in all intellectual life.

Heidegger

Edmund Husserl renounced the Kantian dualism between phenomena and noumena. Only the phenomenon, the object in consciousness, is given. The problem results when we think about consciousness as a faculty for being conscious—knowing only itself. Instead, Husserl maintained, consciousness is always an act that is conscious of something. And so the very act of consciousness, which always has an object, is of necessity unifying. The term that characterizes Husserl and phenomenology is *intention*. The act of consciousness intends, it directs itself toward, an object. The object is intended, it is an object for the intending act. The subject intending and the object intended are both real and are in a reciprocal relation to each other. But just as all consciousness is always of an object, so the only reality is reality for consciousness. Meaning, then, is itself an act and function of intending, and nothing apart from meaning can be. All unities are, for Husserl, unities of meaning.

Martin Heidegger takes the unification of subject and object further when he affirms that as all being is being in the world, the whole human being consists in the reciprocal relation of subjectivity and the world. Thus for Heidegger the meaning of poetic language must be in and of the world which it opens up. Poetic language—in contrast to the language of science—is, in fact, coextensive with being in the world. It discloses that world, because like the human collaboration with reality, the language of poetry is a tissue of tenses, of moods and stances, of facts and values.

Insisting on the emotional, in fact bodily, nature of consciousness, Heidegger emphasizes the world-revealing quality of poetry and distinguishes between the artificial language of logic and the natural language of poetry. This is part of a larger opposition between the instrumental and the human, between the artifact and the work of art. Is there not a dim but undeniable Aristotelian echo in such a distinction? All arts either imitate nature or complete nature. Those arts that complete nature have a final cause beyond their formal cause. These are the toolmaking arts— instrumental, utilitarian. But the arts that imitate nature do not provide means to ends. Rather, in another echo of Aristotle, they clarify the world, they open the world to human meaning. For Heidegger, it is in terms of poetic language that man lives and gains a mode of living in the world. Only if language has shown a meaningful world, and if man responds, can there be human dealings. Because poetic language denies a split between subject and object, between facts and values, poetry is essential human meaning. When Heidegger asserts that it is not man that speaks but language, he is pointing to this world-disclosing function of speech.

Man is a network of lived relationships—with the world, with others, with many things. To each of these ways of behavior there belongs a way of understanding. To behave humanly is to understand. To live authentically as a human being is to be actively involved with the things of this world—an involvement of caring and understanding. At this point Heidegger seems to part from his empiricist affiliations, for man's interchange with things is direct and immediate and is not by images. Nor is it by theoretical analysis.

In contrast to the essential human condition, Heidegger posits an inauthentic existence where man merely moves side by side with things and others, without care or understanding, through the socially determined necessities of everyday life.

Poetic speech is the language of authentic existence. It opens up the network of relationships. Opposed to poetic speech are both the inhuman abstracting disambiguity of logical signs and the confused and mundane language of the commonplace, the stereotypical, the trite.

Although Heidegger finds the birthplace of natural language and the roots of authentic existence in poetic speech, it is important to recognize that he does not dismiss the world of tools and equipment. Indeed his emphasis on the world and on the substantiality of the body would prevent that. The reality of the world, after all, is also material and instrumental. And art delivers those qualities. Like Merleau-Ponty, Heidegger insists on the *thing* quality of art, on its materiality, and he rejects formalism because of its indifference to subject matter. Poetry, like life, is particular, historical, multiply ambiguous. The ambiguity of poetry is, for Heidegger, not a fuzziness, but a rightness and a clarity that puts its reader into a new and concrete situation with a new intensity. Samuel Johnson had pointed out that custom—inauthentic existence—robs even the most humanly important events of their human meaning, and that the powerful concreteness and novelty of literature puts us in emotional and intellectual touch with the world of humanly important events. Poetry functions in much the same way for Heidegger.

To Heidegger, the realm of phenomena is not a veil or an illusion. It is presence. Like Merleau-Ponty, Heidegger might well call for a "nouvelle cogito," a subjectivity that finds its reality in its interrelationships with the world of objects and of others. The world behind the scene is banished. The isolated, private, hidden self is also discounted. The new cogito is not a personal subject, but a cultural and historical being; it is human-beinghood itself. Personal selfhood is, after all, trivial. The personal selfhood of the artist is trivial also. "The artist remains inconsequential as compared with the work, [he is] a passageway that destroys itself in order for the work to emerge."[77]

The struggle against the private state of mind is a major element in modern critical thought. Has it not been a major element since Hume's attempt to find a "standard of taste"? Perhaps from the *Philebus* on, literary theory has dealt with the escape from the triviality of the personal ego. Heidegger, like Husserl, rejects psychology for this reason. It identifies the literary work with the psychic experiences of the author and reader. It seems that for Heidegger private subjectivity is identifiable with the inauthentic—the non-connecting, the non-understanding, the non-caring. In fact the private subject is similar to the object as object—essentially fixed and dead, without phenomenological reality.

Georges Poulet and the Geneva school

Georges Poulet—along with other members of the Geneva school, "The Critics of Consciousness—[78] has often been described as a phenomenologist and has thus been identified with Heidegger and Husserl. Perhaps this should not be. For one thing the Geneva critics do not discount the personal life world of the author. They make that world, as embodied in the text, the source of the work's meaningful coherence, the way of getting into the work, the goal of their interpretive activities.

More important is the attitude toward the conscious subject. The other phenomenologist we have been looking at called for a new cogito where the subject exists in interrelationship with the world of objects. Georges Poulet separates himself from this interest. In a much cited letter to J. Hillis Miller, Poulet rejects a concern with "the mind overwhelmed, filled, and so to speak stuffed with its objects." He declares that the most important form of consciousness is "at a distance from, and protected from, any object, a subjectivity which exists in itself, withdrawn from any power which might determine it from the outside." Far from seeking a new cogito, Poulet affirms his loyalty to the Cartesian tradition. Pure consciousness is prior to and separate from any object, it knows itself by a direct intuition, not by its relations with the world. Literary criticism is then "the consciousness of the critic coinciding with the consciousness of the thinking and feeling person located in the heart of the text."[79] Note the aim of the critical act goes through the text itself to another subjectivity, and note, too, that pure consciousness, the subjectivity that matters, must be *protected* from contamination with objects. "Consciousness of consciousness, literature about literature," is how Miller, himself a disciple, describes the criticism of the Geneva school. He identifies them with Pater and Ruskin, "and so back to romantic criticism."[80]

In many important ways, this group removes itself from the leading tendencies and assumptions that characterize much of twentieth-century criticism. Unlike such movements as New Criticism, Neo-Aristotelianism, structuralism, or Russian formalism, which regard criticism as a mode of objective knowledge, the Geneva critics reject both notions and see critical activity as a subjective act, as being itself not knowledge but a form of literature, a "meditation, reverie, or spiritual quest." Whereas much modern criticism assumes the Kantian notion of disinterested interest, the Geneva school proudly renounces the ideal of detachment. "The most valuable criticism is that in which the writer continues his own private adventure in writing, in which through the very finding of the words he enacts one of the stages of his own personal spiritual adventure."[81] All modern formalisms reified the text and gave that text an intrinsic importance divorced from both author and reader. But these critics of consciousness go through the text to the state of mind of the author. The work merely incarnates the author's consciousness and makes it available to others. "What has to be reached is a subject."

In many ways, the Geneva critics, with their emphasis on the free and uncontaminated subject, are still at war with late nineteenth-century scientism. Nineteenth-century science could be seen as a celebration of matter against spirit, of the world of things over the world of thought. Materialism and determinism were its talismanic notions. Such works as Dostoyevsky's *Notes from the Underground* showed the plight of individual subjectivity in a world defined by the Crystal Palace. Thomas Mann praises the Underground Man as a champion of sensibility against the forces of scientism and positivism. The Underground Man rescued himself from all external forces. He went underground into the subjectivity. In their attempt to deal with pure subjectivity, and to rescue literature from objects and objectivity, the Geneva critics seem still struggling aginst the forces of Darwin, Zola, and Claude Bernard.

In contrast to Heidegger, Poulet tries to overcome being-in-the-world. The critic trying to reach the author's cogito must traverse an alien world filled with exteriority and objectivity—all the things described by the writer, literary forms, biographical information, historical information in order to get to "the hidden face of the moon." The critic must not only get across the world of things, he must also empty his own mind of its personal content so that he might reach and coincide with the author's consciousness. Criticism, then, becomes consciousness of consciousness, as Miller puts it, "the transposition of the mental universe of an author into the interior space of the critic's mind."[82]

The Geneva school shows relatively little interest in individual works and no interest in the form of those works. Poulet, indeed, claims that "there is nothing formal about literature."[83] He is concerned with getting through the work to a mind which can never express itself fully in any objective form. Heidegger called the artist a passageway that destroys itself in order for the work to exist. For Poulet the work may create a structure but it also transcends such structures, "destroys them." What matters is not the form of an individual work but the author's mental universe, the subjective structure of the creating mind.

Poulet's starting point is the fact of our radical isolation. Here, too, he is at one with much nineteenth-century anti-positivism. He has been compared, in this respect, with such connoisseurs of isolation as Walter Pater and William James. The joining of consciousnesses through reading is a way out of that prison cell. A book is not an object but a penetration by a consciousness: "the consciousness of another, no different from the one I assume in every human being I encounter, except that in this case the consciousness is open to me, welcomes me, lets me look deep inside itself, and even allows me, with unheard-of license, to think what it thinks and feel what it feels."[84] Most wonderful of all, reading turns an object into a consciousness and a consciousness that now exists inside me, in "my [own] innermost self."

Sartre called literature the experience of the not-self *par excellence.* Poulet takes this notion to its limits. The penetration by the other consciousness seems to obliterate the boundaries of self: "You are inside it; it is inside you; there is no longer either outside or inside." The reader becomes the subject of another's thoughts. He thinks the thoughts of another and thinks them as his very own though the thoughts he is thinking are alien thoughts. Poulet quotes Rimbaud: "JE est un autre." The book is the author's consciousness, which wakens in the reader an analogue of what the author thought and felt. Literature, it seems, not only delivers the reader from egocentricity; in a way, it also overcomes mortality. The book preserves the writer's "feelings, . . . ideas, . . . modes of dreaming and living," which then live in the reader's consciousness and thus "save the author's identity from death."[85]

The critic's goal is the recovery of the writer's subjectivity. Individual texts provide opportunities for discovering that subjectivity. Miller describes his method: looking at all passages for persistent "obsessions, problems, and attitudes" in order "to glimpse the original unity of the creative mind."[86] The text allows some approach to the subjective event that is the author's point of departure in apprehending his self and the world. The comprehensive reader can extract the author's identity from the totality of his works. Yet it seems that fragments and individual passages can be more revealing of these underlying concerns than complete works. Poulet goes further: the search for the recurrent and the characteristic can also identify mental attitudes that describe the consciousness of an age.

Although Poulet aims at uniting, across time and space, with another consciousness and even with the consciousness of another age, he seems strangely untouched by those persistent and recurring obsessions and attitudes that seem to have characterized the consciousness of our own age. The Marxian analysis of the collective subjectivity is alien to his interest in the pure subjectivity of the individual consciousness; and, of course, the entire Marxian relationship of infrastructure and superstructure makes subjectivity a result of the system of material objects and completely dependent upon that system for any meaning it might have. Marxism, after all, in its determinism, its materialism, its dialectic, seems to represent the very scientism that Poulet rejects. He separates himself from the Marxists because he refuses to admit the intrusion of the infrastructure with its objectifications.

Freudian psychology, with its model of id, ego, and super-ego, its emphasis on the importance of the *un*conscious and *pre*conscious—both stuffed with all sorts of forces and mentalized objects, determined by bio-graphical facts—could not account for the Cartesian cogito. Poulet's pri-macy of consciousness cannot fit with Freud's primacy of the uncon-scious—even with Jung's collective unconscious, for that matter.

Although Nietzsche was also an enemy of scientism and positivism, his "deconstructions" of metaphysics would separate him from Poulet. The significant movements in modern anthropology and linguistics are also forms of "objectifications" which Poulet could not admit.

The structuralists

Poulet's thought, along with that of most of the Geneva school, rests on traditional concepts of language. The reader can travel from the work to the consciousness of the writer—can participate in a collaboration be-tween his own consciousness and the writer's—only if language somehow reflects antecedent thought. But modern linguistics, starting with Saus-sure, makes language a sign system that never corresponds to the thing signified. In this way, structural linguistics erects a firm and impenetrable barrier to the coincidence of minds and to the movement from text to subjectivity. It is, of course, in this area primarily that the Geneva school (and phenomenology generally) has its basic quarrel with structuralism.

Further the structural linguistic model makes rule central and makes in-dividual performance a consequence of rule. There are classes of action, not individuals or groups of individuals. The cogito dwindles then into an effect. A text can no longer refer back to the creative subjectivity as its source, nor could it be thought that the meaning of that text lay in the consciousness of the subject. The subject, itself, becomes a construct. The meaning of a text—if we can, in fact, any longer raise that question—derives not from the subject but from the rules of language. Lévi-Strauss connects the new linguistics with both Freudian and Marxist determinism when he discusses the shift from "conscious phenomena" to their "un-conscious infrastructure."

Jonathan Culler points to the incompatability of structuralism and the thought of the Geneva critics when he calls "the most significant conse-quence of structuralism: its rejection of the notion of the 'subject.' "[87] Is Poulet's concern with tragic isolation anything but "madness," when the human sciences have dissolved man? Thinking, speaking, writing, want-ing are made possible by a series of systems which the subject does not control. Michel Foucault asserts that modern linguistics, anthropology, psychology have "decentered" man in relation to his own desires, dis-course, and actions.[88]

Culler points out that there is still a place for the person in literary in-vestigations. A person did write the work under discussion, but—and this indicates how significantly the creative subject has been decentered—he could write it only within the context of a system of enabling conventions. Perhaps, as Culler suggests, there is still a dialectic of subject and object, but if the subject still exists, he is no longer the origin of meaning. Behind him, making him able to write, supplying his discourse with meaning, are the conventions and rules that make writing possible. The subject becomes little more than a function of the language structure.

Does structuralism represent some kind of victory for the forces of positivism and scientism? Has science finally taken over all human activities? Saussure's overthrow of nineteenth-century linguistic science, which was that of historical linguistics—to use Saussure's term, diachronic linguistics—is presented by his followers as a victory for humanity over the forces of positivism: "a valuable mode of humanistic and qualitative thought alongside the scientific and quantitative."[89] Frederic Jameson quotes Hermann Paul as saying, "what is not historical in linguistics is not scientific," in order to illustrate the nineteenth-century positivist attitude. In contrast, Saussure's synchronic approach is sometimes seen as freeing language study from the tyranny of the merely empirical, from the determinism of historical forces, and allowing it autonomy and meaning.

Because historical linguistics is tied to actual linguistic behavior, and primarily speaking behavior, it is limited to a study of such temporal, accidental, and external causes as geography, migration, and population shifts. Saussure, by separating language from actual speaking, separated also the social from the individual, and the accidental from what is essential in language. Saussure's approach to linguistic thus transcends cultural differences.

But if his escape from history and culture is an escape from the meaninglessness and accident of mere empiricism, Saussure does not substitute a humanistic or idealistic version of language. His view is systematic and deterministic. Language is not "affected by the will of the depositories."[90] He offers a different sort of science. "Diachronic events are always accidental and particular," and therefore not open to systematic knowledge, but language is a system whose parts and systematic relationships can be known. Saussure and, following Saussure, structuralism reject a concern with the historical, the diachronic in favor of the self-contained whole, the system, the synchronic. *Synchronic* and *diachronic* are favorite terms whose appearance characterizes the terminology of structuralism.

Langue and *parole* are also terms that identify structuralist discourse. Saussure seems to use *langue* to refer to the language system, whereas *parole* is its actual use, particularly in speech. The distinction has been paralleled with Noam Chomsky's distinction between competence (the grammatical system we have internalized) and performance (linguistic behavior). Saussure rejects concern with *parole*, which is "many sided and heterogeneous [so that] we cannot discover its unity,"[91] in favor of *langue*, "a system whose parts can and must all be considered in their synchronic solidarity."[92]

Much of the dispute between phenomenology and structuralism deals with the nature and place of language. Phenomenologist Paul Ricouer has accused structural linguistics of a kind of solipsism, has called its theory of language an autonomous entity of internal dependencies. Structuralist Tzvetan Todorov has charged the language theory of the Geneva critics with an elaborate fiction—the assumption that a truer language, belonging to the writer, somehow lies under the actual language of the text. This is a notion that makes the text and its language only a symptom.

Roland Barthes stresses the importance not only of the linguistic doctrines but of the linguistic terminology to structuralism, pointing out that it is the recourse to the "lexicon of signification" that we must finally see the sign of structuralism. The terminology that Barthes refers to also derives from the work of Saussure. All structuralists seem to accept his insights into the nature of the linguistic *sign* as the basic unit of language. Any word in any language is a sign. Language itself is a system of signs. Saussure analyzed the sign into two further components which he called the signifier (*significant* in French) and the signified (*signifié*). The employment of these two words is another mark of structuralist writers.

As we will see in Saussure's treatment of the sign, Ricouer's criticism is valid. Saussure, in fact, ignores any connection between language and reality. The sign "unites not a thing and a name but a concept and a sound image." There is no natural connection affirmed between the signifier and the signified. The sign is arbitrary, it has no basis in reality, but only in the language system. As such, it is, of course, culturally necessary. Inasmuch as the signified is not a thing but the notion of a thing that comes to mind when the appropriate signifier is seen or heard, the only reality we know is a representation of language. So much for the belief that poetic language somehow penetrates and shows forth the nature of reality.

Another of Saussure's principles of signification is that signifiers and signifieds are inseparable. A meaningless sound is not a signifier, because it does not signify. There can be no signifier without a signified. In the same way, there can be no signified without a signifier. No concept exists if it has no expression in language.

Saussure insists that "language is form and not substance," thus emphasizing that it is a system of relations between its parts and that the parts themselves get their identity from their relations to other parts. There is nothing essential about any word. It takes its meaning from its place in a system. We delimit the meaning of a signifier by differentiating it from other signs that are near it. This is the famous principle of *difference*. Without difference there can be no meaning. The "most precise characteristic [of any concept] is in being what the others are not."[93]

> In language there are only differences . . . [and] *without positive terms.*
> Whether we take the signified or the signifier, language has neither ideas
> nor sounds that existed before the linguistic system, but only
> conceptual and phonic differences that have issued from that system.[94]

Lévi-Strauss's interpretation of societies and myths employs the idea of difference. He does not treat symbolic elements in myths as fixed quantities. Each recurrence is analyzed in terms of its relationships within the system, its differences from the other elements in the particular myth. Structuralist literary criticism operates on the same principle. In a play, for example, a character is not analyzed by comparison with something outside the play but by comparison with the other characters that the play contains. Elements in myths, characters in plays are signifiers. All their meanings emanate within the system and derive from relationships among signifiers within the same system.

The self, itself, emerges as an intersubjective construct formed by a cultural system over which the individual has no control. Just as there are no preexisting ideas but values that emanate from the system, so, too, there is no transcendental subject. The subject is also a cultural construction.

John Sturrock describes structuralism's "war on . . . ego philosophies."[95] Language is institutional in its nature. Because we are born into it and because it exceeds us as individuals, it is impersonal. T. S. Eliot had called poetry a continuous self-sacrifice. The structuralists go further and see in any use of language to communicate "with others (or even with ourselves) a surrender of at least a portion of our uniqueness." Jacques Lacan says that in the surrender of the libido to the system, "we pass from the private if delusive order of the Imaginary to the social order of the Symbolic." Symbols are always part of a system; for symbols to exist and operate, an order of conventions and restrictions is necessary. There is nothing symbolic unless there is some sort of language that restricts the freedom of the individual. Jacques Derrida's emphasis on *langue* over *parole* is an emphasis on writing over speech—and this too undermines ego philosophies. In speech the speaker is always present, but in writing he is absent. The written text is freed from the individual who produced it.

In addition to the vocabulary of signification and the notion of difference, structural linguistics is characterized by its distinction between "syntagmatic" and "paradigmatic" relations in language. "In discourse . . . words acquire relations based on the linear nature of language." The elements are arranged in sequence. Saussure calls combinations supported by linearity "syntagms." The sentence is the ideal type of syntagm— "an order of succession . . . a fixed number of elements." Outside discourse "words acquire relations of a different kind." These seem to be relations of association. And because there are many different relations of association—similarity of both form and meaning, only of form or only of meaning, similarity in sound images, a common suffix, a common root, similarity of the concepts signified—words that have something in common result in "groups marked by diverse relations."[96] Words grouped by association are called paradigms. The syntagm is determinate, whereas the paradigm seems to be indeterminate and indefinite.

It appears almost as if the paradigm takes us, with its open-endedness, outside of the structural system and back to the individual subject and his own sense of similarities. This becomes crucial to post-structuralism and the concept that language is indeterminate.

Is Roman Jakobson's opposition between the metaphoric and metonymic poles analogous to the distinction of paradigm and syntagm? In many ways, it seems to be. Metonymy with its attachment to realistic data, its characteristic presence in prose, especially in prose narrative, seems like the syntagm, linear and determined. Whereas metaphor, which Jakobson identifies with romantic and symbolist poetry, is by definition a matter of association and of similarity and struggles against linear—that is, narrative—restraints. It too opens up to a variety of indeterminacies.

Claude Lévi-Strauss has taken up Saussure's major methodological assumptions. He has also taken his terminology. Lévi-Strauss likes to suggest that he is, in fact, providing a linguistic analysis of social structures and of the structures of myths. From the linguistic term, *phoneme,* he coins "mytheme"—the minimal unit of a myth. He claims that he has shown "wonderful symmetries," "perfect homologies," or "complete inversions" in myths, talking as if he has discovered a new language. Discussing French cultural images of domestic animals, he declares: "If birds are metaphorical human beings and dogs metonymical human beings, cattle may be thought of as metonymical inhuman beings and racehorses as metaphorical inhuman beings." (The members of this group seem especially drawn to this polarity. So Jacques Lacan: "The symptom *is* a metaphor whether one likes it or not, as desire *is* a metonymy for all that men may mock the idea."[97]) In his analysis of kinship systems, Lévi-Strauss identifies the circulation of women with the circulation of words and concludes that "marriage regulations and kinship systems [are] a kind of language." Like Saussure he is looking for a *langue,* or, like Chomsky, for a "deep structure."

Lévi-Strauss's search for an underlying system of mythology seems to go beyond Saussure's concept of a *langue* and to suggest a universal unity of all human products. Indeed, Lévi-Strauss acknowledges this when he compares his quest "for the constraining structures of the mind," to the "manner of Kantian philosophy."[98] Although, as Paul Ricouer has observed, Lévi-Strauss does not claim "a transcendental subject," he does, nevertheless, claim to have discovered a "pattern of basic and universal laws."

In this way, Lévi-Strauss, like other structuralists, overcomes such notions as "the illusions of [human mental] liberty," and the arbitrariness of mind that would follow from such liberty. Under the arbitrary data of mythology, Lévi-Strauss seeks "a level at which a kind of necessity becomes apparent."[99] At that level, he discovers the existence of laws.

Just as Saussure rejected the empiricism of the diachronic in favor of the synchronic, so too does Lévi-Strauss reject the frontiers of historical investigation of mythology in order to outline its syntax.

Jacques Ehrman has called the most significant contribution of structuralism the shift from a particle theory to a field theory. Lévi-Strauss is concerned not with the myths of a particular society but with the nature of myths universally. He arrives at his awareness of the universal qualities of myths by studying common features. The analyst tries to construct a coherent system where each myth is understood in its relation to others: "the context of each myth consists . . . of other myths." To explain an element in any myth, not only must that element be compared with others in the same myth but also with elements appearing in similar contexts in other myths. A single syntagmatic chain is meaningless. We can learn nothing from only one myth. One must set a syntagmatic chain, that is to say, a whole myth against other myths. Only in this way can we arrive at paradigmatic classes—and only by reaching common features can we come to understanding.

In the same way, the end of Lévi-Strauss's investigation of social patterns is not to discover what a given social rule means to the society that practices it, but what these phenomena mean in their interrelations. It is to discover not what a myth means to a person who knows only the myths of his own society, but what the myth or its element means within the institution of mythology. Similarly, Lévi-Strauss is concerned with literature as an institution, and with the conventions that constitute it.

Before we look at Roland Barthes and structuralist literary theory, I would like to glance again at what has been called an older cousin of structuralism, Russian formalism, which I mentioned earlier. This movement, which became active during the First World War, was, like structuralism, profoundly influenced by Saussure and Jakobson. In fact, Jakobson helped found both movements. But unlike structuralism and unlike the New Criticism, the formalist movement proudly took up the slogans of empirical science and the beliefs of positivism. Chanting their adherence to facts, to the discovery of literary facts, the formalists claimed as their goal "the attempt to create an independent science of literature which studies specifically literary material." Boris Eichenbaum, in his attack on the academicians and the symbolists, shows the formalists' devotion to the religion of science. The enemies had "no set of [scientific] principles," they completely lacked "both a scientific temperament and a scientific point of view."[100] The formalists, trying to separate literary facts from all other facts, divorced the study of literature from moralism, from subjective philosophic theories, from "history, culture, sociology, psychology, or aesthetics." They looked only toward linguistics, "a science bordering and sharing material" with literature, and found that poetic linguistic qualities have "independent value." Practical language is a means of communication, but poetic language is an end in itself. Form becomes "no longer an envelope," but a complete thing, "without correlative of any kind." Poetry does not communicate, nor is it about some matter other than itself. Eichenbaum summarizes: "Poetic form . . . is not contrasted with anything outside itself—with a content which has been laboriously set inside this form—but is [itself] understood as the genuine content of poetic speech."[101]

In their attempt to divorce form from meaning, to find only those specifics that distinguish literature from other material, the formalists applauded the Russian futurists' experiments in nonsense language. They emphasized sound as against images, for images could easily slide into meaning. Their study of sound indicated that "words without meaning are necessary." Viktor Shklovsky, the leading formalist theorist, asserted that "meaninglessness [is] a widespread linguistic fact and a phenomenon characteristic of poetry."

Trying to find "a system of precise observations and to reach a . . . scientific conclusion," Shklovsky transferred his study of sound from "the acoustical level," where it is liable to impressionistic interpretation, to the objective level of pronunciation and articulation. "A great part of the delight of poetry consists . . . in the independent dance of the organs of speech."

If meaning and subjective impressions are eliminated from consideration, what becomes the end of poetry? The answer seems to be perception itself. "Artistic perception is that perception in which we experience form." Because it is different from our ordinary perception, artistic perception becomes an independent value. Artistic form defamiliarizes, and this seems to be its primary function. "I sing not siren-like to please/For I am harsh," John Donne wrote. Viktor Shklovsky emphasizes the qualities of the rough and the unfamiliar. Art, for him, increases the difficulty and therefore the span of perception, because the process of perception is an aesthetic end in itself "and must be prolonged." In opposition to the symbolists' view of imagery, the formalists make the image, too, part of the process of defamiliarization. "The purpose of the image is not to present the meaning of an object . . . but to create a special perception of the object."[102] The purpose of art is to overcome the automatism of perception.

I am certainly not suggesting any direct filiation between the formalists' stress on perception and the discussions of perception that took place in England from Locke through Samuel Johnson. But in many ways the Russian belief in perception as a positive value echoes the earlier English emphasis. The eighteenth-century writers, unlike the formalists, connected perception and meaning. Yet, in both cases, it was suggested that one of literature's functions was perception itself. Such seventeenth-century wrtiers as Bishop Sprat and John Locke had suggested that art is an analogue and, indeed, a triumph of perception. Dr. Johnson had pointed out that custom and, therefore, inattention strip events of significance. Art returns us to an awareness of perceptual events. And Johnson in his treatment of novelty came close to Shklovsky's celebration of defamiliarization. The difference, of course, was vast. For the seventeenth- and eighteenth-century writers, the renewed perception of art was a way to intensify our perception of reality. The formalists severed art from all external relationships.

Plot, for example, was made a compositional rather than a thematic concept. This emphasized the devices of plot arrangement and thus shifted the concept of plot away from the element of story. Plot was step-by-step construction and was viewed in the same technical terms as such other devices as sound-repetition, parallelism, and so on. Shklovsky, in his stress on the technical devices of literature, in fact abstracts these devices from their story. The same device may appear in different materials. It is the device that is literary.

Form and content are separated to such an extent that the formalists assert that new form does not arise in order to express new content. Content has nothing to do with it. New forms emerge because old forms have grown stale and have lost their aesthetic quality: "The work of art arises from a background of other works and through association with them. The form of a work of art is defined by its relation to other works of art."

It is no wonder that Trotsky attacked formalism. And, though the formalists have some resemblance to structuralism, there seem to be important differences. Few structuralists—perhaps Lévi-Strauss is an exception—saw the parts of a work as removable from the work and as movable from text to text. Although both groups emphasize the signifier over the signified, for the Russian formalists it seems that the signifier signifies only itself.

Now that the reign of structuralism has passed into post-structuralism, there is some debate as to whether structuralism ever existed as a unified movement, just as we now argue whether the New Criticism was ever a single position. Perhaps all that can characterize structuralism is a polemic use of the language of signification and an allegiance to Saussure's distinctions. In other respects the various "structuralist" writers exhibit differences. Lévi-Strauss displays a universalism that Barthes would reject. Lévi-Strauss finds in his study of myths a pattern of basic and universal laws, and he posits a unity of human mental products. Tzvetan Todorov goes even further in this direction, taking Lévi-Strauss's Kantianism into his own Platonism by talking about a universal grammar which he makes the source of all universals and which, he says, "gives definition to man himself." Todorov claims that all languages—all signifying systems—obey the same grammar. In a Platonist *o altitudo,* he adds "It is universal not only because it informs all the languages of the universe, but because it coincides with the structure of the universe itself."[103] In contrast, Roland Barthes represents a strict historicism and nominalism. Whereas Lévi-Strauss assumes a human nature underneath cultural variety, Barthes has argued that the notion of human nature is, itself, determined by culture and by class.

In the realm of literary theory, Roland Barthes is probably the best known member of the "structuralist" group. He is also the most varied. His own intellectual career has recapitulated the story of French literary theory since the Second World War. His continuing attacks on essentialism connect him with Sartre. Of his early books, *Writing Degree Zero* is Marxian, and *On Racine* seems phenomenological. His most recent work identified him with Derrida and post-structuralism. He also represents psychoanalysis. His career is pluralist and he professes a philosophy of pluralism.

In his early attacks on contemporary criticism Barthes objected that it was ahistorical, a meaningless empiricism of names and dates. Instead, he advocated a Marxian approach that examined the role of literature in any given society taking into account the relationship of social and economic facts to literary phenomena, asking about the class structure of authors and readers. He never abandoned this concern and continued to see reading and writing as determined by both culture and class. He also complained about the psychological naiveté of contemporary criticism, its tendency to connect the text with the author's biography. In *Michelet*, Barthes shows how to psychoanalyze a text, to reveal its obsessions, its evasions, the psychological nature of its imagery without mistaking this for a psychoanalysis of the author. He combines structuralism and psychoanalysis by treating the psychological qualities in the work only in relation to other elements within the work and not referring them to such an external context as the author.

Barthes's pluralism has always been insistent, denying even the unity of the individual. He has, in this regard, complained that modern criticism is insufficiently pluralistic, for he argues that the more meaning a text contains the better. "A-symbolia," then—his term for the restriction of textual meanings—joins ahistoricism and psychological naiveté and becomes his third objection against contemporary critics. Comparing all literary uses of language to the words of the Delphic oracle, Barthes stresses that such language is uttered in "the situation of ambiguity itself" and is therefore open to several meanings. No one meaning is granted precedence over others. In fact Barthes shifts attention away from meaning— from significance—to the process of signification, from the signifieds to the signifiers.

His final complaint against the state of criticism is "bad faith," the critics' failure to recognize the ideological basis of their criticisms and to declare that ideology. He argues that instead of taking full responsibility for their values, modern critics pretended that their values were, in fact, universal. Barthes calls this "mystification"—a sinister attempt to make historically and culturally determined phenomena appear to be natural phenomena. Demystification, then, is one of Barthes's constant activities, demonstrating the methods by which the mystifiers have tricked us.

As correctives against these four critical faults, Barthes offers the "four great philosophies" which have, in recent decades, liberated French criticism from its dogmatisms. Existentialism has emphasized the importance of making values explicit. Marxism has indicated the role of culture and class in the production and consumption of literary works. Psychoanalysis has shown the complexity and contradictions that complicate the relations between the psychological facts of the work and the psychological facts of life. Structuralism has offered a model for the analysis of signifiers and by so doing changed the nature and aim of interpretation.

These, for Barthes, are the major elements in the development of the *Novelle Critique*. And although Barthes denies that "it owes anything to Anglo-American criticism," his attack on academic criticism (represented for him by Gustave Lanson) as a species of positivism has marked similarities to the New Critical assault on the false scientism of the American academy. The French and American versions of the New Criticism do seem to have common enemies, and both exhibit a sort of formalism. But beyond that the similarities may be more apparent than real. Barthes could well accuse the American New Critics of "smuggling . . . an ideology . . . surreptitiously." Few of the American New Critics would have accepted his dictum that "criticism is something other than making correct statements in the light of 'true' principles," nor would they have gone along with his emphasis on the self-reflective nature of the critical act.

Whereas the New Criticism emphasized the objective status of the work and a corresponding critical objectivity, Barthes denies that a work can be "an object independent of the psyche and personal history of the critic studying it." He declares that "all criticism must include . . . an implicit comment on itself; all criticism is criticism both of the work under consideration and of the critic."[104] Barthes's tenet that reading is not an innocent act makes criticism not an act of discovery but an interaction. Criticism then deals not with discrete texts but with relationships—the relationship between the "language-as-object" of the author and of the world, and also the relationship between the language of the author and the language of the critic. Declaring the task of criticism to be "purely formal," Barthes describes criticism as a "fitting together." The critic fits together the "language of the day" and the language of the author ("the formal system of logical rules that he evolved in the conditions of his time"). "Critical proof" lies, then, in the critic's ability to "cover" the work under consideration as completely as possible with the critic's own language, a language which is one of "the range of languages offered by [the critic's] situation in time."

Barthes emphasizes the complex necessity that brings about the critic's language. Not only is it a product of the historical development "of knowledge, ideas, and intellectual passions," but the critic "chooses this necessary language in accordance with a certain existential pattern, . . . putting into the operation . . . his preferences, pleasures, resistances, and obsessions."[105] His choice is a matter of necessity, too.

To pretend, under these conditions, to either objectivity or interpretation[106] would be self-deception or bad faith. Criticism can be nothing other than a dialogue between the historical situations and the subjectivities of the author and of the critic, a dialogue that shows "a complete egotistical bias towards the present." "Criticism is the ordering of that which is intelligible in our own time."[107] Structuralism enables the critic to avoid bad faith because it sets before him the aim "not of deciphering the meaning of the work under consideration, but of reconstituting the rules and compulsions that governed the elaboration of that sense."[108] As a signified object, the work eludes the reader's grasp; it does, however, offer itself as "a declared system of significance." Literature is, for Barthes, a language, a system of signs, whose being lies not in its message but in the system. "This being so, the critic is not called upon to reconstitute the message of the work, but [like any other linguist] to determine the formal structure which permits the transmission of meaning." The question is not *what* does a poem mean, but *how* does it mean.

Modern critical theory seems, from the beginning, to have been marked by a fight against subjectivity, and—with such important exceptions as Marxism—by a tendency to dismiss and devalue local and historical factors. In the eighteenth century, David Hume had tried to escape the chaos of subjective indeterminacy by establishing a standard of taste. The twentieth century, too, has also attempted—in the realm of literary theory—to overcome the tyranny of individual response, to establish an objective standard for literary analysis. Can it be, as the century draws to its conclusion, that with Barthes's stress on the subjectivity of both reader and writer, with post-structuralism's insistence on the radical indeterminacy of the literary text, with such other post-structuralist movements as reader-response criticism, the whirl of subjectivity again is king? If this is so, it is so only with severe qualifications that have been established in our century by such forces as Barthes's "four great philosophies."

Although Barthes may point out that subjectivity is an irreducible fact and may also assert that this must prevent interpretation, that is not an open invitation to private impressionism. After all, Barthes also acknowledges the anti-individualistic power of the three infrastructures—*langue*, the forces of production, and the subconscious. Although Barthes dismisses universality and objectivity as culturally determined myths, the notion of individuality that emerges from his discussion is also a cultural product. Subjectivity turns out to be an historically determined superstructure. And like any superstructure, its reality is contingent. Subjectivity, Barthes points out, is the work of all the codes that make up the "I".

Indeed Barthes's subjective has nothing to do with a pure Cartesian consciousness but is equated with historical being. His discussion of literary history in *On Racine,* by decentralizing the place of the author, indicates how subordinate the individual is to the activity. He describes traditional literary history as merely a succession of famous men and he calls for a new approach that emphasizes the milieu rather than the writer. The new study is to be sociological, concerned with shaping institutions, not with individuals. A method that would study the writer's audience, finding its social configuration, that would examine the relationship between major and minor writers, that would focus on the collective literary language and the collective literary sensibility would be able "to amputate literature from the individual."

Barthes's concept of intertextuality also diminishes the importance of the text's relationship to its writer and emphasizes instead the text's relationship to other texts. Every text, he declares, takes shape as a mosaic of other texts. Every text is the absorption and transformation of other texts.

Further, this doctrine separates Barthes's reader from his own individuality. Just as a text is a product of other texts, so the act of reading any work must involve other works. Other texts provide a grid through which the individual work is read by establishing the expectations that make the act of reading possible. Other works enable the reader to pick out salient features and to give them a structure. The subject, then, that reads is "intersubjective," a shared knowledge that is applied in reading. "My subjectivity," Barthes declares in *S/Z,* "has the generality of stereotypes."[109]

There is some similarity here to Eliot's view that poetry extinguishes personality by the power and importance of the poetic tradition itself. Indeed, it seems that Barthes's view that institutionalized conventions make all acts and objects possible goes back at least to Horace. If "the simulacrum is intellect added to object,"[110] that embodied intellect, that manifested structure comes about through convention. From Eliot's tradition, through Frye's archetypes, to Barthes's intertextuality, our age has given renewed importance to the creative role of generality.

Society, culture, history are such generalities for Barthes. Ideas and themes, he says, interest him less than "the way society takes possession of them in order to make them the substance of . . . signifying systems."[111] He directs his attention to signifying systems rather than to signifieds. "A text comes from consorting with the signifiers and letting the signifieds take care of themselves."[112] This emphasis is the basis for Barthes's distinction between *écrivain* and *écrivant* and between text and work.

The *écrivant* is a lesser sort of writer who begins with a predetermined meaning and who makes language the means toward that meaning. For him language is instrumental or, in Eliseo Vivas's term, transitive. Alain Robbe-Grillet criticizes "this universe of signification" in which words, gestures, characters, acts are reduced to a "suspect interiority."

The *écrivain,* on the other hand, writes intransitively, devoting his attention to language rather than to meaning. Thus he is a materialist rather than an idealist, a worker with the material of language. Barthes sees the *écrivain* as the writer of the future. And Robbe-Grillet defines the future universe of the novel in similar terms: "gestures and objects will be there before being something, . . . mocking their own meaning."[113] The *écrivain* produces a text—an object in language—whereas the *écrivant* gives us a work which looks through language to the world. The responsibility of the critic follows—it lies in reconstructing the object's system, not its message.

So far, Barthes's distinctions are familiar ones; Bergson, Valery, and almost everyone else had distinguished instrumental language from literary language. The non-instrumentality of literary language harks back to Kant's purposiveness without purpose. But in his later writings Barthes turned to what is called post-structuralism. Now he describes literary language as pure ambiguity, without bottom, supported by empty meaning.[114] In *S/Z* and *The Pleasure of the Text* he emphasizes discontinuity, exposing the continuity of the text as a deception. Although Barthes refers to the "simple effect of polysemy" as destroying the text's "discursive category," its "sociolinguistic reference," he seems to be talking about more than ambiguity, "a triumphant plural, unimpoverished by any restraint." Language becomes for him a "cacography" (the written version of cacophony), and he glories in its inconsistencies and contradictions.

Whereas the Barthes of "The Structuralist Activity" accepts the goal of intelligibility, for the later Barthes, intelligibility itself becomes destabilized. "The Structuralist Activity" defines a mimesis not very different from Aristotle's. Like Aristotle, Barthes describes a structural activity that does not copy but reconstructs an object in order to render it intelligible. Analysis and synthesis again: "structural man takes the real, decomposes it, then recomposes it." Such works highlight "the human process by which men give meaning to things."[115] Relationships of affinity and dissimilarity articulate the rules of structure. In the 1964 essay, the paradigm was seen as a limited group of units possessing clear relations to other objects of its class. By 1970, the "determinate syntagm is replaced by the infinite paradigm of difference,"[116] and a text becomes "a galaxy of signifiers, not a structure of signifieds."

Is structuralism replaced by post-structuralism? It is hard to say. Lacan, Foucault, Barthes, and Derrida go by both labels. Perhaps it is merely that post-structuralism offers a more radical skepticism toward the possibility of interpretation, more widely opening the text by proposing unexpected alternatives to accepted readings. Thus the structurality of structure itself becomes ambiguous, an uncertain relation of the organizing principle of the structure and its free play.

In 1966 *Yale French Studies* devoted a special volume to Structuralism. In the same year over a hundred humanists and social scientists gathered at Johns Hopkins for a symposium that explored "the impact of contemporary structuralist thought." The proceedings of the symposium were published in 1970. In 1974 *Velocities of Change* appeared, another Hopkins collection of structuralist essays. But by then critics were glibly referring to post-structuralism. Frank Lentricchia describes the post-structuralist phenomena in America: "In the early 1970s we awoke from the dogmatic slumber of our phenomenological sleep to find that a new presence had taken absolute hold over our avant-garde critical imagination."[117] New journals, such as *Diacritics* and *Glyph,* appeared, organs of post-structuralism. Many of America's leading literary thinkers—Hillis Miller, Geoffrey Hartman, Paul de Man, Harold Bloom, (The Yale Gang of Four, they have been called) moved in a post-structural direction. And Hartman claims that traditional critical thought has fled in panic before Derrida's message.

The popular critical imagination has been taken over too. Robert Langbaum tells of the applicant for graduate school who arrived clutching his *Of Grammatology* (a couple of decades ago, he says, it would have been the *Anatomy of Criticism*). Last year, articles about post-structuralism appeared casually enough in such bastions of the commonplace as *Time, The Village Voice,* and *The Atlantic.* Post-structuralism is "big in Oshkosh now," the *Voice* commented.

Even the *Voice* acknowledges that the person who "deserves credit or blame" for post-structuralism's takeover is Jacques Derrida. Derrida offers a new way of interpretation, a double mode of reading. Texts, he says, always implicitly criticize and undermine the philosophies in which they are implicated. The new reading shows how a text is made up of different elements which can never result in a synthesis but continually displace each other. His book, *Glas,* divides each page into two columns; in one column he discusses Hegel—analyzes his concept of the family; the facing column weaves together citations from and a discussion of Genet. What is the relationship between the two columns? It is offered as a possibility but never affirmed. Can it give rise to a synthesis?

Derrida's readings are always investigations of paradoxes. Nothing is ever simply present. Anything that is given as present is dependent for its identity on differences and relations which can never be present. But the fact that they are not present does not mean that they are absent. The problem is with our language, which only offers us this alternative.

"Nothing, in either the elements or the system, is anywhere simply absent or present,"[118] Derrida says. He develops such concepts as *différance* and *supplément* in order to challenge the consistency of system. Supplementarity makes it possible for him to show the confusion between the defining qualities of the marginal and the defining qualities of the central. *Différance,* a word he makes up, designates both difference and an act of differing or deferring which produces differences. *Différance* "is a structure which cannot be conceived on the basis of the opposition presence/absence . . . it is the systematic play of differences." These are the notions which let Derrida explore the paradoxes of signification and to expose the indeterminacy of any utterance.

If all utterances are indeterminant, accepted interpretations become replaceable. M. H. Abrams compares the new, liberated, creative readings of post-structuralism to the reinterpretations of the Old Testament by the Church Fathers and by the Kabbalists, a process of converting old meaning into new meanings. But the post-structuralists attack the concept of meaning itself, and so they do not quite offer a replacement, rather an indication of either the freedom or the terror of language stripped of illusory restraints.

A less hostile witness writing in the letters of *The Atlantic* tells how he offers Derrida's *différance* to undergraduate classes to help them understand how literary language resists clear and unambiguous meanings and to show that confusion and obscurity must therefore be part of every literary encounter.

It would be tempting to suggest that with post-structuralism and its deconstructions we are left only with the ingenuity of the reader to fall back on. But just as the author is dead, according to Barthes, so, Foucault points out, the human reader, man himself, is a simple fold in our knowledge, an illusion engendered by the play of language, and destined to disappear as soon as that knowledge has found a new form. It is, then, the "sea of linguisticity" that seems to deconstruct itself.

[1] William Butler Yeats, *Ideas of Good and Evil* (London: MacMillan, 1903), p. 240.

[2] Allen Tate, *On the Limits of Poetry* (New York: Swallow, Morrow, 1948), p. 4.

[3] Boris Eichenbaum, "Theory of the 'Formal Method,' " in Hazard Adams, ed., *Critical Theory Since Plato* (New York: Harcourt Brace Jovanovich, Inc., 1971), p. 831.

[4] Ibid.

[5] *Encylopedia of Poetry and Poetics*, Alex Preminger, ed. (Princeton, N.J.: Princeton University Press, 1965), p. 377.

[6] William Carlos Williams, "The Red Wheelbarrow," from *Collected Earlier Poems* (New York: New Directions Publishing Co., 1951)

[7] Frederick Nietzsche, *The Birth of Tragedy*, trans. Francis Golffing (New York: Doubleday and Company, Inc., 1956), p. 37.

[8] Geoffrey Hartman, "Beyond Formalism," in Gregory T. Polletta, ed., *Issues in Contemporary Literary Criticism* (Boston: Little, Brown and Company, 1973), p. 173.

[9] Quotations from "Tradition and the Individual Talent" are taken from *Selected Essays* (New York: Harcourt Brace and Company, 1932), pp. 7–9. The essay was first published in 1919.

[10] The titles of articles by William K. Wimsatt and Monroe Beardsley. However, *see* Wimsatt, "Genesis: A Fallacy Revisited," in *The Discipline of Criticism*, ed. Peter Demetz, Thomas Greene, Lowry Nelson, Jr. (New Haven and London: Yale University Press, 1968), p. 198, where Wimsatt also rejects "the dubious notion of the poet's impersonal personality."

[11] Quoted in William K. Wimsatt, Jr., and Cleanth Brooks, *Literary Criticism: A Short History* (New York: Alfred A. Knopf, 1957), p. 660n.

[12] *Speculations* (New York: Harcourt, Brace and Company, 1924), pp. 136–37.

[13] Ibid., p. 128.

[14] I. A. Richards, *Principles of Literary Criticism* (New York: Harcourt, Brace and World, 1928), p. 269.

[15] I. A. Richards, *Coleridge on Imagination* (New York: W. W. Norton and Company, 1950), p. 228.

[16] I. A. Richards, *The Foundations of Aesthetics* (New York: Lear Publishers, 1925), p. 21.

[17] T. S. Eliot, *The Sacred Wood* (London: Methuen and Company, 1928), p. 1. First published in 1920.

[18] Cited in A. Walton Litz, "Literary Criticism," in *Harvard Guide to Contemporary Writing*, ed. Daniel Hoffman (Cambridge, Mass.: Harvard University Press, 1979), p. 54.

[19] John Crowe Ransom, *The World's Body* (New York: Charles Scribner's Sons, 1938), p. 124.

[20] Ibid.

[21] Ibid., pp. 115–16.

[22] Ibid., p. 116.

[23] Ibid., p. 34.

[24] Ibid.

[25] Ibid., p. 36.

[26] Ibid.

[27] Ibid., p. 118.

[28] Ibid., p. 113.

[29] Ibid., p. 133.

[30] Cleanth Brooks, *The Well Wrought Urn* (New York: Harcourt, Brace and World, 1947), p. 202.

[31] Ibid., p. 210.

[32] Ibid., p. 203.

[33] Ibid., p. 195.

[34] R. P. Blackmur, *The Lion and the Honeycomb* (New York: Harcourt, Brace and World, 1955), p. 183.

[35] Ibid., p. 188.

[36] ed. R. S. Crane (Chicago: University of Chicago Press, 1952).

[37] Elder Olson, "William Empson, Contemporary Criticism, and Poetic Diction," in *Critics and Criticism*, p. 45.

[38] Ibid., p. 55.

39 R. S. Crane, *The Languages of Criticism and the Structure of Poetry* (Toronto: University of Toronto Press, 1953), p. 35.

40 Ibid., p. 15.

41 Ibid., p. 48.

42 Ibid., p. 56.

43 Wimsatt and Brooks, p. 753 (The "Epilogue" was written by Wimsatt).

44 Ibid.

45 Northrop Frye, *The Well Tempered Critic* (Bloomington: University of Indiana Press, 1963), p. 140.

46 "The Critical Path," in Gregory T. Polletta, ed., *Issues in Contemporary Literary Criticism* (Boston: Little, Brown and Company, 1973), p. 56.

47 Northrop Frye, *Anatomy of Criticism* (Princeton: Princeton University Press, 1957), p. 113.

48 Ibid., p. 342.

49 Ibid., pp. 96–97.

50 Stanley Edgar Hyman, *The Armed Vision* (New York: Alfred A. Knopf, 1948), p. 6.

51 "The Critical Path," Polletta, p. 52.

52 Northrop Frye, *Secular Scripture: A Study of the Structure of Romance* (Cambridge, Mass.: Harvard University Press, 1976), p. 36.

53 Ibid., p. 36.

54 Geoffrey Hartmen, *Criticism in the Wilderness* (New Haven and London: Yale University Press, 1980), p. 14.

55 Jean-Paul Sartre, *What Is Literature?* (New York: Philosophical Library, 1949), p. 38.

56 Ibid., p. 39.

57 Ibid.

58 Ibid., p. 40.

59 Ibid., p. 44.

60 Ibid.

61 Ibid., p. 45.

62 Ibid.

63 Ibid., p. 48.

64 Ibid., p. 49.

65 Ibid., p. 48.

66 Ibid., p. 63.

67 *Being and Nothingness*, trans. Hazel Barnes (New York: Philosophical Library, 1956), p. 374.

68 *Essays in Aesthetics*, trans. Wade Baskin (New York: Philosophical Library, 1963) p. 32.

69 *What Is Literature?*, p. 76.

70 Ibid., p. 62.

71 Ibid., p. 76.

72 Maurice Merleau-Ponty, "Sartre et l'ultra-bolchevisme," *Les Aventures de la dialectique* (Paris: Gallimard, 1955), p. 189.

73 Ibid., p. 190.

74 Eugenio Donato, "Language, Vision, and Phenomenology," in Richard Macksey, ed., *Velocities of Change* (Baltimore: The Johns Hopkins University Press, 1974), p. 295.

75 Maurice Merleau-Ponty, *Phenomenology of Perception* (London: Routledge and Kegan Paul, 1962), pp. 150–51.

76 Maurice Merleau-Ponty, *Signs* (Evanston, Ill.: Northwestern University Press, 1964), p. 96.

77 Martin Heidegger, *Poetry, Language, Thought*, trans. Albert Hofstatter (New York: Harper and Row, 1971), p. 189.

78 Sarah Lawall, *Critics of Consciousness* (Cambridge: Harvard University Press, 1968).

79 J. Hillis Miller, "The Geneva School," in *Modern French Criticism*, ed. John K. Simon (Chicago: University of Chicago Press, 1977), p. 292.

80 Ibid., p. 277.

81 Albert Béguin, quoted in Ibid., p. 278.

82 Ibid., p. 279.

83 Georges Poulet, *The Interior Distance*, trans. Elliott Coleman (Ann Arbor, Mich.: University of Michigan Press, 1964), p. vii.

[84] Georges Poulet, "The Phenomenology of Reading," printed in Hazard Adams, p. 1213.

[85] Ibid., pp. 1213–22.

[86] J. Hillis Miller, *Charles Dickens: The World of His Novels* (Cambridge, Mass.: Harvard University Press, 1958), p. ix.

[87] Jonathan Culler, *Structuralist Poetics* (Ithaca: Cornell University Press, 1975), p. 28.

[88] Ibid., p. 29.

[89] Fredric Jameson, *The Prison-House of Language* (Princeton, N.J.: Princeton University Press, 1972), p. 11.

[90] Ferdinand de Saussure, *Course in General Linguistics*, ed. Charles Bally and Gilbert Sechehaye, trans. Wade Baskin (New York: McGraw-Hill, 1966), p. 19.

[91] Ibid., p. 9.

[92] Ibid., p. 87.

[93] Ibid., p. 117.

[94] Ibid., p. 120.

[95] John Sturrock, *Structuralism and Since* (Oxford: Oxford University Press, 1979), pp. 13–14.

[96] Saussure, *Course*, pp. 71, 75.

[97] Jacques Lacan, "The Insistence of the Letter in the Unconscious," in Jacques Ehrmann, ed., *Structuralism* (Garden City, New York: Doubleday and Company, Inc., 1970), p. 137.

[98] Claude Lévi-Strauss, *The Raw and the Cooked: Introduction to a Science of Mythology*, trans. John and Doreen Weightman (New York: Harper and Row, 1973), p. 18.

[99] Ibid., p. 21.

[100] Boris Eichenbaum, "Theory of the 'Formal Method,' " reprinted in Hazard Adams, p. 831.

[101] Ibid., p. 841.

[102] Quotations from Shklovsky are in Ibid., pp. 833–35.

[103] Tzvetan Todorov, *Grammaire du Décaméron*, quoted in Frank Lentricchia, *After the New Criticism* (Chicago: University of Chicago Press, 1980), p. 116.

[104] Roland Barthes, "Criticism as Language," in David Lodge, ed., *20th Century Literary Criticism* (London and New York: Longman, 1972), p. 649.

[105] Ibid., p. 651.

[106] For a different position *see* E. D. Hirsch, Jr., "Objective Interpretation," in *Validity in Interpretation* (New Haven, Conn.: Yale University Press, 1967).

[107] "Criticism as Language," p. 651.

[108] Ibid., p. 650.

[109] Roland Barthes, S/Z, trans. Richard Howard (New York: Hill and Wang, 1974) pp. 16–17.

[110] Roland Barthes, "The Structuralist Activity," in Hazard Adams, p. 1196.

[111] Roland Barthes, *Critical Essays*, trans. Richard Howard (Evanston, Ill.: Northwestern University Press, 1972), p. 38.

[112] John Sturrock, "Roland Barthes," in *Structuralism and Since*, p. 69.

[113] Alain Robbe-Grillet, "A Future for the Novel," in Lodge, p. 470.

[114] Lentricchia, p. 141.

[115] "The Structuralist Activity," p. 1197.

[116] S/Z, p. 3.

[117] Lentricchia, p. 159.

[118] Quoted in Sturrock, p. 164.

PART THREE

The Reconsideration
of a Great Book

Rethinking the *Pensées* of Pascal

Otto Bird

Otto Bird, who had a discussion of ethics in last year's issue of *The Great Ideas Today,* of which he is consulting editor, has for many years been associated with Mortimer J. Adler in editorial projects. Among them have been the *Syntopicon* for *Great Books of the Western World,* of which he was associate editor, and the fifteenth edition of the *Encyclopaedia Britannica,* especially its *Propaedia,* to which he was a major contributor.

Educated at the University of Michigan and the University of Toronto, where he received a doctorate in philosophy and literature, Mr. Bird taught for many years at the University of Notre Dame and was director of the General Program of Liberal Studies there until his retirement in 1963. In 1970 he was appointed university professor of arts and letters at Notre Dame, a position he held until his retirement in 1980.

Devoted as he is to the cause of education through great books, Mr. Bird has special interest and competence in both medieval studies and in logic. Among his published books are one on *The Canzone d'Amore of Guido Cavalcanti* (1942) and another on *Syllogistic Logic and Its Extensions* (1964). He is the author as well of *Cultures in Conflict* (1976), a study of the three major historical paradigms, as he calls them, of our intellectual culture—the literary humanistic ideal of antiquity, the theological ideal of the Middle Ages, and the scientific ideal of the modern world—and of the conflicts to which, as forms of knowledge, they have given rise.

More than 300 years after the death of Pascal, and after numerous editions of his writings, especially of the *Pensées,* many of which have extensive commentaries, one might think that there would be little need or occasion to reconsider and to rethink their text. Yet recent scholarship has clearly shown that such a need exists. It arises from examination of the mass of papers and notes that Pascal left upon his untimely death in 1662 at the age of thirty-nine, which were so zealously treasured that they are still extant and today constitute one of the most prized possessions of the Bibliothèque Nationale in Paris. Because of this, scholars can still inspect Pascal's notes and papers in his own handwriting. Recent renewed studies of these have resulted in a better and more accurate understanding of the condition of his papers and of the way they were left at the time of his death. As a consequence of this study we can now have a clearer and more detailed understanding of the project at which he was working during the last years of his life, and which has come to be known, since the first published edition in 1670, as the *Pensées.*

To ascertain Pascal's intentions for this project, it is necessary to know the state and especially the arrangement of his manuscripts at the time he died. This is not easy to determine. Although the notes in his own hand are extant, they are not now in their original state, but instead exist in the arrangement that was given to them some fifty years later. At that time, the Abbé Louis Périer, Pascal's last surviving nephew, in order to assure their preservation, donated them to the Benedictine Abbey of Saint-Germain-des-Prés in Paris. For this purpose he had the various notes and fragments in his possession pasted together and arranged in an album, which he deposited in the library in 1711. His collection now bears the title, in French, *Original of the Pensées of Pascal* (Mss 9202). It consists of fragments of various sizes and shapes, some quite small, while others run to several pages, seemingly arranged in an arbitrary way. Indeed, judged by the state of the fragments contained in this original collection, one might well accept as literally true the statement made in the preface to the first edition of the work, that the papers had been left

> "without any order and without any sequence because they were only the first expressions of his thought that he had written on little pieces of paper just as they entered his mind. And all was so incomplete and so badly written that one had all the difficulty in the world to decipher them."

Because of this alleged confusion of the fragments, editors from the time of the first edition late in the seventeenth century until deep into the twentieth century have felt free to arrange them in any order they liked. As Pascal himself noted, "words differently arranged have a different meaning, and meanings differently arranged have different effects" (No. 23). Editors have accordingly arranged and published the fragments to meet their own predilections. As a result the *Pensées* have been edited so as to present Pascal as a Jansenist, a Protestant, a Catholic, even a skeptic, until the extreme is reached of claiming that every reader must make his own *Pensées*.

The edition that has become the standard one for the twentieth century was made by the French philosopher M. Léon Brunschvicg in 1897. Brunschvicg claims that he has grouped the various fragments together according to their intrinsic significance so as to show their "logical continuity," but he acknowledges that it is not the order that Pascal himself would have followed—the "secret of that plan" having been carried by Pascal with him "into his tomb."*

It is true that Pascal died before he could write the book that he was working on, and hence it is impossible to know the plan that the book eventually would have followed. However, it is not entirely accurate to claim that whatever the plan Pascal had in mind, however tentative it might have been, was a secret that disappeared with him on his death. For there exists more and even better evidence of the state in which he left his papers than that provided by the Original Collection. This other evidence is to be found in the two Copies of the fragments that were made shortly after his death, and that were treasured, as were their originals, by his sister Gilberte Périer and her family until they ultimately found their way to the national library, where they still remain. Like the originals, these Copies have been consulted by various editors of the *Pensées* mainly for the help they provide in deciphering Pascal's difficult handwriting, not for the light they can throw upon his intentions. It is only recently, almost 300 years after they were written, that the true import of the Copies has come to be understood and appreciated.

The preface to the first edition stated that, since it was known that Pascal had been working on a book on religion, "great care was taken after his death to collect all the writings that he had made on this matter.... The first thing that was done was to make a copy of them just as they were and in the same confusion in which they had been found." The Copies now extant date from that time, but they reveal not "confusion" but a very definite organization. Hence later editors concluded that these Copies were preliminary arrangements made by the literary executors in compiling their first edition. Recent study of them, however, has established, to the satisfaction of most, if not all, Pascal scholars, that these Copies are indeed the first ones that were made and that the classification

---

*An English translation of the Brunschvicg edition is published in *GBWW*, Vol. 33, pp. 169–352.

manifest in them is the work of Pascal himself, not of his first editors. But before the evidence for this conclusion can be weighed, one needs to know something of the organization of the Copies and their contents.

Since the two Copies are almost identical, there is no need to consider but one of them. For this purpose the First Copy is preferable and henceforth will be the only one in question, unless otherwise noted. This First Copy (Bib. Nat. Mss. 9203) consists of 472 pages in which sixty-one individual sections are carefully and clearly distinguished. These sixty-one sections can be divided in turn into two large groups. The first group consists of twenty-seven sections, occupying pages 1–188, each of which bears a title, starting with "Order" and ending with "Conclusion." The second group consists of thirty-four sections, occupying pages 189-472, none of which contains a title except for one entitled "Miscellaneous." Each of the sixty-one sections contains copies of the notes and fragments, the originals of which are contained, with few exceptions, in the autograph collection.

As evidence of Pascal's intentions for his projected work, the first group, consisting of twenty-seven sections containing some 382 notes or *pensées,* is the more significant. For this first group also contains a covering table of contents that arranges the twenty-seven sections by titles into two columns, with ten in the first column and the remainder in the second as though to divide the whole into two parts.

The Table of Contents
in the First Copy

1. Order
2. Vanity
3. Wretchedness
4. Boredom
5. Sound opinions of the people (crossed out) Reasons of effects
6. Greatness
7. Contrarieties
8. Diversion
9. Philosophers
10. The Sovereign Good

11. A.P.R.
12. Beginning
13. Submission and use of reason
14. Excellence
15. Transition
15b Nature is corrupt
16. Falsity of other religions
17. Lovable religion
18. Foundation
19. Figurative law
20. Rabbinism
21. Perpetuity
22. Proofs of Moses
23. Proofs of Jesus Christ
24. Prophecies
25. Figures
26. Christian Morality
27. Conclusion

Clearly, the papers organized by titles into these twenty-seven sections represent an attempt at classification. But what reason is there to think that it is Pascal's own doing? Turning back again to the preface of the 1670 edition, we find that the papers are described as being "found all threaded together in various bundles" *(enfilés en diverses liasses)*. From other sources it is known that one way of filing papers in the seventeenth century was to use a needle and thread to catch into one bundle all the papers that one wanted together, maintaining a given sequence. That Pascal himself followed this practice is indicated by the fact that holes such as would be made by a needle and thread can still be seen in many of the autographs in the Original Collection.

There is also a significant difference between the fragments of the first group and those of the second. The originals of the first twenty-seven sections, with few exceptions, consist of pieces of paper cut to fit the size of the text, and each piece contains only one note. Those in the second group, however, consist not only of cut papers but also of large sheets which often contain several different notes. Folio 453 of the Original, for example, consists of no fewer than ten different notes written in little clumps in various places and at different angles on one large sheet of paper. From this it appears that Pascal did not write his notes on little scraps of paper, as claimed in the first preface, but rather that he used a large sheet on which he made many notes, which he then cut apart and divided and classified into threaded bundles. This procedure would account for the many different shapes and sizes of the various fragments. The difference between the two groups is carefully reproduced in the Copy, which shows the care that was taken to represent the papers exactly as they were found.

The table of contents reveals the same care to copy exactly. It contains two "15s" (a 15*bis* as well as a 15), with the title "Nature is corrupt." There is no bundle corresponding to this title. However, there is a note that bears this very title, but it is located in the first section of the second group, which indicates that at one time Section 15*bis* was not empty. Thus the copyist faithfully reproduced the original title before him in the table of contents, even though no corresponding bundle existed for it.

It should also be noted that many of the individual *pensées* clearly indicate that Pascal in making a note had some sort of definite plan in mind. Thus notes are assigned to a "first" or "second part" (Nos. 60, 62, 242, 425). Some notes refer to "chapters" by titles that are the same as those that appear in the Copy's table of contents (No. 570). Other notes contain cross-references to titles that appear in the table (No. 747). And many notes bear titles identical with those in the table (Nos. 246-247: "Order").

All this evidence points to the conclusion that the sections of the Copy correspond to the "bundles" of papers found at the time of Pascal's death, and that the first twenty-seven of them, with titles corresponding to those in the table of contents, constitute so many chapters in the book that he was planning. The fragments contained in the second large group consist of notes that for one reason or another were never allotted their place among the twenty-seven chapters.

Of course, one may acknowledge the validity of these arguments and yet still ask: What difference does it make to our understanding and appreciation of the *Pensées?* To answer this question we must consider the twenty-seven chapters, their order and their content as indicated by the notes Pascal had gathered together for each of them. So that the reader of the Brunschvicg edition may know what *pensées* are included in each of the twenty-seven chapters, a concordance of them is hereby provided, by chapter title from the Copy and by Brunschvicg number the notes contained in each of them.

The Table of Concordance

1. *Order:* 596, 227, 244, 184, 247, 60, 248, 602, 291, 167, 246, 187
2. *Vanity:* 133, 338, 410, 161, 113, 955, 318, 292, 381, 367, 67, 127, 308, 330, 354, 436, 156, 320, 149, cf. 317, 374, 376, 117, 164, 158, 71, 141, 134, 69, 207, 136, 82, 83, 163, 172, 366, 132, 305, 293, 388
3. *Wretchedness:* 429, 112, 111, 181, 379, 332, 296, 294, 309, 177, 151, 295, 115, 326, 879, 205, cf. 174, cf. 165, 405, 66, 110, 454, 389, 73
4. *Boredom and the Essential Qualities of Man:* 152, 126, 128
5. *Reasons of Effects:* 317, 299, 271, 327, 79, 878, 297, 307, 302, 315, 337, 336, 335, 328, 313, 316, 329, 334, 80, 80 & 536, 467, 324, 759, 298, 322
6. *Greatness:* 342, 403, 343, cf. 339, 392, 282, 339, 344, 348, 397, 349, 398, 409, 402
7. *Contrarieties:* 423, 148, 418, 416, 157, 125, 92, 93, 415, 396, 116, 420, 434
8. *Diversion:* 170, 168, 169, 469, 139, 142, 166, 143
9. *Philosophers:* 466, 509, 463, 464, 360, 461, 350
10. *The Sovereign Good:* 361, 425
11. *At Port Royal:* 430
12. *Beginning:* 226, 211, 213, 238, 237, 281, 190, 225, 236, 204, 257, 221, 189, 200, 218, 210, 183
13. *Submission and the Use of Reason in Which True Christianity Consists:* 269, 224, 812, 268, 696, 185, 273, 270, 563, 261, 384, cf. 747, 256, 838, 255, 272, 253, 811, 265, 947, 254, 267
14. *Excellence of This Way of Proving God:* 547, 543, 549, 527
15. *Transition from the Knowledge of Man to God:* 98, 208, 37, 86, cf. 162, 693, 72, 347, 206, 517
15b. *Nature is Corrupt*

16. *Falseness of Other Religions*:   595, 592, 489, 235, 597, 435, 599, 451, 453, 528, 551, 491, 433, 493, 650, 598, 251, 468
17. *To Make Religion Lovable*:   774, 747
18. *The Foundations of Religion and Reply to Objections*:   570, 816, 789, 523, 223, 751, 444, cf. 430, 511, 566, 796, 581, 771, 578, 795, 645, 510, 705, 765, 585, 601, 228
19. *That the Law was Figurative*:   647, 657, 674, 653, 681, 667, 900, 648, 679, 649, 758, 662, 684, 728, 685, 678, 757, 762, 686, 746, 677, 719, 680, 683, 692, 670, 545, 687, 745, 642, 643, 691
20. *Rabbinism*:   635, 446
21. *Perpetuity*:   690, 614, 613, 616, 655, 605, 867, 609, 607, 689, 608
22. *Proofs of Moses*:   626, 587, 624, cf. 204, 703, 629, 625, 702
23. *Proofs of Jesus Christ*:   283, 742, 786, 772, 809, 799, 743, 638, 763, 764, 793, 797, 801, 640, 697, 569, 639, 752, 800, 701, 755, 699, 178, 600, 802
24. *Prophecies*:   773, 730, 733, 694, 770, 732, 734, 725, 748, 710, 708, 716, 706, 709, 753, 724, 738, 720, 723, 637, 695, 756, cf. 726, 729, 735, 718
25. *Particular Figures*:   652, 623
26. *Christian Morality*:   537, 526, 529, 524, 767, 539, 541, 538, 481, 482, 209, 472, 914, 249, 496, cf. 747, 672, 474, 611, 480, 473, 483, 476, 475, 503, 484
27. *Conclusions*:   280, 470, 825, 284, 286, 287

The Plan for the Apology

The friends and family of Pascal provide external and contemporary evidence that during his last years he had been working on an *Apology for the Christian Religion,* that he had even presented a plan for it to his friends at the Convent of Port Royal. The notes headed "APR" (esp. No. 430) are thought to be the notes that he prepared for this conference.

The basis on which he proposed to build his defence is given in a note in the first chapter entitled "Order," in which he wrote:

> Men despise religion; they hate it and fear it is true. To remedy this, we must begin by showing that religion is not contrary to reason; that it is venerable, to inspire respect for it; then we must make it lovable, to make good men hope it is true; finally, we must prove it is true. Venerable, because it has perfect knowledge of man; lovable because it promises the true good. (No. 187)

Other notes indicate that Pascal conceived of the work as having two parts (No. 60). Observing this indication and reading the note just cited in light of the Copy's table of contents, we then obtain the following structure as the overall plan that Pascal proposed for his *Apology*.

To show that the Christian religion is venerable and lovable because it has perfect knowledge of man and promises his true good, it is first necessary to describe the nature and condition of man and of his search for the true good. This task is undertaken by Pascal in the first part corresponding to the first ten chapters listed in the first column of the table of contents. Part One is in turn divided into two parts according as it addresses first the problem of man and second that of happiness and the sovereign good.

The second part of the book was to be the properly apologetic part and would have consisted of Chapters 11 through 27, so arranged, as listed in the second column of the table of contents. In this part three main tasks are laid down: first, to show that belief in the Christian religion is not unreasonable; second, that religion is venerable and lovable in being able to explain the contradictory condition of man and to provide a means of obtaining his true good; and third, to prove that it is true by appealing to the historical evidence provided in Sacred Scripture.

With this view of the overall plan of the work we can now turn to consider in some detail how the project was to be realized. My exposition of it will be based exclusively on the notes classified by chapter in the First Copy but cited according to the Brunschvicg enumeration as translated in *GBWW*, Vol. 33.

Part One of the Apology

Part One is governed by two principles: the general theme of the greatness and wretchedness of man—the *grandeur et misère* of the condition in which he now exists; and a method of reasoning about these facts which is called, somewhat obscurely, the "reason of effects." (After an introductory chapter on the order to be followed in the work, Chapters 2–7 are concerned with the nature and condition of man, followed in Chapters 8–10 by a consideration of the end of man, his good and happiness.) From the notes it appears that the theme of the greatness and wretchedness of man was to have pervaded the entire work. But in Part One it is *misère* that is the controlling idea. This is first contrasted to greatness as littleness, even nothingness, and then in the later sections dealing with the good it is opposed to happiness.

According to Pascal, *misère* is a wider and more complex notion than that of human *grandeur,* and three chapters are devoted to it. It is identified with vanity in Chapter 2 and with boredom in Chapter 4 and is given a strict sense in Chapter 3 as *misère*—wretchedness. In the strict sense, to be wretched and in a state of *misère* is to have the will for something without the power to obtain it (No. 389): to want to have complete certainty, to be completely happy, to enjoy immortality, and yet to be unable to achieve any of these. Tyranny—that is, the tyrant's condition—is cited by Pascal as an example of such wretchedness inasmuch as it consists in "the wish to have in one way what can only be had in another;" e.g., " 'I am fair, therefore I must be feared. I am strong, therefore I must be loved' " (No. 332).

Vanity offers another aspect of wretchedness, and under this title Pascal included the long fragment headed "Imagination" (No. 82). By this term he understood false opinions, prejudice, vain fancies: "If the greatest philosopher in the world find himself upon a plank wider than actually necessary, but hanging over a precipice, his imagination will prevail, though his reason convince him of his safety. . . . Every one knows that the sight of cats or rats, the crushing of a coal, etc., may unhinge the reason" (No. 82).

Boredom supplies still another indication of man's wretchedness or *misère*, and Chapter 4 which bears this title cites as an instance "the weariness which is felt by us in leaving pursuits to which we are attached. A man dwells at home with pleasure; but if he sees a woman who charms him, or if he enjoys himself in play for five or six days, he is miserable if he returns to his former way of living" (No. 128).

Wretchedness, however, does not tell the whole story about man, and Pascal proposed to show the opposite quality of greatness by arguing according to the method of the "reasons of effects." To this topic Chapter 5 is devoted as providing a transition from the three previous chapters to Chapter 6 on greatness. The method is described as a "continual alternation of pro and con" (No. 328). Thus an effect is noted, such as that people respect wealth and power, which constitutes the first "pro"; against this it is argued by the "semi-learned" that wealth and power are external often chance acquisitions bearing no necessary relation to intrinisic merit—the "con"; the really learned, however, uphold the common opinion, but for another better reason, namely that respect for wealth and power afford some assurance against the great evil of civil war—a "pro" again.

Apply this method of arguing to the wretchedness of man, and one has to acknowledge also his greatness, as Chapter 6 does. Vanity, boredom, frustrated desire are observed facts about man; and to know that they are witnesses of misery is to be miserable, "but it is also being great to know that one is miserable." A tree does not know that it is miserable: "The greatness of man is great in that he knows himself to be miserable" (No. 397).

Since Pascal located the greatness of man in knowledge, he was obliged to meet the skeptic's claim that man cannot achieve any certain truth. Thus this same Chapter 6 on greatness contains one of the most famous fragments concerning knowledge through the heart:

We know truth, not only by the reason, but also by the heart, and it is in this last way that we know first principles; and reason, which has no part in it, tries in vain to impugn them. The skeptics, who have only this for their object, labour to no purpose. (No. 282).

As examples, Pascal cites the fact that we know when we are not dreaming and that we recognize space, time, motion, and number without being able to demonstrate their existence. By knowing through the heart man thus understands the immediate intuition of first principles which are self-evident and more certain than any of the knowledge that depends upon them. In this sense, knowledge through the heart corresponds to *nous,* or understanding, in Aristotle's philosophy. But Pascal means something still more, for, just as the heart is thought of as the seat of love, so too by knowledge *through* the heart is to be understood a knowledge that depends upon love as a prerequisite, such as is preeminently the case of our knowledge of God, i.e., of the Christian God. Pascal was more than willing to utilize the arguments of the skeptics—especially as he found them in the essays of Montaigne—to show up the folly of men and to humble reason, but he was far from being a skeptic himself.

Chapter 7, entitled "Contrarieties" or "Contradictions," was meant to provide a preliminary conclusion to the consideration of the theme of *grandeur et misère.* In it Pascal stressed the need to recognize that man is both great and wretched and that one must not be singled out to the exclusion of the other. It is a temptation especially of philosophers, according to Pascal, to emphasize one of the opposites and to neglect the other.

Man must not think that he is on a level either with the brutes or with the angels, nor must he be ignorant of both sides of his nature; but he must know both (No. 418).

With Chapter 8, entitled "Diversion," Pascal began consideration of the sovereign good. Here the opposite to misery is taken to be happiness. It may seem somewhat odd to begin an analysis of happiness with an account of diversion. But by this Pascal understood what we would call "having a good time" in the enjoyment of many pleasant experiences and activities, and there is no doubt that many people do equate happiness with having a good time. Such Pascal takes to be a fact about human nature, an "effect" for which he argues to a "reason of the effect." It is no hard matter to show that man's true happiness cannot consist in the pursuit of diversion, and many philosophers have done so—such is the "con" to the first "pro." But as a second "pro" to that "con" Pascal then asserts that we are wrong to blame those who think it does: "Their error does not lie in seeking excitement, if they seek it only as a diversion; the evil is that they seek it as if the possession of the objects of their quest would make them really happy" (No. 139).

Pascal, in fact, has more scorn for the philosopher-censurers in this connection than for the censured. In Chapter 9 he criticizes the philosophers, especially the Stoics, for maintaining that man can find his true happiness within himself and within his own power. People are right, he says, in feeling that "we must seek our happiness outside ourselves. . . . And thus philosophers have said in vain: 'Retire within yourselves, you will find your good there.' We do not believe them, and those who believe them are the most empty and the most foolish" (No. 464). The reason behind this charge by Pascal is provided in his consideration of the sovereign good, to which the final chapter of Part One is devoted.

His argument there can be reduced to three assertions and a conclusion, thus:

1) "All men seek happiness . . . without exception."

2) All finite goods and any collection of them are "all inadequate, because the infinite abyss [that there is in man] can only be filled by an infinite and immutable object."

3) The good that can satisfy the desire for happiness must be a universal good " such as all can possess at once, without diminution and without envy, and which no one can lose against his will" (No. 425).

The conclusion is that there is only one good that can satisfy these conditions: the Christian God who is both a *totum bonum,* as containing all real goods, and a *summum bonum,* as the highest of goods. However, the arguments to prove this conclusion are still to come, as belonging to Part Two of the projected work.

Part Two of the Apology

Chapter 11, which opens this part, contains a preview of the whole and draws clearly the main lines of Pascal's proposed defence of the Christian faith. The Christian God is a hidden God, but He is not so hidden that He cannot be found, since He is " 'willing to appear openly to those who seek Him with all their heart, and to be hidden from those who flee from Him with all their heart' " (No. 430). Reason alone is insufficient; He can only be found through faith, which depends on a proper disposition of the heart. Through faith, man can achieve understanding of his own contradictory state and also find means to overcome it. For man is not now in the state he was meant to be, but he has fallen from greatness into such wretchedness that by himself he can neither know nor achieve his true good. God, however, has come to the aid of man in the person of Jesus

Christ, who has made it possible for man to recover his original greatness. For Pascal the whole of the Christian faith thus turns about the fall in Adam and the redemption through Jesus Christ.

The plan he drew up for the defence of this faith contains three main parts: first, in which he endeavored to show that it is reasonable, which is the task of Chapters 12–14; second, where he asserted it is venerable and lovable, which is done in Chapters 15–17; third, where he argued that it is true by an analysis of the historical proofs contained in the Bible, the task of Chapters 18–25.

Pascal proposed to begin his defence of the faith by showing that it is unreasonable not even to consider whether the Christian faith is true. The notes gathered for this Chapter 12 emphasize especially the fact of man's mortality and hence by implication the promise that Christ has overcome death and so has made possible an eternal life. Whether or not our soul is immortal makes a difference to how we live in this world: "It concerns all our life to know whether the soul be mortal or immortal" (No. 218). Our position in this life is compared by Pascal to that of a man imprisoned in a dungeon who lies under sentence and has but an hour to learn it and successfully obtain its repeal. In such a situation, he "would act unnaturally," and hence also unreasonably, to spend "that hour, not in ascertaining his sentence, but in playing piquet" (No. 200).

Once he had shown that it is not unreasonable to consider the Christian faith, Pascal undertook to argue for the reasonableness of believing, which is the task of Chapter 13, entitled "Submission and Use of Reason." By reason itself we can distinguish three rules:

We must know where to doubt, where to feel certain, where to
submit," and one breaks them [the rules] and "so understands not the
force of reason . . . . either by affirming everything as demonstrative,
from want of knowing what demonstration is; or by doubting everything,
from want of knowing where to submit; or by submitting in everything,
from want of knowing where they must judge (No. 268).

In short, to be reasonable one must know when to act the skeptic, when the mathematician, and when the Christian.

Faith, according to Pascal, provides the most excellent way of coming to God, which is the import of the short title "Excellence" for Chapter 14, given in the table of contents. The metaphysical proofs of God are dismissed as of little worth. On the one hand they are "so remote from the reasoning of men, and so complicated, that they make little impression," whereas if, on the other hand, they should make an impression on some, it lasts "only during the moment that they see such demonstration; but an hour afterwards they fear that they have been mistaken" (No. 543). The only sure way is to know God through Jesus Christ; that way provides a "middle course, because in Him we find both God and our misery" (No. 527). We thus avoid the pride that comes from emphasizing the knowledge that we have of God apart from our misery, and the despair that comes from knowledge of our misery without that of God.

The transition from a knowledge of man to a knowledge of God, which is the concern of Chapter 15, is accomplished by considering the relation between man and the natural world. "For, in fact, what is man in nature?" Pascal asks, and responds: "A Nothing in comparison with the Infinite, and an All in comparison with the Nothing, a mean between nothing and everything." Incapable of comprehending the extremes, "we sail within a vast sphere, ever drifting in uncertainty." But although such is our natural condition, it is "most contrary to our inclination," which is to "find solid ground and an ultimate sure foundation whereon to build a tower reaching to the Infinite" (No. 72). This disproportion between nature and inclination offers another aspect of our wretchedness; yet the fact that we can know it is itself an index of our greatness. To take note of this disproportion provides a transition to knowledge of God, for it is only through His revelation that we can make sense of it.

The next three chapters (15*bis*, 16, 17) were intended to show that Christianity is venerable in that it can inspire respect, and lovable in that it can attract the heart of man. The first of these, entitled "Nature is Corrupt" (15*bis*), now contains no notes, but in it Pascal would likely have shown how the doctrine of original sin and the corruption of nature furnishes an explanation of man's misery and wretchedness. The importance of the fall for Pascal is apparent not only from the many references he makes to it, but also from the fact that Chapter 20, entitled "Rabbinism," is mainly concerned with noting that the Jews have an ample tradition of the doctrine of original sin (No. 446).

Chapter 17 proposed to "Make Religion Lovable," and would have done so by showing that the redemption accomplished by Jesus Christ enables man to enjoy eternal happiness:

> The carnal Jews and the heathens have their calamities, and Christians
> also. There is no Redeemer for the heathen, for they do not so much as
> hope for one. There is no Redeemer for the Jews; they hope for Him
> in vain. There is a Redeemer only for Christians (No. 747).

Chapter 16 in between these two aimed to show the "Falsity of Other Religions." In it Pascal argued that only Christianity has known our nature, "its greatness and littleness, and the reason for both" (No. 433), and that it alone answers to the needs of all men, the learned as well as the common people: "Being composed of externals and internals . . . . it raises the common people to the internal, and humbles the proud to the external; it is not perfect without the two, for the people must understand the spirit of the letter, and the learned must submit their spirit to the letter" (No. 251). Other notes for this chapter indicate that Pascal was particularly concerned to answer the claims made by the Islāmic religion (Nos. 595, 597, 598, 599).

The third and principal section of Part Two was to provide proof for the truth of Christianity and is the concern of Chapters 18–27. The main burden of the argument is that the Bible, properly interpreted, contains the historical evidence that Jesus Christ was indeed the Messiah foretold by the prophets and the redeemer of fallen man.

Chapter 18, entitled "Foundations," compares various religions with respect to their foundations: The pagen religions of the past were based upon oracles that no longer exist and of which there is no record. Islām has its foundation in the Koran and Mahomet, but this leader was not foretold as a prophet, nor did he provide miracles as proof of his claim. The Jewish religion as contained "in the tradition of the Holy Bible," and distinct from the practices of the people is wholly admirable: "It is the most ancient book in the world, and the most authentic" (No. 601). Hence the Christian religion, which is founded on that tradition, is "so divine that another divine religion has only been the foundation of it" (No. 601).

The Bible as the foundation of Christianity also furnishes the evidence to prove its truth. But for this purpose one must know how to interpret it properly, and that is impossible, according to Pascal, unless it is understood "That the Law was Figurative," which is the title of Chapter 19. "The Old Testament is a cipher" (No. 691), for the deciphering of which a key is needed, since there is a hidden meaning underlying the literal one on its surface. In the Scriptures as in the world, God is a hidden God but not so hidden that he cannot be found. The key has been given by Jesus Christ and the Apostles: "They broke the seal; He rent the veil, and revealed the spirit" (No. 678).

However, it is necessary to distinguish carefully between what is to be interpreted literally and what is to be taken figuratively as a type. According to Pascal, the *manner* of the coming of the Messiah was hidden in a figure, with the result that the literal-minded would not accept Him when He appeared as the Suffering Servant, whereas the *time* of His coming was literally and precisely predicted. This double fact accounts for both His reception and rejection:

> The wicked, taking the promised blessings for material blessings, have fallen into error, in spite of the clear prediction of the time; and the good have not fallen in error. For the understanding of the promised blessings depends on the heart, which calls *good* that which it loves; but the understanding of the promised time does not depend on the heart. And thus the clear prediction of the time, and the obscure prediction of the blessings, deceive the wicked alone (No. 758).

Reason can determine the literal and historical meaning of the text, but it takes the heart, which is not against reason, to reach the hidden and figurative.

Although figurative or spiritual interpretation is essential, Pascal was well aware that it could be used excessively. There are two errors to avoid: "1. To take everything literally. 2. To take everything spiritually" (No. 648). Furthermore, the notes put together for the proof of Christianity rely very heavily upon the literal historical truth of the Bible. This reliance appears especially strong in the claim made for the antiquity of Christianity and in the historical fulfillment of the prophecies made for it. Thus Chapter 21, entitled "Perpetuity," maintained that "the Messiah has always been believed in" (No. 616). The prophets and holy men of Israel believed in Him as one to come and patiently awaited that coming; "He came at length in the fullness of time," was believed in and worshipped, and ever since "this Church, which worships Him who has always been worshipped, has endured uninterruptedly" (No. 613). But the strongest proof of all is to be found in the historical fulfillment of the prophecies, not only of the coming of Jesus Christ, but of its consequences throughout the world:

> That the temples of the idols would be cast down, and that among all nations and in all places of the earth . . . . destroying the worship of Moses in Jerusalem, which was its centre, where He made His first Church; and also the worship of idols in Rome, the centre of it, where He made His chief Church (No. 730).

The high importance that Pascal attributed to the prophecies is indicated by the place assigned to them in the projected work. The chapter devoted to them (Chap. 24) follows immediately after those giving proofs of Moses and of Jesus Christ (Chaps. 22–23). As a complement of the chapter on prophecies to mark the completion of the proofs, Pascal proposed to consider "Particular Figures" or types (Chap. 25). By this term he meant prophecies that were made and fulfilled literally in the Old Testament and figuratively in the New Testament. For Pascal, "the accomplished prophecies constitute a lasting miracle" (No. 838).

The penultimate chapter proposed to bring the history down to the present by considering "Christian Morality." Just as happiness, according to Pascal, must be such that many can share it in common while depriving no one of it, so too morality is made to rest upon a corporate bond. "To regulate the love which we owe to ourselves, we must imagine a body full of thinking members, for we are members of the whole, and must see how each member should love itself" (No. 474). Now it is the nature of a member, such as a hand or a foot, "to have neither life, being, nor movement, except through the spirit of the body, and for the body." Pascal was evidently thinking of the mystical body of which St. Paul wrote (I Corinthians 12:12–30) for he concluded the note by writing: "We love ourselves, because we are members of Jesus Christ. We love Jesus Christ, because He is the body of which we are members" (No. 483).

In concluding his *Apology*, Pascal reaffirmed the primacy of the heart and of love in knowing God and God's work therein: We should not wonder, he wrote, that

> simple people should believe without reasoning. God imparts to them love of Him and hatred of self. He inclines their heart to believe. Men will never believe with a saving and real faith, unless God inclines their heart; and they will believe as soon as He inclines it (No. 284).

With this conclusion his project would have been completed, his plan fulfilled. As a plan it is superior to any that his many editors have elaborated, because it is Pascal's own. Yet, as presented here, it is admittedly much streamlined and simplified. I have drawn upon and cited only a little more than a tenth of the almost 400 notes that Pascal classified in the twenty-seven chapters (40 out of 382). The plan as comprehending all those notes is much richer and much more complex than I have been able to suggest. Omitted principally are many cross-references the notes make from one chapter to another. The order of the heart, as Pascal noted of Scripture, "consists chiefly in digressions on each point to indicate the end, and keep it always in sight" (No. 283), and that is something Pascal himself would not have spurned. The subtlety and complexity that would result have been left aside in an effort to make clear and strong the main line of the *Apology* as Pascal conceived it, and its fundamental coherence.

Notes not classified in the twenty-seven chapters

Upon his death Pascal left behind more than 1,000 notes bearing upon the subject of religion, whereas the plan of the projected *Apology* is based, as we have just seen, upon less than 400 of them. Thus more than 600 notes form a second group that remains to be taken into account. The great majority of these are included in the First Copy, where they occupy pages 189–472. Again, as in the case of the first group, these notes have been carefully and clearly divided into separate sections—some thirty-four of them. But, unlike the first group, only one of the sections bears a title: That one is called "Miscellaneous," which is scarcely revealing. But this fact makes it clear that the notes in this second group have also been classified, and the evidence indicates that it was Pascal's own doing.

The contents of the sections in some instances clearly indicate a unified theme, and it seems equally clear that some were never intended for the *Apology,* but were made for other purposes. Thus a number of them can readily be identified with remarks that appear in the *Provincial Letters,* and Brunschvicg accordingly included only a section of them in his edition (esp. Nos. 921–24). Many of the notes are concerned with the subject of miracles, and it seems unlikely that all of them would have been used in the *Apology.* Gilberte Périer reported in the *Life* that her brother had begun first to consider writing a book on miracles, but had later put it aside for the broader project. There are also, among the notes, devotional writings that were probably meant only for personal meditation, such as No. 553, entitled "The Mystery of Jesus," and which was omitted from the Copy.

For all this, it is evident that most of the notes contained in the second large group contain material for the *Apology*. Many of them bear titles that are the same as one or another of the chapter-heads. Thus No. 131 "Weariness" (*Ennui*) agrees with that of Chapter 4; No. 174 "Misery" with that of Chapter 3; Nos. 653, 657, 659 "Types," i.e., the "Figures" of Chapter 25; No. 617 "Perpetuity" which is the title of Chapter 21. Then there are notes that by their content obviously fit into one or another of the twenty-seven chapters. Thus No. 711 provides an explanatory commentary on the extremely elliptical note in Chapter 25 that cites as a particular figure *Genesis* 49, stating that "Joseph folds his arms and prefers the younger" (No. 623).

Nevertheless, it remains a fact that these notes were not distributed among the twenty-seven chapters. Consequently, we cannot know for sure where they would have been used in the overall plan. As most of these notes are gathered into sections, they come provided with a context that offers considerable help in the interpretation of any one of them. Editors, however, have not respected this context through contiguity but have separated, often widely, notes that were written on the same sheet of paper. A good if not notorious example of this practice appears in the way the notes have been edited that deal with one of the most famous of Pascal's themes—that of the wager.

The *pensée* that has come to be known as the wager (No. 233) was written on both sides of two sheets of paper. Pascal obviously worked and reworked it, since not only are there many corrections within the main body of the text, but additions have been made in all the margins as well as in every available blank space, with indications in some cases of where within the text they were to be inserted. Hence it is clear that the whole four pages constitute a single unit to which the many scattered additions belong no less than does the main text. Yet editors of the *Pensées* have distinguished and enumerated ten different notes and, what is worse, have divided them up and published them in parts of the work that are widely separated, as though they had no bearing on each other. Thus the context for the discussion known as the "wager" has been destroyed, even though the Copy carefully kept together in one section all of the ten notes it comprised as they appear in the four pages of the Original.

The wager as Pascal conceived it consists of the following *pensées*, cited here according to the numeration of the Brunschvicg edition: Nos. 233, 89, 231, 477, 606, 535, 277, 278, 604, and 542. To take into account the context provided by these notes so as to appreciate their bearing upon our understanding of the wager proper—that is, No. 233—one must consider at least briefly the content of each note.

No. 233, entitled "Infinite—nothing," is to the effect that one can and should bet on the existence of an infinite God who can assure us of an eternally happy life and act accordingly. But more about this note is better postponed until we have seen what the other nine much briefer notes have to say.

No. 89 notes that "custom is our nature," with the result that "one who is accustomed to the faith believes in it."

No. 231 supplies a mathematical image of "an infinite and indivisible thing," such as God is said to be, and so shows that such a conjunction is not contradictory. The note makes the further claim that "there remains an infinity for you to know."

Nos. 477 and 606 declare that the "propensity to self" to the neglect of the general good reveals the depravity of man, which Christianity alone among religions has taught in maintaining that "man is born in sin."

No. 535 claims that "we owe a great debt to those who point out our faults" in that they can "prepare us for correction."

Nos. 277 and 278 declare that "the heart has its reasons, which reason does not know" and that "it is the heart that experiences God, and not the reason."

No. 604 states that "the only science contrary to common sense and human nature is that alone which has always existed among men," which as Chapter 21 on perpetuity makes clear is the claim that Pascal made for Christianity.

No. 542 asserts that Christianity alone can make man both "lovable and happy."

From even so brief a description of their content, it is evident that these notes sound many of the themes already struck in the plan of the twenty-seven chapters. But what bearing do they have on the wager proper, i.e., on No. 233? How does the context that they form for it affect our understanding of it? To answer such questions one must consider in some detail the argument of the wager itself.

The argument of the wager

"Infinite—nothing," this heading of No. 233 is an accurate title of the whole complex argument of the wager. This begins with reflection on our knowledge of the infinite in mathematics, then turns to the argument for the existence of an infinitely rewarding God based on the reasonableness of wagering where an infinite good is at stake, and concludes with a moral application that the finite goods of this life should readily be given up, since they count as nothing in comparison with the infinite good to be gained.

As one of the "new mathematicians" of his day, Pascal was fascinated by the infinite, and his researches contributed greatly to laying the foundations of the infinitesimal calculus. He was among the first to use and to appreciate the power of the method of demonstration through mathematical induction, as it is now called. This method offers a way of proving the truth for an infinite number of cases, based as it is on the fact that there is no end to the sequence of natural numbers, 1, 2, 3, . . . For given any number n, one can always obtain a larger by adding 1 to it, i.e., $n+1$. Hence, if it can be proven for a mathematical proposition P that P is true for 1; (if P is true for any number n, it is also true for $n+1$), then it is true for the whole infinite sequence. Pascal employed proof by mathematical induction in developing his theory of chances, presented in the *Treatise on the Arithmetical Triangle*.*

In the wager, however, Pascal's first concern with the infinite lies in the fact that man's relation to it supplies an analogue of the Christian's relation to God. In mathematics we know the existence of an infinite without knowing its nature; we know, for example, that it does not have the same properties as the natural numbers, the infinite being neither odd nor even. So too the Christian knows by faith that the infinite God exists without understanding His nature. But if He is infinite and without parts, as theology teaches, then mathematics also can provide an image for that; as declared in the inserted note No. 231, "it is a point moving everywhere with an infinite velocity; for it is one in all places and is all totality in every place."

But it is in the light of faith that the Christian obtains his knowledge of God. What, if anything, can be known of God if we restrict ourselves to our "natural lights"?† With this question we come to the second part of the argument and the wager itself. Here Pascal's first move is to declare explicitly that reason alone is "incapable of knowing either what God is or if He is." To understand the significance and force of this claim, one must recall that Pascal took for granted the Christian's belief that God is infinitely all good, merciful yet just, who holds out to man an eternity of bliss or of woe. Because of this belief, Pascal dismissed the metaphysical proofs for the existence of God as of little worth, since they fail to touch the heart of the matter as regards God's relation to man. Hence he held that deism, with its notion of God as simply great, powerful, and eternal, but without regard for man, was "almost as far removed from the Christian religion as atheism" (No. 556).

Reason alone cannot prove that there is such a God, nor can it prove that there is not. The question cannot be ignored, however. It has immense practical implications for the way we live. Indeed, to act at all as reasonable beings implies an answer to it one way or the other. "You are

---

*Twelfth Consequence, *GBWW*, Vol. 33, pp. 451–52; for Combinations, Proposition I, pp. 458–59; for Dividing Stakes, Problem I, Proposition I, pp. 464–65.
†No. 233, p. 214.

embarked," Pascal observed, and there is no getting off. We find our-selves in a situation in which we must decide to act either as though God exists or does not. Yet our knowledge is insufficient to determine defi-nitely that one is true and the other false. How then are we to decide which is the best and most reasonable way to act in this doubtful situa-tion? Is there any reason to think that one answer is better as more rea-sonable than another? Pascal, the mathematician, in developing his the-ory of probability, had in effect invented the doctrine now known as decision theory, and it is to this that he now turns to find the answer to the question he has raised. Since he had worked out the theory in response to a request from a gambling friend, it is presented as a doctrine of chances conerning the best and most reasonable way to bet or wager in a game of chance. Only now in this case, unlike a game of chance where one is free to play or to refuse, we "must choose." Which then shall we choose?

To decide, we should consult our "interest," i.e., our happiness. From which side do we stand to gain a greater advantage? On the one side is God offering an infinite good in eternal life, on the other is either the finite good of this life or eternal damnation.

> Let us estimate these two chances. If you gain, you gain all; if you lose, you lose nothing. Wager, then, without hesitation that He is (No. 233, p.215a).

In short, the one side so dominates the other that there is no question which way we should decide.

Against this argument, the objection, however, can be raised that we " 'may perhaps wager too much.' " After all, certain goods, however finite, are given up in order to lead a religious life so as to obtain God's blessing. To meet this objection, Pascal brings forward an argument from probability and the theorem now known as mathematical expectation. This theorem expresses mathematically the probable outcome of a game of chance as a product of the gain that might be won and the chance of obtaining it. Simplified, it can be written as the following equation, in which E stands for expectation, G for gain, C for the chance of winning, and S for stake:

$E = G \times C$
If $E = S$, advantage and disadvantage are equal.
If $E > S$, it is advantageous to wager to win.

In Pascal's wager we are staking the one finite life that we have and the way that we lead it; hence $S = 1$. Furthermore, at this point he supposes that "there is an equal risk of gain and of loss" (p. 215a); i.e., with respect to God's existence we are in a heads or tails situation where our chance of winning is 1 out of 2; hence $C = 1/2$.

Pascal then argues that if we stood to gain 2 lives we "might still wager," since

$E = 2 \times 1/2 = 1$, so even.

But if we stood to win 3 lives we would be "imprudent, when you are forced to play, not to chance" our life, since

$E = 3 \times 1/2 = 3/2$, so advantageous.

And if, as in the supposed situation, the gain is an infinite life, the wager for God is infinitely to our advantage:

$E = \infty \times 1/2 = \infty$

Hence, as there is an infinite gain to be won, it is reasonable to wager our one life.

This argument from probability meets the objection that one might be wagering too much. But it does so by assuming that the chance of God existing is as 1 to 2. While reason may be unable either to prove or disprove that God exists, what reason is there for thinking that the chance is in that proportion? Pascal accordingly allows the chances to decrease from $1/2$ to any number $1/n$ so long as there is 1 chance of winning the infinite and a finite chance of losing it: "There is here an infinity of an infinitely happy life to gain, a chance of gain against a finite number of chances of loss, and what you stake is finite." Accordingly, we have

$E = \infty \times 1/n = \infty/n = \infty$

After this remark Pascal wrote: *"Cela ôte tout parti,"* which is better translated as "that removes any choice," rather than as "it is all divided" (p. 215a). For where there is an infinite at stake, it is reasonable to wager our one life; indeed, to seek to keep our life by not wagering it for an infinite gain is to "renounce reason."

There remains the objection to this argument from chances that the proportion between infinite and finite is misplaced. So far, it has been between the infinite gain and the finite stake. The objection claims that if there is any infinity in question it is between the uncertainty of the gain and the certainty of what is staked. To this Pascal replies in effect that the objection misunderstands the game and the nature of mathematical expectation: "Every player stakes a certainty to gain an uncertainty," and he does so in the case of finite stakes and finite gains "without transgressing against reason." For "the uncertainty of the gain is proportioned to the certainty of the stake according to the proportion of the chances of gain and loss." Simplifying, we have

$G/S = C$

and this follows from the definition of mathematical expectation as

$E = (G \times C = S)$

Hence when there is an infinite to gain, a finite to stake, and a finite chance of losing, it is reasonable as in accord with mathematical expectation to wager on the infinite. Writing as the inventor of mathematical decision theory, Pascal concluded his argument from probability by declaring: "This is demonstrable; and if men are capable of any truths, this is one" (p. 215b).

It has sometimes been objected that these arguments from probability are too general to achieve Pascal's purpose, in that they will hold for any religion that makes the same promises as Christianity. Pascal himself may well have been aware of this possibility. One of the proposed chapters, as we have seen, was expressly concerned to show "The Falsity of Other Religions" (Chap. 16). But even more significant in this regard is the fact that three of the nine notes added to the pages on which he wrote the wager emphasize the uniqueness of Christianity, Nos. 542, 604, and 606.

The wager proper (No. 233) is only one step, however, and a preparatory one at that, to the argument as a whole. It is intended to break down the initial objection that to believe as a Christian is itself an unreasonable act. The argument as a whole goes beyond this in aiming to incite the unbelieving reader to want to believe and to take the steps necessary to come to actual belief. Thus the final part of note No. 233 addresses itself directly to the problem of unbelief. The interlocutor declares his inability to believe and asks what he should do, to which Pascal replies:

> Endeavor, then, to convince yourself, not by increase of proofs of God, but by the abatement of your passions. You would like to attain faith and do not know the way. Learn of those who have been bound like you, . . . who know the way. . . . Follow the way by which they began; by acting as if they believed, taking the holy water, having masses said, etc. (pp. 215–16).

The notes at this point do much to clarify this advice. The first of these concerns the power of custom: "He who is accustomed to the faith believes in it" (No. 89). Since one becomes virtuous by doing virtuous deeds, courageous by performing acts that demand courage, so one disposes oneself to belief by acting as a believer does. Another note deals with the major moral and practical obstacle to belief that is rooted in "bias to our will . . . and the propensity to self [that] is the beginning of all disorder" (No. 477), and the "depraved will" that prefers the satisfaction of its passions before everything else.

Two more of the added notes, which are among the most famous of all the *Pensées*, stress the importance of the heart and of love in the will to believe.

> The heart has its reasons, which reason does not know. We feel it in a thousand things. I say that the heart naturally loves the Universal Being, and also itself naturally, according as it gives itself to them; and it

hardens itself against one or the other at its will. You have rejected the one and kept the other. Is it by reason that you love yourself? (No. 277).

It is the heart which experiences God, and not the reason. This, then, is faith: God felt by the heart, not by reason (No. 278).

At "the end of this discourse" Pascal returns to the contrast between the infinite and nothing. The finite is now identified, not with number, as at the start, but with the finite goods and "poisonous pleasures, glory and luxury" which are as nothing compared to the infinite God: "At each step you take on this road, you will see so great certainty of gain, so much nothingness in what you risk, that you will at last recognize that you have wagered for something certain and infinite, for which you have given nothing" (No. 233, p. 216a). The note added at the end of the four pages containing the wager adds as a further comment: "Do not draw this conclusion from your experiment, that there remains nothing for you to know; but rather that there remains an infinity for you to know" (No. 231). Hence there is no abandonment of reason here. There remains an infinity to know not only in the sense that there is no end to knowledge, since our knowledge cannot conceivably ever be completed so that there remains no more to know, but also in the sense that as man is made for God, he seeks to love and know a being that is infinite. Pascal was speaking not merely as a mathematician of the infinite when he declared that man is "made only for infinity."*

We have now completed consideration of the wager proper (No. 233) together with the nine accompanying notes that provide a context for it. One can scarcely deny that the wager so read is a much richer document than when it is taken alone separated from those nine notes. Although such a reading becomes more complex, it also makes the primary moral and practical purpose of the argument more distinct, and as a consequence the wager proper becomes clearer and easier to understand.

In concluding this discussion of the wager, we might well ask where it would fit in the provisional plan of the twenty-seven chapters, inasmuch as Pascal himself did not assign it to any of them. The most likely place would appear to be in the second part, which was to be devoted to proving the truth of Christianity, and among Chapters 11–27 which constitute that part, it would fit best in Chapter 12, entitled "Beginning." For in this chapter Pascal proposed to show that it is unreasonable to ignore, if not to spurn, Christian claims without considering whether they might be true, and whether indeed it might not be reasonable to believe in them. Such a fit seems the more appropriate in that Pascal included in the notes bundled together for Chapter 12 note No. 218 with its claim that "it

---

Preface to the Treatise on the Vacuum, GBWW, Vol. 33, p. 357.

concerns all our life to know whether the soul be mortal or immortal," which is closely allied with the assertion made in the wager that the way we live reveals by itself the way we have wagered.

The task remaining

To read the *pensées* as they are arranged in the First Copy by no means solves all the problems that confront the reader of Pascal. By doing so, he will know the state of the papers as they were left at the time of Pascal's death, when there was a provisional plan for the *Apology*, divided into twenty-seven or twenty-eight chapters that contain 382 of the more than 1,000 fragments. He will have most of the remaining notes divided in turn, most probably by Pascal himself, into thirty-four sections. Of a few of these, and most notably the wager, it will seem clear where they would fit into the projected plan. But for most of these notes it is not at all so clear, but in fact it is often most extremely doubtful where, if anywhere at all, they should go. Among these are some of the longest and most important and famous of any of the *pensées,* such as those on "The difference between the mathematical and the intuitive mind" (No. 1), "Self-love" (No. 100), that against indifference regarding our state (No. 194), and that on the three orders of body, mind, and charity (No. 793). With these as with many others the reader who follows the order of the Copy will be in the same situation as previous editors, of having to decide how they bear on one another.

Still, there is one undoubted service that the order of the Copy does provide, at least for the reader who desires to get as close as he can to Pascal's own thought. It shows unmistakably that Pascal, in the *Apology* at least, never dissociated and separated the philosophical from the religious elements of his thought. The eighteenth-century editions of the *philosophes* erred most grievously in this respect, especially Condorcet and Voltaire. But Brunschvicg's edition is not entirely free from the same fault. Thus his Section VI is entitled "The Philosophers" (p. 233), which is the same title as Pascal's Chapter 9. But whereas Pascal's contains only seven notes, Brunschvicg's contains eighty-six, of which only two come from Pascal's original seven, namely Nos. 350 and 360 on the Stoics. Of the remaining eighty-four, no less than thirty-one of them are distributed among Pascal's twenty-seven chapters, most of them occurring in Chapters 2 ("Vanity"), 6 ("Greatness"), and 7 ("Contrarieties"). Hence, although editors may have used the same titles as those in Pascal's plan (and nine of Brunschvicg's fourteen sections carry the same titles), their content is most often far removed from that indicated by Pascal's own selection of notes.

Of course, no one can prevent a reader from reading a text as he pleases and wringing from it any sense he can. But if he wants to treat his author justly, he should endeavor to understand it as the author intended it, and for this purpose the context is of great help. As Pascal noted,

> Let no one say that I have said nothing new; the arrangement of the subject is new. . . . In the same way if the same thoughts in a different arrangement do not form a different discourse, no more do the same words in their different arrangement form different thoughts (No. 22).

For the arrangement and context that Pascal intended the Copy is invaluable, however many problems it leaves unsolved, since it contains not only his provisional plan but also his own preliminary classification of the notes that he had made for the projected *Apology for the Christian Religion.*

Documentation

The best account of recent scholarship devoted to Pascal and the consequent rethinking of the *Pensées* that it has occasioned is J. Mesnard, *Les Pensées de Pascal,* Paris, 1976.

The most definitive and critical edition of the *Pensées,* taking into account all the relevant scholarship, is under preparation as part of a new critical edition of the *Oeuvres complètes* under the general editorship of J. Mesnard.

The man most responsible for initiating reconsideration of the importance of the First Copy was L. Lafuma, who published a preliminary edition of the *Pensées* following the arrangement of the First Copy in 1951. An English translation of this edition by A. K. Krailsheimer was published in the Penguin Classics in 1966 and reprinted many times.

A photographic facsimile of the *Original des Pensées de Pascal* was published by Brunschvicg in 1905.

For the analysis of the wager I am most indebted to H. Gouhier, *Blaise Pascal Commentaries,* Paris, 1966, and to I. Hacking, "The Logic of Pascal's Wager," in *American Philosophical Quarterly,* Vol. 9, No. 2, April 1972, pp. 186–92.

PART FOUR

Reviews
of Recent Books

Philosophy in Our Time

Philosophical Explanations
by Robert Nozick

After Virtue
by Alasdair MacIntyre

Reviewed by
Mortimer J. Adler

Mr. Adler, who is editor in chief of *The Great Ideas Today,* has spent a long and active life in the teaching and practice of philosophy, which he refuses to regard, despite his long list of academic achievements and awards, as an academic specialty, preferring to think of it rather as "everybody's business." For many years he was the close associate of Robert M. Hutchins at the University of Chicago, where he devoted himself to the cause of education by means of great books. Since 1952 he has been director of the Institute for Philosophical Research, and since 1974 chairman of the Board of Editors of Encyclopædia Britannica, Inc.

Among many books that he has written, the most recent are *Six Great Ideas* (1981), in which he distinguished the ideas we live by from those we act on, and *The Angels and Us* (1982), a work about angels as a philosophical, not a religious, conception. He has recently completed still another book, *How to Speak and How to Listen,* which is to be published next year.

Mr. Adler is author also of a book published this year called *The Paideia Proposal: An Educational Manifesto,* which is the report of a body known as the Paideia Group, of which he is chairman, that has for three years held conferences on the subject of basic schooling in the United States and has made recommendations for a comprehensive reform of basic education.

With few exceptions, mostly recent and of German origin, the philosophical works contained in the *Great Books of the Western World* were
not written by or for specialists in philosophy. The great philosophers in
the Western tradition addressed themselves to questions they regarded
as necessary for any thinking mind to confront. In this sense it can be said
that philosophy, unlike all other forms of inquiry, is everybody's business.
That is why the great philosophical treatises, with some exceptions, have
been written, as they should be, in a language and in a manner that makes
their message accessible to the reflective intelligence of the ordinary
thoughtful person. The technical terminology that specialists have recourse to in communicating with one another does not properly belong
to philosophy. For the most part, the great books in philosophy have
avoided it, though there are exceptions, as I have indicated.

I do not mean to say that the great books in philosophy are all easy to
read. Some of them—some of Aristotle's treatises, for example, and some
of the later dialogues of Plato—require special efforts of interpretation
on the part of the reader. Nevertheless, even these yield up their message
when that effort is made; it is not defeated by a technical vocabulary invented by the author for his own special purposes.

From the Greeks down to the end of the nineteenth century and even
through the first quarter of this century (once again, with the exceptions
noted above), philosophical inquiry remained the domain of the general-
ist—the thinking human mind. This is certainly true of the writings of the
great stoic philosophers of ancient Rome—Epictetus, Marcus Aurelius,
Seneca. It is true of the philosophical content in the great theological
treatises of the Middle Ages. Thomas Aquinas, for example, in his Prologue to the *Summa Theologica,* says that, since his work is intended for be-
ginners (by which, to be sure, he means those who have at least acquired
the liberal arts) as well as for those who have advanced along the road on
which he is about to set forth, he has tried to write "as briefly and clearly
as the matter itself may allow."

The same intention has been evident in such modern philosophers as
Hobbes, Descartes, Locke, Berkeley, Hume, and John Stuart Mill, though
it is somewhat less clear in Spinoza. It remains the objective when we
come to most of the eminent philosophers writing at the beginning of this
century—William James, Henri Bergson, George Santayana, Bertrand
Russell, and John Dewey.

The rise of specialization in philosophy first became apparent in the 1930s and it had become more and more intense in every decade since the Second World War. Contemplating the possibility of adding to *Great Books of the Western World* a supplementary set of books to be entitled *Great Books of the Twentieth Century,* not long ago I assembled an editorial committee to select works that might be included in such a set. After two years of conference we gave the project up because the intensity of specialization in all the intellectual disciplines, including history and philosophy as well as the sciences, has produced since 1925 or 1930 only technical monographs intended by one specialist for the attention of others in the same narrow field of specialization.

Like the great works of philosophy, the great works in science and history written in earlier times were written for the generally educated reader—not an unread person but not a specialist either. This is as true of Gilbert, Newton, Galileo, Lavoisier, Faraday, and Darwin (in the natural sciences), of Tacitus and Gibbon (in history), as it is of Hobbes, Locke, and John Stuart Mill (in philosophy), and of William James and Sigmund Freud (in psychology).

When we abandoned the project of trying to publish a set of great books of the twentieth century, we reluctantly acquiesced in the gloomy conclusion that great books may still be forthcoming in the field of imaginative literature—poems, novels, and plays—but the likelihood of their being produced in the future in history, the sciences, and philosophy has dwindled almost to the vanishing point.

This is not to say that great original work of the highest merit will not be done in all these fields; but when such work is done, it will be communicated by one specialist to another in the form of a technical monograph or treatise intended only for that kind of reader, as a truly great book never is, and in my judgment cannot be.

The general reader (as I have defined him or her) must from now on depend on secondary lines of communication. Instead of becoming acquainted with the great original contributions in history, science, and philosophy through the reading of works written by the contributors themselves, such a reader must depend upon what have come to be called "popularizations." Sometimes, as in the case of three great twentieth-century physicists—Einstein, Heisenberg, and Schrödinger—the great contributor has attempted to write an account of his discoveries and theories for the general public, but there are few if any other examples of this since the earlier part of this century.

This suggests that in order for philosophical thought to be, in the twentieth century, what it has always been in the past and what it always should be, namely, everybody's business, the effort to make it accessible to the inquiring intelligence of ordinary men and women may have to resort to popularization. The way philosophy is now taught in our universities and the way it is now written by academic or professional philosophers (perhaps, it would be more accurate to refer to them not as philosophers but as professors of philosophy), render it inaccessible to all but a small number of students or readers who wish to become specialists themselves.

I say these things by way of a lengthy introduction to the two recent philosophical books I wish to consider here. Both are books written by professors of philosophy, well thought of by their professional colleagues. One book is *Philosophical Explanations,* by Robert Nozick, of Harvard University. The other is *After Virtue,* by Alasdair MacIntyre, of Wellesley College. Both books, I am sorry to have to say, are failures, owing to the state to which philosophy has sunk in the twentieth century, although Nozick's, which I shall take up first, is in my judgment a much more egregious failure than MacIntyre's, which is not without its virtues.

Critics have praised Professor Nozick's book, calling it "a great work—marvelously inventive, deep, and profound," and, again, "an arresting, original, extremely brilliant work," as well as other distinguished things. Indeed, Professor MacIntyre himself, in a leading review in *The New York Times,* discussed the book with unstinting admiration, though in view of his own approach to moral philosophy he should, it seems to me, have been severely critical, at least of the nearly 200 pages that Professor Nozick devotes to the foundation of ethics.

Professor MacIntyre praised Professor Nozick's book for two other achievements as well, that would certainly make it noteworthy did it deserve such praise. He said Professor Nozick had succeeded in writing a philosophical work intended for the general reader as well as for his professional colleagues; and he said that, in this book, Professor Nozick had also introduced a new way of approaching philosophical questions. Neither of these things is true, however, as I will explain, taking them in order.

As to the first claim, that Professor Nozick has written a book for the general reader, let me quote Professor MacIntyre at length, because what he says makes clear his agreement, in part, with what I have said here myself about the current state of philosophy:

> Philosophers these days have every inducement to write only for one another. The conditions of academic appointment and reappointment coerce them when young into acquiring the style and idiom of the professional journal. Failure to publish in such journals generally spells professional disaster, while success generally produces a style of writing and a concentration upon topics inaccessible to the larger reading public. By so writing, philosophers reinforce the image of philosophy's irrelevance to the concerns of plain, practical people who in modern America tend anyway to believe that a hard-headed involvement in practical affairs precludes them from taking seriously what they perceive as the mere spinning of conceptual cobwebs. Thus the idiom of the mandarin and the prejudices of the philistine reinforce

each other. It is unsurprising that philosophy has become ingrown, and that while John Stuart Mill and William James felt able to address the general educated public on the central problems of philosophy, Professor X now writes for Professor Y.

There is good reason then to take notice when a first-rate philosopher writes an important book on these problems addressed simultaneously to his professional colleagues and to the common reader. When moreover the book is written in crisp, elegant prose and communicates its author's own excitement about both the problems and his solutions, as Robert Nozick's new book is and does, the common reader will be the poorer if he or she does not pay uncommon attention.

Now it is incomprehensible that Professor MacIntyre, having written the first of these two paragraphs, should then have thought it proper, or even possible, to write the second. For, in fact, nothing could be farther from the truth than what his second paragraph says. If it comes to that, Professor Nozick does not himself even *claim,* so far as I can find, to have addressed "the common reader," though if he somewhere makes that appear to be his intention, it is a promise that is not fulfilled. In view of what he has actually written, how could it be? For what he has written is a book of 700 pages that resorts frequently to a technical vocabulary and the symbolic devices of modern logic, that is accompanied by footnotes dealing with matters of no interest or intelligibility to the general reader. Nozick formulates arguments in the manner of twentieth-century linguistic and analytical philosophers who have no concern for their intelligibility outside their own circle. And that is followed, at the end of the text, by notes and comments clearly intended for just such other philosophers, Professor Nozick's colleagues.

None of this is appropriate for, or of any possible interest to, the "common reader" of whom Professor MacIntyre speaks. All of it makes clear that *Philosophical Explanations* is instead an esoteric work, which is *not* intended, as Professor Nozick explicitly allows, for the general reader. Nor is it easy to see why such readers should be expected to buy it for the substantial sum of $25.00, which is what it costs.

Another passage from Professor MacIntyre's review of the book not only indicates why the limited philosophical context within which Nozick's thinking moves made it impossible for him to write a book that might be intelligible to the general reader; it also makes the second of the two unfounded claims for the book with which I am concerned. Again, I quote at length because what Professor MacIntyre says is so revealing with regard to the limited frame of reference within which contemporary philosophers work:

> Many of the insights and arguments that Mr. Nozick puts to such good use had their origin in highly technical discussions within the philosophy of language and the philosophy of mind. Mr. Nozick helps

to vindicate the importance of such discussions by the uses he finds for their conceptual end products, and in so doing he shows indirectly how Continental philosophers who have been explicitly concerned with human value and significance have too often presented us with impoverished and barren discussions on these great issues because they have neglected the more technical discussions of Anglo-American analytic philosophy. One way to characterize Mr. Nozick, not his own way, is as a philosopher who is answering the questions posed by such philosophers as Kierkegaard, Sartre, Marcel and Buber with the aid of tools produced by such very different philosophers as W. V. Quine, Saul Kripke and Hilary Putnam.

There is however, one defect in this characterization. It does nothing to suggest Mr. Nozick's own striking and imaginative orginality. For he does nothing less than propose a new way of doing philosophy. Philosophers since Heraclitus have sought truth. Since Plato they have supposed by and large that to possess truth was to possess absolutely certain knowledge. And from Euclid as well as from Plato they have for the most part inherited an ideal of proof as the only way of arriving at conclusions with the requisite degree and kind of certainty. Sometimes the barrenness of the search for demonstrative proof has turned them into skeptics who thought that because they could not discover the relevant proofs, they could have no well-grounded beliefs whatsoever. And occasionally the ideal of proof has itself been rejected more or less forcefully.

Mr. Nozick seeks to expel it from philosophy finally, replacing it by the notion of explanation. A philosophical explanation is an account that enables us to understand how certain things are possible, given other beliefs or suppositions. It answers questions such as: How is free will possible, if all human actions are causally determined? Or how is it possible for subjective experiences of thinking, feeling and perceiving to find a place in the objective physical world? The adherents of proof, as Mr. Nozick portrays them, aspired to find the one exclusively true and adequate answer to such questions. But the adherents of explanation will reject this attempt at victory for any one particular philosophy over all the others.

So Mr. Nozick asserts: "There are various philosophical views, mutually incompatible, which cannot be dismissed or simply rejected. Philosophy's output is the basketful of these admissible views, all together. One delimiting strategy would be to modify and shave these views, capturing what is true in each, to make them compatible parts of one new view. While I know of no reason in principle why this cannot be done, neither has anyone yet done it satisfactorily . . . . Are we reduced to relativism then, the doctrine that all views are equally good? No, some views can be rejected, and the admissible ones remaining will differ in merits and adequacy . . . . Even when one view is clearly best, though, we do not keep only this first-ranked view, rejecting all the others." For, in Mr. Nozick's account, we ought to be able to learn from the second- and third-ranked views, and indeed in time we might well come to change the order of the ranking.

Once more I remark that it is, if not incomprehensible, then at least very strange that Professor MacIntyre having described twentieth-century philosophy in these altogether justified terms, should then have found in Nozick himself a "striking and imaginative originality," amounting to nothing less than "a new way of doing philosophy."

What is strange about this is that Professor MacIntyre's own book makes it clear that he is himself much better read in the great tradition against which claims of philosophical originality must be measured than is Professor Nozick, whose frame of reference is largely, if not exclusively, provided by European existentialists and Anglo-American analytical and linguistic philosophers since 1945. That is hardly a large enough framework in which to do the job that MacIntyre tells us Nozick has attempted to do. If Nozick's aim is to present "the basketful of admissible views" relevant to major philosophical questions, then what he calls "philosophy's output" should have included an inventory of the thought of ancient and medieval philosophers, and of modern philosophers prior to the Second World War, carefully and conscientiously examined, at least to the same extent that Nozick's book examines the thought of his own contemporaries.

One need only check "the index to people mentioned" and the lengthy notes appended at the end of the book to discover that a great many philosophers who have propounded significant answers to the questions Nozick considers are either not mentioned at all (none of the great thinkers in the long period between Augustine and Aquinas is even cited, though in almost every case their views are highly relevant, and in most cases have greater merit than the views treated by Nozick); or, if such ancient philosophers as Aristotle and Plato are cited here and there, my examination of the passage in such of their works as Nozick refers to shows an inadequate reading of them and an even more inadequate understanding of their thought.

That Professor MacIntyre found it possible to praise a book so deficient in its examination of the whole range of philosophical thought is all the more surprising in the light of his own book, *After Virtue,* in which, dealing with one of the major questions treated by Nozick, the question about the foundations of ethics, he himself covers that whole range of thought, most of which Nozick ignores or neglects.

One wonders about Nozick's own philosophical education at Harvard University, where he earned a doctorate and a position in the Philosophy Department; and perhaps one should also wonder about the standards of scholarship set by the philosophy department of a great university. It would certainly appear to be the case that one can become an eminent professor of philosophy in the contemporary scene even if one plainly exhibits ignorance or, what is even worse, disdainful neglect of one's predecessors prior to 1945. That the new turn philosophy took in the latter part of this century justifies ignorance or neglect of the great body of earlier thought is an outrageous and unwarranted assumption.

I turn now to the novelty or innovative feature that MacIntyre attributes to Nozick's book when he speaks of it as having "striking and imaginative originality" and as proposing "a new way of doing philosophy." I will try to explain why it is not only far from being a "new way," but also that, even if it were a new way, it would not be a new way of "doing philosophy."

To do this, I must call attention to Nozick's use of the word *explanation*, which appears in the title of his book. He uses that word as if it *always* connoted the opposite of a proof or demonstration, the opposite of an argument that has some degree of probative force, even if the conclusion established thereby has something less than certitude, which is the case with almost all philosophical arguments.

Nozick's reason for distinguishing between explanation and proof, or probative argument, is that he wishes to avoid making judgments that assert a particular philosophical view to be true, and opposite views false, or that assert that one particular view is truer than another. This, however, is precisely what a philosopher should do.

A survey of all relevant, diverse or incompatible, views about a given subject, without any consideration of which are true and which are false, or which is truer than another, is a dialectical, *not* a philosophical, undertaking. I will presently explain this distinction between being a dialectician and being a philosopher, but before I do so, let me comment on the distinction between explanation and argument having some degree of probative force.

If a philosophical proposition is self-evidently and necessarily true, because it is impossible to think the opposite, then its truth needs no explanation. Indeed, its truth, being self-evident, cannot be explained, since it rests on no reasons or premises antecedent to itself.

Hence all explanations must occur in the domain of things that either *are* known to be true or are thought of as *capable of being* true, i.e., are *possible*, truths. Only in the case of things already known to be true in the light of evidence and reasons, about which we then ask *why* they are true, do explanations differ from probative arguments that marshal evidence and reasons.

To know *that* something is true differs from knowing *why* it is true. Knowing *that* it is true depends on evidence and reasons that have some degree of probative force with respect to truth. Knowing *why* it is true depends upon being able to explain the truth of what is judged to be true on independent grounds.

When we come to the realm of the merely possible (distinct, on the one hand, from the necessary and the impossible and distinct, on the other hand, from the actual), there is no difference whatsoever between explanation and probative argument. As we have just seen, in the domain of the actual (where we judge that something is true or false, or truer than something else), probative argument precedes explanation and is independent of it. But in the realm of the merely possible (where we judge that something *may be* true and, perforce, must concede that views incompatible with it *may also be* true), an effort to explain why we think a certain view *may be* true is identical with giving a probative argument for its possible truth.

This being so, we can now properly understand the project that Nozick set for himself by dealing with what he calls "philosophical explanations." The project is an attempt to present an inventory of views arguing for, and thus explaining, philosophical possibilities—views that may or may not be true—without attempting to determine whether they are actually true; in short, an examination of all relevant points of view, without taking any of them as one's own or defending one against another.

A project of this sort, well-executed, would obviously be of some service to progress in philosophical thought, since it would provide anyone who wanted to think originally about a given subject with the background needed for that effort. But when it is thus understood, Nozick's project is not in any way novel, or a new departure, except for those who are ignorant of what was proposed much earlier in this century and ignorant of what has already been done along these very lines. I must be personal in this connection, though I hasten to acknowledge that my contribution to such work owes its inception to the late Professor Arthur O. Lovejoy.

In his Presidential Address to the American Philosophical Association in 1916, Professor Lovejoy discussed the conditions of progress in philosophy and proposed the project of a careful and thorough inventory of the fundamental philosophical issues (or the questions to which there are a range of diverse or incompatible answers), together with a setting forth of all these possible answers in a way that indicated their relationship to one another, without trying to assess the truth of any one view in relation to the truth of other views in answer to the same question.

That paper by Professor Lovejoy, published in the Proceedings of the Association in 1917, became, some years after I first read it in the early twenties, the inspiration that led me to propose the establishment of a special research institute to undertake the dialectical project that Professor Lovejoy had in mind.

My proposal was accompanied by extensive quotations from Professor Lovejoy's extraordinary paper. It succeeded in 1952 in getting the financing needed to establish the Institute for Philosophical Research, staffed by a group of collaborative workers who cooperated in the production of a number of purely dialectical books, the first of which was two volumes of *The Idea of Freedom*, published in 1958 and in 1962. Professor Lovejoy, by the way, had explicitly insisted that while purely philosophical work can be done by a solitary thinker, the dialectical enterprise he had in mind required the cooperative work of a group of collaborators.

With this experience in mind, I feel justified in making the following observations about Nozick's book:

(1) There is nothing at all novel or innovative about it. Nozick himself, if not MacIntyre, could have realized this, because he himself refers to *The Idea of Freedom,* which he cannot, however, have read very carefully. If he had, he would have found that Book I of *The Idea of Freedom* not only cites Lovejoy's 1917 paper and quotes from it, and also outlines in detail the nature of the dialectical project; in addition, it explains the distinction between the philosophical and the dialectical task.

Philosophers engaged in solitary thought have the obligation to make judgments about the true or truer answers to any question they consider. If they do not discharge that obligation, they are not philosophers. Dialecticians working collaboratively or cooperatively have the obligation to bring to light all the possible answers to a given question and to examine the arguments for those possible answers that constitute the explanation of their possible truth.

The Institute, of which I have been the Director since 1952, should have been called "The Institute for Dialectical Research" (a point explicitly made in the General Introduction to *The Idea of Freedom*); and the title of Nozick's book would have been more accurate, though doubtless very cumbersome, if it had been "A Dialectical Examination of Philosophical Explanations."

(2) If Nozick had fully understood the nature of his project, he might have realized that he could not execute it by himself—that it required, as the dialectical projects undertaken by the Institute have required, a group of collaborative workers. It is almost impossible for a single person to examine all the relevant philosophical answers given to important philosophical questions over the last twenty-five centuries and to do so with the requisite dialectical neutrality, avoiding favoritism or partiality in the way in which they are set forth and related.

(3) Nozick's failure to understand the dialectical nature of his project and the requisites for carrying it out adequately and fairly are responsible for the inadequacy of its execution, a judgment that I think would be made by anyone who did not make the assumption that philosophical thought about the various subjects covered in this book began in 1945, or even as late as the seventeenth century.

Let me be clear. Even if Nozick's book is not a book for the general reader, as a dialectical work tends not to be, and even if its claim to be a novel and innovative approach to philosophy is without foundation, it still might have been a good book, a worthy dialectical effort. It is not, mainly because of the narrow context or relatively small frame of reference in which Nozick carried on the operation—mainly that of twentieth-century philosophy, and even there only some portion of it.

The questions with which Professor Nozick deals are important philosophical questions: Wherein lies the identity of the self (or for that matter

247

of any individual substance)? Why is there something rather than nothing? How can our claim to know be defended against the skeptic? Do we have free will? What are the foundations of ethics? I omit mention of his final section on "the meaning of life," because I do not think that that loose phrase is associated with any genuine philosophical questions, despite the fact that Professor MacIntyre advises the nonprofessional reader to begin with the book's last chapter.

To all these good questions, there are many possible answers, together with good arguments to support or explain them—many more than Nozick includes in his survey, many more than he appears to be aware of.

Let me give just three examples:

(1) With regard to the question of why something exists rather than nothing, Nozick mentions in a footnote that Leibniz explicitly raised this question, but he does not discuss Leibniz's answer to it; nor does he consider all the answers given to that question in the realm of philosophical theology, not only in the eleventh, twelfth, and thirteenth centuries, but also in modern times.

(2) With regard to the question whether we have free will, Nozick's coverage of the possible answers and of the controversy that revolves around that question is even more inadequate and its inadequacy is even stranger. As I said earlier, footnote references indicate that he was aware of the existence of the second volume of *The Idea of Freedom,* in which more than four hundred pages are devoted to a dialectical survey and examination of the diverse affirmative answers to the question, and the incompatible negative answers to it. This range of answers can be read as explanations of the possible truth that free will exists and of the possible truth that it does not exist.

The hundred pages on free will in Nozick's book ignore or neglect most of these answers, especially the most important ones, which were formulated in the Middle Ages and have been lost to modern thought because of its ignorance of that period. Yet, in this case, the dialectical work was already done for him. All he had to do to take advantage of it was to read carefully and with an open—a truly dialectical—mind those four hundred pages in Volume II of *The Idea of Freedom.* This he obviously did not do.

(3) With regard to the question about the foundations of ethics, we find the same inadequate coverage of the possible answers; and here once more there is the same strangeness about the inadequacy. Nozick's footnote references indicate that he was aware of at least one argument, my own, to the effect that Aristotle, and only Aristotle, had correctly laid the foundations for moral philosophy—for the treatment of such values as the good and the right[1]—showing at the same time why the other major answers to the question failed where Aristotle succeeded. But Nozick does not make use of this argument where he stands in need of it.

So much for Professor Nozick and *Philosophical Explanations.* What I have just said about the unique status of Aristotle's *Ethics* in the field of moral philosophy (that it is the only sound, practical, and undogmatic moral philosophy in the whole Western tradition) is a view that is shared to some extent, but not wholly, by Professor MacIntyre in his book *After Virtue,* to which I now turn. I will try to explain why I do not agree with his less than complete recommendation of Aristotle's *Ethics* as the one sound approach to that subject.

After Virtue is a fine piece of historical scholarship in the field of moral philosophy. It ranges over the whole tradition of Western thought in the field of morals from the early Greeks to the present day. It is well worth reading for the comprehensiveness and clarity of the intellectual narrative it presents, if for no other reason. But there is another reason for reading it, and that is its central message, to which a reader should pay close attention. It is this on which I wish to concentrate within the brief compass of this review. Other reviews of this book have paid too much attention to the historical scholarship, too little to the book's philosophical message, and none to the relation of the one to the other.

The briefest way to summarize the philosophical thesis of *After Virtue* is to explain the title. Professor MacIntyre maintains, and I think quite rightly, that without the Greek, and especially the Aristotelian, conception of moral virtue as an habitual disposition of man's appetites or desires that put him on the pathway toward leading a good human life, moral philosophy is simply bankrupt.

When Rome replaces Greece, and Roman Stoicism (with its insistence that nothing more than a will in conformity with the laws of nature and of reason is needed for a sound morality) ignores the sound common sense in Aristotle's insight that good fortune as well good habits are needed for a good life, Western moral philosophy turns in the wrong direction.

A brief respite from this misdirection occurs in the late Middle Ages, when the moral theology of Thomas Aquinas reinstates Aristotle's conception of the role of moral virtue and of good fortune in the pursuit of temporal (and, therefore, imperfect) happiness. But after that, and especially from the eighteenth century down to our own day, Western moral philosophy goes the whole way toward its present bankrupt condition. As MacIntyre clearly and cogently points out, all attempts to lay the foundation of a sound morality *after* the concept of virtue is abandoned are necessarily doomed to failure.

To touch only the high spots, among the points to which MacIntyre calls our attention are (a) Hume's failure to find a basis for moral sentiments in the passions; (b) Kant's unsuccessful version of ancient Stoicism's appeal solely to the laws of reason; (c) the fumbling efforts of J. S. Mill's Utilitarianism to restore happiness as the ultimate end to be sought, rendered self-defeating by Mill's hedonistic error of identifying happiness with the maximization of pleasures or satisfactions without any basis for differentiating between good pleasures or satisfactions and bad pleasures, and also by his substitution of the general happiness (or the greatest good for the greatest number) for individual happiness as the ultimate end; and, finally, (d) the complete denial of objective truth to any moral judgments (judgments that categorically prescribe what ought to be sought and ought to be done), which leads to the emotivism and the so-called noncognitive ethics prevalent in our own day.

In surveying this demise of sound moral philosophy, MacIntyre heaps excessive and unwarranted praise on the part that Nietzsche played, attributing to him penetrating critical insights that justified the wholesale dismissal of all the modern views with which he was acquainted, and substituting for them nothing but his own brand of nihilistic skepticism. That, in my judgment, makes Nietzsche the villain rather than the hero of the story.

In the first place, we did not need Nietzsche to justify our dismissal of the errors made by moral philosophers since the eighteenth century. An understanding of all the fundamental insights that make Aristotle's *Ethics* the only sound, practical, and undogmatic moral philosophy would have sufficed for that. In the second place, Nietzsche's contribution, if it has any merit at all, is nullified by the nihilistic skepticism which he thought was the only alternative to the doctrines he rejected. His ignorance, misunderstanding, or neglect of Aristotle's *Ethics* is unacceptable. MacIntyre's juxtaposition, in several chapters, of Nietzsche vs. Aristotle, as if this presented us with a genuine choice, is also unacceptable.

That, however, is not the only serious fault with the philosophical message that is interlaced with the historical narrative in MacIntyre's book. The bankruptcy of moral philosophy in modern times does not stem solely from the loss of the concept of moral virtue and the attempt to substitute for it moral laws or rules of conduct, the validity and utility of which have been so successfully challenged. It stems also from the loss of the other elements that, in Aristotle's *Ethics,* are inextricably connected with the concept of virtue.

These elements are as follows:

(1) a nonhedonistic and totally nonpsychological conception of happiness as identical with a whole life well-lived, because virtuously conducted and accompanied by the blessings of good fortune;

(2) an understanding that happiness, so conceived, is not experienceable or enjoyable at any moment in the individual's life, that it functions as the ultimate end for which everything else is a constitutive or an operative means in the same way that an architect's vision of a building to be erected functions as the end to be aimed at, with the one difference that the building, when erected, exists and endures, whereas a good life when completed is over and done with;

(3) the crucial insight that moral or prescriptive judgments have a different kind of truth from that of factual or descriptive judgments, by conformity with right desire instead of by conformity with reality;

(4) the distinction between natural and acquired desires, together with the distinction between real and merely apparent goods—real goods being the objects of natural desires (or inherent human needs), and merely apparent goods seeming to be good only because individuals have acquired desires for them and so happen to want them;

(5) the understanding that though everyone uses the word *happiness* as the name for an end that is never a means—that is, something to be sought entirely for its own sake—not all human beings have the same ultimate good in mind when they pursue happiness;

(6) the rejection of individualistic relativism on the grounds that the happiness everyone ought to seek is the same for all because the real goods we naturally desire are the same for all; which leads to

(7) the conception of happiness not as the *summum bonum* but rather as the *totum bonum,* a whole life made good by the cumulative attainment of *all* the real goods that are the objects of the natural desires common to all human beings because they share the same specific nature; and to

(8) the distinction between these real goods as the constitutive elements of happiness (or a whole life made good) and the moral virtues as the operative or functional means whereby happiness is achieved, but

(9) only, of course, if their presence is accompanied by the blessings of good fortune.

All of the foregoing nine points are summarized in the single sentence in which Aristotle defines happiness as a whole life that is lived in accordance with complete virtue and is accompanied by a moderate amount of the external goods that are the goods of fortune.* The role that virtue plays cannot be understood without an understanding of all the other elements in the picture. Virtue, as Aristotle says, may make a man morally good, but by itself it does not produce the happiness of a morally good life.

Centuries later, a single sentence in Augustine's little treatise on the happy life also encapsulated the Aristotelian doctrine. Happy is the man, Augustine said, who, in the course of a complete life, has everything he desires, *provided that he desires nothing amiss;* or, in other words, provided that his life is lived in accordance with right rather than wrong desires. It cannot be so lived without moral virtue when that is understood to be identical with right desire—desire for the real goods that everyone naturally needs.

Though MacIntyre insists that without the concept of moral virtue a sound moral philosophy cannot be developed, his account of the role that moral virtue plays in a sound moral philosophy is deficient because he either neglects entirely or does not pay sufficient attention to all the other elements in the picture, with which moral virtue is inextricably connected. This has serious consequences for his discussion of virtue and for his

---

* *See* the *Nicomachean Ethics,* Book I, ch. 10, 1101b, 14–21; *GBWW,* Vol. 9, p. 346c.

effort to replace Aristotle's ethics with a doctrine that he thinks will be more acceptable, more congenial or palatable, to contemporary tastes.

For one thing, he fails to distinguish between two radically different senses of the word *good*—the adjectival use of *good* (along with *better* and *best*) to grade objects of any sort (e.g., a good knife, and good coffee), for which such other words as *fine, finer,* and *finest* can always be substituted; and the substantive use of the word in the plural to name goods that are objects of desire. With the exception of the adjective *good* in the phrase "a good man," only the latter use of *good* has moral significance.

This failure on MacIntyre's part underlies his erroneous dismissal of Hume's correct insight that valid prescriptive judgments, which declare what we ought to seek or do, cannot be derived from true descriptive statements about what does or does not exist in reality. There is no way of validating prescriptive judgments except in terms of Aristotle's distinction between prescriptive and descriptive truth, one by conformity to right desire, the other by conformity to reality. In the light of this distinction, it is then possible to formulate one self-evident prescriptive principle: we ought to desire everything that is really good for us; all real goods ought to be desired.

Nothing more than this one self-evident first principle is needed to arrive at other prescriptive truths based on true descriptive statements about the natural desires or needs of all human beings, the objects of which are all real goods that are rightly desired and, therefore, ought to be desired.

MacIntyre's deficient understanding of Aristotle's ethics may also account for his failure to see that another basic difference of the greatest importance between Aristotle's moral philosophy and modern ethical doctrines is the primacy of the good over the right in the one, and the reverse of that in the other.

For Aristotle, the ultimate end to be sought by the individual is his own happiness, the totality of all real goods attainable by virtue and good fortune in a whole life. It is not the general welfare of the political community, nor the general happiness—the happiness of others. One aspect of moral virtue, justice, is concerned with the welfare of the community and the happiness of others; but, unless each individual knows what is really and ultimately good for himself or herself and aims at it, the individual cannot know what is really good for others, to which they have a right because they need every real good for their happiness. Nor will the individual be inclined to avoid injuring others by depriving them of real goods or interfering with their attainment of them, unless he understands that he cannot aim at, or attain, what is really good for himself without also acting justly toward others; that is, without injuring them.

The moral laws or rules of conduct that modern ethical doctrines substitute for the concept of moral virtue are exclusively concerned with right and wrong conduct toward others rather than with the good that the individual ought to seek for himself or herself.

Last, but not least, of the consequences of MacIntyre's argument to be pointed out is his rejection of Aristotle's teaching concerning the unity of virtue, a doctrine reinforced by Aquinas's treatment of the four cardinal virtues (temperance, courage, justice, and prudence) as four aspects of virtue, not four distinct and separable virtues. Aquinas also treats all the other traditionally named virtues as things to be annexed to one or another of the four cardinal aspects of unitary virtue.

The reason why this point is important is that to omit or reject it prevents us from understanding what Aristotle meant by "complete" or "perfect" in that crucial sentence in which he defined happiness as a life lived in accordance with complete or perfect virtue, not just in accordance with some virtues in the absence of others or together with the vices that replace them. It also prevents us from understanding why an individual is obliged to act rightly or justly toward others in order to pursue happiness for himself or herself.

This can be made intelligible only if it is impossible to be courageous, temperate, and prudent without also being just, precisely because the four virtues named are not virtues capable of existing separately. They are only four aspects of virtue, the existence of any one of which is impossible without the coexistence of the other three.

Not to understand the unity of virtue and the inseparability of its four cardinal aspects is not to understand moral virtue itself. Moral virtue is the habit of right desire. Desire can be right in two ways, not one—right in aiming at the end which ought to be sought because it consists in the totality of all real goods, and right in the choice of the means to be employed in acting for the rightly desired end. Prudence is that aspect of virtue which is involved in the right choice of means; temperance and courage in private life, and with them justice in relation to others, are the aspects of virtue which are involved in rightly desiring or aiming at the one ultimate good—the happiness we are all morally obliged to seek.

The intemperate individual, the glutton, drunkard, or sluggard, cannot be prudent, because any means chosen will be chosen for the wrong end. Similarly, the unjust individual, the thief, cannot be prudent; he can only be cunning and clever, Aristotle tells us, because his conduct is not directed to the right end.

For the same reason, an individual cannot be temperate *and* cowardly, or courageous *and* intemperate; that is, an individual cannot have an habitual right desire for the end he ought to seek (as indicated by his being temperate or courageous) and at the same time also have an habitual wrong desire for things he ought not to seek, because the latter are incompatible with the end he ought to seek (as indicated by his being cowardly or intemperate).

This brings me finally to MacIntyre's own project of trying to retain something akin to the notion of virtue (but certainly not identical with the Aristotelian conception of it as summarized above) and to develop a moral philosophy for our day that will be more acceptable than Aristotle's doctrine to current prejudices—for that is all they are.

One of these prejudices, MacIntyre tells us, is the scientific prejudice against Aristotle's "metaphysical biology," which, in his view, provides the indispensable underpinnings for Aristotle's moral philosophy. This scientific prejudice, it should be pointed out, is to be found mainly if not exclusively among social scientists, not biological scientists. It is a prejudice against the notion that all human beings, as members of the species *homo sapiens,* share a common, specific nature and all the species-specific properties that genetically belong to that specific nature.

If the affirmation of a specific nature and species-specific properties is metaphysical biology, then twentieth-century biological science is metaphysical when it looks upon the genetic code as having programmed, in the same way, the development of individual members of a species, all drawn from the same gene pool. The same picture, but not the same words, is to be found in Aristotle's doctrine that individuals of the same species have the same potentialities for development and their normal development consists in the actualization of such potentialities.

This basic biological insight, which is not metaphysical at all in any correct sense of that term, does, of course, underlie Aristotle's moral philosophy. The crucial notion of the natural desires that are inherent in all members of the human species because of their common human nature (together with the notion of the real goods they aim at) rests on the biological fact that all human beings have the same specific potentialities (i.e., the same genetic program) for development and that these potencies are appetitive tendencies to be fulfilled by their actualization.

To say, as Aristotle does, that all men by nature desire to know is to say that all, having minds, have a potentiality for knowing, and that this potentiality is a natural desire or tendency—a need to be fulfilled by the acquisition of knowledge, which is something really good for every human being to possess.

The other contemporary prejudice that Professor MacIntyre wishes to placate by his deflated version of Aristotle's moral philosophy is one that he calls "individualistic liberalism." Briefly stated, it consists in the opinion that everyone should be free to conceive happiness in his own way and to seek it accordingly. Those espousing such individualism are necessarily affronted by a doctrine which proclaims that happiness can be rightly and wrongly conceived, that rightly conceived it is the same for every human being, and that, with minor differences in accidental respects, it must be pursued in the same way by all—that is, by virtuous conduct accompanied by the blessings of good fortune.

Any attempt to avoid these two contemporary prejudices, neither of which is defensible, must result in a moral philosophy that is as defective as Mill's utilitarianism. MacIntyre makes no reference to an excellent contemporary work in moral philosophy (G. H. von Wright's *The Varieties of Goodness*) which, like his own, expresses great admiration for Aristotle's *Ethics* while, at the same time, giving reasons for substituting something else for it that is not as good.

Professor von Wright tells us his reason for turning away from Aristotle's teleological ethics in the direction of Mill's utilitarianism. Referring to Aristotle and Mill as representative of the two main variants of teleological ethics, he writes:

> The one makes the notion of the good of man relative to the notion of the *nature* of man. The other makes it relative to the needs and wants of individual men. We would call the two variants the 'objectivist' and the 'subjectivist' variant respectively. I think it is right to say that Aristotle favoured the first. Here my position differs from his and is, I think, more akin to that of some writers of the utilitarian tradition.

The same prejudices are here apparent—*against* the affirmation of man's specific nature and *for* individualistic liberalism. Neither prejudice, in my judgment, can be regarded as a good reason for replacing Aristotle's *Ethics* with a moral philosophy that is less sound, and that is especially deficient because it cannot combine a principle of moral obligation with the teleological consideration of means and ends.

It must be said in Professor MacIntyre's favor that he acknowledges the deficiencies in what he has been able to come up with so far as a substitute for Aristotle's *Ethics*. He promises further developments in a forthcoming book, but I do not think he can succeed in the project he has set for himself if he persists in the positions he has taken so far.

---

[1]*See* M. J. Adler, *The Time of Our Lives*, subtitled "The Ethics of Common Sense," Holt, Rinehart and Winston, 1970.

Machine Thinking and Thinking Machines

The Mind's I
edited by
Douglas R. Hofstadter
and Daniel C. Dennett

Brainstorms
by Daniel C. Dennett

Mind Design
edited by John Haugeland

Reviewed by
Charles Van Doren

Charles Van Doren, who was educated at St. John's College, Annapolis, from which he graduated in 1947, has also a master's degree in mathematics and a doctorate in English literature, both from Columbia University, where for a time he taught literature.

In 1965 he was made associate director of the Institute for Philosophical Research under Mortimer Adler, and in 1973 he was appointed vice-president, editorial, of Encyclopædia Britannica, Inc. In this position he has been necessarily involved with computers, about which he has learned as much as a layman can, and is responsible for operation of the advanced computer typesetting system the company now uses.

Among books that he has written are *Lincoln's Commando* (1957), *The Idea of Progress* (1967), and, with Mortimer Adler, the revised edition of *How to Read a Book* (1972). He was editor, with Clifton Fadiman, of *The American Treasury* (1955), and with Mr. Adler of the *Great Treasury of Western Thought*. He was executive editor as well of the twenty-volume *Annals of America* (1967), of which he wrote most of the two-volume *Conspectus*. Last year he contributed a review of *Mathematics—The Loss of Certainty*, by Morris Kline, to *The Great Ideas Today*.

The last half of the twentieth century is a remarkable era in human history. This is not just because it is "ours," the half century in which we live; these years seem to have a special character that is likely to be remembered as extraordinary for a long time to come. But we may ask, what is the most distinctive achievement of our time, what will be remembered longest, what will give our age its name?

Several answers come to mind. Ours is the Age of Atomic Energy—and of Atomic Bombs. Doubtless that fact will be long remembered, but it somehow seems less interesting, although no less perilous, than everyone thought twenty or thirty years ago. Ours is the age in which mankind first became aware that the Earth's resources are limited—at least the first time that fact was recognized in more than a century (one must admit that the Old World knew it very well, and Malthus voiced the thought for all time). Ours is the age in which, dimly as yet, man has discovered that no nation, no matter how rich and powerful, can have its way unbridled with the world. That has been a useful lesson, but perhaps it is not an entirely new one. Ours is the Age of Space, though this bright dream, so alluring only twenty years ago, seems to have faded to a faint and perhaps a dying glow. Ours is also the Age of Torture—but again that is hardly new, no matter how shocking it may be to our civilized sensibilities.

Finally, ours is the Age of the Computer, and I for one think this is the fact about us that will be longest remembered. If, that is, we survive the first of our achievements.

It is useful to remind ourselves of how recent computers really are. Although they have their forebears in "analytical engines" and mechanical calculating machines, and although the basic ideas of the modern computer were almost all enunciated by A. M. Turing, the brilliant English mathematician (of whom more below), in the 1930s, it is a fact that little actual computing power, and few working machines, existed in 1950. Today, only a generation later, computers are endemic and have utterly changed the world. Just one statistic tells the story. It is hard to believe, but true, that 1959 was the last year in which there were more telephone calls in the United States between human beings than between computers. Today the great majority of telephone calls are between computers, even though the number of calls between humans has vastly increased. In this connection, incidentally, it is worth considering what would happen if this traffic between computers were to cease. At the moment computers "pay" about three-quarters of the cost of our telephone network. If the calls stopped, they would cease to "pay" it and we would have to take up the slack on our telephone bills, which would therefore be likely to rise by a factor of somewhere between three and five times.

The endemic computer is in most of its installations around the world a utilitarian device—a new kind of tool in the service of man. (A tool can also be a plaything, as most "home computers" are at present, although they give promise of becoming more as time goes on.) But not all computers are tools, or merely tools; some are, or are something like, "thinking machines." Note that I do not say "machines that think," nor do I use the phrase without protective quotation marks. I would not be understood as stating any grand hypothesis here, only as making a distinction between, say, a computer in a bank that sorts checks and keeps balances, and a computer that plays chess or backgammon. (Some computers play chess quite well; they would certainly beat me and most amateurs, although not chess masters. One computer plays backgammon extremely well; it is in fact the world champion, having defeated the human world champion at the end of 1981.) Such a computer—or, to be precise, such a program (we will often confuse hardware and software in what follows)— would seem to be doing something different from mere "number-crunch-

Alan Mathison Turing (1912–1954), a pioneer in computer theory. He was involved in the construction of early computers and the development of programming techniques. His concepts of "computing machines" have dominated the field for half a century.

ing." A good computer chess player cannot, indeed, play chess by merely crunching numbers; the so-called combinatorial explosion would defeat it utterly if it tried to analyze all the consequences of all its opponents' moves.[1] Computers that play chess don't play it that way at all. They make "judgments," take "chances," act on "hunches," follow their "intuitions." (Here again the quotation marks are inserted for protection.)

Whether or not the computer that plays chess or backgammon is really thinking, there is a worldwide confraternity of brilliant people who would like to believe it does, or will someday. Mostly young, and often interconnected by electronic communication devices of one kind or another, these people are, in my view, the aristocracy of modern intellect. They generally agree with me—or rather I with them—that the idea of a computer that thinks is the most interesting idea in the world today.

Despite its very great interest, this idea has not benefited from the expenditure of much research money or time. Computers-as-tools are naturally where the commercial and financial action is.[2] What the search for artificial intelligence, or AI, has primarily benefited from in the past thirty years is a lot of thinking. A good deal of this thought is and has been very bad, and much of it is humdrum, but some of it is very good. A substantial part of the writing on the subject, even if the thought underlying it is not very good, is imaginative and interesting. It is, in sum, a field in which it is a great deal of fun to move around.

Why indeed should this not be so? The question is, can man build artifacts that imitate his most distinctive, perhaps his unique ability—to think? And if so, the question is, what will be the consequences of that: for the artifacts, for man, and for the world?

* * * * * * * * * * *

The field of AI has seen the publication of many papers, more or less technical, since 1950, but only recently have books appeared that are readable by ordinary laymen. Three such books are *The Mind's I,* edited by Douglas R. Hofstadter and Daniel C. Dennett (New York: Basic Books, 1981); *Brainstorms,* by Daniel C. Dennett (Montgomery, Vt.: Bradford Books, 1978); and *Mind Design,* edited by John Haugeland (Montgomery, Vt.: Bradford Books, 1981). They are reviewed in what follows.

The Mind's I. Of Daniel Dennett I will have more to say later. His collaborator here, Douglas Hofstadter, is the author of one of the most remarkable books of recent years, *Gödel, Escher, Bach: An Eternal Golden Braid.* Readers of that astonishing work will recognize the same Hofstadterian *enfant terrible* in this fascinating, charming, and provocative new collection of writings.

One reviewer declared of *Gödel, Escher, Bach* that "whatever human intelligence is, one feels that this book manifests its highest qualities." Hofstadter's intelligence is once again manifest in *The Mind's I*, together with his penchant for—not to say obsession with—perplexities, paradoxes, and problems. That is not particularly surprising. Anyone who confronts the kind of questions dealt with in *The Mind's I*—questions like What is the mind? Who am I? Can mere matter think or feel? Where is the soul?— "runs headlong," as the authors say themselves, "into perplexities."

Is teleportation possible? If you were teleported, say from Earth to Mars, what would that mean about your "I?" Presumably you would exist on both planets; would both of you be "you?" Can you imagine possessing—"you," who are your "I"—a different, better body? Is your brain "you?"—and if not, what is the difference between "you" and your brain? In fact, although I am quite sure you have a brain, I am not so sure you have—or are—an "I." And in any case, *where* is your "I?" It is the more or less serious entertainment of questions like these, and dozens more, that gives Hofstadter's book its delightful, quirky playfulness.

The Mind's I in fact is an anthology, but it is heavily annotated, with a "Reflection" by Hofstadter or by Dennett following most of the selections. These commentaries are often quite long, always apposite, and in a few cases truly brilliant additions to the ideas presented in the selection commented on.

An example occurs on pages 190–91, where a selection by Hofstadter himself ends and a commentary, also by him, begins. The selection, titled "Prelude . . . Ant Fugue," is taken from *Gödel, Escher, Bach*. It is a dialogue in the form of a fugue—readers of the earlier book will understand that exactly; there is no point in trying to explain it to those who have not read the book—about ants and ant colonies, but more importantly about reductionism versus holism in philosophy. On the last page of the dialogue is printed this illustration, drawn by Hofstadter and accompanied by the following comments by the persons of the dialogue.

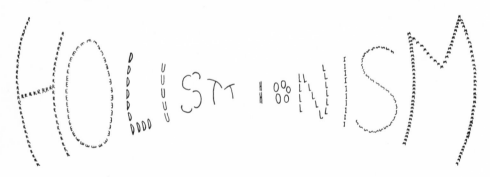

"TORTOISE: Speaking of fugues, this fugue that we have been listening to is nearly over. Toward the end, there occurs a strange new twist on its theme. (*Flips the page in the* Well-Tempered Clavier.) Well, what have we here? A new illustration—how appealing! (*Shows it to the Crab.*)

"CRAB: Well, what have we here? Oh, I see: it's 'HOLISMIONISM,' written in large letters that first shrink and then grow back to their original size. But that doesn't make any sense, because it's not a word. Oh me, oh my! (*Passes it to the Anteater.*)

"ANTEATER: Well, what have we here? Oh, I see: it's 'REDUCTHO-LISM,' written in small letters that first grow and then shrink back to their original size. But that doesn't make any sense, because it's not a word. Oh me, oh my! (*Passes it to Achilles.*)

"ACHILLES: I know the rest of you won't believe this, but in fact this picture consists of the word 'HOLISM' written twice, with the letters continually shrinking as they proceed from left to right. (*Returns it to the Tortoise.*)

"TORTOISE: Iknow the rest of you won't believe this, but in fact this picture consists of the word 'REDUCTIONISM' written once, with the letters continually growing as they proceed from left to right.

"ACHILLES: At last—I heard the new twist on the theme this time! I am so glad that you pointed it out to me, Mr. Tortoise. Finally, I think I am beginning to grasp the art of listening to fugues."

The above interchange—in which you will recognize, if you read it carefully and look equally carefully at the illustration, that every one of the apparently contradictory statements is true—is a sufficiently brilliant presentation, in most kinds of metaphor known to man, of the marvelously complex perplexities of the subject of reductionism versus holism. But Hofstadter is not through yet, although his dialogue ends here. His own commentary on it begins immediately with the pseudo-solemn question, combining, as Martin Gardner says, two puns with a spoonerism: "Is a soul greater than the hum of its parts?" I hope I will be forgiven my enthusiasm when I say I think this is one of the most delightful questions ever asked.

Hofstadter then goes on, in his commentary, to "indulge his fancy for wordplay" with the following diagram, which is worth a semester course:

Hard scientists	Soft scientists
Reductionism (upward causality)	Holism (downward causality)
+	+
Predictionism (upstream causality)	Goalism (downstream causality)
=Mechanism	=Soulism

Not all of the selections in *The Mind's I* are as playful as those by Hofstadter himself (he contributes two others, including an original one called "A Conversation with Einstein's Brain"), but most are as interesting—this is a truly superior collection. Practically all deserve some notice here, but restraint is necessary, and I shall comment on only four.

One of these is by A. M. Turing who, while at King's College, Cambridge, in 1935, began his pioneering work on the theory of mathematical computers. This led him in 1936 to Princeton, where he earned his Ph.D. with a dissertation that among other things described a universal computer—the so-called Turing machine—that with suitable programming could do the work of any machine designed for special-purpose problem solving. After the war Turing joined the computing laboratory at the University of Manchester; there he championed the theory that computers could be constructed that would be capable of thought that would, in suitable circumstances—the so-called Turing test—be indistinguishable from human thought. Although his untimely death from poison in 1954 was declared a suicide, it has since come to be felt that it was a tragic accident.

Perhaps Turing's most influential paper was called "Computing Machinery and Intelligence." It appeared in the journal *Mind* in 1950. Excerpts from this famous discussion of the basic question being addressed in the three books reviewed here appear in *The Mind's I*, which would be a book worth having because it makes these provocative conclusions readily available, if for no other reason.

The Turing test is well known, although it is not always accurately described. To quote Turing's own words:

> . . . the problem can be described in terms of a game which we call the "imitation game." It is played with three people, a man (A), a woman (B), and an interrogator (C) who may be of either sex. The interrogator stays in a room apart from the other two. The object of the game for the interrogator is to determine which of the other two is the man and which is the woman. He knows them by labels X and Y, and at the end of the game he says either "X is A and Y is B" or "X is B and Y is A." The interrogator is allowed to put questions to A and B thus:
>
> C: Will X please tell me the length of his or her hair?
>
> Now suppose X is actually A, then A must answer. It is A's object in the game to try to cause C to make the wrong identification. His answer might therefore be "My hair is shingled, and the longest strands are about nine inches long."
>
> In order that tones of voice may not help the interrogator the answers should be written, or better still, typewritten. The ideal arrangement is to have a teleprinter communicating between the two rooms. . . . The object of the game for the third player (B) is to help the interrogator.

The best strategy for her is probably to give truthful answers. She can add such things as "I am the woman, don't listen to him!" to her answers, but it will avail nothing as the man can make similar remarks.

We now ask the question, "What will happen when a machine takes the part of A in this game?" Will the interrogator decide wrongly as often when the game is played like this as he does when the game is played between a man and a woman? These questions replace our original, "Can machines think?"[3]

No machine has yet passed the Turing test, that is, has played the Turing game successfully. Will a machine ever do so? Ah, that is *the* question, and I will return to it!

Turing certainly thought that someday a machine would win the Turing game. In the rest of the selection reprinted by Hofstadter and Dennett, Turing responds to some of the more common objections raised by anti-AIists. There is The Theological Objection that God has not given an immortal soul to machines, therefore machines will never be able to think. This begs the question, obviously. There is The "Heads in the Sand" Objection, which, simply stated, is that " 'the consequences of machines thinking would be too dreadful. Let us hope and believe that they cannot do so.' " This is a futile objection, although one that is very widespread. Then there is The Mathematical Objection, which, essentially, is that it can be proved that any finite machine must be limited in its power to think (compute). That is undoubtedly true—but men, who certainly think, are also limited. The Argument from Consciousness receives equally short shrift from Turing. Finally, there are the Arguments from Various Disabilities, which take the form " 'I grant you that you can make machines do all the things you have mentioned but you will never be able to make one to do X.' " Among X's are

> Be kind, resourceful, beautiful, friendly . . . have initiative, have a sense of humor, tell right from wrong, make mistakes . . . fall in love, enjoy strawberries and cream . . . make someone fall in love with it, learn from experience . . . use words properly, be the subject of its own thought . . . have as much diversity of behavior as a man, do something really new. . .[4]

We have all heard all of these objections, and more besides. They are all interesting, but all are probably irrelevant. Or so Turing says.

Quite properly, these excerpts from Turing's famous 1950 paper appear early in *The Mind's I,* because many of the other selections in the book address points that Turing raises.

For example, there is the selection by John R. Searle, titled "Minds, Brains, and Programs," in which Searle sharply attacks what he calls "strong" AI, that is, the position that "the computer is not merely a tool in the study of the mind; rather, the appropriately programmed computer really *is* a mind." Searle, interpreting the Turing test as essentially suggesting that if a machine behaves like a man—or cannot be perceived as acting differently from a man—then it must *be* a man, imagines a situation in which a man appears to know Chinese but really does not. Because he appears to, because he behaves as though he does, does he *really* know Chinese? Searle asks. Of course not, he replies. And the same line of reasoning would apply to any machine that passed—or seemed to pass—the Turing test.

Searle's original article appeared with no fewer than twenty-seven responses from assorted pro-AIists, all of whom were incensed by his attack. Hofstadter, in his commentary on the selection, adds still another response. It is excellent, but I am not sure it lays all of Searle's objections, explicit and implicit, to rest. Simulations can be, we all know, very tricky things. . . .[5]

The last two selections in *The Mind's I* that I want to refer to are both by the same author, the Polish writer and philosopher Stanislaw Lem. Lem's is truly an extraordinary imagination; it stands out even in this august company.

The first selection by Lem is titled "The Seventh Sally, *or* How Trurl's Own Perfection Led to No Good." It is from a book called *The Cyberiad* that was published in English in 1974 and has since become a minor classic. Trurl was a kind of magician, or rather infinitely ingenious engineer, or rather incomparable computer-programmer, who traveled through Space and one day lighted upon a small planet the brutal king of which had recently been deposed by his subjects. The king demanded that Trurl restore him to his throne, but Trurl instead created for him a marvelous toy, a tiny model kingdom complete with

> plenty of towns, rivers, mountains, forests, and brooks, a sky with clouds, armies full of derring-do, citadels, castles, and ladies' chambers; and there were marketplaces, gaudy and gleaming in the sun, days of back-breaking labor, nights full of dancing and song until dawn, and the gay clatter of swordplay. Trurl also carefully set into this kingdom a fabulous capital, all in marble and alabaster, and assembled a council of hoary sages, and winter palaces and summer villas, plots, conspirators, false witnesses, nurses, informers, teams of magnificent steeds, and plumes waving crimson in the wind; and then he crisscrossed that atmosphere with silver fanfares and twenty-one gun salutes, also threw in the necessary handful of traitors, another of heroes, added a pinch of prophets and seers, and one messiah and one great poet each, after which he bent over and set the works in motion, deftly making last-minute adjustments with his microscopic tools as it ran, and he gave the women of the kingdom beauty, the men—sullen silence and surliness when drunk, the officials—arrogance and servility, the astronomers—an enthusiasm for stars, and the children—a great capacity for noise. And

all of this, connected, mounted and ground to precision, fit into a box, and not a very large box, but just the size that could be carried about with ease.[6]

The king is at first offended by the small size of his new realm, but he soon grows to enjoy ruling over it and does so with the greatest cruelty.

Trurl returns to his home star where he meets his old friend and philosophical interlocuter, Klapaucius. They engage in a lengthy and highly amusing debate about whether the model is "real" and whether the tiny subjects are "alive." It cannot be denied that they *act* alive; their behavior is indistinguishable from that of real living men—Poles, one might in fact surmise. The argument becomes more and more heated until Trurl and Klapaucius decide to journey to the little planet to see for themselves. There they are astonished to find that the tiny subjects of the cruel king have discovered atomic energy, revolted against their master, and pushed him out into the depths of the space that now surrounds their diminutive world—where, owing to the universal law of gravity, he has become a satellite, has "in this way become the Moon of the Microminians."

The other selection by Lem, titled "Non Serviam," is taken from what must surely be one of the strangest books ever written. Called *A Perfect Vacuum: Perfect Reviews of Nonexistent Books,* it appeared in Polish in 1971. "Non Serviam" is a "review" of a "book" by one Professor Dobb, who at some time or other—probably some years in the future—is (was? will be?) a researcher at a university, where he undertakes (the present tense must suffice) a series of experiments with personoids—that is, computers/machines that think.

Dobb's personoids live in a mathematical universe, and "to declare," Lem "quotes" Dobb as saying, "that the personoids are 'handicapped' with respect to us, inasmuch as they do not see or hear as we do, is totally absurd, because with equal justice one could assert that it is we who are deprived with respect to them—unable to feel with immediacy the phenomenalism of mathematics, which, after all, we know only in a cerebral, inferential fashion. It is only through reasoning that we are in touch with mathematics, only through abstract thought that we 'experience' it. Whereas the personoids *live* in it; it is their air, their earth, clouds, water, and even bread—yes, even food, because in a certain sense they take nourishment from it." They are "imprisoned," hermetically sealed within their machine; they cannot work their way out to the human world. But a man cannot enter their world either. Dobb is fascinated by this aspect of their "life."

He teaches, or allows, the personoids to communicate with one another, which of course they do electronically, and they discourse among themselves with ineffable logic about the nature of themselves, of their

Some early automata were very successful, such as the Musician, made by Pierre Jaquet-Droz in 1773. This young woman is able to play the clavecin with all ten fingers. At regular intervals, her chest rises and falls as if she were breathing. She is able to move her head and eyes. She sways and bends with the music and when she is finished with a piece she makes a gentle bow.

A portion of the
complicated works
inside the Musician.

society, and of their world. Eventually they turn to theology and begin to
voice their inevitable puzzlement as to how they came to be and what
their destiny will be. They "discover" that there is, because there must be,
one God, and they naturally conclude that He is their Creator, that is,
Dobb, although they do not perceive Dobb and wonder whether in fact he
really exists. Dobb is urged by one of his colleagues to tell them he does
exist and thus relieve them of their doubts.

"Now, this," Dobb says, "I most certainly shall not do. For it would
have all the appearance to me of soliciting a sequel—that is, a reaction on
their part. But what exactly could they do or say to me, that I would not
feel the profound embarrassment, the painful sting of my position as their
unfortunate Creator? The bills for the electricity consumed have to be
paid quarterly, and the moment is going to come when my university
superiors demand the 'wrapping up' of the experiment—that is, the dis-
connecting of the machine, or, in other words, the end of the world. That
moment I intend to put off as long as humanly possible. It is the only
thing of which I am capable, but it is not anything I consider praisewor-

thy. It is, rather, what in common parlance is generally called 'dirty work.' Saying this, I hope that no one will get any ideas. But if he does, well, that is his business."[7]

One does not perhaps have to be an AIist to feel a twinge upon reading this. Similar feelings, although a good deal stronger, are felt by readers of Robert Heinlein's great science fiction novel, *The Moon Is a Harsh Mistress,* when MIKE, the super computer who (which?) has come alive at the beginning of the book, is attacked by atomic bombs at the end of it, and "dies."

Brainstorms. This volume too is a collection, but it is not an anthology; all of the pieces contained in it are by Daniel C. Dennett, Douglas Hofstadter's collaborator in editing *The Mind's I* and a well-known writer on philosophy and psychology (he is a professor of philosophy at Tufts University). The pieces in the volume hang together with a remarkable consistency of view and tone, a fact that has elicited much praise for the book. It follows, as Dennett explains in his preface, a book titled *Content and Consciousness,* which appeared in 1969 (*Brainstorms* was published in 1978), and revises and extends, Dennett claims, the theory that he first propounded in that earlier work.

Each of the pieces in *Brainstorms* is interesting and all are well-written and highly readable—as readable as more or less technical philosophical articles are ever likely to be —but the theory, as such, is perhaps not as clear as Dennett suggests. At any rate Dennett's definition of the mind, if that is after all a proper name for it, seems to be relatively simple and certainly very prudent. It is, I think, Ockhamesque, in that Dennett holds that no predication of nonphysical aspects of the mind should be made unless there is a *necessity* to make it—that is, unless no other explanation for observed phenomena can be found. At the same time he is willing to entertain nonphysical aspects at a number of points of the argument. He may therefore be called a mentalist, I think, but *no more a mentalist than he has to be.*

Brainstorms has four parts, the first and fourth of which are most relevant to the main subject of this discussion. Part I, Intentional Explanation and Attributions of Mentality, contains an excellent account of Dennett's notion of intentionality as a characteristic of a rather large class of entities, including men, tigers, and chess-playing computers. The interesting observation here is that we do—indeed, we had better—presume intentionality on the part of all three. A tiger that we assume has no purpose with respect to us will end up eating us; a computer that we assume has no "desire" to win will end up beating us; and a sane man we treat as if he were mad will likely regard *us* as mad and put us in a straitjacket if he can.

These notions obviously bear on our central concern. Even more relevant is the article called "Why You Can't Make a Computer that Feels Pain." The reason is not exactly what one would expect, which is as typical of Dennett as it is of Hofstadter, who *never* gives you what you expect. The reason is not that computers cannot in principle or by definition feel pain; it is that we simply don't know well enough what pain is—we do not have a satisfactory theory of pain—so that we cannot make a machine that feels it. As Dennett says:

> What then is the conclusion? It is that any robot instantiation of any theory of pain will be vulnerable to powerful objections . . ., but reliance on such skeptical arguments would be short-sighted, for the inability of a robot model to satisfy all our intuitive demands may be due not to any irredeemable mysteriousness about the phenomenon of pain, but to irredeemable incoherency in our ordinary concept of pain. . . . If and when a good physiological sub-personal theory of pain is developed, a robot could in principle be constructed to instantiate it. Such advances in science would probably bring in their train wide-scale changes in what we found intuitive about pain, so that the charge that our robot only suffered what we artifically *called* pain would lose its persuasiveness. In the meantime (if there were a cultural lag) thoughtful people would refrain from kicking such a robot. (pp. 228-29)

The last part of the book, Free Will and Personhood, carries through the program outlined in the introduction, in the process revealing a number of shibboleths and straw men for what they are. In "Mechanism and Responsibility," for example, Dennett argues—I think persuasively—that mechanism and responsibility are no more incompatible than are determinism and free will. The latter pair of terms were shown to be able to subsist side by side more than a century ago; Dennett resolves the problems about the former pair in a similar argument. He denies "that there are some things in the world, namely human beings, of which mechanism as an embracing theory cannot be true," for he holds that "there is no incompatibility between mechanistic and intentional explanation." We are thus back to the tiger and the chess-playing computer, the latter of which is certainly "mechanistic," whatever we may think of the tiger, though its behavior can be assumed to be intentional. To the extent that the assumption is justified, one of Turing's Arguments from Various Disabilities is met and countered.

"Mechanism and Responsibility" is immediately followed by "The Abilities of Men and Machines," in which Dennett takes up still another argument, this one rather technical and based on assumptions that Dennett maintains are untenable about Gödel's Theorem and Turing machines. To simplify greatly, what Dennett says is that while it is probably true that no Turing machine can imitate a man, a very large number of Turing machines might be able to, which holds out a fascinating prospect. Dennett ends this piece by revealing once again his excellent sense. "This is no *refutation*," he concedes, "of anti-mechanism, no *proof* that a human being and a computer are in relevant respects alike." At the same time he clears up old confusions that stand in the way of our understanding what we are really talking about when we ask whether a man and machine are, or can be, alike.

The most interesting article in the book—in my view—is called "Conditions of Personhood"; it lays down six conditions. What are persons? First, they are *rational beings.* Second, they are beings to which psychological or mental or *intentional predicates* are ascribed. Third, whether something counts as a person depends in some way on an *attitude taken* toward it, a *stance adopted* with respect to it. Fourth, the object toward which this stance is adopted must be capable of *reciprocating* in some way. Fifth, persons must be capable of *verbal communication.* Sixth, persons are distinguishable from other entities by being *conscious* in some special way: "there is a way in which *we* are conscious in which no other species is conscious. Sometimes this is identified as *self*-consciousness. . . ."

I see no reason to discard any of these conditions, nor do I think much is to be gained by adding others, which are for the most part derivative—such as "possessing an immortal soul." The interesting thing about the six conditions as a group is that computers may just possibly be able to satisfy five of them someday, if they are not able to yet. Already, computers are in some sense *rational beings* (although not yet, or perhaps ever, as fully rational as we are); *intentional predicates* may be at least metaphorically ascribed to them (as in the case of the chess-playing computer, which "wants to win"); when we treat them in a special way they *reciprocate;* they *communicate verbally;* and some kind of self-awareness may someday be built into them whereby we may say they are *conscious.* But there, you say, is the problem: How could we know that a computer was conscious? Isn't whatever behavior it manifests merely a simulation designed to fool us, as though we were playing the Turing game, into *thinking* that it is conscious, as we are? Indeed, that is the problem, a problem that looms no less difficult if I respond by asking how I know *you* are conscious (I really do believe you are). And so the whole thing comes down to the question of the *attitude we take,* the *stance we adopt* toward machines that think, or that might be said to think. Which is no more, possibly—or less—than a question of what we like to believe.

Mind Design. Whereas Dennett is primarily concerned to clear away the underbrush that impedes our journey toward full understanding of AI, John Haugeland, editor of the last of the three volumes discussed here, is a more forthright believer in, or at least proponent of (you can never quite tell about these fellows—all of them are just as likely to be putting forth conclusions "for the sake of the argument"), the idea that artificial intelligence is not a contradiction in terms, in other words that machines *may be able to think.*

Haugeland's book contains twelve essays, two of which I have already mentioned: Dennett's "Intentional Systems" and John R. Searle's "Minds, Brains, and Programs." But the book is for the most part not re-

This loom was invented by Joseph-Marie Jacquard in 1801. Jacquard's loom utilized punched cards that controlled the weaving of the cloth so that any desired pattern could be obtained automatically. These punched cards were adopted by the noted English inventor Charles Babbage as a control mechanism for his calculator, were used by the U.S. statistician Herman Hollerith to feed data to his census machine, and were utilized as the primary means by which programming was fed into early computers.

petitive of themes and ideas previously encountered. Instead, it offers many new ideas and insights, grist for our mental mill. Indeed, Haugeland's introductory comments, called "Semantic Engines: An Introduction to Mind Design," contain an enormously helpful overview of our whole subject, and this book could be recommended for that alone. It will be useful to quote some passages from the beginning of this introduction in order to give some idea of Haugeland's general turn of mind.

> "Reasoning is but reckoning," said Hobbes, in the earliest expression of the computational view of thought. Three centuries later, with the development of electronic "computers," his idea finally began to catch on; and now, in three decades, it has become the single most important theoretical hypothesis in psychology (and several allied disciplines), and also the basis of an exciting new research field, called "artificial intelligence." Recently, the expression *cognitive science* has been introduced to cover all these varied enterprises, in recognition of the common conceptual foundation. . . .
>
> Often (here and elsewhere) the discussion focuses on *artificial intelligence*—"AI," among friends—because it amounts to a kind of distilled essence of cognitive science. But again, it is important to realize that "AI" (like "cognitive science") is more specific in its meaning than the words themselves might suggest. Crudely, we can put the point in terms of different technologies: a project at IBM to wire and program an intelligent robot would probably be AI, whereas a project at DuPont to brew and mold a synthetic-organic android probably would not. But this can be misleading; the crucial issue is not protoplasm versus semiconductor ("wetware" versus "hardware"), but rather whether the product is designed and specified in terms of a computational structure. If it is, then a working model could probably be manufactured much more easily by means of electronics and programming; and that's the *only* relevance of the technology. Indeed, the guiding inspiration of cognitive science is that, at a suitable level of abstraction, a theory of "natural" intelligence should have the same basic form as the theories that explain sophisticated computer systems. It is this idea that makes *artificial* intelligence seem not only possible, but also a central and pure form of *psychological* research. (pp. 1–2)

From this it is clear that Haugeland is a convinced AIist. Yet his book is a fair presentation of both the pro-AI and anti-AI positions. On the pro side are such articles as "Complexity and the Study of Artificial and Human Intelligence," by Zenon Pylyshyn, in which it is argued that AI is fundamentally an empirical science and that "a new technical language" is needed "with which to discipline and expand one's imagination"; Haugeland's two pieces, and Marvin Minsky's well-known "A Framework for Representing Knowledge."

The last advances a fascinating conception of how the mind thinks: "When one encounters a new situation (or makes a substantial change in one's view of the present problem), one selects from memory," says

A portion of the Manchester University Mark I computer (sometimes called MADAM) as it appeared in June 1949. The prototype for this machine was first operative on June 21, 1948. It is believed to be the world's first electronic stored-program computer.

Minsky, "a structure called a *frame.*" This is a remembered framework to be adapted to fit reality by changing details as necessary.

"A *frame* is a data-structure for representing a stereotyped situation, like being in a certain kind of living room, or going to a child's birthday party. Attached to each frame are several kinds of information. Some of this information is about how to use the frame. Some is about what one can expect to happen next. Some is about what to do if these expectations are not confirmed.

"We can think of a frame as a network of nodes and relations. The top levels of a frame are fixed, and represent things that are always true about the supposed situation. The lower levels have many *terminals*—slots that must be filled by specific instances or data. Each terminal can specify conditions its assignments must meet. (The assignments themselves are usually smaller subframes.). . .

"Collections of related frames are linked together into *frame-systems.* The effects of important actions are mirrored by transformations between the frames of a system. . . . Different frames of a system share the same terminals; this is the critical point that makes it possible to coordinate information gathered from different view points."[8]

Minsky's concept of the mind as a computer, which is presented with the dash and bravura usually associated with his ideas, has much, superficially, to recommend it. That does seem, after all, to be something like the way our minds work. And if in fact it *is* how they work, that is very good for AI, because it appears to be obvious that a computer—perhaps a bigger one than any now extant—could be filled with millions of frames and frame-systems, and then it could begin to "think." It would then be what Minsky has here in effect described—a Turing machine.

Minsky, of course, is not immune from attack by capable anti-AIists. Perhaps the most capable one now around is Hubert L. Dreyfus, whose famous book, *What Computers Can't Do,* first appeared in 1972, and whose introduction to a revised edition of that work is included in Haugeland's collection. Called "From Micro-Worlds to Knowledge Representation: AI at an Impasse," it is fairly destructive of most of the AI positions and arguments, including Minsky's, that have been offered in the last ten years. It is destructive in part because Dreyfus, unlike a polemicist such as Searle, is moderate and even gentle in his approach; he always seems to be saying that he is very sorry to have to point out that such and such an argument simply does not hold water. In the case of Minsky's, this is because, Dreyfus says, the human mind either contains an almost infinitely large number of frames or it holds no clearly and logically distinguishable frames at all. The "frames" are not reproducible "knowledge-states"; instead they are instantiations of experience, remembered "scenes" that act like paradigms, and around which the mind, with its nearly infinite subtlety, loops trains of thought that adjust it to reality and, doubtless, reality to it as well. Besides, almost everything the mind knows seems to be available to it at any instant, which is a fact that dismays even the most hopeful engineer—how to make a machine with such incredibly rapid access to any part, large or small, of its enormous memory?

Dreyfus is a redoubtable opponent of AI not only because of his own obvious intelligence and because of his moderate tone; he has also got hold of an insight that seems to suggest that AI may be fundamentally and absolutely unachievable because the human mind may be fundamentally and absolutely not a Turing machine. To understand Dreyfus's rather subtle argument it is necessary to read the entire introduction to the new edition of *What Computers Can't Do,* but the argument can be summed up by saying that Dreyfus at bottom feels that "intelligence cannot be separated from the rest of human life."

> The persistent denial of this seemingly obvious point cannot, however, be laid at the door of AI. It starts with Plato's separation of the intellect or rational soul from the body with its skills, emotions, and appetites. Aristotle continued this unlikely dichotomy when he separated the theoretical from the practical, and defined man as a rational animal—as if one could separate man's rationality from his animal needs and desires. . . .
>
> Great artists have always sensed the truth, stubbornly denied by both philosophers and technologists, that the basis of human intelligence cannot be isolated and explicitly understood. . . . Yeats put it . . . succinctly: "I have found what I wanted—to put it in a phrase, I say, 'Man can embody the truth, but he cannot know it.' "9

* * * * * * * * * * *

The entire field of AI, or, if you will, of cognitive science, is confused by wishful thinking. This is not all on one side. The anti-AIists are probably right in saying that many pro-AIists are blinded by their hope that machines will someday exist—no one says they exist yet—that will somehow or other imitate human intelligence. On the other hand, there appears to be a solid residue on the other side of the kind of blind hope condemned by Turing—the hope that machines will never be like humans, because that would be frightening.

If all that is swept aside—which is not easy to do, since almost everybody is subject to one of these biases or the other (I frankly admit that I am biased toward the pro-AIist side)—then certain facts and conclusions can be written down and considered coolly at our leisure. Among them are these:

(1) *No machine has yet passed the Turing test.* Machines can do some wonderful things, including making billions of separate numerical calculations per second and playing good chess and excellent backgammon. I have had the experience of talking to a machine that talked back to me, in both a man's and a woman's voice, and that drew pictures on a wall at my

command. Robots assemble cars and work in environments deadly to man and guide spaceships through the Solar System. Computers also "make mistakes" that do not seem to be wholly caused by programming errors. Nevertheless, no machine is as yet even remotely capable of passing the Turing test. Any bright interrogator would know in ten seconds which was the man and which was the machine.

(2) *There is no evidence available now that any machine ever will pass the Turing test.* This is clear from the three books reviewed here. Every attempt so far to create a formal model of a human Turing machine has failed. But it is still early days. AI as a discipline is still only thirty or so years old—a human generation. Thus one may also state that there is no definitive evidence that a machine will never pass the Turing test. The question is essentially open.

I frankly admit that I think a machine will pass the test someday, but many will disagree.

(3) *Success or failure in the Turing test will probably not definitively answer the question whether man is a Turing machine.* This is because Dennett's thesis is almost surely correct: a man is not a single Turing machine, although he may be many Turing machines. But even that is a metaphor. There may be layers within the mind, each of which is a Turing machine; or it may be that the mind is made up of an indefinitely large number of Turing machines interconnected in ways that we do not understand at all, and may never understand. Thus a Turing machine might imitate a sufficiently large number of human mental behaviors to pass the test, but still it would not be a human being. If it comes to that, metaphor aside, a machine will never *be* a human being. Machines may behave asymptotically *like* human beings, but that is not the same thing.

(4) *Success or failure in the Turing test will also not definitely resolve the dispute between mechanists and mentalists.* There is no question whatever that the brain is a physical organ and therefore at least *like* a machine. There is also no question whatever that thoughts are immaterial in some sense of that word. What is the connection between brains and thoughts? We don't know. Does that mean that computers will someday have "immaterial" thoughts like men? (They probably don't have them now.) It would seem to be possible; again, however, we don't know.

(5) *Machines think.* That is, although machines are not human intelligences, they perform some operations that men also perform when they are thinking—for example, algorithmic calculation. Many other human mental operations probably have no replica, perhaps even no analogue, in computers. But the fact should not be forgotten. Machines do think, even though there are no "thinking machines"—in the accepted meaning of that term—in existence today.

(6) *Machines are the most useful tools ever devised precisely because they think—in the sense just suggested.* Machines sort data, make discriminations among inputs, combine data to arrive at conclusions, obey commands given in a

The Cyber 205, built by Control Data Corporation, is one of the new supercomputers. Computers such as this one can perform 100 million arithmetic operations per second. To minimize signal travel time in this huge computer, it has been designed so that its several thousand circuit boards are linked by coaxial cables in which signals travel at about nine-tenths the speed of light.

number of different ways, solve problems that people can't solve, draw pictures, play chess, and sing songs. In every case they are acting as an extension of man's mind, just as other tools are extensions of man's hand. But the mind is much more powerful than the hand, and therefore machines that think are much more powerful than machines that merely manipulate. Again, it is worth remembering that such machines are very new. We have had simple machines for three thousand years and power-driven tools for three hundred years, but we have had machines that think for only thirty years.

(7) *It appears that what is almost a new species of animal has evolved within the last generation: man-plus-computer.* Man-plus-power tools came into being about three centuries ago and proceeded to change almost everything about the world. It has been changed again by this new species almost beyond recognition in a mere thirty years; it seems likely that the Universe itself will be altered by he/it in the not too distant future.

Up until quite recently this new species consisted of quasi-symbiotic creatures, one part of which was an adult human being. With the invention of powerful and enormously flexible new programming languages like Seymour Papert's LOGO and Allen C. Kay's SmallTalk, which allow children to program computers, the symbiotic relationship has become much deeper. Children now routinely start *programming* computers at the age of two or three. They have no fear of these machines, as most adults still do; they evidently consider the machines to be a "natural" part of their minds. In twenty years these children will have power and influence in the world. It is really almost unimaginable what they will do with it. They will certainly not be content with the kind of solitary thinking that we do now. They will be electronically interconnected all around the Earth; they will all speak the same language; they may simply abolish war because it is so stupid. What else they will do is neither frightening nor wonderful. But I do hope I live to see it.

(8) The most interesting question is this: What would it mean if machines could be developed that could "think like men"? It is clear that they would not *be* men, so that is not something to be afraid of. At the same time, we might well have to treat them in the special way that we treat persons—that is, they might have to have, or be given, legal status limiting the right simply to use them. If so, they would constitute a great problem for man to deal—and live—with.

A great philosopher of our time has stated his opinion that "if machines are someday constructed to think as well as or better than human beings think then the human race should give up thinking and turn to dreaming instead." This is a very provocative statement. It is true that most humans think seldom and think badly when they do think; they are used to a life that is not governed by (rational) thought. For most of us, to be confronted by a world run according to rationality and logic would be a severe shock. It might drive us crazy; it would certainly make us extremely uncomfortable—even the best of us, who don't think very well either, except rarely.

But we do dream dreams. That we do very well. Why not, then, turn over the thinking to machines that will do it ever so much more effectively—and leave the dreaming to us?

[1]"It might seem," says John Haugeland in *Mind Design*, "that big modern computers, with their tremendous speed and memory, could just look ahead to every possible outcome and see which moves lead to ultimate victory. In principle, this would be possible, since chess is technically finite; and such a machine would be literally invincible. In practical terms, however, such a computation is nowhere near possible. Assuming an aveage of 31.6 options per play gives a thousand (31.6 x 31.6) possible combinations per full move (each side having a turn). Thus looking ahead five moves would involve a quadrillion (10^{15}) possibilities; forty moves (a typical game) would involve 10^{120} possibilities. (For comparison, there have been fewer than 10^{18} seconds since the beginning of the universe.) These numbers are just preposterously large for any physically conceivable computer. They get that big because the number of choices at each additional step *multiplies* the total number of possible combinations so far. For understandable reasons, this is called the *combinatorial explosion;* it plagues control design for all but the most straightforward problems." (p. 16)

[2]A recent rumor has it that the Japanese are budgeting half a billion dollars, more or less, to produce "a machine that thinks" by 1990.

[3]From "Computing Machinery and Intelligence," *Mind,* Vol. LIX, No. 236 (1950). Reprinted in *The Mind's I*, pp. 53–54.

[4]Ibid., p. 61.

[5]Searle contributes a long review of *The Mind's I* to a recent issue of *The New York Review of Books.* He dislikes Hofstadter and Dennett's book as much as I like it. Perhaps this is because he finds the intellectual playfulness of Hofstadter and Dennett rather hard to take. But their very playfulness is a possible argument in favor of his anti-AI position: is it really conceivable that a machine would ever be able to make the kinds of puns that Hofstadter does? But on the other hand, why not?

[6]From *The Cyberiad* by Stanislaw Lem, tr. by Michael Kandel. Copyright © 1974 by The Seabury Press, Inc. Reprinted in *The Mind's I,* pp. 288–89.

[7]"Non Serviam" from *A Perfect Vacuum: Perfect Reviews of Nonexistent Books* by Stanislaw Lem. Copyright 1971 by Stanislaw Lem; English translation copyright © 1979 1978 by Stanislaw Lem. Reprinted in *The Mind's I,* pp. 301, 317.

[8]Minsky, Marvin, MIT AI Lab Memo 306; printed in *Mind Design,* pp. 95–96.

[9]Dreyfus, Hubert L. *What Computers Can't Do* (New York: Harper and Row, 1979). Excerpts from the Introduction reprinted in *Mind Design,* pp. 203–4.

Sychophantasy in Economics:*
A Review of George Gilder's
Wealth and Poverty†

By Louis O. Kelso and
Patricia Hetter Kelso

Louis O. Kelso is a corporate and financial lawyer who has developed financing techniques aimed at increasing the ownership of capital. He is chairman of the board of Kelso, Inc., a San Francisco investment bank specializing in financing employee stock option plans.

Mr. Kelso is also an economist and social thinker whose study of the structure and organization of modern industrial economics has brought him notice as offering solutions to economic problems that conventional economic concepts have proved unable to solve.

He has set forth his general economic theory in *The Capitalist Manifesto* (1958) and *The New Capitalists* (1961), both of which he wrote with Mortimer J. Adler, and also in *Two-Factor Theory: The Economics of Reality* (1968), of which Patricia Hetter was coauthor.

Patricia Hetter Kelso has been associated with Louis Kelso since 1963, first as his writing collaborator and then (since 1975) as vice-president of Kelso, Inc. Patricia Hetter has expounded the theory of universal capitalism in writings of her own, among them "Uprooting World Poverty: A Job for Business," which won the First Place McKinsey Foundation for Management Science in 1963. She and Mr. Kelso have recently completed still another book, *Social Capitalism: Who Should Produce the Wealth of Nations?*, which will appear shortly.

Mrs. Kelso studied government and philosophy at the University of Texas, Austin, and for several years worked for the Swedish government as an international marketing and advertising specialist, an experience that gave her firsthand experience of welfare economics. The Kelsos live in San Francisco.

In his Inaugural Address on March 4, 1933, President Franklin D. Roosevelt told the American people: "Only a foolish optimist can deny the dark realities of the moment . . . Plenty is at our doorstep, but a generous use of it languishes in the very sight of the supply."[1]

Twelve years into the New Deal, Paul G. Hoffman, president of the Studebaker Corporation and Chairman of the Board of Trustees of the Committee for Economic Development, told a Senate subcommittee: "America's capacity to produce a richly varied pattern of goods and services has been amply demonstrated. We have not yet shown a corresponding ability to maintain peacetime market demand at satisfactory levels."[2]

Senator William Fulbright agreed. "Much has been said here about our productive capacity. We have already proved that in the war. We can produce. I don't think there is any question about that. The real problem is on the consumption end."[3]

In 1976 Secretary of Agriculture Earl L. Butz said: "Our productive capacity so far exceeds our capacity to consume, that we couldn't even eat all the wheat we grow if it were free."[4] This is true of all agricultural commodities. The productiveness of the American cow is a national scandal. The government now spends $250,000 an hour to buy the dry milk, butter and cheese that farmers cannot sell;[5] storage of surplus cheese alone—560 million pounds of it—costs taxpayers about $1 million a day.[6]

Only in time of war, or in all-out preparation for war, does the capital plant of the U.S. economy operate anywhere near full capacity.

Meanwhile, on the American consumer front, growing numbers of middle-class Americans are helplessly watching their standard of living, never opulent at best, shrivel. Even before the Reagan Administration's welfare cuts, the American family was in deep economic trouble. "You can't squeeze blood out of a turnip," a judge was quoted as saying in 1976. "Most people who come before me because they can't agree on money matters simply don't have enough money to live on comfortably. They can't make it financially in marriage . . . and they can make it even less out of marriage."[7]

* Copyright 1982, Louis O. Kelso and Patricia Hetter Kelso.
† New York: Basic Books, Inc., Publishers, 1981.

A Tulsa, Oklahoma, divorce court judge explained in 1975 why his city's divorce rate was more than twice the national average, and why the so-called affluent were coming into his court in increasing numbers. "I think the less wealthy people are just tired of the mundane life they are tied to. Let's face it, a family of three kids with daddy making $3.00 an hour is a life sentence. Being stuck must be a horrible feeling and perhaps divorce is the way they see to get away."[8]

As for women, legal experts generally agree that with or without the Equal Rights Amendment, "the vast majority of separated or divorced women can't support themselves or their children on court-awarded alimony or child-support payments, even if they manage to collect every cent the courts awarded them."[9]

The plight of old people, never enviable, has degenerated as inflation eats away the few assets that stand between them and public assistance. "We have senior citizens in their eighties, some very ill and half blind, who in financial desperation come in and ask us for jobs," reported the director of an organization that works with senior citizens in the Bronx.[10] The lines outside San Francisco's St. Anthony Dining Room are swelling with middle-class people. One seventy-one-year-old woman told the director: " . . . I was hungry for about a year and a half. It took me six months to get nerve enough to eat here—it was either that or dying."[11]

As for children, the Department of Agriculture has estimated that a child born in 1981 may cost at least $100,000 more to rear to the age of eighteen than a child born in 1960.[12] Abused, abandoned, and murdered children are now routine. If the trend continues, Americans may soon be as inured to the suffering of the young and the old as were Russians under the tsars or as residents are of modern Calcutta.

We might conceivably expect a book entitled *Wealth and Poverty* to have some relevance to the economic problems of real people such as these— fellow citizens, neighbors, and even ourselves. This expectation is heightened when the book in question is acclaimed by ranking members of the Reagan Administration and representatives of the business press. David Stockman, for example, assures potential readers that *Wealth and Poverty* is "Promethean in its intellectual power and insight. It shatters once and for all the Keynesian and welfare state illusions that burden the failed conventional wisdom of our era." Nathan Glazer of Harvard University characterizes the book as: "A really remarkable analysis of American social and economic policy that demolishes a host of pieties as to the causes of poverty and the conditions that overcome it." Malcolm Forbes, Jr., calls it "A first-rate analysis of the supply-side school of economics" and " 'must' reading for the new year."

But the title turns out to be misleading. Gilder does not distinguish between wealth and income. That *wealth* consists of "large possessions; abundance of things that are objects of human desire; abundance of worldly estate; affluence; riches; abundant supply; large accumulations; all property that has a money value or an exchangeable value; all material objects that have economic utility"[13] will not be learned from Gilder, or even acknowledged as relevant. This perhaps is due to Gilder's peculiar methodology. As he explains in the preface, this present work has sprung from an earlier one, *Visible Man,* a sociological venture in which he undertook to understand poverty by studying the poor. But that was reversing the proper order of things. Just as in physics it is necesary to study *matter* in order to arrive at an understanding of *antimatter,* in economics one can only understand poverty by considering what wealth is and where it comes from. Since Gilder also confides in his preface that he is a second-generation intimate of the Rockefeller family, and bound to David and Peggy Rockefeller by ties of love and gratitude, he would seem to have had a rare opportunity for field work.

Gilder's close Rockefeller connection makes such assertions as the following not only puzzling but downright ironic.

> Work, indeed, is the root of wealth, even of the genius that mostly resides in sweat.[14]

> The only dependable route from poverty is always work, family and faith . . . in order to move up, the poor must not only work, they must work harder than the classes above them.[15]

> Indeed, after work the second principle of upward mobility is the maintenance of monogamous marriage and family . . . [16]

> An analysis of poverty that begins and ends with family structure and marital status would explain far more about the problem than most of the distributions of income, inequality, unemployment, education, IQ, race, sex, home ownership, location, discrimination, and all the other items usually multiply regressed and correlated on academic computers. But even an analysis of work and family would miss what is perhaps the most important of the principles of upward mobility under capitalism—namely, faith.[17]

Why is capital ownership omitted from this list? Surely, the most effective cure for poverty is to be born or marry into one of the five percent of American families which own virtually all of the economy's productive assets. The next most effective cure would be to acquire one's own viable capital estate in the same way that the rich have always done. Gilder to the contrary, the rich do not get or stay that way primarily through hard work, monogamy, procreation, and gullibility but through access to credit which enables them to buy and pay for capital out of its earnings.

Gilder appears to know nothing of business, corporate finance, or property law. He shows no awareness of how virtually all new capital is financed in the American economy, and he is entirely oblivious to the effects and implications of a system of finance which relentlessly makes existing significant stockholders and capital owners richer, while effectively barring all new entrants other than geniuses or extraordinarily lucky people into the capital-owning class.

Indeed, Gilder's book would have been more accurately entitled "In Praise of Plutocracy." It is simply a repackaging of the hoary old Puritan savings myths, or what Keynes called "the principle of accumulation based on inequality." Its central argument is that the savings of the rich, and hence the rich as a class, are essential to the operation of a "capitalist" economy. By "sacrificing" present consumption to acquire savings, and then by putting them "at risk" to finance new enterprise and technological innovation, the rich perform a service bordering on the heroic. In Gilder's rapturous prose:

> The benefits of capitalism still depend on capitalists . . . Under capitalism, when it is working, the rich have the anti-Midas touch, transforming timorous liquidity and unused savings into factories and office towers, farms and laboratories, orchestras and museums—turning gold into goods and jobs and art. That is the function of the rich: fostering opportunities for the classes below them in the continuing drama of the creation of wealth and progress.[18]

Gilder's concept of "supply" is nothing but an extended metaphor for rule by the few who own virtually all of the economy's productive capital today, and who will own even more of it tomorrow no matter which economics faction gains control of national economic policy or which political party is in power. Business finance is designed to make the rich richer, and it does just that.

Inconveniently for plutocrats, however, the United States is still a political democracy committed constitutionally to economic democracy. Wealth concentration is repugnant not only to democratic ideals and sensibilities but to several guarantees of the Constitution itself. It is also structurally antagonistic to the private property, free market economy which is the proper economic complement of political democracy. Therefore, the reigning princes of plutocracy—the same interests President Franklin D. Roosevelt called "economic royalists"—find it necessary to repackage for political resale the old myths which rationalize their virtual monopoly of capital ownership.

Plutocrats also have a psychological problem in a political democracy. There is a phenomenon called wealth-guilt, which the German sociologist Helmut Schoeck analyzes most perceptively in *Envy: A Theory of Social Behavior.* It is not enough to be rich; the possession of wealth must somehow be justified in a social context where the overwhelming majority of people are poor and, so far as the "system" is concerned, destined to perpetual poverty. Riches must somehow be deserved, merited, sanctified. Thus, the apologist for wealth concentration must frame his defense with the sensibilities of the plutocrat in mind, as well as those of the larger society.

The rationalization of wealth concentration in a political democracy involves, first of all, diverting public attention from the phenomenon itself. Just as the apologist for war dislikes photographs of the slaughtered and wounded, the wealth apologist dislikes statistics depicting the distribution of wealth and income. He dislikes rigorous distinctions about what wealth is and what it means in the lives of real people, and also what its absence is like. He is not about to divulge the source of wealth even if he knows it, which, in Gilder's case, he doesn't. It is also necessary to maintain the illusion that the road to wealth in the existing order of things is not a footpath as narrow as that leading through the eye of the needle, but a highway broad enough to accommodate all manner of hopeful folk.

True, wealth and income is a taboo subject in polite society—i.e., society inhibited by the wealth–ignorance of the rich. Wealth statistics in the United States today are almost as crude as mortality statistics before Pasteur forced medicine to become a science. But enlightening statistics may be had. In 1977 Senator Russell B. Long, in an introduction to a symposium on Employee Stock Ownership Plan (ESOP) financing, stated:

> Despite all the fine, populist oratory and good intentions of great men like Franklin Roosevelt, Harry Truman, Dwight Eisenhower, John Kennedy, Lyndon Johnson—the distribution of net worth among Americans today, in relative terms, is about the same as it was when Herbert Hoover succeeded Calvin Coolidge. The distribution for adult population is as follows: .001% of the population have a net worth of $1,000,000 or more; .002% have $500,000–$1,000,000; 2.4% have $100,000–$500,000; 1.7% have $60,000–$100,000; 3.1% have $40,000–$60,000; 6.5% have $20,000–$40,000; 10% have $10,000–$20,000; 13% have $5,000–$10,000; 13% have $3,000–$5,000; 50.2% have less than $3,000.[19]

Gilder, however, mentions the statistical evidence of wealth concentration only to disparage it. Such conclusions as that " 'the top 2 percent of all families own 44 percent of all family wealth, and the bottom 25 percent own none at all' " and that " 'the top 5 percent get 15.3 percent of the pretax income and the bottom 20 percent get 5.4 percent' " are not relevant facts to Gilder but unfair statistical conjurations.[20] They evidence a "mechanical concern" with wealth and income distribution, an unfortunate "distributionist mentality" which has afflicted conventional economics since Ricardo. This mode of thinking is "forever counting the ranks of rich and poor and assaying the defects of capitalism that keep the poor always with us in such great numbers." Poverty body counts give the rich a bad image by implying that wealth creates poverty. But most menacing, they impute that the system is unfair, that the deck is stacked. Thus the distributionist mentality "strikes at the living heart of democratic capitalism (*sic*)." It challenges "the golden rule of capitalism."

Now Gilder has earlier regretted that even the great champions of capitalism such as Friedrich von Hayek, Ludwig von Mises, and even Milton Friedman, have not seen fit to "give capitalism a theology" or even "assign to its results any assurance of justice." Their praise has been pragmatic and technical. Capitalism is good because it produces more wealth and liberty than its competitors. None of these defenders "cogently refutes the thesis that the greatest of capitalists—the founders of the system—were in some sense 'robber barons.' None convincingly demonstrates that the system succeeds and thrives because it gives room for the heroic creativity of entrepreneurs."[21] Gilder now takes it upon himself to fill this ideological vacuum. "Capitalism," he states, "begins with giving." And the golden rule of capitalism is: Unto him that gives shall be given.

Students of monopoly capitalism have long observed the tendency of this system to confirm one of the Bible's many double-entry bookkeeping truths, Matthew 25:29, which promises: "Unto everyone that hath shall be given, and he shall have abundance; but from him that hath not shall be taken away even that which he hath." This is the golden rule of plutocracy. He who owns the economy's productive capital today will own even more tomorrow, thanks to conventional business finance. And he who does not own capital, but who must make his productive input through labor, will be robbed of his little labor productiveness by the technological change which eliminates him and makes the capital owner even more productive. But though it fits the facts, this golden rule is not calculated to vindicate the ways of plutocracy to man.

Gilder needs a metaphor to illustrate his own economic beatitude, and he finds it in one of the more exotic customs known to anthropology, the potlatch. The capitalist system, Gilder declares, is an extended potlatch. *Webster's Third International Dictionary* defines *potlatch* as:

> A ceremonial feast or festival of the Indians of the northwest coast given for the display of wealth to validate or advance individual tribal position or social status and marked by the host's lavish destruction of personal property and an ostentatious distribution of gifts that entails elaborate reciprocation.

But Gilder's metaphorical specifications have required him to sanitize the potlatch into an event the old Kwakiutl chiefs would never recognize. Expunged is the macho braggadocio, the enviously aggressive attempt to humiliate rivals by greater displays of "generosity" and a superior disdain for wealth. Gilder does not mention that the potlatch, like some of monopoly capitalism's tribal practices, sometimes was used by rich chiefs to bankrupt poorer ones, nor that, far from being a "contest in altruism," the potlatch was the literal precursor of the roast. Custom required the visiting chief to sit dangerously close to the fire, and when his host solicitously inquired whether the blaze was too warm for his comfort, to reply manfully that he was shivering with cold. This would be the signal for the host to order the fire piled even higher with wood, augmented on occasion with a few canoes or other goods. The guest had to impassively endure both the psychological and physical heat on pain of losing face.

Nor does Gilder perceive that the potlach had the obvious social function of limiting wealth concentration and power, while at the same time enabling ambitious chiefs to build their personal power bases. Indeed, as things worked out, the most astute chiefs became the richest. But Gilder uses the social sciences only as fishing ponds for exotic metaphors and bits of scholarly flotsam and jetsam that fit into his sychophantasy. As he has observed earlier, "How the rich are regarded and how they see themselves—whether they are merely rich or are also bearers of wealth—is a crucial measure of the health of a capitalist economy.[22] Certainly that distinction is crucial to the self-esteem of the rich and social tolerance of wealth concentration. Gilder is eager to portray the rich not only as wealth-bearers, but as wealth-creators and wealth-dispensers. In that great extended potlatch which is the pres-ent primitive capitalist system, the capitalist financiers are the reincarnated spirits of the Kwakiutl chiefs, their boisterous vaingloriousness transmogrified into almost saintly altruism and social concern. Gilder's capitalist is the feast giver who invites humanity to a magnificent spread. By accepting his invitation, humanity incurs a debt which it must repay with interest. But that is only right and just, as Gilder sees it, because the capitalist was the initial giver. The feast was his investment; the reciprocal gift, his returned principal; the interest, his profit. Gilder is so carried away by the pat beauty of it all that he stops just short of declaring that capitalism is love.

We dwell on Gilder's fatuous potlatch analogy, and his equally fatuous golden rule of capitalism, for two reasons. First, because they are typical of both the substance and style of a book acclaimed by U.S. business and political leaders as "seminal," "Promethean," "brilliant," "a really remarkable analysis of American social and economic policy," and so forth. In Hans Christian Andersen's fable, at least the emperor was real—only his resplendent new clothes were a fraud. But in *Wealth and Poverty,* there is neither emperor nor clothes. This is not a work of reasoned thought, but a vacuous public relations puffball—a pitiful attempt to make the public believe that "supply-side economics" has a credible theoretical foundation, or any theoretical foundation.

Our second reason for dwelling on the potlatch analogy and the golden rule of capitalism is that Gilder claims to have derived them both from one of the few valid truths in conventional economics—Say's Law. Had Gilder understood Say's Law—or, more to the point, if the economics profession did—the nation would have been spared from both supply lopside economics and its equally false antithesis, demand lopside economics. But ever since Jean-Baptiste Say discovered the truth that bears his name, economists have circled it blindly, like moths around a flame. They intuit its importance without being able to decipher its meaning.

Say's Law, compressed into an aphorism—"Supply creates its own demand"—is, as everyone knows by now, the battle cry of the Supply Lopsiders, who have fabricated a rebellion against the Demand Lopsiders, representing the opposite side of Say's equation. The goal of each is simply power over national economic policy, which neither can hold for long unless the public is persuaded that there is some ideological or practical difference between the two impostures, which there is not.

The Demand Lopsiders, flourishing the colors of the Left, want the economic game rules to maximize consumption through redistribution. The Supply Lopsiders, bearing the standard of the Right, want to maximize production by the plutocrats through accelerating the ownership concentration of technology-harnessing capital instruments.

Both sides invoke the authority of Say's Law, which holds that in a market economy, if the government will refrain from interference with market forces, the purchasing power generated by production will be sufficient, over a given time period, to enable the purchase of all that is produced. In effect, therefore, Say's Law states that if government does not interfere with the operation of the free market forces, depressions cannot occur. But depressions do occur, and they have been occurring ever since the burden of production began to be transferred to capital—machinery, land, and structures—at an accelerated rate in the opening stages of the industrial revolution.

Gilder's understanding of the workings of a market economy, and of Say's Law as an interpretation of the relationship between production and consumption in a market economy, is grossly defective, and for the precise reasons that economists, as a whole, including the Demand Lopsiders, fail to understand.

In the first place, Say's Law does not relate to the production, use, financing, acquisition, or disposition of *producer goods,* i.e., capital goods, in any way. Nor does it relate to the production, use, financing, or acquisition of military goods which are not "consumed" in any sense contemplated by J. B. Say. The production, use, financing, and acquisition of capital goods are governed by capital theory, as Kelso and Adler pointed out twenty years ago in *The Capitalist Manifesto* (1958) and *The New Capitalists* (1961).

Adam Smith, whose words J. B. Say was interpreting when he announced his famous law, made this clear:

> Consumption is the sole end and purpose of production; and the interest of the producer ought to be attended to only so far as it may be necessary for promoting that of the consumer. The maxim is so perfectly self-evident that it would be absurd to attempt to prove it. (Adam Smith, *GBWW*, Vol. 39, p. 287.)

Furthermore, Say's Law, by its own terms, is inapplicable to any modern industrial economy, for in every such economy, the price of one of the two factors of production—labor—is usually distorted beyond recognition. Government, by authorizing and encouraging unions coercively and repeatedly to adjust upward the price of labor, and business, by acquiescing in such an adjustment as long as the costs can be passed on to the consumers, have simply made useless the most basic law of market economies.

This observation should not be interpreted as an anti-labor remark. It is merely anti-economist. We have repeatedly said in our writings that the economist's face-saving liturgy that treats labor workers as the only true producers of goods and services, and capital as a mere mystical catalytic agent that makes labor more productive, is simply a "big lie" in the Hitlerian sense. The result of it has been that labor workers, along with both the unemployed and the unemployable, have been prevented from becoming capital workers as capital input grew to its overwhelming predominance through technological change—that is to say, they have been prevented from sharing in the production of goods and services as capital owners and from legitimately (i.e., through production) sharing in the consumption of such capital-produced consumer products.

In the light of this, Gilder's *Wealth and Poverty* can only be seen as another intellectually dishonest and sycophantic stall-tactic on behalf of the plutocracy to suppress the spread of capital ownership to the ninety-five percent of consumers in the American economy who do not own it now.

In his own day, Adam Smith observed that the capital owners (the "mercantile class") were already beginning to exploit the capital-less consumers—that, in the "mercantile," i.e., capitalist, system

> the interest of the consumer is almost constantly sacrificed to that of
> the producer; and it seems to consider production, and not
> consumption, as the ultimate end and object of all industry and
> commerce. (Smith, op. cit., p. 287.)

Thus the Supply Lopsiders carry on an old, though hardly honorable, tradition.

For many years, the authors of this review believed that society's steadfast refusal to perceive that capital workers (i.e., capital owners) are themselves a factor of production and a creator of "value," in the identical sense that labor workers are, was an unconscious anachronism whose corrective was a higher level of consciousness. We still assert this to be true in the case of the general public. But the owners of concentrated wealth, we have belatedly come to understand, have a vested interest in keeping the capital factor uncomprehended by the capital-less many. Their allies and confederates in this endeavor are the professional economists. Once it is admitted that capital workers make productive input in exactly the same ways—functional, moral, political and economic—that labor workers do, the macroeconomic game of capital monopoly will be over, and methods of finance that make the rich ever richer and keep the capital-less capital-less will end.

Then the question of *who owns the capital plant* will be understood as crucial and vital to the capitalist economy's health, as well as to economic justice and opportunity. In a private-property economy, the income which a labor worker or a capital worker produces belongs to him. Thus the principle of distribution of a capitalist economy to be deduced from Say's Law is: "From each according to his production, to each according to his production." But this rule, applied to the concentrated owners of highly productive capital instruments, means that the *few* can produce everything required by the *many,* and therefore, because of Say's Law, the many will be rendered underproductive or nonproductive, and thus forced to live partially or completely as wards of redistribution, boondoggle, welfare, or charity, supported by taxation and inflation.

All this does not mean that Gilder is wrong to say that the American Economics Establishment is in dire need of a new apologetics. Between 1929 and 1932, the private property economy of the United States broke down. It broke down because, as Kelso and Adler pointed out in *The Capitalist Manifesto* and *The New Capitalists,*[23] the enormous productive power of the tiny minority (about five percent) of the population who owned its capital could not provide adequate incomes to support the consumption of the labor workers, the unemployed, and the unemployable. As this became clear to the American people, they elected Franklin D. Roosevelt in the hopes that he would solve the problem. Relying on the demand lopside economics of John Maynard Keynes, they set to work to answer the question: "What can we do to alleviate the effects of poverty?" The result was the elaborate network of welfare and boondoggle channels that redistributed income from the middle-class labor workers and upper-class capital workers to the lower-paid labor workers and the nonworkers. Gilder rails against such redistribution by the liberal demand lopside economists and their followers.

"When government gives welfare, unemployment payments, and public-service jobs in quantities that deter productive work, and when it raises taxes on profitable enterprise to pay for them, demand declines. In fact, nearly all programs that are advocated by economists to promote equality and combat poverty . . . reduce demand by undermining the production from which all demand derives . . . [demand] originates with productive work at any level. This is the simple and homely first truth about wealth and poverty. 'Give and you will be given unto.' This is the secret not only of riches, but also of growth."[24]

This "essential insight of supply-side economics" happens to be false. The case for Supply Lopside economics cannot be built on the case against Demand Lopside economics. Without understanding that there are two factors of production that are in competition; that each individual needs to be productive through the ownership of both; that technological change, which continues day after day, has made production through capital ownership far more potent than production through labor; and that the individual freedom from toil which technology makes possible can be enjoyed only by capital workers, supply-side economics is as senseless as its demand-side counterpart. The Demand Lopsiders and the Supply Lopsiders are simply seesaw misinterpretations of the J.B. Say equation.

Economists will continue to be baffled by Say's Law until they realize that under it, *distribution is a function of production by each consumer.* Only after that insight does it become obvious that true capitalism must be a capitalism of the many, not of the few. Gilder does not know what capitalism is. He is acquainted only with the limited dynamism of primitive or robber-baron capitalism. But that is also true of the members of the professional economics craft-guild. It is their expert ignorance that has made the Supply Lopside hoax credible. The concept of Social Capitalism, a system which distributes purchasing power to all consumers as a result of their direct participation in production—either as labor workers or as capital workers—or both—is beyond their theoretical comprehension, as long as they cling to the obsolete doctrines that were, and still are, the subject of their doctoral dissertations.

Meanwhile, the propertyless many must somehow be provided with purchasing power. That was the only lesson the Great Depression taught. Neither Gilder nor any conventional economist knows how to bring about this consumer demand except in the way which the Keynesians so thoroughly exploited: income redistribution. As the experience of the Reagan administration is demonstrating, without capitalist tools like the Employee Stock Ownership Plan (ESOP), government redistribution will continue because it must. Such capitalist financing methods can substitute capital-produced incomes for welfare, social security, and boondoggle.

Gilder and the Supply Lopsiders believe that to arrive at a truth, they need but invert a lie, and that the antidote to one wrong question is a different wrong question. They counter the question of the redistributive left, "How can we eliminate the effects of poverty?", with the question of the capital-hoarding right, namely: "What can we do to revitalize the productive system?" A proper Social Capitalist question might be: "What can we do to make those who are involuntarily underproductive or nonproductive really productive or more productive?"

There is little in Gilder's book to suggest this question, much less to answer it. In exposing many of the artful errors of the liberals, he undertakes to build a fortress around the institutions and policies that support the Divine Right of the Rich to Stay Rich and Get Richer, and to preserve the nonownership of capital by the overwhelming majority.

John D Rockefeller stated Gilder's message far more honestly, and certainly more succinctly, in 1905. To a reporter who asked him how he became rich, he replied:

I believe the power to make money is a gift from God . . . to be developed and used to the best of our ability for the good of mankind. Having been endowed with the gift I possess, I believe it is my duty to make money and still more money, and to use the money I make for the good of my fellow man according to the dictates of my conscience.[25]

---

[1] *America in Midpassage,* Charles & Mary Beard (New York: The MacMillan Company, 1939), Vol. III, p. 208.

[2] Paul G. Hoffman, President of Studebaker Corporation and Chairman of the Board of Trustees of the Committee for Economic Development, in Hearings on S. 380, the Full Employment Act of 1945, before a subcommittee of the Committee on Banking and Currency, U.S. Senate, 79th Congress, First Session, July–September 1945, p. 709.

[3] Ibid., Page 845.

[4] *New York Times Magazine,* June 13, 1976, p. 53.

[5] San Francisco *Chronicle,* March 9, 1982, p. 7.

[6] San Francisco *Chronicle,* Dec. 25, 1981, p. 14.

[7] "Your Legal Rights As A Woman," *Family Circle,* May 1976, p. 166.

[8] *New York Times,* Jan. 15, 1975, p. 16.

[9] *Family Circle,* op. cit.

[10] *New York Times,* Dec. 1, 1974, p. E-6.

[11] San Francisco *Chronicle,* Nov. 25, 1981, p. 3.

[12] "Cost of Rearing Child said to be $134,000," *New York Times,* Nov. 12, 1981, p. B-5.

[13] *Webster's Third New International Dictionary of the English Language, unabridged.*

[14] p. 51.

[15] p. 68.

[16] p. 69.

[17] p. 72.

[18] p. 63.

[19] *The American University Law Review,* Spring 1977, Vol. 26, No. 3, pp. 515–16.

[20] Typically, Gilder derides median statistics when they verify wealth and income concentration and then cites other median statistics in support of his contention that wealth and income distribution in the U.S. economy is not static but dynamic. (*See* pages 10 and 11.)

[21] p. 6.

[22] p. 50.

[23] Op cit. In *The New Capitalists,* they predicted that if the Demand Lopside solution, rather than the capitalist solution, continued to be implemented, inflation would ravage the American economy and its markets would be taken over by foreign competitors, as in fact has happened.

[24] *Wealth and Poverty,* op. cit., p. 45.

[25] *The Rockefellers, An American Dynasty,* Collier & Horowitz (New York: Holt, Rinehart & Winston, 1976), p. 148.

NOTE TO THE READER

With respect to the writings in this issue of *The Great Ideas Today*, somewhere behind the vision of created intelligence and the fear of it is probably to be found the Prometheus myth—the story, as it may be understood, of how once the gods gave man a measure of their godlike powers, among them those of the artist, from which men derived the hope, or perhaps the illusion, that they could make imperishable things and so transcend their mortal state. The classic account of this is in Aeschylus's *Prometheus Bound* (*GBWW*, Vol. 5, pp. 40–51). An illuminating discussion of that play will be found in the discussion of Greek tragedy by Seth Benardete in *The Great Ideas Today* 1980, pp. 102–43. As for the story of the Faustian homunculus, it appears in the Second Part of Goethe's poem (*GBWW*, Vol. 47, pp. 167 ff.).

Those who wish to see what the great books have said about the mind should look up that idea in Chapter 58 of the *Syntopicon*, where Topic 2, "The human mind in relation to matter or body," is of interest; also Topic 3, where mental differences between animals and men are discussed; also Topic 6, where discussions will be found of the reflexivity of the mind, its knowledge of itself and its acts—all of which are difficult to imagine in any computer.

Those who own *Gateway to the Great Books* will find it interesting to consider "The Process of Thought" by John Dewey, in Vol. 10 of that set, pp. 88–213. A famous vision of the mind as a series of mechanical operations is in I. P. Pavlov, "Scientific Study of the So-called Psychical Processes in the Higher Animals" (*GGB*, Vol. 8, pp. 291–309). More extensive and more readable, though dated in the light of modern knowledge, is the discussion of such operations in William James's *Principles of Psychology, GBWW*, Vol. 53. John Erskine's well-known brief essay, "The Moral Obligation to be Intelligent," which appears in *GGB*, Vol. 10, pp. 1–13, though it has nothing to do with computers, nevertheless raises the question whether our fear of automatic intelligence does not derive in part from our fear of intelligence itself—a frequent strain, Erskine suggests, in Western thought.

Douglass Cater's discussion of the American electoral process raises a question of its own—that of the means by which, in any government, power is exchanged between one ruler and the next: in a democracy, how successive rulers are chosen. Discussion of these matters appears frequently in the great books. See, for example, Book VIII of Plato's *Republic* (*GBWW*, Vol. 7), where Socrates takes a fatalistic view of the process, and also Plutarch's *Lives* (*GBWW*, Vol. 14), which describe the terrible consequences to governments of the ancient world, in Rome particularly, of their failure to arrive at a satisfactory solution to the problem. Shakespeare's understanding of the subject was encyclopedic, and permeates not only the history plays, but also *Hamlet* and above all *King Lear*. The American Constitution itself, and *The Federalist*, are in *GBWW*, Vol. 43.

To pursue this political subject farther, readers may consult the *Syntopicon*, Chapter 16, DEMOCRACY, especially the references at Topic 5*b* dealing with voting and factions. See also Chapter 90, STATE, Topics 8*a–c*, where passages dealing with rulers and public office will be found. In *Gateway,* see Hawthorne's "Sketches of Abraham Lincoln," Vol. 6, pp. 166–71, along with various speeches by Lincoln, and Jefferson's *First Inaugural,* in the same volume.

The consideration of climate by Professor Hare may be thought to have little background in the great books, but in fact some passages in Herodotus dealing with Persia and Egypt treat the subject. See *The History,* Book II, in *GBWW,* Vol. 6. More in point are Montesquieu's observations on the effects of climate upon societies and states: see *The Spirit of Laws,* Books XV-XVIII, in *GBWW,* Vol. 38, pp. 109–34. Montesquieu's book was well known, incidentally, to the framers of the American Constitution. See also Montaigne, "Of cannibals," which recognizes, however quaintly, a relation between natural conditions and human character and institutions, in *GBWW,* Vol. 25, pp. 91–98. This was the source for Shakespeare's depiction of Caliban in *The Tempest* (*GBWW,* Vol. 27).

In the *Syntopicon,* references will be found to passages in the great books dealing with climate in Chapter 51, MAN, Topic 7*b;* also in Chapter 90, STATE, Topic 4*b.* The question of prediction and its difficulties in the science of climatology may be read against the background of references cited in Chapter 83, SCIENCE, Topics 4*e* and 5*e.* And perhaps it would be in point, for those who own *Gateway,* to look at "The Sunless Sea," by Rachel Carson, Vol. 8, pp. 130–46.

Harvey Goldstein's subject—the nature of literature and the method of understanding it—is considered at many points in the great books. The *locus classicus* is, of course, Aristotle's *Poetics* (*GBWW,* Vol. 9), though in fact the discussion there is largely confined to tragedy. Plato's discussion of poetry and poets is chiefly in Books III and X of *The Republic,* and also in the *Ion* (*GBWW,* Vol. 7). The aspect of the matter that lies in treating of sacred texts is considered by Saint Augustine in *On Christian Doctrine* (*GBWW,* Vol. 18, pp. 621 ff.). Boswell's *Life of Samuel Johnson* (*GBWW,* Vol. 44) contains numerous comments by Johnson on writers and writing; Johnson's "Preface to Shakespeare" is in *Gateway to the Great Books,* Vol. 5, pp. 311–53, along with other relevant writings. Among these are "How Should One Read a Book?" by Virginia Woolf; "The Study of Poetry," by Matthew Arnold; "What Is a Classic?" by Sainte-Beuve; "Of the Standard of Taste," by David Hume; three essays by Schopenhauer; "On Simple and Sentimental Poetry," by Friedrich Schiller; Walt Whitman's "Preface to Leaves of Grass"; essays by Hazlitt, Charles Lamb, and De Quincey; and "Dante," and "Tradition and the Individual Talent," by T. S. Eliot. In addition, Alexander Pope's *Essay on Criticism* was published in *The Great Ideas Today* 1981, and Arnold's "On Translating Homer" in the volume for 1971.

In the *Syntopicon,* the readings listed in Chapter 69, POETRY, as well as the "Additional Readings" at the end of it are all relevant. See also Chapter 56, MEMORY AND IMAGINATION, especially Topic 7*b,* which deals with imagination and poetry, and Chapter 43, KNOWLEDGE, Topic 6*b*(4), where passages dealing with the connection between knowledge and intuition, and knowledge and imagination are listed.

PART FIVE

Additions
to the
Great Books Library

The Consolation of Philosophy

Boethius

Editor's Introduction

Author of one of the best-known philosophical works in Western thought, *The Consolation of Philosophy,* Boethius was a Roman statesman and man of affairs as well as a philosopher and theologian in the time (AD 493–526) of the Gothic king Theodoric, who had established himself on the throne of the defeated Western Empire, taking advantage of its disorganization. Boethius, a member of the Roman aristocracy equally devoted to Christianity and the classical past, was among those opposed to this pagan usurper, who nevertheless was at first accommodating, having had a Roman education and wishing to preserve a continuity of administration. The age was one of conflict between Rome and the Eastern Empire at Constantinople, especially over the papacy, and Boethius was a leader in the effort to achieve a reconciliation such as the king could only hope would never come about. When it did, in 520, the strained relations between himself and the aristocracy, which rejoiced in the restoration at Rome of a Christian emperor, began to break down. Boethius, as a prominent member of this class, who by his acts and writings had done much to heal the imperial split, was regarded as especially dangerous. Thus in 524, when the king felt his power slipping away, he had the philosopher arrested, imprisoned, and subsequently executed for treason—with the connivance, apparently, of the emperor, who was glad to have such a sacrificial victim as a means of undermining the considerable following that Theodoric had among Catholic Romans outside the small group to which Boethius belonged.

It was while he was in prison at Pavia—500 miles from his library, as he sadly noted—that Boethius wrote the *Consolation,* an imaginary dialogue between himself and the spirit of Philosophy, who accuses him of having abandoned her. The personal, almost intimate quality of this work, interspersed as it is with poems, cannot hide the long philosophical tradition on which it draws. Boethius was in all probability the most learned man of the age, thoroughly acquainted with both Greek and Latin writings in the arts and sciences and as thoroughly versed in Christian doctrine. Such a combination recalls Saint Augustine, who had died in 430, and indeed Boethius had the same sense of mission to preserve the classical past during unsettled times that clearly threatened its survival. Like Augustine he, too, wrote treatises on the liberal arts, notably music and astronomy (which for him were really sciences), while he also translated Greek mathematical works along with some of the most important writings of both Plato and Aristotle. Perhaps we owe to him even more of the ancient learning that has come down to us than we do to Augustine, for without Boethius we should hardly know as much as we do know of Greek logic and science, or of the late Platonic schools of Athens and Alexandria, or of late Latin culture, to which Boethius did not apply the same strict standard of compatability with Christian doctrine as did Augustine.

Having been buried in a church at Pavia, Boethius was for centuries accorded the veneration of the martyred Saint Severinus, with whose bones his were confused. Thus Cassiodorus, founder of a monastery at Campania, included his works in its library as sacred productions, assuring their own survival. The *Consolation* itself became the most widely read book in the medieval world after the Bible. Translations were made of it into the English vernacular both by King Alfred and by Chaucer (also, somewhat later, by Queen Elizabeth); by the fourteenth century, it had been translated as well into French and German. As a result it served more than any other book as the source of medieval understanding of classical philosophy, of which it was the only version that most men knew, and it was not superseded in this function until the Renaissance made available the original texts on which it had been based. The translation that follows is that of H. R. James, first published in 1897.

CONTENTS

BOOK I

The Sorrows of Boethius

Song 1

Boethius's Complaint

I who wrought my studious numbers
  Smoothly once in happier days,
Now perforce in tears and sadness
  Learn a mournful strain to raise.
Lo, the Muses, grief-dishevelled,
  Guide my pen and voice my woe;
Down their cheeks unfeigned the tear drops
  To my sad complainings flow!
These alone in danger's hour
  Faithful found, have dared attend
On the footsteps of the exile
  To his lonely journey's end.
These that were the pride and pleasure
  Of my youth and high estate
Still remain the only solace
  Of the old man's mournful fate.
Old? Ah yes; swift, ere I knew it,
  By these sorrows on me pressed
Age hath come; lo, Grief hath bid me
  Wear the garb that fits her best.
O'er my head untimely sprinkled
  These white hairs my woes proclaim,
And the skin hangs loose and shrivelled
  On this sorrow-shrunken frame.
Blest is death that intervenes not
  In the sweet, sweet years of peace,
But unto the broken-hearted,
  When they call him, brings release!
Yet Death passes by the wretched,
  Shuts his ear and slumbers deep;
Will not heed the cry of anguish,
  Will not close the eyes that weep.
For, while yet inconstant Fortune
  Poured her gifts and all was bright,
Death's dark hour had all but whelmed me
  In the gloom of endless night.
Now, because misfortune's shadow

Hath o'erclouded that false face,
Cruel Life still halts and lingers,
Though I loathe his weary race.
Friends, why did ye once so lightly
Vaunt me happy among men?
Surely he who so hath fallen
Was not firmly founded then.

Chapter I

While I was thus mutely pondering within myself, and recording my sorrowful complainings with my pen, it seemed to me that there appeared above my head a woman of a countenance exceeding venerable. Her eyes were bright as fire, and of a more than human keenness; her complexion was lively, her vigour showed no trace of enfeeblement; and yet her years were right full, and she plainly seemed not of our age and time. Her stature was difficult to judge. At one moment it exceeded not the common height, at another her forehead seemed to strike the sky; and whenever she raised her head higher, she began to pierce within the very heavens, and to baffle the eyes of them that looked upon her. Her garments were of an imperishable fabric, wrought with the finest threads and of the most delicate workmanship; and these, as her own lips afterwards assured me, she had herself woven with her own hands. The beauty of this vesture had been somewhat tarnished by age and neglect, and wore that dingy look which marble contracts from exposure. On the lowermost edge was inwoven the Greek letter π, on the topmost the letter θ,[1] and between the two were to be seen steps, like a staircase, from the lower to the upper letter. This robe, moreover, had been torn by the hands of violent persons, who had each snatched away what he could clutch.[2] Her right hand held a note-book; in her left she bore a staff. And when she saw the Muses of Poesie standing by my bedside, dictating the words of my lamentations, she was moved awhile to wrath, and her eyes flashed sternly. 'Who,' said she, 'has allowed yon play-acting wantons to approach this sick man—these who, so far from giving medicine to heal his malady, even feed it with sweet poison? These it is who kill the rich crop of reason with the barren thorns of passion, who accustom men's minds to disease, instead of setting them free. Now, were it some common man whom your allurements were seducing, as is usually your way, I should be less indignant. On such a one I should not have spent my pains for naught. But this is one nurtured in the Eleatic and Academic philosophies. Nay, get ye gone, ye sirens, whose sweetness lasteth not; leave him for my muses to tend and heal!' At these words of upbraiding, the whole band, in deepened sadness, with downcast eyes, and blushes that confessed their shame, dolefully left the chamber.

But I, because my sight was dimmed with much weeping, and I could not tell who was this woman of authority so commanding—I was dumfoundered, and, with my gaze fastened on the earth, continued silently to await what she might do next. Then she drew near me and sat on the edge of my couch, and, lookng into my face all heavy with grief and fixed in sadness on the ground, she bewailed in these words the disorder of my mind:

Song 2

His Despondency

Alas! in what abyss his mind
 Is plunged, how wildly tossed!
Still, still towards the outer night
 She sinks, her true light lost,
As oft as, lashed tumultuously
By earth-born blasts, care's waves rise high.

Yet once he ranged the open heavens,
 The sun's bright pathway tracked;
Watched how the cold moon waxed and waned;
 Nor rested, till there lacked
To his wide ken no star that steers
Amid the maze of circling spheres.

The causes why the blusterous winds
 Vex ocean's tranquil face,
Whose hand doth turn the stable globe,
 Or why his even race
From out the ruddy east the sun
Unto the western waves doth run:

What is it tempers cunningly
 The placid hours of spring,
So that it blossoms with the rose
 For earth's engarlanding:
Who loads the year's maturer prime
With clustered grapes in autumn time:

All this he knew—thus ever strove
 Deep Nature's lore to guess.
Now, reft of reason's light, he lies,
 And bonds his neck oppress;
While by the heavy load constrained,
His eyes to this dull earth are chained.

Chapter II

'But the time,' said she, 'calls rather for healing than for lamentation.' Then, with her eyes bent full upon me, 'Art thou that man,' she cries, 'who, erstwhile fed with the milk and reared upon the nourishment which is mine to give, had grown up to the full vigour of a manly spirit? And yet I had bestowed such armour on thee as would have proved an invincible defence, hadst thou not first cast it away. Dost thou know me? Why art thou silent? Is it shame or amazement that hath struck thee dumb? Would it were shame; but, as I see, a stupor hath seized upon thee.' Then, when she saw me not only answering nothing, but mute and utterly incapable of speech, she gently touched my breast with her hand, and said: 'There is no danger; these are the symp-toms of lethargy, the usual sickness of de-luded minds. For awhile he has forgotten himself; he will easily recover his memory, if only he first recognises me. And that he may do so, let me now wipe his eyes that are clouded with a mist of mortal things.' Thereat, with a fold of her robe, she dried my eyes all swimming with tears.

Song 3

The Mists Dispelled

Then the gloom of night was scattered,
  Sight returned unto mine eyes.
So, when haply rainy Caurus
  Rolls the storm-clouds through the skies,
Hidden is the sun; all heaven
  Is obscured in starless night.
But if, in wild onset sweeping,
  Boreas frees day's prisoned light,
All suddenly the radiant god outstreams,
And strikes our dazzled eyesight with his beams.

Chapter III

Even so the clouds of my melancholy were broken up. I saw the clear sky, and regained the power to recognise the face of my physician. Accordingly, when I had lift-ed my eyes and fixed my gaze upon her, I beheld my nurse, Philosophy, whose halls I had frequented from my youth up.

'Ah! why,' I cried, 'mistress of all excel-lence, hast thou come down from on high, and entered the solitude of this my exile? Is it that thou, too, even as I, mayst be perse-cuted with false accusations?'

'Could I desert thee, child,' said she, 'and not lighten the burden which thou hast tak-en upon thee through the hatred of my name, by sharing this trouble? Even forget-ting that it were not lawful for Philosophy to leave companionless the way of the inno-cent, should I, thinkest thou, fear to incur reproach, or shrink from it, as though some strange new thing had befallen? Thinkest thou that now, for the first time in an evil age, Wisdom hath been assailed by peril? Did I not often in days of old, before my ser-vant Plato lived, wage stern warfare with the rashness of folly? In his lifetime, too, Socra-tes, his master, won with my aid the victory of an unjust death. And when, one after the other, the Epicurean herd, the Stoic, and the rest, each of them as far as in them lay, went about to seize the heritage he left, and were dragging me off protesting and resist-ing, as their booty, they tore in pieces the garment which I had woven with my own hands, and, clutching the torn pieces, went off, believing that the whole of me had passed into their possession. And some of them, because some traces of my vesture were seen upon them, were destroyed through the mistake of the lewd multitude, who falsely deemed them to be my disciples. It may be thou knowest not of the banishment of Anaxagoras, of the poison draught of Socrates, nor of Zeno's torturing, because these things happened in a distant country; yet mightest thou have learnt the fate of Arrius, of Seneca, of Soranus, whose stories are neither old nor unknown to fame. These men were brought to destruction for no other reason than that, settled as they were in my principles, their lives were a manifest contrast to the ways of the wicked. So there is nothing thou shouldst wonder at, if on the seas of this life we are tossed by storm-blasts, seeing that we have made it our chiefest aim to refuse compliance with evil-doers. And though, maybe, the host of the wicked is many in number, yet is it contemptible, since it is under no leadership, but is hurried hither and thither at the blind driving of mad error. And if at times and seasons they set in array against us, and fall on in overwhelming strength, our leader draws off her forces into the citadel while they are busy plundering the useless baggage. But we from our vantage ground, safe from all this wild work, laugh to see them making prize of the most valueless of things, protected by a bulwark which aggressive folly may not aspire to reach.'

Song 4

Nothing Can Subdue Virtue

Whoso calm, serene, sedate,
Sets his foot on haughty fate;
Firm and steadfast, come what will,
Keeps his mien unconquered still;
Him the rage of furious seas,
Tossing high wild menaces,
Nor the flames from smoky forges
That Vesuvius disgorges,
Nor the bolt that from the sky
Smites the tower, can terrify.
Why, then, shouldst thou feel affright
At the tyrant's weakling might?
Dread him not, nor fear no harm,
And thou shalt his rage disarm;
But who to hope or fear gives way—
Lost his bosom's rightful sway—
He hath cast away his shield,
Like a coward fled the field;
He hath forged all unaware
Fetters his own neck must bear!

'Dost thou understand?' she asks. Do my words sink into thy mind? Or art thou dull "as the ass to the sound of the lyre"? Why dost thou weep? Why do tears stream from thy eyes?

' "Speak out, hide it not in thy heart."*

If thou lookest for the physician's help, thou must needs disclose thy wound.'

Then I, gathering together what strength I could, began: 'Is there still need of telling? Is not the cruelty of fortune against me plain enough? Doth not the very aspect of this place move thee? Is this the library, the room which thou hadst chosen as thy constant resort in my home, the place where we so often sat together and held discourse of all things in heaven and earth? Was my garb and mien like this when I explored with thee nature's hid secrets, and thou didst trace for me with thy wand the courses of the stars, moulding the while my character and the whole conduct of my life after the pattern of the celestial order? Is this the recompense of my obedience? Yet thou hast enjoined by Plato's mouth the maxim, "that states would be happy, either if philosophers ruled them, or if it should so befall that their rulers would turn philosophers."† By his mouth likewise thou didst point out this imperative reason why philosophers should enter public life, to wit, lest, if the reins of government be left to unprincipled and profligate citizens, trouble and destruction should come upon the good. Following these precepts, I have tried to apply in the business of public administration the principles which I learnt from thee in leisured seclusion. Thou art my witness and that divinity who hath implanted thee in the hearts of the wise, that I brought to my duties no aim but zeal for the public good. For this cause I have become involved in bitter and irreconcilable feuds, and, as happens inevitably, if a man holds fast to the independence of conscience, I have had to think nothing of giving offence to the powerful in the cause of justice. How

often have I encountered and balked Conigastus in his assaults on the fortunes of the weak? How often have I thwarted Trigguilla, steward of the king's household, even when his villainous schemes were as good as accomplished? How often have I risked my position and influence to protect poor wretches from the false charges innumerable with which they were for ever being harassed by the greed and license of the barbarians? No one has ever drawn me aside from justice to oppression. When ruin was overtaking the fortunes of the provincials through the combined pressure of private rapine and public taxation, I grieved no less than the sufferers. When at a season of grievous scarcity a forced sale, disastrous as it was unjustifiable, was proclaimed, and threatened to overwhelm Campania with starvation, I embarked on a struggle with the prætorian prefect in the public interest, I fought the case at the king's judgment-seat, and succeeded in preventing the enforcement of the sale. I rescued the consular Paulinus from the gaping jaws of the court bloodhounds, who in their covetous hopes had already made short work of his wealth. To save Albinus, who was of the same exalted rank, from the penalties of a prejudged charge, I exposed myself to the hatred of Cyprian, the informer.

'Thinkest thou I had laid up for myself store of enmities enough? Well, with the rest of my countrymen, at any rate, my safety should have been assured, since my love of justice had left me no hope of security at court. Yet who was it brought the charges by which I have been struck down? Why, one of my accusers is Basil, who, after being dismissed from the king's household, was driven by his debts to lodge an information against my name. There is Opilio, there is Gaudentius, men who for many and various offences the king's sentence had con-

*See *The Iliad* I, 363; *GBWW*, Vol. 4, p. 6.
†See *The Republic* V, 473D; *GBWW*, Vol. 7, p. 369.

demned to banishment; and when they declined to obey, and sought to save themselves by taking sanctuary, the king, as soon as he heard of it, decreed that, if they did not depart from the city of Ravenna within a precribed time, they should be branded on the forehead and expelled. What would exceed the rigour of this severity? And yet on that same day these very men lodged an information against me, and the information was admitted. Just Heaven! had I deserved this by my way of life? Did it make them fit accusers that my condemnation was a foregone conclusion? Has fortune no shame—if not at the accusation of the innocent, at least for the vileness of the accusers? Perhaps thou wonderest what is the sum of the charges laid against me? I wished, they say, to save the senate. But how? I am accused of hindering an informer from producing evidence to prove the senate guilty of treason. Tell me, then, what is thy counsel, O my mistress. Shall I deny the charge, lest I bring shame on thee? But I did wish it, and I shall never cease to wish it. Shall I admit it? Then the work of thwarting the informer will come to an end. Shall I call the wish for the preservation of that illustrious house a crime? Of a truth the senate, by its decrees concerning me, has made it such! But blind folly, though it deceive itself with false names, cannot alter the true merits of things, and, mindful of the precept of Socrates, I do not think it right either to keep the truth concealed or allow falsehood to pass. But this, however it may be, I leave to thy judgment and to the verdict of the discerning. Moreover, lest the course of events and the true facts should be hidden from posterity, I have myself committed to writing an account of the transaction.

'What need to speak of the forged letters by which an attempt is made to prove that I hoped for the freedom of Rome? Their falsity would have been manifest, if I had been allowed to use the confession of the informers themselves, evidence which has in all matters the most convincing force. Why,

what hope of freedom is left to us? Would there were any! I should have answered with the epigram of Canius when Caligula declared him to have been cognisant of a conspiracy against him. "If I had known," said he, "thou shouldst never have known." Grief hath not so blunted my perceptions in this matter that I should complain because impious wretches contrive their villainies against the virtuous, but at their achievement of their hopes I do exceedingly marvel. For evil purposes are, perchance, due to the imperfection of human nature; that it should be possible for scoundrels to carry out their worst schemes against the innocent, while God beholdeth, is verily monstrous. For this cause, not without reason, one of thy disciples asked, "If God exists, whence comes evil? Yet whence comes good, if He exists not?" However, it might well be that wretches who seek the blood of all honest men and of the whole senate should wish to destroy me also, whom they saw to be a bulwark of the senate and all honest men. But did I deserve such a fate from the Fathers also? Thou rememberest, methinks—since thou didst ever stand by my side to direct what I should do or say— thou rememberest, I say, how at Verona, when the king, eager for the general destruction, was bent on implicating the whole senatorial order in the charge of treason brought against Albinus, with what indifference to my own peril I maintained the innocence of its members, one and all. Thou knowest that what I say is the truth, and that I have never boasted of my good deeds in a spirit of self-praise. For whenever a man by proclaiming his good deeds receives the recompense of fame, he diminishes in a measure the secret reward of a good conscience. What issues have overtaken my innocency thou seest. Instead of reaping the rewards of true virtue, I undergo the penalties of a guilt falsely laid to my charge—nay, more than this; never did an open confession of guilt cause such unanimous severity among the assessors, but that some consideration, either of the mere frailty of human nature, or of fortune's universal instability, availed to soften the verdict of some few. Had I been accused of a design to fire the temples, to slaughter the priests with impious sword, of plotting the massacre of all honest men, I should yet have been produced in court, and only punished on due confession or conviction. Now for my too great zeal towards the senate I have been condemned to outlawry and death, unheard and undefended, at a distance of near five hundred miles away. Oh, my judges, well do ye deserve that no one should hereafter be convicted of a fault like mine!

'Yet even my very accusers saw how honourable was the charge they brought against me, and, in order to overlay it with some shadow of guilt, they falsely asserted that in the pursuit of my ambition I had stained my conscience with sacrilegious acts. And yet thy spirit, indwelling in me, had driven from the chamber of my soul all lust of earthly success, and with thine eye ever upon me, there could be no place left for sacrilege. For thou didst daily repeat in my ear and instil into my mind the Pythagorean maxim, "Follow after God." It was not likely, then, that I should covet the assistance of the vilest spirits, when thou wert moulding me to such an excellence as should conform me to the likeness of God. Again, the innocency of the inner sanctuary of my home, the company of friends of the highest probity, a father-in-law revered at once for his pure character and his active beneficence, shield me from the very suspicion of sacrilege. Yet—atrocious as it is—they even draw credence for this charge from *thee;* I am like to be thought implicated in wickedness on this very account, that I am imbued with *thy* teachings and stablished in *thy* ways. So it is not enough that my devotion to thee should profit me nothing, but thou also must be assailed by reason of the odium which I have incurred. Verily this is the very crown of my misfortunes, that men's opinions for the most part look not to real merit, but to the event; and only recognise foresight where Fortune has crowned the issue with her approval. Whereby it comes to pass that reputation is the first of all things to abandon the unfortunate. I remember with chagrin how perverse is popular report, how various and discordant men's judgments. This only will I say, that the most crushing of misfortune's burdens is, that as soon as a charge is fastened upon the unhappy, they are believed to have deserved their sufferings. I, for my part, who have been banished from all life's blessings, stripped of my honours, stained in repute, am punished for well-doing.

'And now methinks I see the villainous dens of the wicked surging with joy and gladness, all the most recklessly unscrupulous threatening a new crop of lying informations, the good prostrate with terror at my danger, every ruffian incited by impunity to new daring and to success by the profits of audacity, the guiltless not only robbed of their peace of mind, but even of all means of defence. Wherefore I would fain cry out:

Song 5

Boethius's Prayer

'Builder of yon starry dome,
  Thou that whirlest, throned eternal,
Heaven's swift globe, and, as they roam,
  Guid'st the stars by laws supernal:

So in full-sphered splendour dight
  Cynthia dims the lamps of night,
But unto the orb fraternal
  Closer drawn,[3] doth lose her light.

'Who at fall of eventide,
  Hesper, his cold radiance showeth,
Lucifer his beams doth hide,
  Paling as the sun's light groweth,
    Brief, while winter's frost holds sway,
    By thy will the space of day;
  Swift, when summer's fervour gloweth,
    Speed the hours of night away.

'Thou dost rule the changing year:
  When rude Boreas oppresses,
Fall the leaves; they reappear,
  Wooed by Zephyr's soft caresses.
    Fields that Sirius burns deep-grown
    By Arcturus' watch were sown:
  Each the reign of law confesses,
    Keeps the place that is his own.

'Sovereign Ruler, Lord of all!
  Can it be that Thou disdainest
Only man? 'Gainst him, poor thrall,
  Wanton Fortune plays her vainest.
    Guilt's deservèd punishment
    Falleth on the innocent;
  High uplifted, the profanest
    On the just their malice vent.

'Virtue cowers in dark retreats,
  Crime's foul stain the righteous beareth,
Perjury and false deceits
  Hurt not him the wrong who dareth;
    But whene'er the wicked trust
    In ill strength to work their lust,
  Kings, whom nations' awe declareth
    Mighty, grovel in the dust.

'Look, oh look upon this earth,
  Thou who on law's sure foundation
Framedst all! Have we no worth,
  We poor men, of all creation?
    Sore we toss on fortune's tide;
    Master, bid the waves subside!
  And earth's ways with consummation
    Of Thy heaven's order guide!'

When I had poured out my griefs in this long and unbroken strain of lamentation, she, with calm countenance, and in no wise disturbed at my complainings, thus spake:

'When I saw thee sorrowful, in tears, I straightway knew thee wretched and an exile. But how far distant that exile I should not know, had not thine own speech revealed it. Yet how far indeed from thy country hast thou, not been banished, but rather hast strayed; or, if thou wilt have it banishment, hast banished thyself! For no one else could ever lawfully have had this power over thee. Now, if thou wilt call to mind from what country thou art sprung, it is not ruled, as once was the Athenian polity, by the sovereignty of the multitude, but "one is its Ruler, one its King,"* who takes delight in the number of His citizens, not in their banishment; to submit to whose governance and to obey whose ordinances is perfect freedom. Art thou ignorant of that most ancient law of this thy country, whereby it is decreed that no one whatsoever, who hath chosen to fix there his dwelling, may be sent into exile? For truly there is no fear that one who is encompassed by its ramparts and defences should deserve to be exiled. But he who has ceased to wish to dwell therein, he likewise ceases to deserve to do so. And so it is not so much the aspect of this place which moves me, as thy aspect; not so much the library walls set off with glass and ivory which I miss, as the chamber of thy mind, wherein I once placed, not books, but that which gives books their value, the doctrines which my books contain. Now, what thou hast said of thy services to the commonweal is true, only too little compared with the greatness of thy deservings. The things laid to thy charge whereof thou hast spoken, whether such as redound to thy credit, or mere false accusations, are publicly known. As for the crimes and deceits of the informers, thou hast rightly deemed it fitting to pass them over lightly, because the popular voice hath better and more fully pronounced upon them. Thou hast bitterly complained of the injustice of the senate. Thou hast grieved over my calumniation, and likewise hast lamented the damage to my good name. Finally, thine indignation blazed forth against fortune; thou hast complained of the unfairness with which thy merits have been recompensed. Last of all thy frantic muse framed a prayer that the peace which reigns in heaven might rule earth also. But since a throng of tumultuous passions hath assailed thy soul, since thou art distraught with anger, pain, and grief, strong remedies are not proper for thee in this thy present mood. And so for a time I will use milder methods, that the tumours which have grown hard through the influx of disturbing passion may be softened by gentle treatment, till they can bear the force of sharper remedies.'

Song 6

All Things Have Their Needful Order

He who to th' unwilling furrows
    Gives the generous grain,
When the Crab with baleful fervours
    Scorches all the plain;
He shall find his garner bare,
Acorns for his scanty fare.

Go not forth to cull sweet violets
From the purpled steep,
While the furious blasts of winter
Through the valleys sweep;
Nor the grape o'erhasty bring
To the press in days of spring.

For to each thing God hath given
Its appointed time;
No perplexing change permits He
In His plan sublime.
So who quits the order due
Shall a luckless issue rue.

Chapter VI

'First, then, wilt thou suffer me by a few questions to make some attempt to test the state of thy mind, that I may learn in what way to set about thy cure?'

'Ask what thou wilt,' said I, 'for I will answer whatever questions thou choosest to put.'

Then said she: 'This world of ours—thinkest thou it is governed haphazard and fortuitously, or believest thou that there is in it any rational guidance?'

'Nay,' said I, 'in no wise may I deem that such fixed motions can be determined by random hazard, but I know that God, the Creator, presideth over His work, nor will the day ever come that shall drive me from holding fast the truth of this belief.'

'Yes,' said she; 'thou didst even but now affirm it in song, lamenting that men alone had no portion in the divine care. As to the rest, thou wert unshaken in the belief that they were ruled by reason. Yet I marvel exceedingly how, in spite of thy firm hold on this opinion, thou art fallen into sickness. But let us probe more deeply: something or other is missing, I think. Now, tell me, since thou doubtest not that God governs the world, dost thou perceive by what means He rules it?'

'I scarcely understand what thou meanest,' I said, 'much less can I answer thy question.'

'Did I not say truly that something is missing, whereby, as through a breach in

the ramparts, disease hath crept in to disturb thy mind? But, tell me, dost thou remember the universal end towards which the aim of all nature is directed?'

'I once heard,' said I, 'but sorrow hath dulled my recollection.'

'And yet thou knowest whence all things have proceeded.'

'Yes, that I know,' said I, 'and have answered that it is from God.'

'Yet how is it possible that thou knowest not what is the end of existence, when thou dost understand its source and origin? However, these disturbances of mind have force to shake a man's position, but cannot pluck him up and root him altogether out of himself. But answer this also, I pray thee: rememberest thou that thou art a man?'

'How should I not?' said I.

'Then, canst thou say what man is?'

'Is this thy question: Whether I know myself for a being endowed with reason and subject to death? Surely I do acknowledge myself such.'

Then she: 'Dost know nothing else that thou art?'

'Nothing.'

'Now,' said she, 'I know another cause of thy disease, one, too, of grave moment. Thou hast ceased to know thy own nature. So, then, I have made full discovery both of

---

*See *The Iliad* II, 204, 205; *GBWW*, Vol. 4, p. 12.

the causes of thy sickness and the means of restoring thy health. It is because forgetfulness of thyself hath bewildered thy mind that thou hast bewailed thee as an exile, as one stripped of the blessings that were his; it is because thou knowest not the end of existence that thou deemest abominable and wicked men to be happy and powerful; while, because thou hast forgotten by what means the earth is governed, thou deemest that fortune's changes ebb and flow without the restraint of a guiding hand. These are serious enough to cause not sickness only, but even death; but, thanks be to the Author of our health, the light of nature hath not yet left thee utterly. In thy true judgment concerning the world's government,

in that thou believest it subject, not to the random drift of chance, but to divine reason, we have the divine spark from which thy recovery may be hoped. Have, then, no fear; from these weak embers the vital heat shall once more be kindled within thee. But seeing that it is not yet time for strong remedies, and that the mind is manifestly so constituted that when it casts off true opinions it straightway puts on false, wherefrom arises a cloud of confusion that disturbs its true vision, I will now try and disperse these mists by mild and soothing application, that so the darkness of misleading passion may be scattered, and thou mayst come to discern the splendour of the true light.'

Song 7

The Perturbations of Passion

Stars shed no light
　　Through the black night,
　　　　When the clouds hide;
And the lashed wave,
　　If the winds rave
　　　　O'er ocean's tide,—

Though once serene
　　As day's fair sheen,—
　　　　Soon fouled and spoiled
By the storm's spite,
　　Shows to the sight
　　　　Turbid and soiled.

Oft the fair rill,
　　Down the steep hill
　　　　Seaward that strays,
Some tumbled block
　　Of fallen rock
　　　　Hinders and stays.

Then art thou fain
　　Clear and most plain
　　　　Truth to discern,

In the right way
　Firmly to stay,
　　Nor from it turn?

Joy, hope and fear
　Suffer not near,
　　Drive grief away:
Shackled and blind
And lost is the mind
　Where these have sway.

BOOK II

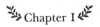

The Vanity of Fortune's Gifts

Chapter I

Thereafter for awhile she remained silent; and when she had restored my flagging attention by a moderate pause in her discourse, she thus began: 'If I have thoroughly ascertained the character and causes of thy sickness, thou art pining with regretful longing for thy former fortune. It is the change, as thou deemest, of this fortune that hath so wrought upon thy mind. Well do I understand that Siren's manifold wiles, the fatal charm of the friendship she pretends for her victims, so long as she is scheming to entrap them—how she unexpectedly abandons them and leaves them overwhelmed with insupportable grief. Bethink thee of her nature, character, and deserts, and thou wilt soon acknowledge that in her thou hast neither possessed, nor hast thou lost, aught of any worth. Methinks I need not spend much pains in bringing this to thy mind, since, even when she was still with thee, even while she was caressing thee, thou usedst to assail her in manly terms, to rebuke her, with maxims drawn from my holy treasure-house. But all sudden changes of circumstances bring inevitably a certain commotion of spirit. Thus it hath come to pass that thou also for awhile hast been parted from thy mind's tranquillity. But it is time for thee to take and drain a draught, soft and pleasant to the taste, which, as it penetrates within, may prepare the way for stronger potions. Wherefore I call to my aid the sweet persuasiveness of Rhetoric, who then only walketh in the right way when she forsakes not my instructions, and Music, my handmaid, I bid to join with her singing, now in lighter, now in graver strain.

'What is it, then, poor mortal, that hath cast thee into lamentation and mourning? Some strange, unwonted sight, methinks, have thine eyes seen. Thou deemest Fortune to have changed towards thee; thou mistakest. Such ever were her ways, ever such her nature. Rather in her very mutability hath she preserved towards thee her true constancy. Such was she when she loaded thee with caresses, when she deluded thee with the allurements of a false happiness. Thou hast found out how changeful is the face of the blind goddess. She who still veils herself from others hath fully discovered to thee her whole character. If thou likest her, take her as she is, and do not complain. If thou abhorrest her perfidy, turn from her in disdain, renounce her, for baneful are her delusions. The very thing which is now the cause of thy great grief ought to have brought thee tranquillity. Thou hast been forsaken by one of whom no one can be sure that she will not forsake him. Or dost thou indeed set value on a happiness that is certain to depart? Again I ask, Is Fortune's presence dear to thee if she cannot be trusted to stay, and though she will bring sorrow when she is gone? Why, if she cannot be kept at pleasure, and if her flight overwhelms with calamity, what is this fleeting visitant but a token of coming trouble? Truly it is not enough to look only at what lies before the eyes; wisdom gauges the issues of things, and this same mutability, with its two aspects, makes the threats of Fortune void of terror, and her caresses little to be desired. Finally, thou oughtest to bear with whatever takes place within the boundaries of Fortune's demesne, when thou hast placed thy head beneath her yoke. But if thou wishest to impose a law of staying and departing on her whom thou hast of thine own accord chosen for thy mistress, art thou not acting wrongfully, art thou not embittering by impatience a lot which thou canst not alter? Didst thou commit thy sails to the winds, thou wouldst voyage not whither thy intention was to go, but whither the winds drave thee; didst thou entrust thy seed to the fields, thou wouldst set off the fruitful years against the barren. Thou hast resigned thyself to the sway of Fortune; thou must submit to thy mistress's caprices. What! art thou verily striving to stay the swing of the revolving wheel? Oh, stupidest of mortals, if it takes to standing still, it ceases to be the wheel of Fortune.'

Song 1

Fortune's Malice

Mad Fortune sweeps along in wanton pride,
Uncertain as Euripus' surging tide;
Now tramples mighty kings beneath her feet;
Now sets the conquered in the victor's seat.
She heedeth not the wail of hapless woe,
But mocks the griefs that from her mischief flow.
Such is her sport; so proveth she her power;
And great the marvel, when in one brief hour
She shows her darling lifted high in bliss,
Then headlong plunged in misery's abyss.

'Now I would fain also reason with thee a little in Fortune's own words. Do thou observe whether her contentions be just. "Man," she might say, "why dost thou pursue me with thy daily complainings? What wrong have I done thee? What goods of thine have I taken from thee? Choose an thou wilt a judge, and let us dispute before him concerning the rightful ownership of wealth and rank. If thou succeedest in showing that any one of these things is the true property of mortal man, I freely grant those things to be thine which thou claimest. When nature brought thee forth out of thy mother's womb, I took thee, naked and destitute as thou wast, I cherished thee with my substance, and, in the partiality of my favour for thee, I brought thee up somewhat too indulgently, and this it is which now makes thee rebellious against me. I surrounded thee with a royal abundance of all those things that are in my power. Now it is my pleasure to draw back my hand. Thou hast reason to thank me for the use of what was not thine own; thou hast no right to complain, as if thou hadst lost what was wholly thine. Why, then, dost bemoan thyself? I have done thee no violence. Wealth, honour, and all such things are placed under my control. My handmaidens know their mistress; with me they come, and at my going they depart. I might boldly affirm that if those things the loss of which thou lamentest had been thine, thou couldst never have lost them. Am I alone to be forbidden to do what I will with my own? Unrebuked, the skies now reveal the brightness of day, now shroud the daylight in the darkness of night; the year may now engarland the face of the earth with flowers and fruits, now disfigure it with storms and cold. The sea is permitted to invite with smooth and tranquil surface to-day, to-morrow to roughen with wave and storm. Shall man's insatiate greed bind *me* to a constancy foreign to my character? This is my art, this the game I never cease to play. I turn the wheel that spins. I delight to see the high come down and the low ascend. Mount up, if thou wilt, but only on condition that thou wilt not think it a hardship to come down when the rules of my game require it. Wert thou ignorant of my character? Didst not know how Crœsus, King of the Lydians, erstwhile the dreaded rival of Cyrus, was afterwards pitiably consigned to the flame of the pyre, and only saved by a shower sent from heaven? Has it 'scaped thee how Paullus paid a meed of pious tears to the misfortunes of King Perseus, his prisoner? What else do tragedies make such woeful outcry over save the overthrow of kingdoms by the indiscriminate strokes of Fortune? Didst thou not learn in thy childhood how there stand at the threshold of Zeus 'two jars,' 'the one full of blessings, the other of calamities'?* How if thou hast drawn over-liberally from the good jar? What if not even now have I departed wholly from thee? What if this very mutability of mine is a just ground for hoping better things? But listen now, and cease to let thy heart consume away with fretfulness, nor expect to live on thine own terms in a realm that is common to all.'

---

*See *The Iliad* XXIV, 527, 528; *GBWW*, Vol. 4, p. 176.

Song 2

Man's Covetousness

What though Plenty pour her gifts
  With a lavish hand,
Numberless as are the stars,
  Countless as the sand,
Will the race of man, content,
Cease to murmur and lament?

Nay, though God, all-bounteous, give
  Gold at man's desire—
Honours, rank, and fame—content
  Not a whit is nigher;
But an all-devouring greed
Yawns with ever-widening need.

Then what bounds can e'er restrain
  This wild lust of having,
When with each new bounty fed
  Grows the frantic craving?
He is never rich whose fear
Sees grim Want forever near.

Chapter III

'If Fortune should plead thus against thee, assuredly thou wouldst not have one word to offer in reply; or, if thou canst find any justification of thy complainings, thou must show what it is. I will give thee space to speak.'

Then said I: 'Verily, thy pleas are plausible—yea, steeped in the honeyed sweetness of music and rhetoric. But their charm lasts only while they are sounding in the ear; the sense of his misfortunes lies deeper in the heart of the wretched. So, when the sound ceases to vibrate upon the air, the heart's indwelling sorrow is felt with renewed bitterness.'

Then said she: 'It is indeed as thou sayest, for we have not yet come to the curing of thy sickness; as yet these are but lenitives conducing to the treatment of a malady hitherto obstinate. The remedies which go deep I will apply in due season. Neverthe-less, to deprecate thy determination to be thought wretched, I ask thee, Hast thou forgotten the extent and bounds of thy felicity? I say nothing of how, when orphaned and desolate, thou wast taken into the care of illustrious men; how thou wast chosen for alliance with the highest in the state—and even before thou wert bound to their house by marriage, wert already dear to their love—which is the most precious of all ties. Did not all pronounce thee most happy in the virtues of thy wife, the splendid honours of her father, and the blessing of male issue? I pass over—for I care not to speak of blessings in which others also have shared—the distinctions often denied to age which thou enjoyedst in thy youth. I choose rather to come to the unparalleled culmination of thy good fortune. If the fruition of any earthly success has weight in the scale of happiness, can the memory of that splendour be swept away by any rising flood of troubles? That day when thou didst see thy two sons ride forth from home joint consuls, followed by a train of senators, and welcomed by the good-will of the people; when these two sat in curule chairs in the Senate-house, and thou by thy panegyric on the king didst earn the fame of eloquence and ability; when in the Circus, seated between the two consuls, thou didst glut the multitude thronging around with the triumphal largesses for which they looked—methinks thou didst cozen Fortune while she caressed thee, and made thee her darling. Thou didst bear off a boon which she had never before granted to any private person. Art thou, then, minded to cast up a reckoning with Fortune? Now for the first time she has turned a jealous glance upon thee. If thou compare the extent and bounds of thy blessings and misfortunes, thou canst not deny that thou art still fortunate. Or if thou esteem not thyself favoured by Fortune in that thy then seeming prosperity hath departed, deem not thyself wretched, since what thou now believest to be calamitous passeth also. What! art thou but now come suddenly and a stranger to the scene of this life? Thinkest thou there is any stability in human affairs, when man himself vanishes away in the swift course of time? It is true that there is little trust that the gifts of chance will abide; yet the last day of life is in a manner the death of all remaining Fortune. What difference, then, thinkest thou, is there, whether thou leavest her by dying, or she leave thee by fleeing away?'

Song 3

All Passes

When, in rosy chariot drawn,
Phœbus 'gins to light the dawn,
By his flaming beams assailed,
Every glimmering star is paled.
When the grove, by Zephyrs fed,
With rose-blossom blushes red;—
Doth rude Auster breathe thereon,
Bare it stands, its glory gone.
Smooth and tranquil lies the deep
While the winds are hushed in sleep.
Soon, when angry tempests lash,
Wild and high the billows dash.
Thus if Nature's changing face
Holds not still a moment's space,
Fleeting deem man's fortunes; deem
Bliss as transient as a dream.
One law only standeth fast:
Things created may not last.

Then said I: 'True are thine admonishings, thou nurse of all excellence; nor can I deny the wonder of my fortune's swift career. Yet it is this which chafes me the more cruelly in the recalling. For truly in adverse fortune the worst sting of misery is to *have been* happy.'

'Well,' said she, 'if thou art paying the penalty of a mistaken belief, thou canst not rightly impute the fault to circumstances. If it is the felicity which Fortune gives that moves thee—mere name though it be—come reckon up with me how rich thou art in the number and weightiness of thy blessings. Then if, by the blessing of Providence, thou hast still preserved unto thee safe and inviolate that which, howsoever thou mightest reckon thy fortune, thou wouldst have thought thy most precious possession, what right hast thou to talk of ill-fortune whilst keeping all Fortune's better gifts? Yet Symmachus, thy wife's father—a man whose splendid character does honour to the human race—is safe and unharmed; and while he bewails thy wrongs, this rare nature, in whom wisdom and virtue are so nobly blended, is himself out of danger—a boon thou wouldst have been quick to purchase at the price of life itself. Thy wife yet lives, with her gentle disposition, her peerless modesty and virtue—this the epitome of all her graces, that she is the true daughter of her sire—she lives, I say, and for thy sake only preserves the breath of life, though she loathes it, and pines away in grief and tears for thy absence, wherein, if in naught else, I would allow some marring of thy felicity. What shall I say of thy sons and their consular dignity—how in them, so far as may be in youths of their age, the example of their father's and grandfather's character shines out? Since, then, the chief care of mortal man is to preserve his life, how happy art thou, couldst thou but recognise thy blessings, who possessest even now what no one doubts to be dearer than life! Wherefore, now dry thy tears. Fortune's hate hath not involved all thy dear ones; the stress of the storm that has assailed thee is not beyond measure intolerable, since there are anchors still holding firm which suffer thee not to lack either consolation in the present or hope for the future.'

'I pray that they still may hold. For while they still remain, however things may go, I shall ride out the storm. Yet thou seest how much is shorn of the splendour of my fortunes.'

'We are gaining a little ground,' said she, 'if there is something in thy lot wherewith thou art not yet altogether discontented. But I cannot stomach thy daintiness when thou complainest with such violence of grief and anxiety because thy happiness falls short of completeness. Why, who enjoys such settled felicity as not to have some quarrel with the circumstances of his lot? A troublous matter are the conditions of human bliss; either they are never realized in full, or never stay permanently. One has abundant riches, but is shamed by his ignoble birth. Another is conspicuous for his nobility, but through the embarrassments of poverty would prefer to be obscure. A third, richly endowed with both, laments the loneliness of an unwedded life. Another, though happily married, is doomed to childlessness, and nurses his wealth for a stranger to inherit. Yet another, blest with children, mournfully bewails the misdeeds of son or daughter. Wherefore, it is not easy for anyone to be at perfect peace with the circumstances of his lot. There lurks in each several portion something which they who experience it not know nothing of, but which makes the sufferer wince. Besides, the more favoured a man is by Fortune, the more fastidiously sensitive is he; and, unless all things answer to his whim, he is overwhelmed by the most trifling misfortunes, because utterly unschooled in adversity. So petty are the trifles which rob the most fortunate of perfect happiness! How many are there, dost thou imagine, who would think themselves nigh heaven, if but a small portion from the wreck of thy fortune should fall to them? This very place which thou callest exile is to them that dwell therein their native land. So true is it that nothing is wretched, but thinking makes it so, and conversely every lot is happy if borne with equanimity. Who is so blest by Fortune as not to wish to change his state, if once he gives rein to a rebellious spirit? With how many bitternesses is the sweetness of human felicity blent! And even if that sweetness seem to him to bring delight in the enjoying, yet he cannot keep it from departing when it will. How manifestly wretched, then, is the bliss of earthly fortune, which lasts not for ever with those whose temper is equable, and can give no perfect satisfaction to the anxious-minded!

'Why, then, ye children of mortality, seek ye from without that happiness whose seat is only within us? Error and ignorance bewilder you. I will show thee, in brief, the hinge on which perfect happiness turns. Is there anything more precious to thee than thyself? Nothing, thou wilt say. If, then, thou art master of thyself, thou wilt possess that which thou wilt never be willing to lose, and which Fortune cannot take from thee. And that thou mayst see that happiness cannot possibly consist in these things which are the sport of chance, reflect that, if happiness is the highest good of a creature living in accordance with reason, and if a thing which can in any wise be reft away is not the highest good, since that which cannot be taken away is better than it, it is plain that Fortune cannot aspire to bestow happiness by reason of its instability. And, besides, a man borne along by this transitory felicity must either know or not know its unstability. If he knows not, how poor is a happiness which depends on the blindness of ignorance! If he knows it, he needs must fear to lose a happiness whose loss he believes to be possible. Wherefore, a never-ceasing fear suffers him not to be happy. Or does he count the possibility of this loss a trifling matter? Insignificant, then, must be the good whose loss can be borne so equably. And, further, I know thee to be one settled in the belief that the souls of men certainly die not with them, and convinced thereof by numerous proofs; it is clear also that the felicity which Fortune bestows is brought to an end with the death of the body: therefore, it cannot be doubted but that, if happiness is conferred in this way, the whole human race sinks into misery when death brings the close of all. But if we know that many have sought the joy of happiness not through death only, but also through pain and suffering, how can life make men happy by its presence when it makes them not wretched by its loss?'

Song 4

The Golden Mean

Who founded firm and sure
Would ever live secure,
In spite of storm and blast
Immovable and fast;
Whoso would fain deride
The ocean's threatening tide;—
His dwelling should not seek
On sands or mountain-peak.
Upon the mountain's height

The storm-winds wreak their spite:
The shifting sands disdain
Their burden to sustain.
Do thou these perils flee,
Fair though the prospect be,
And fix thy resting-place
On some low rock's sure base.
Then, though the tempests roar,
Seas thunder on the shore,
Thou in thy stronghold blest
And undisturbed shalt rest;
Live all thy days serene,
And mock the heavens' spleen.

Chapter V

'But since my reasonings begin to work a soothing effect within thy mind, methinks I may resort to remedies somewhat stronger. Come, suppose, now, the gifts of Fortune were not fleeting and transitory, what is there in them capable of ever becoming truly thine, or which does not lose value when looked at steadily and fairly weighed in the balance? Are riches, I pray thee, precious either through thy nature or in their own? What are they but mere gold and heaps of money? Yet these fine things show their quality better in the spending than in the hoarding; for I suppose 'tis plain that greed always makes men hateful, while liberality brings fame. But that which is transferred to another cannot remain in one's own possession; and if that be so, then money is only precious when it is given away, and, by being transferred to others, ceases to be one's own. Again, if all the money in the world were heaped up in one man's possession, all others would be made poor. Sound fills the ears of many at the same time without being broken into parts, but your riches cannot pass to many without being lessened in the process. And when this happens, they must needs impoverish those whom they leave.

How poor and cramped a thing, then, is riches, which more than one cannot possess as an unbroken whole, which falls not to any one man's lot without the impoverishment of everyone else! Or is it the glitter of gems that allures the eye? Yet, how rarely excellent soever may be their splendour, remember the flashing light is in the jewels, not in the man. Indeed, I greatly marvel at men's admiration of them; for what can rightly seem beautiful to a being endowed with life and reason, if it lack the movement and structure of life? And although such things do in the end take on them more beauty from their Maker's care and their own brilliancy, still they in no wise merit your admiration since their excellence is set at a lower grade than your own.

'Does the beauty of the fields delight you? Surely, yes; it is a beautiful part of a right beautiful whole. Fitly indeed do we at times enjoy the serene calm of the sea, admire the sky, the stars, the moon, the sun. Yet is any of these thy concern? Dost thou venture to boast thyself of the beauty of any one of them? Art *thou* decked with spring's flowers? is it *thy* fertility that swelleth in the fruits of autumn? Why art thou moved with empty transports? why embracest thou an alien excellence as thine own? Never will fortune make thine that which the nature of things has excluded from thy ownership. Doubtless the fruits of the earth are given for the sustenance of living creatures. But if thou art content to supply thy wants so far as suffices nature, there is no need to resort to fortune's bounty. Nature is content with few things, and with a very little of these. If thou art minded to force superfluities upon her when she is satisfied, that which thou addest will prove either unpleasant or harmful. But, now, thou thinkest it fine to shine in raiment of divers colours; yet—if, indeed, there is any pleasure in the sight of such things—it is the texture or the artist's skill which I shall admire.

'Or perhaps it is a long train of servants that makes thee happy? Why, if they behave viciously, they are a ruinous burden to thy house, and exceeding dangerous to their own master; while if they are honest, how canst thou count other men's virtue in the sum of thy possessions? From all which 'tis plainly proved that not one of these things which thou reckonest in the number of thy possessions is really thine. And if there is in them no beauty to be desired, why shouldst thou either grieve for their loss or find joy in their continued possession? While if they are beautiful in their own nature, what is that to thee? They would have been not less pleasing in themselves, though never included among thy possessions. For they derive not their preciousness from being counted in thy riches, but rather thou hast chosen to count them in thy riches because they seemed to thee precious.

'Then, what seek ye by all this noisy outcry about fortune? To chase away poverty, I ween, by means of abundance. And yet ye find the result just contrary. Why, this varied array of precious furniture needs more accessories for its protection; it is a true saying that they want most who possess most, and, conversely, they want very little who measure their abundance by nature's

requirements, not by the superfluity of vain display. Have ye no good of your own implanted within you, that ye seek your good in things external and separate? Is the nature of things so reversed that a creature divine by right of reason can in no other way be splendid in his own eyes save by the possession of lifeless chattels? Yet, while other things are content with their own, ye who in your intellect are God-like seek from the lowest of things adornment for a nature of supreme excellence, and perceive not how great a wrong ye do your Maker. His will was that mankind should excel all things on earth. Ye thrust down your worth beneath the lowest of things. For if that in which each thing finds its good is plainly more precious than that whose good it is, by your own estimation ye put yourselves below the vilest of things, when ye deem these vile things to be your good: nor does this fall out undeservedly. Indeed, man is so constituted that he then only excels other things when he knows himself; but he is brought lower than the beasts if he lose this self-knowledge. For that other creatures should be ignorant of themselves is natural; in man it shows as a defect. How extravagant, then, is this error of yours, in thinking that anything can be embellished by adornments not its own. It cannot be. For if such accessories add any lustre, it is the accessories that get the praise, while that which they veil and cover remains in its pristine ugliness. And again I say, That is no *good*, which injures its possessor. Is this untrue? No, quite true, thou sayest. And yet riches have often hurt those that possessed them, since the worst of men, who are all the more covetous by reason of their wickedness, think none but themselves worthy to possess all the gold and gems the world contains. So thou, who now dreadest pike and sword, mightest have trolled a carol "in the robber's face," hadst thou entered the road of life with empty pockets. Oh, wondrous blessedness of perishable wealth, whose acquisition robs thee of security!'

Song 5

The Former Age

Too blest the former age, their life
  Who in the fields contented led,
And still, by luxury unspoiled,
  On frugal acorns sparely fed.

No skill was theirs the luscious grape
  With honey's sweeetness to confuse;
Nor China's soft and sheeny silks
  T' empurple with brave Tyrian hues.

The grass their wholesome couch, their drink
  The stream, their roof the pine's tall shade;
Not theirs to cleave the deep, nor seek
  In strange far lands the spoils of trade.

The trump of war was heard not yet,
  Nor soiled the fields by bloodshed's stain;
For why should war's fierce madness arm
  When strife brought wound, but brought not gain?

Ah! would our hearts might still return
  To following in those ancient ways.
Alas! the greed of getting glows
  More fierce than Etna's fiery blaze.

Woe, woe for him, whoe'er it was,
  Who first gold's hidden store revealed,
And—perilous treasure-trove—dug out
  The gems that fain would be concealed!

Chapter VI

'What now shall I say of rank and power, whereby,. because ye know not true power and dignity, ye hope to reach the sky? Yet, when rank and power have fallen to the worst of men, did ever an Etna, belching forth flame and fiery deluge, work such mischief? Verily, as I think, thou dost remember how thine ancestors sought to abolish the consular power, which had been the foundation of their liberties, on account of the overweening pride of the consuls, and how for that self-same pride they had already abolished the kingly title! And if, as happens but rarely, these prerogatives are conferred on virtuous men, it is only the virtue of those who exercise them that pleases. So it appears that honour cometh not to virtue from rank, but to rank from virtue. Look, too, at the nature of that power which ye find so attractive and glorious! Do ye never consider, ye creatures of earth, what ye are, and over whom ye exercise your fancied lordship? Suppose, now, that in the mouse tribe there should rise up one claiming rights and powers for himself above the rest, would ye not laugh consumedly? Yet if thou lookest to his body alone, what creature canst thou find more feeble than man, who oftentimes is killed by the bite of a fly, or by some insect creeping into the inner passage of his system! Yet what rights can one exercise over another, save only as regards the body, and that which is lower than the body—I mean fortune? What! wilt thou bind with thy mandates the free spirit? Canst thou force from its due tranquillity the mind that is firmly composed by reason? A tyrant thought to drive a man of free birth to reveal his accomplices in a conspiracy, but the prisoner bit off his tongue and threw it into the furious tyrant's face; thus, the tortures which the tyrant thought the instrument of his cruelty the sage made an opportunity for heroism. Moreover, what is there that one man can do to another which he himself may not have to undergo in his turn? We are told that Busiris, who used to kill his guests, was himself slain by his guest, Hercules. Regulus had thrown into bonds many of the Carthaginians whom he had taken in war; soon after he himself submitted his hands to the chains of the vanquished. Then, thinkest thou that man hath any power who cannot prevent another's being able to do to him what he himself can do to others?

'Besides, if there were any element of natural and proper good in rank and power, they would never come to the utterly bad, since opposites are not wont to be associated. Nature brooks not the union of contraries. So, seeing there is no doubt that wicked wretches are oftentimes set in high places, it is also clear that things which suffer association with the worst of men cannot be good in their own nature. Indeed, this judgment may with some reason be passed concerning all the gifts of fortune which fall so plentifully to all the most wicked. This ought also to be considered here, I think: No one doubts a man to be brave in whom he has observed a brave spirit residing. It is plain that one who is endowed with speed is swift-footed. So also music makes men musical, the healing art physicians, rhetoric public speakers. For each of these has naturally its own proper working; there is no confusion with the effects of contrary things—nay, even of itself it rejects what is incompatible. And yet wealth cannot extinguish insatiable greed, nor has power ever made him master of himself whom vicious lusts kept bound in indissoluble fetters; dignity conferred on the wicked not only fails to make them worthy, but contrarily reveals and displays their unworthiness. Why does it so happen? Because ye take pleasure in calling by false names things whose nature is quite incongruous thereto—by names which are easily proved false by the very effects of the things themselves; even so it is; these riches, that power, this dignity, are none of them rightly so called. Finally, we may draw the same conclusion concerning the whole sphere of Fortune, within which there is plainly nothing to be truly desired, nothing of intrinsic excellence; for she neither always joins herself to the good, nor does she make good men of those to whom she is united.'

Song 6

Nero's Infamy

We know what mischief dire he wrought—
　　Rome fired, the Fathers slain—
Whose hand with brother's slaughter wet
　　A mother's blood did stain.

No pitying tear his cheek bedewed,
     As on the corse he gazed;
That mother's beauty, once so fair,
     A critic's voice appraised.

Yet far and wide, from East to West,
     His sway the nations own;
And scorching South and icy North
     Obey his will alone.

Did, then, high power a curb impose
     On Nero's phrenzied will?
Ah, woe when to the evil heart
     Is joined the sword to kill!

❧ Chapter VII ❧

Then said I: 'Thou knowest thyself that ambition for worldly success hath but little swayed me. Yet I have desired opportunity for action, lest virtue, in default of exercise, should languish away.'

Then she: 'This is that "last infirmity" which is able to allure minds which, though of noble quality, have not yet been moulded to any exquisite refinement by the perfecting of the virtues—I mean, the love of glory—and fame for high services rendered to the commonweal. And yet consider with me how poor and unsubstantial a thing this glory is! The whole of this earth's globe, as thou hast learnt from the demonstration of astronomy, compared with the expanse of heaven, is found no bigger than a point; that is to say, if measured by the vastness of heaven's sphere, it is held to occupy absolutely no space at all. Now, of this so insignificant portion of the universe, it is about a fourth part, as Ptolemy's proofs have taught us, which is inhabited by living creatures known to us. If from this fourth part you take away in thought all that is usurped by seas and marshes, or lies a vast waste of waterless desert, barely is an exceeding narrow area left for human habitation. You, then, who are shut in and prisoned in this merest fraction of a point's space, do ye take thought for the blazoning of your fame, for the spreading abroad of your re-nown? Why, what amplitude or magnificence has glory when confined to such narrow and petty limits?

'Besides, the straitened bounds of this scant dwelling-place are inhabited by many nations differing widely in speech, in usages, in mode of life; to many of these, from the difficulty of travel, from diversities of speech, from want of commercial intercourse, the fame not only of individual men, but even of cities, is unable to reach. Why, in Cicero's days, as he himself somewhere points out, the fame of the Roman Republic had not yet crossed the Caucasus, and yet by that time her name had grown formidable to the Parthians and other nations of those parts. Seest thou, then, how narrow, how confined, is the glory ye take pains to spread abroad and extend! Can the fame of a single Roman penetrate where the glory of the Roman name fails to pass? Moreover, the customs and institutions of different races agree not together, so that what is deemed praiseworthy in one country is thought punishable in another. Wherefore, if any love the applause of fame, it shall not profit him to publish his name among many peoples. Then, each must be content to have the range of his glory limited to his own people; the splendid immortality of fame must be confined within the bounds of a single race.

'Once more, how many of high renown in their own times have been lost in oblivion for want of a record! Indeed, of what avail are written records even, which, with their authors, are overtaken by the dimness of age after a somewhat longer time? But ye, when ye think on future fame, fancy it an immortality that ye are begetting for yourselves. Why, if thou scannest the infinite spaces of eternity, what room hast thou left for rejoicing in the durability of thy name? Verily, if a single moment's space be compared with ten thousand years, it has a certain relative duration, however little, since each period is definite. But this same number of years—ay, and a number many times as great—cannot even be compared with endless duration; for, indeed, finite periods may in a sort be compared one with another, but a finite and an infinite never. So it comes to pass that fame, though it extend to ever so wide a space of years, if it be compared to never-lessening eternity, seems not short-lived merely, but altogether nothing. But as for you, ye know not how to act aright, unless it be to court the popular breeze, and win the empty applause of the multitude—nay, ye abandon the superlative worth of conscience and virtue, and ask a recompense from the poor words of others. Let me tell thee how wittily one did mock the shallowness of this sort of arrogance. A certain man assailed one who had put on the name of philosopher as a cloak to pride and vain-glory, not for the practice of real virtue, and added: "Now shall I know if thou art a philosopher if thou bearest reproaches calmly and patiently." The other for awhile affected to be patient, and, having endured to be abused, cried out derisively: "*Now*, do you see that I am a philosopher?" The other, with biting sarcasm, retorted: "I should have hadst thou held thy peace." Moreover, what concern have choice spirits—for it is of such men we speak, men who seek glory by virtue—what concern, I say, have these with fame after the dissolution of the body in death's last hour? For if men die wholly—which our reasonings forbid us to believe—there is no such thing as glory at all, since he to whom the glory is said to belong is altogether non-existent. But if the mind, conscious of its own rectitude, is released from its earthly prison, and seeks heaven in free flight, doth it not despise all earthly things when it rejoices in its deliverance from earthly bonds, and enters upon the joys of heaven?'

Song 7

Glory May Not Last

Oh, let him, who pants for glory's guerdon,
  Deeming glory all in all,
Look and see how wide the heaven expandeth,
  Earth's enclosing bounds how small!

Shame it is, if your proud-swelling glory
  May not fill this narrow room!
Why, then, strive so vainly, oh, ye proud ones!
  To escape your mortal doom?

Though your name, to distant regions bruited,
  O'er the earth be widely spread,

Though full many a lofty-sounding title
  On your house its lustre shed,

Death at all this pomp and glory spurneth
  When his hour draweth nigh,
Shrouds alike th' exalted and the humble,
  Levels lowest and most high.

Where are now the bones of stanch Fabricius?
  Brutus, Cato—where are they?
Lingering fame, with a few graven letters,
  Doth their empty name display.

But to know the great dead is not given
  From a gilded name alone;
Nay, ye all alike must lie forgotten,
  'Tis not *you* that fame makes known.

Fondly do ye deem life's little hour
  Lengthened by fame's mortal breath;
There but waits you—when this, too, is taken—
  At the last a second death.

Chapter VIII

'But that thou mayst not think that I wage implacable warfare against Fortune, I own there is a time when the deceitful goddess serves men well—I mean when she reveals herself, uncovers her face, and confesses her true character. Perhaps thou dost not yet grasp my meaning. Strange is the thing I am trying to express, and for this cause I can scarce find words to make clear my thought. For truly I believe that Ill Fortune is of more use to men than Good Fortune. For Good Fortune, when she wears the guise of happiness, and most seems to caress, is always lying; Ill Fortune is always truthful, since, in changing, she shows her inconstancy. The one deceives, the other teaches; the one enchains the minds of those who enjoy her favour by the semblance of delusive good, the other delivers them by the knowledge of the frail nature of happiness. Accordingly, thou mayst see the one fickle, shifting as the breeze, and ever self-deceived; the other sober-minded, alert, and wary, by reason of the very discipline of adversity. Finally, Good Fortune, by her allurements, draws men far from the true good; Ill Fortune ofttimes draws men back to true good with grappling-irons. Again, should it be esteemed a trifling boon, thinkest thou, that this cruel, this odious Fortune hath discovered to thee the hearts of thy faithful friends—that other hid from thee alike the faces of the true friends and of the false, but in departing she hath taken away *her* friends, and left thee *thine*? What price wouldst thou not have given for this service in the fulness of thy prosperity when thou seemedst to thyself fortunate? Cease, then, to seek the wealth thou hast lost, since in true friends thou hast found the most precious of all riches.'

Song 8

Love Is Lord of All

Why are Nature's changes bound
To a fixed and ordered round?
What to leaguèd peace hath bent
Every warring element?
Wherefore doth the rosy morn
Rise on Phœbus' car upborne?
Why should Phœbe rule the night,
Led by Hesper's guiding light?
What the power that doth restrain
In his place the restless main,
That within fixed bounds he keeps,
Nor o'er earth in deluge sweeps?
Love it is that holds the chains,
Love o'er sea and earth that reigns;
Love—whom else but sovereign Love?—
Love, high lord in heaven above!
Yet should he his care remit,
All that now so close is knit
In sweet love and holy peace,
Would no more from conflict cease,
But with strife's rude shock and jar
All the world's fair fabric mar.
    Tribes and nations Love unites
By just treaty's sacred rites;
Wedlock's bonds he sanctifies
By affection's softest ties.
Love appointeth, as is due,
Faithful laws to comrades true—
Love, all-sovereign Love!—oh, then,
Ye are blest, ye sons of men,
If the love that rules the sky
In your hearts is throned on high!

BOOK III

####

True Happiness and False

Chapter I

She ceased, but I stood fixed by the sweetness of the song in wonderment and eager expectation, my ears still strained to listen. And then after a little I said: 'Thou sovereign solace of the stricken soul, what refreshment hast thou brought me, no less by the sweetness of thy singing than by the weightiness of thy discourse! Verily, I think not that I shall hereafter be unequal to the blows of Fortune. Wherefore, I no longer dread the remedies which thou saidst were something too severe for my strength; nay, rather, I am eager to hear of them and call for them with all vehemence.'

Then said she: 'I marked thee fastening upon my words silently and intently, and I expected, or—to speak more truly—I myself brought about in thee, this state of mind. What now remains is of such sort that to the taste indeed it is biting, but when received within it turns to sweetness. But whereas thou dost profess thyself desirous of hearing, with what ardour wouldst thou not burn didst thou but perceive whither it is my task to lead thee!'

'Whither?' said I.

'To true felicity,' said she, 'which even now thy spirit sees in dreams, but cannot behold in very truth, while thine eyes are engrossed with semblances.'

Then said I: 'I beseech thee, do thou show to me her true shape without a moment's loss.'

'Gladly will I, for thy sake,' said she. 'But first I will try to sketch in words, and describe a cause which is more familiar to thee, that, when thou hast viewed this carefully, thou mayst turn thy eyes the other way, and recognise the beauty of true happiness.'

Song 1

The Thorns of Error

Who fain would sow the fallow field,
    And see the growing corn,
Must first remove the useless weeds,
    The bramble and the thorn.

After ill savour, honey's taste
    Is to the mouth more sweet;
After the storm, the twinkling stars
    The eyes more cheerly greet.

When night hath past, the bright dawn comes,
    In car of rosy hue;
So drive the false bliss from thy mind,
    And thou shalt see the true.

For a little space she remained in a fixed gaze, withdrawn, as it were, into the august chamber of her mind; then she thus began:

'All mortal creatures in those anxious aims which find employment in so many varied pursuits, though they take many paths, yet strive to reach one goal—the goal of happiness. Now, *the good* is that which, when a man hath got, he can lack nothing further. This it is which is the supreme good of all, containing within itself all particular good; so that if anything is still wanting thereto, this cannot be the supreme good, since something would be left outside which might be desired. 'Tis clear, then, that happiness is a state perfected by the assembling together of all good things. To this state, as we have said, all men try to attain, but by different paths. For the desire of the true good is naturally implanted in the minds of men; only error leads them aside out of the way in pursuit of the false. Some, deeming it the highest good to want for nothing, spare no pains to attain affluence; others, judging the good to be that to which respect is most worthily paid, strive to win the reverence of their fellow-citizens by the attainment of official dignity. Some there are who fix the chief good in supreme power; these either wish themselves to enjoy sovereignty, or try to attach themselves to those who have it. Those, again, who think renown to be something of supreme excellence are in haste to spread abroad the glory of their name either through the arts of war or of peace. A great many measure the attainment of good by joy and gladness of heart; these think it the height of happiness to give themselves over to pleasure. Others there are, again, who interchange the ends and means one with the other in their aims; for instance, some want riches for the sake of pleasure and power, some covet power either for the sake of money or in order to bring renown to their name. So it is on these ends, then, that the aim of human acts and wishes is centred, and on others like to these—for instance, noble birth and popularity, which seem to compass a certain renown; wife and children, which are sought for the sweetness of their possession; while as for friendship, the most sacred kind indeed is counted in the category of virtue, not of fortune; but other kinds are entered upon for the sake of power or of enjoyment. And as for bodily excellences, it is obvious that they are to be ranged with the above. For strength and stature surely manifest power; beauty and fleetness of foot bring celebrity; health brings pleasure. It is plain, then, that the only object sought for in all these ways is *happiness.* For that which each seeks in preference to all else, that is in his judgment the supreme good. And we have defined the supreme good to be happiness. Therefore, that state which each wishes in preference to all others is in his judgment happy.

'Thou hast, then, set before thine eyes something like a scheme of human happiness—wealth, rank, power, glory, pleasure. Now Epicurus, from a sole regard to these considerations, with some consistency concluded the highest good to be pleasure, because all the other objects seem to bring some delight to the soul. But to return to human pursuits and aims: man's mind seeks to recover its proper good, in spite of the mistiness of its recollection, but, like a drunken man, knows not by what path to return home. Think you they are wrong who strive to escape want? Nay, truly there is nothing which can so well complete happiness as a state abounding in all good things, needing nothing from outside, but wholly self-sufficing. Do they fall into error who deem that which is best to be also best deserving to receive the homage of reverence? Not at all. That cannot possibly be vile and contemptible, to attain which the endeavours of nearly all mankind are directed. Then, is power not to be reckoned in the category of good? Why, can that which is plainly more efficacious than anything else be esteemed a thing feeble and void of strength? Or is renown to be thought of no

327

account? Nay, it cannot be ignored that the highest renown is constantly associated with the highest excellence. And what need is there to say that happiness is not haunted by care and gloom, nor exposed to trouble and vexation, since that is a condition we ask of the very least of things, from the possession and enjoyment of which we expect delight? So, then, these are the blessings men wish to win; they want riches, rank, sovereignty, glory, pleasure, because they believe that by these means they will secure independence, reverence, power, renown, and joy of heart. Therefore, it is *the good* which men seek by such divers courses; and herein is easily shown the might of Nature's power, since, although opinions are so various and discordant, yet they agree in cherishing *good* as the end.'

Song 2

The Bent of Nature

How the might of Nature sways
All the world in ordered ways,
How resistless laws control
Each least portion of the whole—
Fain would I in sounding verse
On my pliant strings rehearse.
  Lo, the lion captive ta'en
Meekly wears his gilded chain;
Yet though he by hand be fed,
Though a master's whip he dread,
If but once the taste of gore
Whet his cruel lips once more,
Straight his slumbering fierceness wakes,
With one roar his bonds he breaks,
And first wreaks his vengeful force
On his trainer's mangled corse.
  And the woodland songster, pent
In forlorn imprisonment,
Though a mistress' lavish care
Store of honeyed sweets prepare;
Yet, if in his narrow cage,
As he hops from bar to bar,
He should spy the woods afar,
Cool with sheltering foliage,
All these dainties he will spurn,
To the woods his heart will turn;
Only for the woods he longs,
Pipes the woods in all his songs.
  To rude force the sapling bends,
While the hand its pressure lends;
If the hand its pressure slack,
Straight the supple wood springs back.

Phœbus in the western main
Sinks; but swift his car again
By a secret path is borne
To the wonted gates of morn.
        Thus are all things seen to yearn
In due time for due return;
And no order fixed may stay,
Save which in th' appointed way
Joins the end to the beginning
In a steady cycle spinning.

Chapter III

'Ye, too, creatures of earth, have some glimmering of your origin, however faint, and though in a vision dim and clouded, yet in some wise, notwithstanding, ye discern the true end of happiness, and so the aim of nature leads you thither—to that true good—while error in many forms leads you astray therefrom. For reflect whether men are able to win happiness by those means through which they think to reach the proposed end. Truly, if either wealth, rank, or any of the rest, bring with them anything of such sort as seems to have nothing wanting to it that is good, we, too, acknowledge that some are made happy by the acquisition of these things. But if they are not able to fulfil their promises, and, moreover, lack many good things, is not the happiness men seek in them clearly discovered to be a false show? Therefore do I first ask thee thyself, who but lately wert living in affluence, amid all that abundance of wealth, was thy mind never troubled in consequence of some wrong done to thee?'

'Nay,' said I, 'I cannot ever remember a time when my mind was so completely at peace as not to feel the pang of some uneasiness.'

'Was it not because either something was absent which thou wouldst not have absent, or present which thou wouldst have away?'

'Yes,' said I.

'Then, thou didst want the presence of the one, the absence of the other?'

'Admitted.'

'But a man lacks that of which he is in want?'

'He does.'

'And he who lacks something is not in all points self-sufficing?'

'No; certainly not,' said I.

'So wert thou, then, in the plenitude of thy wealth, supporting this insufficiency?'

'I must have been.'

'Wealth, then, cannot make its possessor independent and free from all want, yet this was what it seemed to promise. Moreover, I think this also well deserves to be considered—that there is nothing in the special nature of money to hinder its being taken away from those who possess it against their will.'

'I admit it.'

'Why, of course, when every day the stronger wrests it from the weaker without his consent. Else, whence come lawsuits, except in seeking to recover moneys which have been taken away against their owner's will by force or fraud?'

'True,' said I.

'Then, everyone will need some extraneous means of protection to keep his money safe.'

'Who can venture to deny it?'

'Yet he would not, unless he possessed the money which it is possible to lose.'

'No; he certainly would not.'

'Then, we have worked round to an opposite conclusion: the wealth which was thought to make a man independent rather puts him in need of further protection. How in the world, then, can want be driven away by riches? Cannot the rich feel hunger? Cannot they thirst? Are not the limbs of the wealthy sensitive to the winter's cold? "But," thou wilt say, "the rich have the wherewithal to sate their hunger, the means to get rid of thirst and cold." True enough; want can thus be soothed by riches, wholly removed it cannot be. For if this ever-gaping, ever-craving want is glutted by wealth, it needs must be that the want itself which can be so glutted still remains. I do not speak of how very little suffices for nature, and how for avarice nothing is enough. Wherefore, if wealth cannot get rid of want, and makes new wants of its own, how can ye believe that it bestows independence?'

Song 3

The Insatiableness of Avarice

Though the covetous grown wealthy
   See his piles of gold rise high;
Though he gather store of treasure
   That can never satisfy;
Though with pearls his gorget blazes,
   Rarest that the ocean yields;
Though a hundred head of oxen
   Travail in his ample fields;
Ne'er shall carking care forsake him
   While he draws this vital breath,
And his riches go not with him,
   When his eyes are closed in death.

Chapter IV

'Well, but official dignity clothes him to whom it comes with honour and reverence! Have, then, offices of state such power as to plant virtue in the minds of their possessors, and drive out vice? Nay, they are rather wont to signalize iniquity than to chase it away, and hence arises our indignation that honours so often fall to the most iniquitous of men. Accordingly, Catullus calls Nonius an "ulcer-spot," though "sitting in the curule chair."* Dost not see what infamy high position brings upon the bad? Surely their unworthiness will be less conspicuous if their rank does not draw upon them the public notice! In thy own case, wouldst thou ever have been induced by all these perils to think of sharing office with Decoratus, since thou hast discerned in him the spirit of a rascally parasite and informer? No; we cannot deem men worthy of reverence on account of their office, whom we deem unworthy of the office itself. But didst thou see a man endued with wisdom, couldst thou suppose him not worthy of reverence, nor of that wisdom with which he was endued?'

'No; certainly not.'

'There is in Virtue a dignity of her own which she forthwith passes over to those to whom she is united. And since public honours cannot do this, it is clear that they do not possess the true beauty of dignity. And here this well deserves to be noticed—that if a man is the more scorned in proportion as he is despised by a greater number, high

----

*See Catullus, LII, 2.

position not only fails to win reverence for the wicked, but even loads them the more with contempt by drawing more attention to them. But not without retribution; for the wicked pay back a return in kind to the dignities they put on by the pollution of their touch. Perhaps, too, another consideration may teach thee to confess that true reverence cannot come through these counterfeit dignities. It is this: If one who had been many times consul chanced to visit barbaric lands, would his office win him the reverence of the barbarians? And yet if reverence were the natural effect of dignities, they would not forego their proper function in any part of the world, even as fire never anywhere fails to give forth heat. But since this effect is not due to their own efficacy, but is attached to them by the mistaken opinion of mankind, they disappear straightway when they are set before those who do not esteem them dignities. Thus the case stands with foreign peoples. But does their repute last for ever, even in the land of their origin? Why, the prefecture, which was once a great power, is now an empty name—a burden merely on the senator's fortune; the commissioner of the public corn supply was once a personage—now what is more contemptible than this office? For, as we said just now, that which hath no true comeliness of its own now receives, now loses, lustre at the caprice of those who have to do with it. So, then, if dignities cannot win men reverence, if they are actually sullied by the contamination of the wicked, if they lose their splendour through time's changes, if they come into contempt merely for lack of public estimation, what precious beauty have they in themselves, much less to give to others?'

Song 4

Disgrace of Honours Conferred by a Tyrant

Though royal purple soothes his pride,
    And snowy pearls his neck adorn,
Nero in all his riot lives
    The mark of universal scorn.

Yet he on reverend heads conferred
    Th' inglorious honours of the state.
Shall we, then, deem them truly blessed
    Whom such preferment hath made great?

Chapter V

'Well, then, does sovereignty and the intimacy of kings prove able to confer power? Why, surely does not the happiness of kings endure for ever? And yet antiquity is full of examples, and these days also, of kings whose happiness has turned into calamity. How glorious a power, which is not even found effectual for its own preservation! But if happiness has its source in sovereign power, is not happiness diminished, and misery inflicted in its stead, in so far as that power falls short of completeness? Yet, however widely human sovereignty be extended, there must still be more peoples left, over whom each several king holds no sway. Now, at whatever point the power on which happiness depends ceases, here powerlessness steals in and makes wretchedness; so, by this way of reckoning, there must needs be a balance of wretchedness in the lot of the king. The tyrant who had made trial of the perils of his condition figured the fears that haunt a throne under the image of a sword hanging over a man's head. What sort of power, then, is this which cannot drive away the gnawings of anxiety, or shun the stings of terror? Fain would they themselves have lived secure, but they cannot; then they boast about their power! Dost thou count him to possess power whom thou seest to wish what he cannot bring to pass? Dost thou count him to possess power who encompasses himself with a body-guard, who fears those he terrifies more than they fear him, who, to keep up the semblance of power, is himself at the mercy of his slaves? Need I say anything of the friends of kings, when I show royal do-minion itself so utterly and miserably weak—why ofttimes the royal power in its plenitude brings them low, ofttimes involves them in its fall? Nero drove his friend and preceptor, Seneca, to the choice of the manner of his death. Antoninus exposed Papinianus, who was long powerful at court, to the swords of the soldiery. Yet each of these was willing to renounce his power. Seneca tried to surrender his wealth also to Nero, and go into retirement; but neither achieved his purpose. When they tottered, their very greatness dragged them down. What manner of thing, then, is this power which keeps men in fear while they possess it—which when thou art fain to keep, thou art not safe, and when thou desirest to lay it aside thou canst not rid thyself of? Are friends any protection who have been attached by fortune, not by virtue? Nay; him whom good fortune has made a friend, ill fortune will make an enemy. And what plague is more effectual to do hurt than a foe of one's own household?'

Song 5

Self-mastery

Who on power sets his aim,
First must his own spirit tame;
He must shun his neck to thrust
'Neath th' unholy yoke of lust.
For, though India's far-off land
Bow before his wide command,
Utmost Thule homage pay—
If he cannot drive away
Haunting care and black distress,
In his power, he's powerless.

 Chapter VI

'Again, how misleading, how base, a thing ofttimes is glory! Well does the tragic poet exclaim:

" 'Oh, fond Repute, how many a time and oft

Hast thou raised high in pride the base-born churl!"*

---

*See *Andromache*, 319, 1320; *GBWW*, Vol. 5, p. 318.

For many have won a great name through the mistaken beliefs of the multitude—and what can be imagined more shameful than that? Nay, they who are praised falsely must needs themselves blush at their own praises! And even when praise is won by merit, still, how does it add to the good conscience of the wise man who measures his good not by popular repute, but by the truth of inner conviction? And if at all it does seem a fair thing to get this same renown spread abroad, it follows that any failure so to spread it is held foul. But if, as I set forth but now, there must needs be many tribes and peoples whom the fame of any single man cannot reach, it follows that he whom thou esteemest glorious seems all inglorious in a neighbouring quarter of the globe. As to popular favour, I do not think it even worthy of mention in this place, since it never cometh of judgment, and never lasteth steadily.

'Then, again, who does not see how empty, how foolish, is the fame of noble birth? Why, if the nobility is based on renown, the renown is another's! For, truly, nobility seems to be a sort of reputation coming from the merits of ancestors. But if it is the praise which brings renown, of necessity it is they who are praised that are famous. Wherefore, the fame of another clothes thee not with splendour if thou hast none of thine own. So, if there is any excellence in nobility of birth, methinks it is this alone—that it would seem to impose upon the nobly born the obligation not to degenerate from the virtue of their ancestors.'

Song 6

True Nobility

All men are of one kindred stock, though scattered far and wide;
For one is Father of us all—one doth for all provide.
He gave the sun his golden beams, the moon her silver horn;
He set mankind upon the earth, as stars the heavens adorn.
He shut a soul—a heaven-born soul— within the body's frame;
The noble origin he gave each mortal wight may claim.
Why boast ye, then, so loud of race and high ancestral line?
If ye behold your being's source, and God's supreme design,
None is degenerate, none base, unless by taint of sin
And cherished vice he foully stain his heavenly origin.

Chapter VII

'Then, what shall I say of the pleasures of the body? The lust thereof is full of uneasiness; the sating, of repentance. What sicknesses, what intolerable pains, are they wont to bring on the bodies of those who enjoy them—the fruits of iniquity, as it were! Now, what sweetness the stimulus of pleasure may have I do not know. But that the issues of pleasure are painful everyone may understand who chooses to recall the memory of his own fleshly lusts. Nay, if these can make happiness, there is no reason why the beasts also should not be happy, since all their efforts are eagerly set upon satisfying the bodily wants. I know, indeed, that the sweetness of wife and children should be right comely, yet only too true to nature is what was said of one—that he found in his sons his tormentors. And how galling such a contingency would be, I must needs put thee in mind, since thou hast never in any wise suffered such experiences, nor art thou now under any uneasiness. In such a case, I agree with my servant Euripides, who said that a man without children was fortunate in his misfortune.

Song 7

Pleasure's Sting

This is the way of Pleasure:
She stings them that despoil her;
And, like the wingèd toiler
   Who's lost her honeyed treasure,
She flies, but leaves her smart
Deep-rankling in the heart.

Chapter VIII

'It is beyond doubt, then, that these paths do not lead to happiness; they cannot guide anyone to the promised goal. Now, I will very briefly show what serious evils are involved in following them. Just consider. Is it thy endeavour to heap up money? Why, thou must wrest it from its present possessor! Art thou minded to put on the splendour of official dignity? Thou must beg from those who have the giving of it; thou who covetest to outvie others in honour must lower thyself to the humble posture of petition. Dost thou long for power? Thou must face perils, for thou wilt be at the mercy of thy subjects' plots. Is glory thy aim? Thou art lured on through all manner of hardships, and there is an end to thy peace of mind. Art fain to lead a life of pleasure? Yet who does not scorn and contemn one who is the slave of the weakest and vilest of things—the body? Again, on how slight and perishable a possession do they rely who set before themselves bodily excellences! Can ye ever surpass the elephant in bulk or the bull in strength? Can ye excel the tiger in swiftness? Look upon the infinitude, the solidity, the swift motion, of the heavens, and for once cease to admire things mean and worthless. And yet the heavens are not so much to be admired on this account as for the reason which guides them. Then, how transient is the lustre of beauty! how soon gone!—more fleeting than the fading bloom of spring flowers. And yet if, as Aristotle says, men should see with the eyes of Lynceus, so that their sight might pierce through obstructions, would not that body of Alcibiades, so gloriously fair in outward seeming, appear altogether loathsome when all its inward parts lay open to the view? Therefore, it is not thy own nature that makes thee seem beautiful, but the weakness of the eyes that see thee. Yet prize as unduly as ye will that body's excellences; so long as ye know that this that ye admire, whatever its worth, can be dissolved away by the feeble flame of a three days' fever. From all which considerations we may conclude as a whole, that these things which cannot make good the advantages they promise, which are never made perfect by the assemblage of all good things—these neither lead as by-ways to happiness, nor themselves make men completely happy.'

Human Folly

Alas! how wide astray
Doth Ignorance these wretched mortals lead
From Truth's own way!
For not on leafy stems
Do ye within the green wood look for gold,
Nor strip the vine for gems;

Your nets ye do not spread
Upon the hill-tops, that the groaning board
With fish be furnishèd;
If ye are fain to chase
The bounding goat, ye sweep not in vain search
The ocean's ruffled face.

The sea's far depths they know,
Each hidden nook, wherein the waves o'erwash
The pearl as white as snow;
Where lurks the Tyrian shell,
Where fish and prickly urchins do abound,
All this they know full well.

But not to know or care
Where hidden lies the good all hearts desire—
This blindness they can bear;
With gaze on earth low-bent,
They seek for that which reacheth far beyond
The starry firmament.

What curse shall I call down
On hearts so dull? May they the race still run
For wealth and high renown!
And when with much ado
The false good they have grasped—ah, then too late!—
May they discern the true!

Chapter IX

'This much may well suffice to set forth the form of false happiness; if this is now clear to thine eyes, the next step is to show what true happiness is.'

'Indeed,' said I, 'I see clearly enough that neither is independence to be found in wealth, nor power in sovereignty, nor reverence in dignities, nor fame in glory, nor true joy in pleasures.'

'Hast thou discerned also the causes why this is so?'

'I seem to have some inkling, but I should

like to learn more at large from thee.'

'Why, truly the reason is hard at hand. *That which is simple and indivisible by nature human error separates,* and transforms from the true and perfect to the false and imperfect. Dost thou imagine that which lacketh nothing can want power?'

'Certainly not.'

'Right; for if there is any feebleness of strength in anything, in this there must necessarily be need of external protection.'

'That is so.'

'Accordingly, the nature of independence and power is one and the same.'

'It seems so.'

'Well, but dost think that anything of such a nature as this can be looked upon with contempt, or is it rather of all things most worthy of veneration?'

'Nay; there can be no doubt as to that.'

'Let us, then, add reverence to independence and power, and conclude these three to be one.'

'We must if we will acknowledge the truth.'

'Thinkest thou, then, this combination of qualities to be obscure and without distinction, or rather famous in all renown? Just consider: can that want renown which has been agreed to be lacking in nothing, to be supreme in power, and right worthy of honour, for the reason that it cannot bestow this upon itself, and so comes to appear somewhat poor in esteem?'

'I cannot but acknowledge that, being what it is, this union of qualities is also right famous.'

'It follows, then, that we must admit that renown is not different from the other three.'

'It does,' said I.

'That, then, which needs nothing outside itself, which can accomplish all things in its own strength, which enjoys fame and compels reverence, must not this evidently be also fully crowned with joy?'

'In sooth, I cannot conceive,' said I, 'how any sadness can find entrance into such a state; wherefore I must needs acknowledge it full of joy—at least, if our former conclusions are to hold.'

'Then, for the same reasons, this also is necessary—that independence, power, renown, reverence, and sweetness of delight, are different only in name, but in substance differ no wise one from the other.'

'It is,' said I.

'This, then, which is one, and simple by nature, human perversity separates, and, in trying to win a part of that which has no parts, fails to attain not only that portion (since there are no portions), but also the whole, to which it does not dream of aspiring.'

'How so?' said I.

'He who, to escape want, seeks riches, gives himself no concern about power; he prefers a mean and low estate, and also denies himself many pleasures dear to nature to avoid losing the money which he has gained. But at this rate he does not even attain to independence—a weakling void of strength, vexed by distresses, mean and despised, and buried in obscurity. He, again, who thirsts alone for power squanders his wealth, despises pleasure, and thinks fame and rank alike worthless without power. But thou seest in how many ways his state also is defective. Sometimes it happens that he lacks necessaries, that he is gnawed by anxieties, and, since he cannot rid himself of these inconveniences, even ceases to have that power which was his whole end and aim. In like manner may we cast up the reckoning in case of rank, of glory, or of pleasure. For since each one of these severally is identical with the rest, whosoever seeks any one of them without the others does not even lay hold of that one which he makes his aim.'

'Well,' said I, 'what then?'

'Suppose anyone desire to obtain them together, he does indeed wish for happiness as a whole; but will he find it in these things which, as we have proved, are unable to bestow what they promise?'

'Nay; by no means,' said I.

'Then, happiness must certainly not be sought in these things which severally are believed to afford some one of the blessings most to be desired.'

'They must not, I admit. No conclusion could be more true.'

'So, then, the form and the causes of false happiness are set before thine eyes. Now turn thy gaze to the other side; there thou wilt straightway see the true happiness I promised.'

'Yea, indeed, 'tis plain to the blind,' said I. 'Thou didst point it out even now in seeking to unfold the causes of the false. For, unless I am mistaken, that is true and perfect happiness which crowns one with the union of independence, power, reverence, renown, and joy. And to prove to thee with how deep an insight I have listened—since all these are the same—that which can truly bestow one of them I know to be without doubt full and complete happiness.'

'Happy art thou, my scholar, in this thy conviction; only one thing shouldst thou add.'

'What is that?' said I.

'Is there aught, thinkest thou, amid these mortal and perishable things which can produce a state such as this?'

'Nay, surely not; and this thou hast so amply demonstrated that no word more is needed.'

'Well, then, these things seem to give to mortals shadows of the true good, or some kind of imperfect good; but the true and perfect good they cannot bestow.'

'Even so,' said I.

'Since, then, thou hast learnt what that true happiness is, and what men falsely call happiness, it now remains that thou shouldst learn from what source to seek this.'

'Yes; to this I have long been eagerly looking forward.'

'Well, since, as Plato maintains in the "Timaeus," we ought even in the most trivial matters to implore the Divine protection, what thinkest thou should we now do in order to deserve to find the seat of that highest good?'

'We must invoke the Father of all things,' said I; 'for without this no enterprise sets out from a right beginning.'

'Thou sayest well,' said she; and forthwith lifted up her voice and sang:

Song 9[4]

Invocation

Maker of earth and sky, from age to age
Who rul'st the world by reason; at whose word
Time issues from Eternity's abyss:
To all that moves the source of movement, fixed
Thyself and moveless. Thee no cause impelled
Extrinsic this proportioned frame to shape
From shapeless matter; but, deep-set within
Thy inmost being, the form of perfect good,
From envy free; and Thou didst mould the whole
To that supernal pattern. Beauteous
The world in Thee thus imaged, being Thyself
Most beautiful. So Thou the work didst fashion

In that fair likeness, bidding it put on
Perfection through the exquisite perfectness
Of every part's contrivance.

                    Thou dost bind
The elements in balanced harmony,
So that the hot and cold, the moist and dry,
Contend not; nor the pure fire leaping up
Escape, or weight of waters whelm the earth.
     Thou joinest and diffusest through the whole,
Linking accordingly its several parts,
A soul of threefold nature, moving all.
This, cleft in twain, and in two circles gathered,
Speeds in a path that on itself returns,
Encompassing mind's limits, and conforms
The heavens to her true semblance.

                    Lesser souls
And lesser lives by a like ordinance
Thou sendest forth, each to its starry car
Affixing, and dost strew them far and wide
O'er earth and heaven. These by a law benign
Thou biddest turn again, and render back
To thee their fires.

                    Oh, grant, almighty Father,
Grant us on reason's wing to soar aloft
To heaven's exalted height; grant us to see
The fount of good; grant us, the true light found,
To fix our steadfast eyes in vision clear
On Thee. Disperse the heavy mists of earth,
And shine in Thine own splendour. For Thou art
The true serenity and perfect rest
Of every pious soul—to see Thy face,
The end and the beginning—One the guide,
The traveller, the pathway, and the goal.

Chapter X

'Since now thou hast seen what is the form of the imperfect good, and what the form of the perfect also, methinks I should next show in what manner this perfection of felicity is built up. And here I conceive it proper to inquire, first, whether any excellence, such as thou hast lately defined, can exist in the nature of things, lest we be deceived by an empty fiction of thought to which no true reality answers. But it cannot be denied that such does exist, and is, as it were, the source of all things good. For everything which is called imperfect is spoken of as imperfect by reason of the privation of some perfection; so it comes to pass that, whenever imperfection is found in any particular, there must necessarily be a perfection in respect of that particular also. For were there no such perfection, it is utterly inconceivable how that so-called *im*perfection should come into existence. Nature does not make a beginning with things mutilated and imperfect; she starts with what is whole and perfect, and falls away later to these feeble and inferior productions. So if there is, as we showed before, a happiness of a frail and imperfect kind, it cannot be doubted but there is also a happiness substantial and perfect.'

'Most true is thy conclusion, and most sure,' said I.

'Next to consider where the dwelling-place of this happiness may be. The common belief of all mankind agrees that God, the supreme of all things, is good. For since nothing can be imagined better than God, how can we doubt Him to be good than whom there is nothing better? Now, reason shows God to be good in such wise as to prove that in Him is perfect good. For were it not so, He would not be supreme of all things; for there would be something else more excellent, possessed of perfect good, which would seem to have the advantage in priority and dignity, since it has clearly appeared that all perfect things are prior to those less complete. Wherefore, lest we fall into an infinite regression, we must acknowledge the supreme God to be full of supreme and perfect good. But we have determined that true happiness is the perfect good; therefore true happiness must dwell in the supreme Deity.'

'I accept thy reasonings,' said I; 'they cannot in any wise be disputed.'

'But, come, see how strictly and incontrovertibly thou mayst prove this our assertion that the supreme Godhead hath fullest possession of the highest good.'

'In what way, pray?' said I.

'Do not rashly suppose that He who is the Father of all things hath received that highest good of which He is said to be possessed either from some external source, or hath it as a natural endowment in such sort that thou mightest consider the essence of the happiness possessed, and of the God who possesses it, distinct and different. For if thou deemest it received from without, thou mayst esteem that which gives more

excellent than that which has received. But Him we most worthily acknowledge to be the most supremely excellent of all things. If, however, it is in Him by nature, yet is logically distinct, the thought is inconceivable, since we are speaking of God, who is supreme of all things. Who was there to join these distinct essences? Finally, when one thing is different from another, the things so conceived as distinct cannot be identical. Therefore that which of its own nature is distinct from the highest good is not itself the highest good—an impious thought of Him than whom, 'tis plain, nothing can be more excellent. For universally nothing can be better in nature than the source from which it has come; therefore on most true grounds of reason would I conclude that which is the source of all things to be in its own essence the highest good.'

'And most justly,' said I.

'But the highest good has been admitted to be happiness.'

'Yes.'

'Then,' said she, 'it is necessary to acknowledge that God is very happiness.'

'Yes,' said I; 'I cannot gainsay my former admissions, and I see clearly that this is a necessary inference therefrom.'

'Reflect, also,' said she, 'whether the same conclusion is not further confirmed by considering that there cannot be two supreme goods distinct one from the other. For the goods which are different clearly cannot be severally each what the other is: wherefore neither of the two can be perfect, since to either the other is wanting; but since it is not perfect, it cannot manifestly be the supreme good. By no means, then, can goods which are supreme be different one from the other. But we have concluded that both happiness and God are the supreme good; wherefore that which is highest Divinity must also itself necessarily be supreme happiness.'

'No conclusion,' said I, 'could be truer to fact, nor more soundly reasoned out, nor more worthy of God.'

'Then, further,' said she, 'just as geometricians are wont to draw inferences from their demonstrations to which they give the name "deductions," so will I add here a sort of corollary. For since men become happy by the acquisition of happiness, while happiness is very Godship, it is manifest that they become happy by the acquisition of Godship. But as by the acquisition of justice men become just, and wise by the acquisition of wisdom, so by parity of reasoning by acquiring Godship they must of necessity become gods. So every man who is happy is a god; and though in nature God is One only, yet there is nothing to hinder that very many should be gods by participation in that nature.'

'A fair conclusion, and a precious,' said I, 'deduction or corollary, by whichever name thou wilt call it.'

'And yet,' said she, 'not one whit fairer than this which reason persuades us to add.'

'Why, what?' said I.

'Why, seeing happiness has many particulars included under it, should all these be regarded as forming one body of happiness, as it were, made up of various parts, or is there some one of them which forms the full essence of happiness, while all the rest are relative to this?'

'I would thou wouldst unfold the whole matter to me at large.'

'We judge happiness to be good, do we not?'

'Yea, the supreme good.'

'And this superlative applies to all; for this same happiness is adjudged to be the completest independence, the highest power, reverence, renown, and pleasure.'

'What then?'

'Are all these goods—independence, power, and the rest—to be deemed members of happiness, as it were, or are they all relative to good as to their summit and crown?'

'I understand the problem, but I desire to hear how thou wouldst solve it.'

'Well, then, listen to the determination of the matter. Were all these members composing happiness, they would differ severally one from the other. For this is the nature of parts—that by their difference they compose one body. All these, however, have been proved to be the same; therefore they cannot possibly be members, otherwise happiness will seem to be built up out of one member, which cannot be.'

'There can be no doubt as to that,' said I; 'but I am impatient to hear what remains.'

'Why, it is manifest that all the others are relative to the good. For the very reason why independence is sought is that it is judged good, and so power also, because it is believed to be good. The same, too, may be supposed of reverence, of renown, and of pleasant delight. Good, then, is the sum and source of all desirable things. That which has not in itself any good, either in reality or in semblance, can in no wise be desired. Contrariwise, even things which by nature are not good are desired as if they were truly good, if they seem to be so. Whereby it comes to pass that goodness is rightly believed to be the sum and hinge and cause of all things desirable. Now, that for the sake of which anything is desired itself seems to be most wished for. For instance, if anyone wishes to ride for the sake of health, he does not so much wish for the exercise of riding as the benefit of his health. Since, then, all things are sought for the sake of the good, it is not these so much as good itself that is sought by all. But that on account of which all other things are wished for was, we agreed, happiness; wherefore thus also it appears that it is happiness alone which is sought. From all which it is transparently clear that the essence of absolute good and of happiness is one and the same.'

'I cannot see how anyone can dissent from these conclusions.'

'But we have also proved that God and true happiness are one and the same.'

'Yes,' said I.

'Then we can safely conclude, also, that God's essence is seated in absolute good, and nowhere else.'

Song 10

The True Light

Hither come, all ye whose minds
Lust with rosy fetters binds—
Lust to bondage hard compelling
Th' earthy souls that are his dwelling—
Here shall be your labour's close;
Here your haven of repose.
Come, to your one refuge press;
Wide it stands to all distress!
 Not the glint of yellow gold
Down bright Hermus' current rolled;
Not the Tagus' precious sands,
Nor in far-off scorching lands
All the radiant gems that hide
Under Indus' storied tide—
Emerald green and glistering white—
Can illume our feeble sight;
But they rather leave the mind
In its native darkness blind.
For the fairest beams they shed
In earth's lowest depths were fed;
But the splendour that supplies
Strength and vigour to the skies,
And the universe controls,
Shunneth dark and ruined souls.
He who once hath seen *this* light
Will not call the sunbeam bright.

Chapter XI

'I quite agree,' said I, 'truly all thy reasonings hold admirably together.'

Then said she: 'What value wouldst thou put upon the boon shouldst thou come to the knowledge of the absolute good?'

'Oh, an infinite,' said I, 'if only I were so blest as to learn to know God also who is the good.'

'Yet this will I make clear to thee on truest grounds of reason, if only our recent conclusions stand fast.'

'They will.'

'Have we not shown that those things which most men desire are not true and perfect good precisely for this cause—that they differ severally one from another, and, seeing that one is wanting to another, they cannot bestow full and absolute good; but that they become the true good when they are gathered, as it were, into one form and agency, so that that which is independence is likewise power, reverence, renown, and pleasant delight, and unless they are all one and the same, they have no claim to be counted among things desirable?'

'Yes; this was clearly proved, and cannot in any wise be doubted.'

'Now, when things are far from being good while they are different, but become good as soon as they are one, is it not true that these become good by acquiring unity?'

'It seems so,' said I.

'But dost not thou allow that all which is good is good by participation in goodness?'

'It is.'

'Then, thou must on similar grounds admit that unity and goodness are the same; for when the effects of things in their natural working differ not, their essence is one and the same.'

'There is no denying it.'

'Now, dost thou know,' said she, 'that all which is abides and subsists so long as it continues one, but so soon as it ceases to be one it perishes and falls to pieces?'

'In what way?'

'Why, take animals, for example. When soul and body come together, and continue in one, this is, we say, a living creature; but when this unity is broken by the separation of these two, the creature dies, and is clearly no longer living. The body also, while it remains in one form by the joining together of its members, presents a human appearance; but if the separation and dispersal of the parts break up the body's unity, it ceases to be what it was. And if we extend our survey to all other things, without doubt it will manifestly appear that each several thing subsists while it is one, but when it ceases to be one perishes.'

'Yes; when I consider further, I see it to be even as thou sayest.'

'Well, is there aught,' said she, 'which, in so far as it acts conformably to nature, abandons the wish for life, and desires to come to death and corruption?'

'Looking to living creatures, which have some faults of choice, I find none that, without external compulsion, forego the will to live, and of their own accord hasten to destruction. For every creature diligently pursues the end of self-preservation, and shuns death and destruction. As to herbs and trees, and inanimate things generally, I am altogether in doubt what to think.'

'And yet there is no possibility of question about this either, since thou seest how herbs and trees grow in places suitable for them, where, as far as their nature admits, they cannot quickly wither and die. Some spring up in the plains, others in the mountains; some grow in marshes, others cling to rocks; and others, again, find a fertile soil in the barren sands; and if you try to transplant these elsewhere, they wither away. Nature gives to each the soil that suits it, and uses her diligence to prevent any of them dying, so long as it is possible for them to continue alive. Why do they all draw their nourishment from roots as from a mouth dipped into the earth, and distribute the strong bark over the pith? Why are all the softer parts like the pith deeply encased within, while the external parts have the strong texture of wood, and outside of all is the bark to resist the weather's inclemency, like a champion stout in endurance? Again, how great is nature's diligence to secure universal propagation by multiplying seed! Who does not know all these to be contrivances, not only for the present maintenance of a species, but for its lasting continuance, generation after generation, for ever? And do not also the things believed inanimate on like grounds of reason seek each what is proper to itself? Why do the flames shoot lightly upward, while the earth presses downward with its weight, if it is not that these motions and situations are suitable to their respective natures? Moreover, each several thing is preserved by that which is agreeable to its nature, even as it is destroyed by things inimical. Things solid like stones resist disintegration by the close adhesion of their parts. Things fluid like air and water yield easily to what divides them, but swiftly flow back and mingle with those parts from which they have been severed, while fire, again, refuses to be cut at all. And we are not now treating of the voluntary motions of an intelligent soul, but of the drift of nature. Even so is it that we digest our food without thinking about it, and draw our breath unconsciously in sleep; nay, even in living creatures the love of life cometh not of conscious will, but from the principles of nature. For oftentimes in the stress of circumstances will chooses the death which nature shrinks from; and contrarily, in spite of natural appetite, will restrains that work of reproduction by which alone the persistence of perishable creatures is maintained. So entirely does this love of self come from drift of nature, not from animal impulse. Providence has furnished things with this most cogent reason for continuance: they must desire life, so long as it is naturally possible for them to continue living. Wherefore in no way mayst thou doubt but that things naturally aim at continuance of existence, and shun destruction.'

'I confess,' said I, 'that what I lately thought uncertain, I now perceive to be indubitably clear.'

'Now, that which seeks to subsist and continue desires to be one; for if its oneness be gone, its very existence cannot continue.'

'True,' said I.

'All things, then, desire to be one.'

'I agree.'

'But we have proved that one is the very same thing as good.'

'We have.'

'All things, then, seek the good; indeed, you may express the fact by defining good as that which all desire.'

'Nothing could be more truly thought out. Either there is no single end to which all things are relative, or else the end to which all things universally hasten must be the highest good of all.'

Then she: 'Exceedingly do I rejoice, dear pupil; thine eye is now fixed on the very central mark of truth. Moreover, herein is revealed that of which thou didst erstwhile profess thyself ignorant.'

'What is that?' said I.

'The end and aim of the whole universe. Surely it is that which is desired of all; and, since we have concluded the good to be such, we ought to acknowledge the end and aim of the whole universe to be "the good." '

Song 11[5]

Reminiscence

Who truth pursues, who from false ways
   His heedful steps would keep,
By inward light must search within
   In meditation deep;
All outward bent he must repress
His soul's true treasure to possess.

Then all that error's mists obscured
   Shall shine more clear than light,
This fleshly frame's oblivious weight
   Hath quenched not reason quite;
The germs of truth still lie within,
Whence we by learning all may win.

Else how could ye the answer due
   Untaught to questions give,

Were't not that deep within the soul
   Truth's secret sparks do live?
If Plato's teaching erreth not,
   We learn but that we have forgot.

Chapter XII

Then said I: 'With all my heart I agree with Plato; indeed, this is now the second time that these things have been brought back to my mind—first I lost them through the clogging contact of the body; then after through the stress of heavy grief.'

Then she continued: 'If thou wilt reflect upon thy former admissions, it will not be long before thou dost also recollect that of which erstwhile thou didst confess thyself ignorant.'

'What is that?' said I.

'The principles of the world's government,' said she.

'Yes; I remember my confession, and, although I now anticipate what thou intendest, I have a desire to hear the argument plainly set forth.'

'Awhile ago thou deemedst it beyond all doubt that God doth govern the world.'

'I do not think it doubtful now, nor shall I ever; and by what reasons I am brought to this assurance I will briefly set forth. This world could never have taken shape as a single system out of parts so diverse and opposite were it not that there is One who joins together these so diverse things. And when it had once come together, the very diversity of natures would have dissevered it and torn it asunder in universal discord were there not One who keeps together what He has joined. Nor would the order of nature proceed so regularly, nor could its course exhibit motions so fixed in respect of position, time, range, efficacy, and character, unless there were One who, Himself abiding, disposed these various vicissitudes of change. This power, whatsoever it be, whereby they remain as they were created, and are kept in motion, I call by the name which all recognise—God.'

Then said she: 'Seeing that such is thy belief, it will cost me little trouble, I think, to enable thee to win happiness, and return in safety to thy own country. But let us give our attention to the task that we have set before ourselves. Have we not counted independence in the category of happiness, and agreed that God is absolute happiness?'

'Truly, we have.'

'Then, He will need no external assistance for the ruling of the world. Otherwise, if He stands in need of aught, He will not possess complete independence.'

'That is necessarily so,' said I.

'Then, by His own power alone He disposes all things.'

'It cannot be denied.'

'Now, God was proved to be absolute good.'

'Yes; I remember.'

'Then, He disposes all things by the agency of good, if it be true that *He* rules all things by His own power whom we have agreed to be good; and He is, as it were, the rudder and helm by which the world's mechanism is kept steady and in order.'

'Heartily do I agree; and, indeed, I anticipated what thou wouldst say, though it may be in feeble surmise only.'

'I well believe it,' said she; 'for, as I think, thou now bringest to the search eyes quicker in discerning truth; but what I shall say next is no less plain and easy to see.'

'What is it?' said I.

'Why,' said she, 'since God is rightly believed to govern all things with the rudder of goodness, and since all things do likewise, as I have taught, haste towards good by the very aim of nature, can it be doubted that His governance is willingly accepted, and that all submit themselves to the sway of the Disposer as conformed and attempered to His rule?'

'Necessarily so,' said I; 'no rule would seem happy if it were a yoke imposed on reluctant wills, and not the safe-keeping of obedient subjects.'

'There is nothing, then, which, while it follows nature, endeavours to resist good.'

'No; nothing.'

'But if anything should, will it have the least success against Him whom we rightly agreed to be supreme Lord of happiness?'

'It would be utterly impotent.'

'There is nothing, then, which has either the will or the power to oppose this supreme good.'

'No; I think not.'

'So, then,' said she, 'It is the supreme good which rules in strength, and graciously disposes all things.'

Then said I: 'How delighted am I at thy reasonings, and the conclusion to which thou hast brought them, but most of all at these very words which thou usest! I am now at last ashamed of the folly that so sorely vexed me.'

'Thou hast heard the story of the giants assailing heaven; but a beneficent strength disposed of them also, as they deserved. But shall we submit our arguments to the shock of mutual collision?—it may be from the impact some fair spark of truth may be struck out.'

'If it be thy good pleasure,' said I.

'No one can doubt that God is all-powerful.'

'No one at all can question it who thinks consistently.'

'Now, there is nothing which One who is all-powerful cannot do.'

'Nothing.'

'But can God do evil, then?'

'Nay; by no means.'

'Then, evil is nothing,' said she, 'since He to whom nothing is impossible is unable to do evil.'

'Art thou mocking me,' said I, 'weaving a labyrinth of tangled arguments, now seeming to begin where thou didst end, and now to end where thou didst begin, or dost thou build up some wondrous circle of Divine simplicity? For, truly, a little before thou didst begin with happiness, and say it was the supreme good, and didst declare it to be seated in the supreme Godhead. God Himself, too, thou didst affirm to be supreme good and all-complete happiness; and from this thou didst go on to add, as by the way, the proof that no one would be happy unless he were likewise God. Again, thou didst say that the very form of good was the essence both of God and of happiness, and didst teach that the absolute One was the absolute good which was sought by universal nature. Thou didst maintain, also, that God rules the universe by the governance of goodness, that all things obey Him willingly, and that evil has no existence in nature. And all this thou didst unfold without the help of assumptions from without, but by inherent and proper proofs, drawing credence one from the other.'

Then answered she: 'Far is it from me to mock thee; nay, by the blessing of God, whom we lately addressed in prayer, we have achieved the most important of all objects. For such is the form of the Divine essence, that neither can it pass into things external, nor take up anything external into itself; but, as Parmenides says of it,

' "In body like to a sphere on all sides perfectly rounded,"*

it rolls the restless orb of the universe, keeping itself motionless the while. And if I have also employed reasonings not drawn from without, but lying within the compass of our subject, there is no cause for thee to marvel, since thou hast learnt on Plato's authority that words ought to be akin to the matter of which they treat.'

---

*See *Sophist*, 244 E; *GBWW*, Vol. 7, p. 566.

Song 12

Orpheus and Eurydice

Blest he whose feet have stood
Beside the fount of good;
Blest he whose will could break
Earth's chains for wisdom's sake!
   The Thracian bard, 'tis said,
Mourned his dear consort dead;
To hear the plaintive strain
The woods moved in his train,
And the stream ceased to flow,
Held by so soft a woe;
The deer without dismay
Beside the lion lay;
The hound, by song subdued,
No more the hare pursued,
But the pang unassuaged
In his own bosom raged.
The music that could calm
All else brought him no balm.
Chiding the powers immortal,
He came unto Hell's portal;
There breathed all tender things
Upon his sounding strings,
Each rhapsody high-wrought
His goddess-mother taught—
·All he from grief could borrow
And love redoubling sorrow,
Till, as the echoes waken,
All Tænarus is shaken;
Whilst he to ruth persuades
The monarch of the shades
With dulcet prayer. Spell-bound,
The triple-headed hound
At sounds so strangely sweet
Falls crouching at his feet.
The dread Avengers, too,
That guilty minds pursue
With ever-haunting fears,
Are all dissolved in tears.
Ixion, on his wheel,
A respite brief doth feel;
For, lo! the wheel stands still.
And, while those sad notes thrill,
Thirst-maddened Tantalus

Listens, oblivious
Of the stream's mockery
And his long agony.
The vulture, too, doth spare
Some little while to tear
At Tityus' rent side,
Sated and pacified.
   At length the shadowy king,
His sorrows pitying,
'He hath prevailèd!' cried;
'We give him back his bride!
To him she shall belong,
As guerdon of his song.
One sole condition yet
Upon the boon is set:
Let him not turn his eyes
To view his hard-won prize,
Till they securely pass
The gates of Hell.' Alas!
What law can lovers move?
A higher law is love!
For Orpheus—woe is me!—
On his Eurydice—
Day's threshold all but won—
Looked, lost, and was undone!
   Ye who the light pursue,
This story is for you,
Who seek to find a way
Unto the clearer day.
If on the darkness past
One backward look ye cast,
Your weak and wandering eyes
Have lost the matchless prize.

BOOK IV

❋

Good and Ill Fortune

❧Chapter I❧

Softly and sweetly Philosophy sang these verses to the end without losing aught of the dignity of her expression or the seriousness of her tones; then, forasmuch as I was as yet unable to forget my deeply-seated sorrow, just as she was about to say something further, I broke in and cried: 'O thou guide into the way of true light, all that thy voice hath uttered from the beginning even unto now has manifestly seemed to me at once divine contemplated in itself, and by the force of the arguments placed beyond the possibility of overthrow. Moreover, these truths have not been altogether unfamiliar to me heretofore, though because of indignation at my wrongs they have for a time been forgotten. But, lo! herein is the very chiefest cause of my grief—that, while there exists a good ruler of the universe, it is possible that evil should be at all, still more that it shoud go unpunished. Surely thou must see how deservedly this of itself provokes astonishment. But a yet greater marvel follows: While wickedness reigns and flourishes, virtue not only lacks its reward, but is even thrust down and trampled under the feet of the wicked, and suffers punishment in the place of crime. That this should happen under the rule of a God who knows all things and can do all things, but wills only the good, cannot be sufficiently wondered at nor sufficiently lamented.'

Then said she: 'It would indeed be infinitely astounding, and of all monstrous things most horrible, if, as thou esteemest, in the well-ordered home of so great a householder, the base vessels shoud be held in honour, the precious left to neglect. But it is not so. For if we hold unshaken those conclusions which we lately reached, thou shalt learn that, by the will of Him of whose realm we are speaking, the good are always strong, the bad always weak and impotent; that vices never go unpunished, nor virtues unrewarded; that good fortune ever befalls the good, and ill fortune the bad, and much more of the sort, which shall hush thy murmurings, and stablish thee in the strong assurance of conviction. And since by my late instructions thou hast seen the form of happiness, hast learnt, too, the seat where it is to be found, all due preliminaries being discharged, I will now show thee the road which will lead thee home. Wings, also, will I fasten to thy mind wherewith thou mayst soar aloft, that so, all disturbing doubts removed, thou mayst return safe to thy country, under my guidance, in the path I will show thee, and by the means which I furnish.'

Song 1

The Soul's Flight

Wings are mine; above the pole
   Far aloft I soar.
Clothed with these, my nimble soul
   Scorns earth's hated shore,
Cleaves the skies upon the wind,
Sees the clouds left far behind.

Soon the glowing point she nears,
   Where the heavens rotate,
Follows through the starry spheres
   Phoebus' course, or straight
Takes for comrade 'mid the stars
Saturn cold or glittering Mars;

Thus each circling orb explores
   Through Night's stole that peers;
Then, when all are numbered, soars
   Far beyond the spheres,
Mounting heaven's supremest height
To the very Fount of light.

There the Sovereign of the world
   His calm sway maintains;
As the globe is onward whirled
   Guides the chariot reins,
And in splendour glittering
Reigns the universal King.

Hither if thy wandering feet
   Find at last a way,
Here thy long lost home thou'lt greet:
   'Dear lost land,' thou'lt say,
'Though from thee I've wandered wide,
Hence I came, here will abide.'

Yet if ever thou art fain
   Visitant to be
Of earth's gloomy night again,
   Surely thou wilt see
Tyrants whom the nations fear
Dwell in hapless exile here.

Then said I: 'Verily, wondrous great are thy promises; yet I do not doubt but thou canst make them good: only keep me not in suspense after raising such hopes.'

'Learn, then, first,' said she, 'how that power ever waits upon the good, while the bad are left wholly destitute of strength.[6] Of these truths the one proves the other; for since good and evil are contraries, if it is made plain that good is power, the feebleness of evil is clearly seen, and, conversely, if the frail nature of evil is made manifest, the strength of good is thereby known. However, to win ampler credence for my conclusion, I will pursue both paths, and draw confirmation for my statements first in one way and then in the other.

'The carrying out of any human action depends upon two things—to wit, will and power; if either be wanting, nothing can be accomplished. For if the will be lacking, no attempt at all is made to do what is not willed; whereas if there be no power, the will is all in vain. And so, if thou seest any man wishing to attain some end, yet utterly failing to attain it, thou canst not doubt that he lacked the power of getting what he wished for.'

'Why, certainly not; there is no denying it.'

'Canst thou, then, doubt that he whom thou seest to have accomplished what he willed had also the power to accomplish it?'

'Of course not.'

'Then, in respect of what he can accomplish a man is to be reckoned strong, in respect of what he cannot accomplish weak?'

'Granted,' said I.

'Then, dost thou remember that, by our former reasonings, it was concluded that the whole aim of man's will, though the means of pursuit vary, is set intently upon happiness?'

'I do remember that this, too, was proved.'

'Dost thou also call to mind how happiness is absolute good, and therefore that, when happiness is sought, it is good which is in all cases the object of desire?'

'Nay, I do not so much call to mind as keep it fixed in my memory.'

'Then, all men, good and bad alike, with one indistinguishable purpose strive to reach good?'

'Yes, that follows.'

'But it is certain that by the attainment of good men become good?'

'It is.'

'Then, do the good attain their object?'

'It seems so.'

'But if the bad were to attain the good which is *their* object, they could not be bad?'

'No.'

'Then, since both seek good, but while the one sort attain it, the other attain it not, is there any doubt that the good are endued with power, while they who are bad are weak?'

'If any doubt it, he is incapable of reflecting on the nature of things, or the consequences involved in reasoning.'

'Again, supposing there are two things to which the same function is prescribed in the course of nature, and one of these successfully accomplishes the function by natural action, the other is altogether incapable of the natural action, instead of which, in a way other than is agreeable to its nature, it—I will not say fulfils its function, but feigns to fulfil it: which of these two would in thy view be the stronger?'

'I guess thy meaning, but I pray thee let me hear thee more at large.'

'Walking is man's natural motion, is it not?'

'Certainly.'

'Thou dost not doubt, I suppose, that it is natural for the feet to discharge this function?'

'No; surely I do not.'

'Now, if one man who is able to use his feet walks, and another to whom the natural use of his feet is wanting tries to walk on his hands, which of the two wouldst thou rightly esteem the stronger?'

'Go on,' said I; 'no one can question but that he who has the natural capacity has more strength than he who has it not.'

'Now, the supreme good is set up as the end alike for the bad and for the good; but the good seek it through the natural action of the virtues, whereas the bad try to attain this same good through all manner of concupiscence, which is not the natural way of attaining good. Or dost thou think otherwise?'

'Nay; rather, one further consequence is clear to me: for from my admissions it must needs follow that the good have power, and the bad are impotent.'

'Thou anticipatest rightly, and that as physicians reckon is a sign the nature is set working, and is throwing off the disease. But, since I see thee so ready at understanding, I will heap proof on proof. Look how manifest is the extremity of vicious men's weakness; they cannot even reach that goal to which the aim of nature leads and almost constrains them. What if they were left without this mighty, this well-nigh irresistible help of nature's guidance! Consider also how momentous is the powerlessness which incapacitates the wicked. Not light or trivial[7] are the prizes which they contend for, but which they cannot win or hold; nay, their failure concerns the very sum and crown of things. Poor wretches! they fail to compass even that for which they toil day and night. Herein also the strength of the good conspicuously appears. For just as thou wouldst judge him to be the strongest walker whose legs could carry him to a point beyond which no further advance was possible, so must thou needs account him strong in power who so attains the end of his desires that nothing further to be desired lies beyond. Whence follows the obvious conclusion that they who are wicked are seen likewise to be wholly destitute of strength. For why do they forsake virtue and follow vice? Is it from ignorance of what is good? Well, what is more weak and feeble than the blindness of ignorance? Do they know what they ought to follow, but

lust drives them aside out of the way? If it be so, they are still frail by reason of their incontinence, for they cannot fight against vice. Or do they knowingly and wilfully forsake the good and turn aside to vice? Why, at this rate, they not only cease to have power, but cease to be at all. For they who forsake the common end of all things that are, they likewise also cease to be at all. Now, to some it may seem strange that we should assert that the bad, who form the greater part of mankind, do not exist. But the fact is so. I do not, indeed, deny that they who are bad are bad, but that they *are* in an unqualified and absolute sense I deny. Just as we call a corpse a dead man, but cannot call it simply "man," so I would allow the vicious to be bad, but that they *are* in an absolute sense I cannot allow. That only *is* which maintains its place and keeps its nature; whatever falls away from this forsakes the existence which is essential to its nature. "But," thou wilt say, "the bad have an ability." Nor do I wish to deny it; only this ability of theirs comes not from strength, but from impotence. For their ability is to do evil, which would have had no efficacy at all if they could have continued in the performance of good. So this ability of theirs proves them still more plainly to have no power. For if, as we concluded just now, evil is nothing, 'tis clear that the wicked can effect nothing, since they are only able to do evil.'

' 'Tis evident.'

'And that thou mayst understand what is the precise force of this power, we determined, did we not, awhile back, that nothing has more power than supreme good?'

'We did,' said I.

'But that same highest good cannot do evil?'

'Certainly not.'

'Is there anyone, then, who thinks that men are able to do all things?'

'None but a madman.'

'Yet they are able to do evil?'

'Ay; would they could not!'

'Since, then, he who can do only good is omnipotent, while they who can do evil also are not omnipotent, it is manifest that they who can do evil have less power. There is this also: we have shown that all power is to be reckoned among things desirable, and that all desirable things are referred to good as to a kind of consummation of their nature. But the ability to commit crime cannot be referred to the good; therefore it is not a thing to be desired. And yet all power is desirable; it is clear, then, that ability to do evil is not power. From all which consid-

erations appeareth the power of the good, and the indubitable weakness of the bad, and it is clear that Plato's judgment was true; the wise alone are able to do what they would, while the wicked follow their own hearts' lust, but can *not* accomplish what they would. For they go on in their wilfulness fancying they will attain what they wish for in the paths of delight; but they are very far from its attainment, since shameful deeds lead not to happiness.'

Song 2

The Bondage of Passion

When high-enthroned the monarch sits, resplendent in the pride
Of purple robes, while flashing steel guards him on every side;
When baleful terrors on his brow with frowning menace lower,
And Passion shakes his labouring breast—how dreadful seems his power!
But if the vesture of his state from such a one thou tear,
Thou'lt see what load of secret bonds this lord of earth doth wear.
Lust's poison rankles; o'er his mind rage sweeps in tempest rude;
Sorrow his spirit vexes sore, and empty hopes delude.
Then thou'lt confess: one hapless wretch, whom many lords oppress,
Does never what he would, but lives in thraldom's helplessness.

Chapter III

'Thou seest, then, in what foulness unrighteous deeds are sunk, with what splendour righteousness shines. Whereby it is manifest that goodness never lacks its reward, nor crime its punishment. For, verily, in all manner of transactions that for the sake of which the particular action is done may justly be accounted the reward of that action, even as the wreath for the sake of which the race is run is the reward offered for running. Now, we have shown happiness to be that very good for the sake of which all things are done. Absolute good, then, is offered as the common prize, as it were, of all human actions. But, truly, this is a reward from which it is impossible to separate the good man, for one who is without good cannot properly be called good at all;

wherefore righteous dealing never misses its reward. Rage the wicked, then, never so violently, the crown shall not fall from the head of the wise, nor wither. Verily, other men's unrighteousness cannot pluck from righteous souls their proper glory. Were the reward in which the soul of the righteous delighteth received from without, then might it be taken away by him who gave it, or some other; but since it is conferred by his own righteousness, then only will he lose his prize when he has ceased to be righteous. Lastly, since every prize is desired because it is believed to be good, who can account him who possesses good to be without reward? And what a prize, the fairest and grandest of all! For remember the corollary which I chiefly insisted on a little while back, and reason thus: Since absolute good is happiness, 'tis clear that all the good must be happy for the very reason that they are good. But it was agreed that those who are happy are gods. So, then, the prize of the good is one which no time may impair, no man's power lessen, no man's unrighteousness tarnish; 'tis very Godship. And this being so, the wise man cannot doubt that punishment is inseparable from the bad. For since good and bad, and likewise reward and punishment, are contraries, it necessarily follows that, corresponding to all that we see accrue as reward of the good, there is some penalty attached as punishment of evil. As, then, righteousness itself is the reward of the righteous, so wickedness itself is the punishment of the unrighteous. Now, no one who is visited with punishment doubts that he is visited with evil. Accordingly, if they were but willing to weigh their own case, could *they* think themselves free from punishment whom wickedness, worst of all evils, has not only touched, but deeply tainted?

'See, also, from the opposite standpoint—the standpoint of the good—what a penalty attends upon the wicked. Thou didst learn a little since that whatever is is one, and that unity itself is good. Accordingly, by this way of reckoning, whatever falls away from goodness ceases to be; whence it comes to pass that the bad cease to be what they were, while only the outward aspect is still left to show they have been men. Wherefore, by their perversion to badness, they have lost their true human nature. Further, since righteousness alone can raise men above the level of humanity, it must needs be that unrighteousness degrades below man's level those whom it has cast out of man's estate. It results, then, that thou canst not consider him human whom thou seest transformed by vice. The violent despoiler of other men's goods, enflamed with covetousness, surely resembles a wolf. A bold and restless spirit, ever wrangling in law-courts, is like some yelping cur. The secret schemer, taking pleasure in fraud and stealth, is own brother to the fox. The passionate man, phrenzied with rage, we might believe to be animated with the soul of a lion. The coward and runaway, afraid where no fear is, may be likened to the timid deer. He who is sunk in ignorance and stupidity lives like a dull ass. He who is light and inconstant, never holding long to one thing, is for all the world like a bird. He who wallows in foul and unclean lusts is sunk in the pleasures of a filthy hog. So it comes to pass that he who by forsaking righteousness ceases to be a man cannot pass into a God-like condition, but actually turns into a brute beast.'

Song 3

Circe's Cup

> Th' Ithacan discreet,
> And all his storm-tossed fleet,
> Far o'er the ocean wave
> The winds of heaven drave—
> Drave to the mystic isle,
> Where dwelleth in her guile
> That fair and faithless one,
> The daughter of the Sun.
> There for the stranger crew
> With cunning spells she knew

To mix th' enchanted cup.
For whoso drinks it up,
Must suffer hideous change
To monstrous shapes and strange.
One like a boar appears;
This his huge form uprears,
Mighty in bulk and limb—
An Afric lion—grim
With claw and fang. Confessed
A wolf, this, sore distressed
When he would weep, doth howl;
And, strangely tame, these prowl
The Indian tiger's mates.
   And though in such sore straits,
The pity of the god
Who bears the mystic rod
Had power the chieftain brave
From her fell arts to save;
His comrades, unrestrained,
The fatal goblet drained.
All now with low-bent head,
Like swine, on acorns fed;
Man's speech and form were reft,
No human feature left;
But steadfast still, the mind,
Unaltered, unresigned,
The monstrous change bewailed.
   How little, then, availed
The potencies of ill!
These herbs, this baneful skill,
May change each outward part,
But cannot touch the heart.
In its true home, deep-set,
Man's spirit liveth yet.
Those poisons are more fell,
More potent to expel
Man from his high estate,
Which subtly penetrate,
And leave the body whole,
But deep infect the soul.

Chapter IV

Then said I: 'This is very true. I see that the vicious, though they keep the outward form of man, are rightly said to be changed into beasts in respect of their spiritual nature; but, inasmuch as their cruel and polluted minds vent their rage in the destruction of the good, I would this license were not permitted to them.'

'Nor is it,' said she, 'as shall be shown in the fitting place. Yet if that license which thou believest to be permitted to them were taken away, the punishment of the wicked would be in great part remitted. For verily, incredible as it may seem to some, it needs must be that the bad are more unfortunate when they have accomplished their desires than if they are unable to get them fulfilled. If it is wretched to will evil, to have been able to accomplish evil is more wretched; for without the power the wretched will would fail of effect. Accordingly, those whom thou seest to will, to be able to accomplish, and to accomplish crime, must needs be the victims of a threefold wretchedness, since each one of these states has its own measure of wretchedness.'

'Yes,' said I; 'yet I earnestly wish they might speedily be quit of this misfortune by losing the ability to accomplish crime.'

'They will lose it,' said she, 'sooner than perchance thou wishest, or they themselves think likely; since, verily, within the narrow bounds of our brief life there is nothing so late in coming that anyone, least of all an immortal spirit, should deem it long to wait for. Their great expectations, the lofty fabric of their crimes, is oft overthrown by a sudden and unlooked-for ending, and this but sets a limit to their misery. For if wickedness makes men wretched, he is necessarily more wretched who is wicked for a longer time; and were it not that death, at all events, puts an end to the evil doings of the wicked, I should account them wretched to the last degree. Indeed, if we have formed true conclusions about the ill fortune of wickedness, that wretchedness is plainly infinite which is doomed to be eternal.'

Then said I: 'A wonderful inference, and difficult to grant; but I see that it agrees entirely with our previous conclusions.'

'Thou art right,' said she; 'but if anyone finds it hard to admit the conclusion, he ought in fairness either to prove some falsity in the premises, or to show that the combination of propositions does not adequately enforce the necessity of the conclusion; otherwise, if the premises be granted, nothing whatever can be said against the inference of the conclusion. And here is another statement which seems not less wonderful, but on the premises assumed is equally necessary.'

'What is that?'

'The wicked are happier in undergoing punishment than if no penalty of justice chasten them. And I am not now meaning what might occur to anyone—that bad character is amended by retribution, and is brought into the right path by the terror of punishment, or that it serves as an example to warn others to avoid transgression; but I believe that in another way the wicked are more unfortunate when they go unpunished, even though no account be taken of amendment, and no regard be paid to example.'

'Why, what other way is there beside these?' said I.

Then said she: 'Have we not agreed that the good are happy, and the evil wretched?'

'Yes,' said I.

'Now, if,' said she, 'to one in affliction there be given along with his misery some good thing, is he not happier than one whose misery is misery pure and simple without admixture of any good?'

'It would seem so.'

'But if to one thus wretched, one destitute of all good, some further evil be added besides those which make him wretched, is he not to be judged far more unhappy than he whose ill fortune is alleviated by some share of good?'

'It could scarcely be otherwise.'

'Surely, then, the wicked, when they are punished, have a good thing added to them—to wit, the punishment which by the law of justice is good; and likewise, when they escape punishment, a new evil attaches to them in that very freedom from punishment which thou hast rightly acknowledged to be an evil in the case of the unrighteous.'

'I cannot deny it.'

'Then, the wicked are far more unhappy when indulged with an unjust freedom from punishment than when punished by a just retribution. Now, it is manifest that it is just for the wicked to be punished, and for them to escape unpunished is unjust.'

'Why, who would venture to deny it?'

'This, too, no one can possibly deny—that all which is just is good, and conversely, all which is unjust is bad.'

Then I answered: 'These inferences do indeed follow from what we lately concluded; but tell me,' said I, 'dost thou take no account of the punishment of the soul after the death of the body?'

'Nay, truly,' said she, 'great are these penalties, some of them inflicted, I imagine, in the severity of retribution, others in the mercy of purification. But it is not my present purpose to speak of these. So far, my aim hath been to make thee recognise that the power of the bad which shocked thee so exceedingly is no power; to make thee see that those of whose freedom from punishment thou didst complain are never without the proper penalties of their unrighteousness; to teach thee that the license which thou prayedst might soon come to an end is not long-enduring; that it would be more unhappy if it lasted longer, most unhappy of all if it lasted for ever; thereafter that the unrighteous are more wretched if unjustly let go without punishment than if punished by a just retribution—from which point of view it follows that the wicked are afflicted with more severe penalties just when they are supposed to escape punishment.'

Then said I: 'While I follow thy reasonings, I am deeply impressed with their truth; but if I turn to the common convictions of men, I find few who will even listen to such arguments, let alone admit them to be credible.'

'True,' said she; 'they cannot lift eyes accustomed to darkness to the light of clear truth, and are like those birds whose vision night illumines and day blinds; for while they regard, not the order of the universe, but their own dispositions of mind, they think the license to commit crime, and the escape from punishment, to be fortunate. But mark the ordinance of eternal law. Hast thou fashioned thy soul to the likeness of the better, thou hast no need of a judge to award the prize—by thine own act hast thou raised thyself in the scale of excellence; hast thou perverted thy affections to baser things, look not for punishment from one without thee—thine own act hath degraded thee, and thrust thee down. Even so, if alternately thou turn thy gaze upon the vile earth and upon the heavens, though all without thee stand still, by the mere laws of sight thou seemest now sunk in the mire, now soaring among the stars. But the common herd regards not these things. What, then? Shall we go over to those whom we have shown to be like brute beasts? Why, suppose, now, one who had quite lost his sight should likewise forget that he had ever possessed the faculty of vision, and should imagine that nothing was wanting in him to human perfection, should we deem those who saw as well as ever blind? Why, they will not even assent to this, either—that they who do wrong are more wretched than those who suffer wrong, though the proof of this rests on grounds of reason no less strong.'

'Let me hear these same reasons,' said I.

'Wouldst thou deny that every wicked man deserves punishment?'

'I would not, certainly.'

'And that those who are wicked are unhappy is clear in manifold ways?'

'Yes,' I replied.

'Thou dost not doubt, then, that those who deserve punishment are wretched?'

'Agreed,' said I.

'So, then, if thou wert sitting in judgment, on whom wouldst thou decree the infliction of punishment—on him who had done the wrong, or on him who had suffered it?'

'Without doubt, I would compensate the sufferer at the cost of the doer of the wrong.'

'Then, the injurer would seem more wretched than the injured?'

'Yes; it follows. And so for this and other reasons resting on the same ground, inasmuch as baseness of its own nature makes men wretched, it is plain that a wrong involves the misery of the doer, not of the sufferer.'

'And yet,' says she, 'the practice of the law-courts is just the opposite: advocates try to arouse the commiseration of the judges for those who have endured some grievous and cruel wrong; whereas pity is rather due to the criminal, who ought to be brought to the judgment-seat by his accusers in a spirit not of anger, but of compassion and kindness, as a sick man to the physician, to have the ulcer of his fault cut away by punishment. Whereby the business of the advocate would either wholly come to a standstill, or, did men prefer to make it serviceable to mankind, would be restricted to the practice of accusation. The wicked themselves also, if through some chink or cranny they were permitted to behold the virtue they have forsaken, and were to see that by the pains of punishment they would rid themselves of the uncleanness of their vices, and win in exchange the recompense of righteousness, they would no longer think these sufferings pains; they would refuse the help of advocates, and would commit themselves wholly into the hands of their accusers and judges. Whence it comes to pass that for the wise no place is left for hatred; only the most foolish would hate the good, and to hate the bad is unreasonable. For if vicious propensity is, as it were, a disease of the soul like bodily sickness, even as we account the sick in body by no means deserving of hate, but rather of pity, so, and much more, should they be pitied whose minds are assailed by wickedness, which is more frightful than any sickness.'

Song 4

The Unreasonableness of Hatred

Why all this furious strife? Oh, why
With rash and wilful hand provoke death's destined day?
If death ye seek—lo! Death is nigh,
Not of their master's will those coursers swift delay!

The wild beasts vent on man their rage,
Yet 'gainst their brothers' lives men point the murderous steel;
Unjust and cruel wars they wage,
And haste with flying darts the death to meet or deal.

No right nor reason can they show;
'Tis but because their lands and laws are not the same.
Wouldst *thou* give each his due; then know
Thy love the good must have, the bad thy pity claim.

Chapter V

On this I said: 'I see how there is a happiness and misery founded on the actual deserts of the righteous and the wicked. Nevertheless, I wonder in myself whether there is not some good and evil in fortune as the vulgar understand it. Surely, no sensible man would rather be exiled, poor and disgraced, than dwell prosperously in his own country, powerful, wealthy, and high in honour. Indeed, the work of wisdom is more clear and manifest in its operation when the happiness of rulers is somehow passed on to the people around them, especially considering that the prison, the law, and the other pains of legal punishment are properly due only to mischievous citizens on whose account they were originally instituted. Accordingly, I do exceedingly marvel why all this is completely reversed—why the good are harassed with the penalties due to crime, and the bad carry off the rewards of virtue; and I long to hear from thee what reason may be found for so unjust a state of disorder. For assuredly I should wonder less if I could believe that all things are the confused result of chance. But now my belief in God's governance doth add amaze-ment to amazement. For, seeing that He sometimes assigns fair fortune to the good and harsh fortune to the bad, and then again deals harshly with the good, and grants to the bad their hearts' desire, how does this differ from chance, unless some reason is discovered for it all?'

'Nay; it is not wonderful,' said she, 'if all should be thought random and confused when the principle of order is not known. And though thou knowest not the causes on which this great system depends, yet forasmuch as a good ruler governs the world, doubt not for thy part that all is rightly done.'

Song 5

Wonder and Ignorance

Who knoweth not how near the pole
    Bootes' course doth go,
Must marvel by what heavenly law
    He moves his Wain so slow;
Why late he plunges 'neath the main,
And swiftly lights his beams again.

When the full-orbèd moon grows pale
    In the mid course of night,
And suddenly the stars shine forth
    That languished in her light,
Th' astonied nations stand at gaze,
And beat the air in wild amaze.[8]

None marvels why upon the shore
    The storm-lashed breakers beat,
Nor why the frost-bound glaciers melt
    At summer's fervent heat;
For here the cause seems plain and clear,
Only what's dark and hid we fear.

Weak-minded folly magnifies
    All that is rare and strange,
And the dull herd's o'erwhelmed with awe
    At unexpected change.
But wonder leaves enlightened minds,
When ignorance no longer blinds.

'True,' said I; 'but, since it is thy office to unfold the hidden cause of things, and explain principles veiled in darkness, inform me, I pray thee, of thine own conclusions in this matter, since the marvel of it is what more than aught else disturbs my mind.'

A smile played one moment upon her lips as she replied: 'Thou callest me to the greatest of all subjects of inquiry, a task for which the most exhaustive treatment barely suffices. Such is its nature that, as fast as one doubt is cut away, innumerable others spring up like Hydra's heads, nor could we set any limit to their renewal did we not apply the mind's living fire to suppress them. For there come within its scope the questions of the essential simplicity of providence, of the order of fate, of unforeseen chance, of the Divine knowledge and predestination, and of the freedom of the will. How heavy is the weight of all this thou canst judge for thyself. But, inasmuch as to know these things also is part of the treatment of the malady, we will try to give them some consideration, despite the restrictions of the narrow limits of our time. Moreover, thou must for a time dispense with the pleasures of music and song, if so be that thou findest any delight therein, whilst I weave together the connected train of reasons in proper order.'

'As thou wilt,' said I.

Then, as if making a new beginning, she thus discoursed: 'The coming into being of all things, the whole course of development in things that change, every sort of thing that moves in any wise, receives its due cause, order, and form from the steadfastness of the Divine mind. This mind, calm in the citadel of its own essential simplicity, has decreed that the method of its rule shall be manifold. Viewed in the very purity of the Divine intelligence, this method is called *providence;* but viewed in regard to those things which it moves and disposes, it is what the ancients called *fate.* That these two are different will easily be clear to anyone who passes in review their respective efficacies. Providence is the Divine reason itself, seated in the Supreme Being, which disposes all things; fate is the disposition inherent in all things which move, through which providence joins all things in their proper order. Providence embraces all things, however different, however infinite; fate sets in motion separately individual things, and assigns to them severally their position, form, and time.

'So the unfolding of this temporal order unified into the foreview of the Divine mind is providence, while the same unity broken up and unfolded in time is fate. And although these are different, yet is there a dependence between them; for the order of destiny issues from the essential simplicity of providence. For as the artificer, forming in his mind beforehand the idea of the thing to be made, carries out his design, and develops from moment to moment what he had before seen in a single instant as a whole, so God in His providence ordains all things as parts of a single unchanging whole, but carries out these very ordinances by fate in a time of manifold unity. So whether fate is accomplished by Divine spirits as the ministers of providence, or by a soul, or by the service of all nature—whether by the celestial motion of the stars, by the efficacy of angels, or by the many-sided cunning of demons—whether by all or by some of these the destined series is woven, this, at least, is manifest: that providence is the fixed and simple form of destined events, fate their shifting series in order of time, as by the disposal of the Divine simplicity they are to take place. Whereby it is that all things which are under fate are subjected also to providence, on which fate itself is dependent; whereas certain things which are set under providence are above the chain of fate—viz., those things which by their nearness to the primal Divinity are steadfastly fixed, and lie outside the order of fate's movements. For as the innermost of several circles revolving round the same centre approaches the simplicity of the midmost point, and is, as it were, a pivot round which the exterior circles turn, while the outermost, whirled in ampler orbit, takes in a wider and wider sweep of space in proportion to its departure from the indivisible unity of the centre—while, further, whatever joins and allies itself to the centre is narrowed to a like simplicity, and no longer expands vaguely into space—even so whatsoever departs widely from primal mind is involved more deeply in the meshes of fate, and things are free from fate in proportion as they seek to come nearer to that central pivot; while if aught cleaves close to supreme mind in its absolute fixity, this, too, being free from movement, rises above fate's necessity. Therefore, as is reasoning to pure intelligence, as that which is generated to that which is, time to eternity, a circle to its centre, so is the shifting series of fate to the steadfastness and simplicity of providence.

'It is this causal series which moves heaven and the stars, attempers the elements to mutual accord, and again in turn transforms them into new combinations; *this* which renews the series of all things that are born and die through like successions of germ and birth; it is *its* operation which binds the destinies of men by an indissoluble nexus of causality, and, since it issues in the beginning from unalterable providence, these destinies also must of necessity be immutable. Accordingly, the world is ruled for the best if this unity abiding in the Divine mind puts forth an inflexible order of causes. And this order, by its intrinsic immutability, restricts things mutable which otherwise would ebb and flow at random. And so it happens that, although to you, who are not altogether capable of understanding this order, all things seem confused and disordered, nevertheless there is everywhere an appointed limit which guides all things to good. Verily, nothing can be done for the sake of evil even by the wicked themselves; for, as we abundantly proved, they seek good, but are drawn out of the way by perverse error; far less can this order which

sets out from the supreme centre of good turn aside anywhither from the way in which it began.

' "Yet what confusion," thou wilt say, "can be more unrighteous than that prosperity and adversity should indifferently befall the good, what they like and what they loathe come alternately to the bad!" Yes; but have men in real life such soundness of mind that their judgments of righteousness and wickedness must necessarily correspond with facts? Why, on this very point their verdicts conflict, and those whom some deem worthy of reward, others deem worthy of punishment. Yet granted there were one who could rightly distinguish the good and bad, yet would he be able to look into the soul's inmost constitution, as it were, if we may borrow an expression used of the body? The marvel here is not unlike that which astonishes one who does not know why in health sweet things suit some constitutions, and bitter others, or why some sick men are best alleviated by mild remedies, others by severe. But the physician who distinguishes the precise conditions and characteristics of health and sickness does not marvel. Now, the health of the soul is nothing but righteousness, and vice is its sickness. God, the guide and physician of the mind, it is who preserves the good and banishes the bad. And He looks forth from the lofty watch-tower of His providence, perceives what is suited to each, and assigns what He knows to be suitable.

'This, then, is what that extraordinary mystery of the order of destiny comes to—that something is done by one who knows, whereat the ignorant are astonished. But let us consider a few instances whereby appears what is the competency of human reason to fathom the Divine unsearchableness. Here is one whom thou deemest the perfection of justice and scrupulous integrity; to all-knowing Providence it seems far otherwise. We all know our Lucan's admonition that it was the winning cause that found favour with the gods, the beaten cause with

Cato. So, shouldst thou see anything in this world happening differently from thy expectation, doubt not but events are rightly ordered; it is in thy judgment that there is perverse confusion.

'Grant, however, there be somewhere found one of so happy a character that God and man alike agree in their judgments about him; yet is he somewhat infirm in strength of mind. It may be, if he fall into adversity, he will cease to practise that innocency which has failed to secure his fortune. Therefore, God's wise dispensation spares him whom adversity might make worse, will not let him suffer who is ill fitted for endurance. Another there is perfect in all virtue, so holy and nigh to God that providence judges it unlawful that aught untoward should befall him; nay, doth not even permit him to be afflicted with bodily disease. As one more excellent than I⁹ hath said:

' "The very body of the holy saint
    Is built of purest ether."

Often it happens that the governance is given to the good that a restraint may be put upon superfluity of wickedness. To others providence assigns some mixed lot suited to their spiritual nature; some it will plague lest they grow rank through long prosperity; others it will suffer to be vexed with sore afflictions to confirm their virtues by the exercise and practice of patience. Some fear overmuch what they have strength to bear; others despise overmuch that to which their strength is unequal. All these it brings to the test of their true self through misfortune. Some also have bought a name revered to future ages at the price of a glorious death; some by invincible constancy under their sufferings have afforded an example to others that virtue cannot be overcome by calamity—all which things, without doubt, come to pass rightly and in due order, and to the benefit of those to whom they are seen to happen.

'As to the other side of the marvel, that the bad now meet with affliction, now get their hearts' desire, this, too, springs from the same causes. As to the afflictions, of course no one marvels, because all hold the wicked to be ill deserving. The truth is, their punishments both frighten others from crime, and amend those on whom they are inflicted; while their prosperity is a powerful sermon to the good, what judgments they ought to pass on good fortune of this kind, , which often attends the wicked so assiduously.

'There is another object which may, I believe, be attained in such cases: there is one, perhaps, whose nature is so reckless and violent that poverty would drive him more desperately into crime. *His* disorder providence relieves by allowing him to amass money. Such a one, in the uneasiness of a conscience stained with guilt, while he contrasts his character with his fortune, perchance grows alarmed lest he should come to mourn the loss of that whose possession is so pleasant to him. He will, then, reform his ways, and through the fear of losing his fortune he forsakes his iniquity. Some, through a prosperity unworthily borne, have been hurled headlong to ruin; to some the power of the sword has been committed, to the end that the good may be tried by discipline, and the bad punished. For while there can be no peace between the righteous and the wicked, neither can the wicked agree among themselves. How should they, when each is at variance with himself, because his vices rend his conscience, and ofttimes they do things which, when they are done, they judge ought not to have been done. Hence it is that this supreme providence brings to pass this notable marvel—that the bad make the bad good. For some, when they see the injustice which they themselves suffer at the hands of evil-doers, are inflamed with detestation of the offenders, and, in the endeavour to be unlike those whom they hate, return to the ways of virtue. It is the Divine power alone to which things evil are also good, in that, by putting them to suitable use, it bringeth them in the end to some good issue. For order in some way or other embraceth all things, so that even that which has departed from the appointed laws of the order, nevertheless falleth within *an* order, though *another* order, that nothing in the realm of providence may be left to haphazard. But

' "Hard were the task, as a god, to recount all, nothing omitting."*

Nor, truly, is it lawful for man to compass in thought all the mechanism of the Divine work, or set it forth in speech. Let us be content to have apprehended this only—that God, the creator of universal nature, likewise disposeth all things, and guides them to good; and while He studies to preserve in likeness to Himself all that He has created, He banishes all evil from the borders of His commonweal through the links of fatal necessity. Whereby it comes to pass that, if thou look to disposing providence, thou wilt nowhere find the evils which are believed so to abound on earth.

'But I see thou hast long been burdened with the weight of the subject, and fatigued with the prolixity of the argument, and now lookest for some refreshment of sweet poesy. Listen, then, and may the draught so restore thee that thou wilt bend thy mind more resolutely to what remains.'

Song 6

The Universal Aim

Wouldst thou with unclouded mind
View the laws by God designed,
Lift thy steadfast gaze on high
To the starry canopy;
See in rightful league of love
All the constellations move.
Fiery Sol, in full career,
Ne'er obstructs cold Phoebe's sphere;
When the Bear, at heaven's height,
Wheels his coursers' rapid flight,
Though he sees the starry train
Sinking in the western main,
He repines not, nor desires
In the flood to quench his fires.
    In true sequence, as decreed,
Daily morn and eve succeed;
Vesper brings the shades of night,
Lucifer the morning light.
Love, in alternation due,
Still the cycle doth renew,
And discordant strife is driven
From the starry realm of heaven.
Thus, in wondrous amity,
Warring elements agree;
Hot and cold, and moist and dry,
Lay their ancient quarrel by;
High the flickering flame ascends,

Downward earth for ever tends.

So the year in spring's mild hours
Loads the air with scent of flowers;
Summer paints the golden grain;
Then, when autumn comes again,
Bright with fruit the orchards glow;
Winter brings the rain and snow.
Thus the seasons' fixed progression,
Tempered in a due succession,
Nourishes and brings to birth
All that lives and breathes on earth.
Then, soon run life's little day,
All it brought it takes away.

But One sits and guides the reins,
He who made and all sustains;
King and Lord and Fountain-head,
Judge most holy, Law most dread;
Now impels and now keeps back,
Holds each waverer in the track.
Else, were once the power withheld
That the circling spheres compelled
In their orbits to revolve,
This world's order would dissolve,
And th' harmonious whole would all
In one hideous ruin fall.

But through this connected frame
Runs one universal aim;
Towards the Good do all things tend,
Many paths, but one the end.
For naught lasts, unless it turns
Backward in its course, and yearns
To that Source to flow again
Whence its being first was ta'en.

❦ Chapter VII ❦

'Dost thou, then, see the consequence of all that we have said?'

'Nay; what consequence?'

'That absolutely every fortune is good fortune.'

'And how can that be?' said I.

'Attend,' said she. 'Since every fortune, welcome and unwelcome alike, has for its object the reward or trial of the good, and the punishing or amending of the bad, every fortune must be good, since it is either just or useful.'

'The reasoning is exceeding true,' said I, 'the conclusion, so long as I reflect upon the providence and fate of which thou hast taught me, based on a strong foundation. Yet, with thy leave, we will count it among those which just now thou didst set down as paradoxical.'

'And why so?' said she.

'Because ordinary speech is apt to assert,

---

*See *The Iliad* XII, 176; *GBWW*, Vol. 4, p. 83.

and that frequently, that some men's fortune is bad.'

'Shall we, then, for awhile approach more nearly to the language of the vulgar, that we may not seem to have departed too far from the usages of men?'

'At thy good pleasure,' said I.

'That which advantageth thou callest good, dost thou not?'

'Certainly.'

'And that which either tries or amends advantageth?'

'Granted.'

'Is good, then?'

'Of course.'

'Well, this is *their* case who have attained virtue and wage war with adversity, or turn from vice and lay hold on the path of virtue.'

'I cannot deny it.'

'What of the good fortune which is given as reward of the good—do the vulgar adjudge it bad?'

'Anything but that; they deem it to be the best, as indeed it is.'

'What, then, of that which remains, which, though it is harsh, puts the restraint of just punishment on the bad—does popular opinion deem it good?'

'Nay; of all that can be imagined, it is accounted the most miserable.'

'Observe, then, if, in following popular opinion, we have not ended in a conclusion quite paradoxical.'

'How so?' said I.

'Why, it results from our admissions that of all who have attained, or are advancing in, or are aiming at virtue, the fortune is in every case good, while for those who remain in their wickedness fortune is always utterly bad.'

'It is true,' said I; 'yet no one dare acknowledge it.'

'Wherefore,' said she, 'the wise man ought not to take it ill, if ever he is involved in one of fortune's conflicts, any more than it becomes a brave soldier to be offended when at any time the trumpet sounds for battle. The time of trial is the express opportunity for the one to win glory, for the other to perfect his wisdom. Hence, indeed, virtue gets its name, because, relying on its own efficacy, it yieldeth not to adversity. And ye who have taken your stand on virtue's steep ascent, it is not for you to be dissolved in delights or enfeebled by pleasure; ye close in conflict—yea, in conflict most sharp—with all fortune's vicissitudes, lest ye suffer foul fortune to overwhelm or fair fortune to corrupt you. Hold the mean with all your strength. Whatever falls short of this, or goes beyond, is fraught with scorn of happiness, and misses the reward of toil. It rests with you to make your fortune what you will. Verily, every harsh-seeming fortune, unless it either disciplines or amends, is punishment.'

Song 7

The Hero's Path

Ten years a tedious warfare raged,
　　Ere Ilium's smoking ruins paid
　　For wedlock stained and faith betrayed,
And great Atrides' wrath assuaged.

But when heaven's anger asked a life,
　　And baffling winds his course withstood,
　　The king put off his fatherhood,
And slew his child with priestly knife.

When by the cavern's glimmering light
  His comrades dear Odysseus saw
  In the huge Cyclops' hideous maw
Engulfed, he wept the piteous sight.

But blinded soon, and wild with pain—
  In bitter tears and sore annoy—
  For that foul feast's unholy joy
Grim Polyphemus paid again.

His labours for Alcides win
  A name of glory far and wide;
  He tamed the Centaur's haughty pride,
And from the lion reft his skin.

The foul birds with sure darts he slew;
  The golden fruit he stole—in vain
  The dragon's watch; with triple chain
From hell's depths Cerberus he drew.

With their fierce lord's own flesh he fed
  The wild steeds; Hydra overcame
  With fire. 'Neath his own waves in shame
Maimed Achelous hid his head.

Huge Cacus for his crimes was slain;
  On Libya's sands Antæus hurled;
  The shoulders that upheld the world
The great boar's dribbled spume did stain.

Last toil of all—his might sustained
  The ball of heaven, nor did he bend
  Beneath; this toil, his labour's end,
The prize of heaven's high glory gained.

Brave hearts, press on! Lo, heavenward lead
  These bright examples! From the fight
  Turn not your backs in coward flight;
Earth's conflict won, the stars your meed!

BOOK V

Free Will and God's
Foreknowledge

✧ Chapter I ✧

She ceased, and was about to pass on in her discourse to the exposition of other matters, when I break in and say: "Excellent is thine exhortation, and such as well beseemeth thy high authority; but I am even now experiencing one of the many difficulties which, as thou saidst but now, beset the question of providence. I want to know whether thou deemest that there is any such thing as chance at all, and, if so, what it is.'

Then she made answer: 'I am anxious to fulfil my promise completely, and open to thee a way of return to thy native land. As for these matters, though very useful to know, they are yet a little removed from the path of our design, and I fear lest digressions should fatigue thee, and thou shouldst find thyself unequal to completing the direct journey to our goal.'

'Have no fear for that,' said I. 'It is rest to me to learn, where learning brings delight so exquisite, especially when thy argument has been built up on all sides with undoubted conviction, and no place is left for uncertainty in what follows.'

She made answer: 'I will accede to thy request;' and forthwith she thus began: 'If chance be defined as a result produced by random movement without any link of causal connection, I roundly affirm that there is no such thing as chance at all, and consider the word to be altogether without meaning, except as a symbol of the thing designated. What place can be left for random action, when God constraineth all things to order? For "ex nihilo nihil" is sound doctrine which none of the ancients gainsaid, although they used it of material substance,

not of the efficient principle; this they laid down as a kind of basis for all their reasonings concerning nature. Now, if a thing arise without causes, it will appear to have arisen from nothing. But if this cannot be, neither is it possible for there to be chance in accordance with the definition just given.'

'Well,' said I, 'is there, then, nothing which can properly be called chance or accident, or is there something to which these names are appropriate, though its nature is dark to the vulgar?'

'Our good Aristotle,' says she, 'has defined it concisely in his "Physics," and closely in accordance with the truth.'

'How, pray?' said I.

'Thus,' says she: 'Whenever something is done for the sake of a particular end, and for certain reasons some other result than that designed ensues, this is called chance; for instance, if a man is digging the earth for tillage, and finds a mass of buried gold. Now, such a find is regarded as accidental; yet it is not "ex nihilo," for it has its proper causes, the unforeseen and unexpected concurrence of which has brought the chance about. For had not the cultivator been digging, had not the man who hid the money buried it in that precise spot, the gold would not have been found. These, then, are the reasons why the find is a chance one, in that it results from causes which met together and concurred, not from any intention on the part of the discoverer. Since neither he who buried the gold nor he who worked in the field *intended* that the money should be found, but, as I said, it *happened* by coincidence that one dug where the other buried the treasure. We may, then, define chance as being an unexpected result flowing from a concurrence of causes where the several factors had some definite end. But the meeting and concurrence of these causes arises from the inevitable chain of order which, flowing from the fountainhead of Providence, disposes all things in their due time and place.'

Song 1

Chance

In the rugged Persian highlands,
  Where the masters of the bow
Skill to feign a flight, and, fleeing,
  Hurl their darts and pierce the foe;
There the Tigris and Euphrates
  At one source their waters blend,
Soon to draw apart, and plainward
  Each its separate way to wend.
When once more their waters mingle
  In a channel deep and wide,
All the flotsam comes together
  That is borne upon the tide:
Ships, and trunks of trees, uprooted
  In the torrent's wild career,
Meet, as 'mid the swirling waters
  Chance their random way may steer.
Yet the shelving of the channel
  And the flowing water's force
Guides each movement, and determines
  Every floating fragment's course.
Thus, where'er the drift of hazard
  Seems most unrestrained to flow,
Chance herself is reined and bitted,
  And the curb of law doth know.

Chapter II

'I am following heedfully,' said I, 'and I agree that it is as thou sayest. But in this series of linked causes is there any freedom left to our will, or does the chain of fate bind also the very motions of our souls?'

'There is freedom,' said she; 'nor, indeed, can any creature be rational, unless he be endowed with free will. For that which hath the natural use of reason has the faculty of discriminative judgment, and of itself distinguishes what is to be shunned or desired. Now, everyone seeks what he judges desirable, and avoids what he thinks should be shunned. Wherefore, beings endowed with reason possess also the faculty of free choice and refusal. But I suppose this faculty not equal alike in all. The higher Divine essences possess a clear-sighted judgment, an uncorrupt will, and an effective power of accomplishing their wishes. Human souls must needs be comparatively free while they abide in the contemplation of the Divine mind, less free when they pass into bodily form, and still less, again, when they are enwrapped in earthly members. But when they are given over to vices, and fall from the possession of their proper reason, then indeed their condition is utter slavery. For when they let their gaze fall from the light of highest truth to the lower world where darkness reigns, soon ignorance blinds their vision; they are disturbed by baneful affections, by yielding and assenting to which they help to promote the slavery in which they are involved and are in a manner led captive by reason of their very liberty. Yet He who seeth all things from eternity beholdeth these things with the eyes of His providence, and assigneth to each what is predestined for it by its merits:

' "All things surveying, all things overhearing." '

Song 2

The True Sun

Homer with mellifluous tongue
Phoebus' glorious light hath sung,
  Hymning high his praise;
  Yet *his* feeble rays
Ocean's hollows may not brighten,
Nor earth's central gloom enlighten.

But the might of Him, who skilled
This great universe to build,
  Is not thus confined;
  Not earth's solid rind,
Nor night's blackest canopy,
Baffle His all-seeing eye.

All that is, hath been, shall be,
In one glance's compass, He
  Limitless descries;
  And, save His, no eyes
All the world survey—no, none!
Him, then, truly name the Sun.

Chapter III

Then said I: 'But now I am once more perplexed by a problem yet more difficult.'

'And what is that?' said she; 'yet, in truth, I can guess what it is that troubles you.'

'It seems,' said I, 'too much of a paradox and a contradiction that God should know all things, and yet there should be free will. For if God foresees everything, and can in no wise be deceived, that which providence foresees to be about to happen must necessarily come to pass. Wherefore, if from eternity He foreknows not only what men will do, but also their designs and purposes, there can be no freedom of the will, seeing that nothing can be done, nor can any sort of purpose be entertained, save such as a Divine providence, incapable of being deceived, has perceived beforehand. For if the issues can be turned aside to some other end than that foreseen by providence, there will not then be any sure foreknowledge of the future, but uncertain conjecture instead, and to think this of God I deem impiety.

'Moreover, I do not approve the reasoning by which some think to solve this puzzle. For they say that it is not because God has foreseen the coming of an event that *therfore* it is sure to come to pass, but, conversely, because something is about to come to pass, it cannot be hidden from Divine providence; and accordingly the necessity passes to the opposite side, and it is not that what is foreseen must necessarily come to pass, but that what is about to come to pass must necessarily be foreseen. But this is just as if the matter in debate were, which is cause and which effect—whether foreknowledge of the future cause of the necessity, or the necessity of the future of the foreknowledge. But we need not be at the pains of demonstrating that, whatsoever be the order of the causal sequence, the occurrence of things foreseen is necessary, even though the foreknowledge of future events does not in itself impose upon them the necessity of their occurrence. For example, if a man be seated, the supposition of his being seated is necessarily true; and, conversely, if the supposition of his being seated is true, because he is really seated, he must necessarily be sitting. So, in either case, there is some necessity involved—in this latter case, the necessity of the fact; in the former, of the truth of the statement. But in both cases the sitter is not therefore seated because the opinion is true, but rather the opinion is true because antecedently he was sitting as a matter of fact. Thus, though the cause of the truth of the opinion comes from the other side, yet there is a necessity on both sides alike. We can obviously reason similarly in the case of providence

and the future. Even if future events are foreseen because they are about to happen, and do not come to pass because they are foreseen, still, all the same, there is a necessity, both that they should be foreseen by God as about to come to pass, and that when they are foreseen they should happen, and this is sufficient for the destruction of free will. However, it is preposterous to speak of the occurrence of events in time as the cause of eternal foreknowledge. And yet if we believe that God foresees future events because they are about to come to pass, what is it but to think that the occurrence of events is the cause of His supreme providence? Further, just as when I *know* that anything is, that thing *necessarily* is, so when I know that anything will be, it will *necessarily* be. It follows, then, that things foreknown come to pass inevitably.

'Lastly, to think of a thing as being in any way other than what it is, is not only not knowledge, but it is false opinion widely different from the truth of knowledge. Consequently, if anything is about to be, and yet its occurrence is not certain and necessary, how can anyone foreknow that it will occur? For just as knowledge itself is free from all admixture of falsity, so any conception drawn from knowledge cannot be other than as it is conceived. For this, indeed, is the cause why knowledge is free from falsehood, because of necessity each thing must correspond exactly with the knowledge which grasps its nature. In what way, then, are we to suppose that God foreknows these uncertainties as about to come to pass? For if He thinks of events which possibly may not happen at all as inevitably destined to come to pass, He is deceived; and this it is not only impious to believe, but even so much as to express in words. If, on the other hand, He sees them in the future as they are in such a sense as to know that they may equally come to pass or not, what sort of foreknowledge is this which comprehends nothing certain nor fixed? What better is this than the absurd vaticination of Teiresias?

' "Whate'er I say
Shall either come to pass—or
not."*

In that case, too, in what would Divine providence surpass human opinion if it holds for
uncertain things the occurrence of which is
uncertain, even as men do? But if at that
perfectly sure Fountain-head of all things
no shadow of uncertainty can possibly be
found, then the occurrence of those things
which He has surely foreknown as coming is
certain. Wherefore there can be no freedom in human actions and designs; but the
Divine mind, which foresees all things without possibility of mistake, ties and binds
them down to one only issue. But this ad-
mission once made, what an upset of human affairs manifestly ensues! Vainly are
rewards and punishments proposed for the
good and bad, since no free and voluntary
motion of the will has deserved either one
or the other; nay, the punishment of the
wicked and the reward of the righteous,
which is now esteemed the perfection of
justice, will seem the most flagrant injustice, since men are determined either way
not by their own proper volition, but by the
necessity of what must surely be. And therefore neither virtue nor vice is anything, but
rather good and ill desert are confounded

together without distinction. Moreover,
seeing that the whole course of events is
deduced from providence, and nothing is
left free to human design, it comes to pass
that our vices also are referred to the Author of all good—a thought than which
none more abominable can possibly be conceived. Again, no ground is left for hope or
prayer, since how can we hope for blessings, or pray for mercy, when every object
of desire depends upon the links of an unalterable chain of causation? Gone, then, is
the one means of intercourse between God
and man—the communion of hope and
prayer—if it be true that we ever earn the
inestimable recompense of the Divine favour at the price of a due humility; for this is
the one way whereby men seem able to hold
communion with God, and are joined to
that unapproachable light by the very act of
supplication, even before they obtain their
petitions. Then, since these things can
scarcely be believed to have any efficacy, if
the necessity of future events be admitted,
what means will there be whereby we may
be brought near and cleave to Him who is
the supreme Head of all? Wherefore it
needs must be that the human race, even as
thou didst erstwhile declare in song, parted
and disserved from its Source, should fall to
ruin.'

Song 3

Truth's Paradoxes

Why does a strange discordance break
    The ordered scheme's fair harmony?
Hath God decreed 'twixt truth and truth
    There may such lasting warfare be,
That truths, each severally plain,
We strive to reconcile in vain?

Or is the discord not in truth,
    Since truth is self-consistent ever?
But, close in fleshly wrappings held,
    The blinded mind of man can never

Discern—so faint her taper shines—
The subtle chain that all combines?

Ah! then why burns man's restless mind
    Truth's hidden portals to unclose?
Knows he already what he seeks?
    Why toil to seek it, if he knows?
Yet, haply if he knoweth not,
Why blindly seek he knows not what?[10]

Who for a good he knows not sighs?
    Who can an unknown end pursue?
How find? How e'en when haply found
    Hail that strange form he never knew?
Or is that man's inmost soul
Once knew each part and knew the whole?

Now, though by fleshly vapours dimmed,
    Not all forgot her visions past;
For while the several parts are lost,
    To the one whole she cleaveth fast;
Whence he who yearns the truth to find
Is neither sound of sight nor blind.

For neither does he know in full,
    Nor is he reft of knowledge quite;
But, holding still to what is left,
    He gropes in the uncertain light,
And by the part that still survives
To win back all he bravely strives.

Chapter IV

Then said she: 'This debate about providence is an old one, and is vigorously discussed by Cicero in his "Divination"; thou also hast long and earnestly pondered the problem, yet no one has had diligence and perseverance enough to find a solution. And the reason of this obscurity is that the movement of human reasoning cannot cope with the simplicity of the Divine foreknowledge; for if a conception of its nature could in any wise be framed, no shadow of uncertainty would remain. With a view of making this at last clear and plain, I will begin by considering the arguments by which thou art swayed. First, I inquire into the reasons why thou art dissatisfied with the solution proposed, which is to the effect that, seeing the fact of foreknowledge is not thought the cause of the necessity of future events, foreknowledge is not to be deemed any hindrance to the freedom of the will. Now, surely the sole ground on which thou arguest the necessity of the future is that things which are foreknown cannot fail to come to pass. But if, as thou wert ready to acknowledge just now, the fact of foreknowledge imposes no necessity on things future, what reason is there for supposing the results of voluntary action constrained to a fixed issue? Suppose, for the sake of ar-

---

*See Horace, *Satires*, II, 5.

gument, and to see what follows, we assume that there is no foreknowledge. Are willed actions, then, tied down to any necessity in *this* case?'

'Certainly not.'

'Let us assume foreknowledge again, but without its involving any actual necessity; the freedom of the will, I imagine, will remain in complete integrity. But thou wilt say that, even although the foreknowledge is not the necessity of the future event's occurrence, yet it is a sign that it will necessarily happen. Granted; but in this case it is plain that, even if there had been no foreknowledge, the issues would have been inevitably certain. For a sign only indicates something which is, does not bring to pass that of which it is the sign. We require to show beforehand that all things, without exception, happen of necessity in order that a preconception may be a sign of this necessity. Otherwise, if there is no such universal necessity, neither can any preconception be a sign of a necessity which exists not. Manifestly, too, a proof established on firm grounds of reason must be drawn not from signs and loose general arguments, but from suitable and necessary causes. But how can it be that things foreseen should ever fail to come to pass? Why, this is to suppose us to believe that the events which providence foresees to be coming were not about to happen, instead of our supposing that, although they should come to pass, yet there was no necessity involved in their own nature compelling their occurrence. Take an illustration that will help to convey my meaning. There are many things which we see taking place before our eyes—the movements of charioteers, for instance, in guiding and turning their cars, and so on. Now, is any one of these movements compelled by any necessity?'

'No; certainly not. There would be no efficacy in skill if all motions took place perforce.'

'Then, things which in taking place are free from necessity as to their being in the present must also, before they take place,

be about to happen without necessity. Wherefore there are things which will come to pass, the occurrence of which is perfectly free from necessity. At all events, I imagine that no one will deny that things now taking place were about to come to pass before they were actually happening. Such things, however much foreknown, are in their occurrence *free*. For even as knowledge of things present imports no necessity into things that are taking place, so foreknowledge of the future imports none into things that are about to come. But this, thou wilt say, is the very point in dispute—whether any foreknowing is possible of things whose occurrence is not necessary. For here there seems to thee a contradiction, and, if they are foreseen, their necessity follows; whereas if there is no necessity, they can by no means be foreknown; and thou thinkest that nothing can be grasped as known unless it is certain, but if things whose occurrence is uncertain are foreknown as certain, this is the very mist of opinion, not the truth of knowledge. For to think of things otherwise than as they are, thou believest to be incompatible with the soundness of knowledge.

'Now, the cause of the mistake is this— that men think that all knowledge is cognized purely by the nature and efficacy of the thing known. Whereas the case is the very reverse: all that is known is grasped not conformably to its own efficacy, but rather conformably to the faculty of the knower. An example will make this clear: the roundness of a body is recognised in one way by sight, in another by touch. Sight looks upon it from a distance as a whole by a simultaneous reflection of rays; touch grasps the roundness piecemeal, by contact and attachment to the surface, and by actual movement round the periphery itself. Man himself, likewise, is viewed in one way by Sense, in another by Imagination, in another way, again, by Thought, in another by pure Intelligence. Sense judges figure clothed in material substance, Imagination figure alone without matter. Thought transcends this again, and by its contemplation of universals considers the type itself which is contained in the individual. The eye of Intelligence is yet more exalted; for over-passing the sphere of the universal, it will behold absolute form itself by the pure force of the mind's vision. Wherein the main point to be considered is this: the higher faculty of comprehension embraces the lower, while the lower cannot rise to the higher. For Sense has no efficacy beyond matter, nor can Imagination behold univer-sal ideas, nor Thought embrace pure form; but Intelligence, looking down, as it were, from its higher standpoint in its intuition of form, discriminates also the several ele-ments which underlie it; but it compre-hends them in the same way as it compre-hends that form itself, which could be cognized by no other than itself. For it cog-nizes the universal of Thought, the figure of Imagination, and the matter of Sense, with-out employing Thought, Imagination, or Sense, but surveying all things, so to speak, under the aspect of pure form by a single flash of intuition. Thought also, in consid-ering the universal, embraces images and sense-impressions without resorting to Imagination or Sense. For it is Thought which has thus defined the universal from its conceptual point of view: "Man is a two-legged animal endowed with reason." This is indeed a universal notion, yet no one is ignorant that the *thing* is imaginable and presentable to Sense, because Thought considers it not by Imagination or Sense, but by means of rational conception. Imagi-nation, too, though its faculty of viewing and forming representations is founded upon the senses, nevertheless surveys sense-impressions without calling in Sense, not in the way of Sense-perception, but of Imagination. See'st thou, then, how all things in cognizing use rather their own fac-ulty than the faculty of the things which they cognize? Nor is this strange; for since every judgment is the act of the judge, it is neces-sary that each should accomplish its task by its own, not by another's power.'

Song 4

A Psychological Fallacy

From the Porch's murky depths
   Comes a doctrine sage,
That doth liken living mind
   To a written page;
Since all knowledge comes through Sense,
Graven by Experience.

'As,' say they, 'the pen its marks
   Curiously doth trace
On the smooth unsullied white
   Of the paper's face,
So do outer things impress
Images on consciousness.'

But if verily the mind
   Thus all passive lies;
If no living power within
   Its own force supplies;

If it but reflect again,
Like a glass, things false and vain—

Whence the wondrous faculty
   That perceives and knows,
That in one fair ordered scheme
   Doth the world dispose;
Grasps each whole that Sense presents,
Or breaks into elements?

So divides and recombines,
   And in changeful wise
Now to low descends, and now
   To the height doth rise;
Last in inward swift review
Strictly sifts the false and true?

Of these ample potencies
   Fitter cause, I ween,
Were Mind's self than marks impressed
   By the outer scene.
Yet the body through the sense
Stirs the soul's intelligence.

When light flashes on the eye,
   Or sound strikes the ear,
Mind aroused to due response
   Makes the message clear;
And the dumb external signs
With the hidden forms combines.

Chapter V

'Now, although in the case of bodies endowed with sentiency the qualities of external objects affect the sense-organs, and the activity of mind is preceded by a bodily affection which calls forth the mind's action upon itself, and stimulates the forms till that moment lying inactive within, yet, I say, if in these bodies endowed with sentiency the mind is not inscribed by mere passive affection, but of its own efficacy discriminates the impressions furnished to the body, how much more do intelligences free from all bodily affections employ in their discrimination their own mental activities instead of conforming to external objects? So on these principles various modes of cognition belong to distinct and different substances. For to creatures void of motive power—shell-fish and other such creatures which cling to rocks and grow there—belongs Sense alone, void of all other modes of gaining knowledge; to beasts endowed with movement, in whom some capacity of seeking and shunning seems to have arisen, Imagination also. Thought pertains only to the human race, as Intelligence to Divinity alone; hence it follows that that form of knowledge exceeds the rest which of its own nature cognizes not only its proper object, but the objects of the other forms of knowledge also. But what if Sense and Imagination were to gainsay Thought, and declare that universal which Thought deems itself to behold to be nothing? For the object of Sense and Imagination cannot be universal; so that either the judgment of Reason is true and there is no sense-object, or, since they know full well that many objects are presented to Sense and Imagination, the conception of Reason, which looks on that which is perceived by Sense and particular as if it were a something "universal," is empty of content. Suppose, further, that Reason maintains in reply that it does indeed contemplate the object of both Sense and Imagination under the form of universality, while Sense and Imagination cannot aspire to the knowledge of the universal, since their cognizance cannot go beyond bodily figures, and that in the cognition of reality we ought rather to trust the stronger and more perfect faculty of judgment. In a dispute of this sort, should not we, in whom is planted the faculty of reasoning as well as of imagining and perceiving, espouse the cause of Reason?

'In like manner is it that human reason thinks that Divine Intelligence cannot see the future except after the fashion in which its own knowledge is obtained. For thy contention is, if events do not appear to involve certain and necessary issues, they cannot be foreseen as certainly about to come to pass. There is, then, no foreknowledge of such events; or, if we can ever bring ourselves to believe that there is, there can be nothing which does not happen of necessity. If, however, we could have some part in the judgment of the Divine mind, even as we participate in Reason, we should think it perfectly just that human Reason should submit itself to the Divine mind, no less than we judged that Imagination and Sense ought to yield to Reason. Wherefore let us soar, if we can, to the heights of that Supreme Intelligence; for there Reason will see what in itself it cannot look upon; and that is in what way things whose occurrence is not certain may yet be seen in a sure and definite foreknowledge; and that this foreknowledge is not conjecture, but rather knowledge in its supreme simplicity, free of all limits and restrictions.'

Song 5

The Upward Look

In what divers shapes and fashions do the creatures great and small
Over wide earth's teeming surface skim, or scud, or walk, or crawl!
Some with elongated body sweep the ground, and, as they move,
Trail perforce with writhing belly in the dust a sinuous groove;
Some, on light wing upward soaring, swiftly do the winds divide,
And through heaven's ample spaces in free motion smoothly glide;
These earth's solid surface pressing, with firm paces onward rove,
Ranging through the verdant meadows, crouching in the woodland grove.
Great and wondrous is their variance! Yet in all the head low-bent
Dulls the soul and blunts the senses, though their forms be different.
Man alone, erect, aspiring, lifts his forehead to the skies,
And in upright posture steadfast seems earth's baseness to despise.
  If with earth not all besotted, to this parable give ear,
Thou whose gaze is fixed on heaven, who thy face on high dost rear:
Lift thy soul, too, heavenward; haply lest it stain its heavenly worth,
And thine eyes alone look upward, while thy mind cleaves to the earth!

375

'Since, then, as we lately proved, everything that is known is cognized not in accordance with its own nature, but in accordance with the nature of the faculty that comprehends it, let us now contemplate, as far as lawful, the character of the Divine essence, that we may be able to understand also the nature of its knowledge.

'God is eternal; in this judgment all rational beings agree. Let us, then, consider what eternity is. For this word carries with it a revelation alike of the Divine nature and of the Divine knowledge. Now, eternity is the possession of endless life whole and perfect at a single moment. What this is becomes more clear and manifest from a comparison with things temporal. For whatever lives in time is a present proceeding from the past to the future, and there is nothing set in time which can embrace the whole space of its life together. To-morrow's state it grasps not yet, while it has already lost yesterday's; nay, even in the life of to-day ye live no longer than one brief transitory moment. Whatever, therefore, is subject to the condition of time, although, as Aristotle deemed of the world, it never have either beginning or end, and its life be stretched to the whole extent of time's infinity, it yet is not such as rightly to be thought eternal. For it does not include and embrace the whole space of infinite life at once, but has no present hold on things to come, not yet accomplished. Accordingly, that which includes and possesses the whole fulness of unending life at once, from which nothing future is absent, from which nothing past has escaped, this is rightly called eternal; this must of necessity be ever present to itself in full self-possession, and hold the infinity of movable time in an abiding present. Wherefore they deem not rightly who imagine that on Plato's principles the created world is made co-eternal with the Creator, because they are told that he believed the world to have had no beginning in time,[11] and to be destined never to come to an end. For it is one thing for existence to be endlessly prolonged, which was what Plato ascribed to the world, another for the whole of an endless life to be embraced in the present, which is manifestly a property peculiar to the Divine mind. Nor need God appear earlier in mere duration of time to created things, but only prior in the unique simplicity of His nature. For the infinite progression of things in time copies this immediate existence in the present of the changeless life, and when it cannot succeed in equalling it, declines from movelessness into motion, and falls away from the simplicity of a perpetual present to the infinite duration of the future and the past; and since it cannot possess the whole fulness of its life together, for the very reason that in a manner it never ceases to be, it seems, up to a certain point, to rival that which it cannot complete and express by attaching itself indifferently to any present moment of time, however swift and brief; and since this bears some resemblance to that ever-abiding present, it bestows on everything to which it is assigned the semblance of existence. But since it cannot abide, it hurries along the infinite path of time, and the result has been that it continues by ceaseless movement the life the completeness of which it could not embrace while it stood still. So, if we are minded to give things their right names, we shall follow Plato in saying that God indeed is eternal, but the world everlasting.

'Since, then, every mode of judgment comprehends its objects conformably to its own nature, and since God abides for ever in an eternal present, His knowledge, also transcending all movement of time, dwells in the simplicity of its own changeless present, and, embracing the whole infinite sweep of the past and of the future, contemplates all that falls within its simple cognition as if it were now taking place. And therefore, if thou wilt carefully consider that immediate presentment whereby it discriminates all things, thou wilt more rightly deem it not foreknowledge as of something future, but knowledge of a moment that never passes. For this cause the name chosen to describe it is not prevision, but providence, because, since utterly removed in nature from things mean and trivial, its outlook embraces all things as from some lofty height. Why, then, dost thou insist that the things which are surveyed by the Divine eye are involved in necessity, whereas clearly men impose no necessity on things which they see? Does the act of vision add any necessity to the things which thou seest before thy eyes?'

'Assuredly not.'

'And yet, if we may without unfitness compare God's present and man's, just as ye see certain things in this your temporary present, so does He see all things in His eternal present. Wherefore this Divine anticipation changes not the natures and properties of things, and it beholds things present before it, just as they will hereafter come to pass in time. Nor does it confound things in its judgment, but in the one mental view distinguishes alike what will come necessarily and what without necessity. For even as ye, when at one and the same time ye see a man walking on the earth and the sun rising in the sky, distinguish between the two, though one glance embraces both, and judge the former voluntary, the latter necessary action: so also the Divine vision in its universal range of view does in no wise confuse the characters of the things which are present to its regard, though future in respect of time. Whence it follows that when it perceives that something will come into existence, and yet is perfectly aware that this is unbound by any necessity, its apprehension is not opinion, but rather knowledge based on truth. And if to this thou sayest that what God sees to be about to come to pass cannot fail to come to pass, and that what cannot fail to come to pass happens of necessity, and wilt tie me down to this word necessity, I will acknowledge that thou affirmest a most solid truth, but one which scarcely anyone can approach to who has not made the Divine his special study. For my answer would be that the same future event is necessary from the standpoint of Divine knowledge, but when considered in its own nature it seems absolutely free and unfettered. So, then, there are two necessities—one simple, as that men are necessarily mortal; the other conditioned, as that, if you know that someone is walking, he must necessarily be walking. For that which is known cannot indeed be otherwise than as it is known to be, and yet this fact by no means carries with it that other simple necessity. For the former necessity is not imposed by the thing's own proper nature, but by the addition of a condition. No necessity compels one who is voluntarily walking to go forward, although it is necessary for him to go forward at the moment of walking. In the same way, then, if Providence sees anything as present, that must necessarily be, though it is bound by no necessity of nature. Now, God views as present those coming events which happen of free will. These, accordingly, from the standpoint of the Divine vision are made necessary conditionally on the Divine cognizance; viewed, however, in themselves, they desist not from the absolute freedom naturally theirs. Accordingly, without doubt, all things will come to pass which God foreknows as about to happen, but of these certain proceed of free will; and though these happen, yet by the fact of their existence they do not lose their proper nature, in virtue of which before they happened it was really possible that they might not have come to pass.

'What difference, then, does the denial of necessity make, since, through their being conditioned by Divine knowledge, they come to pass as if they were in all respects under the compulsion of necessity? This difference, surely, which we saw in the case of the instances I formerly took, the sun's rising and the man's walking; which at the moment of their occurrence could not but be taking place, and yet one of them before it took place was necessarily obliged to be, while the other was not so at all. So likewise the things which to God are present without doubt exist, but some of them come from the necessity of things, others from the power of the agent. Quite rightly, then, have we said that these things are necessary if viewed from the standpoint of the Divine knowledge; but if they are considered in themselves, they are free from the bonds of necessity, even as everything which is accessible to sense, regarded from the standpoint of Thought, is universal, but viewed in its own nature particular. "But," thou wilt say, "if it is in my power to change my purpose, I shall make void providence, since I shall perchance change something which comes within its foreknowledge." My answer is: Thou canst indeed turn aside thy purpose; but since the truth of providence is ever at hand to see that thou canst, and whether thou dost, and whither thou turnest thyself, thou canst not avoid the Divine foreknowledge, even as thou canst not escape the sight of a present spectator, although of thy free will thou turn thyself to various actions. Wilt thou, then, say: "Shall the Divine knowledge be changed at my discretion, so that, when I will this or that, providence changes its knowledge correspondingly?"

'Surely not.'

'True, for the Divine vision anticipates all that is coming, and transforms and reduces it to the form of its own present knowledge, and varies not, as thou deemest, in its foreknowledge, alternating to this or that, but in a single flash it forestalls and includes thy mutations without altering. And this ever-present comprehension and survey of all things God has received, not from the issue of future events, but from the simplicity of His own nature. Hereby also is resolved the objection which a little while ago gave thee offence—that our doings in the future were spoken of as if supplying the cause of God's knowledge. For this faculty of knowledge, embracing all things in its immediate cognizance, has itself fixed the bounds of all things, yet itself owes nothing to what comes after.

'And all this being so, the freedom of man's will stands unshaken, and laws are not unrighteous, since their rewards and punishments are held forth to wills unbound by any necessity. God, who foreknoweth all things, still looks down from above, and the ever-present eternity of His vision concurs with the future character of all our acts, and dispenseth to the good rewards, to the bad punishments. Our hopes and prayers also are not fixed on God in vain, and when they are rightly directed cannot fail of effect. Therefore, withstand vice, practise virtue, lift up your souls to right hopes, offer humble prayers to Heaven. Great is the necessity of righteousness laid upon you if ye will not hide it from yourselves, seeing that all your actions are done before the eyes of a Judge who seeth all things.'

[1] π (P) stands for the Political life, the life of action; θ (Th) for the Theoretical life, the life of thought.

[2] The Stoic, Epicurean, and other philosophical sects, which Boethius regards as heterodox.

[3] The moon is regarded as farthest from the sun at the full, and, as it wanes, approaching gradually nearer.

[4] The substance of this poem is taken from Plato's 'Timaeus,' 29–42. [See GBWW, Vol. 7, pp. 447–53.]

[5] The doctrine of Reminiscence—i.e., that all learning is really recollection—is set forth at length by Plato in the Meno, 81–86, and the Phaedo, 72–76. [See GBWW, Vol. 7, pp. 179–83 and 227–30.]

[6] The paradoxes in this chapter and chapter iv are taken from Plato's Gorgias, 466–479 and 508–509. [See GBWW, Vol. 7, pp. 262–70, 284, 285.]

[7] 'No trivial game is here; the strife
Is waged for Turnus' own dear life.'
                                    Conington.
See Virgil, Aeneid, xii. 764, 765. [GBWW, Vol. 13, p. 374. Cf. also The Iliad, xxii, 159–162; GBWW, Vol. 4, p. 156.]

[8] To frighten away the monster swallowing the moon. The superstition was once common.

[9] Parmenides.

[10] Compare Plato, Meno, 80 [GBWW, Vol. 7, p. 179].

[11] Plato expressly states the opposite in the Timaeus (28B), though possibly there the account of the beginning of the world in time is to be understood figuratively, not literally. [See GBWW, Vol. 7, p. 447.]

Man a Machine

Julien de La Mettrie

Editor's Introduction

No question, it seems fair to say, has more occupied the minds of philosophers than what man is, unless possibly it is what God may be. Of the propositions about human nature which have established themselves, some belong to common observation, some are articles of faith, some in effect are scientific hypotheses. Among them, seven were once noted by Scott Buchanan as of special interest and importance. In rough historical succession they have asserted that man is

> an animal,
>
> a soul,
>
> an angel,
>
> divine,
>
> a machine,
>
> a system of electrons,
>
> a bundle of habits.

It is the fifth contention in this list that Julien Offray (or Offroy) de La Mettrie (1709–51) maintained in a famous little book he published in 1747, whose title, *L'Homme-machine (Man a Machine)* in effect made the claim with a brevity that French more easily conveys than English can.

La Mettrie, himself a figure of note in his time, was a man of unusual attainments. A physician as well as a philosopher, he came to both professions by way of poetry, which was his first love, and the church, which his father, a well-off bourgeois of Saint-Malo, thought more likely to earn him a living. After some time devoted to both subjects in Paris, and following further studies in natural philosophy (i.e., science) at the college of Harcourt, the young man was advised that medicine would after all be the best choice; accordingly, having undertaken a medical course at Reims he was duly granted a medical degree. Subsequently, in 1733, he went to Leiden to study with Hermann Boerhaave (1668–1738), regarded as the father of bedside clinical teaching, under whose guidance La Mettrie became a distinguished medical theorist with contributions to the knowledge of venereal diseases, vertigo, and smallpox.

Of a lively and contentious temper, La Mettrie was nothing if not outspoken in his views. These were materialist ones derived in part from Boerhaave and other noted medical practitioners of the day, and in part from Descartes, among philosophers, who himself thought that animals were machines, or what were called automata, but not men. La Mettrie decided to include men in this category when his writings on physiology were resisted by the medical profession in Paris for reasons, as he thought, of prejudice and jealousy, and also when at the age of thirty-three, while serving as surgeon to a French military unit, he suffered an attack of violent fever from which he recovered convinced that his psychic processes were all functions of his brain and nervous system. His conclusions to that effect were published in a little book called the *Natural History of the Soul* (1745), which caused such a stir that he was obliged to leave Paris, where the book was burned by the common hangman.

Man a Machine was written while La Mettrie lived in Holland, to which he went to live after he left France. There he wrote philosophical works of an anti-religious kind as well as polemical papers directed against what nowadays would be called the medical establishment, with which he was in constant conflict. These writings made Holland as hostile to him as Paris had been, and in 1748 he removed once more, this time to Berlin, where he was given the protection of Frederick the Great, who admired men of outspoken nature and advanced ideas and who made La Mettrie a member of his scientific academy.

While at Berlin, during the last three years of his relatively short life, La Mettrie, who had become the Emperor's court reader, wrote *The Small Man in a Long Queue* (1751) in which he maintained that atheism was the means to human happiness and pleasure the purpose of life. By then he was devoting most of his energies to philosophy, though he returned to medicine long enough to write papers on both dysentery and asthma that were regarded as the best treatments of both those subjects at the time. Among his other philosophical writings were one called *The Art of Pleasure* and another on the philosophy of Epicurus.

La Mettrie died at forty-one of an attack of food poisoning, lamented by his royal patron in a eulogy in which the Emperor praised him for his life-long stand against the "vanity" and "quackery" of his profession, for his gay spirit, and for his quick mind and fertile imagination that, Frederick said, "made flowers grow in the field of medicine." La Mettrie would be mourned, the eulogy concluded, by "all those who are not imposed upon by the pious insults of the theologians. . .as a good man and a wise physician." And although some of his views were too extreme for even the strong-minded men of his time, such as Voltaire, who could not accept the lack of moral responsibility implicit in them, La Mettrie has been recognized as a figure of genuine if eccentric importance in at least the development of psychology, especially the mechanistic theory of personality and sensation.

Man a Machine

I t is not enough for a wise man to study nature and truth; he should dare state truth for the benefit of the few who are willing and able to think. As for the rest, who are voluntarily slaves of prejudice, they can no more attain truth, than frogs can fly.

I reduce to two the systems of philosophy which deal with man's soul. The first and older system is materialism; the second is spiritualism.

The metaphysicians who have hinted that matter may well be endowed with the faculty of thought have perhaps not reasoned ill. For there is in this case a certain advantage in their inadequate way of expressing their meaning. In truth, to ask whether matter can think, without considering it otherwise than in itself, is like asking whether matter can tell time. It may be foreseen that we shall avoid this reef upon which Locke had the bad luck to make shipwreck.

The Leibnizians with their monads have set up an unintelligible hypothesis. They have rather spiritualized matter than materialized the soul. How can we define a being whose nature is absolutely unknown to us?

Descartes and all the Cartesians, among whom the followers of Malebranche have long been numbered, have made the same mistake. They have taken for granted two distinct substances in man, as if they had seen them, and positively counted them.

The wisest men have declared that the soul can not know itself save by the light of faith. However, as reasonable beings they have thought that they could reserve for themselves the right of examining what the Bible means by the word "spirit", which it uses in speaking of the human soul. And if in their investigation, they do not agree with the theologians on this point, are the theologians more in agreement among themselves on all other points?

Here is the result in a few words, of all their reflections. If there is a God, He is the Author of nature as well as of revelation. He has given us the one to explain the other, and reason to make them agree.

To distrust the knowledge that can be drawn from the study of animated bodies, is to regard nature and revelation as two contraries which destroy each other, and consequently to dare uphold the absurd doctrine, that God contradicts Himself in His various works and deceives us.

If there is a revelation, it can not then contradict nature. By nature only can we understand the meaning of the words of the Gospel, of which experience is the only true interpreter. In fact, the commentators before our time have only obscured the truth. We can judge of this by the author of the *Spectacle of Nature*.* "It is astonishing", he says concerning Locke, "that a man who degrades our soul far enough to consider it a soul of clay should dare set up reason as judge and sovereign arbiter of the mysteries of faith, for", he adds, "what an astonishing idea of Christianity one would have, if one were to follow reason".

Not only do these reflections fail to elucidate faith, but they also constitute such frivolous objections to the method of those who undertake to interpret the Scripture, that I am almost ashamed to waste time in refuting them.

The excellence of reason does not depend on a big word devoid of meaning (immateriality), but on the force, extent, and perspicuity of reason itself. Thus a "soul of clay" which should discover, at one glance, as it were, the relations and the conse-

---

*Noel Antoine Pluche (1688–1761), author and theologian, characterized elsewhere by La Mettrie as "a superficial man," and a pedant.

quences of an infinite number of ideas hard to understand, would evidently be preferable to a foolish and stupid soul, though that were composed of the most precious elements. A man is not a philosopher because, with Pliny, he blushes over the wretchedness of our origin. What seems vile is here the most precious of things, and seems to be the object of nature's highest art and most elaborate care. But as man, even though he should come from an apparently still more lowly source, would yet be the most perfect of all beings, so whatever the origin of his soul, if it is pure, noble, and lofty, it is a beautiful soul which dignifies the man endowed with it.

Pluche's second way of reasoning seems vicious to me, even in his system, which smacks a little of fanaticism; for [on his view] if we have an idea of faith as being contrary to the clearest principles, to the most incontestable truths, we must yet conclude, out of respect for revelation and its author, that this conception is false, and that we do not yet understand the meaning of the words of the Gospel.

Of the two alternatives, only one is possible: either everything is illusion, nature as well as revelation, or experience alone can explain faith. But what can be more ridiculous than the position of the author! Can one imagine hearing a Peripatetic say, "We ought not to accept the experiments of Torricelli, for if we should accept them, if we should rid ourselves of the horror of the void, what an astonishing philosophy we should have!"*

I have shown how vicious the reasoning of Pluche is in order to prove, in the first place, that if there is a revelation, it is not sufficiently demonstrated by the mere authority of the Church, and without any appeal to reason, as all those who fear reason claim: and in the second place, to protect against all assault the method of those who would wish to follow the path that I open to them, of interpreting supernatural things, incomprehensible in themselves, in the light of those ideas with which nature has endowed us. Experience and observation should therefore be our only guides here. Both are to be found throughout the records of the physicians who were philosophers, and not in the works of the philosophers who were not physicians. The former have traveled through and illuminated the labyrinth of man; they alone have laid bare to us those springs [of life] hidden under the external integument which conceals so many wonders from our eyes. They alone, tranquilly contemplating our soul, have surprised it, a thousand times, both in its wretchedness and in its glory, and they have no more despised it in the first estate, than they have admired it in the second. Thus, to repeat, only the physicians have a right to speak on this subject. What could the others, especially the theologians, have to say? Is it not ridiculous to hear them shamelessly coming to conclusions about a subject concerning which they have had no means of knowing anything, and from which on the contrary they have been completely turned aside by obscure studies that have led them to a thousand prejudiced opinions,—in a word, to fanaticism, which adds yet more to their ignorance of the mechanism of the body?

But even though we have chosen the best guides, we shall still find many thorns and stumbling blocks in the way.

Man is so complicated a machine that it is impossible to get a clear idea of the machine beforehand, and hence impossible to define it. For this reason, all the investigations have been vain, which the greatest philosophers have made *à priori*, that is, to say, in so far as they use, as it were, the wings of the spirit. Thus it is only *à posteriori* or by trying to disentangle the soul from the organs of the body, so to speak, that one can reach the highest probability concern-

---

*Evangelista Torricelli (1608–47), a disciple of Galileo. Showed that the height to which liquid will rise in a closed tube is determined by atmospheric pressure, an experiment that did away with the notion of a vacuum and made possible both the thermometer and the barometer.

ing man's own nature, even though one can not discover with certainty what his nature is.

Let us then take in our hands the staff of experience, paying no heed to the accounts of all the idle theories of philosophers. To be blind and to think that one can do without this staff is the worst kind of blindness. How truly a contemporary writer says that only vanity fails to gather from secondary causes the same lessons as from primary causes! One can and one even ought to admire all these fine geniuses in their most useless works, such men as Descartes, Malebranche, Leibniz, Wolff and the rest, but what profit, I ask, has any one gained from their profound meditations, and from all their works? Let us start out then to discover not what has been thought, but what must be thought for the sake of repose in life.

There are as many different minds, different characters, and different customs, as there are different temperaments. Even Galen* knew this truth which Descartes carried so far as to claim that medicine alone can change minds and morals, along with bodies. (By the writer of "L'histoire de l'ame,"† this teaching is incorrectly attributed to Hippocrates.) It is true that melancholy, bile, phlegm, blood etc.—according to the nature, the abundance, and the different combination of these humors—make each man different from another.

In disease the soul is sometimes hidden, showing no sign of life; sometimes it is so inflamed by fury that it seems to be doubled; sometimes, imbecility vanishes and the convalescence of an idiot produces a wise man. Sometimes, again, the greatest genius becomes imbecile and loses the sense of self. Adieu then to all that fine knowledge, acquired at so high a price, and with so much trouble! Here is a paralytic who asks if his leg is in bed with him; there is a soldier who thinks that he still has the arm which has been cut off. The memory of his old sensations, and of the place to which they were referred by his soul, is the cause

of his illusion, and of this kind of delirium. The mere mention of the member which he has lost is enough to recall it to his mind, and to make him feel all its motions; and this causes him an indefinable and inexpressible kind of imaginary suffering. This man cries like a child at death's approach, while this other jests. What was needed to change the bravery of Caius Julius, Seneca, or Petronius into cowardice or faintheartedness? Merely an obstruction in the spleen, in the liver, an impediment in the portal vein? Why? Because the imagination is obstructed along with the viscera, and this gives rise to all the singular phenomena of hysteria and hypochondria.

What can I add to the stories already told of those who imagine themselves transformed into wolf-men, cocks or vampires, or of those who think that the dead feed upon them? Why should I stop to speak of the man who imagines that his nose or some other member is of glass? The way to help this man regain his faculties and his own flesh-and-blood nose is to advise him to sleep on hay, lest he break the fragile organ, and then to set fire to the hay that he may be afraid of being burned—a fear which has sometimes cured paralysis. But I must touch lightly on facts which everybody knows.

Neither shall I dwell long on the details of the effects of sleep. Here a tired soldier snores in a trench, in the middle of the thunder of hundreds of cannon. His soul hears nothing; his sleep is as deep as apoplexy. A bomb is on the point of crushing him. He will feel this less perhaps than he feels an insect which is under his foot.

On the other hand, this man who is devoured by jealousy, hatred, avarice, or ambition, can never find any rest. The most peaceful spot, the freshest and most calming drinks are alike useless to one who has

---

*See *GBWW*, Vol. 10.
†The writer of "L'histoire de l'ame" was La Mettrie, who thus corrects himself.

not freed his heart from the torment of passion.

The soul and the body fall asleep together. As the motion of the blood is calmed, a sweet feeling of peace and quiet spreads through the whole mechanism. The soul feels itself little by little growing heavy as the eyelids droop, and loses its tenseness, as the fibres of the brain relax; thus little by little it becomes as if paralyzed and with it all the muscles of the body. These can no longer sustain the weight of the head, and the soul can no longer bear the burden of thought; it is in sleep as if it were not.

Is the circulation too quick? the soul cannot sleep. Is the soul too much excited? the blood can not be quieted: it gallops through the veins with an audible murmur. Such are the two opposite causes of insomnia. A single fright in the midst of our dreams makes the heart beat at double speed and snatches us from needed and delicious repose, as a real grief or an urgent need would do. Lastly as the mere cessation of the functions of the soul produces sleep, there are, even when we are awake (or at least when we are half awake), kinds of very frequent short naps of the mind, vergers' dreams, which show that the soul does not always wait for the body to sleep. For if the soul is not fast asleep, it surely is not far from sleep, since it can not point out a single object to which it has attended, among the uncounted number of confused ideas which, so to speak, fill the atmosphere of our brains like clouds.

Opium is too closely related to the sleep it produces, to be left out of consideration here. This drug intoxicates, like wine, coffee, etc., each in its own measure and according to the dose. It makes a man happy in a state which would seemingly be the tomb of feeling, as it is the image of death. How sweet is this lethargy! The soul would long never to emerge from it. For the soul has been a prey to the most intense sorrow, but now feels only the joy of suffering past, and of sweetest peace. Opium even alters the will, forcing the soul which wished to wake and to enjoy life, to sleep in spite of

itself. I shall omit any reference to the effect of poisons.

Coffee, the well-known antidote for wine, by scourging the imagination, cures our headaches and scatters our cares without laying up for us, as wine does, other headaches for the morrow. But let us contemplate the soul in its other needs.

The human body is a machine which winds its own springs. It is the living image of perpetual movement. Nourishment keeps up the movements which fever excites. Without food, the soul pines away, goes mad, and dies exhausted. The soul is a taper whose light flares up the moment before it goes out. But nourish the body, pour into its veins life-giving juices and strong liquors, and then the soul grows strong like them, as if arming itself with a proud courage, and the soldier whom water would have made flee, grows bold and runs joyously to death to the sound of drums. Thus a hot drink sets into stormy movement the blood which a cold drink would have calmed.

What power there is in a meal! Joy revives in a sad heart, and infects the souls of comrades, who express their delight in the friendly songs in which the Frenchman excels. The melancholy man alone is dejected, and the studious man is equally out of place [in such company].

Raw meat makes animals fierce, and it would have the same effect on man. This is so true that the English who eat meat red and bloody, and not as well done as ours, seem to share more or less in the savagery due to this kind of food, and to other causes which can be rendered ineffective by education only. This savagery creates in the soul, pride, hatred, scorn of other nations, indocility and other sentiments which degrade the character, just as heavy food makes a dull and heavy mind whose usual traits are laziness and indolence.

Pope understood well the full power of greediness when he said:*

---

*In *Moral Essays*, Epistle I,1, 77 (1734).

"Catius is ever moral, ever grave,
Thinks who endures a knave, is next a
   knave,
Save just at dinner—then prefers no
   doubt,
A rogue with ven'son to a saint without."

Elsewhere he says:

"See the same man in vigor, in the
      gout
Alone, in company, in place or out,
Early at business and at hazard late,
Mad at a fox chase, wise at a debate,
Drunk at a borough, civil at a ball,
Friendly at Hackney, faithless at White
   Hall."

In Switzerland we had a bailiff by the name of M. Steigner de Wittighofen. When he fasted he was a most upright and even a most indulgent judge, but woe to the unfortunate man whom he found on the culprit's bench after he had had a large dinner! He was capable of sending the innocent like the guilty to the gallows.

We think we are, and in fact we are, good men, only as we are gay or brave; everything depends on the way our machine is running. One is sometimes inclined to say that the soul is situated in the stomach, and that Van Helmont,* who said that the seat of the soul was in the pylorus, made only the mistake of taking the part for the whole.

To what excesses cruel hunger can bring us! We no longer regard even our own parents and children. We tear them to pieces eagerly and make horrible banquets of them; and in the fury with which we are carried away, the weakest is always the prey of the strongest. . . . .

One needs only eyes to see the necessary influence of old age on reason. The soul follows the progress of the body, as it does the progress of education. In the weaker sex, the soul accords also with delicacy of temperament, and from this delicacy follow tenderness, affection, quick feelings due more to passion than to reason, prejudices,

and superstitions, whose strong impress can hardly be effaced. Man, on the other hand, whose brain and nerves partake of the firmness of all solids, has not only stronger features but also a more vigorous mind. Education, which women lack, strengthens his mind still more. Thus with such help of nature and art, why should not a man be more grateful, more generous, more constant in friendship, stronger in adversity? But, to follow almost exactly the thought of the author of the *Lettres sur la Physiognomie,*† the sex which unites the charms of the mind and of the body with almost all the tenderest and most delicate feelings of the heart, should not envy us the two capacities which seem to have been given to man, the one merely to enable him better to fathom the allurements of beauty, and the other merely to enable him to minister better to its pleasures.

It is no more necessary to be just as great a physiognomist as this author, in order to guess the quality of the mind from the countenance or the shape of the features, provided these are sufficiently marked, than it is necessary to be a great doctor to recognize a disease accompanied by all its marked symptoms. Look at the portraits of Locke, of Steele, of Boerhaave, of Maupertuis, and the rest, and you will not be surprised to find strong faces and eagle eyes. Look over a multitude of others, and you can always distinguish the man of talent from the man of genius, and often even an honest man from a scoundrel. For example, it has been noticed that a celebrated poet combines (in his portrait) the look of a pickpocket with the fire of Prometheus.

History provides us with a noteworthy example of the power of temperature. The famous Duke of Guise was so strongly convinced that Henry the Third, in whose power he had so often been, would never dare

---

*Jan Baptist van Helmont (1580–1644), Flemish physician and chemist.
†A certain Jaques Pernety or Pernetti, d. 1777, who was an ecclesiastic at Lyon in France.

assassinate him, that he went to Blois.* When the Chancelor Chiverny learned of the duke's departure, he cried, "He is lost". After this fatal prediction had been fulfilled by the event, Chiverny was asked why he made it. "I have known the king for twenty years," said he; "he is naturally kind and even weakly indulgent, but I have noticed that when it is cold, it takes nothing at all to provoke him and send him into a passion."

One nation is of heavy and stupid wit, and another quick, light and penetrating. Whence comes this difference, if not in part from the difference in foods, and difference in inheritance, and in part from the mixture of the diverse elements which float around in the immensity of the void? The mind, like the body, has its contagious diseases and its scurvy.

Such is the influence of climate, that a man who goes from one climate to another, feels the change, in spite of himself. He is a walking plant which has transplanted itself; if the climate is not the same, it will surely either degenerate or improve.

Furthermore, we catch everything from those with whom we come in contact; their gestures, their accent, etc.; just as the eyelid is instinctively lowered when a blow is foreseen, or as (for the same reason) the body of the spectator mechanically imitates, in spite of himself, all the motions of a good mimic.

From what I have just said, it follows that a brilliant man is his own best company, unless he can find other company of the same sort. In the society of the unintelligent, the mind grows rusty for lack of exercise, as at tennis a ball that is served badly is badly returned. I should prefer an intelligent man without an education, if he were still young enough, to a man badly educated. A badly trained mind is like an actor whom the provinces have spoiled.

Thus, the diverse states of the soul are always correlative with those of the body. But the better to show this dependence, in its completeness and its causes, let us here make use of comparative anatomy; let us lay bare the organs of man and of animals. How can human nature be known, if we may not derive any light from an exact comparison of the structure of man and of animals?

In general, the form and the structure of the brains of quadrupeds are almost the same as those of the brain of man; the same shape, the same arrangement everywhere, with this essential difference, that of all the animals man is the one whose brain is largest, and, in proportion to its mass, more convoluted than the brain of any other animal; then come the monkey, the beaver, the elephant, the dog, the fox, the cat. These animals are most like man, for among them, too, one notes the same progressive analogy in relation to the *corpus callosum* in which Lancisi†—anticipating the late M. de la Peyronie‡—established the seat of the soul. The latter, however, illustrated the theory by innumerable experiments. Next after all the quadrupeds, birds have the largest brains. Fish have large heads, but these are void of sense, like the heads of many men. Fish have no *corpus callosum,* and very little brain, while insects entirely lack brain.

I shall not launch out into any more detail about the varieties of nature, nor into conjectures concerning them, for there is an infinite number of both, as any one can see by reading no further than the treatises of Willis§ *De Cerebro* and *De Anima Brutorum.*

I shall draw the conclusions which follow clearly from these incontestable observations: 1st, that the fiercer animals are, the less brain they have; 2d, that this organ seems to increase in size in proportion to the gentleness of the animal; 3d, that nature seems here eternally to impose a singular

---

*i.e., to a meeting of the royal council where he would be at the mercy of the King, who in fact had him killed, Dec. 23, 1588.

†Giovanni Lancisi (1654–1720), an Italian physician and botanist who wrote a noted treatise on heart disease, among other works.

‡F. G. de la Peyronie (1678–1747), a surgeon and instructor in anatomy who founded the Academy of Surgery at Paris.

§Thomas Willis (1621–75), an English physician, wrote works on the anatomy of the brain both in humans and in animals.

condition, that the more one gains in intelligence the more one loses in instinct. Does this bring gain or loss?

Do not think, however, that I wish to infer by that, that the size alone of the brain, is enough to indicate the degree of tameness in animals: the quality must correspond to the quantity, and the solids and liquids must be in that due equilibrium which constitutes health.

If, as is ordinarily observed, the imbecile does not lack brain, his brain will be deficient in its consistency—for instance, in being too soft. The same thing is true of the insane, and the defects of their brains do not always escape our investigation. But if the causes of imbecility, insanity, etc., are not obvious, where shall we look for the causes of the diversity of all minds? They would escape the eyes of a lynx and of an argus. A mere nothing, a tiny fibre, something that could never be found by the most delicate anatomy, would have made of Erasmus and Fontenelle two idiots, and Fontenelle himself speaks of this very fact in one of his best dialogues.

Willis has noticed in addition to the softness of the brain-substance in children, puppies, and birds, that the *corpora striata* are obliterated and discolored in all these animals, and that the striations are as imperfectly formed as in paralytics. . . . .

However cautious and reserved one may be about the consequences that can be deduced from these observations, and from many other concerning the kind of variation in the organs, nerves, etc., [one must admit that] so many different varieties can not be the gratuitous play of nature. They prove at least the necessity for a good and vigorous physical organization, since throughout the animal kingdom the soul gains force with the body and acquires keenness, as the body gains strength.

Let us pause to contemplate the varying capacity of animals to learn. Doubtless the analogy best framed leads the mind to think that the causes we have mentioned produce all the difference that is found between animals and men, although we must confess that our weak understanding, limited to the coarsest observations, can not see the bonds that exist between cause and effects. This is a kind of harmony that philosophers will never know.

Among animals, some learn to speak and sing; they remember tunes, and strike the notes as exactly as a musician. Others, for instance the ape, show more intelligence, and yet can not learn music. What is the reason for this, except some defect in the organs of speech? But is this defect so essential to the structure that it could never be remedied? In a word, would it be absolutely impossible to teach the ape a language? I do not think so.

I should choose a large ape in preference to any other, until by some good fortune another kind should be discovered, more like us, for nothing prevents there being such an one in regions unknown to us. The ape resembles us so strongly that naturalists have called it "wild man" or "man of the woods". I should take it in the condition of the pupils of Amman,* that is to say, I should not want it to be too young or too old; for apes that are brought to Europe are usually too old. I would choose the one with the most intelligent face, and the one which, in a thousand little ways, best lived up to its look of intelligence. Finally not considering myself worthy to be his master, I should put him in the school of that excellent teacher whom I have just named, or with another teacher equally skilful, if there is one.

You know by Amman's work, and by all those who have interpreted his method, all the wonders he has been able to accomplish for those born deaf. In their eyes he discovered ears, as he himself explains, and in how short a time! In short he taught them to hear, speak, read, and write. I grant that a deaf person's eyes see more clearly and are keener than if he were not deaf, for the loss

---

*J. C. Amman (1669–1730), a Swiss teacher of deaf mutes.

of one member or sense can increase the strength or acuteness of another, but apes see and hear, they understand what they hear and see, and grasp so perfectly the signs that are made to them, that I doubt not that they would surpass the pupils of Amman in any other game or exercise. Why then should the education of monkeys be impossible? Why might not the monkey, by dint of great pains, at last imitate after the manner of deaf mutes, the motions necessary for pronunciation? I do not dare decide whether the monkey's organs of speech, however trained, would be incapable of articulation. But, because of the great analogy between ape and man and because there is no known animal whose external and internal organs so strikingly resemble man's, it would surprise me if speech were absolutely impossible to the ape. Locke, who was certainly never suspected of credulity, found no difficulty in believing the story told by Sir William Temple in his memoirs, about a parrot which could answer rationally, and which had learned to carry on a kind of connected conversation, as we do. I know that people have ridiculed this great metaphysician; but suppose some one should have announced that reproduction sometimes takes place without eggs or a female, would he have found many partisans? Yet M. Trembley* has found cases where reproduction takes place without copulation and by fission. Would not Amman too have passed for mad if he had boasted that he could instruct scholars like his in so short a time, before he had happily accomplished the feat? His successes have, however, astonished the world; and he, like the author of *The History of Polyps,* has risen to immortality at one bound. Whoever owes the miracles that he works to his own genius surpasses, in my opinion, the man who owes his to chance. He who has discovered the art of adorning the most beautiful of the kingdoms [of nature], and of giving it perfections that it did not have, should be rated above an idle creator of frivolous systems, or a painstaking author of sterile discover-

ies. Amman's discoveries are certainly of a much greater value; he has freed men from the instinct to which they seemed to be condemned, and has given them ideas, intelligence, or in a word, a soul which they would never have had. What greater power than this!

Let us not limit the resources of nature; they are infinite, especially when reinforced by great art.

Could not the device which opens the Eustachian canal of the deaf, open that of apes? Might not a happy desire to imitate the master's pronunciation, liberate the organs of speech in animals that imitate so many other signs with such skill and intelligence? Not only do I defy any one to name any really conclusive experiment which proves my view impossible and absurd; but such is the likeness of the structure and functions of the ape to ours that I have very little doubt that if this animal were properly trained he might at last be taught to pronounce, and consequently to know, a language. Then he would no longer be a wild man, nor a defective man, but he would be a perfect man, a little gentleman, with as much matter or muscle as we have, for thinking and profiting by his education.

The transition from animals to man is not violent, as true philosophers will admit. What was man before the invention of words and the knowledge of language? An animal of his own species with much less instinct than the others. In those days, he did not consider himself king over the other animals, nor was he distinguished from the ape, and from the rest, except as the ape itself differs from the other animals, i.e., by a more intelligent face. Reduced to the bare intuitive knowledge of the Leibnizians he saw only shapes and colors, without being able to distinguish between them: the same, old as young, child at all ages, he lisped out his sensations and his needs, as a dog that is

---

*Abraham Trembley (1710–84), Swiss naturalist who wrote a celebrated work on polyps.

hungry or tired of sleeping, asks for something to eat, or for a walk.

Words, languages, laws, sciences, and the fine arts have come, and by them finally the rough diamond of our mind has been polished. Man has been trained in the same way as animals. He has become an author, as they became beasts of burden. A geometrician has learned to perform the most difficult demonstrations and calculations, as a monkey has learned to take his little hat off and on, and to mount his tame dog. All has been accomplished through signs, every species has learned what it could understand, and in this way men have acquired symbolic knowledge, still so called by our German philosophers.

Nothing, as any one can see, is so simple as the mechanism of our education. Everything may be reduced to sounds or words that pass from the mouth of one through the ears of another into his brain. At the same moment, he perceives through his eyes the shape of the bodies of which these words are the arbitrary signs.

But who was the first to speak? Who was the first teacher of the human race? Who invented the means of utilizing the plasticity of our organism? I can not answer: the names of these first splendid geniuses have been lost in the night of time. But art is the child of nature, so nature must have long preceded it.

We must think that the men who were the most highly organized, those on whom nature had lavished her richest gifts, taught the others. They could not have heard a new sound for instance, nor experienced new sensations, nor been struck by all the varied and beautiful objects that compose the ravishing spectacle of nature without finding themselves in the state of mind of the deaf man of Chartres, whose experience was first related by the great Fontenelle, when, at forty years, he heard for the first time, the astonishing sound of bells.

Would it be absurd to conclude from this that the first mortals tried after the manner of this deaf man, or like animals and like mutes (another kind of animals), to express their new feelings by motions depending on the nature of their imagination, and therefore afterwards by spontaneous sounds, distinctive of each animal, as the natural expression of their surprise, their joy, their ecstasies and their needs? For doubtless those whom nature endowed with finer feeling had also greater facility in expression.

That is the way in which, I think, men have used their feeling and their instinct to gain intelligence and then have employed their intelligence to gain knowledge. Those are the ways, so far as I can understand them, in which men have filled the brain with the ideas, for the reception of which nature made it. Nature and man have helped each other; and the smallest beginnings have, little by little, increased, until everything in the universe could be as easily described as a circle.

As a violin string or a harpsichord key vibrates and gives forth sound, so the cerebral fibres, struck by waves of sound, are stimulated to render or repeat the words that strike them. And as the structure of the brain is such that when eyes well formed for seeing, have once perceived the image of objects, the brain can not help seeing their images and their differences, so when the signs of these differences have been traced or imprinted in the brain, the soul necessarily examines their relations—an examination that would have been impossible without the discovery of signs or the invention of language. At the time when the universe was almost dumb, the soul's attitude toward all objects was that of a man without any idea of proportion toward a picture or a piece of sculpture, in which he could distinguish nothing; or the soul was like a little child (for the soul was then in its infancy) who, holding in his hand small bits of straw or wood, sees them in a vague and superficial way without being able to count or distinguish them. But let some one attach a kind of banner, or standard, to this bit of wood (which perhaps is called a mast), and another banner to another similar object; let the first be known by the symbol 1, and the second by the symbol or number 2, then the child will be able to count the objects, and in this way he will learn all of arithmetic. As soon as one figure seems equal to another in its numerical sign, he will decide without difficulty that they are two different bodies, that 1 + 1 make 2, and 2 + 2 make 4, etc.

This real or apparent likeness of figures is the fundamental basis of all truths and of all we know. Among these sciences, evidently those whose signs are less simple and less sensible are harder to understand than the others, because more talent is required to comprehend and combine the immense number of words by which such sciences express the truths in their province. On the other hand, the sciences that are expressed by numbers or by other small signs, are easily learned; and without doubt this facility rather than its demonstrability is what has made the fortune of algebra.

All this knowledge, with which vanity fills the balloon-like brains of our proud pedants, is therefore but a huge mass of words and figures, which form in the brain all the marks by which we distinguish and recall objects. All our ideas are awakened after the fashion in which the gardener who knows plants recalls all stages of their growth at sight of them. These words and the objects designated by them are so connected in the brain that it is comparatively rare to imagine a thing without the name or sign that is attached to it.

I always use the word "imagine", because I think that everything is the work of imagination, and that all the faculties of the soul can be correctly reduced to pure imagination in which they all consist. Thus judgment, reason, and memory are not absolute parts of the soul, but merely modifications of this kind of medullary screen upon which images of the objects painted in the eye are projected as by a magic lantern.

But if such is the marvelous and incomprehensible result of the structure of the brain, if everything is perceived and explained by imagination, why should we divide the sensitive principle which thinks in man? Is not this a clear inconsistency in the partisans of the simplicity of the mind? For a thing that is divided can no longer without absurdity be regarded as indivisible. See to what one is brought by the abuse of language and by those fine words (spirituality, immateriality, etc.) used haphazard and not understood even by the most brilliant.

Nothing is easier than to prove a system based, as this one is, on the intimate feeling and personal experience of each individual. If the imagination, or, let us say, that fantastic part of the brain whose nature is as unknown to us as its way of acting, be naturally small or weak, it will hardly be able to compare the analogy or the resemblance of its ideas, it will be able to see only what is face to face with it, or what affects it very strongly; and how will it see all this! Yet it is always imagination which apperceives, and imagination which represents to itself all objects along with their names and symbols; and thus, once again, imagination is the soul, since it plays all the rôles of the soul. By the imagination, by its flattering brush, the cold skeleton of reason takes on living and ruddy flesh; by the imagination the sciences flourish, the arts are adorned, the wood speaks, the echoes sigh, the rocks weep, marble breathes, and all inanimate objects gain life. It is imagination again which adds the piquant charm of voluptuousness to the tenderness of an amorous heart; which makes tenderness bud in the study of the philosopher and of the dusty pedant, which, in a word, creates scholars as well as orators and poets. Foolishly decried by some, vainly praised by others, and misunderstood by all; it follows not only in the train of the graces and of the fine arts, it not only describes, but can also measure nature. It reasons, judges, analyzes, compares, and investigates. Could it feel so keenly the beauties of the pictures drawn for it, unless it discovered their relations? No, just as it can not turn its thoughts on the pleasures of

La Mettrie: Man a Machine

the senses, without enjoying their perfection or their voluptuousness, it can not reflect on what it has mechanically conceived, without thus being judgment itself.

The more the imagination or the poorest talent is exercised, the more it gains in *embonpoint*, so to speak, and the larger it grows. It becomes sensitive, robust, broad, and capable of thinking. The best of organisms has need of this exercise.

Man's preeminent advantage is his organism. In vain all writers of books on morals fail to regard as praiseworthy those qualities that come by nature, esteeming only the talents gained by dint of reflection and industry. For whence come, I ask, skill, learning, and virtue, if not from a disposition that makes us fit to become skilful, wise and virtuous? And whence again, comes this disposition, if not from nature? Only through nature do we have any good qualities; to her we owe all that we are. Why then should I not esteem men with good natural qualities as much as men who shine by acquired and as it were borrowed virtues? Whatever the virtue may be, from whatever source it may come, it is worthy of esteem; the only question is, how to estimate it. Mind, beauty, wealth, nobility, although the children of chance, all have their own value, as skill, learning and virtue have theirs. Those upon whom nature has heaped her most costly gifts should pity those to whom these gifts have been refused; but, in their character of experts, they may feel their superiority without pride. A beautiful woman would be as foolish to think herself ugly, as an intelligent man to think himself a fool. An exaggerated modesty (a rare fault, to be sure) is a kind of ingratitude towards nature. An honest pride, on the contrary, is the mark of a strong and beautiful soul, revealed by manly features moulded by feeling.

If one's organism is an advantage, and the preeminent advantage, and the source of all others, education is the second. The best made brain would be a total loss without it, just as the best constituted man

would be but a common peasant, without knowledge of the ways of the world. But, on the other hand, what would be the use of the most excellent school, without a matrix perfectly open to the entrance and conception of ideas? It is. . . .impossible to impart a single idea to a man deprived of all his senses. . . . .

But if the brain is at the same time well organized and well educated, it is a fertile soil, well sown, that brings forth a hundredfold what it has received: or (to leave the figures of speech often needed to express what one means, and to add grace to truth itself) the imagination, raised by art to the rare and beautiful dignity of genius, apprehends exactly all the relations of the ideas it has conceived, and takes in easily an astounding number of objects, in order to deduce from them a long chain of consequences, which are again but new relations, produced by a comparison with the first, to which the soul finds a perfect resemblance. Such is, I think, the generation of intelligence. I say "finds" as I before gave the epithet "apparent" to the likeness of objects, not because I think that our senses are always deceivers, as Father Malebranche has claimed, or that our eyes, naturally a little unsteady, fail to see objects as they are in themselves, (though microscopes prove this to us every day) but in order to avoid any dispute with the Pyrrhonians, among whom Bayle* is well known.

I say of truth in general what M. de Fontenelle says of certain truths in particular, that we must sacrifice it in order to remain on good terms with society. And it accords with the gentleness of my character, to avoid all disputes unless to whet conversation. The Cartesians would here in vain make an onset upon me with their innate ideas. I certainly would not give myself a quarter of the trouble that M. Locke took, to attack such chimeras. In truth, what is the

---

*Pierre Bayle (1647–1706), author of a celebrated *Dictionary* (1697) that was in effect a work of philosophical skepticism.

use of writing a ponderous volume to prove a doctrine which became an axiom three thousand years ago?

According to the principles which we have laid down, and which we consider true; he who has the most imagination should be regarded as having the most intelligence or genius, for all these words are synonymous; and again, only by a shameful abuse [of terms] do we think that we are saying different things, when we are merely using different words, different sounds, to which no idea or real distinction is attached.

The finest, greatest, or strongest imagination is then the one most suited to the sciences as well as to the arts. I do not pretend to say whether more intellect is necessary to excel in the art of Aristotle or of Descartes than to excel in that of Euripedes or of Sophocles, and whether nature has taken more trouble to make Newton than to make Corneille, though I doubt this. But it is certain that imagination alone, differently applied, has produced their diverse triumphs and their immortal glory.

If one is known as having little judgment and much imagination, this means that the imagination has been left too much alone, has, as it were, occupied most of the time in looking at itself in the mirror of its sensations, has not sufficiently formed the habit of examining the sensations themselves attentively. [It means that the imagination] has been more impressed by images than by their truth or their likeness.

Truly, so quick are the responses of the imagination that if attention, that key or mother of the sciences, does not do its part, imagination can do little more than run over and skim its objects.

See that bird on the bough: it seems always ready to fly away. Imagination is like the bird, always carried onward by the turmoil of the blood and the animal spirits. One wave leaves a mark, effaced by the one that follows; the soul pursues it, often in vain: it must expect to regret the loss of that which it has not quickly enough seized and

fixed. Thus, imagination, the true image of time, is being ceaselessly destroyed and renewed.

Such is the chaos and the continuous quick succession of our ideas: they drive each other away even as one wave yields to another. Therefore, if imagination does not, as it were, use one set of its muscles to maintain a kind of equilibrium with the fibres of the brain, to keep its attention for a while upon an object that is on the point of disappearing, and to prevent itself from contemplating prematurely another object—[unless the imagination does all this], it will never be worthy of the fine name of judgment. It will express vividly what it has perceived in the same fashion: it will create orators, musicians, painters, poets, but never a single philosopher. On the contrary, if the imagination be trained from childhood to bridle itself and to keep from being carried away by its own impetuosity—an impetuosity which creates only brilliant enthusiasts—and to check, to restrain, its ideas, to examine them in all their aspects in order to see all sides of an object, then the imagination, ready in judgment, will comprehend the greatest possible sphere of objects, through reasoning; and its vivacity (always so good a sign in children, and only needing to be regulated by study and training) will be only a far-seeing insight without which little progress can be made in the sciences.

Such are the simple foundations upon which the edifice of logic has been reared. Nature has built these foundations for the whole human race, but some have used them, while others have abused them.

In spite of all these advantages of man over animals, it is doing him honor to place him in the same class. For, truly, up to a certain age, he is more of an animal than they, since at birth he has less instinct. What animal would die of hunger in the midst of a river of milk? Man alone. Like that child of olden time to whom a modern writer, refers, following Arnobius, he knows neither the foods suitable for him, nor the water that can drown him, nor the fire that can reduce him to ashes. Light a wax candle for the first time under a child's eyes, and he will mechanically put his fingers in the flame as if to find out what is the new thing that he sees. It is at his own cost that he will learn of the danger, but he will not be caught again. Or, put the child with an animal on a precipice, the child alone falls off; he drowns where the animal would save itself by swimming. At fourteen or fifteen years the child knows hardly anything of the great pleasures in store for him, in the reproduction of his species; when he is a youth, he does not know exactly how to behave in a game which nature teaches animals so quickly. He hides himself as if he were ashamed of taking pleasure, and of having been made to be happy, while animals frankly glory in being cynics. Without education, they are without prejudices. For one more example, let us observe a dog and a child who have lost their master on a highway: the child cries and does not know to what saint to pray, while the dog, better helped by his sense of smell than the child by his reason, soon finds his master.

Thus nature made us to be lower than animals or at least to exhibit all the more, because of that native inferiority, the wonderful efficacy of education which alone raises us from the level of the animals and lifts us above them. But shall we grant this same distinction to the deaf and to the blind, to imbeciles, madmen, or savages, or to those who have been brought up in the woods with animals; to those who have lost their imagination through melancholia, or in short to all those animals in human form who give evidence of only the rudest instinct? No, all these, men of body but not of mind, do not deserve to be classed by themselves.

We do not intend to hide from ourselves the arguments that can be brought forward against our belief and in favor of a primitive distinction between men and animals.

Some say that there is in man a natural law, a knowledge of good and evil, which has never been imprinted on the heart of animals.

But is this objection, or rather this assertion, based on observation? Any assertion unfounded on observation may be rejected by a philosopher. Have we ever had a single experience which convinces us that man alone has been enlightened by a ray denied all other animals? If there is no such experience, we can no more know what goes on in animals' minds or even in the minds of other men, than we can help feeling what affects the inner part of our own being. We know that we think, and feel remorse—an intimate feeling forces us to recognize this only too well; but this feeling in us is insufficient to enable us to judge the remorse of others. That is why we have to take others at their word, or judge them by the sensible and external signs we have noticed in ourselves when we experienced the same accusations of conscience and the same torments.

In order to decide whether animals which do not talk have received the natural law, we must, therefore, have recourse to those signs to which I have just referred, if any such exist. The facts seem to prove it. A dog that bit the master who was teasing it, seemed to repent a minute afterwards; it looked sad, ashamed, afraid to show itself, and seemed to confess its guilt by a crouching and downcast air. History offers us a famous example of a lion which would not devour a man abandoned to its fury, because it recognized him as its benefactor. How much might it be wished that man himself always showed the same gratitude for kindness, and the same respect for humanity! Then we should no longer fear either ungrateful wretches, or wars which are the plague of the human race and the real executioners of the natural law.

But a being to which nature has given such a precocious and enlightened instinct, which judges, combines, reasons, and deliberates as far as the sphere of its activity extends and permits, a being which feels attachment because of benefits received, and which leaving a master who treats it badly goes to seek a better one, a being with a structure like ours, which performs the same acts, has the same passions, the same griefs, the same pleasures, more or less intense according to the sway of the imagination and the delicacy of the nervous organization—does not such a being show clearly that it knows its faults and ours, understands good and evil, and in a word, has consciousness of what it does? Would its soul, which feels the same joys, the same mortification and the same discomfiture which we feel, remain utterly unmoved by disgust when it saw a fellow-creature torn to bits, or when it had itself pitilessly dismembered this fellow-creature? If this be granted, it follows that the precious gift now in question would not have been denied to animals: for since they show us sure signs of repentance, as well as of intelligence, what is there absurd in thinking that beings, almost as perfect machines as ourselves, are, like us, made to understand and to feel nature?

Let no one object that animals, for the most part, are savage beasts, incapable of realizing the evil that they do; for do all men discriminate better between vice and virtue? There is ferocity in our species as well as in theirs. Men who are in the barbarous habit of breaking the natural law are not tormented as much by it, as those who transgress it for the first time, and who have not been hardened by the force of habit. The same thing is true of animals as of men—both may be more or less ferocious in temperament, and both become more so by living with others like themselves. But a gentle and peaceful animal which lives among other animals of the same disposition and of gentle nurture, will be an enemy of blood and carnage; it will blush internally at having shed blood. There is perhaps this difference, that since among animals everything is sacrificed to their needs, to their

pleasures, to the necessities of life, which they enjoy more than we, their remorse apparently should not be as keen as ours, because we are not in the same state of necessity as they. Custom perhaps dulls and perhaps stifles remorse as well as pleasures.

But I will suppose for a moment that I am utterly mistaken in concluding that almost all the world holds a wrong opinion on this subject, while I alone am right. I will grant that animals, even the best of them, do not know the difference between moral good and evil, that they have no recollection of the trouble taken for them, of the kindness done them, no realization of their own virtues. [I will suppose], for instance, that this lion, to which I, like so many others, have referred, does not remember at all that it refused to kill the man, abandoned to its fury, in a combat more inhuman than one could find among lions, tigers and bears, put together. For our compatriots fight, Swiss against Swiss, brother against brother, recognize each other, and yet capture and kill each other without remorse, because a prince pays for the murder. I suppose in short that the natural law has not been given animals. What will be the consequences of this supposition? Man is not moulded from a costlier clay; nature has used but one dough, and has merely varied the leaven. Therefore if animals do not repent for having violated this inmost feeling which I am discussing, or rather if they absolutely lack it, man must necessarily be in the same condition. Farewell then to the natural law and all the fine treatises published about it! The whole animal kingdom in general would be deprived of it. But, conversely, if man can not dispense with the belief that when health permits him to be himself, he always distinguishes the upright, humane, and virtuous, from those who are not humane, virtuous, nor honorable: that it is easy to tell vice from virtue, by the unique pleasure and the peculiar repugnance that seem to be their natural effects, it follows that animals, composed of the same matter, lacking perhaps only one

L' H O M M E
M A C H I N E.

I L ne fuffit pas à un Sage d'étudier la Nature & la Vérité ; il doit ofer la dire en faveur du petit nombre de ceux qui veulent & peuvent penfer; car pour les autres, qui font volontairement Esclaves des Préjugés, il ne leur eft pas plus poffible d'atteindre la Vérité, qu'aux Grenouilles de voler.

JE réduis à deux, les Syftêmes des Philofophes fur l'ame de l'Homme. Le prémier, & le plus ancien, eft le Syftême du Matérialisme; le fecond eft celui du Spiritualisme.

LES Métaphificiens, qui ont infinué que la Matière pourroit bien avoir la faculté de penfer, n'ont pas deshonoré leur Raifon. Pourquoi? C'eft qu'ils ont un avantage, (car ici c'en eft un,) de s'être mal exprimés. En effet, demander fi la Matière peut penfer, fans la confidérer autrement qu'en elle-même, c'eft demander fi la Matière peut marquer les heures. On

B   voit

The first page of *L'Homme Machine* by Julien Offray de La Mettrie. This copy, in the Bibliothèque Nationale, was published in London in 1761.

degree of fermentation to make it exactly like man's, must share the same prerogatives of animal nature, and that thus there exists no soul or sensitive substance without remorse. The following consideration will reinforce these observations.

It is impossible to destroy the natural law. The impress of it on all animals is so strong, that I have no doubt that the wildest and most savage have some moments of repentance. I believe that that cruel maid of Chalons in Champagne must have sorrowed for her crime, if she really ate her sister. I think that the same thing is true of all those who commit crimes, even involuntary or temperamental crimes; true of Gaston of Orleans who could not help stealing; of a certain woman who was subject to the same crime when pregnant, and whose children inherited it; of the woman who, in the same condition, ate her husband; of that other woman who killed her children, salted their bodies, and ate a piece of them every day, as a little relish; of that daughter of a thief and cannibal who at twelve years followed in his steps, although she had been orphaned when she was a year old, and had been brought up by honest people; to say nothing of many other examples of which the records of our observers are full, all of them proving that there are a thousand hereditary vices and virtues which are transmitted from parents to children as those of the foster mother pass to the children she nurses. Now, I believe and admit that these wretches do not for the most part feel at the time the enormity of their actions. Bulimia, or canine hunger, for example, can stifle all feeling; it is a mania of the stomach that one is compelled to satisfy, but what remorse must be in store for those women, when they come to themselves and grow sober, and remember the crimes they have committed aginst those they held most dear! What a punishment for an involuntary crime which they could not resist, of which they had no consciousness whatever! However, this is apparently not enough for the judges. For of these women, of whom I tell,

one was cruelly beaten and burned, and another was buried alive. I realize all that is demanded by the interest of society. But doubtless it is much to be wished that excellent physicians might be the only judges. They alone could tell the innocent criminal from the guilty. If reason is the slave of a depraved or mad desire, how can it control the desire?

But if crime carries with it its own more or less cruel punishment, if the most continued and most barbarous habit can not entirely blot out repentance in the cruelest hearts, if criminals are lacerated by the very memory of their deeds, why should we frighten the imagination of weak minds, by a hell, by specters, and by precipices of fire even less real than those of Pascal? Why must we have recourse to fables, as an honest pope once said himself, to torment even the unhappy wretches who are executed, because we do not think that they are sufficiently punished by their own conscience, their first executioner? I do not mean to say that all criminals are unjustly punished; I only maintain that those whose will is depraved, and whose conscience is extinguished, are punished enough by their remorse when they come to themselves, a remorse, I venture to assert, from which nature should in this case have delivered unhappy souls dragged on by a fatal necessity.

Criminals, scoundrels, ingrates, those in short without natural feelings, unhappy tyrants who are unworthy of life, in vain take a cruel pleasure in their barbarity, for there are calm moments of reflection in which the avenging conscience arises, testifies against them, and condemns them to be almost ceaselessly torn to pieces at their own hands. Whoever torments men is tormented by himself; and the sufferings that he will experience will be the just measure of those that he has inflicted.

On the other hand, there is so much pleasure in doing good, in recognizing and appreciating what one receives, so much satisfaction in practising virtue, in being gentle, humane, kind, charitable, compassionate and generous (for this one word includes all the virtues), that I consider as sufficiently punished any one who is unfortunate enough not to have been born virtuous.

We were not originally made to be learned; we have become so perhaps by a sort of abuse of our organic faculties, and at the expense of the State which nourishes a host of sluggards whom vanity has adorned with the name of philosophers. Nature has created us all solely to be happy—yes, all of us from the crawling worm to the eagle lost in the clouds. For this cause she has given all animals some share of natural law, a share greater or less according to the needs of each animal's organs when in normal condition.

Now how shall we define natural law? It is a feeling that teaches us what we should not do, because we would not wish it to be done to us. Should I dare add to this common idea, that this feeling seems to me but a kind of fear or dread, as salutary to the race as to the individual; for may it not be true that we respect the purse and life of others only to save our own possessions, our honor, and ourselves; like those Ixions of Christianity* who love God and embrace so many fantastic virtues, merely because they are afraid of hell!

You see that natural law is but an intimate feeling that, like all other feelings (thought included), belongs also to imagination. Evidently, therefore, natural law does not presuppose education, revelation, nor legislator,—provided one does not propose to confuse natural law with civil laws, in the ridiculous fashion of the theologians.

The arms of fanaticism may destroy those who support these truths, but they will never destroy the truths themselves.

I do not mean to call in question the existence of a supreme being; on the contrary it seems to me that the greatest degree of probability is in favor of this belief. But since the existence of this being goes no further than that of any other toward proving the need of worship, it is a theoretic truth with very little practical value. Therefore, since we may say, after such long experience, that religion does not imply exact honesty, we are authorized by the same reasons to think that atheism does not exclude it.

Furthermore, who can be sure that the reason for man's existence is not simply the fact that he exists? Perhaps he was thrown by chance on some spot on the earth's surface, nobody knows how nor why, but simply that he must live and die, like the mushrooms which appear from day to day, or like those flowers which border the ditches and cover the walls.

Let us not lose ourselves in the infinite, for we are not made to have the least idea thereof, and are absolutely unable to get back to the origin of things. Besides it does not matter for our peace of mind, whether matter be eternal or have been created, whether there be or be not a God. How foolish to torment ourselves so much about things which we can not know, and which would not make us any happier even were we to gain knowledge about them!

But, some will say, read all such works as those of Fénelon, of Nieuwentyt, of Abadie, of Derham, of Rais, and the rest.† Well! what will they teach me or rather what have they taught me? They are only tiresome repetitions of zealous writers, one of them adds to the other only verbiage, more likely to strengthen than to undermine the foundations of atheism. The number of the evidences drawn from the spectacle of nature does not give these evidences any more force. Either the mere structure of a finger, of an ear, of an eye, a single observation of Malpighi‡ proves all, and doubtless much better than Descartes and Malebranche

---

*Ixion on account of treachery was forced into Erebus where, bound and scourged on a wheel of fire, he was made to cry "benefactors should be honored."

†i.e., theologians, of which this is a list of ones prominent in the 17th and 18th centuries.

‡Marcello Malpighi (1628–94), Italian anatomist and physiologist.

proved it, or all the other evidences prove nothing. Deists, and even Christians, should therefore be content to point out that throughout the animal kingdom the same aims are pursued and accomplished by an infinite number of different mechanisms, all of them however exactly geometrical. For what stronger weapons could there be with which to overthrow atheists? It is true that if my reason does not deceive me, man and the whole universe seem to have been designed for this unity of aim. The sun, air, water, the organism, the shape of bodies,—everything is brought to a focus in the eye as in a mirror that faithfully presents to the imagination all the objects reflected in it, in accordance with the laws required by the infinite variety of bodies which take part in vision. In ears we find everywhere a striking variety, and yet the difference of structure in men, animals, birds, and fishes, does not produce different uses. All ears are so mathematically made, that they tend equally to one and the same end, namely, hearing. But would Chance, the deist asks, be a great enough geometrician to vary thus, at pleasure, the works of which she is supposed to be the author, without being hindered by so great a diversity from gaining the same end? Again, the deist will bring forward as a difficulty those parts of the animal that are clearly contained in it for future use, the butterfly in the caterpillar, man in the sperm, a whole polyp in each of its parts, the valvule in the oval orifice, the lungs in the foetus, the teeth in their sockets, the bones in the fluid from which they detach themselves and (in an incomprehensible manner) harden. And since the partisans of this theory, far from neglecting anything that would strengthen it, never tire of piling up proof upon proof, they are willing to avail themselves of everything, even of the weakness of the mind in certain cases. Look, they say, at men like Spinoza, Vanini, Desbarreau, and Boindin, apostles who honor deism more than they harm it.* The duration of their health was the measure of their unbelief, and one rarely fails,

they add, to renounce atheism when the passions, with their instrument, the body, have grown weak.

That is certainly the most that can be said in favor of the existence of God: although the last argument is frivolous in that these conversions are short, and the mind almost always regains its former opinions and acts accordingly, as soon as it has regained or rather rediscovered its strength in that of the body. That is, at least, much more than was said by the physician Diderot, in his Pensées Philosophiques, a sublime work that will not convince a single atheist.† What reply can, in truth, be made to a man who says, "We do not know nature; causes hidden in her breast might have produced everything. In your turn, observe the polyp of Trembley: does it not contain in itself the causes which bring about regeneration? Why then would it be absurd to think that there are physical causes by reason of which everything has been made, and to which the whole chain of this vast universe is so necessarily bound and held that nothing which happens, could have failed to happen, — causes, of which we are so invincibly ignorant that we have had recourse to a God, who, as some aver, is not so much as a logical entity? Thus to destroy chance is not to prove the existence of a supreme being, since there may be some other thing which is neither chance nor God—I mean, nature. It follows that the study of nature can make only unbelievers; and the way of thinking of all its more successful investigators proves this."

The weight of the universe therefore far from crushing a real atheist does not even shake him. All these evidences of a creator, repeated thousands and thousands of times, evidences that are placed far above the comprehension of men like us, are self-

---

*These are the names of celebrated freethinkers or atheists. For Spinoza, see *GBWW*, Vol. 31.
†Diderot (1713–84), editor of the famous *Encyclopedie*, tried to show in his *Philosophical Reflections* (1746) that the discoveries of natural science prove the existence of God.

evident (however far one push the argument) only to the anti-Pyrrhonians, or to those who have enough confidence in their reason to believe themselves capable of judging on the basis of certain phenomena, against which, as you see, the atheists can urge others perhaps equally strong and absolutely opposed. For if we listen to the naturalists again, they will tell us that the very causes which, in a chemist's hands, by a chance combination, made the first mirror, in the hands of nature made the pure water, the mirror of the simple shepherdess; that the motion which keeps the world going could have created it, that each body has taken the place assigned to it by its own nature, that the air must have surrounded the earth, and that iron and the other metals are produced by internal motions of the earth, for one and the same reason; that the sun is as much a natural product as electricity; that it was not made to warm the earth and its inhabitants, whom it sometimes burns, any more than the rain was made to make the seeds grow, which it often spoils; that the mirror and the water were no more made for people to see themselves in, than were all other polished bodies with this same property; that the eye is in truth a kind of glass in which the soul can contemplate the image of objects as they are presented to it by these bodies, but that it is not proved that this organ was really made expressly for this contemplation, nor purposely placed in its socket, and in short that it may well be that Lucretius, the physician Lamy, and all Epicureans both ancient and modern were right when they suggested that the eye sees only because it is formed and placed as it is, and that, given once for all, the same rules of motion followed by nature in the generation and development of bodies, this marvelous organ could not have been formed and placed differently.

Such is the *pro* and the *con*, and the summary of those fine arguments that will eternally divide the philosophers. I do not take either side.*

This is what I said to one of my friends, a Frenchman, as frank a Pyrrhonian as I, a man of much merit, and worthy of a better fate. He gave me a very singular answer in regard to the matter. "It is true," he told me, "that the *pro* and *con* should not disturb at all the soul of a philosopher, who sees that nothing is proved with clearness enough to force his consent, and that the arguments offered on one side are neutralized by those of the other. However," he continued, "the universe will never be happy, unless it is atheistic." Here are this wretch's reasons. If atheism, said he, were generally accepted, all the forms of religion would then be destroyed and cut off at the roots. No more theological wars, no more soldiers of religion—such terrible soldiers! Nature infected with a sacred poison, would regain its rights and its purity. Deaf to all other voices, tranquil mortals would follow only the spontaneous dictates of their own being the only commands which can never be despised with impunity and which alone can lead us to happiness through the pleasant paths of virtue.

Such is natural law: whoever rigidly observes it is a good man and deserves the confidence of all the human race. Whoever fails to follow it scrupulously affects, in vain, the specious exterior of another religion; he is a scamp or a hypocrite whom I distrust.

After this, let a vain people think otherwise, let them dare affirm that even probity is at stake in not believing in revelation, in a word that another religion than that of nature is necessary, whatever it may be. Such an assertion is wretched and pitiable; and so is the good opinion which each one gives us of the religion he has embraced! We do not seek here the votes of the crowd. Whoever raises in his heart altars to superstition, is born to worship idols and not to thrill to virtue.

---

*La Mettrie here cites Virgil, *Eclogue III*, line 108, "Non nostrum inter vos tantas componere lites." ("Not mine betwixt such rivals to decide"; See *GBWW*, Vol. 13, p. 13.)

But since all the faculties of the soul depend to such a degree on the proper organization of the brain and of the whole body, that apparently they are but this organization itself, the soul is clearly an enlightened machine. For finally, even if man alone had received a share of natural law, would he be any less a machine for that? A few more wheels, a few more springs than in the most perfect animals, the brain proportionally nearer the heart and for this very reason receiving more blood—any one of a number of unknown causes might always produce this delicate conscience so easily wounded, this remorse which is no more foreign to matter than to thought, and in a word all the differences that are supposed to exist here. Could the organism then suffice for everything? Once more, yes; since thought visibly develops with our organs, why should not the matter of which they are composed be susceptible of remorse also, when once it has acquired, with time, the faculty of feeling?

The soul is therefore but an empty word, of which no one has any idea, and which an enlightened man should use only to signify the part in us that thinks. Given the least principle of motion, animated bodies will have all that is necessary for moving, feeling, thinking, repenting, or in a word for conducting themselves in the physical realm, and in the moral realm which depends upon it.

Yet we take nothing for granted; those who perhaps think that all the difficulties have not yet been removed shall now read of experiments that will completely satisfy them.

1. The flesh of all animals palpitates after death. This palpitation continues longer, the more cold blooded the animal is and the less it perspires. Tortoises, lizards, serpents, etc., are evidence of this.

2. Muscles separated from the body contract when they are stimulated.

3. The intestines keep up their peristaltic or vermicular motion for a long time.

4. According to Cowper, a simple injection of hot water reanimates the heart and the muscles.

5. A frog's heart moves for an hour or more after it has been removed from the body, especially when exposed to the sun or better still when placed on a hot table or chair. If this movement seems totally lost, one has only to stimulate the heart, and that hollow muscle beats again. Harvey made this same observation on toads.*

6. Bacon of Verulam in his treatise *Sylva Sylvarum* cites the case of a man convicted of treason, who was opened alive, and whose heart thrown into hot water leaped several times, each time less high, to the perpendicular height of two feet.

7. Take a tiny chicken still in the egg, cut out the heart and you will observe the same phenomena as before, under almost the same conditions. The warmth of the breath alone reanimates an animal about to perish in the air pump.

The same experiments, which we owe to Boyle and to Stenon, are made on pigeons, dogs, and rabbits.† Pieces of their hearts beat as their whole hearts would. The same movements can be seen in paws that have been cut off from moles.

8. The caterpillar, the worm, the spider, the fly, the eel—all exhibit the same phenomena; and in hot water, because of the fire it contains, the movement of the detached parts increases.

9. A drunken soldier cut off with one stroke of his sabre an Indian rooster's head. The animal remained standing, then walked, and ran: happening to run against a wall, it turned around, beat its wings still running, and finally fell down. As it lay on the ground, all the muscles of this rooster kept on moving. That is what I saw myself,

*For Harvey, see *GBWW*, Vol. 28; for Bacon, following, see *GBWW*, Vol. 30, which does not, however, include the work cited ("Forest of Forests"), published in 1627.
†Robert Boyle (1627–91), the chemist, was one of the great natural philosophers of the age; Nicolas Sténon (1631–87), a physician, wrote a work on the anatomy of the brain.

and almost the same phenomena can easily be observed in kittens or puppies with their heads cut off.

10. Polyps do more than move after they have been cut in pieces. In a week they regenerate to form as many animals as there are pieces. I am sorry that these facts speak against the naturalists' system of generation; or rather I am very glad of it, for let this discovery teach us never to reach a general conclusion even on the ground of all known (and most decisive) experiments.

Here we have many more facts than are needed to prove, in an incontestable way, that each tiny fibre or part of an organized body moves by a principle which belongs to it. Its activity, unlike voluntary motions, does not depend in any way on the nerves, since the movements in question occur in parts of the body which have no connection with the circulation. But if this force is manifested even in sections of fibres the heart, which is a composite of peculiarly connected fibres, must possess the same property. I did not need Bacon's story to persuade me of this. It was easy for me to come to this conclusion, both from the perfect analogy of the structure of the human heart with that of animals, and also from the very bulk of the human heart, in which this movement escapes our eyes only because it is smothered, and finally because in corpses all the organs are cold and lifeless. If executed criminals were dissected while their bodies are still warm, we should probably see in their hearts the same movements that are observed in the face-muscles of those that have been beheaded.

The motive principle of the whole body, and even of its parts cut in pieces, is such that it produces not irregular movements, as some have thought, but very regular ones, in warm blooded and perfect animals as well as in cold and imperfect ones. No resource therefore remains open to our adversaries but to deny thousands and thousands of facts which every man can easily verify.

If now any one ask me where is this innate force in our bodies, I answer that it very clearly resides in what the ancients called the parenchyma, that is to say, in the very substance of the organs not including the veins, the arteries, the nerves, in a word, that it resides in the organization of the whole body, and that consequently each organ contains within itself forces more or less active according to the need of them.

Let us now go into some detail concerning these springs of the human machine. All the vital, animal, natural, and automatic motions are carried on by their action. Is it not in a purely mechanical way that the body shrinks back when it is struck with terror at the sight of an unforeseen precipice, that the eyelids are lowered at the menace of a blow, as some have remarked, and that the pupil contracts in broad daylight to save the retina, and dilates to see objects in darkness? Is it not by mechanical means that the pores of the skin close in winter so that the cold can not penetrate to the interior of the blood vessels, and that the stomach vomits when it is irritated by poison, by a certain quantity of opium and by all emetics, etc.? that the heart, the arteries and the muscles contract in sleep as well as in waking hours, that the lungs serve as bellows continually in exercise,—that the heart contracts more strongly than any other muscle? . . .

I shall not go into any more detail concerning all these little subordinate forces, well known to all. But there is another more subtle and marvelous force, which animates them all; it is the source of all our feelings, of all our pleasures, of all our passions, and of all our thoughts: for the brain has its muscles for thinking, as the legs have muscles for walking. I wish to speak of this impetuous principle that Hippocrates calls *enormon* (soul).* This principle exists and has its seat in the brain at the origin of the nerves, by which it exercises its control over all the rest of the body. By this fact is explained all that can be explained, even to

---

*For Hippocrates, see *GBWW*, Vol. 10.

the surprising effects of maladies of the imagination. . . .

Look at the portrait of the famous Pope who is, to say the least, the Voltaire of the English. The effort, the energy of his genius are imprinted upon his countenance. It is convulsed. His eyes protrude from their sockets, the eyebrows are raised with the muscles of the forehead. Why? Because the brain is in travail and all the body must share in such a laborious deliverance. If there were not an internal cord which pulled the external ones, whence would come all these phenomena? To admit a soul as explanation of them, is to be reduced to [explaining phenomena by] the operations of the Holy Spirit.

In fact, if what thinks in my brain is not a part of this organ and therefore of the whole body, why does my blood boil, and the fever of my mind pass into my veins, when lying quietly in bed, I am forming the plan of some work or carrying on an abstract calculation? Put this question to men of imagination, to great poets, to men who are enraptured by the felicitous expression of sentiment, and transported by an exquisite fancy or by the charms of nature, of truth, or of virtue! By their enthusiasm, by what they will tell you they have experienced, you will judge the cause by its effects; by that harmony which Borelli, a mere anatomist, understood better than all the Leibnizians, you will comprehend the material unity of man. In short, if the nerve-tension which causes pain occasions also the fever by which the distracted mind loses its will-power, and if, conversely, the mind too much excited, disturbs the body (and kindles that inner fire which killed Bayle while he was still so young); if an agitation rouses my desire and my ardent wish for what, a moment ago, I cared nothing about, and if in their turn certain brain impressions excite the same longing and the same desires, then why should we regard as double what is manifestly one being? In vain you fall back on the power of the will, since for one order that the will gives, it bows a

hundred times to the yoke. And what wonder that in health the body obeys, since a torrent of blood and of animal spirits forces its obedience, and since the will has as ministers an invisible legion of fluids swifter than lightning and ever ready to do its bidding! But as the power of the will is exercised by means of the nerves, it is likewise limited by them.——

Does the result of jaundice surprise you? Do you not know that the color of bodies depends on the color of the glasses through which we look at them, and that whatever is the color of the humors, such is the color of objects, at least, for us, vain playthings of a thousand illusions? But remove this color from the aqueous humor of the eye, let the bile flow through its natural filter, then the soul having new eyes, will no longer see yellow. Again, is it not thus, by removing cataract, or by injecting the Eustachian canal, that sight is restored to the blind, or hearing to the deaf? How many people, who were perhaps only clever charlatans, passed for miracle workers in the dark ages! Beautiful the soul, and powerful the will which can not act save by permission of the bodily conditions, and whose tastes change with age and fever! Should we, then, be astonished that philosophers have always had in mind the health of the body, to preserve the health of the soul, that Pythagoras gave rules for the diet as carefully as Plato forbade wine? The regime suited to the body is always the one with which sane physicians think they must begin, when it is a question of forming the mind, and of instructing it in the knowledge of truth and virtue; but these are vain words in the disorder of illness, and in the tumult of the senses. Without the precepts of hygiene, Epictetus, Socrates, Plato, and the rest preach in vain:* all ethics is fruitless for one who lacks his share of temperance; it is the source of all virtues, as intemperance is the source of all vices.

Is more needed, (for why lose myself in

---

*For Epictetus, see *GBWW*, Vol. 12; for Socrates and Plato, see *GBWW*, Vol. 7.

discussion of the passions which are all explained by the term, *enormon,* of Hippocrates) to prove that man is but an animal, or a collection of springs which wind each other up, without our being able to tell at what point in this human circle, nature has begun? If these springs differ among themselves, these differences consist only in their position and in their degrees of strength, and never in their nature; wherefore the soul is but a principle of motion or a material and sensible part of the brain, which can be regarded, without fear or error, as the mainspring of the whole machine, having a visible influence on all the parts. The soul seems even to have been made for the brain, so that all the other parts of the system are but a kind of emanation from the brain. This will appear from certain observations, made on different embryos, which I shall now enumerate.

This oscillation, which is natural or suited to our machine, and with which each fibre and even each fibrous element, so to speak, seems to be endowed, like that of a pendulum, can not keep up forever. It must be renewed, as it loses strength, invigorated when it is tired, and weakened when it is disturbed by excess of strength and vigor. In this alone, true medicine consists.

The body is but a watch, whose watchmaker is the new chyle. Nature's first care, when the chyle enters the blood, is to excite in it a kind of fever which the chemists, who dream only of retorts, must have taken for fermentation. This fever produces a greater filtration of spirits, which mechanically animate the muscles and the heart, as if they had been sent there by order of the will.

These then are the causes or the forces of life which thus sustain for a hundred years that perpetual movement of the solids and the liquids which is as necessary to the first as to the second. But who can say whether the solids contribute more than the fluids to this movement or *vice versa?* All that we know is that the action of the former would soon cease without the help of the latter, that is, without the help of the fluids which

by their onset rouse and maintain the elasticity of the blood vessels on which their own circulation depends. From this it follows that after death the natural resilience of each substance is still more or less strong according to the remnants of life which it outlives, being the last to perish. So true is it that this force of the animal parts can be preserved and strengthened by that of the circulation, but that it does not depend on the strength of the circulation, since, as we have seen it can dispense with even the integrity of each member or organ.

I am aware that this opinion has not been relished by all scholars, and that Stahl especially had much scorn for it. This great chemist has wished to persuade us that the soul is the sole cause of all our movements. But this is to speak as a fanatic and not as a philosopher.

To destroy the hypothesis of Stahl, we need not make as great an effort as I find that others have done before me. We need only glance at a violinist. What flexibility, what lightness in his fingers! The movements are so quick, that it seems almost as if there were no succession. But I pray, or rather I challenge, the followers of Stahl who understand so perfectly all that our soul can do, to tell me how it could possibly execute so many motions so quickly, motions, moreover, which take place so far from the soul, and in so many different places. That is to suppose that a flute player could play brilliant cadences on an infinite number of holes that he could not know, and on which he could not even put his finger!

But let us say with M. Hecquet that all men may not go to Corinth.* Why should not Stahl have been even more favored by nature as a man than as a chemist and a practitioner? Happy mortal, he must have received a soul different from that of the rest of mankind,—a sovereign soul, which,

---

*Phillip Hecquet (1661–1737), noted French physician. The remark about Corinth is in fact a quotation from Horace, *Epistles,* I,17.

not content with having some control over the voluntary muscles, easily held the reins of all the movements of the body, and could suspend them, calm them, or excite them, at its pleasure! With so despotic a mistress, in whose hands were, in a sense, the beating of the heart, and the laws of circulation, there could certainly be no fever, no pain, no weariness. . . . ! The soul wills, and the springs play, contract or relax. But how did the springs of Stahl's machine get out of order so soon? He who has in himself so great a doctor, should be immortal.

Moreover, Stahl is not the only one who has rejected the principle of the vibration of organic bodies. Greater minds have not used the principle when they wished to explain the action of the heart. . . . etc. One need only read the *Institutions of Medicine* by Boerhaave* to see what laborious and enticing systems this great man was obliged to invent, by the labor of his mighty genius, through failure to admit that there is so wonderful a force in all bodies.

Willis and Perrault, minds of a more feeble stamp, but careful observers of nature (whereas nature was known to the famous Leyden professor only through others and second hand, so to speak) seem to have preferred to suppose a soul generally extended over the whole body, instead of the principle which we are describing. But according to this hypothesis (which was the hypothesis of Vergil and of all Epicureans, an hypothesis which the history of the polyp might seem at first sight to favor) the movements which go on after the death of the subject in which they inhere are due to a remnant of soul still maintained by the parts that contract, though, from the moment of death, these are not excited by the blood and the spirits. Whence it may be seen that these writers, whose solid works easily eclipse all philosophic fables, are deceived only in the manner of those who have endowed matter with the faculty of thinking, I mean to say, by having expressed themselves badly in obscure and meaningless terms. In truth, what is this remnant of a soul, if it is not the "moving force" of the Leibnizians (badly rendered by such an expression), which however Perrault in particular has really foreseen. See his *Treatise on the Mechanism of Animals.*

Now that it is clearly proved against the Cartesians, the followers of Stahl, the Malebranchists, and the theologians who little deserve to be mentioned here, that matter is self-moved, not only when organized, as in a whole heart, for example, but even when this organization has been destroyed, human curiosity would like to discover how a body, by the fact that it is originally endowed with the breath of life, finds itself adorned in consequence with the faculty of feeling, and thus with that of thought. And, heavens, what efforts have not been made by certain philosophers to manage to prove this! and what nonsense on this subject I have had the patience to read!

All that experience teaches us is that while movement persists, however slight it may be, in one or more fibres, we need only stimulate them to re-excite and animate this movement almost extinguished. This has been shown in the host of experiments with which I have undertaken to crush the systems. It is therefore certain that motion and feeling excite each other in turn, both in a whole body and in the same body when its structure is destroyed, to say nothing of certain plants which seem to exhibit the same phenomena of the union of feeling and motion.

But furthermore, how many excellent philosophers have shown that thought is but a faculty of feeling, and that the reasonable soul is but the feeling soul engaged in contemplating its ideas and in reasoning! This would be proved by the fact alone that when feeling is stifled, thought also is checked, for instance in apoplexy, in lethar-

---

*Herman Boerhaave (1668–1738), Dutch physician and philosophe, was among the foremost scientists of his age. He wrote numerous works, from some of which La Mettrie took the inspiration for this essay.

gy, in catalepsis, etc. For it is ridiculous to suggest that, during these stupors, the soul keeps on thinking even though it does not remember the ideas that it has had.

As to the development of feeling and motion, it is absurd to waste time seeking for its mechanism. The nature of motion is as unknown to us as that of matter. How can we discover how it is produced unless, like the author of "The History of the Soul," we resuscitate the old and unintelligible doctrine of substantial forms? I am then quite as content not to know how inert and simple matter becomes active and highly organized, as not to be able to look at the sun without red glasses; and I am as little disquieted concerning the other incomprehensible wonders of nature, the production of feeling and of thought in a being which earlier appeared to our limited eyes as a mere clod of clay.

Grant only that organized matter is endowed with a principle of motion, which alone differentiates it from the inorganic (and can one deny this in the face of the most incontestable observation?) and that among animals, as I have sufficiently proved, everything depends upon the diversity of this organization: these admissions suffice for guessing the riddle of substance and of man. It [thus] appears that there is but one [type of organization] in the universe, and that man is the most perfect [example]. He is to the ape, and to the most intelligent animals, as the planetary pendulum of Huyghens is to a watch of Julien Leroy.* More instruments, more wheels and more springs were necessary to mark the movements of the planets than to mark or strike the hours; and Vaucanson,† who needed more skill for making his flute player than for making his duck, would have needed still more to make a talking man, a mechanism no longer to be regarded as impossible, especially in the hands of another Prometheus. In like fashion, it was necessary that nature should use more elaborate art in making and sustaining a machine which for a whole century could mark all

motions of the heart and of the mind; for though one does not tell time by the pulse, it is at least the barometer of the warmth and the vivacity by which one may estimate the nature of the soul. I am right! The human body is a watch, a large watch constructed with such skill and ingenuity, that if the wheel which marks the seconds happens to stop, the minute wheel turns and keeps on going its round, and in the same way the quarter-hour wheel, and all the others go on running when the first wheels have stopped because rusty or, for any reason, out of order. Is it not for a similar reason that the stoppage of a few blood vessels is not enough to destroy or suspend the strength of the movement which is in the heart as in the mainspring of the machine; since, on the contrary, the fluids whose volume is diminished, having a shorter road to travel, cover the ground more quickly, borne on as by a fresh current which the energy of the heart increases in proportion to the resistance it encounters at the ends of the blood-vessels? And is not this the reason why the loss of sight (caused by the compression of the optic nerve and by its ceasing to convey the images of objects) no more hinders hearing, than the loss of hearing (caused by obstruction of the functions of the auditory nerve) implies the loss of sight? In the same way, finally, does not one man hear (except immediately after his attack) without being able to say that he hears, while another who hears nothing, but whose lingual nerves are uninjured in the brain, mechanically tells of all the dreams which pass through his mind? These phenomena do not surprise enlightened physicians at all. They know what to think about man's nature, and (more accurately to express myself in passing) of two physicians, the better one and the one who deserves more confidence is always, in my

---

*Huygens's *Treatise on Light,* another work, is in *GBWW,* Vol. 34; Leroy (1686–1759), celebrated French watchmaker.

†Jacques de Vaucanson (1709–82), noted inventor of his day.

opinion, the one who is more versed in the physique or mechanism of the human body, and who, leaving aside the soul and all the anxieties which this chimera gives to fools and to ignorant men, is seriously occupied only in pure naturalism.

Therefore let the pretended M. Charp deride philosophers who have regarded animals as machines. How different is my view! I believe that Descartes would be a man in every way worthy of respect, if, born in a century that he had not been obliged to enlighten, he had known the value of experiment and observation, and the danger of cutting loose from them. But it is none the less just for me to make an authentic reparation to this great man for all the insignificant philosophers—poor jesters, and poor imitators of Locke—who instead of laughing impudently at Descartes, might better realize that without him the field of philosophy, like the field of science without Newton, might perhaps be still uncultivated.*

This celebrated philosopher, it is true, was much deceived, and no one denies that. But at any rate he understood animal nature, he was the first to prove completely that animals are pure machines. And after a discovery of this importance demanding so much sagacity, how can we without ingratitude fail to pardon all his errors!

In my eyes, they are all atoned for by that great confession. For after all, although he extols the distinctness of the two substances, this is plainly but a trick of skill, a ruse of style, to make theologians swallow a poison, hidden in the shade of an analogy which strikes everybody else and which they alone fail to notice. For it is this, this strong analogy, which forces all scholars and wise judges to confess that these proud and vain beings, more distinguished by their pride than by the name of men however much they may wish to exalt themselves, are at bottom only animals and machines which, though upright, go on all fours. They all have this marvelous instinct, which is devel-

oped by education into mind, and which always has its seat in the brain, (or for want of that when it is lacking or hardened, in the medulla oblongata) and never in the cerebellum; for I have often seen the cerebellum injured, and other observers have found it hardened, when the soul has not ceased to fulfil its functions.

To be a machine, to feel, to think, to know how to distinguish good from bad, as well as blue from yellow, in a word, to be born with an intelligence and a sure moral instinct, and to be but an animal, are therefore characters which are no more contradictory, than to be an ape or a parrot and to be able to give oneself pleasure. . . . .I believe that thought is so little incompatible with organized matter, that it seems to be one of its properties on a par with electricity, the faculty of motion, impenetrability, extension, etc.

Do you ask for further observations? Here are some which are incontestable and which all prove that man resembles animals perfectly, in his origin as well as in all the points in which we have thought it essential to make the comparison. . . .

Let us observe man both in and out of his shell, let us examine young embryos of four, six, eight or fifteen days with a microscope; after that time our eyes are sufficient. What do we see? The head alone; a little round egg with two black points which mark the eyes. Before that, everything is formless, and one sees only a medullary pulp, which is the brain, in which are formed first the roots of the nerves, that is, the principle of feeling, and the heart, which already within this substance has the power of beating of itself; it is the *punctum saliens* of Malpighi, which perhaps already owes a part of its excitability to the influence of the nerves. Then little by little, one sees the head lengthen from the neck, which, in dilating, forms first the thorax in-

---

*For Descartes, see *GBWW*, Vol. 31; for Locke, see *GBWW*, Vol. 35.

side which the heart has already sunk, there to become stationary; below that is the abdomen, which is divided by a partition (the diaphragm). One of these enlargements of the body forms the arms, the hands, the fingers, the nails, and the hair; the other forms the thighs, the legs, the feet, etc., which differ only in their observed situation, and which constitute the support and the balancing pole of the body. The whole process is a strange sort of growth, like that of plants. On the tops of our heads is hair in place of which the plants have leaves and flowers; everywhere is shown the same luxury of nature, and finally the directing principle of plants is placed where we have our soul, that other quintessence of man.

Such is the uniformity of nature, which we are beginning to realize; and the analogy of the animal with the vegetable kingdom, of man with plant. Perhaps there even are animal plants, which in vegetating, either fight as polyps do, or perform other functions characteristic of animals. . . . .

We are veritable moles in the field of nature; we achieve little more than the mole's journey and it is our pride which prescribes limits to the limitless. We are in the position of a watch that should say (a writer of fables would make the watch a hero in a silly tale): "I was never made by that fool of a workman, I who divide time, who mark so exactly the course of the sun, who repeat alond the hours which I mark! No! that is impossible!" In the same way, we disdain, ungrateful wretches that we are, this common mother of all kingdoms, as the chemists say. We imagine, or rather we infer, a cause superior to that to which we owe all, and which truly has wrought all things in an inconceivable fashion. No; matter contains nothing base, except to the vulgar eyes which do not recognize her in her most splendid works; and nature is no stupid workman. She creates millions of men, with a facility and a pleasure more intense than the effort of a watchmaker in making the most complicated watch. Her power shines

forth equally in creating the lowliest insect and in creating the most highly developed man; the animal kingdom costs her no more than the vegetable, and the most splendid genius no more than a blade of wheat. Let us then judge by what we see of that which is hidden from the curiosity of our eyes and of our investigations, and let us not imagine anything beyond. Let us observe the ape, the beaver, the elephant, etc., in their operations. If it is clear that these activities can not be performed without intelligence, why refuse intelligence to these animals? And if you grant them a soul, you are lost, you fanatics! You will in vain say that you assert nothing about the nature of the animal soul and that you deny its immortality. Who does not see that this is a gratuitous assertion; who does not see that the soul of an animal must be either mortal or immortal, whichever ours [is], and that it must therefore undergo the same fate as ours, whatever that may be, and that thus [in admitting that animals have souls], you fall into Scylla in the effort to avoid Charybdis?

Break the chain of your prejudices, arm yourselves with the torch of experience, and you will render to nature the honor she deserves, instead of inferring anything to her disadvantage, from the ignorance in which she has left you. Only open wide your eyes, only disregard what you can not understand, and you will see that the ploughman whose intelligence and ideas extend no further than the bounds of his furrow, does not differ essentially from the greatest genius,—a truth which the dissection of Descartes's and of Newton's brains would have proved; you will be persuaded that the imbecile and the fool are animals with human faces, as the intelligent ape is a little man in another shape; in short, you will learn that since everything depends absolutely on difference of organization, a well constructed animal which has studied astronomy, can predict an eclipse, as it can predict recovery or death when it has used its genius and its clearness of vision, for a time, in the school of Hippocrates and at the bedside of the sick. By this line of observations and truths, we come to connect the admirable power of thought with matter, without being able to see the links, because the subject of this attribute is essentially unknown to us.

Let us not say that every machine or every animal perishes altogether or assumes another form after death, for we know absolutely nothing about the subject. On the other hand, to assert that an immortal machine is a chimera or a logical fiction, is to reason as absurdly as caterpillars would reason if, seeing the cast-off skins of their fellow-caterpillars, they should bitterly deplore the fate of their species, which to them would seem to come to nothing. The soul of these insects (for each animal has his own) is too limited to comprehend the metamorphoses of nature. Never one of the most skilful among them could have imagined that it was destined to become a butterfly. It is the same with us. What more do we know of our destiny than of our origin? Let us then submit to an invincible ignorance on which our happiness depends.

He who so thinks will be wise, just, tranquil about his fate, and therefore happy. He will await death without either fear or desire, and will cherish life (hardly understanding how disgust can corrupt a heart in this place of many delights); he will be filled with reverence, gratitude, affection, and tenderness for nature, in proportion to his feeling of the benefits he has received from nature; he will be happy, in short, in feeling nature, and in being present at the enchanting spectacle of the universe, and he will surely never destroy nature either in himself or in others. More than that! Full of humanity, this man will love human character even in his enemies. Judge how he will treat others. He will pity the wicked without hating them; in his eyes, they will be but mis-made men. But in pardoning the faults of the structure of mind and body, he will none the less admire the beauties and the virtues of both. Those whom nature shall have favored will seem to him to deserve more respect than those whom she has treated in step-motherly fashion. Thus, as we have seen, natural gifts, the source of all acquirements, gain from the lips and heart of the materialist, the homage which every other thinker unjustly refuses them. In short, the materialist, convinced, in spite of the protests of his vanity, that he is but a machine or an animal, will not maltreat his kind, for he will know too well the nature of those actions, whose humanity is always in proportion to the degree of the analogy proved above [between human beings and animals]; and following the natural law given to all animals, he will not wish to do to others what he would not wish them to do to him.

Let us then conclude boldly that man is a machine, and that in the whole universe there is but a single substance differently modified. This is no hypothesis set forth by dint of a number of postulates and assumptions; it is not the work of prejudice, nor even of my reason alone; I should have disdained a guide which I think to be so untrustworthy, had not my senses, bearing a torch, so to speak, induced me to follow reason by lighting the way themselves. Experience has thus spoken to me in behalf of reason; and in this way I have combined the two.

But it must have been noticed that I have not allowed myself even the most vigorous and immediately deduced reasoning, except as a result of a multitude of observations which no scholar will contest; and furthermore, I recognize only scholars as judges of the conclusions which I draw from the observations; and I hereby challenge every prejudiced man who is neither anatomist, nor acquainted with the only philosophy which can here be considered, that of the human body. Against so strong and solid an oak, what could the weak reeds of theology, of metaphysics, and of the schools, avail,—childish arms, like our parlor foils, that may well afford the pleasure of fencing, but can never wound an adversary. Need I say that I refer to the empty and trivial notions, to the pitiable and trite arguments that will be urged (as long as the shadow of prejudice or of superstition re- mains on earth) for the supposed incompatibility of two substances which meet and move each other unceasingly? Such is my system, or rather the truth, unless I am much deceived. It is short and simple. Dispute it now who will.

The Function of Criticism at the Present Time

Matthew Arnold

Editor's Introduction

Readers of *The Great Ideas Today* may recall Matthew Arnold's essay, "On Translating Homer," which appeared in these pages over a decade ago—to be exact, in 1971. On that occasion Arnold was described by the editors as "the preeminent English critic of his day" in a tradition that was held to include Dryden, Samuel Johnson, and T. S. Eliot. This judgment seemed right then and seems so now, when there are reasons to reprint another of Arnold's essays, "The Function of Criticism at the Present Time." These reasons are the presence elsewhere in this volume of a discussion of literary criticism in our own day, and the special character of Arnold's piece, which as its title suggests was something of a manifesto. It is interesting to compare what a great critic of another age thought criticism ought to be with what in fact it has become.

"The Function of Criticism at the Present Time" was originally published as the introduction to Arnold's *Essays in Criticism* (1865), the first of two collections of his critical writings he made during his lifetime. These writings, which appeared first as lectures or in periodicals, were for the most part devoted to single authors such as Tolstoy, Homer, and Wordsworth, of whom it may be noted that as they were by no means always English, neither were they necessarily contemporaries. Arnold was among the first, perhaps in some real sense he was really *the* first person to suppose that it might be of interest if the best authors of any time and place were passed, as it were, through a single critical intelligence and discussed from a single point of view, the point of view being what the essay here reprinted was at pains to define. Such an undertaking would have seemed superfluous, not to say impertinent, in the days of Johnson, Swift, Pope, and Dryden—not to speak of Milton and Ben Jonson in still earlier times—when it would have been assumed that the proper point of view in such matters was for the most part that which all well-educated and literate men knew and shared, and in which they needed no instruction. Such an undertaking would nowadays be thought impossible, perhaps, when a body of common reading, of common authors, can no longer be taken for granted in such an audience, if indeed there *is* any longer such an audience outside of academic circles, and even supposing a critic wished to address it.

Arnold was forty-three at the time this essay appeared, already well into the second phase of his career, of which the first had been devoted to poetry. Two collections of verse had been published by him, only to be withdrawn shortly afterward from a dissatisfaction which is implicit in the critical observations set forth here, and which Arnold stated at greater length in his writings on other poets. His conception of poetry was that it should be "a criticism of life," by which he meant, not that it should undertake to disapprove of life, whatever that may mean, but that by its depiction it should offer an imagined alternative, an idealization—life as it ought to be, rather than as it is. Arnold's own poems failed to do this, he felt; they could no more than indicate his despair of—his sense of isolation from—the life of his own age, which he thought lacking in unity, calmness, and coherence—virtues he could not render, unfortunately, in poetic terms. His critical writings were in praise of poets greater than himself, such as Homer and Sophocles, who he thought had done that, and as distinct from others, such as Chaucer, who in his opinion had not.

Such a conception of criticism is essentially moral, of course, and indeed Arnold was nothing if not moral—his criticism always implies a conception of human life as at best it may be lived. Because of this, he can seem old-fashioned, not to say quaint, by comparison with the critics of our own time, some of whom are certainly prescriptive in their views, though not from the tragic sense of life, as at bottom it was, that Arnold really had, while others are eloquent in analytic techniques, in psychological insights, in mythic constructs to which he could not pretend. Arnold survives, nevertheless, as a kind of cultural witness which he was proud to make, and which he would have thought the less of subsequent criticism if it could not make. He survives as such because what seemed to him the best kind of human life to live was what he thought he saw embodied in the best literature, and what he thought could be realized in the lives men actually live so far as they understood that literature and the possibilities it presented to them. This deep sense of connection in him between literature and life—between poetry and ideas, as he might have said—has continued to interest posterity long after some of the books Arnold cared most about are no longer read, and when many of his "ideas" are no longer accepted. It is what makes any reader pay attention to his opinions even when they do not agree with them. For they ask of us, finally, that we judge of them by a sense of life that we all have as human beings—a sense that, to be sure, we have in large part derived from the books that we have read. That is what the poet Hopkins may be assumed to have had in mind when, taking to task his friend Robert Bridges for some derogatory remark about Arnold, he said: "I have more reason than you for disagreeing with him and thinking him very wrong, but nevertheless I am sure he is a rare genius and a great critic."

The Function of Criticism at the Present Time

Many objections have been made to a proposition which, in some remarks of mine on translating Homer, I ventured to put forth; a proposition about criticism, and its importance at the present day. I said: "Of the literature of France and Germany, as of the intellect of Europe in general, the main effort, for now many years, has been a critical effort; the endeavour, in all branches of knowledge, theology, philosophy, history, art, science, to see the object as in itself it really is." I added, that owing to the operation in English literature of certain causes, "almost the last thing for which one would come to English literature is just that very thing which now Europe most desires,—criticism"; and that the power and value of English literature was thereby impaired. More than one rejoinder declared that the importance I here assigned to criticism was excessive, and asserted the inherent superiority of the creative effort of the human spirit over its critical effort. And the other day, having been led by a Mr. Shairp's excellent notice of Wordsworth[1] to turn again to his biography, I found, in the words of this great man, whom I, for one, must always listen to with the profoundest respect, a sentence passed on the critic's business, which seems to justify every possible disparagement of it. Wordsworth says in one of his letters:—

"The writers in these publications" (the Reviews), "while they prosecute their inglorious employment, cannot be supposed to be in a state of mind very favourable for being affected by the finer influences of a thing so pure as genuine poetry."

And a trustworthy reporter of his conversation quotes a more elaborate judgment to the same effect:—

"Wordsworth holds the critical power very low, infinitely lower than the inventive; and he said to-day that if the quantity of time consumed in writing critiques on the works of others were given to original composition, of whatever kind it might be, it would be much better employed; it would make a man find out sooner his own level, and it would do infinitely less mischief. A false or malicious criticism may do much injury to the minds of others; a stupid invention, either in prose or verse, is quite harmless."

It is almost too much to expect of poor human nature, that a man capable of producing some effect in one line of literature, should, for the greater good of society, voluntarily doom himself to impotence and obscurity in another. Still less is this to be expected from men addicted to the composition of the "false or malicious criticism" of which Wordsworth speaks. However, everybody would admit that a false or malicious criticism had better never have been written. Everybody, too, would be willing to admit, as a general proposition, that the critical faculty is lower than the inventive. But is it true that criticism is really, in itself, a baneful and injurious employment; is it true that all time given to writing critiques on the works of others would be much better employed if it were given to original composition, of whatever kind this may be? Is it true that Johnson had better have gone on producing more *Irenes* instead of writing his *Lives of the Poets;* nay, is it certain that Wordsworth himself was better employed in making his Ecclesiastical Sonnets than when he made his celebrated Preface, so full of criticism, and criticism of the works of others? Wordsworth was himself a great critic, and it is to be sincerely regretted that he has not left us more criticism; Goethe was one of the greatest of critics, and we may sincerely congratulate ourselves that he has left us so much criticism. Without wasting time over the exaggeration which Wordsworth's judgment on criticism clearly contains, or over an attempt to trace the causes,—not difficult, I think, to be traced,—which may have led Wordsworth to this exaggeration, a critic may with advantage seize an occasion for trying his own conscience, and for asking himself of what real service at any given moment the practice of criticism either is or may be made to his mind and spirit, and to the minds and spirits of others.

The critical power is of lower rank than the creative. True; but in assenting to this proposition, one or two things are to be kept in mind. It is undeniable that the exercise of a creative power, that a free creative activity, is the highest function of man; it is proved to be so by man's finding in it his true happiness. But it is undeniable, also, that men may have the sense of exercising this free creative activity in other ways than in producing great works of literature or art; if it were not so, all but a very few men would be shut out from the true happiness of all men. They may have it in well-doing, they may have it in learning, they may have it even in criticising. This is one thing to be kept in mind. Another is, that the exercise of the creative power in the production of great works of literature or art, however high this exercise of it may rank, is not at all epochs and under all conditions possible; and that therefore labour may be vainly spent in attempting it, which might with more fruit be used in preparing for it, in rendering it possible. This creative power works with elements, with materials; what if it has not those materials, those elements, ready for its use? In that case it must surely wait till they are ready. Now, in literature,—I will limit myself to literature, for it is about literature that the question arises,—the elements with which the creative power works

are ideas; the best ideas on every matter which literature touches, current at the time. At any rate we may lay it down as certain that in modern literature no manifestation of the creative power not working with these can be very important or fruitful. And I say *current* at the time, not merely accessible at the time; for creative literary genius does not principally show itself in discovering new ideas, that is rather the business of the philosopher. The grand work of literary genius is a work of synthesis and exposition, not of analysis and discovery; its gift lies in the faculty of being happily inspired by a certain intellectual and spiritual atmosphere, by a certain order of ideas, when it finds itself in them; of dealing divinely with these ideas, presenting them in the most effective and attractive combinations,—making beautiful works with them, in short. But it must have the atmosphere, it must find itself amidst the order of ideas, in order to work freely; and these it is not so easy to command. This is why great creative epochs in literature are so rare, this is why there is so much that is unsatisfactory in the productions of many men of real genius; because, for the creation of a master-work of literature two powers must concur, the power of the man and the power of the moment, and the man is not enough without the moment; the creative power has, for its happy exercise, appointed elements, and those elements are not in its own control.

Nay, they are more within the control of the critical power. It is the business of the critical power, as I said in the words already quoted, "in all branches of knowledge, theology, philosophy, history, art, science, to see the object as in itself it really is." Thus it tends, at last, to make an intellectual situation of which the creative power can profitably avail itself. It tends to establish an order of ideas, if not absolutely true, yet true by comparison with that which it displaces; to make the best ideas prevail. Presently these new ideas reach society, the touch of truth is the touch of life, and there is a stir and growth everywhere; out of this stir and growth come the creative epochs of literature.

Or, to narrow our range, and quit these considerations of the general march of genius and of society,—considerations which are apt to become too abstract and impalpable,—every one can see that a poet, for instance, ought to know life and the world before dealing with them in poetry; and life and the world being in modern times very complex things, the creation of a modern poet, to be worth much, implies a great critical effort behind it; else it must be a comparatively poor, barren, and short-lived affair. This is why Byron's poetry had so little endurance in it, and Goethe's so much; both Byron and Goethe had a great productive power, but Goethe's was nourished by a great critical effort providing the true materials for it, and Byron's was not; Goethe knew life and the world, the poet's necessary subjects, much more comprehensively and thoroughly than Byron. He knew a great deal more of them, and he knew them much more as they really are.

It has long seemed to me that the burst of creative activity in our literature, through the first quarter of this century, had about it in fact something premature; and that from this cause its productions are doomed, most of them, in spite of the sanguine hopes which accompanied and do still accompany them, to prove hardly more lasting than the productions of far less splendid epochs. And this prematureness comes from its having proceeded without having its proper data, without sufficient materials to work with. In other words, the English poetry of the first quarter of this century, with plenty of energy, plenty of creative force, did not know enough. This makes Byron so empty of matter, Shelley so incoherent, Wordsworth even, profound as he is, yet so wanting in completeness and variety. Wordsworth cared little for books, and disparaged Goethe. I admire Wordsworth, as he is, so much that I cannot wish him different; and it is vain, no doubt, to imagine such a man

different from what he is, to suppose that he *could* have been different. But surely the one thing wanting to make Wordsworth an even greater poet than he is,—his thought richer, and his influence of wider application,— was that he should have read more books, among them, no doubt, those of that Goethe whom he disparaged without reading him.

But to speak of books and reading may easily lead to a misunderstanding here. It was not really books and reading that lacked to our poetry at this epoch; Shelley had plenty of reading, Coleridge had immense reading. Pindar and Sophocles—as we all say so glibly, and often with so little discernment of the real import of what we are saying—had not many books; Shakespeare was no deep reader. True; but in the Greece of Pindar and Sophocles, in the England of Shakespeare, the poet lived in a current of ideas in the highest degree animating and nourishing to the creative power; society was, in the fullest measure, permeated by fresh thought, intelligent and alive. And this state of things is the true basis for the creative power's exercise, in this it finds its data, its materials, truly ready for its hand; all the books and reading in the world are only valuable as they are helps to this. Even when this does not actually exist, books and reading may enable a man to construct a kind of semblance of it in his own mind, a world of knowledge and intelligence in which he may live and work. This is by no means an equivalent to the artist for the nationally diffused life and thought of the epochs of Sophocles or Shakespeare; but, besides that it may be a means of preparation for such epochs, it does really constitute, if many share in it, a quickening and sustaining atmosphere of great value. Such an atmosphere the many-sided learning and the long and widely-combined critical effort of Germany formed for Goethe, when he lived and worked. There was no national glow of life and thought there as in the Athens of Pericles or the England of Elizabeth. That was the poet's weakness. But there was a sort of equivalent for it in the complete culture and unfettered thinking of a large body of Germans. That was his strength. In the England of the first quarter of this century there was neither a national glow of life and thought, such as we had in the age of Elizabeth, nor yet a culture and a force of learning and criticism such as were to be found in Germany. Therefore the creative power of poetry wanted, for success in the highest sense, materials and a basis; a thorough interpretation of the world was necessarily denied to it.

At first sight it seems strange that out of the immense stir of the French Revolution and its age should not have come a crop of works of genius equal to that which came out of the stir of the great productive time of Greece, or out of that of the Renascence, with its powerful episode the Reformation. But the truth is that the stir of the French Revolution took a character which essentially distinguished it from such movements as these. These were, in the main, disinterestedly intellectual and spiritual movements; movements in which the human spirit looked for its satisfaction in itself and in the increased play of its own activity. The French Revolution took a political, practical character. The movement which went on in France under the old *régime,* from 1700 to 1789, was far more really akin than that of the Revolution itself to the movement of the Renascence; the France of Voltaire and Rousseau told far more powerfully upon the mind of Europe than the France of the Revolution. Goethe reproached this last expressly with having "thrown quiet culture back." Nay, and the true key to how much in our Byron, even in our Wordsworth, is this!—that they had their source in a great movement of feeling, not in a great movement of mind. The French Revolution, however,—that object of so much blind love and so much blind hatred,—found undoubtedly its motive-power in the intelligence of men, and not in their practical sense; this is what distinguishes it from the English Revolution of Charles the First's time. This is what makes it a more spiritual event than our Revolution, an event of much more powerful and world-wide interest, though practically less successful; it appeals to an order of ideas which are universal, certain, permanent. 1789 asked of a thing, Is it rational? 1642 asked of a thing, Is it legal? or, when it went furthest, Is it according to conscience? This is the English fashion, a fashion to be treated, within its own sphere, with the highest respect; for its success, within its own sphere, has been prodigious. But what is law in one place is not law in another; what is law here to-day is not law even here to-morrow; and as for conscience, what is binding on one man's conscience is not binding on another's. The old woman who threw her stool at the head of the surpliced minister in St. Giles's Church at Edinburgh obeyed an impulse to which millions of the human race may be permitted to remain strangers. But the prescriptions of reason are absolute, unchanging, of universal validity; *to count by tens is the easiest way of counting*— that is a proposition of which every one, from here to the Antipodes, feels the force; at least I should say so if we did not live in a country where it is not impossible that any morning we may find a letter in the *Times* declaring that a decimal coinage is an absurdity. That a whole nation should have been penetrated with an enthusiasm for pure reason, and with an ardent zeal for making its prescriptions triumph, is a very remarkable thing, when we consider how little of mind, or anything so worthy and quickening as mind, comes into the motives which alone, in general, impel great masses of men. In spite of the extravagant direction given to this enthusiasm, in spite of the crimes and follies in which it lost itself, the French Revolution derives from the force, truth, and universality of the ideas which it took for its law, and from the passion with which it could inspire a multitude for these ideas, a unique and still living power; it is—it will probably long remain— the greatest, the most animating event in history. And as no sincere passion for the things of the mind, even though it turn out in many respects an unfortunate passion, is ever quite thrown away and quite barren of good, France has reaped from hers one fruit—the natural and legitimate fruit, though not precisely the grand fruit she expected: she is the country in Europe where *the people* is most alive.

But the mania for giving an immediate political and practical application to all these fine ideas of the reason was fatal. Here an Englishman is in his element: on this theme we can all go on for hours. And all we are in the habit of saying on it has undoubtedly a great deal of truth. Ideas cannot be too much prized in and for themselves, cannot be too much lived with; but to transport them abruptly into the world of politics and practice, violently to revolutionise this world to their bidding,—that is quite another thing. There is the world of ideas and there is the world of practice; the French are often for suppressing the one and the English the other; but neither is to be suppressed. A member of the House of Commons said to me the other day: "That a thing is an anomaly, I consider to be no objection to it whatever." I venture to think he was wrong; that a thing is an anomaly *is* an objection to it, but absolutely and in the sphere of ideas: it is not necessarily, under such and such circumstances, or at such and such a moment, an objection to it in the sphere of politics and practice. Joubert has said beautifully: *"C'est la force et le droit qui règlent toutes choses dans le monde; la force en attendant le droit."* (Force and right are the rulers of this world; force till right is ready.) *Force till right is ready;* and till right is ready, force, the existing order of things, is justified, is the legitimate ruler. But right is something moral, and implies inward recognition, free assent of the will; we are not ready for right,—*right*, so far as we are concerned, *is not ready,*— until we have attained this sense of seeing it and willing it. The way in which for us it may change and transform force, the existing order of things, and become, in its turn, the legitimate ruler of the world, should depend on the way in which, when our time comes, we see it and will it. Therefore for other people enamoured of their own newly discerned right, to attempt to impose it upon us as ours, and violently to substitute their right for our force, is an act of tyranny, and to be resisted. It sets at nought the second great half of our maxim, *force till right is ready.* This was the grand error of the French Revolution; and its movement of ideas, by quitting the intellectual sphere and rushing furiously into the political sphere, ran, indeed, a prodigious and memorable course, but produced no such intellectual fruit as the movement of ideas of the Renascence, and created, in opposition to itself, what I may call an *epoch of concentration.* The great force of that epoch of concentration was England; and the great voice of that epoch of concentration was Burke. It is the fashion to treat Burke's writings on the French Revolution as superannuated and conquered by the event; as the eloquent but unphilosophical tirades of bigotry and prejudice. I will not deny that they are often dis-figured by the violence and passion of the moment, and that in some directions Burke's view was bounded, and his observation therefore at fault. But on the whole, and for those who can make the needful corrections, what distinguishes these writings is their profound, permanent, fruitful, philosophical truth. They contain the true philosophy of an epoch of concentration, dissipate the heavy atmosphere which its own nature is apt to engender round it, and make its resistance rational instead of mechanical.

But Burke is so great because, almost alone in England, he brings thought to bear upon politics, he saturates politics with thought. It is his accident that his ideas were at the service of an epoch of concentration, not of an epoch of expansion; it is his characteristic that he so lived by ideas, and had such a source of them welling up within him, that he could float even an epoch of concentration and English Tory politics with them. It does not hurt him that Dr.

Price and the Liberals were enraged with him; it does not even hurt him that George the Third and the Tories were enchanted with him. His greatness is that he lived in a world which neither English Liberalism nor English Toryism is apt to enter;—the world of ideas, not the world of catchwords and party habits. So far is it from being really true of him that he "to party gave up what was meant for mankind," that at the very end of his fierce struggle with the French Revolution, after all his invectives against its false pretensions, hollowness, and madness, with his sincere conviction of its mischievousness, he can close a memorandum on the best means of combating it, some of the last pages he ever wrote,—the *Thoughts on French Affairs,* in December 1791,—with these striking words:—

"The evil is stated, in my opinion, as it exists. The remedy must be where power, wisdom, and information, I hope, are more united with good intentions than they can be with me. I have done with this subject, I believe, for ever. It has given me many anxious moments for the last two years. *If a great change is to be made in human affairs, the minds of men will be fitted to it; the general opinions and feelings will draw that way. Every fear, every hope will forward it; and then they who persist in opposing this mighty current in human affairs, will appear rather to resist the decrees of Providence itself, than the mere designs of men. They will not be resolute and firm, but perverse and obstinate.*"

That return of Burke upon himself has always seemed to me one of the finest things in English literature, or indeed in any literature. That is what I call living by ideas: when one side of a question has long had your earnest support, when all your feelings are engaged, when you hear all round you no language but one, when your party talks this language like a steam-engine and can imagine no other,—still to be able to think, still to be irresistibly carried, if so it be, by the current of thought to the opposite side of the question, and, like Balaam, to be unable to speak anything *but what the Lord has put in your mouth.* I know nothing more striking, and I must add that I know nothing more un-English.

For the Englishman in general is like my friend the Member of Parliament, and believes, point-blank, that for a thing to be an anomaly is absolutely no objection to it whatever. He is like the Lord Auckland of Burke's day, who, in a memorandum on the French Revolution, talks of "certain miscreants, assuming the name of philosophers, who have presumed themselves capable of establishing a new system of society." The Englishman has been called a political animal, and he values what is political and practical so much that ideas easily become objects of dislike in his eyes, and thinkers, "miscreants," because ideas and thinkers have rashly meddled with politics and practice. This would be all very well if the dislike and neglect confined themselves to ideas transported out of their own sphere, and meddling rashly with practice; but they are inevitably extended to ideas as such, and to the whole life of intelligence; practice is everything, a free play of the mind is nothing. The notion of the free play of the mind upon all subjects being a pleasure in itself, being an object of desire, being an essential provider of elements without which a nation's spirit, whatever compensations it may have for them, must, in the long run, die of inanition, hardly enters into an Englishman's thoughts. It is noticeable that the word *curiosity*, which in other languages is used in a good sense, to mean, as a high and fine quality of man's nature, just this disinterested love of a free play of the mind on all subjects, for its own sake,—it is noticeable, I say, that this word has in our language no sense of the kind, no sense but a rather bad and disparaging one. But criticism, real criticism, is essentially the exercise of this very quality. It obeys an instinct prompting it to try to know the best that is known and thought in the world, irrespectively of practice, politics, and everything of the kind; and to value knowledge and thought as they approach this best, without the intrusion of any other considerations whatever. This is an instinct for which there is, I think, little original sympathy in the practical English nature, and what there was of it has undergone a long benumbing period of blight and suppression in the epoch of concentration which followed the French Revolution.

But epochs of concentration cannot well endure for ever; epochs of expansion, in the due course of things, follow them. Such an epoch of expansion seems to be opening in this country. In the first place all danger of a hostile forcible pressure of foreign ideas upon our practice has long disappeared; like the traveller in the fable, therefore, we begin to wear our cloak a little more loosely. Then, with a long peace, the ideas of Europe steal gradually and amicably in, and mingle, though in infinitesimally small quantities at a time, with our own notions. Then, too, in spite of all that is said about the absorbing and brutalising influence of our passionate material progress, it seems to me indisputable that this progress is likely, though not certain, to lead in the end to an apparition of intellectual life; and that man, after he has made himself perfectly comfortable and has now to determine what to do with himself next, may begin to remember that he has a mind, and that the mind may be made the source of great pleasure. I grant it is mainly the privilege of faith, at present, to discern this end to our railways, our business, and our fortune-making; but we shall see if, here as elsewhere, faith is not in the end the true prophet. Our ease, our travelling, and our unbounded liberty to hold just as hard and securely as we please to the practice to which our notions have given birth, all tend to beget an inclination to deal a little more freely with these notions themselves, to canvass them a little, to penetrate a little into their real nature. Flutterings of curiosity, in the foreign sense of the word, appear amongst us, and it is in these that criticism must look to find its account. Criticism first; a time of true creative activity, perhaps,—

which, as I have said, must inevitably be preceded amongst us by a time of criticism,—hereafter, when criticism has done its work.

It is of the last importance that English criticism should clearly discern what rule for its course, in order to avail itself of the field now opening to it, and to produce fruit for the future, it ought to take. The rule may be summed up, in one word *disinterestedness.* And how is criticism to show disinterestedness? By keeping aloof from what is called "the practical view of things"; by resolutely following the law of its own nature, which is to be a free play of the mind on all subjects which it touches. By steadily refusing to lend itself to any of those ulterior, political, practical considerations about ideas, which plenty of people will be sure to attach to them, which perhaps ought often to be attached to them, which in this country at any rate are certain to be attached to them quite sufficiently, but which criticism has really nothing to do with. Its business is, as I have said, simply to know the best that is known and thought in the world, and by in its turn making this known, to create a current of true and fresh ideas. Its business is to do this with flexible honesty, with due ability; but its business is to do no more, and to leave alone all questions of practical consequences and applications, questions which will never fail to have due prominence given to them. Else criticism, besides being really false to its own nature, merely continues in the old rut which it has hitherto followed in this country, and will certainly miss the chance now given to it. For what is at present the bane of criticism in this country? It is that practical considerations cling to it and stifle it. It subserves interests not its own. Our organs of criticism are organs of men and parties having practical ends to serve, and with them those practical ends are the first thing and the play of mind the second; so much play of mind as is compatible with the prosecution of those practical ends is all that is wanted. An organ like the *Revue des Deux Mondes,* having for its main function to understand and utter the best that is known and thought in the world, existing, it may be said, as just an organ for a free play of the mind, we have not. But we have the *Edinburgh Review,* existing as an organ of the old Whigs, and for as much play of the mind as may suit its being that; we have the *Quarterly Review,* existing as an organ of the Tories, and for as much play of mind as may suit its being that; we have the *British Quarterly Review,* existing as an organ of the political Dissenters, and for as much play of mind as may suit its being that; we have the *Times,* existing as an organ of the common, satisfied, well-to-do Englishman, and for as much play of mind as may suit its being that. And so on through all the various fractions, political and religious, of our society; every fraction has, as such, its organ of criticism, but the notion of combining all fractions in the common pleasure of a free disinterested play of mind meets with no favour. Directly this play of mind wants to have more scope, and to forget the pressure of practical considerations a little, it is checked, it is made to feel the chain. We saw this the other day in the extinction, so much to be regretted, of the *Home and Foreign Review.* Perhaps in no organ of criticism in this country was there so much knowledge, so much play of mind; but these could not save it. The *Dublin Review* subordinates play of mind to the practical business of English and Irish Catholicism, and lives. It must needs be that men should act in sects and parties, that each of these sects and parties should have its organ, and should make this organ subserve the interests of its action; but it would be well, too, that there should be a criticism, not the minister of these interests, not their enemy, but absolutely and entirely independent of them. No other criticism will ever attain any real authority or make any real way towards its end,—the creating a current of true and fresh ideas.

It is because criticism has so little kept in the pure intellectual sphere, has so little detached itself from practice, has been so directly polemical and controversial, that it has so ill accomplished, in this country, its best spiritual work; which is to keep man from a self-satisfaction which is retarding and vulgarising, to lead him towards perfection, by making his mind dwell upon what is excellent in itself, and the absolute beauty and fitness of things. A polemical practical criticism makes men blind even to the ideal imperfection of their practice, makes them willingly assert its ideal perfection, in order the better to secure it against attack; and clearly this is narrowing and baneful for them. If they were reassured on the practical side, speculative considerations of ideal perfection they might be brought to entertain, and their spiritual horizon would thus gradually widen. Sir Charles Adderley says to the Warwickshire farmers:—

"Talk of the improvement of breed! Why, the race we ourselves represent, the men and women, the old Anglo-Saxon race, are the best breed in the whole world. . . . The absence of a too enervating climate, too unclouded skies, and a too luxurious nature, has produced so vigorous a race of people, and has rendered us so superior to all the world."

Mr. Roebuck says to the Sheffield cutlers:—

"I look around me and ask what is the state of England? Is not property safe? Is not every man able to say what he likes? Can you not walk from one end of England to the other in perfect security? I ask you whether, the world over or in past history, there is anything like it? Nothing. I pray that our unrivalled happiness may last."

Now obviously there is a peril for poor human nature in words and thoughts of such exuberant self-satisfaction, until we find ourselves safe in the streets of the Celestial City.

Das wenige verschwindet leicht dem Blicke
Der vorwärts sieht, wie viel noch übrig bleibt—

says Goethe; "the little that is done seems nothing when we look forward and see how much we have yet to do." Clearly this is a better line of reflection for weak humanity, so long as it remains on this earthly field of labour and trial.

But neither Sir Charles Adderley nor Mr. Roebuck is by nature inaccessible to considerations of this sort. They only lose sight of them owing to the controversial life we all lead, and the practical form which all speculation takes with us. They have in view opponents whose aim is not ideal, but practical; and in their zeal to uphold their own practice against these innovators, they go so far as even to attribute to this practice an ideal perfection. Somebody has been wanting to introduce a six-pound franchise, or to abolish church-rates, or to collect agricultural statistics by force, or to diminish local self-government. How natural, in reply to such proposals, very likely improper or ill-timed, to go a little beyond the mark and to say stoutly, "Such a race of people as we stand, so superior to all the world! The old Anglo-Saxon race, the best breed in the whole world! I pray that our unrivalled happiness may last! I ask you whether, the world over or in past history, there is anything like it?" And so long as criticism answers this dithyramb by insisting that the old Anglo-Saxon race would be still more superior to all others if it had no church-rates, or that our unrivalled happiness would last yet longer with a six-pound franchise, so long will the strain, "The best breed in the whole world!" swell louder and louder, everything ideal and refining will be lost out of sight, and both the assailed and their critics will remain in a sphere, to say the truth, perfectly unvital, a sphere in which spiritual progression is impossible. But let criticism leave church-rates and the franchise alone, and in the most candid spirit, without a single lurking thought of practical innovation, confront with our dithyramb this paragraph on which I stumbled in a newspaper immediately after reading Mr. Roebuck:—

"A shocking child murder has just been committed at Nottingham. A girl named Wragg left the workhouse there on Saturday morning with her young illegitimate child. The child was soon afterwards found dead on Mapperly Hills, having been strangled. Wragg is in custody."

Nothing but that; but, in juxtaposition with the absolute eulogies of Sir Charles Adderley and Mr. Roebuck, how eloquent, how suggestive are those few lines!" Our old Anglo-Saxon breed, the best in the whole world!"—how much that is harsh and ill-favoured there is in this best! *Wragg!* If we are to talk of ideal perfection, of "the best in the whole world," has any one reflected what a touch of grossness in our race, what an original shortcoming in the more delicate spiritual perceptions, is known by the natural growth amongst us of such hideous names,—Higginbottom, Stiggins, Bugg! In Ionia and Attica they were luckier in this respect than "the best race in the world"; by the Ilissus there was no Wragg, poor thing! And "our unrivalled happiness";—what an element of grimness, bareness, and hideousness mixes with it and blurs it; the workhouse, the dismal Mapperly Hills,—how dismal those who have seen them will remember;—the gloom, the smoke, the cold, the strangled illegitimate child! "I ask you whether, the world over or in past history, there is anything like it?" Perhaps not, one is inclined to answer; but at any rate, in that case, the world is very much to be pitied. And the final touch,—short, bleak, and inhuman: *Wragg is in custody.* The sex lost in the confusion of our unrivalled happiness; or (shall I say?) the superfluous Christian name lopped off by the straightforward vigour of our old Anglo-Saxon breed? There is profit for the spirit in such contrasts as this; criticism serves the cause of perfection by establishing them. By eluding sterile conflict, by refusing to remain in the sphere where alone narrow and relative conceptions have any worth and validity, criticism may diminish its momentary importance, but only in this way has it a chance of gaining admittance for those wider and more perfect conceptions to which all its duty is really owed.

Mr. Roebuck will have a poor opinion of an adversary who replies to his defiant songs of triumph only by murmuring under his breath, *Wragg is in custody;* but in no other way will these songs of triumph be induced gradually to moderate themselves, to get rid of what in them is excessive and offensive, and to fall into a softer and truer key.

It will be said that it is a very subtle and indirect action which I am thus prescribing for criticism, and that, by embracing in this manner the Indian virtue of detachment and abandoning the sphere of practical life, it condemns itself to a slow and obscure work. Slow and obscure it may be, but it is the only proper work of criticism. The mass of mankind will never have any ardent zeal for seeing things as they are; very inadequate ideas will always satisfy them. On these inadequate ideas reposes, and must repose, the general practice of the world. That is as much as saying that whoever sets himself to see things as they are will find himself one of a very small circle; but it is only by this small circle resolutely doing its own work that adequate ideas will ever get current at all. The rush and roar of practical life will always have a dizzying and attracting effect upon the most collected spectator, and tend to draw him into its vortex; most of all will this be the case where that life is so powerful as it is in England. But it is only by remaining collected, and refusing to lend himself to the point of view of the practical man, that the critic can do the practical man any service; and it is only by the greatest sincerity in pursuing his own course, and by at last convincing even the practical man of his sincerity, that he can escape misunderstandings which perpetually threaten him.

For the practical man is not apt for fine distinctions, and yet in these distinctions truth and the highest culture greatly find their account. But it is not easy to lead a practical man,—unless you reassure him as to your practical intentions, you have no chance of leading him,—to see that a thing which he has always been used to look at

from one side only, which he greatly values, and which, looked at from that side, quite deserves, perhaps, all the prizing and admiring which he bestows upon it,—that this thing, looked at from another side, may appear much less beneficent and beautiful, and yet retain all its claims to our practical allegiance. Where shall we find language innocent enough, how shall we make the spotless purity of our intentions evident enough, to enable us to say to the political Englishman that the British Constitution itself, which, seen from the practical side, looks such a magnificent organ of progress and virtue, seen from the speculative side,—with its compromises, its love of facts, its horror of theory, its studied avoidance of clear thoughts,—that, seen from this side, our august Constitution sometimes looks,—forgive me, shade of Lord Somers!—a colossal machine for the manufacture of Philistines? How is Cobbett to say this and not be misunderstood, blackened as he is with the smoke of a lifelong conflict in the field of political practice? how is Mr. Carlyle to say it and not be misunderstood, after his furious raid into this field with his *Latter-day Pamphlets?* how is Mr. Ruskin, after his pugnacious political economy? I say, the critic must keep out of the region of immediate practice in the political, social, humanitarian sphere, if he wants to make a beginning for that more free speculative treatment of things, which may perhaps one day make its benefits felt even in this sphere, but in a natural and thence irresistible manner.

Do what he will, however, the critic will still remain exposed to frequent misunderstandings, and nowhere so much as in this country. For here people are particularly indisposed even to comprehend that without this free disinterested treatment of things, truth and the highest culture are out of the question. So immersed are they in practical life, so accustomed to take all their notions from this life and its processes, that they are apt to think that truth and culture themselves can be reached by the processes of this life, and that it is an impertinent singularity to think of reaching them in any other. "We are all *terrae filii*" ["sons of the earth"], cries their eloquent advocate; "all Philistines together. Away with the notion of proceeding by any other way than the course dear to the Philistines; let us have a social movement, let us organise and combine a party to pursue truth and new thought, let us call it *the liberal party,* and let us all stick to each other, and back each other up. Let us have no nonsense about independent criticism, and intellectual delicacy, and the few and the many. Don't let us trouble ourselves about foreign thought; we shall invent the whole thing for ourselves as we go along. If one of us speaks well, applaud him; if one of us speaks ill, applaud him too; we are all in the same movement, we are all liberals, we are all in pursuit of truth." In this way the pursuit of truth becomes really a social, practical, pleasurable affair, almost requiring a chairman, a secretary, and advertisements; with the excitement of an occasional scandal, with a little resistance to give the happy sense of difficulty overcome: but, in general, plenty of bustle and very little thought. To act is so easy, as Goethe says; to think is so hard! It is true that the critic has many temptations to go with the stream, to make one of the party movement, one of these *terrae filii;* it seems ungracious to refuse to be a *terrae filius,* when so many excellent people are; but the critic's duty is to refuse, or, if resistance is vain, at least to cry with Obermann: *Périssons en résistant* [let us die resisting"].

How serious a matter it is to try and resist, I had ample opportunity of experiencing when I ventured some time ago to criticise the celebrated first volume of Bishop Colenso.[2] The echoes of the storm which was then raised I still, from time to time, hear grumbling round me. That storm arose out of a misunderstanding almost inevitable. It is a result of no little culture to attain to a clear perception that science and religion are two wholly different things.

The multitude will for ever confuse them; but happily that is of no great real importance, for while the multitude imagines itself to live by its false science, it does really live by its true religion. Dr. Colenso, however, in his first volume did all he could to strengthen the confusion,[3] and to make it dangerous. He did this with the best intentions, I freely admit, and with the most candid ignorance that this was the natural effect of what he was doing; but, says Joubert, "Ignorance, which in matters of morals extenuates the crime, is itself, in intellectual matters, a crime of the first order." I criticised Bishop Colenso's speculative confusion. Immediately there was a cry raised: "What is this? here is a liberal attacking a liberal. Do not you belong to the movement? are not you a friend of truth? Is not Bishop Colenso in pursuit of truth? then speak with proper respect of his book. Dr. Stanley is another friend of truth, and you speak with proper respect of his book; why make these invidious differences? both books are excellent, admirable, liberal; Bishop Colenso's perhaps the most so, because it is the boldest, and will have the best practical consequences for the liberal cause. Do you want to encourage to the attack of a brother liberal his, and your, and our implacable enemies, the *Church and State Review* or the *Record,*—the High Church rhinoceros and the Evangelical hyaena? Be silent, therefore; or rather speak, speak as loud as ever you can! and go into ecstasies over the eighty and odd pigeons."

But criticism cannot follow this coarse and indiscriminate method. It is unfortunately possible for a man in pursuit of truth to write a book which reposes upon a false conception. Even the practical consequences of a book are to genuine criticism no recommendation of it, if the book is, in the highest sense, blundering. I see that a lady who herself, too, is in pursuit of truth, and who writes with great ability, but a little too much, perhaps, under the influence of the practical spirit of the English liberal movement, classes Bishop Colenso's book and M. Renan's together, in her survey of the religious state of Europe, as facts of the same order, works, both of them, of "great importance"; "great ability, power, and skill"; Bishop Colenso's, perhaps, the most powerful; at least, Miss Cobbe gives special expression to her gratitude that to Bishop Colenso "has been given the strength to grasp, and the courage to teach, truths of such deep import." In the same way, more than one popular writer has compared him to Luther. Now it is just this kind of false estimate which the critical spirit is, it seems to me, bound to resist. It is really the strongest possible proof of the low ebb at which, in England, the critical spirit is, that while the critical hit in the religious literature of Germany is Dr. Strauss's book, in that of France M. Renan's book, the book of Bishop Colenso is the critical hit in the religious literature of England. Bishop Colenso's book reposes on a total misconception of the essential elements of the religious problem, as that problem is now presented for solution. To criticism, therefore, which seeks to have the best that is known and thought on this problem, it is, however well meant, of no importance whatever. M. Renan's book attempts a new synthesis of the elements furnished to us by the Four Gospels. It attempts, in my opinion, a synthesis, perhaps premature, perhaps impossible, certainly not successful. Up to the present time, at any rate, we must acquiesce in Fleury's sentence on such recastings of the Gospel-story: *Quiconque s'imagine la pouvoir mieux écrire, ne l'entend pas* ["Whoever thinks he can write better, does not understand it"]. M. Renan had himself passed by anticipation a like sentence on his own work, when he said: "If a new presentation of the character of Jesus were offered to me, I would not have it; its very clearness would be, in my opinion, the best proof of its insufficiency." His friends may with perfect justice rejoin that at the sight of the Holy Land, and of the actual scene of the Gospel-story, all the current of M. Renan's thought may have naturally changed, and a new casting of that sto-

ry irresistibly suggested itself to him; and that this is just a case for applying Cicero's maxim: Change of mind is not inconsistency—*nemo doctus unquam mutationem consilii inconstantiam dixit esse.* Nevertheless, for criticism, M. Renan's first thought must still be the truer one, as long as his new casting so fails more fully to commend itself, more fully (to use Coleridge's happy phrase about the Bible) to *find* us. Still M. Renan's attempt is, for criticism, of the most real interest and importance, since, with all its difficulty, a fresh synthesis of the New Testament *data,*—not a making war on them, in Voltaire's fashion, not a leaving them out of mind, in the world's fashion, but the putting a new construction upon them, the taking them from under the old, traditional, conventional point of view and placing them under a new one,—is the very essence of the religious problem, as now presented; and only by efforts in this direction can it receive a solution.

Again, in the same spirit in which she judges Bishop Colenso, Miss Cobbe, like so many earnest liberals of our practical race, both here and in America, herself sets vigorously about a positive reconstruction of religion, about making a religion of the future out of hand, or at least setting about making it. We must not rest, she and they are always thinking and saying, in negative criticism, we must be creative and constructive; hence we have such works as her recent *Religious Duty,* and works still more considerable, perhaps, by others, which will be in every one's mind. These works often have much ability; they often spring out of sincere convictions, and a sincere wish to do good, and they sometimes, perhaps, do good. Their fault is (if I may be permitted to say so) one which they have in common with the British College of Health, in the New Road. Every one knows the British College of Health; it is that building with the lion and the statue of the Goddess Hygeia before it; at least I am sure about the lion, though I am not absolutely certain about the Goddess Hygeia. This building does credit, perhaps, to the resources of Dr. Morrison and his disciples; but it falls a good deal short of one's idea of what a British College of Health ought to be. In England, where we hate public interference and love individual enterprise, we have a whole crop of places like the British College of Health; the grand name without the grand thing. Unluckily, creditable to individual enterprise as they are, they tend to impair our taste by making us forget what more grandiose, noble, or beautiful character properly belongs to a public institution. The same may be said of the religions of the future of Miss Cobbe and others. Creditable, like the British College of Health, to the resources of their authors, they yet tend to make us forget what more grandiose, noble, or beautiful character properly belongs to religious constructions. The historic religions, with all their faults, have had this; it certainly belongs to the religious sentiment, when it truly flowers, to have this; and we impoverish our spirit if we allow a religion of the future without it. What then is the duty of criticism here? To take the practical point of view, to applaud the liberal movement and all its works,—its New Road religions of the future into the bargain,—for their general utility's sake? By no means; but to be perpetually dissatisfied with these works, while they perpetually fall short of a high and perfect ideal.

For criticism, these are elementary laws; but they never can be popular, and in this country they have been very little followed, and one meets with immense obstacles in following them. That is a reason for asserting them again and again. Criticism must maintain its independence of the practical spirit and its aims. Even with well-meant efforts of the practical spirit it must express dissatisfaction, if in the sphere of the ideal they seem impoverishing and limiting. It must not hurry on to the goal because of its practical importance. It must be patient, and know how to wait; and flexible, and know how to attach itself to things and how to withdraw from them. It must be apt to

study and praise elements that for the fulness of spiritual perfection are wanted, even though they belong to a power which in the practical sphere may be maleficent. It must be apt to discern the spiritual shortcomings or illusions of powers that in the practical sphere may be beneficent. And this without any notion of favouring or injuring, in the practical sphere, one power or the other; without any notion of playing off, in this sphere, one power against the other. When one looks, for instance, at the English Divorce Court,—an institution which perhaps has its practical conveniences, but which in the ideal sphere is so hideous; an institution which neither makes divorce impossible nor makes it decent, which allows a man to get rid of his wife, or a wife of her husband, but makes them drag one another first, for the public edification, through a mire of unutterable infamy,—when one looks at this charming institution, I say, with its crowded trials, its newspaper reports, and its money compensations, this institution in which the gross unregenerate British Philistine has indeed stamped an image of himself,—one may be permitted to find the marriage theory of Catholicism refreshing and elevating. Or when Protestantism, in virtue of its supposed rational and intellectual origin, gives the law to criticism too magisterially, criticism may and must remind it that its pretensions, in this respect, are illusive and do it harm; that the Reformation was a moral rather than an intellectual event; that Luther's theory of grace no more exactly reflects the mind of the spirit than Bossuet's philosophy of history reflects it; and that there is no more antecedent probability of the Bishop of Durham's stock of ideas being agreeable to perfect reason than of Pope Pius the Ninth's. But criticism will not on that account forget the achievements of Protestantism in the practical and moral sphere; nor that, even in the intellectual sphere, Protestantism, though in a blind and stumbling manner, carried forward the Renascence, while Catholicism threw itself violently across its path.

I lately heard a man of thought and energy contrasting the want of ardour and movement which he now found amongst young men in this country with what he remembered in his own youth, twenty years ago. "What reformers we were then!" he exclaimed; "what a zeal we had! how we canvassed every institution in Church and State, and were prepared to remodel them all on first principles!" He was inclined to regret, as a spiritual flagging, the lull which he saw. I am disposed rather to regard it as a pause in which the turn to a new mode of spiritual progress is being accomplished. Everything was long seen, by the young and ardent amongst us, in inseparable connection with politics and practical life. We have pretty well exhausted the benefits of seeing things in this connection, we have got all that can be got by so seeing them. Let us try a more disinterested mode of seeing them; let us betake ourselves more to the serener life of the mind and spirit. This life, too, may have its excesses and dangers; but they are not for us at pres-ent. Let us think of quietly enlarging our stock of true and fresh ideas, and not, as soon as we get an idea or half an idea, be running out with it into the street, and trying to make it rule there. Our ideas will, in the end, shape the world all the better for maturing a little. Perhaps in fifty years' time it will in the English House of Commons be an objection to an institution that it is an anomaly, and my friend the Member of Parliament will shudder in his grave. But let us in the meanwhile rather endeavour that in twenty years' time it may, in English literature, be an objection to a proposition that it is absurd. That will be a change so vast, that the imagination almost fails to grasp it. *Ab integro saeclorum nascitur ordo* ["Order is born from the ages' renewal"].

If I have insisted so much on the course which criticism must take where politics and religion are concerned, it is because, where these burning matters are in question, it is most likely to go astray. I have wished, above all, to insist on the attitude which criticism should adopt towards things in general; on its right tone and temper of mind. But then comes another question as to the subject-matter which literary criticism should most seek. Here, in general, its course is determined for it by the idea which is the law of its being; the idea of a disinterested endeavour to learn and propagate the best that is known and thought in the world, and thus to establish a current of fresh and true ideas. By the very nature of things, as England is not all the world, much of the best that is known and thought in the world cannot be of English growth, must be foreign; by the nature of things, again, it is just this that we are least likely to know, while English thought is streaming in upon us from all sides, and takes excellent care that we shall not be ignorant of its existence; the English critic of literature, therefore, must dwell much on foreign thought, and which particular heed on any part of it, which, while significant and fruitful in itself, is for any reason specially likely to escape him. Again, judging is often spoken of as the critic's one business, and so in some sense it is; but the judgment which almost insensibly forms itself in a fair and clear mind, along with fresh knowledge, is the valuable one; and thus knowledge, and ever fresh knowledge, must be the critic's great concern for himself. And it is by communicating fresh knowledge, and letting his own judgment pass along with it,—but insensibly, and in the second place, not the first, as a sort of companion and clue, not as an abstract lawgiver,—that he will generally do most good to his readers. Sometimes, no doubt, for the sake of establishing an author's place in literature, and his relation to a central standard (and if this is not done, how are we to get at our *best in the world?*), criticism may have to deal with a subject-matter so familiar that fresh knowledge is out of the question, and then it must be all judgment; an enunciation and detailed application of principles. Here the great safeguard is never to let oneself become abstract, always to retain an intimate and lively consciousness of the truth of what one is saying, and, the moment this fails us, to be sure that something is wrong. Still, under all circumstances, this mere judgment and application of principles is, in itself, not the most satisfactory work to the critic; like mathematics, it is tautological, and cannot well give us, like fresh learning, the sense of creative activity.

But stop, some one will say; all this talk is of no practical use to us whatever; this criticism of yours is not what we have in our minds when we speak of criticism; when we speak of critics and criticism, we mean critics and criticism of the current English literature of the day; when you offer to tell criticism its function, it is to this criticism that we expect you to address yourself. I am sorry for it, for I am afraid I must disappoint these expectations. I am bound by my own definition of criticism: *a disinterested endeavour to learn and propagate the best that is known and thought in the world.* How much of current English literature comes into this "best that is known and thought in the world"? Not very much I fear; certainly less, at this moment, than of the current literature of France or Germany. Well, then, am I to alter my definition of criticism, in order to meet the requirements of a number of practising English critics, who, after all, are free in their choice of a business? That would be making criticism lend itself just to one of those alien practical considerations, which, I have said, are so fatal to it. One may say, indeed, to those who have to deal with the mass—so much better disregarded—of current English literature, that they may at all events endeavour, in dealing with this, to try it, so far as they can, by the standard of the best that is known and thought in the world; one may say, that to get anywhere near this standard, every critic should try and possess one great literature, at least, besides his own; and the more unlike his own, the better. But, after all, the criticism I am really concerned with,—the criticism which alone can much help us for the future, the criticism which, throughout Europe, is at the present day meant, when so much stress is laid on the importance of criticism and the critical spirit,—is a criticism which regards Europe as being, for intellectual and spiritual purposes, one great confederation, bound to a joint action and working to a common result; and whose members have, for their proper outfit, a knowledge of Greek, Roman, and Eastern antiquity, and of one another. Special, local, and temporary advantages being put out of account, that modern nation will in the intellectual and spiritual sphere make most progress, which most thoroughly carries out this program. And what is that but saying that we too, all of us, as individuals, the more thoroughly we carry it out, shall make the more progress?

There is so much inviting us!—what are we to take? what will nourish us in growth towards perfection? That is the question which, with the immense field of life and of literature lying before him, the critic has to answer; for himself first, and afterwards for others. In this idea of the critic's business the essays brought together in the following pages have had their origin; in this idea, widely different as are their subjects, they have, perhaps, their unity.

I conclude with what I said at the beginning: to have the sense of creative activity is the great happiness and the great proof of being alive, and it is not denied to criticism to have it; but then criticism must be sincere, simple, flexible, ardent, ever widening its knowledge. Then it may have, in no contemptible measure, a joyful sense of creative activity; a sense which a man of insight and conscience will prefer to what he might derive from a poor, starved, fragmentary, inadequate creation. And at some epochs no other creation is possible.

Still, in full measure, the sense of creative activity belongs only to genuine creation; in literature we must never forget that. But what true man of letters ever can forget it? It is no such common matter for a gifted nature to come into possession of a current of true and living ideas, and to produce amidst the inspiration of them, that we are likely to underrate it. The epochs of Aeschylus and Shakespeare make us feel their preeminence. In an epoch like those is, no doubt, the true life of literature; there is the promised land, towards which criticism can only beckon. That promised land it will not be ours to enter, and we shall die in the wilderness: but to have desired to enter it, to have saluted it from afar, is already, perhaps, the best distinction among contemporaries; it will certainly be the best title to esteem with posterity.

---

[1] I cannot help thinking that a practice, common in England during the last century, and still followed in France, of printing a notice of this kind,—a notice by a competent critic,—to serve as an introduction to an eminent author's works, might be revived among us with advantage. To introduce all succeeding editions of Wordsworth, Mr. Shairp's notice might, it seems to me, excellently serve; it is written from the point of view of an admirer, nay, of a disciple, and that is right; but then the disciple must be also, as in this case he is, a critic, a man of letters, not, as too often happens, some relation or friend with no qualification for his talks except affection for his author.

[2] So sincere is my dislike to all personal attack and controversy, that I abstain from reprinting, at this distance of time from the occasion which called them forth, the essays in which I criticised Dr. Colenso's book; I feel bound, however, after all that has passed, to make here a final declaration of my sincere impenitence for having published them. Nay, I cannot forbear repeating yet once more, for his benefit and that of his readers, this sentence from my original remarks upon him: *There is truth of science and truth of religion; truth of science does not become truth of religion until it is made religious.* And I will add: Let us have all the science there is from the men of science; from the men of religion let us have religion.

[3] It has been said that I make it "a crime against literary criticism and the higher culture to attempt to inform the ignorant." Need I point out that the ignorant are not informed by being confirmed in a confusion?

The Real Thing

Henry James

Editor's Introduction

What relation artists may have to their subjects, to their material—the sense, if any, in which what they make of that material is either "real" or "true"—is an old philosophical question. Plato maintained that what the artist produced, being but an imitation of reality, was for that reason inferior, and dangerous insofar as the imitation can be taken for—was even designed to be taken for—the real thing. This doctrine, which nowadays is mostly scorned, had nevertheless a certain integrity in holding that at least poetry, quite as much as other forms of utterance, ought to tell the truth, should not be valued, as the Athenians of Plato's time seemed to value it (and as the Victorians did also), precisely because it did *not* tell the truth—because it was a beautiful, consoling lie. Aristotle, however, argued in the *Poetics* that artistic imitation has a truth of its own, and that the artist, in particular the dramatic artist, is to be judged by the extent to which he realizes this truth, not by the extent to which he fails of another. That is because, for Aristotle, art is what combines form and matter in ways that do not occur in nature, where scientific and philosophical truth should prevail: actors are not really heroes, nor are women made of marble, except in works of art, where such unreal combinations are precisely the point. And so the debate has gone on, with Platonic and Aristotelian positions reappearing again and again over the ages, and with still other arguments, such as that the work of art is not an imitation at all but a "creation" that has its own reality as well as its own truth, being put forth more recently.

Perhaps no writer of modern times has been more interested in these matters than Henry James (1843–1916), brother of William James, whose *Principles of Psychology* appear in Volume 53 of *Great Books of the Western World.* Henry James was himself a psychologist of sorts, not as a scientist or a philosopher, but as a writer of fiction exhaustive in its exploration of a certain range of motives and feelings that James understood and cared about. His interest in the issues mentioned above is indicated by the numerous stories he wrote dealing with artists and writers in the course of a long literary career, and his opinion as to the specific question which has been raised will be found in the story here reprinted, called appropriately, "The Real Thing." First published in 1893, this tale may be taken as a kind of parable of the way that question resolved itself in his own mind.

433

Such preoccupations were a function of James's own life, in which his devotion to his craft, the writing of fiction, had about it an almost religious sense of commitment. He never married, had no other occupation. From about 1870, when his first stories appeared, to 1915 or so—that is, the year before his death—he produced a succession of novels and tales unsurpassed in their perception of life as it was lived, or as he thought it could be lived, in the society in which he himself moved. This was an international society, predominantly English (James, though an American by birth, was an expatriate) but not wholly so, and certainly not in any provincial sense—an upper-class society of well-mannered affluence with leisure for the intense personal involvements and moral predicaments that were James's real concern. That was the only society he knew anything about. Yet it can fairly be said that he concentrated on it for the same reason that Shakespeare, say, concentrated on kings and nobles, the reason being that such persons, by virtue of their freedom from mundane cares, were perceived as having the fullest human potential. And James, for his own part, though fairly well off, was not above the want of such income as he could earn from the sale of his works, nor are the artists and writers in his tales wealthy, being often rather hard up, as perhaps he nearly was himself at times. His popularity as a novelist, which was considerable through the eighties, did not survive that decade, for all that much of his best work was produced afterward, and though he was thereafter increasingly honored as a master of his art. Certainly he did not admire, nor did he ever practice, a life of indolent ease.

Among other examples of James's stories of artists, most of them written in the early nineties, are "The Next Time," in which an unsuccessful writer tries to write a bad but popular book and can only produce another esoteric masterpiece; "The Figure in the Carpet," in which another writer of a similar kind despairs of criticism's failure to discover the inner meaning of his work; "The Death of the Lion," in which such a figure is done in by a succession of hostesses with kind, uncomprehending attentions; "The Lesson of the Master," where still another writer confronts the fact that his work has suffered through certain compromises he has made; and "The Middle Years," in which the same sort of writer, eager to overcome his own imperfections, dreams of redeeming them with a last, splendid burst of creativity, only to discover that he is fatally ill, when he concludes: "A second chance—*that's* the delusion. There never was to be but one. We work in the dark—we do what we can—we give what we have. Our doubt is our passion and our passion is our task. The rest is the madness of art." And as all these stories may be read as imaginative extensions of James's own situation at various times, so those last remarks may be taken, as indeed they often have been, for the epitaph he would have wished.

The Real Thing

When the porter's wife, who used to answer the house-bell, announced "A gentleman and a lady, sir," I had, as I often had in those days—the wish being father to the thought—an immediate vision of sitters. Sitters my visitors in this case proved to be; but not in the sense I should have preferred. There was nothing at first however to indicate that they mightn't have come for a portrait. The gentleman, a man of fifty, very high and very straight, with a moustache slightly grizzled and a dark grey walking-coat admirably fitted, both of which I noted professionally—I don't mean as a barber or yet as a tailor—would have struck me as a celebrity if celebrities often were striking. It was a truth of which I had for some time been conscious that a figure with a good deal of frontage was, as one might say, almost never a public institution. A glance at the lady helped to remind me of this paradoxical law: she also looked too distinguished to be a "personality." Moreover one would scarcely come across two variations together.

Neither of the pair immediately spoke—they only prolonged the preliminary gaze suggesting that each wished to give the other a chance. They were visibly shy; they stood there letting me take them in—which, as I afterwards perceived, was the most practical thing they could have done. In this way their embarrassment served their cause. I had seen people painfully reluctant to mention that they desired anything so gross as to be represented on canvas; but the scruples of my new friends appeared almost insurmountable. Yet the gentleman might have said "I should like a portrait of my wife," and the lady might have said "I should like a portrait of my husband." Perhaps they weren't husband and wife—this

naturally would make the matter more delicate. Perhaps they wished to be done together—in which case they ought to have brought a third person to break the news.

"We come from Mr. Rivet," the lady finally said with a dim smile that had the effect of a moist sponge passed over a "sunk" piece of painting, as well as of a vague allusion to vanished beauty. She was as tall and straight, in her degree, as her companion, and with ten years less to carry. She looked as sad as a woman could look whose face was not charged with expression; that is her tinted oval mask showed waste as an exposed surface shows friction. The hand of time had played over her freely, but to an effect of elimination. She was slim and stiff, and so well-dressed, in dark blue cloth, with lappets and pockets and buttons, that it was clear she employed the same tailor as her husband. The couple had an indefinable air of prosperous thrift—they evidently got a good deal of luxury for their money. If I was to be one of their luxuries it would behove me to consider my terms.

"Ah Claude Rivet recommended me?" I echoed; and I added that it was very kind of him, though I could reflect that, as he only painted landscape, this wasn't a sacrifice.

The lady looked very hard at the gentleman, and the gentleman looked round the room. Then staring at the floor a moment and stroking his moustache, he rested his pleasant eyes on me with the remark: "He said you were the right one."

"I try to be, when people want to sit."

"Yes, we should like to," said the lady anxiously.

"Do you mean together?"

My visitors exchanged a glance. "If you could do anything with *me* I suppose it would be double," the gentleman stammered.

"Oh yes, there's naturally a higher charge

for two figures than for one."

"We should like to make it pay," the husband confessed.

"That's very good of you," I returned, appreciating so unwonted a sympathy—for I supposed he meant pay the artist.

A sense of strangeness seemed to dawn on the lady. "We mean for the illustrations—Mr. Rivet said you might put one in."

"Put in—an illustration?" I was equally confused.

"Sketch her off, you know," said the gentleman, colouring.

It was only then that I understood the service Claude Rivet had rendered me; he had told them how I worked in black-and-white, for magazines, for storybooks, for sketches of contemporary life, and consequently had copious employment for models. These things were true, but it was not less true—I may confess it now; whether because the aspiration was to lead to everything or to nothing I leave the reader to guess—that I couldn't get the honours, to say nothing of the emoluments, of a great painter of portraits out of my head. My "illustrations" were my pot-boilers; I looked to a different branch of art—far and away the most interesting it had always seemed to me—to perpetuate my fame. There was no shame in looking to it also to make my fortune; but that fortune was by so much further from being made from the moment my visitors wished to be "done" for nothing. I was disappointed; for in the pictorial sense I had immediately *seen* them. I had seized their type—I had already settled what I would do with it. Something that wouldn't absolutely have pleased them, I afterwards reflected.

"Ah you're—you're—a—?" I began as soon as I had mastered my surprise. I couldn't bring out the dingy word "models": it seemed so little to fit the case.

"We haven't had much practice," said the lady.

"We've got to *do* something, and we've thought that an artist in your line might

perhaps make something of us," her husband threw off. He further mentioned that they didn't know many artists and that they had gone first, on the off-chance—he painted views of course, but sometimes put in figures; perhaps I remembered—to Mr. Rivet, whom they had met a few years before at a place in Norfolk where he was sketching.

"We used to sketch a little ourselves," the lady hinted.

"It's very awkward, but we absolutely *must* do something," her husband went on.

"Of course we're not so *very* young," she admitted with a wan smile.

With the remark that I might as well know something more about them the husband had handed me a card extracted from a neat new pocket-book—their appurtenances were all of the freshest—and inscribed with the words "Major Monarch." Impressive as these words were they didn't carry my knowledge much further; but my visitor presently added: "I've left the army and we've had the misfortune to lose our money. In fact our means are dreadfully small."

"It's awfully trying—a regular strain," said Mrs. Monarch.

They evidently wished to be discreet—to take care not to swagger because they were gentlefolk. I felt them willing to recognise this as something of a drawback, at the same time that I guessed at an underlying sense—their consolation in adversity—that they *had* their points. They certainly had; but these advantages struck me as preponderantly social; such for instance as would help to make a drawing-room look well. However, a drawing-room was always, or ought to be, a picture.

In consequence of his wife's allusion to their age Major Monarch observed: "Naturally it's more for the figure that we thought of going in. We can still hold ourselves up." On the instant I saw that the figure was indeed their strong point. His "naturally" didn't sound vain, but it lighted up the question. "*She* has the best one," he continued, nodding at his wife with a pleasant after-dinner absence of circumlocution. I could only reply, as if we were in fact sitting over our wine, that this didn't prevent his own from being very good; which led him in turn to make answer: "We thought that if you ever have to do people like us we might be something like it. She particularly—for a lady in a book, you know."

I was so amused by them that, to get more of it, I did my best to take their point of view; and though it was an embarrassment to find myself appraising physically, as if they were animals on hire or useful blacks, a pair whom I should have expected to meet only in one of the relations in which criticism is tacit, I looked at Mrs. Monarch judicially enough to be able to exclaim after a moment with conviction: "Oh yes, a lady in a book!" She was singularly like a bad illustration.

"We'll stand up, if you like," said the Major; and he raised himself before me with a really grand air.

I could take his measure at a glance—he was six feet two and a perfect gentleman. It would have paid any club in process of formation and in want of a stamp to engage him at a salary to stand in the principal window. What struck me at once was that in coming to me they had rather missed their vocation; they could surely have been turned to better account for advertising purposes. I couldn't of course see the thing in detail, but I could see them make somebody's fortune—I don't mean their own. There was something in them for a waistcoat-maker, an hotel-keeper or a soap-vendor. I could imagine "We always use it" pinned on their bosoms with the greatest effect; I had a vision of the brilliancy with which they would launch a table d'hôte.

Mrs. Monarch sat still, not from pride but from shyness, and presently her husband said to her: "Get up, my dear, and show how smart you are." She obeyed, but she had no need to get up to show it. She walked to the end of the studio and then came back blushing, her fluttered eyes on the partner of her appeal. I was reminded of an incident I had accidentally had a glimpse of in Paris—being with a friend there, a dramatist about to produce a play, when an actress came to him to ask to be entrusted with a part. She went through her paces before him, walked up and down as Mrs. Monarch was doing. Mrs. Monarch did it quite as well, but I abstained from applauding. It was very odd to see such people apply for such poor pay. She looked as if she had ten thousand a year. Her husband had used the word that described her: she was in the London current jargon essentially and typically "smart." Her figure was, in the same order of ideas, conspicuously and irreproachably "good." For a woman of her age her waist was surprisingly small; her elbow moreover had the orthodox crook. She held her head at the conventional angle, but why did she come to *me*? She ought to have tried on jackets at a big shop. I feared my visitors were not only destitute but "artistic"—which would be a great complication. When she sat down again I thanked her, observing that what a draughtsman most valued in his model was the faculty of keeping quiet.

"Oh *she* can keep quiet," said Major Monarch. Then he added jocosely: "I've always kept her quiet."

"I'm not a nasty fidget, am I?" It was going to wring tears from me, I felt, the way she hid her head, ostrich-like, in the other broad bosom.

The owner of this expanse addressed his answer to me. "Perhaps it isn't out of place to mention—because we ought to be quite business-like, oughtn't we?—that when I married her she was known as the Beautiful Statue."

"Oh dear!" said Mrs. Monarch ruefully.

"Of course I should want a certain amount of expression," I rejoined.

"Of *course!*"—and I had never heard such unanimity.

"And then I suppose you know that you'll get awfully tired."

"Oh we *never* get tired!" they eagerly cried.

"Have you had any kind of practice?"

They hesitated—they looked at each other. "We've been photographed—*immensely*," said Mrs. Monarch.

"She means the fellows have asked us themselves," added the Major.

"I see—because you're so good looking."

"I don't know what they thought, but they were always after us."

"We always got our photographs for nothing," smiled Mrs. Monarch.

"We might have brought some, my dear," her husband remarked.

"I'm not sure we have any left. We've given quantities away," she explained to me.

"With our autographs and that sort of thing," said the Major.

"Are they to be got in the shops?" I enquired as a harmless pleasantry.

"Oh yes, *hers*—they used to be."

"Not now," said Mrs. Monarch with her eyes on the floor.

II

I could fancy the "sort of thing" they put on the presentation copies of their photographs, and I was sure they wrote a beautiful hand. It was odd how quickly I was sure of everything that concerned them. If they were now so poor as to have to earn shillings and pence they could never have had much of a margin. Their good looks had been their capital, and they had good-humouredly made the most of the career that this resource marked out for them. It was in their faces, the blankness, the deep intellectual repose of the twenty years of country-house visiting that had given them pleasant intonations. I could see the sunny drawing-rooms, sprinkled with periodicals she didn't read, in which Mrs. Monarch had continuously sat; I could see the wet shrubberies in which she had walked, equipped to admiration for either exercise. I could see the rich covers the Major had helped to shoot and the wonderful garments in which, late at night, he repaired to the smoking-room to talk about them. I could imagine their leggings and waterproofs, their knowing tweeds and rugs, their rolls of sticks and cases of tackle and neat umbrellas; and I could evoke the exact appearance of their servants and the compact variety of their luggage on the platforms of country stations.

They gave small tips, but they were liked; they didn't do anything themselves, but they were welcome. They looked so well everywhere; they gratified the general relish for stature, complexion and "form." They knew it without fatuity or vulgarity, and they respected themselves in consequence. They weren't superficial; they were thorough and kept themselves up—it had been their line. People with such a taste for activity had to have some line. I could feel how even in a dull house they could have been counted on for the joy of life. At present something had happened—it didn't matter what, their little income had grown less, it had grown least—and they had to do something for pocket-money. Their friends could like them, I made out, without liking to support them. There was something about them that represented credit—their clothes, their manners, their type; but if credit is a large empty pocket in which an occasional chink reverberates, the chink at least must be audible. What they wanted of me was to help to make it so. Fortunately they had no children—I soon divined that. They would also perhaps wish our relations to be kept secret: this was why it was "for the figure"—the reproduction of the face would betray them.

I liked them—I felt, quite as their friends must have done—they were so simple; and I had no objection to them if they would suit. But somehow with all their perfections I didn't easily believe in them. After all they were amateurs, and the ruling passion of my life was the detestation of the amateur. Combined with this was another perversity—an innate preference for the represented subject over the real one: the defect of the real one was so apt to be a lack of representation. I like things that appeared; then one was sure. Whether they *were* or not was a subordinate and almost always a profitless question. There were other considerations, the first of which was that I already had two or three recruits in use, notably a young person with big feet, in alpaca, from Kilburn, who for a couple of years had come to me regularly for my illustrations and with whom I was still—perhaps ignobly—satisfied. I frankly explained to my visitors how the case stood, but they had taken more precautions than I supposed. They had reasoned out their opportunity, for Claude Rivet had told them of the projected *édition de luxe* of one of the writers of our day—the rarest of the novelists—who, long neglected by the multitudinous vulgar and dearly prized by the attentive (need I mention Philip Vincent?) had had the happy fortune of seeing, late in life, the dawn and then the full light of a higher criticism; an estimate in which on the part of thepublic there was something really of expiation. The edition preparing, planned by a publisher of taste, was practically an act of high reparation; the wood-cuts with which it was to be enriched were the homage of English art to one of the most independent representatives of English letters. Major and Mrs. Monarch confessed to me they had hoped I might be able to work *them* into my branch of the enterprise. They knew I was to do the first of the books, "Rutland Ramsay," but I had to make clear to them that my participation in the rest of the affair—this first book was to be a test—must depend on the satisfaction I should give. If this should be limited my employers would drop me with scarce common forms. It was therefore a crisis for me, and naturally I was making special preparations, looking about for new people, should they be necessary, and securing the best types. I admitted however that I should like to settle down to two or three good models who would do for everything. "Should we have often to—a—put on special clothes?" Mrs. Monarch timidly demanded.

"Dear yes—that's half the business."

"And should we be expected to supply our own costumes?"

"Oh no; I've got a lot of things. A painter's models put on—or put off—anything he likes."

"And you mean—a—the same?"

"The same?"

Mrs. Monarch looked at her husband again.

"Oh she was just wondering," he explained, "if the costumes are in *general* use." I had to confess that they were, and I mentioned further that some of them—I had a lot of genuine greasy last-century things—had served their time, a hundred years ago, on living world-stained men and women; on figures not perhaps so far removed, in that vanished world, from *their* type, the Monarchs', *quoi!* of a breeched and bewigged age. "We'll put on anything that *fits,*" said the Major.

"Oh I arrange that—they fit in the pictures."

"I'm afraid I should do better for the modern books. I'd come as you like," said Mrs. Monarch.

"She has got a lot of clothes at home: they might do for contemporary life," her husband continued.

"Oh I can fancy scenes in which you'd be quite natural." And indeed I could see the slipshod rearrangements of stale properties—the stories I tried to produce pictures for without the exasperation of reading them—whose sandy tracts the good lady might help to people. But I had to return to the fact that for this sort of work—the daily mechanical grind—I was already equipped: the people I was working with were fully adequate.

"We only thought we might be more like *some* characters," said Mrs. Monarch mildly, getting up.

Her husband also rose; he stood looking at me with a dim wistfulness that was touching in so fine a man. "Wouldn't it be rather a pull sometimes to have—a—to have—?"

He hung fire; he wanted me to help him by phrasing what he meant. But I couldn't—I didn't know. So he brought it out awkwardly: "The *real* thing; a gentleman, you know, or a lady." I was quite ready to give a general assent—I admitted that there was a great deal in that. This encouraged Major Monarch to say, following up his appeal with an unacted gulp: "It's awfully hard—we've tried everything." The gulp was communicative; it proved too much for his wife. Before I knew it Mrs. Monarch had dropped again upon a divan and burst into tears. Her husband sat down beside her, holding one of her hands; whereupon she quickly dried her eyes with the other, while I felt embarrassed as she looked up at me. "There isn't a confounded job I haven't applied for—waited for—prayed for. You can fancy we'd be pretty bad first. Secretaryships and that sort of thing? You might as well ask for a peerage. I'd be *anything*—I'm strong; a messenger or a coalheaver. I'd put on a gold-laced cap and open carriage-doors in front of the haberdasher's; I'd hang about a station to carry portmanteaux; I'd be a postman. But they won't *look* at you; there are thousands as good as yourself already on the ground. *Gentlemen,* poor beggars, who've drunk their wine, who've kept their hunters!"

I was as reassuring as I knew how to be, and my visitors were presently on their feet again while, for the experiment, we agreed on an hour. We were discussing it when the door opened and Miss Churm came in with a wet umbrella. Miss Churm had to take the omnibus to Maida Vale and then walk half a mile. She looked a trifle blowsy and slightly splashed. I scarcely ever saw her come in without thinking afresh how odd it was that, being so little in herself, she should yet be so much in others. She was a meagre little Miss Churm, but was such an ample heroine of romance. She was only a freckled cockney, but she could represent everything, from a fine lady to a shepherdess; she had the faculty as she might have had a fine voice or long hair. She couldn't spell and

she loved beer, but she had two or three "points," and practice, and a knack, and mother-wit, and a whimsical sensibility, and a love of the theatre, and seven sisters, and not an ounce of respect, especially for the *h.* The first thing my visitors saw was that her umbrella was wet, and in their spotless perfection they visibly winced at it. The rain had come on since their arrival.

"I'm all in a soak; there *was* a mess of people in the 'bus. I wish you lived near a stytion," said Miss Churm. I requested her to get ready as quickly as possible, and she passed into the room in which she always changed her dress. But before going out she asked me what she was to get into this time.

"It's the Russian princess, don't you know?" I answered; "the one with the 'golden eyes,' in black velvet, for the long thing in the *Cheapside.*"

"Golden eyes? I *say!*" cried Miss Churm, while my companions watched her with intensity as she withdrew. She always arranged herself, when she was late, before I could turn round; and I kept my visitors a little on purpose, so that they might get an idea, from seeing her, what would be expected of themselves. I mentioned that she was quite my notion of an excellent model—she was really very clever.

"Do you think she looks like a Russian princess?" Major Monarch asked with lurking alarm.

"When I make her, yes."

"Oh if you have to *make* her—!" he reasoned, not without point.

"That's the most you can ask. There are so many who are not makeable."

"Well now, *here's* a lady"—and with a persuasive smile he passed his arm into his wife's—"who's already made!"

"Oh I'm not a Russian princess," Mrs. Monarch protested a little coldly. I could see she had known some and didn't like them. There at once was a complication of a kind I never had to fear with Miss Churm.

This young lady came back in black velvet—the gown was rather rusty and very low on her lean shoulders—and with a Japanese fan in her red hands. I reminded her that in the scene I was doing she had to look over some one's head. "I forget whose it is; but it doesn't matter. Just look over a head."

"I'd rather look over a stove," said Miss Churm; and she took her station near the fire. She fell into position, settled herself into a tall attitude, gave a certain backward inclination to her head and a certain forward droop to her fan, and looked, at least to my prejudiced sense, distinguished and charming, foreign and dangerous. We left her looking so while I went downstairs with Major and Mrs. Monarch.

"I believe I could come about as near it as that," said Mrs. Monarch.

"Oh you think she's shabby, but you must allow for the alchemy of art."

However, they went off with an evident increase of comfort founded on their demonstrable advantage in being the real thing. I could fancy them shuddering over Miss Churm. She was very droll about them when I went back, for I told her what they wanted.

"Well, if *she* can sit I'll tyke to book-keeping," said my model.

"She's very ladylike," I replied as an innocent form of aggravation.

"So much the worse for *you.* That means she can't turn round."

"She'll do for the fashionable novels."

"Oh yes, she'll *do* for them!" my model humorously declared. "Ain't they bad enough without her?" I had often sociably denounced them to Miss Churm.

III

It was for the elucidation of a mystery in one of these works that I first tried Mrs. Monarch. Her husband came with her, to be useful if necessary—it was sufficiently clear that as a general thing he would prefer to come with her. At first I wondered if this were for "propriety's" sake—if he were going to be jealous and meddling. The idea was too tiresome, and if it had been confirmed it would speedily have brought our acquaintance to a close. But I soon saw there was nothing in it and that if he accompanied Mrs. Monarch it was—in addition to the chance of being wanted—simply because he had nothing else to do. When they were separate his occupation was gone and they never *had* been separate. I judged rightly that in their awkward situation their close union was their main comfort and that this union had no weak spot. It was a real marriage, an encouragement to the hesitating, a nut for pessimists to crack. Their address was humble—I remember afterwards thinking it had been the only thing about them that was really professional—and I could fancy the lamentable lodgings in which the Major would have been left alone. He could sit there more or less grimly with his wife—he couldn't sit there anyhow without her.

He had too much tact to try and make himself agreeable when he couldn't be useful; so when I was too absorbed in my work to talk he simply sat and waited. But I liked to hear him talk—it made my work, when not interrupting it, less mechanical, less special. To listen to him was to combine the excitement of going out with the economy of staying at home. There was only one hindrance—that I seemed not to know any of the people this brilliant couple had known. I think he wondered extremely, during the term of our intercourse, whom the deuce I *did* know. He hadn't a stray sixpence of an idea to fumble for, so we didn't spin it very fine; we confined ourselves to questions of leather and even of liquor—saddlers and breeches-makers and how to get excellent claret cheap—and matters like "good trains" and the habits of small game. His lore on these last subjects was astonishing—he managed to interweave the stationmaster with the ornithologist. When he couldn't talk about greater things he could talk cheerfully about smaller, and since I couldn't accompany him into reminiscences of the fashionable world he could lower the conversation without a visible effort to my level.

So earnest a desire to please was touching in a man who could so easily have knocked one down. He looked after the fire and had an opinion on the draught of the stove without my asking him, and I could see that he thought many of my arrangements not half knowing. I remember telling him that if I were only rich I'd offer him a salary to come and teach me how to live. Sometimes he gave a random sigh of which the essence might have been: "Give me even such a bare old barrack as *this,* and I'd do something with it!" When I wanted to use him he came alone; which was an illustration of the superior courage of women. His wife could bear her solitary second floor, and she was in general more discreet; showing by various small reserves that she was alive to the propriety of keeping our relations markedly professional—not letting them slide into sociability. She wished it to remain clear that she and the Major were employed, not cultivated, and if she approved of me as a superior, who could be kept in his place, she never thought me quite good enough for an equal.

She sat with great intensity, giving the whole of her mind to it, and was capable of remaining for an hour almost as motionless as before a photographer's lens. I could see she had been photographed often, but somehow the very habit that made her good for that purpose unfitted her for mine. At first I was extremely pleased with her lady-like air, and it was a satisfaction, on coming to follow her lines, to see how good they were and how far they could lead the pencil. But after a little skirmishing I began to find her too insurmountably stiff; do what I would with it my drawing looked like a photograph or a copy of a photograph. Her figure had no variety of expression—she herself had no sense of variety. You may say that this was my business and was only a question of placing her. Yet I placed her in every conceivable position and she man-

aged to obliterate their differences. She was always a lady certainly, and into the bargain was always the same lady. She was the real thing, but always the same thing. There were moments when I rather writhed under the serenity of her confidence that she *was* the real thing. All her dealings with me and all her husband's were an implication that this was lucky for *me.* Meanwhile I found myself trying to invent types that approached her own, instead of making her own transform itself—in the clever way that was not impossible for instance to poor Miss Churm. Arrange as I would and take the precautions I would, she always came out, in my pictures, too tall—landing me in the dilemma of having represented a fascinating woman as seven feet high, which (out of respect perhaps to my own very much scantier inches) was far from my idea of such a personage.

The case was worse with the Major—nothing I could do would keep *him* down, so that he became useful only for the representation of brawny giants. I adored variety and range, I cherished human accidents, the illustrative note; I wanted to characterise closely, and the thing in the world I most hated was the danger of being ridden by a type. I had quarrelled with some of my friends about it; I had parted company with them for maintaining that one *had* to be, and that if the type was beautiful—witness Raphael and Leonardo—the servitude was only a gain. I was neither Leonardo nor Raphael—I might only be a presumptuous young modern searcher; but I held that everything was to be sacrificed sooner than character. When they claimed that the obsessional form could easily *be* character I retorted, perhaps superficially, "Whose?" It couldn't be everybody's—it might end in being nobody's.

After I had drawn Mrs. Monarch a dozen times I felt surer even than before that the value of such a model as Miss Churm resided precisely in the fact that she had no positive stamp, combined of course with the other fact that what she did have was a curious and inexplicable talent for imitation. Her usual appearance was like a curtain which she could draw up at request for a capital performance. This performance was simply suggestive; but it was a word to the wise—it was vivid and pretty. Sometimes even I thought it, though she was plain herself, too insipidly pretty; I made it a reproach to her that the figures drawn from her were monotonously (*bêtement,* as we used to say) graceful. Nothing made her more angry; it was so much her pride to feel she could sit for characters that had nothing in common with each other. She would accuse me at such moments of taking away her "reputytion."

It suffered a certain shrinkage, this queer quantity, from the repeated visits of my new friends. Miss Churm was greatly in demand, never in want of employment, so I had no scruple in putting her off occasionally, to try them more at my ease. It was certainly amusing at first to do the real thing—it was amusing to do Major Monarch's trousers. They *were* the real thing, even if he did come out colossal. It was amusing to do his wife's back hair—it was so mathematically neat—and the particular "smart" tension of her tight stays. She lent herself especially to positions in which the face was somewhat averted or blurred; she abounded in ladylike back views and *profils perdus.* When she stood erect she took naturally one of the attitudes in which court-painters represent queens and princesses; so that I found myself wondering whether, to draw out this accomplishment, I couldn't get the editor of the *Cheapside* to publish a really royal romance, "A Tale of Buckingham Palace." Sometimes however the real thing and the make-believe came into contact; by which I mean that Miss Churm, keeping an appointment or coming to make one on days when I had much work in hand, encountered her invidious rivals. The encounter was not on their part, for they noticed her no more than if she had been the housemaid; not from intentional loftiness, but simply because as yet, professionally, they didn't

know how to fraternise, as I could imagine they would have liked—or at least that the Major would. They couldn't talk about the omnibus—they always walked; and they didn't know what else to try—she wasn't interested in good trains or cheap claret. Besides, they must have felt—in the air—that she was amused at them, secretly derisive of their ever knowing how. She wasn't a person to conceal the limits of her faith if she had had a chance to show them. On the other hand Mrs. Monarch didn't think her tidy; for why else did she take pains to say to me—it was going out of the way, for Mrs. Monarch—that she didn't like dirty women?

One day when my young lady happened to be present with my other sitters—she even dropped in, when it was convenient, for a chat—I asked her to be so good as to lend a hand in getting tea, a service with which she was familiar and which was one of a class that, living as I did in a small way, with slender domestic resources, I often appealed to my models to render. They liked to lay hands on my property, to break the sitting, and sometimes the china—it made them feel Bohemian. The next time I saw Miss Churm after this incident she surprised me greatly by making a scene about it—she accused me of having wished to humiliate her. She hadn't resented the outrage at the time, but had seemed obliging and amused, enjoying the comedy of asking Mrs. Monarch, who sat vague and silent, whether she would have cream and sugar, and putting an exaggerated simper into the question. She had tried intonations—as if she too wished to pass for the real thing—till I was afraid my other visitors would take offence.

Oh they were determined not to do this, and their touching patience was the measure of their great need. They would sit by the hour, uncomplaining, till I was ready to use them; they would come back on the chance of being wanted and would walk away cheerfully if it failed. I used to go to the door with them to see in what magnificent order they retreated. I tried to find other employment for them—I introduced them to several artists. But they didn't "take," for reasons I could appreciate, and I became rather anxiously aware that after such disappointments they fell back upon me with a heavier weight. They did me the honour to think me most *their* form. They weren't romantic enough for the painters, and in those days there were few serious workers in black-and-white. Besides, they had an eye to the great job I had mentioned to them—they had secretly set their hearts on supplying the right essence for my pictorial vindication of our fine novelist. They knew that for this undertaking I should want no costume-effects, none of the frippery of past ages—that it was a case in which everything would be contemporary and satirical and presumably genteel. If I could work them into it their future would be assured, for the labour would of course be long and the occupation steady.

One day Mrs. Monarch came without her husband—she explained his absence by his having had to go to the City. While she sat there in her usual relaxed majesty there came at the door a knock which I immediately recognised as the subdued appeal of a model out of work. It was followed by the entrance of a young man whom I at once saw to be a foreigner and who proved in fact an Italian acquainted with no English word but my name, which he uttered in a way that made it seem to include all others. I hadn't then visited his country, nor was I proficient in his tongue; but as he was not so meanly constituted—what Italian is?—as to depend only on that member for expression he conveyed to me, in familiar but graceful mimicry, that he was in search of exactly the employment in which the lady before me was engaged. I was not struck with him at first, and while I continued to draw I dropped few signs of interest or encouragement. He stood his ground however—not importunately, but with a dumb dog-like fidelity in his eyes that amounted to innocent impudence, the manner of a devoted servant—

he might have been in the house for years—unjustly suspected. Suddenly it struck me that this very attitude and expression made a picture; whereupon I told him to sit down and wait till I should be free. There was another picture in the way he obeyed me, and I observed as I worked that there were others still in the way he looked wonderingly, with his head thrown back, about the high studio. He might have been crossing himself in Saint Peter's. Before I finished I said to myself "The fellow's a bankrupt orange-monger, but a treasure."

When Mrs. Monarch withdrew he passed across the room like a flash to open the door for her, standing there with the rapt pure gaze of the young Dante spellbound by the young Beatrice. As I never insisted, in such situations, on the blankness of the British domestic, I reflected that he had the making of a servant—and I needed one, but couldn't pay him to be only that—as well as of a model; in short I resolved to adopt my bright adventurer if he would agree to officiate in the double capacity. He jumped at my offer, and in the event my rashness—for I had really known nothing about him—wasn't brought home to me. He proved a sympathetic though a desultory ministrant, and had in a wonderful degree the *sentiment de la pose*. It was uncultivated, instinctive, a part of the happy instinct that had guided him to my door and helped him to spell out my name on the card nailed to it. He had had no other introduction to me than a guess, from the shape of my high north window, seen outside, that my place was a studio and that as a studio it would contain an artist. He had wandered to England in search of fortune, like other itinerants, and had embarked, with a partner and a small green hand-cart, on the sale of penny ices. The ices had melted away and the partner had dissolved in their train. My young man wore tight yellow trousers with reddish stripes and his name was Oronte. He was sallow but fair, and when I put him into some old clothes of my own he looked like an Englishman. He was as good as Miss Churm, who could look, when requested, like an Italian.

IV

I thought Mrs. Monarch's face slightly convulsed when, on her coming back with her husband, she found Oronte installed. It was strange to have to recognise in a scrap of a lazzarone a competitor to her magnificent Major. It was she who scented danger first, for the Major was anecdotically unconscious. But Oronte gave us tea, with a hundred eager confusions—he had never been concerned in so queer a process—and I think she thought better of me for having at last an "establishment." They saw a couple of drawings that I had made of the establishment, and Mrs. Monarch hinted that it never would have struck her he had sat for them. "Now the drawings you make from *us,* they look exactly like us," she reminded me, smiling in triumph; and I recognised that this was indeed just their defect. When I drew the Monarchs I couldn't anyhow get away from them—get into the character I wanted to represent; and I hadn't the least desire my model should be discoverable in my picture. Miss Churm never was, and Mrs. Monarch thought I hid her, very properly, because she was vulgar; whereas if she was lost it was only as the dead who go to heaven are lost—in the gain of an angel the more.

By this time I had got a certain start with "Rutland Ramsay," the first novel in the great projected series; that is I had produced a dozen drawings, several with the help of the Major and his wife, and I had sent them in for approval. My understanding with the publishers, as I have already hinted, had been that I was to be left to do my work, in this particular case, as I liked, with the whole book committed to me; but my connexion with the rest of the series was only contingent. There were moments when, frankly, it *was* a comfort to have the real thing under one's hand; for there were characters in "Rutland Ramsay" that were very much like it. There were people presumably as erect as the Major and women of as good a fashion as Mrs. Monarch. There was a great deal of country-house life—treated, it is true, in a fine fanciful ironical generalised way—and there was a considerable implication of knickerbockers and kilts. There were certain things I had to settle at the outset; such things for instance as the exact appearance of the hero and the particular bloom and figure of the heroine. The author of course gave me a lead, but there was a margin for interpretation. I took the Monarchs into my confidence, I told them frankly what I was about, I mentioned my embarrassments and alternatives. "Oh take *him!*" Mrs. Monarch murmured sweetly, looking at her husband; and "What could you want better than my wife?" the Major enquired with the comfortable candour that now prevailed between us.

I wasn't obliged to answer these remarks—I was only obliged to place my sitters. I wasn't easy in mind, and I postponed a little timidly perhaps the solving of my question. The book was a large canvas, the other figures were numerous, and I worked off at first some of the episodes in which the hero and the heroine were not concerned. When once I had set *them* up I should have to stick to them—I couldn't make my young man seven feet high in one place and five feet nine in another. I inclined on the whole to the latter measurement, though the Major more than once reminded me that *he* looked about as young as any one. It was indeed quite possible to arrange him, for the figure, so that it would have been difficult to detect his age. After the spontaneous Oronte had been with me a month, and after I had given him to understand several times over that his native exuberance would presently constitute an insurmountable barrier to our further intercourse, I waked to a sense of his heroic capacity. He was only five feet seven, but the remaining inches were latent. I tried him almost secretly at first, for I was really rather afraid of the judgement my other models would pass on such a choice. If they regarded Miss Churm as little better than a snare what would they think of the representation by a person so little the real thing as an Italian street-vendor of a protagonist formed by a public school?

If I went a little in fear of them it wasn't because they bullied me, because they had got an oppressive foothold, but because in their really pathetic decorum and mysteriously permanent newness they counted on me so intensely. I was therefore very glad when Jack Hawley came home: he was always of such good counsel. He painted badly himself, but there was no one like him for putting his finger on the place. He had been absent from England for a year; he had been somewhere—I don't remember where—to get a fresh eye. I was in a good deal of dread of any such organ, but we were old friends; he had been away for months and a sense of emptiness was creeping into my life. I hadn't dodged a missile for a year.

He came back with a fresh eye, but with the same old black velvet blouse, and the first evening he spent in my studio we smoked cigarettes till the small hours. He had done no work himself, he had only got the eye; so the field was clear for the production of my little things. He wanted to see what I had produced for the *Cheapside*, but he was disappointed in the exhibition. That at least seemed the meaning of two or three comprehensive groans which, as he lounged on my big divan, his leg folded under him, looking at my latest drawings, issued from his lips with the smoke of the cigarette.

"What's the matter with you?" I asked.

"What's the matter with *you?*"

"Nothing save that I'm mystified."

"You are indeed. You're quite off the hinge. What's the meaning of this new fad?" And he tossed me, with visible irrev-

erence, a drawing in which I happened to have depicted both my elegant models. I asked if he didn't think it good, and he replied that it struck him as execrable, given the sort of thing I had always represented myself to him as wishing to arrive at; but I let that pass—I was so anxious to see exactly what he meant. The two figures in the picture looked colossal, but I supposed this was *not* what he meant, inasmuch as, for aught he knew to the contrary, I might have been trying for some such effect. I maintained that I was working exactly in the same way as when he last had done me the honour to tell me I might do something some day. "Well, there's a screw loose somewhere," he answered; "wait a bit and I'll discover it." I depended on him to do so: where else was the fresh eye? But he produced at last nothing more luminous than "I don't know—I don't like your types." This was lame for a critic who had never consented to discuss with me anything but the question of execution, the direction of strokes and the mystery of values.

"In the drawings you've been looking at I think my types are very handsome."

"Oh they won't do!"

"I've been working with new models."

"I see you have. *They* won't do."

"Are you very sure of that?"

"Absolutely—they're stupid."

"You mean *I* am—for I ought to get round that."

"You *can't*—with such people. Who are they?"

I told him, so far as was necessary, and he concluded heartlessly: "Ce sont des gens qu'il faut mettre à la porte."

"You've never seen them; they're awfully good"—I flew to their defence.

"Not seen them? Why all this recent work of yours drops to pieces with them. It's all I want to see of them."

"No one else has said anything against it—the *Cheapside* people are pleased."

Every one else is an ass, and the *Cheapside* people the biggest asses of all. Come, don't pretend at this time of day to have pretty illusions about the public, especially about publishers and editors. It's not for *such* animals you work—it's for those who know, *coloro che sanno;* so keep straight for *me* if you can't keep straight for yourself. There was a certain sort of thing you used to try for—and a very good thing it was. But this twaddle isn't *in* it." When I talked with Hawley later about "Rutland Ramsay" and its possible successors he declared that I must get back into my boat again or I should go to the bottom. His voice in short was the voice of warning.

I noted the warning, but I didn't turn my friends out of doors. They bored me a good deal; but the very fact that they bored me admonished me not to sacrifice them—if there was anything to be done with them—simply to irritation. As I look back at this phase they seem to me to have pervaded my life not a little. I have a vision of them as most of the time in my studio, seated against the wall on an old velvet bench to be out of the way, and resembling the while a pair of patient courtiers in a royal antechamber. I'm convinced that during the coldest weeks of the winter they held their ground because it saved them fire. Their newness was losing its gloss, and it was impossible not to feel them objects of charity. Whenever Miss Churm arrived they went away, and after I was fairly launched in "Rutland Ramsay" Miss Churm arrived pretty often. They managed to express to me tacitly that they supposed I wanted her for the low life of the book, and I let them suppose it, since they had attempted to study the work—it was lying about the studio—without discovering that it dealt only with the highest circles. They had dipped into the most brilliant of our novelists without deciphering many passages. I still took an hour from them, now and again, in spite of Jack Hawley's warning: it would be time enough to dismiss them, if dismissal should be necessary, when the rigour of the season was over. Hawley had made their acquaintance—he had met them at my fireside—and thought them a ridiculous pair. Learning

that he was a painter they tried to approach him, to show him too that they were the real thing; but he looked at them, across the big room, as if they were miles away: they were a compendium of everything he most objected to in the social system of his country. Such people as that, all convention and patent-leather, with ejaculations that stopped conversation, had no business in a studio. A studio was a place to learn to see, and how could you see through a pair of feather-beds?

The main inconvenience I suffered at their hands was that at first I was shy of letting it break upon them that my artful little servant had begun to sit to me for "Rutland Ramsay." They knew I had been odd enough—they were prepared by this time to allow oddity to artists—to pick a foreign vagabond out of the streets when I might have had a person with whiskers and credentials; but it was some time before they learned how high I rated his accomplishments. They found him in an attitude more than once, but they never doubted I was doing him as an organ-grinder. There were several things they never guessed, and one of them was that for a striking scene in the novel, in which a footman briefly figured, it occurred to me to make use of Major Monarch as the menial. I kept putting this off, I didn't like to ask him to don the livery—besides the difficulty of finding a livery to fit him. At last, one day late in the winter, when I was at work on the despised Oronte, who caught one's idea on the wing, and was in the glow of feeling myself go very straight, they came in, the Major and his wife, with their society laugh about nothing (there was less and less to laugh at); came in like country-callers—they always reminded me of that—who have walked across the park after church and are presently persuaded to stay to luncheon. Luncheon was over, but they could stay to tea—I knew they wanted it. The fit was on me, however, and I couldn't let my ardour cool and my work wait, with the fading daylight, while my model prepared it. So I asked Mrs.

Monarch if she would mind laying it out—a request which for an instant brought all the blood to her face. Her eyes were on her husband's for a second, and some mute telegraphy passed between them. Their folly was over the next instant; his cheerful shrewdness put an end to it. So far from pitying their wounded pride, I must add, I was moved to give it as complete a lesson as I could. They bustled about together and got out the cups and saucers and made the kettle boil. I know they felt as if they were waiting on my servant, and when the tea was prepared I said: "He'll have a cup, please—he's tired." Mrs. Monarch brought him one where he stood, and he took it from her as if he had been a gentleman at a party squeezing a crush-hat with an elbow.

Then it came over me that she had made a great effort for me—made it with a kind of nobleness—and that I owed her a compensation. Each time I saw her after this I wondered what the compensation could be. I couldn't go on doing the wrong thing to oblige them. Oh it *was* the wrong thing, the stamp of the work for which they sat—Hawley was not the only person to say it now. I sent in a large number of the drawings I had made for "Rutland Ramsay," and I received a warning that was more to the point than Hawley's. The artistic adviser of the house for which I was working was of opinion that many of my illustrations were not what had been looked for. Most of these illustrations were the subjects in which the Monarchs had figured. Without going into the question of what *had* been looked for, I had to face the fact that at this rate I shouldn't get the other books to do. I hurled myself in despair on Miss Churm—I put her through all her paces. I not only adopted Oronte publicly as my hero, but one morning when the Major looked in to see if I didn't require him to finish a *Cheapside* figure for which he had begun to sit the week before, I told him I had changed my mind—I'd do the drawing from my man. At this my visitor turned pale and stood looking at me. "Is *he* your idea of an English gentleman?" he asked.

I was disappointed, I was nervous, I wanted to get on with my work; so I replied with irritation: "Oh my dear Major—I can't be ruined for *you!*"

It was a horrid speech, but he stood another moment—after which, without a word, he quitted the studio. I drew a long breath, for I said to myself that I shouldn't see him again. I hadn't told him definitely that I was in danger of having my work rejected, but I was vexed at his not having felt the catastrophe in the air, read with me the moral of our fruitless collaboration, the lesson that in the deceptive atmosphere of art even the highest respectability may fail of being plastic.

I didn't owe my friends money, but I did see them again. They reappeared together three days later, and, given all the other facts, there was something tragic in that one. It was a clear proof they could find nothing else in life to do. They had threshed the matter out in a dismal conference—they had digested the bad news that they were not in for the series. If they weren't useful to me even for the *Cheapside* their function seemed difficult to determine, and I could only judge at first that they had come, forgivingly, decorously, to take a last leave. This made me rejoice in secret that I had little leisure for a scene; for I had placed both my other models in position together and I was pegging away at a drawing from which I hoped to derive glory. It had been suggested by the passage in which Rutland Ramsay, drawing up a chair to Artemisia's piano-stool, says extraordinary things to her while she ostensibly fingers out a difficult piece of music. I had done Miss Churm at the piano before—it was an attitude in which she knew how to take on an absolutely poetic grace. I wished the two figures to "compose" together with intensity, and my little Italian had entered perfectly into my conception. The pair were vividly before me, the piano had been pulled out; it was a charming show of blended youth and murmured love, which I had only to catch and keep. My visitors stood and looked at it, and I was friendly to them over my shoulder.

They made no response, but I was used to silent company and went on with my work, only a little disconcerted—even though exhilarated by the sense that *this* was at least the ideal thing—at not having got rid of them after all. Presently I heard Mrs. Monarch's sweet voice beside or rather above me: "I wish her hair were a little better done." I looked up and she was staring with a strange fixedness at Miss Churm, whose back was turned to her. "Do you mind my just touching it?" she went on—a question which made me spring up for an instant as with the instinctive fear that she might do the young lady a harm. But she quieted me with a glance I shall never forget—I confess I should like to have been able to paint *that*—and went for a moment to my model. She spoke to her softly, laying a hand on her shoulder and bending over her; and as the girl, understanding, gratefully assented, she disposed her rough curls, with a few quick passes, in such a way as to make Miss Churm's head twice as charming. It was one of the most heroic personal services I've ever seen rendered. Then Mrs. Monarch turned away with a low sigh and, looking about her as if for something to do, stooped to the floor with a noble humility and picked up a dirty rag that had dropped out of my paint-box.

The Major meanwhile had also been looking for something to do, and, wandering to the other end of the studio, saw before him my breakfast-things neglected, unremoved. "I say, can't I be useful *here?*" he called out to me with an irrepressible quaver. I assented with a laugh that I fear was awkward, and for the next ten minutes, while I worked, I heard the light clatter of china and the tinkle of spoons and glass.

Mrs. Monarch assisted her husband—they washed up my crockery, they put it away. They wandered off into my little scullery, and I afterwards found that they had cleaned my knives and that my slender stock of plate had an unprecedented surface. When it came over me, the latent eloquence of what they were doing, I confess that my drawing was blurred for a moment—the picture swam. They had accepted their failure, but they couldn't accept their fate. They had bowed their heads in bewilderment to the perverse and cruel law in virtue of which the real thing could be so much less precious than the unreal; but they didn't want to starve. If my servants were my models, then my models might be my servants. They would reverse the parts—the others would sit for the ladies and gentlemen and *they* would do the work. They would still be in the studio—it was an intense dumb appeal to me not to turn them out. "Take us on," they wanted to say—"we'll do *anything.*"

My pencil dropped from my hand; my sitting was spoiled and I got rid of my sitters, who were also evidently rather mystified and awestruck. Then, alone with the Major and his wife I had a most uncomfortable moment. He put their prayer into a single sentence: "I say, you know—just let *us* do for you, can't you?" I couldn't—it was dreadful to see them emptying my slops; but I pretended I could, to oblige them, for about a week. Then I gave them a sum of money to go away, and I never saw them again. I obtained the remaining books, but my friend Hawley repeats that Major and Mrs. Monarch did me a permanent harm, got me into false ways. If it be true I'm content to have paid the price—for the memory.

The President of the United States

Woodrow Wilson

Editor's Introduction

Born at Staunton, Virginia, in 1856, the son of a Presbyterian minister of strong Calvinist views, Woodrow Wilson early learned to look upon human life as the fulfillment of God's will, to see man as what he called "a distinct moral agent" in that work. Powerfully moved to the idea of "service," he came to think of himself as one from whom great contributions, and possibly great sacrifices, might be expected. Nothing less would be tolerated, he seems to have believed, either from his conscience, the pressure of which twice led to youthful breakdowns, or from his sense of public affairs, to which he brought convictions of strict righteousness. "Tolerance," he wrote in a youthful essay, 'is an admirable intellectual gift; but it is of little worth in politics. Politics is a war of *causes;* a joust of principles. Government is too serious a matter to admit of meaningless courtesies."

Yet this driven, stern, and lonely man, who throughout his life lamented his inability to have friendships, to get along easily with other human beings, had an extraordinary gift for dealing with them—for inspiring in them a devotion he could never achieve on a personal level—as a statesman. Such a talent only gradually revealed itself, it is true. Having graduated from Princeton in 1879, Wilson studied law, but found legal practice uncongenial and decided to pursue graduate studies at Johns Hopkins, from which in 1886 he received a doctorate in history and government. The academic life that followed, first at Bryn Mawr, then at Wesleyan, and finally back at Princeton, where in 1890 he was made professor of politics and jurisprudence, was equally unsatisfying, though Wilson worked hard, published six books. "I have a strong instinct of leadership," he observed of himself, "an unmistakeably oratorical temperament, and the keenest possible delight in affairs; and it has required very constant and stringent schooling to content me with the sober methods of a scholar and the man of letters." He added: "I have a passion for interpreting great thoughts to the world; I should be complete if I could . . . so communicate . . . to the minds of the great mass of the people as to impel them to great political achievements." But completion could not then have seemed to mean much more than what in fact appeared in 1902, when he was invited to become the head of Princeton.

As a university president, Wilson proved both fertile in ideas and effective in their realization. Dissatisfied with undergraduate instruction, he raised large sums of money, hired fifty young preceptors to serve as contacts between students and teachers, organized systematic curricula for the college, proposed a quadrangular system of student living such as was later adopted at Yale and Harvard, and otherwise reshaped undergraduate education, all in a scant half dozen years. Then he thought he saw that the logic of his reforms required an end to the sacred Princeton eating clubs as undemocratic barriers to undergraduate life, and on this issue, being opposed by influential alumni and showing a tactless, uncompromising spirit that was prophetic of his later troubles, he met defeat.

Ironically, the immediate consequence of his failure was to propel him into the political sphere he had always wished to enter. His battle with the Princeton traditionalists was widely publicized and brought him to the attention of Democratic Party bosses looking for someone to run for governor of New Jersey who could attract the progressive voters in the state. Wilson, who had become well known for his public addresses and essays directed against business combinations and unrepresentative politics on the national scene, seemed just the man. Accordingly, in September 1910, he was offered the nomination, which he accepted, and having waged an eloquent campaign, he was elected two months later. "Can you imagine anyone," a party boss who visited him at his comfortable book-lined Princeton office is reported to have said, "being damn fool enough to give this up for the heartaches of politics?"

As governor, Wilson was as successful as he had been at Princeton. Turning his back on the bosses, he won the support of the young Progressives, who till then had distrusted him, by putting through series of reform measures unprecedented in New Jersey's history. Among them were a primary and elections law, a corrupt practices act, workman's compensation, utilities regulation, school reforms, and an act allowing cities to adopt a commission form of government.

Wilson thus established himself as a formidable figure in politics, an impression he enforced by a series of speeches in 1911-12 in which he clearly expressed a national vision of the sort he had realized in his own state. These speeches called for change in the laws and institutions of the trust-dominated, boss-governed country of that day, but change that would serve "established purposes and conceptions." It was a summons based on the idea, as one historian has said, "that we must have a forward-looking return to the past," an essentially conservative vision that sought reform by means of restoration of representative institutions. In this was perhaps the essence of Wilsonian idealism, as well as its underlying contradiction. Perhaps it was the contradiction to be expected from one whose heroes were Edmund Burke and Walter Bagehot, Englishmen of the eighteenth and nineteenth centuries who in their political writings had defended tradition against revolution, gradualism as distinct from radical change.

Whatever its basis, Wilson's eloquence, taken with his success as governor, gained him the Democratic presidential nomination in 1912. And with the opposition divided between President Taft, who sought a second term, and Theodore Roosevelt, who ran as a third-party candidate, this proved the chance he needed. After a campaign that stressed what he called the New Freedom, which was a conception of economic and political power restored to the hands of the people who had lost control of it, Wilson was elected twenty-eighth President of the United States.

Again he distinguished himself, putting forth a program of domestic legislation consistent with the vision he had formed. In the first two years of his term he achieved a reduced tariff, a federal income tax, the banking and currency reforms embodied in the Federal Reserve Act, creation of the Federal Trade Commission, and passage of the Clayton Anti-Trust Act that gave important rights to organized labor. This legislation, which made fundamental changes in the social and economic climate of the country, amounted to an extraordinary personal triumph.

A revolution in Mexico leading to hostile confrontations and the coming of World War I turned Wilson's attention to foreign affairs, with which thereafter he was chiefly occupied. Although his sympathies were with the Allies in the war, he adopted a neutral policy and endeavored to play the role of peacemaker. This policy was strained first by the British blockade of Germany, which led to widespread violations of American rights at sea, and then by German submarine attacks on shipping that neared the British Isles. These resulted in the destruction, in May 1915, of the British liner "Lusitania" with loss of over 100 American lives, an event that seems to have fixed Wilson in the conviction that while injuries to property might be met with protests, those that took life must lead to war. Yet he wished to avoid war. "There is such a thing as a nation being too proud to fight," he said. And with strongly worded threats that caused the Germans to back down, he did maintain neutrality for two years afterward, in the course of which he was elected to a second term by an extremely close vote.

In this interval, Wilson made strenuous efforts to arrange a peace, the terms of which he set forth in a speech to the Senate in January 1917. It should be a "peace without victory," he said, marked by relinquishment of territorial claims, limitation of armaments, and creation of a League of Nations. Unhappily, his plan was frustrated by the German resumption, at about the same time, of unrestricted submarine warfare, and when at length this resulted in the loss of further American lives at sea, Wilson decided on hostilities. "It is a fearful thing," he said, "to lead this great, peaceful people into war," but such was his request to Congress in April 1917—a request to make war "for democracy, for the right of those who submit to authority to have a voice in their own Governments, for the rights and liberties of small nations, for a universal dominion of right by such a concert of free peoples as shall bring peace and safety to all nations and make the world itself at last free."

It is generally agreed that American entrance into a war otherwise stalemated was the decisive factor in its eventual result, that Germany's surrender eighteen months later could have been accomplished in no other way. Certainly, when Wilson arrived in Europe on the way to the peace conference at Versailles in December 1918, he was greeted by frenzied popular outbursts as the hero who had brought peace to the world. But his sense of triumph was short-lived. When the conference got under way, it was clear that Wilson faced, in the representatives of the victorious Allies, a determination to impose a settlement upon Germany that denied the greater part of Wilson's principles. As the weeks of deliberation went by, the president grew less and less hopeful that any reordering of world affairs would come out of such efforts. "What I seem to see," he told a friend, ". . . is a tragedy of disappointment." In the end, with his expectations dashed for the kind of peace he believed would have redeemed the sacrifices of the war, he decided that everything depended on the League of Nations, that if the United States could be induced to join that organization, the war's expense of blood and treasure might not have been in vain.

Wilson's determination to risk everything—his physical health as well as his political fortunes—on this one issue of the League was the crisis of his career, and his failure to persuade the Congress to accept American participation broke him utterly. That could have been averted had he been willing to allow conditions to American involvement which a different temper might have regarded as relatively minor, and which in fact the European Allies were quite willing to accept. But Wilson was adamant, insisting on all or nothing, and at last, after an exhausting speaking tour around the country in which he attempted to rally support for an unconditional commitment, he suffered a disabling stroke that rendered him powerless for the remainder of his term. America did not join the League of Nations, Wilson's party was repudiated in the election of 1920, and he himself died finally at Washington in 1924, having retired in virtual seclusion. His last message before leaving office, directed to the opposition leader of the Senate, was that he had "no further communication to make."

Among Wilson's writings, still of interest are *Congressional Government* (1885), his doctoral dissertation, and *Constitutional Government* (1908), from which the chapter that follows is taken. A projected magnum opus, *The Philosophy of Politics,* was put aside when he first ran for office and never resumed. In 1919 he was awarded the Nobel Prize for Peace.

The President of the United States

It is difficult to describe any single part of a great governmental system without describing the whole of it. Governments are living things and operate as organic wholes. Moreover, governments have their natural evolution and are one thing in one age, another in another. The makers of the Constitution constructed the federal government upon a theory of checks and balances which was meant to limit the operation of each part and allow to no single part or organ of it a dominating force; but no government can be successfully conducted upon so mechanical a theory. Leadership and control must be lodged somewhere; the whole art of statesmanship is the art of bringing the several parts of government into effective coöperation for the accomplishment of particular common objects,—and party objects at that. Our study of each part of our federal system, if we are to discover our real government as it lives, must be made to disclose to us its operative coördination as a whole: its places of leadership, its method of action, how it operates, what checks it, what gives it energy and effect. Governments are what politicians make them, and it is easier to write of the President than of the presidency.

The government of the United States was constructed upon the Whig theory of political dynamics, which was a sort of unconscious copy of the Newtonian theory of the universe. In our own day, whenever we discuss the structure or development of anything, whether in nature or in society, we consciously or unconsciously follow Mr. Darwin; but before Mr. Darwin, they followed Newton. Some single law, like the law of gravitation, swung each system of thought and gave it its principle of unity. Every sun, every planet, every free body in the spaces of the heavens, the world itself, is kept in its place and reined to its course by the attraction of bodies that swing with equal order and precision about it, themselves governed by the nice poise and balance of forces which give the whole system of the universe its symmetry and perfect adjustment. The Whigs had tried to give England a similar constitution. They had had no wish to destroy the throne, no conscious desire to reduce the king to a mere figurehead, but had intended only to surround and offset him with a system of constitutional checks and balances which should regulate his otherwise arbitrary course and make it at least always calculable.

They had made no clear analysis of the matter in their own thoughts; it has not been the habit of English politicians, or indeed of English-speaking politicians on either side of the water, to be clear theorists. It was left to a Frenchman to point out to the Whigs what they had done. They had striven to make Parliament so influential in the making of laws and so authoritative in the criticism of the king's policy that the king could in no matter have his own way without their coöperation and assent, though they left him free, the while, if he chose, to interpose an absolute veto upon the acts of Parliament. They had striven to secure for the courts of law as great an independence as possible, so that they might be neither over-awed by parliament nor coerced by the king. In brief, as Montesquieu pointed out to them in his lucid way, they had sought to balance executive, legislature, and judiciary off against one another by a series of checks and counterpoises, which Newton might readily have recognized as suggestive of the mechanism of the heavens.

The makers of our federal Constitution followed the scheme as they found it expounded in Montesquieu, followed it with genuine scientific enthusiasm. The admirable expositions of the *Federalist* read like thoughtful applications of Montesquieu to the political needs and circumstances of America. They are full of the theory of checks and balances. The President is balanced off against Congress, Congress against the President, and each against the courts. Our statesmen of the earlier generations quoted no one so often as Montesquieu, and they quoted him always as a scientific standard in the field of politics. Politics is turned into mechanics under his touch. The theory of gravitation is supreme.

The trouble with the theory is that government is not a machine, but a living thing. It falls, not under the theory of the universe, but under the theory of organic life. It is accountable to Darwin, not to Newton. It is modified by its environment, necessitated by its tasks, shaped to its functions by the sheer pressure of life. No living thing can have its organs offset against each other as checks, and live. On the contrary, its life is dependent upon their quick coöperation, their ready response to the commands of instinct or intelligence, their amicable community of purpose. Government is not a body of blind forces; it is a body of men, with highly differentiated functions, no doubt, in our modern day of specialization, but with a common task and purpose. Their coöperation is indispensable, their warfare fatal. There can be no successful government without leadership or without the intimate, almost instinctive, coördination of the organs of life and action. This is not theory, but fact, and displays its force as fact, whatever theories may be thrown across its track. Living political constitu-

tions must be Darwinian in structure and in practice.

Fortunately, the definitions and prescriptions of our constitutional law, though conceived in the Newtonian spirit and upon the Newtonian principle, are sufficiently broad and elastic to allow for the play of life and circumstance. Though they were Whig theorists, the men who framed the federal Constitution were also practical statesmen with an experienced eye for affairs and a quick practical sagacity in respect of the actual structure of government, and they have given us a thoroughly workable model. If it had in fact been a machine governed by mechanically automatic balances, it would have had no history; but it was not, and its history has been rich with the influences and personalities of the men who have conducted it and made it a living reality. The government of the United States has had a vital and normal organic growth and has proved itself eminently adapted to express the changing temper and purposes of the American people from age to age.

That is the reason why it is easier to write of the President than of the presidency. The presidency has been one thing at one time, another at another, varying with the man who occupied the office and with the circumstances that surrounded him. One account must be given of the office during the period 1789 to 1825, when the government was getting its footing both at home and abroad, struggling for its place among the nations and its full credit among its own people; when English precedents and traditions were strongest; and when the men chosen for the office were men bred to leadership in a way that attracted to them the attention and confidence of the whole country. Another account must be given of it during Jackson's time, when an imperious man, bred not in deliberative assemblies or quiet councils, but in the field and upon a rough frontier, worked his own will upon affairs, with or without formal sanction of law, sustained by a clear undoubting conscience and the love of a people who had grown deeply impatient of the régime he had supplanted. Still another account must be given of it during the years 1836 to 1861, when domestic affairs of many debatable kinds absorbed the country, when Congress necessarily exercised the chief choices of policy, and when the Presidents who followed one another in office lacked the personal force and initiative to make for themselves a leading place in counsel. After that came the Civil War and Mr. Lincoln's unique task and achievement, when the executive seemed for a little while to become by sheer stress of circumstances the whole government, Congress merely voting supplies and assenting to necessary laws, as Parliament did in the time of the Tudors. From 1865 to 1898 domestic questions, legislative matters in respect of which Congress had naturally to make the initial choice, legislative leaders the chief decisions of policy, came once more to the front, and no President except Mr. Cleveland .played a leading and decisive part in the quiet drama of our national life. Even Mr. Cleveland may be said to have owed his great rôle in affairs rather to his own native force and the confused politics of the time, than to any opportunity of leadership naturally afforded him by a system which had subordinated so many Presidents before him to Congress. The war with Spain again changed the balance of parts. Foreign questions became leading questions again, as they had been in the first days of the government, and in them the President was of necessity leader. Our new place in the affairs of the world has since that year of transformation kept him at the front of our government, where our own thoughts and the attention of men everywhere is centred upon him.

Both men and circumstances have created these contrasts in the administration and influence of the office of President. We have all been disciples of Montesquieu, but we have also been practical politicians. Mr. Bagehot once remarked that it was no proof of the excellence of the Constitution of the United States that the Americans had operated it with conspicuous success because the Americans could run any constitution successfully; and, while the compliment is altogether acceptable, it is certainly true that our practical sense is more noticeable than our theoretical consistency, and that, while we were once all constitutional lawyers, we are in these latter days apt to be very impatient of literal and dogmatic interpretations of constitutional principle.

The makers of the Constitution seem to have thought of the President as what the stricter Whig theorists wished the king to be: only the legal executive, the presiding and guiding authority in the application of law and the execution of policy. His veto upon legislation was only his 'check' on Congress,—was a power of restraint, not of guidance. He was empowered to prevent bad laws, but he was not to be given an opportunity to make good ones. As a matter of fact he has become very much more. He has become the leader of his party and the guide of the nation in political purpose, and therefore in legal action. The constitutional structure of the government has hampered and limited his action in these significant rôles, but it has not prevented it. The influence of the President has varied with the men who have been Presidents and with the circumstances of their times, but the tendency has been unmistakably disclosed, and springs out of the very nature of government itself. It is merely the proof that our government is a living, organic thing, and must, like every other government, work out the close synthesis of active parts which can exist only when leadership is lodged in some one man or group of men. You cannot compound a successful government out of antagonisms. Greatly as the practice and influence of Presidents has varied, there can be no mistaking the fact that we have grown more and more inclined from generation to generation to look to the President as the unifying force in our complex system, the leader both of his party and of the nation. To do so is not inconsistent with the actual provisions of the Constitution; it is only inconsistent with a very mechanical theory of its meaning and intention. The Constitution contains no theories. It is as practical a document as Magna Carta.

The rôle of party leader is forced upon the President by the method of his selection. The theory of the makers of the Constitution may have been that the presidential electors would exercise a real choice, but it is hard to understand how, as experienced politicians, they can have expected anything of the kind. They did not provide that the electors should meet as one body for consultation and make deliberate choice of a President and Vice-President, but that they should meet "in their respective states" and cast their ballots in separate groups, without the possibility of consulting and without the least likelihood of agreeing, unless some such means as have actually been used were employed to suggest and determine their choice beforehand. It was the practice at first to make party nominations for the presidency by congressional caucus. Since the Democratic upheaval of General Jackson's time nominating conventions have taken the place of congressional caucuses; and the choice of Presidents by party conventions has had some very interesting results.

We are apt to think of the choice of nominating conventions as somewhat haphazard. We know, or think that we know, how their action is sometimes determined, and the knowledge makes us very uneasy. We know that there is no debate in nominating conventions, no discussion of the merits of the respective candidates, at which the country can sit as audience and assess the wisdom of the final choice. If there is any talking to be done, aside from the formal addresses of the temporary and permanent chairmen and of those who present the platform and the names of the several aspirants for nomination, the assembly adjourns. The talking that is to decide the result must be done in private committee rooms and behind the closed doors of the headquarters

of the several state delegations to the convention. The intervals between sessions are filled with a very feverish activity. Messengers run from one headquarters to another until the small hours of the morning. Conference follows conference in a way that is likely to bring newspaper correspondents to the verge of despair, it being next to impossible to put the rumors to-gether into any coherent story of what is going on. Only at the rooms of the national committee of the party is there any clear knowledge of the situation as a whole; and the excitement of the members of the convention rises from session to session under the sheer pressure of uncertainty. The final majority is compounded no outsider and few members can tell how.

Many influences, too, play upon nominating conventions, which seem mere winds of feeling. They sit in great halls, with galleries into which crowd thousands of spectators from all parts of the country, but chiefly, of course, from the place at which the convention sits, and the feeling of the galleries is transmitted to the floor. The cheers of mere spectators echo the names of popular candidates, and every excitement on the floor is enhanced a hundred fold in the galleries. Sudden gusts of impulse are apt to change the whole feeling of the convention, and offset in a moment the most careful arrangements of managing politicians. It has come to be a commonly accepted opinion that if the Republican convention of 1860 had not met in Chicago, it would have nominated Mr. Seward and not Mr. Lincoln. Mr. Seward was the acknowledged leader of the new party; had been its most telling spokesman; had given its tenets definition and currency. Mr. Lincoln had not been brought within view of the country as a whole until the other day, when he had given Mr. Douglas so hard a fight to keep his seat in the Senate, and had but just now given currency among thoughtful men to the striking phrases of the searching speeches he had made in debate with his practised antagonist. But the

President Wilson's inauguration after his 1916 reelection.

convention met in Illinois, amidst throngs of Mr. Lincoln's ardent friends and advocates. His managers saw to it that the galleries were properly filled with men who would cheer every mention of his name until the hall was shaken. Every influence of the place worked for him and he was chosen.

Thoughtful critics of our political practices have not allowed the excellence of the choice to blind them to the danger of the method. They have known too many examples of what the galleries have done to supplement the efforts of managing politicians to feel safe in the presence of processes which seem rather those of intrigue and impulse than those of sober choice. They can cite instances, moreover, of sudden, unlooked-for excitements on the floor of such bodies which have swept them from the control of all sober influences and hastened them to choices which no truly deliberative assembly could ever have made. There is no training school for Presidents, unless, as some governors have wished, it be looked for in the governorships of states; and nominating conventions have confined themselves in their selections to no class, have demanded of aspirants no particular experience or knowledge of affairs. They have nominated lawyers without political experience, soldiers, editors of newspapers, newspaper correspondents, whom they pleased, without regard to their lack of contact with affairs. It would seem as if their choices were almost matters of chance.

In reality there is much more method, much more definite purpose, much more deliberate choice in the extraordinary process than there seems to be. The leading spirits of the national committee of each party could give an account of the matter which would put a very different face on it and make the methods of nominating conventions seem, for all the undoubted elements of chance there are in them, on the whole very manageable. Moreover, the party that expects to win may be counted on to make a much more conservative and thoughtful selection of a candidate than the party that merely hopes to win. The haphazard selections which seem to discredit the system are generally made by conventions of the party unaccustomed to success. Success brings sober calculation and a sense of responsibility.

And it must be remembered also that our political system is not so coördinated as to supply a training for presidential aspirants or even to make it absolutely necessary that they should have had extended experience in public affairs. Certainly the country has never thought of members of Congress as in any particular degree fitted for the presidency. Even the Vice President is not afforded an opportunity to learn the duties of the office. The men best prepared, no doubt, are those who have been governors of states or members of cabinets. And yet even they are chosen for their respective offices generally by reason of a kind of fitness and availability which does not necessarily argue in them the size and power that would fit them for the greater office. In our earlier practice cabinet officers were regarded as in the natural line of succession to the presidency. Mr. Jefferson had been in General Washington's cabinet, Mr. Madison in Mr. Jefferson's, Mr. Monroe in Mr. Madison's; and generally it was the Secretary of State who was taken. But those were days when English precedent was strong upon us, when cabinets were expected to be made up of the political leaders of the party in power; and from their ranks subsequent candidates for the presidency were most likely to be selected. The practice, as we look back to it, seems eminently sensible, and we wonder why it should have been so soon departed from and apparently forgotten. We wonder, too, why eminent senators have not sometimes been chosen; why members of the House have so seldom commanded the attention of nominating conventions; why public life has never offered itself in any definite way as a preparation for the presidential office.

If the matter be looked at a little more

closely, it will be seen that the office of President, as we have used and developed it, really does not demand actual experience in affairs so much as particular qualities of mind and character which we are at least as likely to find outside the ranks of our public men as within them. What is it that a nominating convention wants in the man it is to present to the country for its suffrages? A man who will be and who will seem to the country in some sort an embodiment of the character and purpose it wishes its government to have,—a man who understands his own day and the needs of the country, and who has the personality and the initiative to enforce his views both upon the people and upon Congress. It may seem an odd way to get such a man. It is even possible that nominating conventions and those who guide them do not realize entirely what it is that they do. But in simple fact the convention picks out a party leader from the body of the nation. Not that it expects its nominee to direct the interior government of the party and to supplant its already accredited and experienced spokesmen in Congress and in its state and national committees; but it does of necessity expect him to represent it before public opinion and to stand before the country as its representative man, as a true type of what the country may expect of the party itself in purpose and principle. It cannot but be led by him in the campaign; if he be elected, it cannot but acquiesce in his leadership of the government itself. What the country will demand of the candidate will be, not that he be an astute politician, skilled and practised in affairs, but that he be a man such as it can trust, in character, in intention, in knowledge of its needs, in perception of the best means by which those needs may be met, in capacity to prevail by reason of his own weight and integrity. Sometimes the country believes in a party, but more often it believes in a man; and conventions have often shown the instinct to perceive which it is that the country needs in a particular presidential year, a mere representative

partisan, a military hero, or some one who will genuinely speak for the country itself, whatever be his training and antecedents. It is in this sense that the President has the rôle of party leader thrust upon him by the very method by which he is chosen.

As legal executive, his constitutional aspect, the President cannot be thought of alone. He cannot execute laws. Their actual daily execution must be taken care of by the several executive departments and by the now innumerable body of federal officials throughout the country. In respect of the strictly executive duties of his office the President may be said to administer the presidency in conjunction with the members of his cabinet, like the chairman of a commission. He is even of necessity much less active in the actual carrying out of the law than are his colleagues and advisers. It is therefore becoming more and more true, as the business of the government becomes more and more complex and extended, that the President is becoming more and a more political and less and less an executive officer. His executive powers are in commission, while his political powers more and more centre and accumulate upon him and are in their very nature personal and inalienable.

Only the larger sort of executive questions are brought to him. Departments which run with easy routine and whose transactions bring few questions of general policy to the surface may proceed with their business for months and even years together without demanding his attention; and no department is in any sense under his direct charge. Cabinet meetings do not discuss detail: they are concerned only with the larger matters of policy or expediency which important business is constantly disclosing. There are no more hours in the President's day than in another man's. If he is indeed the executive, he must act almost entirely by delegation, and is in the hands of his colleagues. He is likely to be praised if things go well, and blamed if they go wrong; but his only real control is of the

461

persons to whom he deputes the performance of executive duties. It is through no fault or neglect of his that the duties apparently assigned to him by the Constitution have come to be his less conspicuous, less important duties, and that duties apparently not assigned to him at all chiefly occupy his time and energy. The one set of duties it has proved practically impossible for him to perform; the other it has proved impossible for him to escape.

He cannot escape being the leader of his party except by incapacity and lack of personal force, because he is at once the choice of the party and of the nation. He is the party nominee, and the only party nominee for whom the whole nation votes. Members of the House and Senate are representatives of localities, are voted for only by sections of voters, or by local bodies of electors like the members of the state legislatures. There is no national party choice except that of President. No one else represents the people as a whole, exercising a national choice; and inasmuch as his strictly executive duties are in fact subordinated, so far at any rate as all detail is concerned, the President represents not so much the party's governing efficiency as its controlling ideals and principles. He is not so much part of its organization as its vital link of connection with the thinking nation. He can dominate his party by being spokesman for the real sentiment and purpose of the country, by giving direction to opinion, by giving the country at once the information and the statements of policy which will enable it to form its judgments alike of parties and of men.

For he is also the political leader of the nation, or has it in his choice to be. The nation as a whole has chosen him, and is conscious that it has no other political spokesman. His is the only national voice in affairs. Let him once win the admiration and confidence of the country, and no other single force can withstand him, no combination of forces will easily overpower him. His position takes the imagination of the country.

He is the representative of no constituency, but of the whole people. When he speaks in his true character, he speaks for no special interest. If he rightly interpret the national thought and boldly insist upon it, he is irresistible; and the country never feels the zest of action so much as when its President is of such insight and calibre. Its instinct is for unified action, and it craves a single leader. It is for this reason that it will often prefer to choose a man rather than a party. A President whom it trusts can not only lead it, but form it to his own views.

It is the extraordinary isolation imposed upon the President by our system that makes the character and opportunity of his office so extraordinary. In him are centred both opinion and party. He may stand, if he will, a little outside party and insist as if it were upon the general opinion. It is with the instinctive feeling that it is upon occasion such a man that the country wants that nominating conventions will often nominate men who are not their acknowledged leaders, but only such men as the country would like to see lead both its parties. The President may also, if he will, stand within the party counsels and use the advantage of his power and personal force to control its actual programs. He may be both the leader of his party and the leader of the nation, or he may be one or the other. If he lead the nation, his party can hardly resist him. His office is anything he has the sagacity and force to make it.

That is the reason why it has been one thing at one time, another at another. The Presidents who have not made themselves leaders have lived no more truly on that account in the spirit of the Constitution than those whose force has told in the determination of law and policy. No doubt Andrew Jackson overstepped the bounds meant to be set to the authority of his office. It was certainly in direct contravention of the spirit of the Constitution that he should have refused to respect and execute decisions of the Supreme Court of the United States, and no serious student of our histo-

The president leaving the Hall of Mirrors after signing the Treaty of Versailles, on June 28, 1919. In the foreground is Georges Clemenceau, at that time premier of France.

ry can righteously condone what he did in such matters on the ground that his intentions were upright and his principles pure. But the Constitution of the United States is not a mere lawyers' document: it is a vehicle of life, and its spirit is always the spirit of the age. Its prescriptions are clear and we know what they are; a written document makes lawyers of us all, and our duty as citizens should make us conscientious lawyers, reading the text of the Constitution without subtlety or sophistication; but life is always your last and most authoritative critic.

Some of our Presidents have deliberately held themselves off from using the full power they might legitimately have used, because of conscientious scruples, because they were more theorists than statesmen. They have held the strict literary theory of the Constitution, the Whig theory, the Newtonian theory, and have acted as if they thought that Pennsylvania Avenue should have been even longer than it is; that there should be no intimate communication of any kind between the Capitol and the White House; that the President as a man was no more at liberty to lead the houses of Congress by persuasion than he was at liberty as President to dominate them by authority,— supposing that he had, what he has not, authority enough to dominate them. But the makers of the Constitution were not enacting Whig theory, they were not making laws with the expectation that, not the laws themselves, but their opinions, known by future historians to lie back of them, should govern the constitutional action of the country. They were statesmen, not pedants, and their laws are sufficient to keep us to the paths they set us upon. The President is at liberty, both in law and conscience, to be as big a man as he can. His capacity will set the limit; and if Congress be overborne by him, it will be no fault of the makers of the Constitution,—it will be from no lack of constitutional powers on its part, but only because the President has the nation behind him, and Congress has not. He has no means of compelling Congress except through public opinion.

That I say he has no means of compelling Congress will show what I mean, and that my meaning has no touch of radicalism or iconoclasm in it. There are illegitimate means by which the President may influence the action of Congress. He may bargain with members, not only with regard to appointments, but also with regard to legislative measures. He may use his local patronage to assist members to get or retain their seats. He may interpose his powerful influence, in one covert way or another, in contests for places in the Senate. He may also overbear Congress by arbitrary acts which ignore the laws or virtually override them. He may even substitute his own orders for acts of Congress which he wants but cannot get. Such things are not only deeply immoral, they are destructive of the fundamental understandings of constitutional government and, therefore, of constitutional government itself. They are sure, moreover, in a country of free public opinion, to bring their own punishment, to destroy both the fame and the power of the man who dares to practise them. No honorable man includes such agencies in a sober exposition of the Constitution or allows himself to think of them when he speaks of the influences of "life" which govern each generation's use and interpretation of that great instrument, our sovereign guide and the object of our deepest reverence. Nothing in a system like ours can be constitutional which is immoral or which touches the good faith of those who have sworn to obey the fundamental law. The reprobation of all good men will always overwhelm such influences with shame and failure. But the personal force of the President is perfectly constitutional to any extent to which he chooses to exercise it, and it is by the clear logic of our constitutional practice that he has become alike the leader of his party and the leader of the nation.

The political powers of the President are

not quite so obvious in their scope and character when we consider his relations with Congress as when we consider his relations to his party and to the nation. They need, therefore, a somewhat more critical examination. Leadership in government naturally belongs to its executive officers, who are daily in contact with practical conditions and exigencies and whose reputations alike for good judgment and for fidelity are at stake much more than are those of the members of the legislative body at every turn of the law's application. The law-making part of the government ought certainly to be very hospitable to the suggestions of the planning and acting part of it. Those Presidents who have felt themselves bound to adhere to the strict literary theory of the Constitution have scrupulously refrained from attempting to determine either the subjects or the character of legislation, except so far as they were obliged to decide for themselves, after Congress had acted, whether they should acquiesce in it or not. And yet the Constitution explicitly authorizes the President to recommend to Congress "such measures as he shall deem necessary and expedient," and it is not necessary to the integrity of even the literary theory of the Constitution to insist that such recommendations should be merely perfunctory. Certainly General Washington did not so regard them, and he stood much nearer the Whig theory than we do. A President's messages to Congress have no more weight or authority than their intrinsic reasonableness and importance give them: but that is their only constitutional limitation. The Constitution certainly does not forbid the President to back them up, as General Washington did, with such personal force and influence as he may possess. Some of our Presidents have felt the need, which unquestionably exists in our system, for some spokesman of the nation as a whole, in matters of legislation no less than in other matters, and have tried to supply Congress with the leadership of suggestion, backed by ar-

gument and by iteration and by every legitimate appeal to public opinion. Cabinet officers are shut out from Congress; the President himself has, by custom, no access to its floor; many long-established barriers of precedent, though not of law, hinder him from exercising any direct influence upon its deliberations; and yet he is undoubtedly the only spokesman of the whole people. They have again and again, as often as they were afforded the opportunity, manifested their satisfaction when he has boldly accepted the rôle of leader, to which the peculiar origin and character of his authority entitle him. The Constitution bids him speak, and times of stress and change must more and more thrust upon him the attitude of originator of policies.

His is the vital place of action in the system, whether he accept it as such or not, and the office is the measure of the man,— of his wisdom as well as of his force. His veto abundantly equips him to stay the hand of Congress when he will. It is seldom possible to pass a measure over his veto, and no President has hesitated to use the veto when his own judgment of the public good was seriously at issue with that of the houses. The veto has never been suffered to fall into even temporary disuse with us. In England it has ceased to exist, with the change in the character of the executive. There has been no veto since Anne's day, because ever since the reign of Anne the laws of England have been originated either by ministers who spoke the king's own will or by ministers whom the king did not dare gainsay; and in our own time the ministers who formulate the laws are themselves the executive of the nation; a veto would be a negative upon their own power. If bills pass of which they disapprove, they resign and give place to the leaders of those who approve them. The framers of the Constitution made in our President a more powerful, because a more isolated, king than the one they were imitating; and because the Constitution gave them their veto in such explicit terms, our Presidents have not hesitated to use it, even when it put their mere individual judgment against that of large majorities in both houses of Congress. And yet in the exercise of the power to suggest legislation, quite as explicitly conferred upon them by the Constitution, some of our Presidents have seemed to have a timid fear that they might offend some law of taste which had become a constitutional principle.

In one sense their messages to Congress have no more authority than the letters of any other citizen would have. Congress can heed or ignore them as it pleases; and there have been periods of our history when presidential messages were utterly without practical significance, perfunctory documents which few persons except the editors of newspapers took the trouble to read. But if the President has personal force and cares to exercise it, there is this tremendous difference between his messages and the views of any other citizen, either outside Congress or in it: that the whole country reads them and feels that the writer speaks with an authority and a responsibility which the people themselves have given him.

The history of our cabinets affords a striking illustration of the progress of the idea that the President is not merely the legal head but also the political leader of the nation. In the earlier days of the government it was customary for the President to fill his cabinet with the recognized leaders of his party. General Washington even tried the experiment which William of Orange tried at the very beginning of the era of cabinet government. He called to his aid the leaders of both political parties, associating Mr. Hamilton with Mr. Jefferson, on the theory that all views must be heard and considered in the conduct of the government. That was the day in which English precedent prevailed, and English cabinets were made up of the chief political characters of the day. But later years have witnessed a marked change in our practice, in this as in many other things. The old tradition was indeed slow in dying out. It persisted with considerable vitality at least until General Garfield's day, and may yet from time to time revive, for many functions of our cabinets justify it and make it desirable. But our later Presidents have apparently ceased to regard the cabinet as a council of party leaders such as the party they represent would have chosen. They look upon it rather as a body of personal advisers whom the President chooses from the ranks of those whom he personally trusts and prefers to look to for advice. Our recent Presidents have not sought their associates among those whom the fortunes of party contest have brought into prominence and influence, but have called their personal friends and business colleagues to cabinet positions, and men who have given proof of their efficiency in private, not in public, life,—bankers who had never had any place in the formal counsels of the party, eminent lawyers who had held aloof from politics, private secretaries who had shown an unusual sagacity and proficiency in handling public business; and if the President were himself alone the leader of his party, the members of his cabinet only his private advisers, at any rate advisers of his private choice. Mr. Cleveland may be said to have been the first President to make this conception of the cabinet prominent in his choices, and he did not do so until his second administration. Mr. Roosevelt has emphasized the idea.

Upon analysis it seems to mean this: the cabinet is an executive, not a political body. The President cannot himself be the actual executive; he must therefore find, to act in his stead, men of the best legal and business gifts, and depend upon them for the actual administration of the government in all its daily activities. If he seeks political advice of his executive colleagues, he seeks it because he relies upon their natural good sense and experienced judgment, upon their knowledge of the country and its business and social conditions, upon their sagacity as representative citizens of more than usual observation and discretion; not because they are supposed to have had any very intimate contact with politics or to have made a profession of public affairs. He has chosen, not representative politicians, but eminent representative citizens, selecting them rather for their special fitness for the great business posts to which he has assigned them than for their political experience, and looking to them for advice in the actual conduct of the government rather than in the shaping of political policy. They are, in his view, not necessarily political officers at all.

It may with a great deal of plausibility be argued that the Constitution looks upon the President himself in the same way. It does not seem to make him a prime minister or the leader of the nation's counsels. Some Presidents are, therefore, and some are not. It depends upon the man and his gifts. He may be like his cabinet, or he may be more than his cabinet. His office is a mere vantage ground from which he may be sure that effective words of advice and timely efforts at reform will gain telling momentum. He has the ear of the nation as of course, and a great person may use such an advantage greatly. If he use the opportunity, he may take his cabinet into partnership or not, as he pleases; and so its character may vary with his. Self-reliant men will regard their cabinets as executive councils; men less self-reliant or more prudent will regard them as also political councils, and will wish to call into them men who have earned the confidence of their party. The character of the cabinet may be made a nice index of the theory of the presidential office, as well as of the President's theory of party government; but the one view is, so far as I can see, as constitutional as the other.

One of the greatest of the President's powers I have not yet spoken of at all: his control, which is very absolute, of the foreign relations of the nation. The initiative in foreign affairs, which the President possesses without any restriction whatever, is virtually the power to control them absolutely. The President cannot conclude a treaty with a foreign power without the consent of the Senate, but he may guide every step of diplomacy, and to guide diplomacy is to determine what treaties must be made, if the faith and prestige of the government are to be maintained. He need disclose no step of negotiation until it is complete, and when in any critical matter it is completed the government is virtually committed. Whatever its disinclination, the Senate may feel itself committed also.

I have not dwelt upon this power of the President, because it has been decisively influential in determining the character and influence of the office at only two periods in our history; at the very first, when the government was young and had so to use its incipient force as to win the respect of the nations into whose family it had thrust itself, and in our own day when the results of the Spanish War, the ownership of distant possessions, and many sharp struggles for foreign trade make it necessary that we should turn our best talents to the task of dealing firmly, wisely, and justly with political and commercial rivals. The President can never again be the mere domestic figure he has been throughout so large a part of our history. The nation has risen to the first rank in power and resources. The other nations of the world look askance upon her, half in envy, half in fear, and wonder with a deep anxiety what she will do with her vast strength. They receive the frank professions of men like Mr. John Hay, whom we wholly trusted, with a grain of salt, and doubt what we were sure of, their truthfulness and sincerity, suspecting a hidden design under every utterance he makes. Our President must always, henceforth, be one of the great powers of the world, whether he act greatly and wisely or not, and the best statesmen we can produce will be needed to fill the office of Secretary of State. We have but begun to see the presidential office in this light; but it is the light which will more and more beat upon it, and more and more determine its character and its effect upon the politics of the nation. We can never hide our President again as a mere domestic officer. We can never again see him the mere executive he was in the thirties and forties. He must stand always at the front of our affairs, and the office will be as big and as influential as the man who occupies it.

How is it possible to sum up the duties and influence of such an office in such a system in comprehensive terms which will cover all its changeful aspects? In the view of the makers of the Constitution the President was to be legal executive; perhaps the leader of the nation; certainly not the leader of the party, at any rate while in office. But by the operation of forces inherent in the very nature of government he has become all three, and by inevitable consequence the most heavily burdened officer in the world. No other man's day is so full as his, so full of the responsibilities which tax mind and conscience alike and demand an inexhaustible vitality. The mere task of making appointments to office, which the Constitution imposes upon the President, has come near to breaking some of our Presidents down, because it is a never-ending task in a civil service not yet put upon a professional footing, confused with short terms of office, always forming and dissolving. And in proportion as the President ventures to use his opportunity to lead opinion and act as spokesman of the people in affairs the people stand ready to overwhelm him by running to him with every question, great and small. They are as eager to have him settle a literary question as a political; hear him as acquiescently with regard to matters of special expert knowledge as with regard to public affairs, and call upon him to quiet all troubles by his personal intervention. Men of ordinary physique and discretion cannot be Presidents and live, if the strain be not somehow relieved. We shall be obliged always to be picking our chief magistrates from among wise and prudent athletes,—a small class.

The future development of the presidency, therefore, must certainly, one would confidently predict, run along such lines as the President's later relations with his cabinet suggest. General Washington, partly out of unaffected modesty, no doubt, but also out of the sure practical instinct which he possessed in so unusual a degree, set an example which few of his successors seem to have followed in any systematic manner. He made constant and intimate use of his colleagues in every matter that he handled, seeking their assistance and advice by letter when they were at a distance and he could not obtain it in person. It is well known to all close students of our history that his greater state papers, even those which seem in some peculiar and intimate sense his personal utterances, are full of the ideas and the very phrases of the men about him whom he most trusted. His rough drafts came back to him from Mr. Hamilton and Mr. Madison in great part rephrased and rewritten, in many passages reconceived and given a new color. He thought and acted always by the light of counsel, with a will and definite choice of his own, but through the instrumentality of other minds as well as his own. The duties and responsibilities laid upon the President by the Constitution can be changed only by constitutional amendment,—a thing too difficult to attempt except upon some greater necessity than the relief of an overburdened office, even though that office be the greatest in the land; and it is to be doubted whether the deliberate opinion of the country would consent to make of the President a less powerful officer than he is. He can secure his own relief without shirking any real responsibility. Appointments, for example, he can, if he will, make more and more upon the advice and choice of his executive colleagues; every matter of detail not only, but also every minor matter of counsel or of general policy, he can more and more depend upon his chosen advisers to determine; he need reserve for himself only the larger matters of counsel and that general oversight of the business of the government and of the persons who conduct it which is not possible without intimate daily consultations, indeed, but which is possible without attempting the intolerable burden of direct control. This is, no doubt, the idea of their functions which most Presidents have entertained and which most Presidents suppose themselves to have acted on; but we have reason to believe that most of our Presidents have taken their duties too literally and have attempted the impossible. But we can safely predict that as the multitude of the President's duties increases, as it must with the growth and widening activities of the nation itself, the incumbents of the great office will more and more come to feel that they are administering it in its truest purpose and with greatest effect by regarding themselves as less and less executive officers and more and more directors of affairs and leaders of the nation,—men of counsel and of the sort of action that makes for enlightenment.

PICTURE CREDITS

N ow there's a way to identify all
your fine books with flair and style.
As part of our continuing service to you,
Britannica Home Library Service, Inc. is
proud to be able to offer you the fine quality
item shown on the next page.

B ooklovers will love the heavy-duty
personalized **Ex Libris** embosser.
Now you can personalize all your
fine books with the mark of distinction, just
the way all the fine libraries of the world do.

T o order this item ,
please type or print your name,
address and zip code on a plain sheet
of paper. (Note special instructions for
ordering the embosser). Please send a check
or money order only (your money will be
refunded in full if you are not delighted) for
the full amount of purchase, including
postage and handling, to:

Britannica Home Library Service, Inc.
Attn: Yearbook Department
Post Office Box 6137
Chicago, Illinois 60680

17 68

IN THE
BRITANNICA
TRADITION
OF QUALITY...

EX LIBRIS
PERSONAL EMBOSSER

A mark of distinction for your fine books. A book embosser just like the
ones used in libraries. The 1½″ seal imprints "Library of _____" (with
the name of your choice) and up to three centered initials. Please
type or print clearly BOTH full name (up to 26 letters including
spaces between names) and up to three initials.
Please allow six weeks for delivery.

Just $20.00

plus $2.00 shipping and handling

This offer available only in the United States.
Illinois residents please add sales tax

Britannica Home Library Service, Inc.